TWENTIETH CENTURY
POLITICAL THOUGHT

TWENTIETH CENTURY
POLITICAL THOUGHT

Edited by

JOSEPH S. ROUCEK

Philosophical Library
New York

Printed in the United States of America

Dedicated to

BOYD B. RAKESTRAW

Associate Director, Extension Division
University of California

PREFACE

There is no doubt that the complexity of modern social life, even more complicated by World War II, and by the international problems on a global scale, makes the task of political theory particularly difficult. In its search for absolute truth and its efforts to square itself completely with the facts of political and social life, political theory has been one of the chief occupations of outstanding thinkers and of their interpreters and critics.

This interest has broadened during the last century and a half. With the popularization of the ideals of democracy, more and more people from the lower ranks of society have been granted the right—in some cases, only theoretically—to make their political opinions effective. At any rate, whether or not the masses have any political rights, the modern rulers, from Churchill and Roosevelt to Hitler and Stalin, must always be aware of the existence of the masses, and they must operate their political machineries in such a way that these masses are made to feel that "theirs is the will." The most important aspect of this process of social control, the manipulations of ideologies, is nothing else but the utilization of political creeds, philosophies and ideologies, for the mobilization of mass movements.

It is true that the history of mankind is also the history of the wars of ideologies, exemplified, for instance, by the blood struggle between Catholicism and Protestantism in the sixteenth century. But the present world conflict differs from any in the past. Our modern era has produced a class of intellectuals well trained in ideologies and capable of carrying on the warfare of ideas on a level never before attained. Furthermore, the amazing advances in science and technology of the past hundred years have challenged innumerable traditions, upset many fixed beliefs, and produced a unique totalitarian character of the intellectual struggle, so that today there is not a single system of thought which is not influenced by the present war of ideologies.

Furthermore, we must notice that the whole problem of political theory is related, broadly speaking, to the whole field of social sciences and that, in a narrower sense, it is a problem of increasingly growing importance when we consider the mass character of our civilization, the growing improvements of our means of communication, the growing bitterness of social struggles for the distribution and control of power in internal and international affairs, and the recent discoveries in the field of propaganda as the means of persuasion in politics.

There is no question whatsoever that there is a definite need for the present text, prepared in collaboration with capable and well-known specialists. The vast bulk of monographs and specialized studies exploring various aspects of that enormous field, known as Political Thought (Political Theory, Political Philosophy, Social Philosophy, Social Thought, and similar studies) has now become so great that even the specialist cannot keep up with its expanse, and the man in the street is overwhelmed by it— even if he hears only a small part of its conclusions. Growing accumulation of such data, not to speak of the interpretative data as well as the advancement of such recent disciplines as The Sociology of Knowledge and the "new" field of Semantics, make it impossible for one person to become expert in very many different branches even in his own general field. The book demonstrates that there is a periodic need for some integration of the ever-widening range of highly specialized field of knowledge —a problem introduced by the overwhelming quality of the floods of ever new, and sometimes reputable, printed matter.

The present volume is a harvest of examinations aiming to synthesize, summarize, and re-interpret the crop of ripening studies of the available knowledge on the most important trends in Political Thought in America and abroad, which has sorted a widely scattered material, assembled related products, and prepared them for consumption in a readable form. Each chapter is designed to bring into sharp focus the main trends involved in the topic.

The editor is particularly proud of being able to secure the present co-authors as his collaborators. Surely, a disposition of a single author to be panoramic is a notable eccentricity in our age of specialization. Thus, the willingness to collaborate in a democratic method on a text by several co-authors has become, within the last two decades, a more respectable practice.

The volume, it is hoped, will be used not only as a text, but also will be found useful by the lay reader as an informative introduction to the main cross-currents in political ideologies of the present century.

JOSEPH S. ROUCEK

CO-AUTHORS

ANDERSON, G. ARNOLD
Iowa State College & Harvard
University

BARNES, HARRY ELMER
formerly Smith College & New
School for Social Research

BURDETTE, FRANKLIN L.
Butler University

CAVE, FLOYD A.
San Francisco State College

CLYDE, PAUL H.
Duke University

DAVIS, HAROLD E.
Office of Coordinator of Inter-
American Affairs

EHRENPREIS, WIKTOR J.
"Poland Fights"

FELLMAN, DAVID
University of Nebraska

HOOVER, GLENN E.
Mills College

IRISH, MARIAN D.
Florida State College for Women

KALIJARVI, THORSTEN V.
University of New Hampshire

MENDIZABAL, A.
New School for Social Research

MORGENTHAU, HENRY J.
University of Chicago

PETTEE, G. S.
formerly Harvard University

PORTNER, STUART
National Archives; Editor: *Military Affairs*

POTTER, PITMAN B.
Oberlin College; Editor: *American Journal of International Law*

RADER, MELVIN
University of Washington

RODEE, CARLTON C.
University of Southern California

ROSSI, JOSEPH
University of Wisconsin

ROUCEK, JOSEPH S.
Hofstra College

RUMNEY, J.
Newark University

SANDELIUS, W. E.
University of Kansas

SCHERMERHORN, F. A.
Baldwin-Wallace College

SELL, F. C.
Mount Holyoke College

SIBLEY, M. Q.
University of Illinois

WEEKS, O. DOUGLAS
University of Texas

WILSON, FRANCIS G.
University of Illinois

TABLE OF CONTENTS

TWENTIETH CENTURY
POLITICAL THOUGHT

CHAPTER I

EVOLUTIONARY SOCIALISM, SYNDICALISM, GUILD SOCIALISM AND ANARCHISM

GLENN E. HOOVER

In Western Europe and the United States, Marxian socialism had reached the peak of its prestige and power by 1914. In those areas it never completely recovered from the effects of the First World War. Oddly enough, however, that same war enshrined Marxian socialism in the Moscow Kremlin as the state doctrine of the U.S.S.R. Questions raised by the war split the socialist parties of some of the warring nations, and completely disrupted the Second International, with which these parties were affiliated. Outside of Russia, Maxian socialism has never regained its importance, either as an ideology or as a political force.

Although the major socialist parties prior to 1914 were all professedly Marxian, some of their doctrines had been seriously questioned, both by party members and the socialistic sponsors of other radical movements. Some of these critics shared the objectives of the Marxians but differed from them either in their analysis of existing evils, or the immediate policies to be pursued. Others differed with the Marxians over the ultimate form of the regime which they hoped to establish, and particularly on the role to be played by the political state in a socialist society.

As Marxian socialism developed, particularly in its stronghold Germany, it assumed the character of a predominantly political movement, aiming at the state ownership and control of all means of production and distribution, with the possible exception of land. The ownership and control of agricultural land presented difficulties which most of the socialist parties preferred to ignore, lest any program they adopted might alienate peasant support. The dominant role assigned to the political state by the Marxian parties aroused the fear, among both radicals and conservatives, that the triumph of the socialist parties might lead to what is now called a totalitarian state.

THE REVISIONIST MOVEMENT

Marxism is discussed in another chapter, and here we need only recall that, as interpreted by his followers, it assumed the ultimate catastrophic downfall of capitalism, an event which was to mark the end of the revolutionary struggle of the proletariat. In so far as the Marxian doctrine was expressed in the Communist Manifesto—the only one of Marx's writings which was ever widely read—it further declared that the workers "had nothing to lose but their chains," and continued with the somewhat inconsistent prediction that the misery of the workers would increase.

It was unfortunate for Marx's reputation as a prophet that the Manifesto was published in January, 1848, a year in which the economic and political conditions of Europe seemed to justify reckless predictions. The monarchy in France was indeed overthrown, and certain liberal constitutions were granted in other European countries. On the other hand, the Hungarian revolt was suppressed by the Austrian and Russian armies, and with the end of the depression which had precipitated these revolutionary events, Europe became conservative again, and "the "brave boasts of 1848" came to sound a little hollow.

What has been called "the marvellous Nineteenth Century" seemed determined to give the lie to Marxian predictions. Europe prospered; the suffrage was extended in many lands, even to the poorest of the male workers; the nationalist sentiments

---

[1] The disintegration of the revolutionary movement which followed the failure of the uprisings in 1848, and the effect of these defeats on Marx and Engels are well described in Edmund Wilson, *To The Finland Station* (New York: Harcourt Brace), 1940.

of the workers prevailed over their international sympathies, and the proletariat of France, Germany, Britain and Italy toyed with the idea that they might derive some advantage from the imperialistic policies of their governments. The workers showed little disposition to form an international brotherhood and they suspected that if revolutions were attempted they might lose much more than their "chains" with which Marx had so picturesquely endowed them.

For some time after, events had set a different course than the Marxians had predicted. Most of the socialist parties accepted the doctrine of "Das Kapital" as "all but verbally inspired." [2] Organizations are always reluctant to alter their creeds and considerable time must run after the creeds are outworn before they will be formally altered.

The leader in the movement to revise the Marxian doctrine was Edouard Bernstein. His loyalty to the socialist movement could not be questioned. When Bismarck's Anti-Socialist Law of 1878 forced the German movement underground, he went to Switzerland, where for ten years he served as editor of the party organ which was smuggled over the German frontier. When, at the instance of the German government, he was forced to leave Switzerland, he moved the paper to London, where he remained for thirteen years. While there he became the friend of Friedrich Engels, the collaborator and benefactor of the always impoverished Marx. He returned to Germany in 1901 and served for several sessions in the Reichstag.

Although Bernstein never ceased to be a professing socialist, and always retained his high regard for Marx, he resented the tendency of certain socialists to look upon Marx's writings as certain of his contemporaries looked upon the Bible, The Koran, or the Book of Mormon. He questioned some of the Marxian theories and he disliked all talk about "the dictatorship of the proletariat", which, to him, was incompatible with the growing strength of the democratic traditions in Western

---

[2] Bertrand Russell, *Proposed Roads to Freedom* (New York: Henry Holt, 1919), p. 27.

Europe. He believed such phrases only aroused needless opposition to the socialist program.[3]

Bernstein also urged the discontinuance of such clichés as "expropriating the expropriators", as that implied the taking of private property without compensation, which he believed violated sound ethical principles. He believed too, that the socialist doctrines should be made acceptable to patriots who resented the slogan that "the proletarian has no fatherland." His residence in England had also made him aware that the workers were far from being a homogeneous mass. He recognized that the interests of the high paid, skilled workers were often, in the short run at least, in conflict with the interests of the unskilled, and he concluded that for the socialists to rely on too great a degree of working class solidarity was to rely on a broken reed.[4]

Bernstein's chief attack, however, was directed against the "theory of increasing misery" and the prediction of the decline of the middle class. These were matters of fact, rather than vague theory, and he devoted himself to the accumulation of evidence that on these points Marx was wrong. His old friend, Karl Kautsky, felt impelled to lead the orthodox in the suppression of this heresy, which was formally repudiated by the German Social Democratic Party. Despite this official repudiation the German movement lost its original revolutionary ardor, and Bertrand Russell is of the opinion that Bernstein's revisionist movement "at last conquered the bulk of the party." [5]

While Bernstein was leading the Revisionist Movement in Germany, Jean Jaurès (1859-1914) was laboring to make Marxian socialism acceptable to the patriotic citizens of France. He was not distinguished as a theoretician, but his scholarship, his great eloquence and his unquestioned honesty helped to create a strong and unified party. Although nominally Marxian, it was sufficiently moderate to enable it to win adherents even among the French peasants, long noted for their "rugged individualism."

---

[3] Edouard Bernstein, *Evolutionary Socialism* (New York: Huebsch, 1909), p. 146.
[4] *Ibid.*, p. 103.
[5] Bertrand Russell, *Proposed Roads to Freedom* (New York: Holt, 1919), p. 27.

Jaurès worked hard for peace and international solidarity and, for his pains, was shot by a patriotic fanatic at the outbreak of the First World War. He must be given the major part of the credit—or the blame—for modifying Marxian doctrine so that it could win support from Frenchmen of all classes.

THE FABIAN SOCIALISTS

While Bernstein in Germany and Jaurès in France were moderating the policies of their respective socialist parties from within, a group of socialists in London, organized as the Fabian Society, did even more to free the socialist movement from complete subservience to Marxian doctrine. The Fabian Society was organized the year that Marx died (1883), but its purpose was not to do him honor. It was predominantly a "white collar" and "high brow" organization, and soon enrolled an unusual group of young men, including George Bernard Shaw, Sidney Webb and H. G. Wells. These were later to be among the foremost literary celebrities of our time.

The name of the Fabian Society is significant for it derives from the Roman general, Fabius Cunctator ("delayer"), who was first condemned and later praised for his patient maneuvering in his campaign against Hannibal. The way in which the Fabian program and languuage differed from that of Marx in his Communist Manifesto days is shown by the following sections from the "Basis" of their society, to which new members were to subscribe:

"The Fabian Society consists of socialists.

"It therefore aims at the reorganization of Society by the emancipation of Land and Industrial Capital from individual ownership, and the vesting of them in the community for the general benefit. In this way only, can the natural and acquired advantages of the country be equitably shared by the whole people.

"The Society accordingly works for the extinction of private property in land, with equitable consideration of established expectations, and due provision as to the tenure of the home and the homestead; for the transfer to the community, by constitutional methods, of all such industries as can be conducted socially; and for the establishment, as the governing consideration in the regulation of production, distribution and service, of the common good instead of private profit." (From the version adopted in 1919.) [6]

The Fabian Society never tried to secure a large membership, and its importance derived from the distinguished character of its leaders and the excellence of its publications. Of the 212 numbered Tracts published from the beginning of the Society to 1924, Sidney Webb (now Lord Passfield) wrote 43, and G. B. Shaw wrote 14. In addition, each has written books which were published by or in coooperation with the Society, of which the best known is *Fabian Essays in Socialism*, edited by Shaw, which ran into several editions.

The evolutionary and non-Marxian character of Fabian socialism was frankly acknowledged by Shaw, who always reminded his readers that it was a constitutional movement which the most respectable citizen might join, if only he had intelligence enough. He recalls that in the *Fabian Essays,* Marx and the Marxian theory of value, so important to the orthodox, were not even mentioned. Most of the Fabian leaders had read Marx but there is no reason to believe that they were influenced in any way by his life or his work. Instead of playing with phrases such as "the class struggle", "abolishing the wages system", "expropriating the expropraitors", etc. they popularized "the inevitability of gradualness" and they contributed much toward giving the socialist movement in Britain its non-Marxian and non-revolutionary character. [7]

SOCIALISM IN THE UNITED STATES

The socialist movement in the United States has always been essentially an evolutionary one. Although some of the many parties that have arisen have professed their adherence to Marxian doctrine, they have been essentially parties of protest, and have never seriously contemplated the "seizure of power", either by building a majority party or by "direct action."

---

[6] Edward R. Pease, *The History of the Fabian Society, rev. ed.* (International Publishers, New York, 1926), p. 259.

[7] A brilliant and humorous account of the development of Fabian socialism, and its relation to the Marxian variety is to be found in Bernard Shaw, *The Intelligent Woman's Guide to Socialism* (New York: Brentano's, 1928), pp. 465-470.

The American socialist movement has never been able to win the trade union support which contributed so largely to the strength of the socialist parties in Europe. In part this was due to the fact that Samuel Gompers, who dominated the American Federation of Labor until his death in 1924, was violently hostile to socialism. His jibe that "socialism bears the same relation to economics that astrology bears to astronomy" probably continues to reflect the opinion of most of the leaders of organized labor in the United States. By and large they refuse their support to any "third party" movement and support the capitalistic system, asking only for "a fair day's pay for a fair day's work", and more recently, for the recognition of "the right of collective bargaining."

The peaceful platitudes employed to express the general "aims" of American unionists are not based on any fundamental objection to violence. On the contrary, strikes and labor disputes in the United States have resulted in more bloodshed than in any other country in the world, with the possible exception of Czarist Russia. However, to kill a "scab", a company policeman or even a National Guardsman is no indication at all of a desire to start a revolution. So long as classes are reasonably fluid in the United States, property reasonably distributed and the real income of workers relatively high, even professed socialists will be reluctant to overthrow our economic system. Perhaps the recent voluntary dissolution of the Communist Party in the United States is an admission by the most ardent of our Marxians that any American changes in the direction of socialism must result from a peaceful and evolutionary process.

SYNDICALISM

The word syndicalism derives from the French word *syndicat* (trade union). As now employed it means the theories and programs of those revolutionists who would utilize the economic power of industrial unions to destroy capitalism and organize a socialist society. Unlike other radical ideologies, it grew out of the organized labor movement. Usually some theory is first developed, and then an organization is formed to popularize it, but with syndicalism the organization came first. It is of distinctly working-class origin, whereas Marxism, according to Bertrand Russell, is "middle class" and anarchism—surprisingly enough—is of aristocratic origin.[8]

The movement gained its greatest strength in France, where, by the beginning of the present century, syndicalist ideas dominated the Confédération Générale du Travail, which was roughly comparable in structure to the American Federation of Labor. It drew its support from those who dreaded the unlimited powers of the state—even a socialist one—and from those who had lost hope in political socialism. They believed that the workers' political power—ineffective at best—could be exerted only on election days, whereas their economic power could be used continuously, and with crushing effect.

The methods favored by the syndicalists were the strike, boycott, the label and sabotage. The boycott and the union label are devices employed by even the most conservative unions, and the strike too is an accepted weapon. However, the syndicalists used the strike not to secure some concessions, but to hasten the destruction of the capitalist system and to establish the rule of the proletariat.

Sabotage is also a word of French origin which is traced to *sabot* (wooden shoe), and its present meaning may derive either from the practice of throwing a wooden shoe into a machine to disrupt operations, or to the slow and clumsy movements which result from wearing wooden shoes. As presently employed, the term is wider in scope than the Scotch expression "ca' canny" (go cautiously) or the more familiar "soldiering", the connotation of which should not, perhaps, be stressed in time of war. The term was also applied to the deliberate destruction of productive equipment and other acts which have always been forbidden by both common and statutory law.

The syndicalist policies of the French trade unions brought them into sharp conflict with their government on several occasions. In the railway strike of 1910, the government headed by

---

[8] Bertrand Russell, *Proposed Roads to Freedom* (New York: Holt, 1919), p. 70.

M. Briand, a professed socialist, arrested the Strike Committee, called all the railway workers to the colors under the French military service law, replaced strikers with soldiers, and completely defeated the unions. Thereafter they directed their propaganda against militarism and nationalism. From their experience they concluded that both must be destroyed before their revolution could be carried through.

The syndicalist movement in the United States was represented by the Industrial Workers of the World (I. W. W.) which was first organized by socialists in 1905. Three years later it embarked on a program aimed at organizing all workers into industrial unions, preferably "one big union", which would then employ the syndicalist tactics of strike, sabotage, etc. It never had a large membership and was never so strong as its enemies feared it to be. However, in the mills and camps of the Northwest, in the grain states, and among the immigrants of certain Eastern cities, it organized workers who had been neglected by the older unions. When the authorities attempted to prevent their propaganda activities, the "free speech" fights which resulted were often more dramatic than their strikes, and they aroused an opposition which was often fanatical and panicky.

Before and during the First World War, the I. W. W. was anti-militarist. It opposed the entrance of the United States into the war, and after we became a belligerent, it organized and sponsored strikes which hindered the war effort. The Federal government promptly answered with the arrest of 166 of the leaders, 93 of whom, including their leader, "Big Bill" Haywood, were convicted and sentenced. After the war, several states, led by Idaho in 1917, enacted so-called "Criminal Syndicalism Laws", and prosecutions continued. In California alone, from 1919 to 1924, 531 individuals were indicted, 164 convicted and 128 were sentenced for terms of from one to fourteen years.

As a result of the relentless opposition of the various states, and disagreement over organizational forms and tactics, the I. W. W. "splintered" into ineffective units. Many of its leaders became active in the newly formed Communist party and the "One Big Union" became but a legendary rebel in the history of American

labor. It led the way in organizing Negroes, immigrants and unskilled workers, and its arguments for industrial unionism may
have helped the C. I. O. to organize the mass production industries. It marked the flood-tide of revolutionary unionism in the
United States. With the passing of the I. W. W., the American
unions entered the more profitable but less heroic era of "collective
bargaining", and their eyes lost the vision of the workers' utopia.

GUILD SOCIALISM

Fashions change in the realm of radical thought, and if no
new aims or tactics can be discovered, the old ones must at least
be given new names. Moreover a certain insularity of mind makes
it advisable to give native names to any foreign doctrines that
may be imported. For these and other reasons, many British workers in the first quarter of the present century who had lost their
faith in political action and governmental ownership, developed
what they called Guild Socialism.

The movement was originally a reactionary one in the sense
that many of its pioneers hoped to restore the medieval guilds,
with certain modifications necessitated by modern conditions.
Ideas of this sort had been popularized by the eloquent critics
of modern industrialism, Carlyle and Ruskin, both of whom believed that the "way out" was the "way back." [9] The spectacular
revival of the Roman Catholic Church in England during the last
half of the Nineteenth Century contributed to the idealization of
Medieval institutions, including the guilds. The well-known Catholic writers, G. K. Chesterton and Hilaire Belloc looked wist-
fully at the economic institutions which prevailed when the
Church was at the height of its power, and they were indefatigable in their denunciation of collectivism, which they thought
would result inevitably in the "servile state."

In 1915 the National Guilds League was formed as a propaganda body. It never had more than five hundred members but
these included such effective writers and speakers as R. H. Tawney, Bertrand Russell, H. N. Brailsford and G. D. H. Cole. The

---

[9] Niles Carpenter, *Guild Socialism* (New York: Appleton, 1922), p. 46.

League issued numerous pamphlets of high quality and published a monthly paper. Various members wrote books expounding the new doctrine, contributed articles to newspapers and periodicals and furnished speakers for unions and other interested groups. Like the Fabian Society, from which it drew some of its members, it created an intellectual ferment quite out of proportion to its numbers. The experience of both organizations shows that a very small group with brains and the gift of expression can influence an entire nation and even the whole of the literate world.

The pro-guild sentiment in the established trade unions led to the organization of guilds which were to operate as business units. These organizations of craftsmen were to furnish their own capital and management, and by eliminating the entrepreneur, were to distribute to their working members what would otherwise have gone to those who performed the entrepreneuric functions. The largest of such organizations was the National Building Guild which ultimately absorbed most of the local guilds in the house-building industry. At the close of the war, when the government housing scheme became operative, several of these guilds were the low bidders on public housing projects. So long as the government advanced funds as the work progressed they were able to operate, but when they were compelled to operate on their own credit and capital, they were soon forced into bankruptcy. With the collapse of the building guilds, the attempt of the English workers to give practical life to their guild socialist ideas came to an end.

The guild movement failed not only because of the difficulty of securing capital and credit, but because it soon became divided over the desirability of remaking Britain after the Soviet pattern. Another dispute arose over the "social credit" scheme associated with the name of Major C. H. Douglas. The fact that the guild movement could appeal to such divergent groups as Catholic medievalists and revolutionary unionists was an original source of strength, but in the long run the heterogeneity of its supporters was an element of weakness. Guild socialism survived only in the realm of the mind, but in this realm it exerts a continuing influence on the British workers, strengthening their opposition to "statism", and making them wary of any socialist program which would concentrate all economic power in the hands of the government.

ANARCHISM

Anarchism is the least understood—or rather the most misunderstood—of all the revolutionary ideologies. The popular conceptions of it are generally inaccurate and frequently grotesque. Although some of its leading exponents, such as Prince Kropotkin and Count Tolstoy, are among the most admirable characters which the revolutionary movements have produced, the name of their philosophy is still used to frighten the timid and the naïve. The reason for this confusion is that the anarchist movement has been fed by many streams and the word "anarchist" must be given a meaning broad enough to apply to all who apply the term to themselves.

In the absence of an accepted definition of anarchism we shall summarize the points on which the anarchists have found the most general agreement. They include the following:

1. The social, moral and economic evils of the modern world are intolerable, but they can neither be cured nor alleviated by any action of the state, which is always an instrument of personal or class domination.
2. Human nature is essentially good, but is corrupted by evil institutions, chiefly the state and the Church.
3. The division of labor and other forms of economic cooperation should always be on a voluntary basis.
4. The new society can only result from a revolutionary change in the individual, his institutional environment, or both.

Many beliefs and doctrines which cannot be called anarchistic nevertheless have contributed to the formulation of anarchism in its modern form. For instance, the belief in the Golden Age—widely held by the ancients—has suggested to many that the evil and injustice which they observed could be traced to political and social institutions. A quaint but typical expression of this belief is found in the writings of Chuang Tzu, a Chinese philosopher who lived about 300 B.C. He wrote:

The people have certain natural instincts:—to weave and clothe themselves, to till and feed themselves. These are common to all humanity, and all are agreed thereon. Such instincts are called "Heaven-sent".

And so in the days when natural instincts prevailed, men moved quietly and gazed steadily. . . . All things were produced, each for its own proper sphere. Birds and beasts multiplied; trees and shrubs grew up. The former might be led by the hand; you could climb up and peep into the raven's nest. For then man dwelt with birds and beasts, and all creation was one. There were no distinctions of good and bad men. Being all equally without knowledge, their virtue could not go astray. Being all equally without evil desires, they were in a state of natural integrity, the perfection of human existence.

But when Sages appeared, tripping up people over charity and fettering them with duty to their neighbor, doubt found its way into the world. And then, with their gushing over music and fussing over ceremony, the empire became divided against itself.[10]

The nostalgic character of anarchist thought is particularly prevalent in Spain. There the peasants, anarchists included, seem to yearn for the good old days of the era of Spanish dominance, a more recent period which Spaniards consider their Golden Age (Siglo de Oro). It has also been suggested that Spanish peasants who describe themselves as anarchists, would welcome some such free and communal life as is found among the Berber tribesmen of North Africa.[11]

Hostility to the state, particularly to the coercive features of it, is the core of anarchist doctrine, but it is also found in many of the more exalted and heretical religious sects which flourished during the later Middle Ages. Many of them believed the State to be sinful by nature, and their members were discouraged from serving in the army or performing any of the duties usually required of citizens. Some of them, such as The Brothers and Sisters of the Free Spirit, showed distinct anarchistic tendencies. Their doctrine of freedom extended to relations between the sexes, and led to their ruthless extermination, although their influence can be traced to later sects which developed in France,

---

[10] "Musings of a Chinese Mystic," in *The Wisdom of the East Series*, edited by L. Cranmer-Byng and Dr. S. A. Kapadiat (London: John Murray, 1906), p. 67.
[11] Gerald Brenan, *The Spanish Labyrinth* (New York: Macmillan, 1943), Ch. VIII.

Belgium, Germany and Switzerland. The opposition to bearing arms, still manifested by the Mennonites, the Dukhobors and similar Christian sects, is in line with the older tradition.

The doctrine that an individual should be free, even from state control, also drew support from the anti-monarchists of the Sixteenth and Seventeenth Centuries, some of whom insisted that an individual may rightfully determine for himself if a tyrant should be destroyed. The Diggers and The Levellers in England in the Seventeenth Century subscribed to a doctrine of natural rights which were inherent in the individual and therefore not subject to state limitation. This opinion was shared by many of the French Encyclopedists, and is embodied in the oft-quoted distich of Diderot:

> La nature n'a fait ni serviteurs ni maitres
> Je ne veux ni donner ni recevoir des lois.

It reappears in part in the belief of the Physiocrats in the Natural Order, and through the writings of Adam Smith was given wide currency in the world of English letters.

The anarchist doctrine that each individual has rights of which he cannot be justly deprived by any government, is clearly stated in our Declaration of Independence. In the Constitution which was later adopted, and especially in the Bill of Rights which was promptly attached to it, certain matters were designated as outside the scope of governmental regulation. The Fathers of our Constitution were not only concerned with setting up the machinery of our national government, but they were perhaps equally concerned with limiting its power and preserving what they thought were the rights of the individual, not only as against individual tyrants, but even against the majority. They, like the anarchists, feared that the majority might prove to be the most implacable of tyrants.

In the present century, the self-styled anarchists are pretty largely concentrated in workers' organizations. Before the rise of Fascism in Italy and Spain, they gave a distinct flavor to the labor movement in those countries, and in Spain, they were active in organizing the unsuccessful resistance to Franco in the recent civil war in which the Spanish Republic was overthrown. The importance of anarchism in the Latin countries of Europe is usually attributed to the influence of Bakunin, the Russian anarchist nobleman who competed with Karl Marx for leadership of the revolutionary workers' movement in Europe, and to Proudhon, a French writer who is reputed to have been the first to make anarchism a conscious mass movement.

Anarchism has always been primarily an exotic movement in the United States. Its propaganda has been carried on chiefly by Spaniards, Russians and Italians, and has been largely directed to their own nationality groups. Somewhat earlier a distinguished German anarchist, Johann Most, published an anarchist paper in New York, but the work among German immigrants was pretty largely destroyed when certain anarchist leaders were convicted of participation in the Haymarket riots in Chicago in 1886.

In the decades before the first World War the two most active anarchist propagandists in this country were Emma Goldman and Alexander Berkman, who with other radicals of Russian extraction were deported to Russia in 1919. Even the indefatigable and somewhat gullible Joint Committee of the New York Legislature, in the red-baiting days of 1920, reported on American anarchism as follows:

In the United States the activities of the anarchists played no significant part in the development of the radical movement until the outbreak of the war. Their numbers were not great and were confined largely to the foreign elements of the working class, notably the Italians, Spanish and Russians.[12]

Although no important organization has ever formally subscribed to the anarchist doctrines, some of these doctrines, such as atheism, are widely held. Practically all the recognized anarchist leaders with the exception of Count Leo Tolstoy, have been materialists and atheists, and it is hardly a coincidence that anti-clerical sentiments are most prevalent in France, Spain and Italy, where the anarchist movements have been the most active. The anti-clericals have at times been extremely influential in the Latin states of Europe, and more recently in Mexico. Probably only a few of the anti-clericals agree with the anarchists that "religion

---

[12] New York State, *Revolutionary Radicalism* (Albany, 1920), Vol. I, p. 843.

is the opium of the people", for many of them are deists in the Nineteenth Century tradition and some are even professing Catholics. However, in any mass struggle against the established church, the atheistic doctrines to which anarchists so generally subscribe have been widely disseminated.

Anti-clericalism has never reached significant proportions in countries such as the United States, where no religious sect has succeeded in establishing dominance. Even here, however, the religious indifference of the masses, so often reported by Church leaders, must encourage anarchists in their belief that atheism will ultimately find general acceptance. It is one of their doctrines to which the "rich and well-born" subscribe as readily as the poor, and some believe it is more prevalent in the higher strata of society than in the lower.

The hostility to all forms of state interference, although an essential of the anarchist faith, is held by many who would indignantly deny that they approved of any anarchistic doctrine whatsoever. In the nations which still adhere to a relatively free economy, the opposition to regimentation and state interference is now led by business men and liberals, many of whom use arguments to which every anarchist would subscribe. Fortunately the supporters of the various "liberty leagues" who regard Washington and the White House as the source of all their woe are comfortably unaware of the presence of their ideological bed-fellows. It is, however, one of the paradoxes of our time that the anti-state doctrines, which the anarchists propagated so ineffectually, are now disseminated on a grand scale by that very class which the anarchists hoped to destroy.

BIBLIOGRAPHY

BEER, M. *History of British Socialism.* London: G. Bell & Sons, 1929. This is the standard work on the history of British socialism. It contains an objective treatment of the Fabian Society and shows how British socialism evolved into a movement.

BERNSTEIN, EDOUARD. *Evolutionary Socialism.* New York: Huebsch, 1909. The author was the leader in the "revisionist" movement which aimed at the modification or rejection of many of the theories of Marx.

BRENAN, GERALD. *The Spanish Labyrinth.* New York: Macmillan, 1943. This book gives an excellent account of the Anarchist movement in Spain, the country in which it has won the greatest popular support.

BRISSENDEN, PAUL F. *The I. W. W.* New York: Columbia University Press, 1936. The definitive work on the I. W. W. to date of publication.

CARPENTER, NILES. *Guild Socialism.* New York: Appleton, 1922. This is an objective account of the Guild Socialist movement in Great Britain.

COLE, G. D. H. *Self Government In Industry.* London: Bell, 1920. An argument for guild socialism by one who was its foremost advocate in Great Britain.

EASTMAN, MAX. *Stalin's Russia and The Crisis In Socialism.* New York: Norton, 1940. A profound criticism of Marxism by an able veteran of the American Socialist movement.

KROPOTKIN, P. *Fields, Factories and Workshops.* New York: Nelson, 1912. The author, a Russian prince converted to Anarchism, applies his philosophy to the economic problems of our times.

LAIDLER, HARRY W. *A History of Socialist Thought.* New York: Crowell, 1927. A sympathetic and objective treatment of socialist thinkers from the earliest times to date.

LEVINE, LOUIS. *Syndicalism In France.* New York: Longmans, Green, 1914. The standard work on this subject by a competent American scholar.

NOMAD, MAX. *Apostles of Revolution.* Boston: Little, Brown & Co., 1939. Contains brilliant chapters on three anarchists, Bakunin, Nechayev, and Johann Most.

PEASE, EDWARD R. *The History of the Fabian Society,* rev. ed. New York: International Publishers, 1926. The story of the Society by one of the veteran Fabians.

RUSSELL, BERTRAND. *Proposed Roads To Freedom.* New York: Henry Holt, 1919. A brilliant discussion of socialism, anarchism and syndicalism by a distinguished English philosopher.

SHAW, BERNARD. *The Intelligent Woman's Guide To Socialism.* New York: Brentano's, 1928. A brilliant presentation of a non-Marxian brand of socialism which can only be described as Shavian.

TOLSTOI, LEV NIKOLAEVICH. *What Then Must We Do?* Oxford Press, 1936. The social program of the greatest Christian Anarchist of our time.

CHAPTER II

SOVIET COMMUNISM

The historical theory insists that the "material" conditions of life, taken as a whole, *primarily* determine historical events.

MELVIN RADER

THE MATERIALISTIC INTERPRETATION OF HISTORY

Although my primary purpose is to present an objective interpretation of the political doctrines of the Union of Soviet Socialist Republics, my account would be largely unintelligible without a summary of the underlying interpretation of history. This historical and political body of doctrine consists essentially of the theories of Karl Marx and Friedrich Engels as interpreted and extended by Nicolai Lenin (Vladimir Ilyich Ulianov) and Joseph Stalin (Joseph Djugashvili).

Nothing is more fundamental in determining the behaviour of a community than the way it obtains its living and the kind of living it obtains. Although the theory recognizes other "material conditions", such as the biological and the geographical, the economic factor is regarded as the most fundamental.

In contrast to thorough-going economic determinists, Maxists believe that culture and economics are dialectically interactive and interdependent, and that a *purely* economic explanation is an illegitimate abstraction from the concrete fullness of history. Although art, morality, science, religion, politics, etc., are based on the productive system, they react upon one another and upon the economic foundation. Thus there is an interaction of unequal forces, of which the economic is much the more powerful and decisive, but not alone active.

All history, except in the most primitive society and the future communist system, is dominated by economic class conflicts: between freeman and slave, patrician and plebian, lord and serf, guild master and journeyman, or wage earner and capitalist. These conflicts reach a fierce crescendo in the transition from one form of society to another, for example, in the supplanting of feudalism by capitalism. Revolution is the destruction of the rule of one class through the appropriation of political and economic power by another class.

In modern industrial countries there are at least five classes: peasants, petty bourgeoisie, capitalist bourgeoisie, landed aristocracy, and proletariat. The fundamental class struggle, however, is being waged by the proletariat and the capitalist bourgeoisie. Other classes, although they complicate and retard the division into these two great hostile camps, are subordinate to the major contestants.

There are five *main* stages in the development of class relations and the productive system in human history: primitive communism, slavery, feudalism, capitalism, and, in the future, a return, at a higher level, to communism. These stages are not sharply demarcated; they overlap and interpenetrate, and development through every stage is not necessarily inevitable. Marx and Engels, for example, expressed the belief that, under some circumstances, Russia might be able to realize socialism without passing through the advanced stages of capitalism.[1]

This phase of the theory was developed by Lenin, who opposed the more conventional interpretation of Marxism, that it necessarily envisages a uniform evolution in every country, passing through the stages of small competitive capitalism, to large-scale monopoly capitalism, and finally on to socialism. Lenin, in contrast, insisted that the crisis of capitalism is world-wide and the old order will burst apart at "the weakest links in the chain". These links are not necessarily in the more advanced capitalistic countries but perhaps in the more backward and dependent areas

[1] *Cf.* Soloman F. Bloom, *The World of Nations* (New York: Columbia University Press, 1941), XII; and Marx, *Selected Works* (New York: International Publishers, 1935), II, pp. 667-685.

that have suffered most from international warfare and imperialistic exploitation. Upon the basis of this interpretation, Lenin believed that Russia would be in the vanguard of the revolutionary movement.

In its most general aspects, however, the transition from capitalism to socialism is said to conform to a universal pattern of mutation. Marx and his Russian disciples, basing themselves on Hegel's *Logic*, maintain that insignificant and imperceptible quantitative changes, at certain nodal points, are transformed into basic qualitative changes. "Every metal," for example, "has its temperature of incandescence and fusion; every liquid its definite freezing and boiling point at a given pressure . . . ; and finally also every gas has its critical point at which it can be liquified by pressure and cooling." [2] Likewise, such mutations occur in organic growth and evolution; and the development from feudalism to capitalism, or from capitalism to socialism, represents profound mutation in the social sphere. The fallacy of political reformism is to overlook this law of development: it expects to modify, little by little, the structure of capitalism, and fails to realize that, at a certain point, the whole system becomes unstable, enters into grim conflict with opposing forces, and becomes radically transformed in the ensuing revolutionary struggle.

The transformation from one form of society to another not only involves a revolutionary change in class relations but, largely as a consequence of this economic transformation, a profound change in politics, art, religion, philosophy, science, and morality. The dominant ideas and institutions of any society are the ideas and institutions of the dominant economic class. The historian, mindful of these facts, should look to the productive system for the primary causes of cultural transformations.

This system can be analyzed into two main components: first, the "productive forces"—the human labor power, machinery, materials, and techniques embodied in the processes of production; and second, the "productive relations"—the class structure expressed in the control of industry and the distribution of wealth.

---

[2] Engels, *Dialectics of Nature* (New York: International Publishers, 1940), p. 30.

The historical process is determined mainly by the tendency of the productive forces to develop more rapidly than the productive relations. A profound disequilibrium ultimately results: the class institutions act as "fetters" upon the developing techniques. When the crisis reaches an intense pitch of suffering and conflict, the class which suffers most from this disequilibrium finally by revolutionary action destroys the fetters of the old society and establishes its own order upon the basis of new productive relations.

CULTURE AND IDEOLOGY

Critics have often misunderstood the role of culture and ideology in the Marxian-Soviet theory of history. Hence this phase of historical materialism must be stated in a little more detail.

According to the theory, the system of production determines the general character of political, social, and cultural processes. Human beings, however, are often unaware of the material roots of their ideas and activities. They fancy that what they do and believe is the result of pure thought, and do not enquire into the profound conditioning effect of their material environment.

When a concept is caused mainly by economic and material forces, but appears to the mind which entertains it as an idea springing directly from the intellect itself and from the pre-existing stock of ideas—it is called by the Marxists an "ideological concept." Idealists, and indeed most historians, fail to recognize the very great extent to which ideas are thus economically conditioned. They think of philosophy, morals, religion, law, and other forms of culture as having an independent history, whereas these have no history, no development *in and of themselves*, but only as part of a vast social process.

Since nature and society are conceived as an integrated and interrelated evolving whole, any aspect of that whole—including economics, politics, religion, art, etc.—cannot be understood in isolation. The Marxian-Soviet theorists preserve the Hegelian doctrine that no "thing" taken in isolation is wholly real and that no proposition taken in isolation is wholly true. But whereas for Hegel the totality, within which truth and reality are found, is the rational system of an all-embracing Absolute Mind, for the Marxists this totality is a nexus of material entities and evolving organisms, eventuating, at the highest level, in conscious and collective human development: in the historical process which has become conscious in the minds of its creators.

One must not conclude that, because this theory denies an independent development to the various cultural spheres, it also denies them any effect upon history. Although brought into existence mainly by economic factors, an ideology "may react on its environment and even on its own causes." [3]

The subtlety of Marx's theory is indicated by his doctrine of the non-uniformity of historical development. Although all phases of the historical process are interdependent, their rates of change vary, and progress in one phase may be attended by decadence in another. For example, capitalist production, even in its progressive and expanding phase, is "hostile to certain branches of spiritual production, such as art and poetry." Hence we cannot make "the lower sphere the measure of the higher one".[4]

THE THEORY OF THE STATE

Marx and Lenin, in contrast to Hegel who contended that the State alone provides a just balance between the contending interests in society, maintained that it is primarily an organ of class domination. Stated baldly, its chief function is the creation of an "order" which legalizes and perpetuates the oppression of one or more classes by another.

The nature of the State is indicated by its origin. The earliest type of economy—hunting, fishing, and gathering—called for relatively few tools, and these were produced and used by communal family groups, which gradually expanded into gentile clans. Since there was no surplus wealth, society was not divided

---

[3] Marx and Engles, *Correspondence* (New York: International Publishers, 1936), p. 512.

[4] Marx, *Theorien über den Mehrwert* (Berlin, Dietz, 1923), I, pp. 381-2; and Marx and Engels, *Historisch-Kritische Gesamtausgabe* (Berlin, Marx-Engels, Verlag, 1927), I, p. 218. See also the Soviet theorist, Mikhail Lifshitz, *The Philosophy of Art of Karl Marx* (New York, Critic's Group, 1938), pp. 68-69.

into rich and poor, exploiters and exploited. Because of the extremely low level of productive forces, however, this was a destitute state of human life, and its abolition, although characterized by the rise of a master class, was a major step in human progress.[5] The change came with the development of the productive forces. As pasturage and agriculture gradually developed an economic surplus accumulated, individual family life and private property were introduced, the rich began to dominate the poor and the males to dominate the females. The State then arose to enforce the control by the privileged class.

In ancient times, the State guaranteed the rule of masters over slaves, and in feudal times, the dominance of lords over serfs; in our own society, its main function has been, first, to secure to the capitalist class the possession of the means of production, and second, to compete with other States, perhaps by means of war, in acquiring a larger share of raw materials and markets throughout the world. The coercive agents for achieving this dominance, the police and the military force, are at the very roots of the State.

Since the State protects the interests of the ruling class, there must be severe limits upon democracy, particularly when the existing order is severely threatened. Marx and Lenin pointed to the bloody liquidation of the Paris Commune, the first proletarian government, as terrifying evidence that governments become grimly dictatorial when the class structure of society is seriously threatened.

When an economy is prosperously expanding, the ruling class can afford to make concessions to the workers, and something like a balance of power between contending classes, may temporarily be achieved. The role of the State under these circumstances is, within limits, to moderate the collisions between classes rather than to repress the subject classes. But eventually, and especially

---

[5] *Cf.* the article by L. A. Leontiev and other leading Soviet economists, "Political Economy in the Soviet Union," *Science and Society,* vol. viii, no. 2 (Spring, 1944), pp. 115-6. This article also discounts the influence of the form of the family upon primitive communism.

during crises, the coercive dominance of the ruling class will plainly assert itself.

The coercive dominance of the ruling class is achieved not only within the domestic economy but also within colonial territories. "Imperialism," Marx declared, "is the most prostitute and the ultimate form of State power" under capitalism.[6] This phase of Marxian theory was worked out much more fully by Lenin. He believed that capitalism has entered its final "imperialistic stage," in which its contradictions have become fully manifest. In his famous book, *Imperialism: The Highest Stage of Capitalism* (1916), he analyzes the rise and development of capitalistic monopolies (cartels, syndicates, trusts, etc.), and the correlative increase in the power and scope of "finance capital"—or, in other words, of the great investment bankers. Industrial and finance capital are being united under a single directorate, and are now working in close cooperation with the capitalistic State, which has become increasingly militarized and bureaucratic. These changes usher in the era of tariffs, quotas, artificial price-fixing, and restrictive trade agreements, in consequence of which the expanding productive forces come into ever intenser conflict with the forms of capitalistic concentration. In the attempt to find a way out of this impasse, the monopolists feverishly search for cheaper labor, raw materials, and new markets; and the nations, controlled by these capitalistic interests, enter into a fierce imperialistic struggle for a division and a redivision of areas to exploit. The conflict inevitably culminates in world war, which deepens the crisis and prepares the way for proletarian revolution.

In general, the force making for such revolutionary change, as we have seen, is the conflict between the dynamic productive forces and the static class relations. Political power is directly implicated in this conflict, because the State is the primary agency which enforces class stratification. The proletariat, in its revolutionary drive to change the class basis of society, must therefore capture the organs of political domination. Victory will be won only after protracted struggle and perhaps many defeats.

---

[6] Marx, *The Civil War in France* (New York: International Publishers, 1933), p. 39.

Socialists and Communists waged a bitter feud over the question whether the transition to socialism need be violent. The theorists of the Second International, such as Bernstein, maintained that the change can take place peacefully, and sought support in such pronouncements as Marx's famous speech at Amsterdam on the Morrow of the Hague Congress of the First International (1872). The spokesmen of the Third International, such as Lenin, argued that the transition cannot occur without a violent struggle against the entrenched forces of privilege, and emphasized passages in Marx and Engels which bear out this view. Both sides obtained a certain amount of comfort and support from the original Marxian texts.

After the revolution, according to both Marx and Lenin, there will still be a difficult and perhaps long transitional period before a communist society can be securely established. This is the "socialist" phase of collectivist construction, sometimes called the "first stage of communism," before a world-wide classless society has been achieved. In this transitional period, armies and police forces must be maintained, and repression must be sternly exercised, to combat the threats of counter-revolution and war and to insure disciplined advance toward complete communism. The State takes the form of "the dictatorship of the proletariat."

Although a great deal has been written by later theorists and critics concerning the meaning of this phrase, Marx and Engels used it but rarely. It is used frequently, however, by Lenin and Stalin. In essence, it means the unmasked, coercive rule of the proletarian class, but in form this rule can be as democratic as the safety of the new revolutionary regime, which Marx, Lenin, and Stalin believed should be preserved *at all costs*.

Very little is said in the original Marxian texts about the nature of a socialist State, but it is indicated that the existing political machinery must be fundamentally transformed.[7] Political and economic institutions will more completely interpenetrate, and the workers, through their representatives and communal councils, will determine public policy. The political organization of the

---

[7] *Cf.* Marx, *The Civil War in France* (New York: International Publishers, 1933), section iii.

Paris Commune is considered the model of a new proletarian State.

Lenin insisted that the Revolution necessarily demands a complete shattering of the bourgeois State apparatus, and that a new Soviet State, based upon worker's councils ("soviets"), and directed by a single vanguard party of disciplined members, must take its place. Unlike Marx, he was in a position to carry his ideals into execution. Features of the original Soviet system, as organized under Lenin's leadership, were unity of legislative and executive power, representation not only of localities but also of vocations, and indirect election of higher Soviets. These features were substantially changed by the 1936 Constitution, which abolished indirect election, broadened the franchise, and organized representation upon the basis of nationalities and regions rather than vocations.

According to the Marxian theory, which was accepted by the Soviet State, the economic system under the workers' control will be reorganized upon the principle, not of production for profit, but socially planned production for use. Industry will be in the hands of the government or non-profit making cooperatives. The full productive capacity of society, no longer fettered by an obsolete profit system, will be employed to meet common human needs. Step by step, the remnants of class-stratification will be eliminated.

As long as there is economic scarcity and the need for special incentives, however, there must be a system of differential wages adjusted to the productivity of the workers. The principle of distribution will be based on the motto of Saint Simon: "From each according to his capacity, to each what he produces." The unequal incomes, however, will be controlled in the public interest and supplemented by a larger number of social services, such as public schools, public medicine, old age and accident insurance, etc.

When the era of abundance has been securely established, a more generous system of distribution can be inaugurated. The new principle will be the ideal of Louis Blanc: "From each according to his ability, to each according to his need." This will be the communist stage of uncoerced cooperative production and widest equalitarian sharing. When all the springs of cooperative wealth are thus gushing freely, industry will serve the all-round development of the individual, and mankind will pass from "the realm of necessity into the realm of freedom."

Socialism or "the first stage of communism" will thus gradually develop into "the second stage of communism," the cooperative commonwealth organized upon a worldwide basis. When the last remnants of the old class antagonisms have disappeared, political coercion will be unnecessary. Genuine freedom—political, economic, and intellectual—will be realized, and the coercive State will "wither away." Conflicts will no doubt continue, but they will involve the peaceful clash of minds rather than the violent contest of arms.[8]

THE SOVIET UNION IN TRANSITION

The above summary represents the classical heritage of Marxian-Leninist theory, which has served as the basis for launching the great Soviet experiments. Recent events, however, have involved profound modifications in this body of doctrine.

Even before Lenin's death in January, 1924, an intense struggle was brewing between Leon Trotsky and Joseph Stalin. Trotsky, a brilliant Jew and a Menshevik, had been Vice-President of the first Soviet during the abortive Russian Revolution of 1905. Subsequently he lived in exile until after the March Revolution of 1917, and joined the Bolsheviks only at that late date. After the October Revolution, he won a distinguished reputation as Foreign Minister, diplomatic negotiator at Brest Litovsk, and, above all, as organizer and commander of the Red Army. From the beginning, he espoused a theory of "permanent revolution," according to which revolutionary action in any one country is merely a stage in world-wide revolution. Internationalism, he was convinced, is the necessary foundation of all advance; and the attempt to achieve socialism nationally—even in as big a country

---

[8] Cf. Marx, *Critique of the Gotha Programme* (New York: International Publishers, 1933), and Lenin, *The State and Revolution* (New York: International Publishers, 1932), for the basic political theory.

as Russia—would necessarily mean a retrogression to a lower economic stage.

Stalin is a man of very different calibre and belief. Reared as a Georgian, his outlook has been comparatively provincial, and he has never lived outside of Russia. From the outset he has been a Bolshevik, and, relatively speaking, a nationalist. His first important publication was a defense of the concept of nationalism ("Marxism and the National Question," 1913), and his first official post in the Soviet Government was as People's Commissar for Nationalities, a position in which his lifelong interest in nationalism could find expression. When Lenin died, he was in the exceedingly strategic position of being General Secretary of the Communist Party.

After a struggle of several years duration that profoundly shook the Party, he won a decisive victory over the Trotskyist opposition, perhaps chiefly because he was master of the Party machine. Although Trotsky found powerful allies in such men as Kamenev, Zinoviev, Radek, and Bukharin, he was driven into exile, and most of his collaborators ultimately faced the firing squad. It required, however, the great treason trials and purges to achieve the liquidation of the Trotskyist opposition, which evidently employed all the ruses of conspiracy and secret insurrection against Stalin's regime. Even in exile, until his assassination in 1940 in Mexico, Trotsky continued his anti-Stalinist agitation, and his followers tried to form the nucleus of a "Fourth International", which includes the "Socialist Workers' Party of America" and a similar group in England. These Parties are still maintaining the Trotskyist thesis that present-day Russia is being ruled by a bureaucratic caste system inimical to the "Leninist ideals" of socialism and world revolution.

The fundamental policies of Stalin can be indicated only in the broadest outline. Whereas Trotsky clamored for world revolution as indispensable to socialist construction, Stalin instituted the great five-year plans to demonstrate that socialism can be built in a single country. For the first time in history, the economic system of a great nation was brought under the control of a single plan. A daring program was evolved by the Central Planning Commission in Moscow to transform a backward and semi-feudal country into an industrialized and socialist commonwealth.

Under the successive five-year plans, three colossal revolutions have been carried out. First, an agricultural revolution substituted large-scale collective and mechanized farming in place of small-scale individual methods. Second, an industrial revolution rapidly built up "heavy industries", such as iron and steel and machine-making plants, and thereby achieved a swift extension and mechanization of Soviet industry. Third, a military revolution resulted from the technical mobilization of virtually the whole population for total warfare, and from the primary stress upon defense industries, which expanded two or three times more rapidly than industry as a whole.

Perhaps no leader but Stalin had the icy nerves and steel determination to achieve a socialist planned economy at the cost of such a drastic uprooting of humanity as necessarily attended this program; but without such profound changes the Soviet Union could not have survived the Second World War and, in consequence, the Axis might have imposed its will upon all nations.

While Stalin's administration was thus building socialism in a single country, his nationalism also found expression in the creation of a new type of "multi-national State". According to a definition he formulated as early as 1913, "a nation is an historically evolved, stable community of language, territory, economic life, and psychological make-up manifested in a community of culture." [9] Upon the basis of this definition, he distinguished various national areas within the borders of Russia, such as Georgia, White Russia, Lithuania, the Ukraine, etc. He maintained that culture within the workers' State should be national in form and socialist in content, with wide autonomy for national regions within the Union. In pursuance of this ideal, the Soviet Government has encouraged a remarkable diversity of language and folk culture. Even backward tribes, which formerly had no written language, have been supplied with native alphabets, grammars, and written literature. The changes introduced into the Soviet Consti-

---

[9] Stalin, *Marxism and the National Question* (New York, International Publishers, 1942), p. 12.

tution in February, 1944, granting to each constituent republic the right to engage in diplomatic relations with foreign nations and to maintain separate military contingents, represent a further expression of the multi-national policy of the Soviet Union. All such "autonomy", of course, is within a socialist economy integrated by a monolithic Party and by comprehensive planning agencies.

The new Soviet nationalism has also found expression in the dissolution of the Communist International, the greatly intensified appreciation of Russian history and national traditions, the upsurge of patriotism during Russia's struggle against the Axis armies, and the encouragement of political accord and cultural interchange among the Slavic peoples. This nationalism, however, is not to be interpreted as a reversion to Czarist imperialism and pan-Slavism, nor as a new form of "red imperialism" driving toward future wars. There is no good evidence that Soviet nationalism is counter-revolutionary or anti-international, nor that it is contrary to Stalin's fundamental policy of building "socialism in a single country". Although doubtless the leaders of the Soviet Union would like to see socialism spread, they evidently do not intend to promote this objective by violent revolutionary interventionism or militarist expansion. After the Second World War, they will wish to rebuild their shattered cities and farms and to resume the great tasks of socialist construction.[10]

Within the limits imposed by a disciplined one-party government, the Soviet Union has moved toward a broad social and economic democracy. Especially remarkable is the extended conception of human rights embodied in the Soviet Constitution—the right to remunerative work, provision for motherhood, rest and holidays, free public education, free public medicine, economic and social security, etc., without distinction of race, sex, or class. Also noteworthy, in the opinion of a number of observers, is the amount of Soviet "self-criticism", in the form of public discussion within trade unions, cooperative societies, agricultural col-

---

[10] For corroboration of this interpretation of Soviet nationalism, see the excellent article by Heinz H. F. Eulau, "The New Soviet Nationalism," *Annals of the American Academy of Political and Social Science*, vol. 232, March, 1944, pp. 25-32.

lectives, and various other types of association. Perhaps most important of all has been the wide sharing of culture: the rapid liquidation of illiteracy, the multiplication of schools, the vast increase in the circulation of books, the widespread development of technical skills, and the mushroom growth of art and music circles, theatrical groups, and scientific societies.

It is well to remember that the Soviet system is highly dynamic, and that the announced ideal of its leaders is human freedom achieved on a cooperative basis ("the second stage of communism"). Such undemocratic features as the secret police, the monolithic Party control, and "the disease of orthodoxy" in respect to Marxian and Party doctrines, it is profoundly to be hoped, will prove to be transitory. In the words of Beatrice Webb, they may turn out to be "the growing pains of a new social order which has struggled into existence in a hostile world." [11] There are indications, such as the conciliatory attitude toward the Russian Orthodox Church and the renewed appreciation of Russian history and national traditions, that Soviet thought and practice are becoming more tolerant and conservative; but there is no good reason, according to such a seasoned observer as Maurice Hindus, to think that the Soviet Union is departing from socialism.

If we turn from domestic policy to foreign relations, we again find that the Soviet Union is evolving. The fundamental goal of the Soviet diplomacy, during the difficult years of the rise of fascism, was defense through collective security, a policy which found expression in Litvinov's able presentation at Geneva of the thesis that "peace is indivisible." After the counter-policy of appeasement had been pushed to ruinous extremes at Munich, the Soviet Union found itself isolated, and attempted for some time to remain out of the War while building up buffer areas against attack. This phase of isolationism was cancelled by the Nazi invasion, and Russia has learned at heavy cost the same lesson of interdependence that America has learned.

As a member of the United Nations, the Soviet Union is now pledged to a policy of democratic internationalism. This

---

[11] Sidney and Beatrice Webb, *The Truth About Soviet Russia* (New York: Longmans, Green, 1942), p. 75.

policy has been expressed by the Soviet government's adherence
to the Atlantic Charter, by the Anglo-Soviet treaty of mutual assistance of May 26, 1942, by the agreements reached at the Moscow and Teheran Conferences, and by such authoritative statements as Stalin's speech on the occasion of the twenty-fifth anniversary of the Soviet regime. On the latter occasion, Stalin outlined the program of action of the Anglo-Soviet-American coalition as follows: "Abolition of racial exclusiveness; equality of
nations and integrity of their territories; liberation of enslaved
nations and restoration of their sovereign rights; the right of every
nation to arrange its affairs as it wishes; economic aid to nations
that have suffered and assistance to them in attaining their material welfare; restoration of democratic liberties; destruction of
the Hitlerite regime." [12] This statement should be supplemented
by the joint declaration of Roosevelt, Churchill, and Stalin at
Teheran: "We recognize fully the supreme responsibility resting
upon us and all the nations to make a peace which will command
good will from the overwhelming masses of the peoples of the
world and banish the scourge and terror of war for many generations."

CRITIQUES OF MARXIAN-SOVIET THEORY

Turning now from the exposition of Communist theory to
the criticisms directed against it, we find a prodigious volume
of controversial literature, too vast to be more than briefly indicated.

The "materialistic interpretation of history" has been attacked by innumerable critics. Although originally inspired by
Marx, Werner Sombart has denied the entire historical-economic
thesis of Marxism, maintaining that non-economic interests, such
as the religious and the political, have on the whole held the
primacy in history. Max Weber and Ernest Troeltsch have similarly contended that religion has exercised a more originative
and independent causal role than Marxism admits. Likewise, Rudolf Stammler has maintained the relative independence of legal

---

[12] *Soviet War Documents,* Washington, Embassy of the Union of Soviet Socialist
Republics, December, 1943, p. 38.

systems, which he believes profoundly condition the whole economic order. Georges Sorel and Hendrik de Man have insisted that myths, ideals, and heroic attitudes often play a more important role than economic processes. Max Lerner believes that Marxists have not been sufficiently aware of the irrational elements in human motivation: folk traditions, nationalistic sentiments, racial prejudices, group neuroses, subconscious or semiconscious impulses.

Among the critics of Marxian methodology, Karl Mannheim contends that Marx and the Communists have never faced the problem of knowledge in all its depth and complexity and have been too prone to think of their own science as an exception to the historical relativism and conditionality of human thought. Similarly, Beatrice and Sidney Webb have complained of "the disease of orthodoxy," the tendency to insist upon the letter of Marxism and the rigid adherence to "the Party line."

Another criticism, urged by John Dewey among others, is that Communist methods are not compatible with Communist objectives, since the tactics of dictatorship and violence inevitably pervert and infect the goal of a peaceful cooperative commonwealth. Somewhat similar was the fear expressed after the Bolshevik Revolution by the famous socialist theorist, Karl Kautsky, and the equally famous German revolutuionist, Rosa Luxemburg, that the policy of dictatorship, as exercised under Lenin's leadership, would stifle the democratic aspirations and creative spontaneity of the Russian people. The English Fabians, prominent among whom are Sidney and Beatrice Webb, Bernard Shaw, and R. H. Tawney, have criticized the Marxian and Leninist thesis that class struggle is the inherent dynamic of revolutionary change and have regarded the transition to socialism as the peaceful culmination of democratic and evolutionary processes. Likewise many social democrats such as Eduard Bernstein have rejected the Marxian concepts of class struggle and favored collaboration with all "progressive forces." Incidentally, even Stalin has favored such broad cooperation in achieving victory over the Axis and in organizing the Peace.

A considerable number of critics, such as the American

liberal, Alfred M. Bingham, have maintained that Marxists underestimate the strength and power of the middle class. Whereas small entrepreneurs and independent tradesmen have dwindled in number as Marx predicted, there has been a considerable increase of skilled and professional workers: lawyers, teachers, engineers, technicians, civil service employees, and especially administrators. James Burnham accordingly has concluded that we are confronted not by a proletarian but by a "managerial" revolution, whereby a new "class" of political and industrial bureaucrats are consolidating their power. A kindred type of criticism, formulated by Robert Michels, Gaetano Mosca, and Vilfredo Pareto, regards the classless ideal of Marxian Communism as essentially Utopian. They argue that the proletarian revolution merely substitutes one type of ruling élite for another, and that the primary object of every élite including the Communist is to maintain its own power and privilege.

Various other criticisms, such as the economic polemics of Eugene von Böhm-Bawerk, Achille Loria, and Ludwig von Mises, lie outside of the purview of an essay devoted to political theory.

All of these criticisms, of course, have been vigorously contested, and their truth or falsity can be ascertained only in the light of careful scrutiny. But whatever may be one's final reaction to them, one cannot deny the immense influence of Soviet Communism upon human action. No social philosophers, ancient or modern, have exercised a vaster influence than Marx, Lenin, and Stalin, and the Soviet system represents by far the most significant social innovation of the present Century. This system, moreover, is in rapid transition, and there is good reason to hope that Russia is advancing toward a new, more comprehensive type of democracy.

SELECTED BIBLIOGRAPHY

ADAMS, H. P. *Karl Marx in His Earlier Writings*. London: Allen and Unwin, 1940. An excellent objective survey of Marx's earlier works, some of which are not available in English.

BLOOM, SOLOMON F. *The World of Nations: A Study of the National Implications in the Work of Karl Marx*. New York: Columbia University Press, 1941. Indicates that Marx took account of national peculiarities.

BOBER, MANDELL MORTON. *Karl Marx's Interpretation of History.* Cambridge: Harvard University Press, 1927. Interprets Marx as an economic determinist.

CHANG, SHERMAN H. M. *The Marxian Theory of the State.* Philadelphia: University of Pennsylvania Press, 1931. A comprehensive study.

DALLIN, D. J. *Soviet Russia's Foreign Policy.* New Haven: Yale University Press, 1942; and *Russia and Postwar Europe.* New Haven: Yale University Press, 1943. Scholarly account of Soviet policy in world affairs.

Encyclopaedia of the Social Sciences. New York: Macmillan, 1930-1935. Consult the captions Bolshevism, Materialism, Russian Revolution, Socialism, Marx, Lenin, Trotsky, Stalin, etc.

EULAU, HEINZ H. F. "The New Soviet Nationalism," *Annals of the American Academy of Political and Social Science,* vol. 232, March, 1944, pp. 25-32. Excellent brief interpretation.

HINDUS, MAURICE. *Mother Russia.* New York: Doubleday, Doran, 1943. Remarkable for its concrete and human understanding of the Russian people.

History of the Communist Party of the Soviet Union. New York: International Publishers, 1939. Official Communist Party publication covering the period from 1883 to 1937. The important section on dialectical and historical materialism was written by Stalin.

HOOK, SIDNEY. *Towards the Understanding of Karl Marx.* New York: John Day, 1933; and *From Hegel to Marx.* New York: Reynal and Hitchcock, 1936. Studies by the leading pragmatic interpreter of Marx.

KOHN, HANS. *Nationalism in the Soviet Union.* New York: Columbia University Press, 1933. An authoritative study. For more recent developments, should be supplemented by Eulau, cited above.

LENIN, V. I. *Selected Works.* New York: International Publishers, 1935 ff. Twelve volumes containing the most important of Lenin's writings. See especially *The State and Revolution* and *Imperialism: The Highest Stage of Capitalism.*

MARX, KARL, AND ENGELS, FRIEDRICH. *Historisch-Kritische Gesamtausgabe.* Frankfurt, Marx-Engels Archive, 1927 ff. Most complete and authoritative edition of the works of Marx and Engels. Recent volumes have been issued in Moscow, Russia.

MARX, KARL AND ENGELS, FRIEDRICH. *Correspondence: 1846-1895: A Selection with Commentary and Notes.* New York: International Publishers, 1936. Throws much light upon Marxism and its historical and biographical setting.

MARX, KARL. *Selected Works.* New York: International Publishers, 1933. A two-volume, annotated compilation of the basic shorter works of Marx and Engels prepared by the Marx-Engels-Lenin Institute, Moscow.

MEHRING, FRANZ. *Karl Marx: The Story of His Life.* New York: Covici-Friede, 1935. The classic biography.

PARES, BERNARD. *History of Russia.* New York: Knopf, 1926; and *Russia.* New York: Penguin Books, 1943. Excellent for the background and history of the Soviet system.

ROSENBERG, ARTHUR. *A History of Bolshevism from Marx to the First Five Years' Plan.* New York: Oxford University Press, 1934. The narrative is presented against the general background of European history.

SOMMERVILLE, JOHN. "Dialectical Materialism," in Dagobert D. Runes (editor), *Twentieth Century Philosophy.* New York: Philosophical Library, 1943. A sympathetic, able summary of Soviet philosophy.

STALIN, JOSEPH. *Leninism,* two volumes. New York: International Publishers, 1928-1933; anl *Marxism and the National Question.* New York: International Publishers, 1942. Stalin's most important theoretical pronouncements.

TROTSKY, LEON. *The History of the Russian Revolution.* New York: Simon and Shuster, 1936; and *The Revolution Betrayed.* New York: Doubleday, Doran, 1937. Written with skill and verve, and with barbs for his enemies.

WEBB, SIDNEY AND BEATRICE. *Soviet Communism: A New Civilization,* revised edition. New York: Scribner's, 1937; and *The Truth About Soviet Russia.* New York: Longmans, Green, 1942. Sympathetic, documented, and comprehensive interpretation by two famous British socialists.

WILSON, EDMUND. *To the Finland Station.* New York: Harcourt, Brace, 1940. Vivid account of the development of socialist thought, including Marx, Engels, Lenin, and Trotsky.

CHAPTER III

SOCIOLOGICAL CONTRIBUTIONS TO POLITICAL THEORY

HARRY ELMER BARNES

I. THE SOCIOLOGICAL APPROACH TO THE STUDY OF THE STATE

The relation of sociology to political theory is fairly obvious. Sociology is the general and comprehensive science of society. Political science is one of the special social sciences; the one which concentrates upon a study of the state. The state is one of the most important social institutions which develop out of the general matrix of society as a whole. Sociology is concerned with the origin and growth of society and with the rise and nature of all social institutions. Hence, its approach to a study of the state is more all-inclusive and generic than is that of political science. Before men created the state they had to adapt themselves to socialized methods of living in primitive communities. More than 99 per cent of human existence had passed before men lived in what may be technically regarded as political society. Hence, from the standpoint of both sociological and chronological perspective, a knowledge of sociology is essential to any profound grasp of the nature of the state and political activities. Professor Franklin H. Giddings stated this point very cogently when he wrote that "to teach the theory of the state to men who have not learned the first principles of sociology, is like teaching astronomy or therodynamics to men who have not learned the Newtonian Laws of Motion." [1] Political control is only one form of social control, and the latter broad field is the peculiar subject-matter of sociology.

---

[1] F. H. Giddings. *Principles of Sociology* (New York: Macmillan, 1896), p. 37.

II. Sociological Conceptions of the State

While, as we shall see later on, the sociologists are by no means in agreement as to what the state should do, there is a reasonable unanimity among them as to the nature of the state. They regard it as one of the primary institutions of society, in company with economic, religious and educational institutions. It is unique among these primary institutions, at least in historic times, in being vested with supreme authority in enforcing its dicta and purposes. Before the rise of the state, religion exerted this type of absolute authority, and the traditional struggle between church and state, which long antedated the traditional medieval conflict, was an inevitable by-product of the transition from an ultimate social control based upon recourse to supernatural power to one founded upon secular dominion. In our day, the latter has won almost as complete a victory as did the former in primitive times.

In the earlier stages of the development of sociology, those writers who looked upon society as a social organism, such as Paul Lillienfeld, Albert Schäffle, René Worms and Herbert Spencer, regarded the state as the brain or directive organ of society. In the next generation of sociologists, leaders like Lester F. Ward, Giddings and L. T. Hobhouse, conceived of the state as the supreme and mature form of human association. Perhaps the best statement of this point of view is that set forth by Giddings:

The chief purposive organization of civil society is the state, through which the social mind dominates the integral community, prescribes forms and obligations to all minor purposive associations, and shapes the social composition. Coordinating all activities and relations, the state maintains conditions under which all its subjects may live, as Aristotle said, "a perfect and self-sufficing life." [2]

Elaborating upon this general position in regard to the nature of the state, such writers as Gustav Ratzenhofer, A. W. Small and A. F. Bentley, offered one of the most practical and useful conceptions of the state, namely, the idea that the state is the final arbiter or umpire of the social process, controlling and di-

---

[2] F. H. Giddings. *Descriptive and Historical Sociology* (New York: Macmillan, 1906), p. 509.

recting the conflicts and struggles of lesser social groups and interests. These conflicts and struggles of interest groups are the most dynamic force in modern social development. But, without control and direction by the state, anarchy and chaos would result. It is the function of the state both to conserve the dynamic impulses in social conflict and, at the same time, to insure order and coherence in social life.

III. SOCIOLOGICAL ATTITUDES TOWARDS SOCIAL CONTROL

One of the most important contributions which sociology has made to political theory is to be found in the analysis of the ultimate controls over group and individual activity. Political scientists are wont to regard the control of conduct as primarily a matter of political authority and the exercise thereof by governmental and legal agents. They stress law as the fundamental item in social control. The sociologists admit that, today, law is the most potent and direct type of social control, but they offer a far broader and more comprehensive analysis of the whole problem, indicating among other things, that law itself is a reflection of group attitudes, past and present. They also call attention to the fact that society was controlled by non-political forces during the greater portion of man's existence on the planet, the state and government being relatively recent products of social evolution.

The earliest and basic foundations of social control are to be found in customs, folkways, and mores, a subject studied and expounded with great thoroughness by writers such as W. G. Sumner, Julius Lippert, Friedrich Ratzel, Edward Westermarck and others. The classic work on the subject is, of course, William Graham Sumner's immortal *Folkways*. In their trial-and-error efforts to maintain sheer existence, men in any given community develop certain habitual ways of handling the outstanding problems of living. These became customs and folkways. When handed down from generation to generation they became social habits. In time, men consciously contemplated this mass of social habits and rationalized their origin and significance. When they reached this level of conscious appraisal and approval they came to be mores, which determine the rightness and acceptability of all social behavior in any given group.

In time, certain of the more elemental and highly cherished mores evolved into our fundamental or primary institutions, such as family life and ideals, economic institutions, government, religion, or our relations with the supposed supernatural world, and education, or the means of handing on the accepted mores and institutions.

Public opinion, or community sentiment, which still remains a more fundamental and persuasive method of social control than governmental edicts, is an outgrowth and reflection of social customs, folkways, mores and institutions. The content of public opinion is determined thereby and public opinion derives its force and power from the devotion, often fanatical, of the group to its folkways.

Not only do social habits and their reflection in public opinion control a far wider and more diversified field of conduct than government and law, but the latter lose much of their realism and potency unless they are in close accord with public opinion. In every case, laws originally grow out of the pressure of public opinion, and laws become dead letters only as the result of changes in public opinion, which leave earlier legislation stranded without the active approval of public sentiment. Laws will rarely be supported enthusiastically or enforced with success unless they accord fairly well with the prevailing content of public opinion.

Since public opinion is a more fundamental source of social control than political authority, special significance attaches to the sociological studies of public opinion by such writers as Giddings, E. A. Ross, Trotter, Graham Wallas, Emile Durkheim, Ferdinand Tönnies and Walter Lippmann. Durkheim has especially emphasized the way in which social pressure and social thinking dominate individual thought and conduct. Trotter and LeBon have emphasized the essentially irrational character of a great deal of public opinion, especially that originating in herd impulses and in the psychic life of crowds. Wallas has given special attention to the potency of symbolism in mass thinking and has shown how modern politicians exploit the magic power of symbols to dominate the thought and action of voters. Lippmann has clearly indicated that, even when contemporary public opinion is relatively rational, it is rarely based upon a sufficient command of the facts to provide assured guidance for effective social control and political conduct. If the state, government and legislation reflect public opinion, it follows that they cannot efficiently serve contemporary needs until we create an intelligent and informed public opinion through more realistic and cogent social education.

It is here that an important contribution has been made by sociologists to the relation of education to social control and political reconstruction. Men like Jesse H. Newlon, George S. Counts and others have laid special emphasis upon our failure to provide an adequate and cogent educational foundation for democracy. For over a hundred years we have been teaching little potential democrats the type of subject-matter originally devised for the instruction of children of a decadent feudal nobility or the rising bourgeoisie of the early modern towns. Hence, as the above writers point out, we need not be surprised at the current crisis in democracy, when we have a public opinion lamentably ill-equipped to wrestle with the problems of the twentieth century. This thesis of the indispensable nature of a truly democratic education to the creation of an efficient democracy has been the life contribution to American education of John Dewey, and Dewey's doctrines have been most effectively popularized by William H. Kilpatrick. A comprehensive review of the social ideas of American educators has been provided by Merle Curti.

The most irrational type of public opinion is that which grows out of herd impulses and the psychological attitudes of crowds. Trotter has given us our best study of the powerful and intolerant character of the psychology of the human herd, which becomes especially fanatical and overpowering in wartime. LeBon, Scipio Sighele and others launched the study of crowd psychology and indicated its dangers for democracy, especially in legislative debate and in political campaigns. Under the influence of crowd psychology, human actions are prone to be irrational, intolerant, and ill considered, and, hence, very poorly adapted to the understanding and direction of the complicated issues of contemporary life. These problems of crowd psychology and their relation to political and other forms of group activity have been studied in terms of a more up-to-date psychology by such writers as Everett Dean Martin.

Our contemporary means of communication, the daily newspaper, the telephone, telegraph, movies and radio, have tended to reduce whole populations to essentially a crowd psychological state, especially in periods of public excitement. Hence, the need for careful study of crowd psychology and the social therapy which will increase the degree of rationality in group reactions to public problems. There can be no effective handling of the problems of our day by a crowd-minded electorate or an administration dominated by crowd controls.

These new instruments of communication have not only reduced whole populations to the mental level of crowds, but they have made far more potent and prevalent what we customarily call propaganda, namely, the deliberate effort to influence the thinking and conduct of individuals and groups to predetermined ends. Such sociologists as F. E. Lumley, William Albig, Leonard Dobb and others, have given special attention to the relation of propaganda to contemporary public life and have pointed out its striking challenge to the democratic process in our day. A socially-minded educator, Clyde R. Miller, who shares the views of Dewey and Counts, created an Institute for the analysis of propaganda, designed as a social therapeutic to aid in revamping democracy, but it was submerged under a wave of war-hysteria.

These are only a few of the ways in which sociology has contributed to a better understanding of the breadth and diversity of social control, but they will suffice to indicate how sterile must be any form of political theory which studies human behavior and political problems solely in terms of the political frame of reference.

IV. SOCIOLOGICAL INTERPRETATIONS OF THE ORIGINS AND EVOLUTION OF THE STATE

The sociological contributions to political origins and development falls into two fields: (1) The development of the state out of other forms of associated life; (2) the stages through which political evolution has passed.

Aristotle once remarked that man is by nature a political animal. Viewed literally, this is not true, for it ignores society. What Aristotle really meant was that man is a social animal, and this is obviously true. If man has not been inherently social, he never could have developed political life. One of the most important contributions of sociology to social and political origins has been its emphasis upon this natural sociability of man and the institutional products of this great gregarious trait. There have been numerous sociological contributions to the explanation of the foundations of human sociability, such as the emphasis upon sympathy by Adam Smith, Alexander Sutherland and Giddings, the stress on cooperation by Prince Kropotkin and Jacques Novicow, the notion of the gregarious instinct underlined by William Macdougal and Trotter, Giddings' doctrine of the "consciousness of kind", Gabriel Tarde's conception of imitation, and the like. We need not here review this interesting and often controversial literature. All we need point out is that human association, in general, antedated political society by hundreds of thousands of years. Man was dominated during this long period by habit and custom. After this long training in associated life, he slowly developed these crystalized and cherished social habits which we now know of as institutions, among them the state and government.

When one realizes the social origin of all institutions, including the state, it becomes clearly apparent that no one can have any clear understanding of political origins without previous sociological training and decent acquaintance with the factors that promote human sociability and bring into being the primary institutions of human society. Political origins can be understood only when viewed against the broader panorama of generic so-

cial origins. We may now turn to a consideration of some sociological views of the evolution of the state and government.

Down to well past the middle of the 19th century it was
generally believed by scholars that the earliest form of government was a patriarchal tribal society, like that portrayed in the
Bible as pertaining among the early Hebrews. This point of view
was most comprehensively and authoritatively expounded by Sir
Henry Sumner Maine in his *Ancient Law*. The notion of primitive patriarchy was assaulted by J. J. Bachhofen in his work on
The Mother Right in 1860. He contended that a matriarchal society, dominated by females, preceded the patriarchal stage so
thoroughly studied by Maine. This general position was accepted
and elaborated in the *Ancient Society* of Lewis Henry Morgan.
This book was the most influential study of political evolution
for a generation following its appearance in 1877.

We cannot here go into the elaborate details of Morgan's
theory of political evolution. Suffice it to say that Morgan believed that the earliest form of human society was a pre-kinship
type of horde, without fixed family relations. This was followed
by the maternal clan which, in turn, gave way to the paternal
gens that crystalized into patriarchal society as envisaged by
Maine. All forms of kinship or gentile society, of which the patriarchal was the latest, were supplanted by the rise of civil society
or the state, which first came into being in early Oriental times,
as a product of the mastery of metals, the art of writing and
other epoch-making inventions. Along with this outline of social
and political evolution, Morgan postulated successive stages of
savagery and barbarism, each associated rather precisely with a
characteristic type of material culture. This idea that a maternal
system preceded paternal dominion has been defended in our day
by Robert Briffault in his elaborate book, *The Mothers*.

The dogma of maternal priority and of the orderly evolution and inevitable sequence of social stages has been overthrown
by critical ethnology, though much of substantial merit remains
in Morgan's emphasis upon the close interrelation between material culture, inventions and property, on the one hand, and social
and political evolution, on the other. This attack upon Morgan's

views has been led by Franz Boaz and his disciples. It is best systematized by one of the latter, Robert H. Lowie, who summarizes the newer point of view in his *Primitive Society*.

To sum up. There is no fixed succession of maternal and paternal descent; Sibless tribes may pass directly into the matrilineal or the patrilineal conditions; if the highest civilizations emphasize the paternal side of the family, so do many of the lowest; and the social history of particular people cannot be reconstructed from any generally valid scheme of evolution but only in the light of its known and probable cultural relations with neighboring peoples.[3]

If ethnology has given to sociology the accepted ideas of pre-political evolution, the sociologists themselves assuredly provided the substantial explanation of the origins of the state, or civil society. According to this view, the state, in any literal sense, began at the close of primitive society. It was created as the result of the wars between primitive groups, which led to the conquest of some by others and the consequent establishment of political authority through force. The oldest form of civil society were the early city states of oriental antiquity, which later developed into monarchies and the great oriental empires, from Egypt to Rome.

The sociologist who first systematized this doctrine was an Austrian-Pole, Ludwig Gumplowicz, whose famous work on the *Struggle of Races* appeared in 1883. Of course, earlier writers, such as Polybius, Bodin, Hobbes, Hume, and Adam Ferguson has anticipated this notion, but Gumplowicz rounded it out, gathered an immense body of illustrative material, and gave the notion currency in both Europe and America. It is now generally accepted by students of social and political evolution, though Kropotkin and Novicow have indicated how cooperative activities and economic factors amply supplemented war and conflict in the creation of the state.

It should be made clear, however, that there was no sharp break between pre-political and civil society. Many primitive groups have developed fairly elaborate political relationships, including kingdoms and occasional empires. But even here there is evidence of the intervention of war and conquest.

---

[3] R. H. Lowie. *Primitive Society* (New York: Boni and Liveright), 1920, p. 185.

Sociologists have done much to clarify the sequence of political stages since the origins of the state. For example, Guillaume De Greef held that political evolution is essentially a process of gradual transition from despotic authority to voluntary contract. Franz Oppenheimer suggested the following stages: primitive feudal states, maritime states, mature feudal states, and constitutional states. Hobhouse contended that political life rested first upon kinship, then upon authority and, finally, upon citizenship. Perhaps more valuable than any of these grandiose evolutionary demarcations have been such careful sociological studies of actual political development as W. Christie MacLeod's *Origin and History of Politics.*

On the basis of these various studies, the sociologists have given us a pretty clear picture of political evolution. This has been, essentially, as follows: Pre-political society has existed without systematic kinship relations and has been both maternal and paternal, when any kinship systems have existed. There is no evidence that one type was earlier than the other or that there was any uniform sequence from one to another. Between primitive society, whether on a kinship basis or not, and formal civil society or the state, there was an intervening stage known as feudalism which rested upon personal relationships between the governing and governed elements. Civil society or the state has been founded primarily upon territorial residence and the control of such vital economic items as property. The first states were the antique city-states, followed by the ancient monarchies and empires. After the reversion to feudalism in the middle ages the modern national state made its appearance. The national state has passed through three main stages to date: (1) the absolutistic or tyrannical; (2) the representative, and (3) the democratic, the latter being a late and radical form of representative government. It is contended by many that the territorial basis of the state and government will ultimately be supplanted by a functional framework, founded upon vocational associations like labor unions. Syndicalism has espoused such a notion in theory, and Soviet Russia has installed it quite extensively in practice. Whatever the future course of political evolution, it should be evident that sociology has given us a clear picture of political evolution down to date. The few political scientists who have given any special attention to political evolution, such as Edward Jenks and E. M. Sait, have gained much from the panorama of political evolution supplied by the sociologists.

V. SOCIOLOGICAL CONCEPTIONS OF THE MAKE-UP OF THE STATE

The political scientists have long contended that the indispensable elements in any state are a population, a territory and sovereign power. But the political scientists have done little to indicate the relation of the type of population and territory to the character of the state or to explain what makes possible any such thing as sovereign power in political society. The sociologists have given attention to exactly these matters and have also suggested other elements in the state, in addition to population, territory and sovereignty.

It is to sociology that we owe the origin of the scientific study of population problems, which is known as demography and deals with such matters as birth and death rates, fertility and fecundity, vitality classes, and the like. Through such studies as these we are able to get a clear picture of the character of any political population at any given time and to provide the basis for prediction as to probable future trends in population changes. Such data and trends are of immense value to statesman. For example, a sharply falling rate of population growth, an abnormally high death rate, extensive illness and the like, are an indication of social decadence and ample cause for alarm on the part of political leaders. There can be no powerful nation which is not a healthy nation, and the slowing down of population growth may be particularly dangerous to any state surrounded by neighbors whose population is growing rapidly. The pressure of a rapidly growing population upon a limited means of subsistence is among the more potent provocations of international friction and war. As Simonds and Emeny have pointed out, the struggle between "have and have not" nations is far more real than the popular conception of a clash between freedom and dictatorship. These vital facts of population situations and trends have been studied with accuracy and insight by such sociologists as P. E. Levasseur, Francesco Nitti, Arthur Newsholme, A. L. Bowley, W. F. Willcox, Maxim Kovalesky, C. D. Wright, D. F. Durand, W. B. Bailey, W. S. Thompson, E. B. Reuter and many others.

But it is not only the quantity of the population that counts. The quality is, in some ways, even more significant. A hundred thousand superior persons can create a better society than ten million degenerates, morons and weaklings. One of the great problems of contemporary statesmanship is the improvement of the quality of the population. The only scientific proposal which has been put forward to achieve this result is what we call eugenics, founded a generation ago by Sir Francis Galton and vigorously promulgated in our generation by his disciple, Karl Pearson, in England, and by Charles B. Davenport, S. J. Holmes, Fredrick Osborne and others in U. S. The eugenic program is of special relevance in our own day, when the complicated problems of modern life demand an ever improved and superior level of human ability. This fact has been amply emphasized by Otto Ammon, G. Vacher de Lapouge, A. A. Tenney, F. H. Hankins and others.

One of the main aberrations in political science has been the acceptance of a racial interpretation of political ability and achievement, especially the hypothesis of the superior political ability of the white race and of the unique Anglo-saxon and Germanic political genius. Such vagaries have been elaborately described and exposed by Hankins and other scientific students of race problems. There is no ground for assuming any unique political capacity on the part of any race, and the facts of history, if literally and superficially interpreted, would seem to offer much evidence as to the political backwardness of the Germans, who were not able to achieve political unification until near the close of the 19th century.

To the average political scientist, the element of territory in the state implies primarily a map with certain boundaries enclosing a given number of square miles. There is little intimation that a hundred thousand square miles in one part of the world has different implications for political life from the same area in a different part of the planet. To political science, territory is primarily an area in which to raise a flag, to erect government buildings and to police with civilian officers and armies.

In dealing with the territorial basis of the state, the sociologists go to the works of the anthropogeographers, who deal with such vital factors as economic resources, topography, routes of travel and communication, climate and climatic changes, strategic position and cultural contacts. A. R. Cowan and H. J. Mackinder have indicated the bearing of strategic positions and key regions upon political power. In the more sophisticated form of geo-politics, this notion has exerted a large influence upon Nazi strategy. Leon Metchnikoff has made it clear why early civilization first sprang up in the great river basins of antiquity. Edmond Demolins and Jean Brunhes have shown us how important natural routes of travel and trade have been in producing political prosperity and supremacy. Frédéric LePlay and Patrick Geddes have emphasized the basic character of natural geographic regions and have shown the advantages of political conformity to such areas. Julius Hann and Ellsworth Huntington have made it clear the extensive effects of climate and climatic changes upon the physical vitality and economic resources of nations. All of these varied geographical factors which affect the social population, and, therefore, political life, have been organized and appraised in the comprehensive works on human geography by such masters as Friedrich Ratzel, Camille Vallaux, Paul Vidal de la Blanche, Jean Brunhes and Russell Smith.

The Belgian sociologist, De Greef, has even suggested that political boundaries are not real boundaries of a state. The latter are the ever-shifting equilibrium of pressures on either side of the formal legal and military boundaries. Changing conditions will shift the real social boundaries, even if they might at one time have coincided with the political boundaries of the state. We shall recur to this important thesis later.

Sovereignty has always occupied a prominent place in political theory, but the political scientists have rarely gone further than a mere definition of the term, as for example in J. W. Burgess' classic statement that sovereignty is "the original, absolute, unlimited power (of the state) over the individual subject and over all association of subjects". Political scientists have but infrequently considered whether sovereignty actually exists, and, if so, how it is that any such absolute power arises and operates. These latter questions are precisely the ones which sociology examines.

Some sociologists, such as Spencer, Novicow, De Greef, and Bentley, contend that the political notion of absolute sovereignty is a mere legal fiction. But the more usual sociological approach to sovereignty has been an examination of its genesis and character. This attitude has been well stated by Giddings:

Let us pass now from these conceptions of sovereignty to the social fact of sovereignty; and let us ask whether we are justified in assuming that the fact has at all times been one and the same fact, or whether sovereignty itself may have been a variable, an evolutionary, phenomenon, created by and in turn creating varying moods of human feelings, varying attitudes of will and consequently varying conceptions and speculations. This is a question which I suspect the student of political science as such or the jurist as such may be unable to answer. It is, I venture to think, a sociological question; and I believe that the answer to it, if found at all, must be found through ways of looking at social facts and processes that are acquired only through some sociological training.[4]

Giddings holds that the only realistic conception of sovereignty is "the dominant human power, individual and pluralistic, in a politically organized and politically independent population". He contends that there are four forms of sovereignty which are, broadly speaking, the chronological stages in its development, namely, personal sovereignty; the sovereignty of a superior class which gains dominion through social, economic or religious prestige; the mass sovereignty of unlimited majority rule; and the ascendency of a collective opinion and collective will to which the public defers. A similar approach to the problem is supported by Ludwig Stein. J. R. Commons and Achille Loria have offered an economic interpretation of sovereignty, associating it with the rise of private property and the growth of capitalism. In his *Social*

[4] F. H. Giddings. "Sovereignty and Government," *Political Science Quarterly,* vol. xxi, p. 7.

Control, Ross has given us a socio-psychological account of sovereignty, developing the idea that, as society advances, public opinion and other psychic forces grow in influence at the expense of the sheer physical force of the state.

All in all, the sociologists have established the fact that political sovereignty is not original, absolute, universal or unlimited, that political power of any sort is rarely supreme in any society, that sovereignty is derivative rather than original, that it arises from social, economic and psychic forces, and that it can be fruitfully studied only in its social setting and in the light of the evolution of the state within society. In short, sovereignty is a sociological rather than a political or legal phenomenon, however important the determination of the legal superior may be in concrete instances for practical juristic purposes in the courtroom.

Of very great importance is the sociological insistence that we must go beyond population, territory and sovereign power, if we are to envisage all the vital elements of the state. The sociologists lay special stress upon the importance of economic factors, particularly property, in political activity. Here they follow the general line of analysis taken by such early statesman as John Adams, James Madison, Daniel Webster, and John Calhoun. The sociological position is that the state is the umpire of social conflicts and that these conflicts arise chiefly out of economic interests and the distribution of property; as Madison put it, out of the "various and unequal distribution of property". The thesis of the complete economic determination of political life has been defended by such writers as Gumplowicz, Oppenheimer and Loria. Less extreme and perhaps more tenable is the conception of Ratzenhofer, Small and Bentley, who look upon political activity as primarily a matter of adjusting the struggles between conflicting interests in society.

Other sociologists, notably Max Weber, have held that psychological and ethical forces underlie the economic and control the strength and operation of the latter. Weber contended that, while Protestantism stimulated and encouraged capitalism in Western Europe, a different set of psychic and ethical factors in India and China discouraged its development there, though the

economic background was markedly similar to that which lay
back of the growth of capitalism in early modern Europe. The
same point of view has been upheld, with more critical reservations, by Ernst Troeltsch, R. H. Tawney and Thorstein Veblen.
We have already, in our discussion of social control, indicated
the emphasis placed by some sociologists upon psychological factors in the state, demonstrating that political control always depends upon the underlying and ultimate social control exerted
through various intellectual and emotional forces.

VI. The Types of States and Governments

The sociological contribution to the analysis of the various
forms of the state and government falls into two modes of approach. The first is a sociological classification of states and the
second is a sociological analysis of the forms traditionally accepted
by political science, such as monarchy, aristocracy and democracy.
In general, sociologists have no great respect for the traditional
classifications offered by political science. This attitude is well expressed by Bentley:

> Set opposite to all these various forms of psychical interpretation,
> we have a dead political science. It is a formal study of the most exter-
> nal characteristics of governing institutions. It loves to classify govern-
> ments by incidental attributes, and when all is said and done it cannot
> classify them much better now than by lifting up bodily Aristotle's mon-
> archies, aristocracies and democracies which he found significant for Greek
> institutions, and using them for measurements of all sorts and conditions
> of modern government. And since nobody can be very sure but that the
> United States is really a monarchy under the classification or England
> really a democracy, the classification is not entitled to great respect. Nor
> do the classifications that make the fundamental distinction between
> despotism and republics fair much better. They lose all sight of the con-
> tent of the process in some trick point about the form.[5]

Since the fundamental purpose of the state and government
is to adjust and compromise the conflicts among social interests,
the only realistic classification of states and governments must
be one which relates to the technique employed in bringing about

---

[5] A. F. Bentley. *The Process of Government* (Chicago :University of Chicago
Press, 1908), p. 162.

this adjustment. Bentley has also cogently stated this proposition:

Whenever and wherever we study the process of government, we never get away from the group and class activities, and when we get these group activities properly stated we come to see that the differences between governments are not fundamental differences or differences of principle, but that they are strictly differences of technique for the func- tioning of the interests, that they are adopted because of group needs, and that they will continue to be changed in accord with group needs.[6]

The superficiality of conventional classifications of states and governments has also been emphasized by Giddings in his theory of "protocracy", namely, the contention that, whatever the name or type of state and government, the few always rule. The ablest and most alert minority always rise to the top and dominate political society, even in democracies. All governments are, thus, "protocracies," whether monarchial, aristocratic or democratic. A similar position was maintained by Vilfredo Pareto who held that all governments, past and present, have been oligarchies of the élite existing more by the use of force than by reason. If abil- ity fades from the governing class, then the élite among the formally governed will seize control and adopt the residues essen- tial for maintaining themselves in power. The successful statesman follows the precept of Machiavelli, namely, to talk profusely about eternal justice and then act as if there were none of it.

We may now look briefly at some typical sociological classi- fications of the state. Comte contended that there are only two fundamental types of states—a theocracy, in which the temporal power is subordinate to the spiritual, and a sociocracy, where the temporal and spiritual power are properly coordinated. Spencer also could see only two main types of states, the military, fash- ioned primarily for war and extremely authoritarian, and the in- dustrial state, set up chiefly for productive industry and implying democratic politics, extensive civil liberties and extreme limita- tion of state activities. He predicted the possibility of an ethical state in the future, devoid of war and exploitation and devoted to the furtherance of cultural interests. Bagehot also envisaged two types of states, one based upon authoritative control for mili-

---

[6] *Ibid.*, p. 320.

tary efficiency and the other a representative government founded
on the principle of free discussion. Ratzenhofer and Small thought
of two types of states, the "conquest-state", based upon the subjection of one group by another through physical force, and the
"culture-state", in which political control is more liberal and is
colored by more extensive industrial development. While accepting monarchy and aristocracy as satisfactory classifications for
earlier types of the state, Ward held that we must differentiate
three types of democracy. The first is a physiocracy, or extreme
individualism; the second plutocracy, or the control of the state
by organized and predatory wealth; and the third, which lies
ahead of us, is sociocracy, or the control of society by social scientists who seek to accelerate social progress by following out the
laws of sociology. Ross would differentiate political regimes according to the groups which control them:

When the priest guides it we call it *clericalism*. When the fighting
caste is referred to, we call it *militarism*. When the initiative lies with
the minions of the state, we call it *officialdom*. The leadership of moneyed
men is *capitalism*. That of men of ideas is *liberalism*. The reliance of
men upon their own wisdom and strength is *individualism*. These distinctions I need hardly add, are far deeper than distinctions like aristocracy,
monarchy, republic, which relate merely to the form of government.[7]

The sociologists have also made an important contribution
in examining and qualifying the conventional views about the
traditional forms of the state and governments. For example,
Giddings insists that the majority can never rule, even in so-
called radical democracies. The able few will always control. As
he puts it:

The few always dominate. . . . Invariably the few rule, more or
less arbitrarily, more or less drastically, more or less extensively. Democracy, even the most radical democracy, is only that state of politically
organized mankind in which the rule of the few is least arbitrary and
most responsible, least drastic and most considerate.[8]

Sociologists, such as Hobhouse, have shown that merely
giving a name to a form of state, means little or nothing. For

---

[7] E. A. Ross. *Social Control* (New York: Macmillan, 1904), pp. 78-79.
[8] F. H. Giddings. *The Responsible State* (Boston: Houghton, Mifflin, 1918), pp.
19-20.

example, to call a form of state democracy is a mere sham unless we bring into being those conditions which make democracy possible. We cannot expect to have a real democracy so long as we have an uninformed public opinion, political grafters, economic inequalities and imperialistic foreign policies. The same point of view is defended by Ludwig Stein and Charles H. Cooley. All of these writers agree that we can have a pure democracy only in small states. Elsewhere, we must rely upon representative government through republican organization. Small has laid special stress upon the fact that, even if we could have political democracy, it would mean little or nothing without economic democracy. He says that our present, so-called capitalistic democracy is really a combination of "lottery and famine". True democracy must make full provision for social justice and equality of opportunity in the way of a livelihood and economic security. In this contention he is upheld by C. A. Ellwood and most enlightened sociologists.

Now that democracy is being threatened by totalitarianism, it may be well to point out that eminent sociologists have foreshadowed or given their benediction to this form of the state as the only solution for the complex problems of our day. Among such writers are Werner Sombart, and Hans Fryer in Germany, the Italian-Swiss, Pareto, and Othmar Spann in Austria. We find a qualified support of this attitude in the idea of a managerial revolution, as envisaged by Lawrence Dennis and James Burnham in the United States.

VII. Sociological Conceptions of the Process of Government

Far and away the most important contribution which sociology has made to political theory is the sociological conception of the process of government. This rests upon the fundamental hypothesis, amply supported by the facts, that the state is not made up of individuals but of groups with definite interests, so far mainly economic. This notion of political society has been cogently stated by Bentley, whose thinking was primarily influenced by that of Ratzenhofer and Small.

There is no group without its interest. And interest as the term will be used in this work, is the equivalent of a group. We may speak also of an interest group or of a group interest, again merely for the sake of clearness and expression. The group and the interest are not separate. . . .

As for political questions under any society in which we are called upon to study them, we shall never find a group interest of the society as a whole. We shall always find that the political interest and activities of any given group—and there are no political phenomena except group phenomena—are directed against other activities of men who appear in other groups, political or other. The phenomena of political life which we study will always divide the society in which they occur, along lines which are very real, though of varying degrees of definiteness. The society itself is nothing other than the complex of the groups that compose it.[9]

Following out this point of view, the sociologists understand clearly enough that the essential process of government is the adjustment of the conflicts between these interest groups. The most comprehensive analysis of this fundamental position was presented by Ratzenhofer and adapted to the English-speaking public by Professor Small. In this way, the sociologists exposed the shallowness of the frequent implication of political science that government is a sort of pietistic organization which functions for the good of the governed. According to the political point of view, for example, log-rolling is looked upon as a pathological and degenerate form of political activity. From the standpoint of sociological analysis it is, on the contrary, the very essence of government. This fact has been lucidly expounded by Bentley:

Log rolling is a term of opprobrium. This is because it is used mainly with reference to its grosser forms. . . . Log rolling is, however, in fact, the most characteristic legislative process . . . and when we have reduced the legislative process to the play of group interests, then log rolling, or give and take, appears as the very nature of the process. It is compromise, not in the abstract moral form, which philosophers can sagely discuss, but in the practical form with which every legislator who gets results through government is acquainted. It is trading. It is the adjustment of interests. . . . There was never a time in the history of the

---

[9] Bentley, *op cit.*, pp. 211-12, 222.

American congress when legislation was conducted in any other way.[10]

In order to provide greater honesty, directness and efficiency in this process of adjusting group conflicts through government, the more enlightened sociologists recommend the abandonment of the old archaic territorial form of representation and the substitution of vocational or professional representation. In such a system, the various professions and occupations would directly elect their representatives in legislative bodies. This need for this reform has been argued with special eloquence by H. A. Overstreet. Until it is introduced, the lobby will, as Pendleton Herring and H. L. Childs have amply demonstrated, continue to be the third and most powerful house in any legislature.

Against this background we can readily understand the sociological interpretation of political parties. The latter always represent either some powerful interest group or a combination of interest groups which seek some common end. In spite of all the graft and corruption which attend the conflict of political parties, their struggles are the most dynamic force in a democratic state. This fact has been well stated by Ward:

The vigorous interaction of the two forces, which look so much like antagonism, strife and struggle, transforms force into energy and energy into power, and build political and social structures. And after they are constructed, the same influences transform them, and it is this that constitutes social progress. Political institutions—the laws of every country—are the products of this political synergy, the crystalized acts of legislative bodies created by political bodies.[11]

At the same time, sociologists have been alert to point out the dangers in party government, especially its threat to democracy. Wallas, in his *Human Nature in Politics,* has shown how clever manipulators of party symbols and catch-words are able to control, manipulate and betray the masses in political campaigns. Giddings has contended that political parties always result in oligarchy, due to the fact that the few always dominate, even in the democratic government. The most powerful summary

---

[10] *Ibid.,* pp. 370-71.

[11] L. F. Ward. "The Sociology of Political Parties," *American Journal of Sociology,* vol. xiii, pp. 440-41.

of the anti-democratic tendencies of political parties has been
provided by Robert Michels, in his extended study, *Political Parties*. According to Michels, the masses are stupid and lacking in
initiative. The alert few naturally come to the top as leaders in
any political party. In the beginning, they may seek to serve the
masses. But in due time they build up a political organization, and
slowly but surely the organization becomes the end rather than
the means of political life. In the end, a corrupt and self-seeking
oligarchy is the inevitable outcome of party life even in a democracy. In short, democracies cannot exist without parties, but
parties inevitably kill off democracies.

VIII. SOCIOLOGICAL THEORIES OF THE PROVINCE OF THE STATE

Since sociologists have written over a number of generations
and have been drawn from every class in modern society it is
natural that they would reflect different class and group attitudes towards the desirable degree of state activity. But they are
united in one thing, namely, in that their criterion of the desirable degree of state activity is the alleged relation of the latter
to social well-being and human progress. The sociological views
about the province of the state have varied all the way from
anarchism to extreme collectivism.

The outstanding sociological exponent of anarchism was the
Russian writer, Kropotkin, who advocated an anarchistic society
controlled by voluntary cooperation, dispensing entirely with the
coercive political state. Novicow did not go quite so far as Kropotkin, but he stood for that extreme degree of individualism
which limits the state to the role of a collective policeman, devoted solely to the protection of the persons and property of citizens. Almost as extreme and far more influential was Spencer,
the classical sociological protagonist of individualism. In his *Social
Statics* and his *Man vs. State* Spencer argued that the sphere of
government should be limited to the protection of persons and
property from domestic and foreign attack and to insuring the
freedom and enforcement of contract. The state should, as Spencer
put it, concern itself entirely with "Negative Regulation". Spen-

cer's views were vastly influential for decades. As late as 1905, Justice Oliver Wendell Holmes accused his majority colleagues on the Supreme Court of being dominated by Spencer's ideas, and in 1912 Spencer's books were reprinted to confound the supporters of Theodore Roosevelt's "Bull Moose" party. Spencer's ideas were given currency in America in the lucid and dogmatic writings of his disciple, Sumner, particularly in the latter's terse little work, *What the Social Classes Owe to Each Other.*

At the opposite extreme from such individualism was the cordiality of such sociologists as Comte, Ward, Hobhouse, Schäffle, Stein and Small to extensive state activity. They believed that the complicated problems of our day, in an age of industrialism, require an extended degree of state intervention and control. No absolute position can be taken, since the degree and type of collectivism recommended must depend upon a sociological study of the conditions in any state at any time, in order to determine the degree of regulation which is necessary. In case such a study seemed to indicate the need for even a socialistic regime these writers would not flinch. The most extreme advocates of state intervention among sociologists are those who have fallen under the spell of Marxism and Fascist Totalitarianism. The Marxists believe that the state must control economic life completely in the early stages of the socialist revolution, but contemplate the ultimate withering away of political activity and the establishment of a cooperative and classless commonwealth. The Fascist totalitarians, however, look forward to an unlimited and permanent dominion of the state over all aspects of human life. In his *A New Social Philosophy* Sombart has bitterly attacked the traditional sociological view of the state as merely the umpire of the social process.

The majority of the sociologists refuse to accept any dogmatic and absolute position as to the role of the state. This must depend upon the circumstances in any society at any time. They take what is called an eclectic position. This attitude has been well stated by Ross:

It is idle to attempt to lay down definitely the proper functions of the state, because its scope should depend upon such variables as the trend of social relationships, the development of the social mind, the advances of technique, the talent available for government, etc.[12]

The same general attitude is adhered to by Cooley:

We must take the relative point of view and hold that the sphere of government operations is not, and should not be fixed but varies with the social condition at large. Hard-and-fast theories of what the state may best be and do, whether restrictive or expansive, we may well regard with distrust. It is by no means impossible that the whole character of the political state and its relation to the rest of life is undergoing change of an unforseeable kind which will eventually make our present dogmas on this point seem quite obsolete.[13]

The events of the generation since Cooley wrote these words afford ample confirmation of the sagacity of his concluding sentence.

Durkheim has made an interesting and helpful suggestion, namely, that the government should go far in determining those general policies which affect the well-being of the citizens, but should delegate expert administration to technically equipped professional groups, a point of view which is generally known as administrative syndicalism. This solution would seek to combine both state responsibility and expert government.

Their attitudes towards state activity have naturally colored the position taken by sociologists in regard to the relation of the state to social evolution. Writers like Spencer and Sumner believe that social evolution, like organic evolution, is automatic and that government intervention would only impede and frustrate the processes of nature. Ward and the collectivists believe that, while social evolution may have been automatic down to modern times, the social sciences have now given us the information by means of which we can effect a short cut to desirable social goals which could be otherwise attained only through centuries of wasteful and unchartered automatic evolution.

Sociologists have given much attention to revolution. Most of them agree that revolutions are a wasteful and violent method of securing social progress, but at times they seem necessary. The great danger lies in a counter-revolution which may destroy the benefits secured through revolutionary measures.

[12] E. A. Ross. *Principles of Sociology* (New York: Century, 1930), p. 624.
[13] C. H. Cooley. *Social Organization* (New York: Scribner, 1909), p. 403.

Sociologists are generally agreed that it is the conservatives rather than the radicals who produce revolutions. By their adamant and senseless opposition to all change, the conservatives bring about a condition which makes violent revolution the only alternative to fatal stagnation. LeBon, Ellwood, Crane Brinton, T. H. P. Edwards, and P. A. Sorokin have given special attention to revolution. Sorokin believes that we are now in the midst of a generation of revolutions which will ultimately bring about a transition from our present sensate culture to a future ideational civilization.

The sociologists naturally take a relativistic attitude towards liberty. The degree of liberty which can and should exist is not absolute but is determined by the circumstances prevailing in any country at any given time. The more mature and homogenous any society, the greater the amount of liberty which may be expected and desired. Great differences in culture and economic possessions in any state are deadly to liberty, as likewise is the existence of international chaos and the threat of constant war.

The sociologists have ruthlessly destroyed the idea that there is any such thing as a natural right, existing anterior to man and society. All rights are the product of social experiences and the social process. As Hobhouse, Giddings and Cooley have stated, the only defensible type of natural right is one which will promote the social welfare of a given country at any specific period. Giddings has fruitfully emphasized the fact that states and communities, as well as individuals, have natural rights.

IX. SOCIOLOGICAL ATTITUDES TOWARDS AND INTERNATIONAL RELATIONS.

Sociological notions of the social value of war have differed widely. Gumplowicz and other social Darwinists have contended that war is a highly constructive and dynamic factor in human society, comparable to the struggle for existence in the biological world. On the other hand, Novicow, G. F. Nicolai and other internationalists have contended that war has always been a social evil and that the claims for its social services, even in the remote past, have been grossly exaggerated. Such writers as Giddings,

E. C. Hayes and Stein have taken any eclectic attitude. They admit the past contributions of war to political consolidation and the like, but hold that it is now a dangerous anachronism. But all schools of sociologists agree that there is no hope of ending war until we provide general social and cultural conditions compatible with world peace. The sociologists, especially Sorokin, have been very helpful in emphasizing the social and economic causes of war.

Sociologists also differ in their attitudes towards imperialism. John Fiske, Benjamin Kidd and Giddings have defended imperialism as a means of extending the higher cultures to backward areas. This attitude has been violently assailed by Hobhouse and Sumner, who contended that imperialism is incompatible with democracy, liberty and peace. It promotes poverty and intolerance at home and war abroad.

A number of sociologists have given special attention to the problem of international organization. Hobhouse, Stein, J. H. W. Stuckenberg and Wallas have emphasized the need for a strong international organization, perhaps a world state, as the only sufficient means of ending the menace of war. The most extreme and forceful proponent of this point of view has been the English publicist, H. G. Wells.

An important contribution to international relations and world peace has been made by De Greef, in his sociological theory of frontiers. He distinguishes between mere political frontiers, as established by accident or as the outcome of wars, and social frontiers, which are the everchanging result of social pressures exerted by national groups. They are an unstable equilibrium. Peace can be preserved only when we develop some type of international organization which will periodically adjust the political or military frontiers to the underlying and dynamic social frontiers.

X. Conclusion.

We have in the preceding pages given only the most casual representative sampling of some leading sociological contributions to political theory. Limitations of space prevented anything more than this. In fact, the writer devoted a book of over 250 pages to this subject and even this volume is only a skeleton digest of a larger unpublished work of over a 1000 pages which, in itself, cannot be regarded as much more than an adroit sampling of sociological writings on political theory. But even the few pages in this chapter will indicate the degree to which sociology has, or at least may, broaden out the perspective of political theory.

We may, in conclusion, mention the fact that sociology has done much to clarify the history of political theory by making it clear that every stage and type of political theory has been no more or less than a reflection and rationalization of an existing culture, political community or individual complexes. Giddings, for example, used to point out how Machiavelli reflected the conspiratal society of early modern Italy. But Giddings' own sociology was equally a rationalization of a buoyant and imperialistic America, at the turn of the century. This important notion has especially been cultivated by Karl Mannheim and other exponents of the sociology of knowledge.

REFERENCES

ALBIG, WILLIAM. *Public Opinion*. New York: Macmillian, 1939. Best study of propaganda and censorship.

BARNES, H. E. *Sociology and Political Theory*. New York: Knopf, 1924. Only comprehensive treatment of this subject.

BARNES, H. E. AND BECKER, H. F. *Contemporary Social Theory*. New York: Appleton-Century, 1940. Most complete and up-to-date summary.

BEARD, C. A. *The Economic Basis of Politics*. New York: Knopf, 1922. Brilliant little book, by dean of American Political Science.

BENTLEY, A. F. *The Process of Government*. Chicago: University of Chicago Press 1908. Best sociological analysis.

COKER, F. A. *Organismic Theories of the State*. New York: Longmans, 1910. Standard book on subject.

COOLEY, C. H. *Social Organization*. New York: Scribner, 1909. Pioneer work on primary groups and democracy.

COUNTS, G. S. *The Prospect of American Democracy*. New York: Day, 1938. Best single work on democracy.

CURTI, M. E. *The Social Ideas of American Educators*. New York: Scribner, 1935. Excellent historical survey.

DE GREEF, G. J. *La Structure générale des Sociétés*. Brussels: Larcier, 1907-08, 3 vols. Noted for social theory of frontiers.

ELLWOOD, C. A. *Sociology in its Psychological Aspects*. New York: Appleton, 1912. The pioneer book in the field.

GIDDINGS, F. H. *Democracy and Empire*. New York: Macmillian, 1900. Vigorous defense of imperialism.

————. *The Responsible State*. Boston: Houghton, Mifflin, 1918. Brief sociological theory of politics, written under influence of war hysteria.

HANKINS, F. H. *The Racial Basis of Civilization*. New York: Knopf, 1926. The best sociological treatment of race.

HERTZLER, J. O. *Social Institution*. New York: McGraw-Hill, 1929. Good introduction.

HOBHOUSE L. T. *Social Evolution and Political Theory*. New York: Col. Univ. Pr. 1918. A classic work.

HOLMES, S. J. *The Eugenics Predicament*. New York: Harcourt Brace, 1933. Some analysis.

KARE, F. B. *American Social Psychology*. New York: McGraw-Hill, 1932.

LOWIE, R. H. *Primitive Society*. New York: Boni and Liveright, 1920. Best statement of critical school.

MACLEOD, W. C. *The Origin and History of Politics*. New York: Wiley, 1931. Best history of politics.

MANHEIM, KARL. *Ideology and Utopia*. Standard book on sociology of knowledge.

MICHELS, ROBERT. *Political Parties*. New York: Hearts Int. Lib. 1915. Most original work on subject.

NEWLON, J. H. *Education for democracy in our Time*. New York: McGraw-Hill, 1939. A suggestive work.

OPPENHEIMER, FRANZ. *The State*. Indianapolis: Bobbs Merril, 1914. Good economic interpretation.

OSBORNE FREDERICK. *Preface to Eugenics*. New York: Harper, 1940. Splendid introduction.

OVERSTREET, H. A. *"The Government of Tomorrow"*. The Forum (Vol. LIV). Brilliant exposition of occup. repr.

PARETO, VILFREDO. *The Mind in Society*. New York: Harcourt-Brace, 1935, 4 vols. A vast and much discussed book.

PARSONS, TALCOTT. *The Structure of Social Action*. New York: McGraw-Hill, 1937. Good summary of theoretical sociology.

ROSS, E. A. *Social Control*. New York: Macmillan, 1904. A pioneer and brilliantly written book.

SMALL, A. W. *General Sociology*. Chicago: University of Chicago Press, 1905. Ratzenhofer in American dress.

SOMBART, WERNER. *A New Social Philosophy*. Princeton: Princeton University Press, 1937. Famous economist historian supports totalitarianism.

SOROKIN, P. A. *Social and Cultural Dynamics*. New York: American Book Co., 4 vols., 1937. Voluminous and learned work.

SPENCER, HERBERT. *The Study of Sociology*. New York: Appleton, 1933. Classic introduction to the field.

STERN, B. J., and LOUIS HENRY MORGAN. *Social Evolutionist*. Chicago: Chicago University Press, 1931. Good study of Morgan's ideas.

SUMNER, W. G. *What Social Classes Owe to Each Other*. New York: Harper, 1883. Classic statement of laissez-faire philosophy.

————. *Folkways*. Boston: Ginn, 1907. A monumental study of folkways.

THOMAS, FRANKLIN. *The Environmental Basis of Society*. New York: Century, 1925. Best summary of writings in this field.

THOMPSON, W. S. *Population Problems*. New York: McGraw-Hill, 1935. Best manual in field.

TROTTER, WILFRED. *Instincts of the Herd in Peace and War*. London: Unwin, 1916. Brilliant essay.

WEBER, MAX. *The Protestant Ethic, and the Spirit of Capitalism*. New York: Scribner, 1930. An epoch-making book.

WALLAS, GRAHAM. *Human Nature in Politics*. Boston: Houghton Mifflin, 1908. Pioneer work in realistic political psychology.

CHAPTER IV

RECENT NATIONALISM, PAN-NATIONALISM AND IMPERIALISM

O. DOUGLAS WEEKS

National consciousness has been described as the most important force in modern times. It has transcended and pervaded much of the political thought of the 19th and 20th centuries. Religion has yielded to it, and class consciousness, also a vital force, has been subordinated to it.[1] Its principal manifestations may be found in the philosophies of nationalism, pan-nationalism, and modern imperialism, which have constituted essentially a single body of thought. Nationalism, which may be defined as the formulization or rationalization of national consciousness, occupies the first place in this trilogy, because pan-nationalism and modern imperialism have been, for the most part, its mere projections. During the last half-century the phenomena which these terms represent have loomed larger, have assumed new and more extreme forms, and have become more intimately associated. A wide variety of new nationalistic leaders and movements have made their appearance, serious attempts have been made to solve the perplexing problems of conflicting nationalisms, and many objective analyses and interpretations have been undertaken by a growing number of interested scholars.

THE NATURE OF NATIONALISM; ITS DEMOCRATIC ORIGIN

National consciousness and nationalism on the part of the masses are world-wide facts today. The nationalism of a particular people is a more or less dogmatic, accepted philosophy, ideology, or body of beliefs with respect to the nation or nationality, its

---

[1] Walter Sulzbach. *National Consciousness* (Washington: American Council on Public Affairs, 1943), p. 1.

relationships with and attitudes toward other nations and nationalities, and its rights and privileges in the world at large. The nation or nationality around which the ideology is built may be characterized as the result of a complex set of conditions—geographical (homeland), ethnical (race or *Volk*), traditional (myths and customs), historical (heroic or memorable events), linguistic (common language), political (presence or absence of statehood and peculiar political institutions), social (distinctive social organization), and economic (economic theory, structure, possessions or needs)—which surround a given people and which mark it as different from other well-defined peoples. The dynastic origin of many modern states has meant that statehood and nationality have frequently not coincided. Modern nationalism has, therefore, inevitably sought full expression in unified and independent statehood. Hence, politically divided nations have desired union in a single state; politically subject nationalities have demanded separation and self-determination; and colonial peoples have struggled for self-government and independence. Thus nationalism may take various forms, which makes analysis difficult. Particular nationalisms may be readily examined and explained, but nationalism as an all-embracing term is less susceptible of satisfactory definition.

Most present-day students of national consciousness and nationalism are agreed that they represent essentially a mass state of mind of comparatively recent origin among the majority of peoples and are the result of a variety of convergent causes produced by the conditions of modern civilization. Carlton J. H. Hayes, a leading American authority on nationalism, has emphasized that the development of commerce, industrialism, and capitalism during the last few centuries has meant the progressive drawing together of the lives of peoples and has accentuated a unity of feeling within them and a sense of difference between them. This has brought in its wake the modern sovereign state with its centralized government, which has fostered the growth of national consciousness and nationalism and has served as the chief vehicle

of their expression.[2]   As Hans Kohn has pointed out, however, the
sovereign state was the creation of the absolute monarchs of the
16th and 17th centuries, whose motives were more dynastic than
national.   It remained, therefore, for the French Revolution and
the later revolutionary movements it inspired to transfer sovereignty from the king to the people with the result that supreme
allegiance or loyalty was given to the nation rather than to its
ruler. National consciousness and nationalism, then, were born
of mass consciousness and the democratic idea that the state belonged to the masses of the nation as a whole.[3] In the words of
Friedrich Meinecke, noted German student of nationalism, *"Es ist
also kein Zufall, dasz der Ära des modernen Nationalgedankens
eine Ära individualistischer Freiheitsregungen unmittelbar voran-
geht. Die Nation trank gleichsam das Blut der freien Persönlich-
keit zu erheben."* [4] National consciousness had previously existed,
but it had been more or less vague and rather the exclusive possession of an aristocracy or intelligentsia which assumed to be the
chief carriers or spokesmen of whatever national tradition there
may have been. Thus the elite had been the nation, but now the
role was assumed by the *Volk*.[5] Hence, France in her great revolution, Hayes and others contend, was the first to realize a truly
democratic nationalism, which later spread in varying degrees
throughout and beyond Europe, and which strongly colored all nationalistic movements until late in the 19th century. Aside from
France, however, the liberal nation—states of Western Europe—
notably the United Kingdom and the Scandinavian and low countries—, because of their deep-rooted systems of representative
government, built up the strongest traditions of liberal nationalism

---

[2] Carlton J. H. Hayes. "Nationalism," *Encyclopaedia of the Social Sciences,* XI,
240; Roy V. Peel and Joseph S. Roucek (Eds.), *Introduction to Politics* (New
York: Thomas Y. Crowell Co.), 1941, ch. 6.

[3] Hans Kohn. "The Nature of Nationalism." *American Political Science Review,*
XXXIII, 1939, pp. 1001-1021.

[4] Friedrich Meinecke. *Weltbürgertum und Nationalstaat, Studien zur Genesis des
deutsches Nationalstaates,* 7th Ed. (Munich: R. Oldenbourg Verlag, 1928), p. 9.

[5] Frederick Hertz. "Wesen und Werden der Nation" in *Nation und Nationalität*
(Karlsruhe: G. Braun Verlag, 1927), pp. 1-88.

within themselves. Outside Europe, the same may be said of the United States and the self-governing dominions of the British Empire.

Since about 1880, however, as the spirit of nationalism became more active in Eastern Europe and the Orient and had to be adjusted to peoples living under a wide variety of circumstances and lacking democratic traditions, the liberal ingredient has diminished. Moreover, with the industrialization of Western and Central Europe, the United States, and Japan, the greater nations became rivals and regarded smaller or less advanced peoples as their lawful prey. Thus dawned the age of economic nationalism and modern imperialism which served to dilute whatever liberal content there may have been in the national spirits of some of these states so far as the outside world was concerned.[6] More will be said of this later.

NON-LIBERAL EUROPEAN THEORIES OF NATIONALISM

The birth of democratic national consciousness did not altogether terminate the leadership of an elite, for in the case of many nationalities the nationalism of the masses was more the result of the propaganda of a persistent intelligentsia than a product of spontaneous popular action. In some instances, no doubt, the effect was to create national consciousness for which there was little real justification. German nationalism, which owed much of its origin to the democratic impulses of the French Revolutionary age, came more and more to be identified, due to the influence of Herder, Hegel, Fichte, the German organismic thinkers, the German Pan-Nationalists, and many intellectual leaders who came later, with a mystical *Volksgeist*, whose mysterious ways were supposedly revealed clearly only to the governing masters of the people. Reactionaries, conservatives, and anti-democrats in other countries—French *Réactionnaires* and Integral Nationalists: Edmund Burke, Thomas Carlyle, and Lord Hugh Cecil in Great Britain; and fascists of various types in Italy and else-

---

[6] Carlton J. H. Hayes. *Essays on Nationalism* (New York: The Macmillan Company, 1926); *The Historical Evolution of Modern Nationalism* (New York: Richard R. Smith, 1930).

where—have in a wide variety of ways sought to find in some elite a harnessing and directing power over national consciousness.[7] To them, uncontrolled mass nationalism, like democracy, was a crude, dangerous, and disintegrating force. Even students of the psychological bases of nationalism and national leadership, like Roberto Michels, viewed the masses in all countries as inert and as dough in the hands of their leaders. All nations, Michels affirmed, were subject to the "iron law of oligarchy". The leadership of democracies, no less than that of autocratic and aristocratic regimes, creates nationalistic concepts, myths, and stereotypes, impresses them upon the people, and rules by their constant reiteration.[8]

Italian Fascism and German Nazism have made the most of these ideas. In them, nationalism appears in its most malignant and exaggerated forms. Their glorification of the chosen race, *Volk,* nation, or state and its relegation to realms beyond reason and morality, their justification of the most ruthless military aggression, their enthronement of an elite among their own people as well as the peoples they have conquered, and their totalitarian and autarchic economies are well enough known and are dealt with at length elsewhere in the present volume. Their ideologies were anticipated earlier in the present century in other countries by groups like the French Integral Nationalists, they have strongly influenced the rulers of fascist or near-fascist regimes in other states, notably those of present-day Spain and Japan, and they are reflected in the pronouncements and deeds of quisling governments in France, Norway, and other occupied countries. These

---

[7] Consult: Lord Hugh Cecil. "National Instinct, the Basis of Social Institutions," in *Burnett House Papers,* No. 9. (London: Oxford University Press, 1926) ; and William C. Buthman. *The Rise of Integral Nationalism in France* (New York: Columbia University Press, 1939).

[8] Roberto Michels: *Der Patriotismus, Prolegomena zu seiner Soziologischen Analyse* (Munich: Dunker und Hamblot, 1929) ; *Political Parties: A Sociological Study of the Oligarchical Tendencies of Modern Democracy,* translated from the French (New York: Hearst's International Library Co.), 1915.

philosophies are amply stated in the writings of Mussolini, Hitler, and their many literary assistants.[9]

While the influence of the French Revolution was slight in Russia, a well-defined philosophy of nationalism took shape in the 19th century to which Slavophils, advocates of Pan-Slavism, and liberals like Paul M. Milyoukov contributed. The international emphasis of Marxian Socialism and the general character of the Soviet regime have been treated elsewhere. Suffice it to say here that, in line with Marxian ideology, the nation had no intrinsic value for Lenin, for he regarded it as merely an instrument in the struggle of the world proletariat for power. He took into account the survival power of nationalism, however, and was willing to recognize it and use it so as it might aid in the world struggle to establish communism. The Soviet Union has always nominally extended equality, national privileges, and the right of secession to its peoples. With the advent of Stalin to supreme leadership, the international viewpoint of Lenin was shifted to one of "socialism in a single country". Thus the experiment of Communism was to be carried to complete success within the Soviet Union itself. Under this new emphasis the five-year plans were launched, and the new nationalism was defined in terms of admiration for new factories, collective farms, power plants, mines, and cities. This new nationalism became the cornerstone of Soviet domestic and foreign policies. The words "patriotism" and "Fatherland" were revived along with the old folksongs and classic literature. More recently, the liquidation of the Third International, cooperation with the Western allies in the struggle against Germany, and Russia's own heroic defense are indications of a full rebirth and intensification of Russian nationalism, and may result eventually in something more nearly akin to the liberal nationalisms of the West.[10]

[9] W. H. McGovern. *From Luther to Hitler* (Boston: Houghton Mifflin Co.), 1941.
[10] Hans Kohn. *Nationalism in the Soviet Union,* translated from the German. (New York: Columbia University Press, 1933) ; *Nationalism.* A Report by a Study Group of Members of the Royal Institute of International Affairs (London: Oxford University Press, 1939), ch. V; Samuel N. Harper. *The Government of the Soviet Union* (New York: Van Nostrand), 1938, ch. XI; N. Lenin. *Ueber die nationale Frage,* 2 vols. (Berlin: Rewohlt Verlag, 1931) ; Joseph Stalin. *Leninism,* 2 vols. (London: Allen and Unwin, 1932-1933).

Pan-Nationalism and Imperialism

Pan-nationalism describes a variety of movements which represent projections or extensions of nationalistic movements, but with many differences in origin and purpose. Pan-Germanism in its earliest form was little more than a nationalistic movement to bring all Germans under a single state, but it later developed into German imperialism and paved the way for the Napoleonic aspirations of Hitler. Pan-Slavism, on the other hand, began as a cultural and mutual-assistance movement among the various Slavic peoples, but was later largely absorbed in Tsarist imperialism and has recently been seemingly resurrected by Soviet Russia as a part of her policy toward her Slavic neighbors to the West. Anglo-Saxonism and Pan-Hispanism emphasized, until recently at least, only the cultural kinship, respectively, of the English and Spanish-speaking peoples. Other so-called pan-movements of a hemispheric, geographical, or religious character have been only incidentally nationalistic in their implications or have even run counter to nationalistic aspirations.[11]

Imperialism has appeared in many forms and has been variously defined. While it is much older than modern nationalism and under certain circumstances is not its inevitable accompaniment, the fact remains that, since the advent of the latter, imperialism has usually been one of its manifestations and has largely become its tool or servant. In general, imperialism embraces varying types of conquest, absorption, domination, or penetration of peoples and territories by stronger powers and has been motivated by the ambitions of dynasts, militarists, religionists, agriculturists, merchants, capitalistic investors, industrialists, nationalists, pan-nationalists, missionaries of "superior civilizations", protagonists of politico-economic ideologies, and seekers of *Lebensraum* for peoples whose homelands lacked necessary natural resources and economic opportunities for growing populations. The many forms of imperialism have embodied various combinations of these motivations. Nationalism enters most potently into imperialism, perhaps, when the aim is to unify a nation

---

[11] Hans Kohn. "Pan-Movements," *Encyclopaedia of the Social Sciences*, XI, 544.

under a single state organization, to free co-nationals held by other states, to hold peoples who try to secede, and to subdue other peoples for the purpose of enhancing the domain, power, wealth, or prestige of the aggressor nation. These purposes all appear in the nationalistic movements of the last century and a half, but some of them have been most loudly espoused to explain the recent aggressions of Germany, Italy, and Japan.

While the state usually figures prominently in all types of imperialism, political annexation of new territories is not always the main object of imperialistic expansions. Particularly since the rise of modern industrialism with its insatiable quest for raw materials and markets, new types of control have developed which are more economic than political. Economic domination, however, almost inevitably leads to some form of political intervention to back it up, whether it be outright annexation or the establishment of leaseholds, protectorates, spheres of influence or whatnot. The imperialism of the great Western powers between 1870 and 1914 usually involved the penetration or annexation of non-contiguous, overseas colonies inhabited largely by "backward" peoples. Much was said about the assumption of the "white man's burden", whatever the real motives, but national prestige and an urge for a place in the imperialistic sun came nearer the true explanation, and behind that lay the real motive of economic gain, which often proved to be elusive for nations as a whole, however much it may have profited a few of their capitalistic investors. While the newer imperialisms of Italy and Japan have been similar in that they have involved the conquest of non-contiguous territories and "inferior" peoples, the acquisition of natural resources lacking in their homelands and more living space for teeming populations has figured much more prominently. In the case of Nazi Germany, although imperialistic mastery of a great portion of the earth has been the ultimate grandiose aspiration, the more immediate aim has been that of subjecting the territories of contiguous European states to the stern regimen of the "master race" in order to provide it with adequate *Lebensraum* and opportunity to fulfill its destiny. Finally, it may be added, that however loudly the Communists,

particularly those of Soviet Russia, may have condemned nationalism and imperialism as the products of capitalism, it is not difficult to discern these old wolves in the new sheep's clothing of
Soviet national policy and the Third International. Dynasticism,
liberalism, fascism, and communism in varying degrees and differing forms have embraced imperialism.[12]

Self-Determination vs. Imperialism

Nationalism is not only the breeder of modern imperialism,
but it is also the chief factor in the revolt against that imperialism. The emergence of national consciousness among many
European peoples may be traced to the desire to be rid of the
yoke of Napoleon or to overthrow the dynastic state system which
the Congress of Vienna attempted to revive after Napoleon and
which either divided or subjugated nations so as to deny them
self-determination as unified and independent national states. The
unification of Germany and Italy in the 19th century and the
appearance of many new national states during that century and
as a result of World War I are cases in point. The birth of new
nationalisms may be noted in the 18th century revolt of the American colonies against British imperialism, the liberation of the
Spanish colonies in the 19th century, and the rise of national
consciousness and of independence movements among Oriental
peoples in the late 19th and 20th centuries.

Viscount Bryce and Woodrow Wilson were outstanding
later exponents of self-determination for subject nationalities.
So far as Europe and America were concerned, Bryce thought
of nationalism as the upward struggle of democracy and self-
determination to attain the twin principles of liberty and nationality. He appreciated, however, the many obstacles confronting
the realization of such a liberal dream for all peoples. He did
not believe that all races or nationalities were of equal importance,
even though each nationality may have a unique contribution to
make to a world civilization and should be allowed some sort of

---

[12] Consult: F. L. Schuman. *International Politics*, 3rd Ed. (New York: McGraw-
Hill Book Co., Inc., 1941), Book Three.

freedom to do so.[13] President Wilson, unlike Bryce, did not fully anticipate or entirely comprehend all the complexities attending the application of the doctrine of self-determination which he espoused and defended on a world stage during and immediately after the first World War, and yet, for all its faults, the Versailles peace arrangement, for which Wilson shared responsibility, went farther than any previous international agreements in recognizing and establishing the principle at least in Central Europe. However dismal the failure to realize Wilson's ideals may now seem to have been, his championship of the cause of liberal self-determination gave it a prominence and assured it a measure of success in international politics which will not be permanently erased. Events since 1919 fully demonstrate that it is futile for every nationality, however small, to attain or maintain complete independent statehood. Autonomous status within larger states or federations would seem more practicable for many of them. In the free world of the future, nationalism may stand a better chance of survival and make a more valuable contribution to civilization by sacrificing its urge for expression in nominally independent but actually ineffectual sovereignty. Many of the current proposals for post-war reorganization of the national state system reflect this thought.

It is possible here to mention only two or three of the experiments in self-determination which followed World War I. Czechoslovakia, without doubt, stands out as the most successful. Despite certain divisions of an historical and economic nature between the Czechs and the Slovaks and the presence of large German, Magyar, Polish, and Ukrainian minorities, the existence of a strong middle class and the able leadership of Masaryk and Benes produced a real national unity and a satisfactory parliamentary democracy. These men have been aptly called the Washington and Hamilton of Czechoslovakia. Although modern Czech nationalism was originally inspired by the great Czech historian, Palacký, Masaryk, his disciple, translated it into reality as the

---

[13] Viscount Bryce. "The Principle of Nationality and Its Applications," in *Essays and Addresses in War Time* (New York: The Macmillan Co., 1918).

founder of the new state, and Benes was the latter's chief collaborator and successor in the presidency. Masaryk emphasized
the fact that Czechoslovakia was not a mere artificial creation
made possible by the fortunes of war. Her claims to an independent national existence, he believed, were fully justified by
her past history, past leadership, mature culture, and economic
development. Masaryk's nationalism was a deliberate and discerning love of his nation as opposed to a belief in it right or wrong.
Benes largely accepted the ideas of Masaryk and strove to maintain his nation's independence to the last.[14]

Yugoslavian and Roumanian nationalism present a somewhat different pattern. Both peoples had vague memories of
long past unity and independence, and both were divided for
centuries under alien jurisdiction, the respective fragments having developed different traditions and varied economic organization. When Serbia was expanded into Yugoslavia and Roumania's
frontiers were greatly extended at the end of World War I, national unity was scarcely realized in either. In Yugoslavia fundamental division was reflected in two rival political leaders—
Nicholas Pashitch and Stephen Raditch, who upheld, respectively,
the aspirations of the Serbs and the Croats. Long a figure in the
politics of Serbia, Pashitch was primarily a Serbian patriot, who
fought the federalist demands of the Croats and sought to establish a strongly centralized government under Serbian control.
He may be said to have been primarily responsible for the creation of the Yugoslav kingdom. Radich, equally inspired by a
loyalty to Croatia, fought the centralizing policies of Pashitch.
In the end, dictatorship under the King resulted. Largely peasant
and lacking a virile middle class, it may truthfully be said that
Yugoslavia was, to a great extent, devoid of the elements which
help to develop a true philosophy of nationalism. A somewhat

---

[14] T. G. Masaryk. *The Making of a State* (New York: Stokes, 1927); Edward
Benes. *My War Memoirs* (Boston: Houghton Mifflin, 1928); *Democracy Today
and Tomorrow* (New York: The Macmillan Co., 1939).

similar picture is presented by Roumania, a country also largely peasant, with a national-minded ruling class.[15]

Nationalism Beyond Europe

Europe has been pre-eminently the cradle of nationalism. Nationalistic movements in other parts of the world have drawn their ideas from Europe and have arisen to a considerable extent from defense motives inspired by a desire to be rid of European tutelage and encroachment. In differing degrees this has been true of the development of nationalism in the Western Hemisphere and in Asia. In the Americas, more or less harsh colonial subjection produced an attitude of revolt and a separation dividing peoples closely connected by ties of blood and tradition, which resulted in independent statehood under which a sense of distinctive nationalism later emerged. In Asia, the impact of Western imperialism, the resulting desire of the Asiatic to compete with or to be free of the foreigner, and the importation of European ideas of the nation and the state produced a spirit of nationalism which has served to Europeanize Japan in a measure, to unite China, and to build up in India a considerable unity of resistance. Except for Japan, allegiance wider than that to group or locality has been, in the past, more often religious and cultural than political. Western ideas of the state and nation have been brought in by native leaders, but they have flourished in a distinct atmosphere and have been expressed in terms peculiar to the peoples among whom they have taken root.

In Latin-America, geography, the general nature of the movements for independence, and the presence of proportionately large indigenous populations have determined the character of nationalism. Far-flung and widely separated areas caused the disintegration of early attempts at continental union and have

[15] Joseph S. Roucek. *The Politics of the Balkans* (New York: McGraw-Hill, 1939); Robert William Seton-Watson. *The Rise of Nationality in the Balkans* (London: Constable, 1917); Wesley M. Gewehr. *The Rise of Nationalism in the Balkans* (New York: Henry Holt, 1931); David Mitrany. *Greater Rumania: A Study in National Ideals* (New York: Hodder and Stoughton, 1917); *The Land and Peasant in Roumania* (London: Oxford University Press, 1930); *The Effect of the War in Southeastern Europe* (New Haven: Yale University Press, 1936).

since worked against it. The independence movements were largely inspired by small upper-classes and were not coördinated. Varying degrees of assimilation of the native population, economic bondage, and political oligarchy have prevented the full development of mass nationalism. The influx of diverse foreign elements has had a disintegrating influence. Dramatic national leaders have appeared in Latin-America from time to time, but no very consistent bodies of nationalistic philosophy have been developed. By and large, nationalism, except in a few countries, is still in an aristocratic stage.[16]

Japanese nationalism represents a strange combination of traditional and European elements. Of all peoples of the Orient, the Japanese have always been the most unified. Perhaps among no people have nationality, nationalism, religion, state, government, and social life been so closely intertwined. Long isolation and peculiar institutional development have been largely responsible. Moreover, unlike most Asiatic peoples, the Japanese have so far been free of invading and subjugating conquerors. To them the nation and state are as one with the Emperor acting as head of both and serving as a kind of father to a huge patriarchal family, with internal society following a hierarchal pattern. When contact with Western civilization came in the middle of the 19th century, the Japanese rapidly adjusted themselves to it, absorbing readily what fitted in best with their traditional ways. Fundamental economic changes came along with a limited adoption of Western parliamentary institutions, but the essential authoritarianism of the past survived and was further bolstered up by Prussian and later by Fascist and Nazi conceptions of nationalism and the state. This was particularly true with regard to the fundamental Japanese belief in their own national superiority. The perpetuation of a military oligarchy, the lack of natural resources, and the demands of modern industrialization, led Japan into a philosophy and policy of imperialism which caused

---

[16] *Nationalism,* A Report by a Study Group of Members of the Royal Institute of International Affairs (London: Oxford University Press, 1939), pp. 125-133.

the development of her grandiose scheme for conquering and exploiting Asia.[17]

The nationalism of modern China has been the outgrowth of a desire to be free of European and of Japanese control. It took shape near the beginning of the present century in two conflicting movements: (1) reaction against all things foreign as exemplified in the Boxer Rebellion of 1900; and (2) acceptance and absorption of Western ideas in order to grow strong and throw off encroachment. The later movement began with the founding of the Kuomintang, or Chinese Nationalist Party, in 1911 by Sun Yat-sen. The Revolution of 1912 was its first expression, and the later work of the Kuomintang under its founder and his successor, Chiang K'ai-shek, has brought Chinese nationalism to its present state of development. Sun Yat-sen's writings contain the embodiment of present-day accepted Chinese nationalistic philosophy; his *San Min Chu I* constitutes the official ideology. The policies of Chiang K'ai-shek, since he became master of the Kuomintang and leader of the national government in 1927, represents the dominant rightist official interpretation of *San Min Chu I*. *San Min Chu I* embodies "three principles of government for the benefit of the people"—nationalism, democracy, and economic collectivism. The first principle involves cultivating state allegiance, opposing foreign economic exploitation, and growing toward democracy. Democracy, the second principle, must be rooted in the old democratic spirit of China and gradually attained nationally under the tutelage of a strong central government and single party. The third principle, economic collectivism, must be attained in a pragmatic way, neither wholly liberal nor communistic. Finally, a China thus modernized and strengthened, could lead Asia and the world to a true cosmopolitanism.[18]

---

[17] *Ibid.*, pp. 160-162; Robert Karl Reischaur. *Japan, Government—Politics* (New York: Thomas Nelson and Sons, 1939); *The Tanaka Memorial* (San Francisco: Chinese National Salvation Publicity Bureau).

[18] Sun Yat-sen. *San Min Chu I* (Shanghai: The Commercial Press, Inc., 1932); Paul M. A. Linebarger. *The China of Chiang K'ai-shek* (Boston: World Peace Foundation, 1941).

The traditional disunity of India and its fundamental causes are too well-known to require discussion here. For fifty years before 1914 a philosophy of nationalism was in the process of formation, but it was largely developed by and confined to a narrow upper-class circle of intellectuals and others who had absorbed Western thought. The Indian National Congress, which is today the central organ of Indian nationalism and predominantly Hindu, was created in 1885 under British inspiration, and at first confined its objectives to the reform of the provincial legislatures in order to allow greater Indian representation and to a demand for Indianization of the Civil Service. Since 1914, however, with the progress of industrialization and education, the reluctance of the British to grant substantial autonomy, and the appearance of powerful mass leadership, the National Congress has moved intermittently toward demands for dominion status and, finally, for outright independence.

Three leaders who have profoundly influenced the development of a conscious Indian nationalism may be mentioned— Rabindranath Tagore, Mohandas K. Gandhi, and Pandit Jawaharlal Nehru. Tagore was a great poet, author, and educator, who emphasized cultural nationalism as opposed to political nationalism of the Western type which he regarded as "a gregarious demand for the exclusive enjoyment of the good things of the earth". This materialistic spirit crushes the moral and spiritual values of a people. India's battle is one of the spirit which will restore her ancient culture and fuse her peoples. Gandhi also has sought to eliminate the nationalistic influences of the West, but in the opinion of Tagore he dissipated his moral force in political adventures. And yet, as a great mass leader, he has been largely responsible for carrying the Indian nationalist movement to the people. While Gandhi clings to old-fashioned Hindu customs and favors a return to a simple society of handicraft industries, his principal associate, Pandit Jawaharlal Nehru, seeks to establish India as a modern nation-state with a socialist economy. He, along with other Indian leaders, minimizes the serious obstacles to Indian unity which the British are inclined to over-emphasize, namely, the gulf between Hindus and Moslems, the

Hindu caste system, the lack of a national consciousness among the peasantry and the proletariat, and the absence of a common language.[19]

SELECTED BIBLIOGRAPHY

BARKER, ERNEST. *National Character and the Factors in its Formation.* London: Harper and Brothers, 1927. An analysis of race, geography, economic conditions, law and government, religion, language and literature, and education as factors in natioalism with special reference to England.

DEMIASHKEVICH, MICHAEL. *The National Mind—English, French, German.* New York: American Book Company, 1938. An attempt to analyze the mass minds and behavior patterns of three great nations in an approach to the problem of national leadership.

HAYES, CARLTON J. H. *Essays on Nationalism.* New York: The Macmillan Company, 1926. A significant general analysis of nationalism as a philosophy and as an historical movement.

HAYES, CARLTON J. H. "Nationalism—Historical Development," *Encyclopaedia of the Social Sciences,* XI, p. 240. An excellent summary of Hayes' findings on the historical aspects of nationalism.

HAYES, CARLTON J. H. *The Historical Evolution of Modern Nationalism.* New York: Richard R. Smith, 1931. A consideration of five types of nationalism advanced by groups of influential political philosophers during the past two centuries.

KOHN, HANS. *A History of Nationalism in the East,* translated from the German by Margaret M. Green. London: Routledge, 1929. An authoritative work on the development of the national idea in Egypt, Turkey, Arabia, Persia, Afghanistan, and India.

KOHN, HANS. *Nationalism in the Soviet Union,* translated from the German. New York: Columbia University Press, 1933. A study of the conflict between the international and national aspects of thought and of the problem of nationalities in the Soviet Union.

KOHN, HANS. *The Idea of Nationalism.* New York: Macmillan, 1944. The outstanding work of recent years.

KOHN, HANS. "Pan-Movements," *Encyclopaedia of the Social Sciences,* XI, 544. An excellent summary of the history and nature of the principal pan-nationalist and other pan-movements. Note attached bibliography.

LENIN, N. *Uber die nationale Frage,* 2 vols. Berlin: Rewohlt Verlag, 1930-31. Extracts from the speeches and writings of Lenin on nationalism with an introduction in the form of a reprint of Joseph Stalin's "Der Leninismus und die nationale Frage."

LINEBARGER, PAUL M. A. *The China of Chiang K'ai-shek, A Political Study.* Boston: World Peace Foundation, 1941. A thorough presentation and explanation of the political system and nationalistic theories of China by a well-qualified writer.

---

[19] Hans Kohn. *A History of Nationalism in the East* (New York: Harcourt, Brace, and Co., 1929), ch. XII; R. Palme Dutt. *India Today* (London: Victor Gollancz, Ltd., 1940); Jawaharlal Nehru. *Toward Freedom* (New York: The John Day Co., 1941); Rabindranath Tagore. *Nationalism* (New York: The Macmillan Company, 1917).

MASARYK, THOMAS GARRIGUE. *The Making of a State.* New York: Frederick A. Stokes Company, 1927. Masaryk's own story of the founding of Czechoslovakia and a presentation of his philosophy of nationalism.

MCGOVERN, WILLIAM MONTGOMERY. *From Luther to Hitler.* Boston: Houghton Mifflin Co., 1941. An indispensable study of the sources and nature of the Fascist-Nazi philosophy.

MEINECKE, FRIEDRICH. *Weltbürgertum und Nationalstaat, Studien zur Genesis des deutschen Nationstaates,* 7th ed. Munich: R. Oldenbourg Verlag, 1928. The outstanding work on the history of German nationalism with expositions of the principal philosophers who have developed it.

MERRIAM, CHARLES EDWARD. *The Making of Citizens.* Chicago: The University of Chicago Press, 1931. The summary volume of an important series, "Studies in the Making of Citizens," dealing with conceptions of nationalism and civic training in France, Germany, England, Italy, Soviet Russia, Austria-Hungary, Switzerland, and the United States, under the general editorship of Professor Merriam.

MICHELS, ROBERTO. *Der Patriotismus: Prolegomena zu seiner sociologischen Analyse.* Munich: Dunker und Humblot, 1929. A psychological approach to nationalism.

Nation und Nationalität, first supplementary volume of *Jahrbuch für Soziologie for 1927.* Karlsruhe: G. Braun Verlag, 1927. An important series of five significant essays on nationalism by Austrian, Dutch, German, and Hungarian scholars, including "Wessen und Werden der Nation" by Friedrich Hertz.

Nationalism, A Report by a Study Group of Members of the Royal Institute of International Affairs. London: Oxford University Press, 1939. An excellent survey of nationalistic movements with an analysis of the nature and causes of nationalism.

PINSON, KOPPEL S. *A Bibliographical Introduction to Nationalism.* New York: Columbia University Press, 1935. An indispensable tool for students of nationalism.

REISCHAUER, ROBERT KARL. *Japan, Government-Politics.* New York: Thomas Nelson and Sons, 1939. An excellent analysis of the political philosophy, government, and practical politics of Japan.

ROUCEK, JOSEPH S. *The Politics of the Balkans.* New York: McGraw-Hill 1939. An up-to-date survey of Balkan politics which emphasizes the nature of nationalism.

SCHUMAN, FREDERICK L. *International Politics,* 3rd. Ed. New York: McGraw-Hill Book Co., Inc., 1941. An up-to-date study of the Western state system in transition. Book III is largely concerned with imperialism.

SULZBACH, WALTER. *National Consciousness.* Washington: American Council on Public Affairs, 1943. A very serviceable study of the factors making for nationalism and national consciousness.

CHAPTER V

FASCISM

MARIAN D. IRISH

Fascism belongs particularly to Italy and to Benito Mussolini in the years between 1919 and 1944 but it is also a universal movement in the interim of the first two great world wars of the twentieth century. Called by many names it may everywhere be identified by a certain uniformity in ideology, psychology and political technique. In its most accomplished form, it is a one-party system controlled by a personal dictator, operating in a totalitarian state which has combined nineteenth century nationalism in politics with twentieth century collectivism in economics. In this form it was once the government of Germany, Turkey, Spain as well as Italy. In somewhat lesser degree, a single party ruled the people of Austria, Bulgaria, Greece and Portugal. Hungary, Roumania, Yugoslavia, Latvia and Lithuania, although retaining multiple parties, also became strictly authoritarian.

As a manifestation of attitude rather than actual institutionalization, the tendency to enhance the power of the executive at the expense of the legislature was to be found even in so-called democratic countries. As minority parties or dissenting groups, fascists were organized by 1939 in France, England, Norway, Ireland, Denmark, Holland, Sweden and the United States. These "movements" apparently had no single causation for they were found in the victorious as well as the defeated states of 1919; in strong and powerful and rich states, and in weak and small and poor states, in states where popular sovereignty was tradition and in states where dictatorships have been perpetual. Fascism, however, has certain things in common. First, the ingredients of hatred are mixed according to the particular circumstances of the state concerned; the fascist hates communism, liberalism and internationalism. Secondly, fascism is rampant nationalism and this may involve, again depending on local conditions, racialism, religious bigotry, anti-semitism. Thirdly, fascism is anti-intellectual, grossly emotional, chauvinistic, always aggressive, full of sound and fury and force.

FASCISM IN THE UNITED STATES

In the United States where the depression bred many groups of malcontents, some persons of high rank in government, a few tycoons in business, even dignitaries of the church became leaders of fascist cohorts. The rank and file of the American fascists, however, were generally the "rabble", who frustrated in their own lines of endeavor apparently found vicarious excitement and compensation in organizations to suppress other individuals. Religious bigotry, anti-Semitic and anti-Catholic, seems the predominant motive of the American fascist, although most of the "Christian" bunds have also been anti-communist, anti-liberal, anti-New Deal and anti-alien. In the period just before the World War II there were many such groups in the United States although it is somewhat difficult to determine which of these were genuinely fascist and which were motivated directly or indirectly by the several Axis propaganda agencies in the country. Thus, the hyphenated nationalist groups which joined the American First movement and subsequently the Peace Now movement were probably supported in large measure by Berlin and Rome.

Most of the American fascist leaders at the outbreak of the War in 1939 were crack-pots or demagogues who ranted and raved the doctrines of sedition in the name of patriotism. Typical was Joe McWilliams, one-time national commander of the Christian Mobilizers, who boasted more than once that when he became the American *Fuhrer* he would down all dissident opinion, run the government like a factory and ship all Jews to Madagascar![1] Of quite different character, a better fascist and one much more dangerous to American democracy was Lawrence

---

[1] *Life Magazine.* 16:15, Jan. 17, 1944.

Dennis, eminently intellectual product of Harvard University with practical experience in the Department of State and Wall Street. Dennis's specialty was softening the people for a "palace revolution" which he pretended not to advocate but to anticipate. Two of his books, *The Coming American Fascism* and the *Dynamics of War and Revolution* present a brilliant and plausible exposition of "government by the elite".[2]

FASCISM IN ITALY: CHRONOLOGY

In this chapter we are not concerned with these anti-constitutional attacks against the government led by persons who would themselves like to be in power the better to implement their particular fanaticism. We shall consider here only the *ex post facto* philosophy of the Italian fascists who did accomplish their revolution and who under Il Duce had twenty years of license to develop a systematic rationalization of party dictatorship and corporate government.

Italian fascism dates from several events. In March, 1919, the renegade Socialist editor of *Il Popolo d'Italia* summoned the first meeting of the *Fascio di combattimento,* fifty or so ex-socialists and ex-soldiers in Milan. Similar meetings shortly took place in other Italian cities, a sort of spontaneous combustion of malcontent. In the elections of May, 1921 the Fascists obtained 35 seats in the Chamber of Deputies, their first official participation in the government they were soon to abolish. In November, 1921, the Milan *Fasci* joined with other groups throughout the country to form a national party, *Partito Nazionale Fascista,* accepting Benito Mussolini as leader. In July, 1922, when the first Facta cabinet resigned, Mussolini openly declared the Fascists were a revolutionary party unwilling to support the existing government of Italy. In October, 1922, the Fascists made their famous March on Rome which was stopped short of civil insurrection by the King's appointment of Mussolini as Prime Minister. In the

---

[2] Lawrence Dennis. *The Coming American Fascism* (New York: Harpers, 1936); *The Dynamics of War and Revolution* (privately printed by the *Weekly Foreign Letter,* New York, 1940).

April elections of 1924, the Fascists, receiving the largest number of votes, under the Acerbo Electoral Law, were automatically given two-thirds membership of the Chamber. In the same year, in protest generally against the Fascist reign of terror and specifically against the Matteotti murder, in imitation of the ancient Aventine secession, the Socialists, Populists and Liberals withdrew from the government leaving only a rump parliament of fascists and conservatives. From 1925, the Italian government was entirely fascist under the personal dictatorship of Mussolini.

There are many explanations both negative and positive for this sequence of events in Italy. On the negative side, it must be conceded that the practice of parliamentary government was never particularly popular in Italy, was virtually in disgrace by 1919. The *Statuto* providing for responsible parliamentary government had been suddenly thrust upon the country without due respect for the autocratic and despotic character of all previous Italian politics. Moreover, it ignored the illiteracy and political inexperience of the Italian people although democracy postulates a constant and intelligent interest by the majority in the formulation of the general will. Because Italian intervention had been championed largely by outside pressure groups, the legislature which had early tended toward pacifism was seldom called during the war years. The government operated mostly by decree powers of the ministry and even in matters of finance and international relations the legislature was seldom allowed the privilege of debate. Once having lost its powers and prestige, the Chamber of Deputies was never able to recover its rightful authority as the representative agency of the people.

The mechanics of parliamentary government were further deadlocked in post-war Italy by the introduction of universal male suffrage and proportional representation. In the parliament of 1921 there were at least 12 distinct parties no one of which could possibly command a majority performance. The largest party was the Marxian Socialist but its members were more accustomed to direct action than political conniving. The party second in size, the *Popolari,* was Catholic, Socialist and Agrarian. These two parties, workers and peasants, respectively were opposed to vested economic interests, against industrial employers on one hand and landed proprietors on the other. Whether socialism was ever a serious menace in Italy is still a matter of acrimonious debate among the surviving Italian politicians who were contemporaries in post-war Italy. But the mere arithmetic of the parliamentary situation in 1921 (more than half of the Chamber of Deputies sat to the left of the Democratic Liberals) implied the impotence of constitutional democratic government in Italy. Obviously the democratic process could not be utilized immediately by any right-wing minority so long as the proletariat maintained its mathematical majority. And the Fascists were in a hurry to hold political power for themselves alone; perforce they were revolutionary.

Whether fascism at the outset was a mass movement or a middle-class manoeuvre is difficult to determine, but certainly it tried to incorporate the many dissident elements in post-war Italy. Always displaying the symbols of martial victory, the fascists summoned the world-war veterans to redeem their country from the defeatism of Versailles. To the workers the Fascists promised government protection for collective bargaining and legislation guaranteeing maximum hours and minimum wages. To the industrialists the Fascists offered relief at once from sabotage, strikes and insubordinate syndicalism. For the people in general, they generously mixed a compound of social security and nationalism that was bound to appease as well as to excite. To the individual, they promised relief from political responsibility, guaranteeing that the burden of participating in government would be removed from the great majority! To everyone they bespoke the glory that was the Roman Empire and the grandeur that was the Roman Church.

Because Italian fascism was compelled to appeal to so many different groups in the country it was impolitic to tie the movement to any particular philosophy. Hence the early writings in Italy all insist upon the "realism" of fascism which denied the validity of any doctrine that can not be tested successfully in immediate application. Said Mussolini himself in the early days (March 23, 1921), "We do not believe in dogmatic programs

. . . . We permit ourselves the luxury of being aristocrats and democrats; conservatives and progressives; reactionaries and revolutionaries; legalitarians and illegalitarians according to the circumstances of time, place, atmosphere—in a word, of history, in which we are constrained to live and act." [3] Following his chief, Rocco, Minister of Justice affirmed, "Fascism above all is action and sentiment." [4] Even Gentile, the noted philosopher who became Mussolini's first Minister of Education, was content to explain that fascism was a return to the Mazzinian slogan "Thought and Action"; subsequently, while still maintaining that fascism could not be analyzed as a series of political formulae he insisted that it contained a logical system. [5] At any rate, for the first few years the fascists found it good strategy to play upon the emotions rather than to appeal to the reason of the Italian people.

MUSSOLINI

Indeed Fascism was at first not so much a political philosophy as the projection of a personality. The person was Benito Mussolini and much of the doctrinal development of Italian fascism is the rationalization of his biography. He was born in rural Romagna, the son of a blacksmith inn-keeper with republican syndicalist leanings. His mother was the village school mistress, a pious woman, ambitious that her sons be a cut above the rough and revolutionary countryman who was their father. Accordingly, Benito received a teacher's diploma at the age of 18 and for a brief period in an otherwise adventurous life, he was pedagogue in an elementary school in Emilia. Dismissed for dancing, drinking and disagreeing in politics with the Mayor, he spent the next decade as a manual laborer and free agent wandering in Switzerland, Germany, France, Austria, Italy, in

---

[3] Herbert L. Matthews. *The Fruits of Fascism* (New York: Harcourt, Brace, 1943), p. 16. Many times quoted.
[4] Alfredo, Rocco. *The Political Doctrine of Fascism, International Conciliation,* 1926, #223.
[5] Giovanni Gentile. "The Philosophical Basis of Fascism," *Foreign Affairs,* VI (Jan., 1928), p. 290.

and out of many prisons and universities depending on whether his interest in revolutionary socialism was active or merely academic at the time.

Returning to Italy after years of exile, Mussolini, the socialist agitator, became editor in 1910 of a weekly entitled *The Class War* (*La Lotta di Classe*). His editorial policy of pacifism and outright advocacy of sabotage within a year put him back in jail, for 1911 was the year of the Tripolitan War. Released from jail, with the prestige of a martyr, he became editor of the socialist paper in Milan, *Avanti*, from which position he was shortly forced to resign because of his chauvinistic editorial policy! This time, however, because he was on the side of the powers existing, instead of going back to prison, he got financial backing for a new newspaper, *Popolo d'Italia*, which became the chief organ of allied intervention. When Italy went to war the great interventionist reached the front ranks as a private but the explosion of a trench mortar soon retired him to the home front. Here, as editor of *Popolo d'Italia*, the wounded hero resumed his verbal fight for *Italia irridenta* without which he would have had little editorial material since both socialism and intervention had proved personally unprofitable.

Mussolini's outlook on life was partly conditioned by early environment but on the whole he seems to have adopted Nietzsche's watchword, "Live dangerously." Following lucky hunches, egotistic and ambitious, he seized his opportunities whenever he saw them. Believing in the validity of practicality, he capitalized upon his inconsistencies while still maintaining the courage of his convictions. There is no doubt that in his youth he was an omniverous reader but he claimed never to have put his faith in books, perhaps because he himself was a scrivener. Likewise though he attended many schools, he never attached his name to any particular teacher, perhaps because he himself was once a teacher.

Nevertheless though Mussolini denies all charges of plagiary, he should acknowledge many familiar sources in the footnotes to his fascism. In his *Autobiography* he does pay respects to few of his mentors: to William James, the American pragmatist; to

George Sorel, the French syndicalist; to Nietzsche, German creator of superman; to Pareto, the Italian sociologist who observed
the importance of the imponderable; to Machiavelli, his hero.[6]
In 1924 when Mussolini went to Bologna for an honorary degree, he wrote a brief thesis on *The Prince* of Machiavelli, thus
to demonstrate the identity between his own life and the doctrine
of Machiavelli. Accepting Machiavelli's pessimistic judgment of
men, Mussolini closely follows the argument of *The Prince* in the
"pre-ordained" anti-thesis between the State and the Individual.
He was already quite positive that "representative systems belong
more to the machinery of politics than to ethics" and that popular sovereignty was never more than an abstraction. As he observed, " referendum works excellently when it is a question of
a village fountain, but when the supreme interests of a people
are in question even the most ultra-democratic governments are
careful not to refer matters to the judgment of the people itself". . . .[7]

Because Mussolini has insisted that the essence of fascism
is faith and not reason, instinct and not doctrine, the intellectual
sources of Italian fascism remain rather sparse and meager. Not
until fascism became a *fait accomplish* was it strategic or feasible
to add *thought* to *action*. The most definitive source of information is a brief essay entitled *Political and Social Doctrine of
Fascism*. This appeared first in 1932 in the *Italian Encyclopaedia*
and has been widely reprinted under the acknowledged author-
ship of *Il Duce* although it is rumored in academic circles that
credit should probably be given to Gentile rather than Mussolini.
Giovanni Gentile, as Minister of Education under fascism, has
occasionally produced philosophical articles expounding the spiritual and ethical possibilities of fascism. Likewise the academic
Palmieri has contributed various touches of idealism and "pure

[6] W. K. Stewart. "The Mentors of Mussolini," *American Political Science Review*,
XXII (November, 1928), pp. 22-43. Curiously he makes no mention of Hegel,
Marx and Lenin although these too must have conditioned the intellectual back-
ground of the ex-socialist.

[7] Margherita Sarfatti. *Life of Benito Mussolini* (New York: Stokes, 1926), p.
129.

thought" to an otherwise sordid system. Mussolini himself never accepted neo-Hegelianism but found it sufficiently expedient to give it semi-official sanction, particularly in the period when he was working for the Concordat between the Italian state and the Roman papacy.

The *Political Doctrine of Fascism* by Alfredo Rocco, Minister of Justice, is a concise and logical piece of writing, the most able exposition from a legal standpoint though it perforce is thin and written too soon to be actually authoritative on the corporate state. The official historiographer is Gioacchino Volpe who published his "History of Fascism" in 1934 along with a reprint of Mussolini's encyclopaedia essay. The most prolific propagandist however was Virginio Gayda who held no official position either in the government or in the party but who as editor of *Il Giornale d'Italia* had tremendous popular influence. Blustering, brilliant and bombastic, daily and Sunday, Gayda wrote his editorials, announcing, explaining, defending the gaudy imperialism of the "New Caesar". Here then are the motley "philosophers" of fascism: Gentile, Palmieri, Rocco, Volpe and Gayda, pedagogists and journalists turned politicians and professional theorists of the state; these are the "elite" who, giving credence to the ideas of Mussolini, with him contrived a fascist ideology.

REPUDIATES PACIFISM

First of all, Fascism "believes neither in the possibility nor the utility of perpetual peace ... . and repudiates the doctrines of pacifism".[8]

In world affairs Mussolini called himself a political realist whose foreign policy would be determined by "a precise consideration of international forces, their relations and inevitable changes".[9] Mussolini knew that Italy could not act as a first-rate power until it ceased to belong to the category of "have-not" nations; thus it became the historic mission of the Fascist re-

---

[8] Benito Mussolini. *Political and Social Doctrine of Fascism,* printed in translation in *International Conciliation,* #306, 1935.

[9] Benito Mussolini's speech quoted in *New York Times,* May 26, 1935.

gime "to square our resources with our aims, our measures with
our rights, our forces with our will",[10] a mission which could not
come to fruition except by wars of conquest. Steeped in Sorelian-
ism, Mussolini was fortuitously able to idealize militaristic necessity in terms of heroics and ethics; "War alone brings up to its
highest tension all human energy and puts the stamp of nobility
upon the peoples who have the courage to meet it." [11] Thus the
men of Italy made war on Abyssinia in the name of civilization
and reached the epitome of human exaltation as they released
the clouds of poison gas on the hordes of the Negus.

As in international relations so also within the country does
the Fascist make violence a regular policy of the state. Force in
action is the very prerequisite of government and power the pre-
rogative of the state. By force the Fascists came to power and
this was right since a counter-revolutionary minority could not
hope to control a parliamentary government by purely peaceable
tactics.

Brought up in an anarchist-syndicalist atmosphere from the
days of his youth Mussolini had learned the efficacy of direct
action. Yet he never ruled by force alone; rather he looked upon
force "as an episode, not a system".[12] The ex-editor and political
propagandist also appreciated the more insidious ways of psychological persuasion.

STATISM

The core of fascist philosophy is the concept of the absolute
and totalitarian state. The state is not purely an idealistic abstraction but is possessed of organic and ethic substance. Fascism
is opposed to the "atomistic theory of the state", that is to the
democratic idea that the state being the sum of the individual citizens should be activated by the greatest number. Fascism, taking
a historio-biological approach to politics, discovers that the body

---

[10] Roberto Cantalupo. "Fascism in Italian History," *Foreign Affairs,* IV (October,
1925), p. 61.

[11] Benito Mussolini. "Political and Social Doctrine of Fascism." *International
Conciliation,* 1935, #306.

[12] Sarfatti, *op. cit.,* p. 37.

politic was conceived in the past and will reach maturity in the future. Society is not just a collection of individuals but must be considered as a succession of generations. The state embodies the general will and the ultimate purpose of the past, the present, and the future. As it is superior to the individual, so it may also transcend the immediate interest of this whole contemporary generation if they fail to comprehend the imminent destiny of the Italian nation.

The Myth of Nationalism

Mussolini entirely rejects the economic determination of Marxism, substituting the myth of nationalism as the all-important factor in history. He himself boasted on this point, "We have created our myth. The myth is a faith, it is passion. It is not necessary that it shall be a reality . . . Our myth is the greatness of the Nation" (Naples, 1922).[13] There is no doubt that Italian fascism was tremendously influenced by the Roman tradition, by the Renaissance, by the Mazzinian *Risorgimento*. The history of the Italian people since "the Fall of Rome" has been one of vain-glorious ambition frustrated by impotent politics and poor economics. In all their despair and bitterness, however, they retained a strong feeling for the primacy of Rome and it was upon this emotion that Mussolini's Fascists capitalized for their own purposes. Transported by the mystical nature of the absolute state, the patriotic citizen submissively accepted the fascist dictatorship. It is to be noted here that racialism did not enter to any extent into this myth of nationalism, for the Roman myth is essentially cosmopolitan. Thus Italian fascism was never particularly anti-semitic. On the other hand, because Italian fascism was the conscious exaltation of one nation above all others in history, fascism was scarcely a commodity for export.

Traditionalism

Nationalism is of course bolstered by traditionalism. The appeal to history was psychologically practical; yet Mussolini had

---

[13] Herman Finer. *Mussolini's Italy* (New York: Henry Holt, 1935), p. 218.

no intention of burying Italy in the dead past. He was deferent
to those institutions which time had tested, the family, the church,
the monarchy, but he did not hold that tradition alone could determine that which should be immutable and inviolable. As he
looked backward, he saw that history offered a panorama of
hierarchies. It was the duty of the Fascist to preserve those values
of past hierarchies "which have not lost their usefulness", to graft
new elements of life to the trunk of such hierarchies, to prepare
the way for new hierarchies.[14]

TOTALITARIANISM

It is to be noted that the fascist state possesses more than
juridical personality; it is the total life of the nation and hence
the span of its absolute control comprehends all social activity. It
regulates as of right the economic order, organizes the corporate
state, enforces the collaboration of capital and labor, controls production and distribution in agriculture and industry. In support
of its temporal power it exalts the church as an allied institution
of spiritual authoritarianism. It invades even the privacy of the
family putting bounties on fertility as a matter of public policy
to increase the man-power which the state will need for its industrial and imperialistic armies. With its emphasis on tradition
and historical continuity it promotes cultural conformity.

THE CORPORATE STATE

The corporate state is the fascist denial of Marxianism. "The
nation is a moral, political and economic unity integrally embodied in the fascist state." [15] Mussolini repudiates the materialism of socialism and rejects the proposition that the economic
motive is the all-important force in the transformation of society.
Whether or not fascism began as a reaction from the middle
class, Mussolini presumed that fascism was "the march of Italy",
which should under no circumstances be impeded by the action

---

[14] Sarfatti, op. cit., p. 289. Fascist organ Gerarchia ("Hierarchy"), in the first
number of the Review. Written by Mussolini.
[15] Basic principle affirmed in the Charter of Labor, 1927.

of any individual group or class. As he explained it, the citizen in the corporate state is valuable only because of his work and thought for the state and not because he is aged 21 and can vote.[16] The individual is judged by his capacity to contribute to the welfare of the state and his right to participate in public affairs is determined by the measure of his productivity. This is the rationalization of functional rather than territorial representation in the corporate state.

Though ostensibly anti-socialist the Charter of Labor equally disapproves of *laissez-faire* capitalism, "the corporate state regards private initiative in the field of production as the most useful and efficient instrument to further the interest of the Nation". But, "since private enterprise is a function of import to the nation, its management is responsible to the state for general policies of production". Private initiative is tolerated but "where political interests of the State are involved", the State may intervene. Ten years later when Italy was engaged in war. Mussolini indicated how far intervention might go when the government took over the management of all key-industries. "Key industries" were defined as those which "owing to their nature, the volume of their production and their decisive importance in the event of war are outside the bounds of private economy". These in short were: the heavy industries which were producing war goods; banking and credit which had from the outset been under state control; foreign trade which likewise from the beginning has been a function of the state.[17] Thus it is obvious the role of capital under fascism is quite different from the part it plays in democratic government. At least it may be said that private profits are not the index of capitalism in fascist Italy.

LABOR IN THE CORPORATE STATE

Labor viewed as a social duty, is far from free in the fascist state. Organized in syndicates recognized by the state and subject to state control, both employers and employees enter into

---

[16] Benito Mussolini. *My Autobiography* (New York: Scribners, 1938), ch. 12.

[17] Mussolini's speech, *New York Times*, May 24, 1936.

collective·bargaining to determine such questions as wages, hours of work and discipline. These collective contracts are enforced as law by special labor courts set up by the state. All industrial disputes, individual or general, arising out of these contracts or any other controversy involving labor issues, are similarly settled in these labor courts. Strikes and lock-outs are both prohibited for these will show up production and deprive the state of its rightful prosperity. In the corporate state, capital and labor must collaborate; they have equal rights and equal duties, neither is free, both must serve the state.

The Charter of Labor in 1927 presents little more than the platitudes of the corporate state. Not for several years were the structural details even indicated in the political blue-prints. In November 1933 Mussolini announced to the newly created National Council of Corporations that "the capitalistic mode of production has been superseded and with it the theory of economic liberalism".[18] The corporate state was created "to increase the wealth, political power and well being of the Italian people". One year later, he declared (Nov. 10, 1934) "today the great corporate machinery is set in motion". Twenty-two categories of production had been designated each representing a particular branch of economic activity, its membership including all the employers and workers concerned with that industry together with certain representatives of the fascist party and government. Whereas the syndicates were arranged at first instance in local communities the corporations were truly national in character, organs *per se* of the state. Thus the Council of Corporations was to operate "in the economic fields the Grand Council and Militia operate in the political field". The chamber of deputies with its territorial representation had become an anachronism.

The "Social Factor" in Fascism

Mussolini from time to time found it politically expedient to stress the "social factor" in corporativism. In the Labor Charter

---

[18] *The Corporate State,* speeches by Benito Mussolini (Vallechi Editore, Firenze, 1936), p. 11.

there was more than a modicum of socialism, of state protection for the proletariat in the form of public employment services, workmens' compensation, motherhood insurance, health insurance, unemployment insurance, technical training of workers, industrial safety and sanitation, etc. In his many speeches to the workers, he frequently promised fair wages, decent homes, work guaranteed, want abolished eventually in the state of plenty. Whether actually the workers standard of living was improved under fascism is a moot question; the nayes seem to have it, but theoretically at least labor was accorded its fair share in the corporate state.[19]

AUTARCHIE

Whatever standard of living corporativism promised the whole people of Italy for the future, the immediate object was to increase the power of the Italian state in international relations. This Mussolini himself frankly and smugly admitted, although his explanation, as usual, was couched in lofty idealism "Imperialism is the eternal and immutable law of life. It is at bottom nothing other than the need, the desire and the will to expansion which every individual and every live and vital people possess." [20] To a state that is bent on imperialistic expansion, autarchie becomes the prerequisite of success; hence economic self-sufficiency becomes the goal of the fascist state. Thus corporativism which might in time of peace have become the implement of state socialism in Italy was always geared for war. As a military measure, fascism stimulated agricultural production, cut down on unessential imports, substituted home-made for imported products, developed hydro-electric power, explored oil mineral resources. After her unfortunate experience with League sanctions in the Abyssinian War, more than ever was it necessary for Italy "to realize in the shortest possible time the maximum

---

[19] For a realistic and scholarly study of "higher social justice" in application, see Carl Schmidt, *The Corporate State in Action* (New York: Oxford University Press, 1939).

[20] Finer, *op. cit.,* p. 180.

possibility of autonomy in the economic life of the nation".[21]
Pax Romana was a myth; fascism conditioned by Italian economy
and demography had to be belligerent. It is ironical that fascism
was defeated on the battlefield.

REPUDIATION OF DEMOCRACY

A nation that is primarily a fighting organization not only
acquiesces in the ideal of force in action but necessarily accepts
the practice of dictatorship. In any army, discipline and obedience
are required of the rank and file. Certainly a people in arms
out to conquer the world must take orders without question from
Il Duce. On this point Mussolini is brutally cynical; like Machiavelli he has no faith in the intelligence of his countrymen. Fascism
"affirms the immutable, beneficial and fruitful inequality of mankind".[22] The title of the official Fascist Review, *Gerarchia* ("Hierarchy"), chosen by Mussolini was in itself an affront to democracy
and the challenge of Fascism. "Above all, he who talks of 'hierarchy' in reality takes up a fighting position against all those who
tend—in spirit or in life—to lower or destroy the necessary ranks
of society."[23]

Fascism combats the whole complex system of democratic
ideology. It flatly repudiates the doctrine of popular sovereignty
returning to the older juridical concept of state sovereignty.
Holding that universal suffrage is a meaningless mechanical process, nevertheless, it admits that the people do possess an "instinctive discernment of what is necessary for the wealth of race".[24]
It may be politics therefore to allow the people some expression
of opinion through plebescites although as a regular routine the
great mass of citizens are not suitable advocates of the general
will. As the hero-worshipping Rocco observes, the capacity to

[21] Matthews, *op. cit.*, quoted by, p. 229.

[22] Mussolini. *Political and Social Doctrines of Fascism.*

[23] Sarfatti, *op. cit.*, p. 289. Mussolini in the first number of *Gerarchia.*

[24] Rocco, *op. cit.*

ignore individual interests in favor of society and history is a rare gift.[25]

Because the fascist party was at first a small minority albeit the *elite* it was necessary to compel the obdeience of the whole people by force. Government administered by a minority, however, is always a precarious and transitional solution even when the administrators are in principle identified with the higher interests of the nation. Hence, Gini observes, it was correct for Mussolini to anticipate the consent of the majority since popular government is always more stable. Force was the immediate prerequisite for the external forms of obedience; indoctrination was the next step to secure the inward rational consent of the people.[26] Gentile makes much the same sort of rationalization for fascist propaganda. The individual must be made conscious of the fact that his spiritual life is identified with the corporate state which thus becomes "the peoples state . . . the democratic state par excellence".

The philosophical justification for the fascist dictatorship is a combination of Nietzsche's superman and Pareto's elite. Mussolini became head of the government because at a weak moment in Italian history he was the strongest man on the scene of political action. He was not the choice of the people, the wisest nor the bravest man in the land. He was simply an opportunist who happened also to be a political genius. Thus Italian fascism is inextricably mixed with the biography of Mussolini; what part is personal and which is national only the historian can tell at a much later date. No less a scholar than Finer closes his study of *Mussolini's Italy* with this judgment, "The fascist system depends on a genius and with his passage it must pass."

Granting the political ability of *Il Duce* it is nevertheless difficult to see why the people believed that the Fascist party constituted the total "elite" of Italy. Arrogant self-selection seems to have been the only sanction for "the aristocracy of action"

[25] Rocco, *op. cit.*

[26] Corrodo Gini. "Scientific Basis of Fascism," *Political Science Quarterly*, XLII (March, 1927), pp. 99.

that sat in the Grand Council. Rocco wrote vaguely of a class born to rule because of natural intelligence, rare intuition and cultural preparation. Yet it is obvious that the political racketeers who operated the fascist government belonged to no such *elite*. Evidently the fascist government could propagandize the idea of the "ethic state" without ever confusing politics with anything but politics.

The Italian citizen was forced to conform to the practical implications of a government headed by superman, assisted by the elite. If individual initiative was encouraged it was simply because the fascist recognized that this seemed to obtain the best social results with the least effort. Liberty for the individual, meaning *laissez faire* on the part of the government, has no justification in corporativism where state and individual "are inseparable terms of a necessary synthesis".[27] The citizen is free in so far as he can identify his personal ambitions with the will of the state. Only by complete abnegation, by the sacrifice of his particular interest to the greater good of the state, can the individual develop his own personality to its fullest extent and achieve his immortality in the spiritual life of the nation. Or in less lofty terms, the good fascist citizen is "a soldier bound to all the rest of the army, a molecule who feels and pulsates with the entire organism". For an individual to talk of his "individual rights" is presumptuous; he must first perform his social duties".

Fascism and the Church

Mussolini himself has professed that fascism is a religious conception. The mystical and transcendental attributes of the nation have given it a god-like character which the citizen must worship. Again it was particularly fortuitous that the Roman tradition enhanced both the temporal and spiritual claims of Italian fascism. The Treaty and Concordat of 1929, officially terminating the long "tension" between the church and state, was a stunning victory for the fascists. The Church was exceedingly useful to fascism because the majority of the Italian people were

---

[27] Gentile, *op. cit.*

Catholics. To recognize the Roman Catholic Church as the established church of Italy, to give its catechism a regular place in public instruction, to give civil effect to religious marriage and to leave the question of divorce to the Church, these were small matters when the large consideration was the "imponderable", *Il Duce* and the Pontiff in temporal and spiritual accord, the Roman question settled "in a definite and irrevocable form". Moreover, recognition of the Roman Catholic Church as the true religion of Italy did not alter the fascist appeal to faith in the "imminent conscience of the nation". With the Lateran pact in his pocket, within a short time, Mussolini again made it clear that in totalitarianism, the Church retained none of its sovereignty, whereas "the Fascist State claims in full its character of ethicality; it is Catholic, but it is Fascist; indeed, above all, exclusively, essentially Fascist".[28]

CRITICISM AND EVALUATION

There are many Italian critics of fascism but after Matteotti's murder, few remained in Italy and dared to voice their opposition aloud. Some chose and were able to leave the country; this was particularly true among that class called "intelligentsia" who valued their freedom of thought beyond any material gain which Mussolini could promise. Uncompromising foes of fascism, from their vantage points in evile they pressed their attacks on Mussolini's regime. In this country alone, three university professors, Max Ascoli, Antonio Borgese and Gaetana Salvemini, have been largely responsible for the adverse opinion of fascism held generally from the outset in academic circles.[29] It is obvious that they have not written with the usual detachment of scholars but rather with avowed prejudice and purpose, to destroy the myth of fascism. Individually in their several works, they have amassed incontrovertible data to prove the fundamental mendacity of Mussolini. Thus they deny that fascism saved Italy from Bolshevism and with an accumulation

---

[28] Finer, *op. cit.*, p. 460, May 14, 1929.

[29] See bibliography for selected works of Ascoli, Borgese and Salvemini.

of reputable references show that the industrial unrest was already abated when Mussolini made his March on Rome. Likewise they attack the validity of fascism on purely practical grounds, claiming "it doesn't work". With impressive supporting facts, they charge that the standard of living was actually lowered by Mussolini, that the peasants and workers were both unhappy and worse off than before, that morals were bad and morale was low, that fascist government was no more than systematic terrorism.

The most articulate and powerful spokesman of the antifascist forces has been Count Carlo Sforza now acknowledged leader of the liberal democratic movement in occupied Italy. A politician and statesman of pre-fascist Italy his appraisal of fascism has been essentially realistic. He too sums up the fascist regime as one colossal lie which has gained not one iota of truth by countless reiteration. Like Finer he views the rise and fall of fascism in the character of Mussolini. Condescending, almost sympathetic, he regards Mussolini as a second-rate journalist with a flare for writing brilliantly and superficially on the thousand affairs of the day but who, on coming to power, was overwhelmed by the complexity of political phenomena which he had never quite comprehended. This "pathetic disproportion between the legend artificially created about a man raised to the rank of a demi-god and the actual capacities of this same man" is the tragic explanation of the fascist fiasco that ended in the "insane war of 1940".[30]

The academic bystander who is charged with a scholarly review of fascism can not presume to pass judgment with such swift passion. On the other hand in attempting to evaluate a political theory which acknowledges for itself no sanctions except empiricism and pragmatism, it seems only fair to use as criterion the success or failure of its institutions. This too is no simple proposition for fascism in operation not only departed in many respects from its own rationalizations of government but apparently there was neither consistency nor constancy in any

---

[30] Count Carlo Sforza. *Contemporary Italy* (New York: Dutton, 1944), p. 298.

of its practices. As every dictatorship must be sensitive to the winds of popular sentiment so Mussolini's program veered in many directions, following no single course; because it had to be opportunistic, it was ineffectual in the long run. Thus in the summer of 1942 when the Italian government surrendered to the United Nations, the proof was indubitable that after twenty years of fascist dictatorship, Mussolini's Italy was conspicuously lacking in economic prosperity and military power. Moreover, from the sad fate of Mussolini, it seems probable that the Italian people were only too willing to dispense with that rare hero who had been self-chosen Il Duce.

In conclusion, however, it should be observed that the defeat of fascism was caused mainly by events on the material plane. Whether fascism as a philosophy will continue to have any validity for the Italians after the war is still to be determined. Even at this writing it is not clear that the Italian people if free to set up their next form of government would be motivated by the multiple will for individual freedom; the utility of the corporate state (removed from fascist politicians) may yet be a significant factor in the processes of reconstruction. Moreover, it does not seem so assured as Sforza would hope that the Italian people would readily accept European interdependence as a political principle; it may well be that the "myth of Rome" will survive to sustain a more potent nationalism when this war is over.

SELECTED BIBLIOGRAPHY

ASCOLI, MAX AND FEILER. *Fascism for Whom.* New York: W. W. Norton, 1938.

BORGESE, G. A. *Goliath; The March of Fascism.* New York: Viking Press, 1938. (Strictly anti-fascist.)

CANTALUPO, ROBERT. "Fascism in Italian History,"*Foreign Affairs,* 4:61-71, 1925. (Officially approved by Mussolini.)

COKER, FRANCIS. *Recent Political Thought.* New York: Appleton, 1934. Excellent chapters on Fascist ideology by an outstanding authority on modern political theory.

EBENSTEIN, WILLIAM. "Fascist Italy." *American Book,* 1939.

FINER, HERMAN. *Mussolini's Italy.* New York: Henry Holt, 1935. (Favorable account of Mussolini's Italy, complete with historical background, biographical material, including a critical exposition of Fascist theories and Fascist institutions—by an eminent British student of public administration.)

FLORINSKY, MICHAEL. *Fascism and National Socialism.* New York: MacMillan, 1936.

Fortune. July, 1934, Vol. 10.

GENTILE, GIOVANNI. "The Philosophic Basis of Fascism." *Foreign Affairs*, 6:290-304, 1928.

GINI, CORRODO. "Scientific Basis of Fascism." *Political Science Quarterly*, 42-99-115, 1927.

LOEWENSTEIN, KARL. "Militant Democracy and Fundamental Rights," *American Political Science Review*, 31:417-432, 638-658, 1937.

MATTHEWS, HERBERT L. *The Fruits of Fascism.* New York: Harcourt, Brace, 1943. (By the former head of the N. Y. *Times* Rome Bureau, "This book seeks reasons and causes and effects"; is definitely good reportage.)

MUSSOLINI, BENITO. *My Autobiography.* New York: Scribners, 1938. (Foreward by Richard Washborn Child.) (At least the author writes from first hand observation and experience! If Italian Fascism is no more than "'corporeal projection of a successful personality", here is the essence of the political theory involved.)

MUSSOLINI, BENITO. "Political and Social Doctrines of Fascism," *International Conciliation,* #306, 1935. (Reprinted from the *Italian Encyclopedia,* 1932 ed.)

MUSSOLINI, BENITO. *The Corporate State.* Vallechi Editore Firenze, 1936.

ROCCO, ALFRED. "The Political Doctrine of Fascism." *International Conciliation,* 1926, #223.

SALVEMINI, GAETANO. *The Fascist Dictatorship in Italy.* Holt, 1927; *Under the Axe of Fascism.* Toronto: Macmillan, 1936. Informative and critical, by Italy's outstanding scholar in exile.

SARFATTI, MARGHERITA. *The Life of Benito Mussolini.* New York: Frederick Stokes, 1926. From the Italian of Margherita Sarfatti with a preface by Benito Mussolini, translated by Frederick Whyte. (Mussolini says in his *Preface,* "This book pleases me." Written by a hero-worshipper, valuable for the many verbatim remarks from Mussolini's early writings and speeches as Socialist and Fascist.)

SCHMIDT, CARL T. *The Corporate State in Action.* New York: Oxford University Press, 1939.

SCHNEIDER, H. *Making Fascists.* Chicago: University of Chicago Press, 1929. Mainly a study of fascist propaganda techniques.

SCHNEIDER, HERBERT W. *Source Book of European Governments.* New York: Van Nostrand, 1937. Section on Fascist Government. (A good collection of documents.)

SFORZA, COUNT CARLO. *European Dictatorships.* Brentananos, 1932; *The Real Italians.* Columbia, 1941; *Contemporary Italy.* Dutton, 1944. Realistic attacks on fascist politics by the well-known Italian statesman in exile.

SPEARMAN, DIANA. *Modern Dictatorship.* New York, Columbia, 1939.

STEWART, W. K. "The Mentors of Mussolini." *American Political Science Review,* 22:843-869, 1928.

SWABEY, MARIE. "The Leading Myths of Our Time." *Ethics,* 49:169-186, 1939.

SPENCER, HENRY R. *Government and Politics of Italy.* Yonkers: World Book Company, 1932. Concise but not recently revised.

STEINER, ARTHUR. *Government in Fascist Italy.* New York: McGraw-Hill, 1938. Mainly a study of the Fascist Government in operation, a judicious account by a good political scientist.

CHAPTER VI

RACISM

DAVID FELLMAN

THE DISTINCTION BETWEEN RACE AND RACISM

Racism is one of the most explosive elements of contemporary political thought. Whatever form it may take, it embodies the notion that some allegedly identifiable collection of human beings is naturally and inherently superior to others. The distinguishing characteristics of groups are variously and often curiously described, by some in terms of such purely physical and measurable phenomena as the cephalic index or hair form, and by others in terms of purely cultural traits, such as language or form of government. There is an equally wide range of values which are taken as the indicia of superiority, including such items as military prowess, mechanical efficiency, an asserted passion for freedom, and an assumed freedom from passion. Whatever a race may be, and in whatever respects it is supposed to be unique, the racist asserts that his group is biologically and therefore everlastingly superior. This is the essence of racism.

It is much more difficult to assign to the term "race" a specific connotation. It is, as Ernest Barker has suggested, a "Protean term",[1] and it is employed indiscriminately to label groups from many different points of view. Thus, race is used by some to denote a linguistic group, or a number of different peoples whose languages are believed to stem from some common source. It is also taken as synonymous with a political entity, such as a state or nation, and hence some writers refer loosely to the "French race" or the "English race". Those who use the term

---

[1] Ernest Barker, *National Character* (New York: Harper, 1927), p. 19.

with scientific care, however, as anthropologists or biologists,
use race as a zoological term to classify and describe groups of
people according to measurable physical characteristics which
are believed to be hereditary in character.[2] These characteristics
include skin color, eye color and form, hair color and form, shape
of the nose, stature and head form. The anthropologist insists
that race must be distinguished from language and culture which
are elements of learned behavior having no biological foundation.
For the scientist, race is a useful field of study which is concerned with the problem of the genetic constitution of groups,
and through which their migrations, contacts and biological cross-
ings may be described.

UNIVERSALITY OF RACIST DOCTRINES

Racist thought is rampant all over the modern world. The
doctrines of racial purity and superiority lie at the core of Nazi
ideology, which has visions of a peace "founded by the victorious
sword of a people of overlords which puts the world into the
service of a higher culture".[3] The militant nationalism and expansionism of Japan is built upon a national racial myth.[4] As
a matter of political expediency, the contemporary German brand
of racism was officially proclaimed in Fascist Italy, warmed over
by obedient journalists and party hacks.[5] In Africa, the line between white and black is the fundamental political and social
fact. Speaking of South Africa, Millin writes that "the gulf be-

[2] See: Alexander A. Goldenweiser, *Anthropology* (New York: Crofts, 1937), p.
13.

[3] A. Hitler, *Mein Kampf* (New York: Reynal & Hitchcock, 1940), p. 599.

[4] A convenient summary of Japanese racist thought will be found in C. S. Braden,
"Japanese Imperialism and Religion," *Amerasia,* II (Nov., 1938), 148-156. See
also: S. L. Gulick, *Evolution of the Japanese* (New York: Revell, 1903), Chap.
XIII; W. M. McGovern, *Modern Japan* (London: Unwin, 1920), pp. 123-133;
P. S. Reinsch, *Intellectual and Political Currents in the Far East* (New York:
Houghton, Mifflin, 1911), Chap. VII; H. S. Quigley, *Japanese Government and
Politics* (New York: Century, 1932), Chap. V; W. H. Chamberlin, *Japan over
Asia* (Boston: Little, Brown, 1938), Chap. X; D. C. Holtom, *Modern Japan and
Shinto Nationalism* (Chicago: University of Chicago Press, 1943).

[5] M. Agronsky, "Racism in Italy." *Foreign Affairs,* XVII (Jan., 1939), pp. 391-401.

tween black and white is so wide, so terrible and irreducible, that, by contrast, no other division seems of fundamental consequence".[6] In much of Latin America no formal color line exists, and in a few places, notably Brazil and the smaller countries of the West Indies and the Southern Caribbean, relations between races are cordial to the point of large-scale intermarriage. Nevertheless, social distinctions based upon economic and cultural lines follow racial groupings, and a strong desire to be white is noted by observers.[7] In the American South every important phase of social and political life is shaped by the relations of black and white.[8] The world over, sharp and painful lines are drawn in racist language between colors and between various shades of same color, between old settlers and new immigrants, between upper and lower classes, between religious groups, and between urban and rural populations. Even in the field of artistic and literary criticism, it is quite common to find facile explanations of the art of a Degas, the music of a Wagner, or the novels of a Dostoievski, in terms of assumed inherent qualities of a French "racial genius", a German "racial soul", and a Russian "racial conscience".[9]

Manifestly, the sentiments provoked by racist preachments are very powerful. They are strong enough to keep a diversified and politically contentious population in the American South within the confines of a single party. The Nazi appeal to blood

---

[6] Sarah G. Millin, *The South Africans* (New York: Boni & Liveright, 1927), p. 125. See also: R. L. Buell, *The Native Problem in Africa* (New York: Macmillan, 1928); I. D. MacCrone, *Race Attitudes in South Africa* (London: Oxford University Press, 1937); Isaac Fisher, "Black and White in Certain Parts of West Africa," *Annals of the American Academy,* CXL (Nov., 1928), 319-330.

[7] L. L. and J. S. Bernard, "The Negro in Relation to other Races in Latin America," *Annals,* CXL (Nov., 1928), 306-318; James Bryce, *South America: Observations and Impressions* (New York: Macmillan, 1914); Cedric Dover, *Half-Caste* (London: Secker & Warburg, 1937); Donald Pierson, *Negroes in Brazil* (Chicago: University of Chicago Press, 1942), esp. Chap. VIII.

[8] Paul Lewinson, *Race, Class, and Party* (New York: Oxford Press, 1932).

[9] An excellent collection of illustrations drawn from many sources will be found in Jacques Barzun, *Race, A Study in Modern Superstition* (New York: Harcourt, Brace, 1937), Chaps. I and V, and pp. 301-321.

was triumphant in the Saar and the Sudetenland against the claims of highly treasured competing values. The color line led to the unification of warring white groups in South Africa, Boer and Briton, within the framework of a unitary state.[10] Both occupational and religious loyalties have, in various places, been forced to give ground against the appeal to racial pride. It shapes the immigration, expulsion, and propagation policies of nations. It strengthens the claims of chauvinistic nationalists and rationalizes the case for imperialists. Racism has an important part in shaping private and public employment and educational policies. It is everywhere an important calculation for politicians in quest of power.

THE ROOTS OF RACISM

Considering how many theories are to be found in the voluminous literature on the subject, it may well be that there is no single explanation for the tremendous appeal which racism seems to make in the contemporary world. In its broadest terms, it should be noted that racism offers a very simple, convenient, mystical explanation or justification of almost anything, and saves one the trouble of facing unpleasant realities or of thinking through complex problems.[11] Man as a rationalizing creature picks up his arguments wherever he can find them, and the more flexible and undefined they are, the more popular they are apt to be. For example, in early American colonial history, an intensely religious community found a moral justification for slavery in the discovery that Negroes are a congenitally inferior race, after the process of conversion had made the ownership of one Christian by another embarrassing; after all, property is prop-

---

[10] See E. M. Sait, *Political Institutions: A Preface* (New York: Appleton-Century, 1938), pp. 396-8.

[11] E. A. Ross, *Social Psychology* (New York: Macmillan, 1914), p. 3, states that racism is "the cheap explanation tyros offer for any collective trait that they are too stupid or too lazy to trace to its origin in the physical environment, the social environment, or historical conditions". For similar, oft-quoted comments see: Walter Bagehot, *Physics and Politics* (New York: Appleton, 1901), p. 3; John Stuart Mill, *Principles of Political Economy* (New York: Appleton, 1880), Vol. I, p. 403.

erty, and deserves a good argument.[12] German racists talked for
years about the "Yellow Peril", and contemptuously characterized
the Japanese as "undermen", "trained monkeys", and "yellow
devils",[13] but when it became expedient to bring Japan into the
Axis, it was soon discovered by German "race scientists" that
the Japanese were Aryans after all. Thus, also, while Mussolini
assured Ludwig in 1932 that there was no room for anti-semitism
in Italy,[14] the pressure of the senior member of the Axis led to
the belated discovery that Italy's handful of Jews presented a
very serious problem requiring a root—and—branch solution in
the approved totalitarian way.

Furthermore, racism is flattering and reassuring to those
who believe in it. No matter how morally inadequate, or ineffi-
cient, or stupid, or unsuccessful a racist may be, he can always
find tremendous satisfaction in the comfortable knowledge that
he is nevertheless a superior person because of his ineradicable,
inborn traits. On the other hand, the most blameless and desirable
members of an allegedly inferior race can never atone for the
crime of having chosen the wrong parents. In a penetrating
analysis of the idea of white superiority in the American South,
Dollard writes:

"In the North a man may have a prestige position because he has
money, or is learned, or is old; the novelty in the South is that one
has prestige solely because one is white. The gain here is very simple.
It consists in the fact that a member of the white caste has an automatic
right to demand forms of behavior from Negroes which serve to increase his own self-esteem." [15]

The present vogue of racist thought may also be traced to
the fact that it is couched in the terminology of science, in an
age which attaches a special sanctity to anything smacking of the

---

[12] See M. W. Jernegan, *Laboring and Dependent Classes in Colonial America,*
1607-1783 (University of Chicago Press, 1931), pp. 24-43.

[13] For a choice collection of German statements to this effect see: Anton Pettenkofer, "Hitler Means to Destroy Japan," *Asia,* XLI (Nov., 1941), pp. 653-660.

[14] Emil Ludwig, *Talks with Mussolini* (Boston: Little, Brown, 1933), pp. 69-70.
Mussolini declared: "National pride has no need of the delirium of race."

[15] John Dollard, *Caste and Class in a Southern Town* (New Haven: Yale University Press, 1937), pp. 173-4.

scientific, and which has been deeply impressed with the findings of biology and physiological psychology, with their emphasis upon the organic aspects of mental behavior. The racist writers pose as ethnologists, sociologists, biologists and anthropologists; they count, measure, weigh, describe, photograph and correlate in the most approved fashions, and presume to reach their conclusions from the irresistible pull of objective evidence.

It seems to be generally agreed that the doctrine of racial superiority is also rooted in a fundamental tendency of group behavior which Sumner called ethnocentrism.[16] According to this view, a group of people living together and sharing a common culture tends to regard itself as the center of the universe, with a pride in its own standards, values and habits, which it seeks to preserve at all costs. The result is the development of an in-group psychology which regards members of other groups with fear and hatred, both of which are automatic and elemental emotional responses.[17] It is to be noted, furthermore, that discovery and exploration, coupled with the conditions of modern communication and transportation, have led to group contacts more numerous than ever before in history. There is therefore a much greater awareness of the existence of foreign groups, and particularly of groups sharply different, physically and culturally, from the white European.[18]

Finally, the strength of racism may be found in the fact that it is related to some of the most powerful emotional attitudes and intellectual currents of our times. Pre-eminent among them is the sentiment of nationalism, which has undoubtedly contributed heavily to the intensity of racial animosities. It has

---

[16] William Graham Sumner, *Folkways* (Boston: Ginn & Co., 1907), pp. 13-15.

[17] A good brief description of in-group, out-group psychology will be found in E. R. Clinchy, "Prejudice and Minority Groups," in F. J. Brown and J. S. Roucek, eds., *Our Racial and National Minorities* (New York: Prentice-Hall, 1937), Chap. XII. On this point see also: S. A. Queen and J. R. Gruener, *Social Pathology* (New York: Crowell, 1940), Chap. XVI.

[18] See: Franz Boas, *The Mind of Primitive Man* (New York: Macmillan, 1938, rev. ed.), p. 29; F. G. Detweiler, "The Rise of Race Antagonisms," *American Journal of Sociology*, XXXVII (March, 1932), pp. 738-747.

been pointed out that the feeling of racial unity is a result, not a cause, of the consciousness of common origins and destiny which comes with the development of political unity.[19] The mystical aspects of racism suggest that it is also linked up with the traditions of the romantic movement.[20] The emphasis of racism upon group survival, its acceptance of survival as a test of fitness, and its ruthless attitude toward alien groups suggest an appropriation of popular and crude generalizations derived from Warwinian theories of evolution.[21] It is also noted that racial prejudice tends to support a class or caste society by assigning the lower classes an immutable, natural status of inferiority, and hence is an expression of conservatism and a useful tool for resisting social change.[22] Furthermore, racism is associated with etatist, authoritarian and anti-democratic currents of contemporary political thought, for it denies the democratic principle of human equality, and by identifying race with class conflict, it seeks to exalt the power of the state and lodge it securely in the hands of the favored classes.

In its broadest terms, prejudice against minorities is not a novel thing; men have hated each other and slaughtered each other in the past for all sorts of reasons. The racist approach

---

[19] C. J. H. Hayes, *Essays on Nationalism* (New York: Macmillan, 1926), Chap. VII; F. H. Hankins, "Race as a Factor in Political Theory," in C. E. Merriam and H. E. Barnes, eds., *History of Political Theories: Recent Times* (New York: Macmillan, 1924), pp. 508-510.

[20] Ernest Seillière, *Le comte de Gobineau et l'aryanisme historique* (Paris, Plon, 1903), Introduction; Hans Kohn, *Revolutions and Dictatorships* (Cambridge: Harvard University Press, 1941), Chap. VII; R. D. Butler, *The Roots of National Socialism* (New York: Dutton, 1942), Chap. II.

[21] For the connection between social Darwinism and racism see: W. M. McGovern, *From Luther to Hitler* (Boston: Houghton, Mifflin, 1941), Chap. X; Jacques Barzun, *Darwin, Marx, Wagner* (Boston: Little, Brown, 1941), pp. 100-109.

[22] G. Landtman, *The Origin of the Inequality of the Social Classes* (London: Paul, Trench, Trubner, 1938); R. E. Park, "The Bases of Race Prejudice," *Annals*, CXL (Nov., 1928), pp. 11-20; E. B. Reuter, *The American Race Problem* (New York: Crowell, 1927), pp. 31-35; H. A. Miller, "Race and Class Parallelism," *Annals, ut supra*, 2, writes: "What we really mean by higher and lower races are higher and lower classes, and the only thing that race has to do with it is as an advertising label before which it is difficult to be blindfolded."

is simply more in tune with contemporary folklore than some of the divisive stratagems utilized in the past. Benedict has pointed out that in studying racial persecution, it is persecution and not race that must be investigated. She writes:

"If civilized men expect to end prejudice—whether religious or racial—they will have to remedy major social abuses, in no way connected with religion or race, to the common advantage. Whatever reduces conflict, curtails irresponsible power, and allows people to obtain a decent livelihood will reduce race conflict. Nothing less will accomplish the task." [23]

In other words, the problem which racism poses is co-extensive with the whole range of human experience.

The Strands of Racism

A glance at some of the early writers will suggest the various purposes which racist thought can serve and the techniques and terminologies which are employed. First of all, it has been used as a class doctrine. Thus the Comte de Boulainvilliers, while investigating the history of his family, published a book in 1727 in which he concluded that the members of the ancient French nobility were descendants of the Franks or Germans, who had conquered the native Celtic or Gallic population and remained as feudal lords. He thought that the Franks were superior mentally, and were therefore the guardians of political liberty; the King, by allying himself with the Third Estate, descendants of the conquered race, destroyed the feudal system and set up a despotism. On the other hand, the Abbé Sieyès, writing in 1789, showed how accommodating this idea can be by defending the French Revolution as an effort on the part of the Third Estate to regain the status it had enjoyed before the Frankish invasion. [24]

---

[23] Ruth Benedict, *Race: Science and Politics* (New York: Modern Age, 1940), p. 237.

[24] Henri de Boulainvilliers, *Histoire de l'ancien Gouvernement de la France* (Paris, 1727, transl. by C. Forman, London, 1739); Emmanuel Sieyès, *Qu'est-ce que le tiers état?* (Paris, 1888, ed. by E. Champion).

The most influential of the early writers who used racism as a class doctrine was Count Arthur de Gobineau, whose famous *Essai sur l'inégalité des races humaines* (1853-55) [25] served as an inspiration for much of the race mysticism that followed him. Royalist, journalist and polished diplomat, student of the religions and philosophies of Asia, Gobineau wrote as a conservative Catholic opposed to democracy. His fundamental thesis was that mankind consists of a number of distinct races, each possessing its own hereditary physical, mental and emotional characteristics, unaffected by environment or education. He believed that the white race was superior to all others, but that among its sub-groups the greatest was the Aryan.[26] In ancient times the Aryans were the Germanic people, and in the modern era are best represented by the aristocrats of France and England, and to a lesser degree by those of Germany. Gobineau thought that all the great civilizations of the past arose from conquest, especially by Aryans, and a subsequent partial mixture of races, but that too much racial amalgamation leads not only to racial degeneration, but also to a decline in the quality of civilization itself. He expressed great concern for his noble Aryan race, which was suffering from too much intermarriage with the lower classes.

Another approach to an attempted explanation of class in terms of race was developed by a group of investigators who approached the problem from the point of view of Darwinian social selectionism and physical anthropology. Pre-eminent among them were Paul Broca and Georges Vacher de Lapouge in France and

---

[25] Translated as *The Inequality of Human Races,* by Adrian Collins (New York: Putnam, 1915).

[26] The term "Aryan" was popularized by the great philologist, the German Professor Max Müller, who, in describing the similarities of a group of languages, including English, German, Latin, Greek and Sanscrit, ventured the suggestion that there had been an original Aryan language spoken by an Aryan race. Müller later vigorously denied the racist conclusions drawn from this hypothesis: "To me an ethnologist who speaks of Aryan race, Aryan blood, Aryan eyes and hair, is as great a sinner as a linguist who speaks of a dolichocephalic dictionary or a brachycephalic grammar." *Biographies of Words and the Home of the Aryans* (London: Longmans, Green, 1888), p. 120.

Alfred Otto Ammon in Germany.[27] These men measured skulls in
large numbers and arrived at the general conclusion that tall
blond dolichocephalics (long-heads) were more numerous in
the cities and the upper classes. Ammon's explanation was that
the tall blond dolichocephalics possess more initiative, adven-
turousness and energy, and have a greater capacity for a higher
culture; they therefore gravitated, in the struggle for existence,
into the upper classes and into the cities, while the brachy-
cephalics, being more simple and docile, stayed in the country.
Lapouge identified the superior tall blond dolichocephalics with
the Aryans, and while he did not believe that there were pure
races in a thoroughly mixed Europe, he did maintain that the
Aryan element of its population was superior, and that its higher
social status was due to inherent qualities and not to conquest.

Other writers found racism useful as a nationalistic tool of
praise and disparagement, especially following the Franco-Prussian War of 1870. Quatrefages discovered that the Prussians
were essentially an Asiatic race, and Broca held that since the
French were predominantly broad-headed, they had larger and
better brains. Historians developed the thesis that French civilization had matured independently of Germanic sources.[28] German writers were of course quick to respond with comparable
notions of German superiority.[29]

---

[27] Broca, *Mémoires d'anthropologie* (Paris, 1871-1888); Ommon, *Anthropologische
Untersuchungen ueber die Wehrpflichtigen in Baden* (Hamburg, 1890), *Die na-
türliche Auslese beim Menschen* (Jena, 1893), *Die Gesellschaftsordnung und
ihre natürlichen Grundlagen* (Jena, 1895), "Histoire d'une idée. L'anthroposo-
ciologie," *Revue internationale de sociologie*, VI (1898), pp. 145-181; Lapouge,
"The Fundamental Laws of Anthroposociology," *Journal of Political Economy*,
VI (1897), pp. 54-92, *Les Sélections sociales* (Paris, 1896), *Race et milieu social*
(Paris, 1909). Similar studies were made by Collignon, Durand de Gros and
Muffang in France, Livi in Italy, Houzé in Belgium, Ripley and Closson in the
United States. For bibliography, see: *Revue internationale de sociologie*, VI, pp.
177-179.

[28] Armand de Quatrefages, *La race prussiene* (Paris, 1871), trans. by I. Innes
(London, 1872); Broca, *op. cit.* For a distinguished example of nationalistic
history writing see: Fustel de Coulanges, *Histoire des institutions politiques de
l'ancienne France* (Paris: Hachette, 1889-92, new ed., 6 vols.).

[29] Paul de Lagarde, *Deutsche Schriften* (Göttingen, 1878-1881); Heinrich Dries-
mans, *Kulturgeschichte der Rasseninstinkte* (Leipzig, 1899-1901).

Still another approach to racist dogmas came through the study of eugenics. Thus, a considerable number of English and American writers took the position that men are not only fundamentally and inherently unequal, but that their differences are hereditary.[30] Woods found that there were twenty-five geniuses among some eight hundred members of royal families; Ellis concluded that the upper classes of England, including 4½% of the population, contributed 63% of the geniuses of the country, while the working classes, with 84% of the population, gave the country only 12% of its geniuses; similar observations were made by Galton, Cattell and Clarke.[31] Summarizing the results of extensive intelligence testing, Terman concluded that the upper social classes in America contributed most of the children of superior intelligence.[32] This group drew the general inference that class structure is natural and good and must be accepted, and that accordingly education ought to be adjusted to the needs and abilities of each class. Furthermore, as was so eloquently argued by Stoddard, they believed that the superior stocks do not neces-

---

[30] Karl Pearson, *National Life from the Standpoint of Science* (London: Black, 1901), *The Scope and Importance to the State of the Science of National Eugenics* (New York: Macmillan, 1911), "On the Inheritance of Mental and Moral Characters in Man," *Biometrika*, III (1904), pp. 131-190; W. C. D. Whetham,, *Heredity and Society* (New York: Longmans, Green, 1912); E. Huntington and L. F. Whitney, *The Builders of America* (New York: Morrow, 1927); P. Popenoe and R. H. Johnson, *Applied Eugenics* (New York: Macmillan, 1918); H. H. Goddard, *The Kallikak Family* (New York: Macmillan, 1912); H. E. Walter, *Genetics* (New York: Macmillan, 1913); M. F. Guyer, *Being Well-Born* (Indianapolis: Bobbs-Merrill, 1927); C. B. Davenport, *Heredity in Relation to Eugenics* (New York: Holt, 1911).

[31] F. A. Woods, *Mental and Moral Heredity in Royalty* (New York: Holt, 1906), p. 301; Havelock Ellis, *A Study of British Genius* (London: Hurst & Blackett, 1904), Chap. III; Francis Galton, *Hereditary Genius* (New York: Appleton, 1871, rev. ed.), *English Men of Science* (London: Macmillan, 1874); J. M. Cattell, *American Men of Science* (New York: Science Press, 1921, 3rd ed.), pp. 781-790; E. L. Clarke, *American Men of Letters, their Nature and Nurture* (New York: Columbia, 1916). See also: W. T. J. Gun, *Studies in Hereditary Ability* (London: Allen & Unwin, 1928).

[32] L. M. Terman, *The Measurement of Intelligence* (Boston: Houghton, Mifflin, 1916), p. 96. See also: C. C. Brigham, *A Study of American Intelligence* (Princeton University Press, 1923); N. J. Lennes, *Whither Democracy?* (New York: Harper, 1927); C. S. Yoakum and R. M. Yerkes, *Army Mental Tests* (New York: Holt, 1920).

sarily survive in the process of social selection and competion, for, because of existing conditions and policies, the inferior stocks not only survive but are overbreeding. To prevent what these writers like to call a "progressive deterioration" of the population, the state must step in with a positive program, embracing such items as compulsory sterilization of the unfit, birth control, reduction of social services which encourage the unfit to breed, and positive policies which will stimulate marriages and the birth of children among superior folks.[33] Some of these writers also drew racist conclusions from their findings.[34]

GERMAN RACISM

The stronghold of racist ideology in the contemporary world is undoubtedly Germany, where the idea of an innately superior master-race is the cornerstone of high state policy. Here Gobineau's doctrines soon commanded a wide following and evoked a tremendous amount of racist literature.[35] One of the most influential of the German racists was Houston Stewart Chamberlain, an aristocratic English expatriate, and son-in-law of Wagner, who published his powerfully-written *Foundations of the Nineteenth Century* in 1899.[36] He believed that racial differences are obvious, as a matter of immediate experience, and that these dif-

---

[33] T. Lothrop Stoddard, *The Rising Tide of Color* (New York: Scribner's, 1920), *The Revolt against Civilization* (New York: Scribner's, 1922); E. M. East, *Heredity and Human Affairs* (New York: Scribner's, 1927).

[34] Galton believed there were great mental differences among races, *Hereditary Genius*, pp. 327-8. Pearson thought that the white man is infinitely superior to all other races, pointing out that in thousands of years the Negroes of Africa failed to produce a civilization "in the least comparable with the Aryan." *National Life from the Standpoint of Science*, p. 19.

[35] Wagner and his Bayreuth group were enthusiastic Gobinists. A *Gobineau Vereinigung* was organized under the presidency of Professor K. L. Schemann in 1894. For glorifications of the tall, blue-eyed blonde in this period see: Theodor Poesche, *Die Arier* (Jena, 1878); Carl Penka, *Origines ariacae* (Vienna, 1883), *Die herkunst der Arier* (Vienna, 1886). *Inter alia*, Penka believed that tall blondes are instinctively Protestant!

[36] References are to the English translation by John Lees, New York and London: John Lane, 1911, 2 volumes. By permission of Dodd, Mead & Co.

ferences, physical and mental, determine every man's personality. Not only is the white race superior to the black and yellow races, but there are superior and inferior sub-groups within the white race, of which he identified four principle ones, the Jews, the ancient Greeks, the ancient Romans and the modern Teutons. The Jews he bitterly denounced as a cold, egoistic and materialistic people who, through intermarriage, were polluting the Aryan race. In the absence of historical proofs he resorted to what he called "scientific psychology" to demonstrate that Christ was not of Jewish descent and that Paul must have had at least a Hellenic mother, because he had an "un-Jewish intellect".[37] Chamberlain was more generous with the Greeks and Romans of antiquity, but he thought that the Greek city-states were tainted with democracy, self-love and slavery,[38] and that the Romans were weak in the intellectual and artistic fields. Both made the mistake of losing their early vigor through race mixture with alien stocks.

The great race of the modern world, and the greatest of all historic races, is the Teutonic or Germanic, whose mission is to regenerate civilization. "It is only shameful indolence of thought, or disgraceful historical falsehood, that can fail to see in the entrance of the Germanic tribes into the history of the world the rescuing of agonising humanity from the clutches of the everlastingly bestial." [39] He described the ideal Teuton ecstatically, pointing to "the great radiant heavenly eyes, the golden hair, the gigantic stature, the symmetrical muscular development, the lengthened skull (which an ever-active brain, tortured by longing, had changed from the round lines of animal contentedness and extended towards the front), the lofty countenance, required by an elevated spiritual life as the seat of its expression".[40]

---

[37] *Ibid.*, II, p. 57, I, p. 206.

[38] *Ibid.*, I, p. 61.

[39] *Ibid.*, I, p. 495.

[40] *Ibid.*, I, p. 535.

Teutonic blood, he maintained, is responsible for the civilization of the last eight hundred years, with its special genius for religion, culture and organic unity. The greatness of each nation depends upon the proportion of real Teutonic blood in its population, for "the less Teutonic a land is, the more uncivilized it is".[41] But, having identified the aristocrats of Europe as Teutons, he had to face the obvious fact that not all of them were blonde and long-headed, for many of them had dark skins and broad skulls. This facile writer found it rather easy to include these contrasting physical types within his Teutonic theory. He simply brushed aside all the findings and principles of physical anthropology, which he accepted at the outset as valid, and evolved a theory of "rational anthropology", according to which all people who have Teutonic characteristics, such as a capacity for loyalty and a passion for independence, are Teutons.[42] In other words, a Teuton is anyone Chamberlain thinks is a Teuton.[43]

Recent German writers have made a greater show of utilizing the methodology and terminology of scientific anthropology and biology. Using the term "race" somewhat more precisely, they measure and describe people in terms of body build, height, skin, eye and hair color, and group them into races, but they also assume that each race has definite and inherent emotional and intellectual as well as physical qualities. Perhaps the most influential writer in this group, and one who may be regarded as typical, is Hans Günther. His racial interpretation of European history, supported by a profusion of pictures, maps, charts and

---

[41] *Ibid.*, II, p. 188.

[42] *Ibid.*, I, pp. 522-552.

[43] His leading immediate follower was Ludwig Woltmann, founder in 1902 of the *Politische Anthropologische Revue,* and author of: *Politische Anthropologie* (Eisenach, 1903), *Die Germanen und die Renaissance in Italien* (Leipzig, 1905), *Die Germanen in Frankreich* (Jena, 1907). Woltmann's "research" consisted principally in studying the portraits of great men in the art galleries of Europe. All persons who appeared to have any of the assumed characteristics of Nordics he labelled Teutonic, and concluded that nearly all the great figures of European history were Nordics, including Leonardo, Dante, Napoleon and Julius Caesar!

footnotes, has attracted a great deal of attention.[44] Defining a race as "a human group which is marked off from every other human group through its own proper combination of bodily and mental characteristics, and in turn produces only its like",[45] Günther found five races in Europe: Nordic, Mediterranean, Dinaric, Alpine and East Baltic. Nordic man invariably possesses all the qualities which are highly regarded in our civilization, including truthfulness, judgment, energy, practicality, boldness, competitiveness, prudence, reserve, steadfastness, dutifulness, knightliness, individualism, humor, fairness, trustworthiness, sublimity, heroism, tenderness, cleanliness, creativeness and military prowess.[56]

A similar "scientific" analysis of the other races yields much less flattering generalizations. The Alpine race, while reflective and hard working, is narrow-minded, selfish, sullen, envious, suspicious, and materialistic, has a distaste for leadership, and an inclination towards mediocrity, mass organization, criminality and the democratic theory of equality. The Mediterranean race is passionate, excitable, talkative, crafty, lazy, and volatile, lacking in foresight and a sense of law and order, strongly sexual, and given to criminality. Dinaric man comes off a little better, but he lacks foresight and leadership and the Nordic's spiritual urge

---

[44] H. F. K. Günther, *Rassenkunde Europas* (Munich, 1926, 2d ed.), translated as *The Racial Elements of European History*, by G. C. Wheeler (New York: Dutton, 1928). Other leading writers in this group include: Eugene Fischer, F. Lentz, *Grundriss der menschlichen Erblichkeitslehre und Rassenhygiene* (Munich, 1921), translated as *Human Heredity*, by E. and C. Paul (New York: Macmillan, 1931); Herman Gauch, *Neue Grundlagen zur Rassensforschung* (Leipzig, 1933), translated as *New Foundations for Research into Social Race Problems* (Berlin, 1933); E. von Eickstedt, *Grundlagen der Rassenpsychologie* (Stuttgart, 1936); Ludwig Schemann, *Die Rasse in den Geistes-wissenschaften* (Munich, 1928); H. W. Siemens, *Grundzüge der Vererbungslehre* (Munich, 1926), translated as *Race Hygiene and Heredity*, by L. F. Barker (London & New York: Appleton, 1926); Alfred Rosenberg, *Der Mythus des 20. Jahrhunderts* (Munich, 1930), *Blut und Ehre* (Munich, 1935). For a revealing view of Hitler's race theories see: Hermann Rauschning, *The Voice of Destruction* (New York: Putnam's, 1940), Chap. XVI. See also: Ernest Hamburger and others, *Le Droit Raciste d' l'assaut de la Civilisation* (New York: Maison Française, 1943).

[45] *Ibid.*, p. 3.

[46] *Ibid.*, pp. 51-56.

to conquest, and is inclined to be rough and uncouth. The East
Baltic is a confused, rambling dreamer, visionary and irresolute,
without any real creative power or individuality, very revengeful
and brutal, given to violent changes of disposition, and lacking
in cleanliness.[47] These are all natural and fixed characteristics
incapable of being affected by environment.

In a startling and sweeping restatement of the main currents
of European history, Günther develops the notion that the cultures of Europe and Asia, even those of ancient Rome and
Greece, were due to Nordic conquests, and that the early cultures
declined when the Nordic stock degenerated through intermarriage. Only countries having a dominant Nordic element are
capable of a high civilization, and this, he believes, is especially
true for Germany.

AMERICAN RACISM

There were some writers in the United States before the
Civil War who elaborated racist ideas, particularly in defense of
slavery. Starting with the premise that the human races must
have been polygenetic in origin, they assigned to the Negro a
distinct origin and a permanently inferior type.[48] The bulk of
American racist literature has been of more recent vintage, and is
couched in the language of modern biology, psychology and anthropology. In general, American racists, along with some contemporary English writers,[49] believe in the fixity of racial types
and in Nordic, Anglo-Saxon or Teutonic superiority; they assert

---

[47] *Ibid.,* pp. 56-63.

[48] Samuel G. Morton, *Crania Americana* (Phila., 1839); J. C. Nott, *Types of
Mankind* (Phila., 1854), *Indigenous Races of the Earth* (Phila., 1857); John
Campbell, *Negromania* (Phila., 1851). See Charles E. Merriam, *A History of
American Political Theories* (New York: Macmillan, 1926), Chap. VI.

[49] J. M. Robertson, *The Germans* (London, 1916); Grant Allen, *Anglo-Saxon
Britain* (London, 1901); Isaac Taylor, *Origin of the Aryans* (London, 1895);
Lord Charles Beresford, "The Future of the Anglo-Saxon Race," *North American
Review,* CLXXI (Dec., 1900), pp. 802-810; Sidney Low, "Personal Recollec-
tions of Cecil Rhodes," *Nineteenth Century,* LI (May, 1902), pp. 828-840. Na-
tionalistic-minded historians, such as J. R. Green and J. A. Froude, and romantic
writers, such as Thomas Carlyle and Charles Kingsley, accepted some form of
Anglo-Saxonism or Teutonism.

that race mixture leads to degeneration and the decay of civilizations; and they advocate immigration restrictions, eugenic and educational policies, and political reforms calculated to assure a predominant place in society for the tall, blue-eyed, long-headed blonde type.[50]

A striking illustration of American racism is found in the first four chapters of John W. Burgess' *Political Science and Comparative Constitutional Law*,[51] the greatest treatise in systematic political science published in this country in his day. According to Burgess, the Teutonic nations are "the political nations par excellence", and their peculiar creation is the national state.[52] He argued that in any nationally composite state where the Teutonic element is dominant, it should never surrender the balance of political power, though it should exercise its power with "justice and moderation". He also believed that the Teutonic nations have a "mission" to carry modern political organization into those parts of the world which are inhabited by unpolitical and barbaric races, for "there is no human right to the status of a barbarian".[53]

The persuasive Nordic apology written by Madison Grant

---

[50] The leading title include: Alfred P. Schultz, *Race or Mongrel* (Boston, 1908); William S. Sadler, *Long Heads and Round Heads* (Chicago, 1918); William Roscoe Thayer, *Out of Their Own Mouths* (New York, 1917); Charles W. Gould, *America, A Family Matter* (New York, 1922); Carl C. Brigham, *A Study of American Intelligence* (Princeton, 1923); Clinton S. Burr, *America's Race Heritage* (New York, 1922); T. Lothrop Stoddard, *The Revolt against Civilization* (New York, 1922), *The Rising Tide of Color* (New York, 1920); Madison Grant, *The Passing of the Great Race* (New York, 1916); Henry F. Osborn, *Man Rises to Parnassus* (New York, 1927); G. E. Woodberry, *Lectures on Race Power in Literature* (New York, 1905); Homer Lea, *The Day of the Saxon* (New York, 1912); A. E. Wiggam, *The Fruit of the Family Tree* (Indianapolis, 1924). For convenient summaries of American racism consult: Frank H. Hankins, *The Racial Basis of Civilization* (New York: Knopf, 1926), Chap. VII, and George A. Dorsey, "Race and Civilization," in C. A. Beard, ed., *Whither Mankind* (New York: Longmans, Green, 1929), Chap. X.

[51] Boston: Ginn & Co., 1890, 2 volumes.

[52] *Ibid.*, I, pp. 31-37. He admitted that the Teuton went through a period of education and training in the Empire, but "education can only develop what already exists in seed and germ."

[53] *Ibid.*, I, pp. 44-46.

is typical of more recent American racist books.[54] Expressing the
belief that the great lesson of "the science of race" is the im-
mutability not only of bodily characters, but of "psychical pre-
dispositions and impulses" as well, Grant held that race "lies at
the base of all the phenomena of modern history." [55] Thus,
through universal suffrage and equality of rights, democracy tends
to undermine the native American aristocracy which, because of
its superior qualities, should rule the nation. Race crossing is always bad, for "the result of the mixture of two races, in the long
run, gives us a race reverting to the more ancient, generalized
and lower type".[56] His general theme is that the tall, blue-eyed
long-headed Nordic is superior to all other racial types. The Nordic is "the white man par excellence"; the world over, his is a
"a race of soldiers, sailors, adventurers, and explorers, but above
all, of rulers, organizers, and aristocrats".[57] He is quite sure that
all the great figures of European history, including Dante, Ra-
phael, Titian, Michelangelo and Leonardo, were Nordics.[58]

SCIENTIFIC ANTHROPOLOGY

The doctrines of the racists have received their most powerful refutation in the writings of modern scientific anthropologists.
"All reputable anthropologists," says Hooton, "condemn the malignant nonsense about racial psychology which is preached and
published by those who try to justify the oppression of ethnic
minorities. Political theories about race are nothing more than
instruments of propaganda, devised for the child minds of totalitarian populations." [59] For the anthropologist race is a purely
physical concept descriptive of groups of men from the stand-

---

[54] The Passing of the Great Race (New York: Scribner's, 1916).

[55] Ibid., pp. xv, xvii.

[56] Ibid., pp. 15-16.

[57] Ibid., pp. 150, 198.

[58] Ibid., p. 191.

[59] E. A. Hooton, Twilight of Man (New York: Putnam's, 1939), p. 129.

point of their common hereditary physical traits. Goldenweiser has pointed out, however, that race is also a state of mind and an attitude, an irrational concept tied up with "emotional backgrounds, traditions, the urge of self-interest, the forces of group psychology", and that it is "the province of garbled facts, special pleading, prejudice, conceit, jealousy, and selfishness".[60]

Anthropologists emphasize the face that culture cannot be explained by race. The cultural characteristics of a people are related to time, place and circumstance, and have nothing to do with biological inheritance, so far, at least, as the available evidence indicates. Everywhere, man demonstrates a capacity for religion, art, leadership, organization and invention.[61] The student of human culture, says Goldenweiser, finds "the basic differences between the shrewd and intelligent, on the one hand, and the stupid and gullible, on the other, with all the intervening gradations" everywhere he goes.[62] Boas has suggested that "if we were to select the most intelligent, imaginative, energtic and emotionally stable third of mankind, all races would be represented".[63]

Hooton has summarized what he considers the consensus of scientific anthropological opinion on the subject of race.[64] A race is a physical division of mankind having similar anatomical features of an hereditary character. There is no single physical criterion for distinguishing races, and none of the criteria of bod-

---

[60] Alexander A. Goldenweiser, *History, Psychology, and Culture* (New York: Knopf, 1933), pp. 389, 397, 411.

[61] See: A. L. Kroeber, *Anthropology* (New York: Harcourt, Brace, 1923), Chap. IV; Ruth Benedict and Gene Weltlish, *The Races of Mankind* (New York: Public Affairs Committee, Inc., 1943).

[62] *Anthropology*, p. 32. See also: Robert H. Lowie, *An Introduction to Cultural Anthropology* (New York: Farrar & Rinehart, 1940, 2d ed.), p. 9.

[63] Franz Boas, *Anthropology and Modern Life* (New York: Norton, 1932, rev. ed.), p. 79. See also: Ralph Linton, *The Study of Man* (New York: Appleton-Century, 1936), Chap. III; Edward Sapir, *Language* (New York: Harcourt, Brace, 1921), Chap. X; J. C. Prichard, *The Natural History of Man* (London: Baillière, 1855, 4th ed.), Book III.

[64] *Apes, Men, and Morons* (New York: Putnam, 1937), Chap. XII.

ily form and structure is impervious to environmental influences,
such as climate, diet, exercise and altitude.[45] As yet, anthropologists have found no relationship between any physical criterion
of race and mental capacity, whether in individuals or groups.
It is possible that races may differ' psychologically, with respect
to tastes, temperament, even intellect, but there is as yet no scientific proof. 'Race is not synonymous with language, culture or
nationality. 'As yet, physical anthropologists cannot grade races
on an evolutionary scale; each race has a mixture of advanced
and primitive characteristics. There are no pure races in any
civilized country, for contemporary races have interbred for many
thousands of years; at best, there may be a little racial purity in
remnants of savage groups living in isolation. It is demonstrable
that most existing races have a composite origin. It is also established that hybridization, even between the most diverse races,
does not result in a decrease of fertility or lessened vitality, and
that there is no degeneration if the parents are normal.[66] Finally,
within every race there is great individual variation with regard
to physical features and mental capacity.[67] "Each racial type runs
the gamut from idiots and criminals to geniuses and statesmen.
. . . There are no racial monopolies either of human virtues or
of vices." [68]

---

[65] On this point consult the impressive studies of Franz Boas: *Changes in Bodily
Form of Descendants of Immigrants* (Washington: Government Printing Office,
1911); "The Head-Forms of Italians as Influenced by Heredity and Environment,"
American Anthropologist, N. S., XV (1913), pp. 163-188; *The Mind of Primitive Man* (New York: Macmillan, 1938, rev. ed.), Chap. V; *Race, Language
and Culture* (New York: Macmillan, 1940), pp. 60-148. See also: H. L. Shapiro,
Migration and Environment (New York: Oxford Press, 1939).

[66] "Every civilized group of which we have record has been a hybrid group, a
fact which disposes effectively of the theory that hybrid peoples are inferior to
pure-bred ones." Ralph Linton, *The Study of Man*, p. 34.

[67] Thus, the German anthropologist, Felix von Luschan, measured the cephalic
indices of over 1200 Jews, and found that their range was from 65 to 98, a range
as wide as that of the human race. "Die anthropologische Stellung der Juden,"
*Korrespondenzblatt der Deutschen Gesellschaft für Anthropologie, Ethnologie und
Urgeschichte*, XXIII (1892), pp. 94-100.

[68] *Apes, Men and Morons*, p. 154. In 1928, the American Anthropological Association unanimously repudiated and condemned racism. The text of the resolution will be found in *Science*, LXXXIX (Jan 13, 1939), p. 30.

Scientific anthropology denies the notion advanced by many racists that primitive man is a "self-evident" proof of inherent racial inequality.[69] Summarizing in 1938 the results of forty years of careful study, Franz Boas states: "There is no fundamental difference in the ways of thinking of primitive and civilized man. A close connection between race and personality has never been established." [70] Boas recapitulates the vast body of available evidence, and concludes that there is no basis for calculating the mental ability of any group, whether primitive or not, in terms of brain size, hair, pigmentation, or any other physical characters, and particularly, that it is impossible to describe races in terms of remoteness from the animal, for the features which are specifically human appear with varying intensity in various races. He maintains that the mental processes of primitive man and civilized man are essentially the same, measured in terms of such fundamental activities as the inhibition of impulses, the power of attention, logical thinking and originality.[71] Furthermore, the similarities of fundamental culture traits—such as the producing of fire by friction, the boiling of food, the use of tools, the concepts of space, time and form, the belief in the supernatural— suggest their independence of race and language. Experience indicates that members of most races, when placed in a certain culture, can participate in it, as is shown by the highly educated Indians in North and South America, the modern Chinese and Japanese, and successful Negroes in the United States.

Anthropologists also insist that notions of group superiority usually contain an unexamined assumption as to what the criteria of superiority really are. The mere fact that two groups are dif-

---

[69] See: Goldenweiser, *Early Civilization* (New York: Knopf, 1929), pp. 3-15, for an excellent discussion of the assumed biological and psychological inferiorities of the primitive races.

[70] *The Mind of Primitive Man,* p. v.

[71] On the complexity of the thought processes of primitive man, see also: Paul Radin, *Primitive Man as Philosopher* (New York: Appleton-Century, 1927); George F. Murdock, *Our Primitive Contemporaries* (New York: Macmillan, 1934); Melville J. Herskovitz, *The Economic Life of Primitive Peoples* (New York: Knopf, 1940); Margaret Mead, ed., *Cooperation and Competition Among Primitive Peoples* (New York: McGraw-Hill, 1937).

ferent, as compared with each other, whether in terms of physical appearance or culture, does not necessarily lead to the conclusion that one is superior to the other, unless one group starts with the assumption that its standards are the basis of the comparison. Thus, it has been pointed out that while our white civilization is superior in terms of science and philosophy, it is doubtful whether this is true for religion, ethics, art and political organization; if morality means living according to a code of behavior, then most primitive people are more moral than we are.[72] In fact, Sapir has suggested that a genuine culture is "inherently harmonious, balanced, self-satisfactory," ideally one "in which nothing is spiritually meaningless, in which no important part of the general functioning brings with it a sense of frustration, of misdirected or unsympathetic effort". Viewed in this light, the ethnologist "cannot but admire the well-rounded life of the average participant in the civilization of a typical American Indian tribe; the firmness with which every part of that life—economic, social, religious, and aesthetic—is bound together into a significant whole in respect to which he is far from a passive pawn; above all, the molding role, oftentimes definitely creative, that he plays in the mechanism of his culture".[73]

The findings of modern scientific anthropology are consistent with and supported by the teachings of a wider world of scholarship. Biologists point out that while the influence of genetic factors upon group and class differences is highly speculative, the influence of environment is obviously very great, and that the differences between individuals are infinitely more significant than any actual differences between races.[74] Hogben has unhesi-

---

[72] Goldenweiser, *History, Psychology, and Culture,* pp. 410-411.

[73] E. Sapir, "Culture, Genuine and Spurious," *American Journal of Sociology,* XXIX (Jan., 1924), pp. 401, 413-414.

[74] H. J. Muller, *Out of the Night; a Biologist's View of the Future* (New York: Vanguard, 1935), Chap. VI; C. H. Waddington, *An Introduction to Modern Genetics* (New York: Macmillan, 1939), Chap. XV; J. S. Huxley and A. C. Haddon, *We Europeans* (New York: Harper, 1936); W. E. Castle, "Biological and Social Consequences of Race-Crossing," *American Journal of Physical Anthropology,* IX (1936), pp. 145-156; J. B. S. Haldane, *Heredity and Politics* (London: Allen & Unwin, 1938).

tatingly asserted, as a professional biologist, that all the knowledge now available as to the relationship between the physical characteristics and cultural capabilities of human communities could be written on the back of a postage stamp.[75] In a recent essay on the concept of race, Julian Huxley, after reviewing the evidence, concludes that under the circumstances, it is desirable that the very term "race", as applied to man, should be dropped from scientific and general vocabulary.[76] Migration and crossing have produced such a fluid state of affairs that no clear-cut term is descriptive of present conditions. He maintains that until a method is invented for distinguishing between the effects of social environment and genetic constitution, nothing of scientific value can be said about genetic differences in intelligence, initiative and aptitude.

Similarly, distinguished studies by competent psychologists, Garth, Freeman, Klineberg, Anastasi, have demonstrated that groups have no characteristic or inherent psychological differences, and that there is nothing in the mentality of any group which, because of its biological heredity, renders it incapable of acquiring the culture of the community in which it lives.[77] Many sociologists have accepted and elaborated upon the thesis that change and progress result from racial amalgamation, a point of view which denies the familiar racist theory that race mixture leads to degeneration.[78] Sociologists have also called attention to the similarities in fundamental customs and beliefs all

---

[75] Lancelot Hogben, "Preface on Prejudices," in Cedric Dover, *Half-Caste,* p. 9.

[76] J. S. Huxley, *Man Stands Alone* (New York: Harper, 1941), Chap. IV.

[77] T. R. Garth, *Race Psychology* (New York: McGraw-Hill, 1931); F. S. Freeman, *Individual Differences* (New York: Holt, 1934); Otto Klineberg, *Race Differences* (New York: Harper, 1935); Anne Anastasi, *Differential Psychology* (New York: Macmillan, 1937).

[78] Ludwig Gumplowicz, *Der Rassenkampf* (Innsbruck, 1883); Gustav Ratzenhofer, *Wesen und Zweck der Politik* (Leipzig, 1893); F. H. Giddings, *Principles of Sociology* (New York, 1896); Lester F. Ward, *Pure Sociology* (New York, 1903); Franz Oppenheimer, *The State* (Indianapolis, 1914). See also: D. R. Young, *American Minority Peoples* (New York: Harper, 1932); L. Adamic, *From Many Lands* (New York: Harper, 1940); C. F. Wittke, *We Who Built America* (New York: Prentice-Hall, 1940).

over the world, a fact which, if proved, makes race distinctions seem quite inconsequential.[79]

CONCLUSION

It cannot be said that racist ideas persist because no efforts have been made to combat them. Despite the tremendous amount of scientific research and historical writing on the subject, however, the shibboleths of racism are still paraded and widely accepted as basic truths. Thus, the notion that the American Negro is biologically inferior is still accepted by very many people, in spite of the impressive body of evidence which calls attention to the incredible handicaps imposed upon him by a hostile white society.[80] The worst forms of anti-semitism still exist, in the face of the many studies now available which demonstrate the fact that Jews are a collection of human beings who are shaped, as all people are, by the forces of their environment, their attitudes and activities being conditioned by their eternal status as

---

[79] Adolf Bastian, *Ethnische Elementargedanken in der Lehre vom Menschen* (Berlin, 1895); Herbert Spencer, *Principles of Sociology* (New York, 1893); E. B. Tylor, *Primitive Culture* (New York, 1874); Lewis H. Morgan, *Ancient Society* (New York, 1877); J. G. Frazer, *The Golden Bough* (London & New York, 1911-1919); E. Durkheim, *The Elementary Forms of the Religious Life* (London, 1915); L. Lévy-Bruhl, *Primitive Mentality* (New York, 1923); W. Wundt, *Elements of Folk Psychology* (New York, 1916); W. G. Sumner and A. G. Keller, *The Science of Society* (New Haven, 1927). Consult: R. H. Lowie, *The History of Ethnological Theory* (New York: Farrar & Rinehart, 1937).

[80] See: Donald Young, ed., *The American Negro, Annals,* CXL (Nov., 1928); Dollard, *Caste and Class in a Southern Town;* E. B. Reuter, *The American Race Problem* (New York: Crowell, 1927); B. W. Doyle, *The Etiquette of Race Relations in the South* (University of Chicago Press, 1937); C. J. Johnson, *The Negro in American Civilization* (New York: Holt, 1930); M. J. Herkovitz, *The American Negro: A Study in Racial Crossing* (New York: Kopf, 1928); E. T. Thompson, ed., *Race Relations and the Race Problem* (Durham, Duke University Press, 1939).

a wandering, persecuted alien minority.[81] Racial prejudices are manifestly deeply-rooted in the contemporary world.

Nevertheless, objective analysis has laid bare the basic faults of the racist position. In a systematic summary, Barzun has listed the principal objections to racism: its inconsistencies, its lack of proof of causation, its mysticism, elusiveness and obscurantism, its statistical fallacies, its duplicity of motives, its rhetorical and tautological devices, its tendency toward absolutism.[82] The racist explanation of differences in human performance, says Toynbee, is "either an ineptitude or a fraud." [83] This does not imply that all groups are the same, at any given moment of history, nor that group pride in achievement is necessarily wrong. It is possible, however, to point to a great tradition without attributing it to the possession of unique, immutable genes and blood.[84]

Indeed, history furnishes many examples of philosophies and political systems which had no place for racist assumptions. Both the Alexandrian and Roman Empires accommodated various and diverse human groups. The philosophy of the Stoics

---

[81] For recent titles see: I. Graeber and S. H. Britt, *Jews in a Gentile World* (New York: Macmillan, 1942); H. M. Valentin, *Antisemitism* (New York: Viking, 1936); Maurice Samuel, *The Great Hatred* (New York: Knopf, 1940); L. J. Levinger, *Anti-Semitism Yesterday and Tomorrow* (New York: Macmillan, 1936); Council for Democracy, *Nazi Poison* (New York, 1941); Herman Bernstein, *The Truth About the Protocols of Zion* (New York: Covici-Friede, 1935); Jacques Maritain, *A Christian Looks at the Jewish Question* (New York: Longmans, Green, 1939); S. A. Fineberg, *Overcoming Anti-Semitism* (New York: Harper, 1943).

[82] *Race, A Study in Modern Superstition,* pp. 278-284. For other readable discussions of racism of a critical character, not previously cited, see: Paul Radin, *The Racial Myth* (New York: McGraw-Hill, 1934); Eugene Pittard, *Race and History* (New York: Knopf, 1926); Jean Finot, *Race Prejudice* (London: Constable, 1906); Friedrich Hertz, *Race and Civilization* (New York: Macmillan, 1928); Theophile Simar, *Étude Critique sur la Fondation de la Doctrine des Races* (Brussels: Lamertin, 1922); M. F. Ashley Montagu, *Man's Most Dangerous Myth: The Fallacy of Race* (New York: Columbia Univ. Press, 1942).

[83] A. J. Toynbee, *A Study of History* (London: Oxford University Press, 1934), Vol. I, p. 245.

[84] See, for example, G. E. G. Catlin, *The Anglo-Saxon Tradition* (London: Paul, Trench, Trubner, 1939).

and of early Christianity accepted the implications of the idea of the brotherhood of man. The rationalism of the eighteenth century and the ideologies of the French and Russian Revolutions deny the racist position. The spirit of modern science at its best is patently anti-racist. The long history of man is strewn with the corpses of now-forgotten creeds which denied the essential dignity and worth of all human life. Perhaps racism will some day be interred among them.

SELECTED BIBLIOGRAPHY

BARZUN, JACQUES, *Race, A Study in Modern Superstition* (New York: Harcourt, Brace, 1937). Particularly effecti vein showing in how many fields of thought racist ideas appear, as in those of literary and artistic criticism.

BENEDICT, RUTH, *Race: Science and Politics* (New York: Modern Age, 1940). A lucid summary of the main stream of racist thought and of available scientific information on the subject, written by a first-rate anthropologist.

BOAS, FRANZ, *The Mind of Primitive Man* (New York: Macmillan, 1938, rev. ed.). A classic analysis of the essential humanity of man, written by the dean of American anthropologists, and revised in the light of a life-time of study.

CHAMBERLAIN, HOUSTON STEWART, *Foundations of the Nineteenth Century,* translated by John Lees (New York & London: John Lane, 1911). A powerfully written statement of the point of view of modern German racism.

DOLLARD, JOHN, *Caste and Class in a Southern Town* (New Haven: Yale University Press, 1937). A case study of race relations in an American southern community, with emphasis upon the more subtle aspects of such relations. A superb study.

GOBINEAU, ARTHUR DE, *The Inequality of Human Races,* translated by Adrian Collins (New York: Putnam, 1915). A highly influential book by one of the "founding fathers" of racism in modern times.

GRANT, MADISON, *The Passing of the Great Race* (New York: Scribner's, 1916). A characteristic statement of the racist point of view by an American writer in which stock racist assumptions are warmed over to fit the American scene.

GUNTHER, HANS F. K., *The Racial Elements of European History,* translated by G. C. Wheeler (New York: Dutton, 1928). A typical example of the "science of race" as set forth by the contemporary German school of "anthropologists".

HANKINS, FRANK H., *The Racial Basis of Civilization* (New York: Knopf, 1926). A critical analysis of racist doctrines by a competent American sociologist, with special reference to Teutonism and Nordicism.

HOOTON, E. A., *Apes, Men, and Morons* (New York: Putnam, 1937), Chap. XII. A concise summary of the point of view of scientific anthropologists today on the subject of race.

HUXLEY, J. S., and HADDON, A. C., *We Europeans* (New York: Harper, 1936). An examination of contemporary racism from the point of view of modern biology.

KLINEBERG, OTTO, *Race Differences* (New York: Harper, 1935). One of several outstanding analyses of racism from the standpoint of psychological research.

McGOVERN, WILLIAM M., *From Luther to Hitler* (Boston: Houghton, Mifflin, 1941), Chap. X. An examination of the ideological backdrop of racism from the point of view of social Darwinism.

BRADEN, C. S., "Japanese Imperialism and Religion," *Amerasia,* II (Nov., 1938), pp. 148-156. A concise summary of Japanese racism, with many quotations from Japanese sources, particularly school text-books.

DETWEILER, F. G., "The Rise of Race Antagonisms," *American Journal of Sociology,* XXXVII (March, 1932), pp. 738-747. Traces the growth of race prejudice as a phenomenon of group contacts.

PARK, R. E., "The Bases of Race Prejudice," *Annals of the American Academy,* CXL (Nov., 1928), pp. 11-20. A sociological analysis of the roots of racial prejudice.

SAPIR, E., "Culture, Genuine and Spurious," *American Journal of Sociology,* XXIX (Jan., 1924), pp. 401-429. A brilliant defense of the genuineness of the culture of "primitive man."

CHAPTER VII

NAZIISM

HANS J. MORGENTHAU

If a political philosophy is a coherent system of thought intent upon justifying before ethics and reason a certain political program and certain political institutions, Naziism has not developed a political philosophy. What passes as the political philosophy of Naziism is a conglommeration of fragments of ideas, often inconsistent with each other, always vague and capable of contradictory interpretations, and hence adaptable to the exigencies of changing political conditions. Its intellectual quality is low, and its literary style is crude. Its appeal is to emotions rather than to reason.

It is not by accident that these are the general characteristics of the political philosophy of Naziism. On the one hand, they grow out of the particular political conditions under which the doctrine of Naziism originated. On the other hand, they bear the mark of the disdain for reason, which characterizes the Nazi movement.

Political philosophies, such as liberalism or communism, which appeal to one clearly defined social group, the middle classes or the proletariat, can afford to develop a coherent doctrine which reflects faithfully the conditions, interests and aspirations of this particular group. Naziism does not appeal to any social group in particular, but to certain elements in all groups. Since the conditions, interests and aspirations of these groups are largely contradictory, a political doctrine, which intends to appeal to all of them at the same time, cannot fail to be itself incoherent and contradictory. While, however, pre-Nazi political philosophy would have regarded such inconsistency a serious weakness, Naziism, in so far consistent with its general philosophic assumptions, sees in it an actual virtue.[1]

NAZIISM—A POLITICAL RELIGION

For the tradition of Western civilization, man is a rational being. It is upon this rationality, which is the common possession of all men, that the possibility of universal truth, binding upon all men, is founded. Naziism is essentially anti-intellectualist and irrationalist. Naziism has a low opinion of the common man. The masses are by their very nature stupid, sullen, ignorant, irresolute, swayed by emotions. It is for the elite and their leader to impose their will upon the masses and to give directions to their blind instincts. If such is the nature of the common man, a political philosophy, instead of being a rational system appealing to reason, becomes an instrument, cleverly and unscrupulously managed by the elite, for molding mind and will of the masses. Ideas become truly weapons, that is, weapons of propaganda, and the standard to which they must comply is no longer truth but effectiveness. It, then, is quite irrelevant whether a political idea is true, precise, and consistent with others. A lie is to be preferred if only it is capable of bringing about the desired political result.[2]

It follows from the same anti-intellectualist premises that Naziism has no use for elucidation and development of its political doctrine by discussion. Since political doctrine is an instrument for the domination of the masses, it must ask unquestioned acceptance. If it would allow the masses to debate its merits and to improve upon it, it would put into jeopardy the very objectives for which it is used.

In sum, Naziism is less a political philosophy than a political religion. It has in Hitler its saviour, in S. A., S. S. and party its sacred orders, in *Mein Kampf* its bible, in the immutable

---

[1] *Mein Kampf* (New York: Reynal and Hitchcock, 1940), p. 283 *et seq.*, Vol. II, Chapters V, VI, VII, XI.

[2] *Mein Kampf*, pp. 230 *et seq.*, 313; *The Speeches of Adolf Hitler* (London, New York, Toronto: Oxford University Press, 1942), pp. 62, 863.

twenty-five points of the party program its catechism, in the racial community its mystical body. It has its miracles and rituals, its apostles, martyrs and saints.[3] With genuine religion it has in common that it derives its claim to acceptance not from the truthfulness of its suppositions, which is verifiable by experience, but from authority, and, furthermore, that its claim to acceptance is absolute and not subject to critical doubt. It differs from genuine religion in that its manipulators are not supposed to believe in it, that it constantly changes according to the exigencies of the political situation, and, finally and most important, that its avowed objective is not to establish relationships between the individual and supernatural forces, but to establish and perpetuate the political power of a self-appointed elite over the masses of humanity.

THE ARISTOCRACY OF RACE [4]

According to democratic tradition, all men are born equal. It is the most fundamental tenet of the political philosophy of Naziism that men are not born equal. By equality is of course meant not actual equality in ability and achievement, but equality in individual worth and, hence, legal status. It is the latter that Naziism denies. It asserts the value of personality against the supremacy of mere numbers which is regarded as the constitutive principle of democracy. Individuals, as well as groups of individuals, such as nations, differ not only in their intellectual and psychological traits which may be important for their social and economic position, but also in those qualities which determine their political and legal status. Naziism sees each nation divided into two groups: those who are born to rule, and those who are born to be ruled. The same distinction is made on a world-wide scale: there are nations whose destiny it is to rule, and there are others who are preordained to serve. This political status is determined by one's blood or race.

---

[3] *The Speeches of Adolph Hitler*, pp. 137, 138, 158, 159, 405 *et seq.*, 1458, 1543, 1559, and innumerable other passages. *Cf.* also *Mein Kampf*, p. 573 *et seq.*

[4] *Mein Kampf*, Vol. I, Chapter XI, Vol. II, Chapters II, IV.

The racial doctrine of Naziism has little, if any, connection with the findings of biology and anthropology. "Blood," in the Nazi doctrine, is essentially a mystical entity, a substance which creates life in all its biological, psychological and cultural manifestations, and it is the kind of blood flowing in one's veins, which will determine the kind of life one is to lead. Nothing can escape the determining influence of "blood". Physical appearance and character no less than political convictions and attitudes are determined by race. Religion, art, science are functions of "blood". Race and "blood" become synonomous with soul and vital energy. In the concepts, materialistic and mystical at the same time, of race, blood, and soil, the concepts of "nature" and of the "folk spirit" of the German Romantic school find their resurrection.[5]

This race concept of Naziism has three distinctive characteristics. First, it advances a biological interpretation of history, culture, and politics. Hegel had found the determining element in the Spirit, Marx had found it in economic conditions, others had found it in religion, in the nation, or in ideas in general. For Naziism, biological characteristics are both the source and the outer manifestations of morality, culture, and personal worth. Tell me what your, your parents', and your grandparents' biological characteristics are, and I will tell you what kind of a man you are. Race, then, becomes the yardstick by which the worth of the individual is measured. Race explains his personality, and whatever he is, sees and does, is explained in the light of his membership in a certain race.

It is a further belief of the race doctrine of Naziism that racial characteristics are constant. They are today what they

[5] A popular school of thought sees in the political philosophy of Naziism only the logical consummation of the age-old tradition of German political thought. It is indeed obvious that with respect to many of its tenets, such as the emphasis upon will and emotions as over against reason, the glorification of the state and the disdain for the individual as such, the worship of power pure and simple, the political philosophy of Naziism builds upon foundations laid by the German tradition. Yet one looks in vain in the pre-Nazi tradition of German political thought for the intellectual crudeness, the moral nihilism and the pseudo-religious fervor, which characterize Nazi political thought. In other words, Naziism brutalizes and vulgarizes certain traits which are part of the tradition of German political thought.

were two thousand years ago. Race seems to be a kind of primordial biological fact which is completely impervious to the influences of physical and social environment. What holds true for the race as such is also true for the individual member of the race. For him race is a kind of fate into which he is born and from which he cannot escape. Education may be able to make him race-conscious, that is, proudly aware of the race to which he belongs and contemptuous of the others. Yet it cannot alter the biological fact of race, from which all individual qualities stem.

It can, however, impress upon the members of the race the importance of racial purity. The belief in it is the third distinctive characteristic of the racial doctrine of Naziism, and it is difficult to over-emphasize its bearing upon Nazi theory and practice. When a higher and a lower race mix, it is, according to the Nazi doctrine, strangely enough the contribution of the inferior race which dominates the mixture. Consequently, the superior race decays. Since racial characteristics as such remain constant, race mixture becomes the deadly danger against which the higher race must guard.

The race, which throughout history has proved itself to be superior to all others, is the Aryan or Nordic race. Whatever is valuable in ancient and modern culture was created by members of the Nordic race. Whatever good there is in the creation of an inferior race, such as Christianity or Marxism, is due to the contribution made by members of the Nordic race. All history is envisaged as a struggle between the Nordic and inferior races. Thus the decadence of France, for instance, is attributed, on the one hand, to the destruction of the Nordic element, as represented in the nobility, through the religious wars and the Revolution, and, on the other hand, to the infiltration of Negro blood into the body of metropolitan France. Similarly, the struggle between Germans and Slavs is explained as a struggle between the master race of the Nordics and the half-barbaric peoples of the East.

The race doctrine fulfilled for the political practice of Naziism a four-fold function. First, it integrated the German people into a new community transcending the traditional cleavages into political, social, and religious groupings. Second, it set up, within the traditional German community itself, a zone of racial contamination, comprehending minorities and individual dissenters of all kinds, in the destruction of which the newly discovered racial community could experience its own superiority. Furthermore, it established the claim to world-wide conquest as a mission to be fulfilled by the master race. Finally, it created and justified in the totalitarian state the political organization through which this triple function of integration, elimination, and conquest was to be accomplished.

THE TRANSFORMATION OF NATIONALISM

The dominant principle of political integration from the middle of the nineteenth century to the advent of the Nazi movement had been nationalism. Germany and Italy became unified nations under the guidance of this principle. The independence movements of the Finns, the Poles, the Czechs, the Hungarians, and the Balkan peoples drew inspiration and justification from the same source. The principle of national self-determination was made by the peace settlements of Versailles and Saint-Germain, the basis for what was believed to be an enduring peace.

Yet the triumph of the national principle in 1919 made obvious its limitations as a principle of political integration. Its consistent application gave rise to economic difficulties, such as the division of economic units (Silesia) and the creation of political units without economic foundation (Austria). It gave rise also to political and military difficulties, such as the atomization of the Danube Valley and the separation of East Prussia from the bulk of Germany through the Polish Corridor. Finally, political and military considerations prevented the national principle from being applied to all cases where its logic would have required its application. Thus, Austria was artificially maintained as an independent state and prevented from uniting with Germany, and the Sudetenland, predominantly settled by Germans, was made part of Czechoslovakia.

These weaknesses and inconsistencies gave the Nazis the opportunity of using the national principle as a weapon with which to destroy the territorial order which was based upon this self-same principle of nationality. In order to be able to do this, the Nazis transformed the national principle by interpreting the concept of nation in terms of race.

Throughout the nineteenth century nationalism was intimately connected with the liberal movement. In a sense the principle of national self-determination was simply the principle of individual self-determination, that is, of individual liberty, transferred to a group of individuals who have certain characteristics in common. The cry for national self-determination is but the collective echo of the cry for individual liberty. The political goal of the individual was essentially identical with the goal of the national group, that is, freedom from oppression by autocratic government. Consequently, membership in a nation was a matter of individual choice; the nation, in the words of Renan, is "a daily plebiscite". This goal of individual and collective freedom was furthermore in harmony with the economic interests of the middle classes which were the main supporters and beneficiaries of liberal nationalism.

The post-war conditions which determined the growth of Naziism altered completely the political, social, and economic implications of nationalism. To the Nazis at least, liberal nationalism no longer seemed to have sufficient strength, in the face of powerful disintegrating influences, to integrate Germany into a working political community. Versailles turned the national principle against Germany whose territorial losses were justified by it. More especially, the Republic of Weimar, which identified itself with the idea of liberal nationalism, was also identified with the German defeat of 1918 and the Treaty of Versailles growing out of it, as well as with the political and economic disappointments of the post-war period. For all these reasons, the value of the traditional national principle as a political weapon became doubtful in the eyes of the German nationalists. Furthermore, the lower strata of the middle classes were economically proletarized under the impact of inflation and unemployment. Because of this, they could no longer derive satisfaction from their separate existences as individual shop-keepers or employees. Nor could they find compensation, as in former times, in the idea of the national state, as it was repre-sented by the Republic of Weimar. They gave up the indi-vidualistic aspirations of liberalism for the realization of which the economic and social realities offered no opportunity, and gave the libertarian aspirations of nationalism a collectivist turn against the destructive forces inside and outside Germany and in favor of the suffering true Germans. They were able to do this by making nationalism identical with racism. Thus it be-came possible to transform the struggle for national liberation at the same time into a revolutionary struggle inside Germany and into a struggle for conquest on a world-wide scale.

THE NATIONALIST SOCIALIST COMMUNITY

The constitutive principle of the nation was then no longer the free choice of the individual on the basis of cultural pref-erences but certain biological characteristics which once and for-ever divided each nation into two hostile camps. The pseudo-religious energies engendered by liberal nationalism could thus be directed against any objective within or without the political frontiers, which was stigmatized as racially inferior or at least hostile to the master race.

Whereas in liberal political philosophy the individual is the center around whose worth and aspirations the political system revolves, the racial community now takes this central place. Life, liberty and happiness of the individual amount to nothing as compared with the existence, safety, and greatness of the community. "Germany will live even if we must die," and "The common good comes before individual advancement" become the slogans of the new collectivist creed. By merging his individuality with the mystical body of the racial community, the individual would regain the awareness of his worth, which he had lost in the turmoil of national humiliation, social dis-integration, and economic insecurity. The dissensions between capital and labor, city and farm, government and parliament, the Right and the Left, seemed to disappear once it was discovered that the members of all these warring groups were united in the greater community of the race. This community would solve the political, economic and social problems with which these groups had struggled in vain, by leading its members back to the source of all strength and wisdom, the mainspring of the race itself: "Blood and soil." The mystical communion with "blood and soil," whose processes escape rational analysis, becomes thus the key to the solution of all the problems which the Republic of Weimar had not been able to solve.

The racist interpretation of history, its fusion with the nationalist tradition, and the emergence of a new racially determined collectivism provided Naziism with a number of political and propagandistic weapons which, ingeniously used, decided the struggle for domestic power in favor of the Nazis and brought them very close to victory over their foreign enemies as well.

Naziism has never developed a consistent or even intelligible economic program; its intellectual deficiencies are nowhere more glaring than here. While it opposed the socialist parties, the labor unions, and the republican program of social reform, it appealed to the proletarized members of the middle classes and to the unemployed members of the laboring class in the name of socialism. While it proclaimed the principle of social revolution, it applied for and received the moral and financial support of those who sought through this support to buy protection against social revolution and even social reform. National Socialist collectivism showed a way out of these dilemmas. Since the traditional social, economic and political conflicts, to which terms such as socialism, capitalism, class struggle and the like refer, have been superseded by the struggle between races, the traditional conflicts are interpreted in the light of this struggle. Thus Naziism is opposed to capital, but not to the racially good, that is, Germanic capital which is creative and benevolent, but to the racially evil, that is, Jewish and international capital which is parasitic and destructive. Thus Naziism is in favor of socialism, but of the racially good, that is, German variety which manifests itself in service for the racial community and finds its noblest expression in the Prussian Army and the state of Frederick the Great. On the other hand, Naziism is hostile to Marxian, that is, Jewish socialist values allegiance to an international class higher than loyalty to the racial community. Thus Naziism can be against and in favor of socialism and against and in favor of capitalism at the same time and by the same formula placate, and through common opposition to the same enemy unite, antagonistic groups.

Similarly Naziism is able at once to oppose and defend Christianity. It opposes the racially contaminated type of Christianity, which is internationalist, unheroic and pacifist. Yet it defends and promotes German Christendom which glorifies the manly virtues, cultivates the combative instincts and expresses the deepest aspirations of the racial soul.

Furthermore, the reduction of all domestic conflict to racial ones makes it possible strictly and definitely to localize the conflicting principles and interests in biologically determined and therefore easily identifiable groups. Hence, whenever a conflict arises, the German race is on the side of the angels, and the Jews and other "racial degenerates" are on the side of the devil, and once the problem is posed in such terms, the solution presents no intellectual or physical difficulties. When the Nazis call the Jewish question the key to the solution of all the problems of the age, they show, beyond the immediate propagandistic purpose, a clear awareness of the decisive function which National Socialist collectivism fulfills for their political theory and practice.

The idea of racial community not only destroys the concept of the national state as the main instrumentality of political integration in the domestic field; it also has a revolutionary effect upon the relations between states. From the collapse of the Holy Alliance to the advent of Naziism, the principle of non-intervention determined the attitude of a government with regard to the domestic affairs of other governments. Naziism replaces this principle by the idea of intervention on a dual basis. Since the biological fact of race supersedes the free choice of nation-

ality as the principle of political integration, the members of the
German race, wherever they live and whatever their nationality,
are the racial comrades of the members of the German race
living within the German boundaries. They owe allegiance to
the German government, in which the racial community finds its
political manifestation, and confronted with a conflict between
loyalty to the nation of their choice and allegiance to the racial
community, they must give precedence to the latter.

It is furthermore the mission of the master race to bring
racial salvation to the peoples of the earth by freeing them from
the domination of racially inferior groups and establishing the
dominance of the master race. Hence, disruptive interference,
on the basis of racial distinctions, in the domestic affairs of other
nations, corresponds as a technique of political conquest to the
substitution of the struggle between races for the traditional
conflicts on the domestic scene. Ultimately, the distinction between domestic and international affairs tends to be obliterated,
and social and political conflicts everywhere appear as phases
of a gigantic struggle between races for supremacy.

The Totalitarian State [6]

It follows from the postulate of the racial inequality of men
and from its particular manifestation in the National Socialist
community that within a certain territory only the members of
the superior race can enjoy political rights. Yet the political
hierarchy, based upon racial excellence, does not end there.
Within the superior race, a fundamental triple distinction must
be made between the masses, which have no inborn racial consciousness nor political judgment of their own and are therefore
the mere raw material for political leadership; the relatively
small group of the elite, a political aristocracy and sacred order
in one which, because of its racial qualities, is predestined to
lead the masses, to imbue them with racial consciousness, to
show them the political goals, and to use them for the realization of these goals; finally, the leader, the incarnation of the

---

[6] *Mein Kampf,* Vol. II, Chapters II, IV, VIII, IX, XI.

racial spirit itself, statesman and saviour in one, who, drawing strength and wisdom from the mystical sources of blood and soil, guides with unfailing instinct the destinies of the racial community.

While according to democratic political thought the ultimate power rests with the people to whom the political leaders and public officials are responsible, Naziism reverses the distribution of power and responsibility between people and government. Naziism conceives of the relationship between government and people essentially in military terms, and Hitler himself has referred to the army as the model of political organization.[7] Consequently, the fullness of political power is vested in the political leader who delegates part of it to his "political soldiers", that is, the members of the political oligarchy, the Nazi party. The leader is politically responsible to nobody and morally responsible only to his racial conscience, the Germanic god or the German people as the embodiment of the racial spirit. The members of the party are politically responsible to the leader from whom they derive their political power. The people as such, while providing at times ideological justification for the exercise of political power by the elite, have disappeared as the seat of autonomous political power and the receptacle of political responsibility. Under such premises, the popular election of public officials and the determination of policies by majority vote become absurd relics of a by-gone age which believed in the rational nature and the individual worth of the common man.

It also follows from these premises that the traditional dichotomy between state and society, that is, the spheres of government action and of individual freedom, becomes obsolete. In pre-Nazi political philosophy, even in the doctrine of the absolute monarchy at least as a matter of principle, the government has only as much power as the constitution and the laws of the land permit it to have. As for the rest, the people are free to do as they please. In Nazi doctrine the concept of law

---

[7] *Mein Kampf*, pp. 384 *et seq.*, 620; *The Speeches of Adolf Hitler*, pp. 442, 556, 789.

loses its character as an objective rule of conduct to which government and people alike are subject. Legal rules now are mere instrumentalities of political domination which assure to the party dictatorship the element of order without which no organization can function, and which furthermore are used as a means of coercion by which recalcitrant members of the community are brought into line. Law is used and interpreted according to the political exigencies of the hour; beyond this usefulness as a political instrumentality it has no objective, rational value at all. "Law is what benefits the German people," and what benefits the German people is determined by the supreme decision of the leader.

The supreme will of the leader, far from being restrained by an objective rule of law, is the absolute source and measure of governmental power. He determines how far the power of the party shall extend, what spheres of individual endeavor it shall control and by what means. This absence of legal restraint makes the power of the state potentially limitless, that is, total. The very nature of the leadership principle makes it actually so.

The doctrine of democracy starts with the assumption that all citizens are potentially capable of arriving at the right political decision and that, consequently, nobody has a monopoly of political wisdom to which, at least potentially, the others would not have access. It follows from this premise that all citizens have an equal right to hold and express their own opinion on any matter political or otherwise and to propagandize for it with the final aim of making it the dominant one. "The best test of truth is the power of the thought to get itself accepted in the competition of the market." Philosophic relativism, political pluralism, the protection of minorities of all kinds and with respect to all kinds of activities are therefore the earmarks of democratic theory and practice.

Naziism, on the contrary, recognizes only one truth, political and otherwise, that is, the truth which emanates from the leader's supernatural insight and wisdom. Consequently, non-conformism is more than mere dissension but a sacrilegious revolt against the "voice of the blood" through which the genius of the race makes itself known. Since "Hitler is always right," he has not only the right but the obligation to impose what he has found to be right upon the passive and confused mind of the masses and to destroy the heretic who dares to dissent in thought, word or action. Totalitarianism is therefore not by accident the distinguishing characteristic of the Nazi state. The power of the state, as represented in the leader, is total since no legal restraint puts limits to the exercise of governmental power. In its actual exercise, the power of the state regulates, controls, and circum-. scribes all activities of the individual, be they political, religious, artistic, educational, economic, or of the most intimate personal nature. Government, society and the individual merge into one gigantic political organization which as the totalitarian state forms the political counterpart to what the racial community is in the biological and spiritual sphere.[8]

THE CULT OF VIOLENCE

The principle of organization through which the totalitarian state molds the racial community for its purposes is coercion, intellectual and physical, and the traditional agencies of the state are transformed into instruments of coercion. The party which in pre-Nazi doctrine was an instrumentality in the competitive struggle for political power now becomes the monopolistic keeper and dispenser of the political gospel, an army of "political soldiers" who have to see to it that the political decision of the leader is transformed into the political action of the "racial

---

[8] Much has been made by some writers of the apparent subordination in Nazi philosophy of the state to the race (see, for instance, *Mein Kampf*, p. 592 *et seq.*), and of the apparent opposition, especially emphasized by the official Nazi philosopher Rosenberg, of Naziism to the state worship of Hegel. Closer analysis, however, shows that this element in Nazi political thought fulfilled a useful political function while the Nazi movement stood in revolutionary opposition to the legitimate government representing the state, and needed a legitimation superior to the legality of the established order. As soon as the Nazi movement had conquered the state and state and race had become identical, the subordination of state to race lost all political meaning in domestic affairs. It was, however, still useful for the ideological justification of state action and as a means of undermining the authority of foreign governments and of dissolving the national coherence of foreign states. As a check upon the total power of the state, it has never had any importance.

comrades". The universities are no longer busy discovering new truths but fulfill the public function of imbuing the public with the political truths already discovered by the leader. They become, like primary and secondary education, press, radio, and official religion, agencies of governmental propaganda and, since the state keeps them under monopolistic control, of intellectual coercion.

These instrumentalities of intellectual coercion are, however, implemented by an instrumentality of physical coercion, that is, the political police. Its functions illuminate another distinctive element of Nazi political thought, that is, the estimation of organized physical violence not as a necessary evil but as a positive good. Pre-Nazi political thought considers physical violence, especially in its organized form, an evil which to eliminate is one of the main tasks of civilized governments. Hence, pre-Nazi political thought is pacifist with respect to foreign affairs and upholds the ideal of government by discussion and law in domestic affairs.

This abhorrence of the use of force, concomitant with the ascendancy of the commercial spirit, is for Naziism an unmistakable sign of weakness, of intellectual and physical decadence. The racially healthy man, the blonde hero, finds enjoyment in the demonstration of his physical superiority. The soldier is the ideal man, warfare the ideal occupation. The history of nations as well as of individuals is the story of an unending struggle for power, which, sometimes fought with non-physical means, is always ready to transform itself into the use of individual and organized violence. In this clash of hostile forces the stronger reveals himself as such and establishes his claim to rule. Domestic strife and international war are the selective principles through which the hierarchy of the strong over the weak is created and put to the ever-renewed test of actual combat. Since, as we have seen, this hierarchy is of the very essence of the social and political order, as conceived by Nazi philosophy, the hidden will of nature and of racial destiny becomes manifest in combat and war. War, then, is not only inevitable but even desirable. Far from shunning it, the master race which as such claims the right to rule the world, must concentrate the national effort upon preparation for it in order to be able to prove the justice of its claim. In the same way in which the totalitarian state of Naziism finds its ultimate aim in the victorious war, the political philosophy of Naziism culminates in the glorification of war.[9]

BIBLIOGRAPHY

Primary Sources

BAYNES, N. H. *The Speeches of Adolf Hitler* (New York: Oxford University Press, 1942).

CHANDLER, A. R. *The Clash of Political Ideals* (New York: D. Appleton, 1940).

CHILDS, H. L. *The Nazi Primer* (New York: Harper, 1938).

COOLE, W. W., and POTTER, M. F. *Thus Speaks Germany* (London: George Rutledge, 1941).

HITLER, A. *Mein Kampf* (New York: Reynal and Hitchcock, 1940).

SALES, RAOUL DE ROUSSY DE. *My New Order* (New York: Reynal and Hitchcock, 1941).

Secondary Sources

ABEL, T. *Why Hitler Came Into Power* (New York: Prentice-Hall, 1938).

BRADY, R. A. *The Spirit and Structure of German Fascism* (London: Victor Gollancz, 1937).

BUTLER, ROHAN D'O. *The Roots of National Socialism* (New York: E. P. Dutton, 1942).

DEWEY, JOHN. *German Philosophy and Politics* (New York: G. P. Putnam, 1942).

ERMATH, FRITZ. *The New Germany* (Washington: Digest Press, 1936).

FLORIN, J., and HERZ, JOHN H. "Bolshevist and National Socialist Doctrines of International Law," *Social Research,* Vol. 7 (1940), pp. 1-31.

FLORINSKY, M. T. *Fascism and National Socialism* (New York: Macmillan, 1936).

HEIMANN, E. *Communism, Fascism or Democracy?* (New York: W. W. Norton, 1938).

KOLNAI, A. *The War Against the West* (New York: The Viking Press, 1938).

LASSWELL, H. D. "The Psychology of Hitlerism," *Political Quarterly,* Vol. 4 (1933), pp. 373-384.

LICHTENBERGER, H. *The Third Reich* (New York: The Greystone Press, 1937).

McGOVERN, W. M. *From Luther to Hitler* (Cambridge: Houghton Mifflin, 1941).

MAYER, C. "On the Intellectual Origin of National Socialism," *Social Research,* Vol. 9 (1942), pp. 225-247.

MORGENTHAU, H. J. "National Socialist Doctrine of World Organization," *Proceedings of the Seventh Conference of Teachers of International Law and Related Subjects* (Washington, 1941), pp. 103-108.

NEUMANN, FRANZ. *Behemoth* (New York: Oxford University Press, 1942).

---

[9] *Mein Kampf,* pp. 221 *et seq.,* 728 *et seq.,* Vol. II, Chapter IX; *The Speeches of Adolf Hitler,* pp. 185, 196, 197.

NIEBUHR, R. "The Germans and the Nazis," *The Nation,* Vol. 154 (1942), pp. 398-400.

OAKESHOTT, M. *The Social and Political Doctrines of Contemporary Europe* (New York: Macmillan, 1942).

PREUSS, L. "Racial Theory and National Socialist Political Thought," *The Southwestern Social Science Quarterly,* Vol XV (1934), pp. 103-118.

RAUSCHNING, H. *The Revolution of Nihilism* (New York: Alliance Book Corporation, 1939).

————. *The Voice of Destruction* (New York: G. P. Putnam, 1940).

SABINE, G. H. *A History of Political Theory* (New York: Henry Holt, 1937).

SALES, RAOUL DE ROUSSY DE. "What Makes a German," *Atlantic Monthly,* Vol. 169 (1942), pp. 335-344.

SANTAYANA, G. *Egotism in German Philosophy* (New York: C. Scribner, 1916).

SCHUMANN, F. L. "The Political Theory of German Fascism," *American Political Science Review,* Vol. 28 (1934), pp. 210-232.

————. *The Nazi Dictatorship* (New York: Alfred A. Knopf, 1936).

SNYDER, L. L. *From Bismarck to Hitler* (Williamsport: The Bayard Press, 1935).

VIERECK, P. *Metapolitics* (New York: Alfred A. Knopf, 1941).

CHAPTER VIII

THE QUESTION OF SOVEREIGNTY AND RECENT TRENDS OF JURISTIC THOUGHT

WALTER E. SANDELIUS

It has been asserted that all the major wars of the last few centuries have turned upon the question of political sovereignty. There is much truth in this way of stating the central political problem of succeeding generations and different times. As the great war of these days neared its dynamic climax and conclusion, it seems altogether likely that in the settlements to come we shall be no less concerned than in times past, it may be we shall be more than ever concerned, with debates about national sovereignty.

These debates will not be a matter merely of logic-chopping phrases and abstruse notions. They will be a testimony to the realities of national and international forces in conflict, heavy as these will be with economic dispute and contention of interests along both national and other than national lines. The crisis of national sovereignty in these days obviously is part with, and essence of, the larger conflict of a world in revolution.

The time of political and economic crisis, however, is never the hey-day of juristic thinking. Such a time may serve to disintegrate established ways of juristic thinking. It may underscore the validity of certain of the newer trends of legal thought and development already under way. But just as a very special function of legal institutions is to conserve the social gains that already have been made, so the systematic formulation of legal philosophies will tend to reflect rather the basic norms in the long-run developments of community, than those eruptive forces that play when social orders change.

For evidence of juristic thought, therefore, such as can be considered to be anything more than a pretended philosophy of law, there is little to be gained from the sifting, for example, of the pseudo-juristic literature of the Nazi state. This pretended legal reasoning is too full of unsettled revolutionary and counter-revolutionary force to have any real meaning as jurisprudence. The same, by and large, remains true—though to far less degree —of corresponding developments in the great Soviet State. In Russia, indeed, legal procedures of recent growth have a great deal to show, that ought to be of interest also to the western communities, yet the time seems premature for any advanced degree here of systematic legal philosophy.

The enduring political thought of Ancient Greece came at the end of what was best in Greek civilization. While the political—which includes the juridical—thinking is always part of the creative, yet in the vanguard of social change philosophy hardly is to be distinguished as such. In the Western democracies that now represent civilization, it is not the last decade so much, but the last half century to which we must look for the significant trends in juristic development.

What these trends are would require a large tome to explore. We shall try here to gather up some of them, with some degree of reference to the conception of sovereignty, such as is assigned to this chapter.

Now, whatever may be said as to the reality, always, of the problem of sovereignty, is not the share of attention that is given to this concept, in the recent schools of legal thought, one of altogether diminishing importance? To answer this question it will be necessary to characterize these schools rather broadly.

I. *Analytical jurisprudence considered together with a brief statement of the origin of the idea of sovereignty and of its relation to comparative jurisprudence.*

The first use of the word, sovereignty, as a term in political discussion is commonly accredited to Jean Bodin, who in the sixteenth century supported the claims of the rising nation-state, defending in particular the position of the French monarchy. Sovereignty as the embodiment of a supreme authority, however, has been the subject of controversy wherever society has been sufficiently organized to encourage political speculation whatsoever. The Greeks, the Romans, the writers of the Middle Ages all sensed, in some sort, the central position which this concept occupies in political theory, and many of the ablest thinkers of succeeding generations in the West have devoted considerable effort to its exposition.

Wherever men live together, in more or less of community, there is bound to arise also clash of interests and conflict of wills. There is presupposed some principle ordering their relations. The source in which that principle finds its force has been denoted the sovereign. Depending upon the point of view, the attributes of sovereignty are many and varied. Practically every social science, at one time or another, has claimed sovereignty as a subject falling within its particular province of investigation. The legalist, the historian, the philosopher, the economist, the psychologist, and the sociologist have all entered the play. From the juristic standpoint, a recent tendency of importance in the United States has been the attempt to unify the divergent approaches to the subject, making a broader, more inclusive view of the science of law. This phase is a contribution of the so-called sociological school, headed in this country, it might be said, by the late Justice Holmes and by Roscoe Pound.

Concerning ourselves essentially with sovereignty in a juristic sense, it is to be kept in mind of course that any categorizing of the several directions pursued into the problem of sovereignty, and of its relation to jurisprudence, necessarily varies with the viewpoint of the individual observer. It has become, in fact, rather the fashion of the hour to attribute everything that may appear in any social or moral outlook whatsoever entirely to the social, or the historic background of the observer, and accordingly to discount any notion at all of an abiding validity of whatever it is that may appear. This extreme of relativism ends in a complete denial of any possibility of true science in these matters. It represents, we may think, one of the unfortunate vagaries of the time we live in. In its worst excesses it has brought fruits such as may be seen for example in the fascistic philosophies of today. There is, however, no space to include here an analysis of the influence of personal experience upon the individual jurist.

These speculations apart, there appear commonly, in one terminology or another, the following classifications of juristic schools: (1) the analytical or Austinian, (2) the historical, (3) the philosophical, (4) the pluralistic, and (5) the sociological. Many writers accord the "pure" jurisprudence of Hans Kelsen a special category. Any such classification is to some extent arbitrary, and even more so is the putting of a writer in any one of the categories when in reality he may evince characteristics of several. Professor Kelsen, for example, shows certain similarities to the Austinians. Sir Henry Maine, one of the earlier representatives of the historical school, finds himself conceding a strong position also to the analytical point of view. In general, however, the various viewpoints concerned here may be included among the above-mentioned schools.

In the war of theories the analytical approach, which has become identified with the name of John Austin, in an important sense stands alone against the field. The conception of national sovereignty, which may be so largely attributed to this way of thinking in the jurisprudence of recent democracy, has achieved its best formulation near the end of the nineteenth and the beginning of the twentieth centuries, perhaps, at the hands of A. V. Dicey in England, Esmein in France, and W. W. Willoughby in the United States.

The analytical school may be regarded as having been fathered by Jean Bodin, though Bodin has his place also in the genesis of the historical method. His *De Republica,* written to justify the supremacy of the King of France in the new national state, incorporates all the essentials of Austinianism. Sovereignty, he says, is supreme power over the internal affairs of a nation. It is an ultimate authority over all citizens and subjects, an authority above and beyond law, because law is but the creation of the sovereign. The sovereign cannot be bound by his own will. Nor can he be restrained by the will of any preceding sovereign authority. It is the sovereign's function to order the legal relations of his subjects as he sees fit. He can make, abrogate or change law subject to the approval of none.

Yet in the laying down of these dicta, Bodin was mindful of the natural limitations upon man, for we find him saying that the sovereign must not attempt to transgress the laws of God, of nature, and of nations. In speaking of the law of nations he would include certain rules which we today would gather up under the head of constitutional law. Later, however, we find him asserting that the sovereign is not bound by the laws of nations should those laws be opposed to the laws of God and nature. It is in these latter, then, that the final authority resides, and it is in this respect of limitation that Bodin differs most notably from the later analytical jurists. Bodin's sovereign is supreme, yet limited. The later theorists displayed no such reluctance to accept the logical consequences of the absolutistic conception of sovereignty.

Analytical jurisprudence achieved its fullest and most rigid formulation in England. Hobbes, Bentham, Austin, Lewis, and Holland all contributed to its development there. Although there is some question as to the justice of so doing, the classic enunciation of analytical jurisprudence is attributed to John Austin, the nineteenth century English lawyer. It is rather largely of Austin's making that law in the English-speaking communities so generally has been thought of as the command of a political superior to a political inferior. The political superior is the sovereign, the sole and unlimited source of law. The criterion of sovereignty, however, is not in the making of law, so much as in the authority to say what is and what is not law. The legislator is he, not by whose authority the law was first made, but by whose authority it continues to be law.

The sway of sovereignty is in no wise restricted by the existence of natural laws, international law, or constitutional law. These are not laws properly speaking, not positive laws in the Austinian sense, but at best rules of positive morality. Laws of nature are not the essence of legal right. They are not commands of a political superior to a political inferior. The same holds true of the law set by one sovereign to another. Sovereignty to be meaningful must be applied only within the limits of the state organization. Constitutional law is regarded in only a slightly more favorable light as being law. This, according to Austin, is a compound of positive morality and positive law— law so far as the "individuals and small aggregates composing the sovereign number" are concerned, morality so far as the collective sovereignty is concerned.

Among the analytical jurists may be listed also Dicey as the most eminent of recent Austinianism in England, Hegel, Seydel, and Jellinek in Germany, Esmein in France, and Willoughby and Garner in the United States. These agreed with Austin that sovereignty is supreme power, inalienable and indivisible.

Dicey, improving upon Austin, distinguished in a significant way between political and legal sovereignty. In England, Parliament, "the King in Parliament," was said to be the *legal* sovereign, absolute in the legal sphere, while *politically* it was limited by the electoral power responsible for the constituency of Parliament. The courts in their regard for law and legal sovereignty had no concern in their judicial function with the limitations politically imposed by the electorate, any more than with the more broadly limiting conditions of, say, history, climate or some eternal science. Dicey's distinction was meant, not to divide sovereignty, but to mark off two quite separate spheres of ultimacy. In this it must be said that, for the limited purposes of a strictly national system of legality, and so long as there were no serious issues as to whom the legal sovereign actually did represent, he succeeded in making a very clear formulation of the modern Austinianism.

Also Willoughby and Garner have each a significant point of departure from Austin, the former in that he supports the claim of constitutional law as law proper, and the latter in rendering a like service for international law. The contention of Professor Willoughby is that Austin reduced constitutional law to the level of positive morality, due to his failure to recognize a distinction between the state and the government. The government is but the representative of the state, he argued, and must conduct itself in accordance with constitutional laws, while these emanate from the sovereign will of the state itself. Professor Garner rejects the fundamental principle of Austin that, in order to be recognized as law, the rule necessarily is backed by a sovereign power, and so must issue from a political superior to a political inferior; Garner accepts international law as law in its own right. Though the Austinian emphasis upon physical sanction as the necessary support of law seems to him too narrow, yet domestic law he would regard as of the essence of sovereign will.

There is no space here to include a statement of the significant contributions to this general viewpoint of Jellinek in Germany and of Esmein in France.

II. *The Historical School*

The historical school commanded a support as widespread as that of the analytical school during the past century. Its most outstanding leaders have been Savigny in Germany, Maine in England, and perhaps Carter in the United States. A distinguished representative of the twentieth century was the Russian savant, Sir Paul Vinogradoff, who so largely gave himself to England.

In point of time Savigny was the principal originator of the method and viewpoint of history in jurisprudence. The core of the view achieved is, according to Savigny, "that every age creates its world not for itself and arbitrarily, but in close communion with the whole past. In consequence every age must recognize something that is given, which is necessary and free at the same time; necessary because not dependent upon the arbitrary will of the present; free because as little dependent upon a foreign command, but rather produced by the high nature of the people as a constantly growing and developing body." The historical school "ascribes the great weight to the recognition of the living connection which knits the present to the past." But this is not to be interpreted as making light of "the value and independence of each age".

Along with all the other social institutions, law is to be regarded as the product of the past. More specifically Savigny finds the source of law in the general spirit of the people. This general spirit or consciousness is "the spirit of the people living and working in common in all the individuals, which gives birth to positive law, which therefore is to the consciousness of each individual not accidentally but necessarily one and the same". As emanation of a basic consensus, law is not made so much as found. It resides in and grows with the human race itself. As particular segments of the human race residing in different nations have different characteristics, so do the systems of law which appertain to these differ from each other. Law, therefore, is not the arbitrary command of a supreme and unlimited sovereign, but a product of the common consciousness of the whole community. An investigation of primitive law is believed to establish this conception beyond dispute.

Whereas Savigny's method may be regarded as a fusion of the philosophical and the historical, that of Sir Henry Maine, father of the English historical school, is comparative and historical. Maine admitted the applicability, in large part, of the Austinian doctrine of sovereignty to modern systems of law, but only exceptionally to the institutions and mores of primitive man. In the matter of practical attitude toward the growing democracy of his day, Maine's historicism influenced him, probably, in the direction of his conservative bias.

For Jude Carter, American representative among historical jurists, there can be no question as to the unreality of Austin's theory. All law, he maintains, is but custom, and all the acts of legislatures, past and future, are no more than a "mere fringe on the body of law".

The late Sir Paul Vinogradoff adds a new emphasis, that of applying the historical method to various legal systems with a view to discovering inter-system similarities, differences, and influences of one upon another. As summarized by Dean Pound, "Where the historical school saw in the history of law the unfolding of a single idea, [Vinogradoff] saw a succession of ideas, giving rise to a succession of types. . . . The central point of his contention was that historical types are the foundation of a theory of law."

III. *Philosophical Schools*

According to Professor C. E. Merriam there are three phases in the development of the philosophical schools: (1) the natural law school of the eighteenth century; (2) the metaphysical school of the nineteenth century; (3) the social-philosophical school of the twentieth century, of which in turn there are three branches—the social utilitarians, the neo-Kantians, and the neo-Hegelians.

(1) The idea of natural law was given expression first by the Greek Stoics and carried over by the Romans among whom it reached its zenith in the writings of Cicero. "Speaking broadly," says Lord Bryce, "the law of nature represented to the Romans that which is conformable to reason, to the best side of human nature, to an elevated morality, to practical good sense, to general convenience. It is simple and rational as opposed to that which is artificial or arbitrary. It is universal as opposed to that which is local or national. It is superior to all other law because it belongs to mankind as mankind . . ." Natural law recognizes no subordination to the will of an earthly sovereign. On the contrary, it demands obedience from all mortals, high and low alike. The canonists of the Middle Ages, likewise Bodin, Grotius, and Blackstone, all postulated a natural law. The dominance of the analytical, historical and sociological schools of modern times have not been able to suppress the defenders of this point of view. Bryce asks, "Who can say that an idea so ancient, in itself so simple, yet capable of taking many aspects, an idea which has had so varied a history and so wide a range of influence, may not have a career reserved for it in the long future which still lies before the human race?" In 1910 Joseph Charmont published his book, *La renaissance de droit naturel*, betokening a revival of natural law theory. Recent statements by so advanced a relativist as Harold Laski testify to the hold that is retained, with one variation or another, by this age-old conception.

(2) The metaphysical jurisprudence differs from the natural law school in that it seeks an ideal element, a principle, about which all law and legality may be constructed rather than

a whole body of natural laws. It agrees with the natural law theorists in regarding law as found, not made. Though on the whole, lightly regarded by him, Dean Pound credits the metaphysical school with fixing the "lines of the ethical interpretation of legal history", and "giving content to the idea of freedom which historical jurists postulate as unfolding in legal development".

An outstanding representative of this point of view, whose immediate influence extends well into the twentieth century, is Thomas Hill Green, Oxford idealist, exponent of the philosophy of ethical self-realization. The ideal critique which is to be applied to law and legal institutions, says Green, is that which fosters self-realization of the members of society. The ethical value "of the institutions of civil life lies in their operation as giving reality to the capacities of will and reason and enabling them to be really exercised". The function of law is not so much to mould the citizen in a moral form as to remove all possible hindrances to his self-directed development. Morality is to be aided, in fact *can* be fostered, by the state not directly but only indirectly. This metaphysical idealism has its affinities with the social utilitarianism, of Rudolf von Jhering for example (to be mentioned later), yet differs from the latter in its emphasis upon the moral nature of the ultimate responsibility of the individual for himself.

(3) It may be agreed with Dean Pound that the development of jurisprudence in the twentieth century has taken two main directions, one philosophical, the other sociological. The first may be denoted the social-philosophical school. One phase of it is the social utilitarianism the leader of which is Rudolf von Jhering, and which gets its name to distinguish it from the individual utilitarianism of Bentham. Jhering conceived of the purpose of law as the protection of individual and social interests that lie back of all legal right. The theory of interests, Professor Merriam tells us, has gone a long way toward superseding the theory of natural rights. The social utilitarians, in any case, are more nearly akin to the analytical jurists than to the historical, for they conceive of law as a conscious product. It has been

suggested that this may be due in large measure to the strong movement of social reform in Germany in the latter part of the nineteenth century, arousing there a new faith in the ability of man to design his own environment. The Austinian conception of law as sovereign will, however, is replaced by the idea of dominant legal purpose.

Another late nineteenth century, philosophical kind of reaction against the historical school, which retains moreover its force and influence to the present, is the neo-Kantian school of Rudolf Stammler, its founder and leader. Stammler attempted to set up a universally valid method of evaluation upon the justice attained by law, but with reference to this ideal element of the law he imposed restrictions of time and place. The quest was for relative justice, for the "ideal of an epoch", with emphasis upon the social nature of justice.

A third type of social philosophical jurisprudence is the neo-Hegelianism of Joseph Kohler. Law, to Kohler, is the product of the composite cultural forces of an age. By Kultur, Kohler means the whole conquest by society of nature—human and material. The neo-Hegelians differ from Hegel in one notable respect. Whereas Hegel held that law, while representing an historical force, is arrived at deductively, Kohler and followers proceed empirically, having recourse to history, anthropology and ethnology. Although law is a cultural phenomenon, the view here is that it can be consciously modified to meet the needs of the present. Law is relative to the flux of civilization. Always it reflects the entire culture, interpreted as extending beyond the material and economic to include also, for example, the ethical and religious views which the law reflects. "The law establishes the channels through which the stream of culture flows." Law is not the command of the sovereign; it is the expression of the general view of life.

Leon Duguit, influential twentieth century French jurist, would fit perhaps equally well with the group of pluralistic thinkers later considered, or with the sociological school, though we include him here with the social philosophical school. Duguit is the recognized champion of the conception of objective law.

It has been said of him that he attempts what Compte attempted for philosophy, "to emancipate it from theology and metaphysics."

Whereas in the analytical view law is subjective as being the command of the sovereign, the theory of objective law would deny any validity at all to the concept of state sovereignty. The state is not sovereign, the state is in no sense a person, according to Duguit. Only the individual is a person. The consciousness of the state is no more than the consciousness of all the people who compose it. "The state is only the manifestation of a force and it may be defined as the man or the group of men who in fact in a given society are materially stronger than the others, or as the simple fact of the differentiation between the governor and the governed." Political power "is a fact which has in itself no character of legitimacy or illegitimacy, . . . the product of social evolution."

The doctrine of national sovereignty advanced by Esmein falsely assumes, says Duguit: (1) an exact correspondence which in fact is often non-existent between state and nation; and (2) oneness and indivisibility—the suppression in the national territory of all groups exercising independent control, in a way that no longer has any near correspondence to the facts. The law exists without the sovereign and above the state, above the rulers and the ruled, a rule which is compulsory on one and on the other. "If there is such a thing as sovereignty of the state it is juristically limited by this rule of law." Nor is law based on the natural right of the individual, because so-called natural right is only metaphysical affirmation. Law is not a power of the community any more than it is power of the individual. Law is objective, an expression of the fact of social solidarity. It is based upon and evolves together with social solidarity. In order to be law it must enhance the solidarity of the community. Community, however, is relative. Community is local, national and international. There is community of the working man, of the industrialist, of the churchman, of innumerable groups, in addition to that of the state which is only one of these. Law is a seemless web governing all these, "a rule of conduct in perpetual

evolution, resulting from continually changing forms of the social solidarity, and varying constantly to time and place."

In practical life the term "public service" may be substituted for social solidarity, for that which conduces to the one
conduces to the other. What is "public service?" "Any activity
that has to be governmentally regulated and controlled because
it is indispensable to the realization and development of social
solidarity is a public service so long as it is of such a nature that
it cannot be assured save by governmental intervention." If the
objective facts of social solidarity demand a rule, then it is the
function of government to declare the law accordingly. There
is nowhere to be found some final authority with exclusive right
to adjust law to need. Sovereignty in a true sense resides in a
principle, not in a state or person. Leftist groups as well as internationalists have been much interested in the jurisprudence of
Duguit.

IV. *International Positivism—Pure Jurisprudence*

The various approaches to the problem of sovereignty and
law have engendered a confusion of concepts in which the terms
sovereignty and law have numerous meanings arrived at by as
many methods. To Hans Kelsen this represents an anarchical
state of affairs much to be deprecated. He sets out, therefore,
to establish a pure science of jurisprudence, in which only those
conclusions will be acceptable which conform to the requirements
of strict juristic logic. All other considerations are to be waved
aside. Historical, political and social facts are to be regarded
as having no relevance to the strict science of jurisprudence.

Kelsen sees two attributes of sovereignty which have remained constant throughout most of the history of its discussion. These are its exclusive residence in the state as subject,
and its characteristic possession of supreme authority. Kelsen
here gives little heed to the protests of the pluralists. The property of enjoying recognition as the highest authority can belong,
he thinks, only to an over-ruling norm, one which logically cannot itself be overruled and which constitutes, therefore, the original and final source of authority.

Central to the understanding of this theory is the purely
juristic concept of the state. The state, in this sense, is no more
or less than the sum of legal relations of a society; it is the whole
ordering of relationships on the basis of the highest norm. Thus
the identification of law and state attributes the possession of
sovereignty to the law itself, for the exclusive residence of sovereignty in the state as subject has been accepted as a basic fact.
Once arrived at this conclusion becomes, for Kelsen, universally
valid, for his construction of a juristic science contains only those
logical relationships which are pertinent to every legal organization, no matter the time or place. Older theories which conceived the state as superior to the law have no validity for the
reason that a juristic science must by its nature exclude every
consideration outside of the legal sphere.

Confining himself strictly to the frame of reference indicated Kelsen finds fault with almost every other juristic school on
one score or another. Discarded is the proposition that purpose be
regarded as the important criterion of law, for the state, and
therefore the law—since the two are identified, must be complete
within itself; law is its own purpose. Similarly, as regards the
conception of positive law, legal positivism here simply refers to
the self-contained nature of law as contrasted with social, moral,
and other extra-law systems. The relevance of any item for
juristic consideration depends solely upon the ability of that
item to fit within the tight confines of the purely logical construction erected upon the juristic premise.

The essential element in legality, says Kelsen, is the fact
of obligation, the fact that anyone ought to do this or that. Why
he should do so is not important for the fact of obligation as
such. This kind of reasoning exalts duty for duty's sake. The
essence of state organization is obedience.

At this point Kelsen momentarily drops his role as jurist
to suggest an answer to the obvious question of how may be
determined the merit of an obligation. While this issue has no
relevance to the juristic premise as such, it would appear that
"outside of jurisprudence, the justification of a legal order" lies
in "its ability to explain most simply relationships in social fact".

This insistence upon jurisprudence as a logical system leads naturally to the assertion that there is no difference in principle between municipal and international law. Legal systems are concerned with the ordering of legal relationships, and the body of norms which characterize the state have no more reality than those which pertain to inter-state relationships. The usual distinction between municipal and international law, namely, that the former has for its object persons while the latter applies to states, is accordingly rejected. In both cases the concern is simply with legal relationships. It is maintained indeed that the subjects of international law are not states at all but individual persons. The world is of one legal system, not of several. To the objection that international law is enforced by no physical sanction, we are reminded that sovereignty inheres in the law itself, and that there are many examples of law that prevail without coercive sanction.

The point of view which supports the primacy of municipal law, says Kelsen, derives from the philosophic outlook that is purely subjective, that of the self, which recognizes no equal. The state recognizes no authority superior to its own. In this point of view international law has strength only in so far as states will to limit themselves. This is the auto-limitation theory of Jellinek.

The primacy of international law springs from just the opposite philosophical orientation, the objective. It begins with the whole, with a world spirit, and works down to the part, the individual person. In this system the state, no less than the individual, is part of the whole and, therefore, subordinate in importance to the whole. That law which reaches the greatest share of the whole supplies the most basic norm and has first claim, namely, the international rule. The logic of the subjective point of view Kelsen would see as leading to an eventual negation of all law, except only in so far as individuals may choose to limit themselves. The hope for world peace rests with the objective conception, and this, Kelsen believes, eventually will come to prevail.

Critics of Kelsen impute to this attempt to establish a pure juridical science a reversion to the analytical frame of mind. In order to give "clarity and rigor" to legal phenomena, exclusion is made of all ideas of interpretation and application, such as inform the law with living principle. Law by its nature must defy such mathematical formulation if it is to be anything but meaningless formality. Precisely those doubts and difficulties which the pure jurists put aside for extra juridical consideration are those which, in fact, give real body and vigor to a science of law.

Kelsen's pupil, Verdross, while concurring with Kelsen's views on the primacy of international law, retains more of the traditional concept of sovereignty as an earmark of the state. He does not, however, support the notion of sovereignty as the mark of an all powerful, unlimited state. Sovereignty is viewed as the creation of international law itself, and as such the mark of a full-fledged political community, the state, which is immediately subordinate to international law. Thus is the position of the state contrasted with that of persons or groups within the state, such as commonly are not direct subjects of international law. The monism of Kelsen has undergone considerable modification.

V. *Political Pluralism*

Pluralism as a political philosophy of this century is less alive today than it was two decades ago. Representing a tendency to discount the importance of the state among social institutions, and emphatically to deny the concept of state sovereignty, its influence has waned with the clearly increasing dominance of the state. Harold Laski, who in his earlier writings became a chief contender for this point of view, shows in his later production a decided shift in the direction of increased emphasis upon the state, even upon the coercive aspect of the political process. The evolving nature of the Soviet state as, despite its federalistic form, a highly integrated power complex, while also it has represented with great influence that social outlook to which pluralism has made its own signal contribution, may have had something to do with the evident weakening of the pluralistic school. Yet by and large it has done service of no small share in keeping the modern state to a sense of its responsibilities.

On the juristic side of pluralism the roots extend many centuries back in the annals of legal philosophy. We need not trace here, in the writings of Althusius, and much later of Gierke in Germany, and of the English historian Maitland, the progress of the conception of real personality of the corporation as a legal entity and a living community not dependent for its life upon the state. Suffice it to recall in this abbreviated space Maitland's own words, written in the late nineteenth century, concerning the lesser corporation as a real, not a fictitious, personality: "My organized group shall be a sovereign state." This conception had marked influence later upon the writings of the Dutch jurist, Krabbe, and on those of Leon Duguit. But we have chosen to discuss these in a somewhat different connection. It is rather the non-legalistic defense of the rights of the church by Figgis in England, of group personality by Miss Follett in this country, and of the human individual by the invigorating attack of Harold Laski, which in its criticism of the irresponsible state has challenged attention.

VI. *Sociological Schools*

When Auguste Compte invented the new science of sociology, he set loose a host of implications for every branch of social science and especially for the several branches considered as a whole. The tendency toward synthesis has had its effect upon juristic science no less than elsewhere. Jurisprudence has come to be regarded not as a separate, isolated field for investigation, such as Austin or Kelsen with all their valuable contribution tried to make it, but as fairly integrated with the whole purview of social forces. Dean Pound says, "In the present century jurists have become conscious that the distinctions between the several social sciences are necessitated not by the nature of things, but simply by the requirements of division of labour."

As the emphasis has changed from one approach to another in the study of sociology, so has the sociological interpretation of law evolved. Four phases in this development have been distinguished: (1) the mechanical stage, (2) the biological, (3) the psychological, and (4) the stage of unification which today is already dominant although still in the course of further growth. The exponents of the mechanical phase attempted to give law, regarded as product of social forces, the precision and certainty of mathematics.

The next step made use of biological analogies and principles, holding that the system of law most suited to man's evolution will survive in the competitive struggle. In the general struggle of men and groups of men law is born and nurtured. The appropriate law forces out the incapable law. Experience has resulted in the natural selection of those laws and legal systems best adapted to foster man's growth. This view, however, is regarded as having put too much stress on the study of primitive man for the sufficient explanation of advanced communities.

The third stage in the advancement of the sociological slant emphasizes the importance of psychological phenomena such as appear in the facts of social imitation and of group personality. Finally has come a tendency to unite, for the juristic purpose, these approaches and points of view. In the United States the leadership in this has included notably the late Justice Holmes and Dean Pound.

Pound would found a theory of law upon social interests. "The task is one of satisfying human demands, of securing interests or satisfying claims or demands with the least of friction and the least waste, whereby the means of satisfaction may be made to go as far as possible." The law must strike a balance between social and individual interests, and the theory of law must consider not only the making of law but the administration as well. Pound's point of view is essentially a functional one.

The eminent Dutch sociological jurist, Krabbe, expounds "the sovereignty of law". Sovereignty resides in law, the actual force of which, derives from a "sense of right" which extends through the community generally and that to some degree is manifest in all its members. This sense of right Krabbe defines as "a universal human impulse which calls forth a specific reaction with respect to our own behavior and that of other men". The purpose of law is to adjust the conflict of interests within the community. Krabbe's view shows considerable similarity to that of Pound, but Pound has little concern with the notion of sovereignty, while Krabbe is at pains to deny the sovereignty of the nation-state in the interest of rights both of the lesser groups and of the larger international community, and of the common sense of right there evident.

The chief traits evinced by the sociological jurisprudence are well summed up by Professor Merriam: (1) an interest more in the working of the law than in the abstract content of the rule, (2) an emphasis on the social nature of law and faith in its improvement through intelligent effort, (3) stress rather upon the social purpose of law than upon its sanction, (4) regard for legal precept as rather a guide than an inflexible rule of conduct, (5) some lack of philosophic unity, yet a capacity for adjustment to varying needs and points of view.

VII. *Present Trends*

Contemporary jurisprudence tends to minimize the analysis and investigation of abstract conceptions such as more largely characterized earlier modes of thought in this sphere. Just what is the nature of law and what its source would appear as of less importance than the matter of how it functions and what can be done to improve its conformity with the counsel of a common sense experience. The result is to concentrate upon problems of juristic reform and upon the improvement of legal application. Included here are the issues of restatement of law in an attempt to improve its form, of devising an effective instrument for ascertaining the social facts pertinent to the processes of law, of an expansion of social justice, and of individualizing the application of law to the unique case.

The reaction against excessive formalism in jurisprudence is doubtless a healthy trend. Yet care must be taken lest reaction be carried too far and jurisprudence develop into mere categories of rule of thumb. Adequate concern for the working of law would imply a criterion of social ethics, and such a one must depend upon *all* our knowledge of the nature of man and of the processes of society.

As for the future of the concepts of sovereignty and juristic law, in a world ravaged by war, the same causes that once produced these notions assuredly are preparing again the way for a new order among men, such as at least will change, if not deepen, the guiding conceptions of legal growth. More than mere principles of political organization compel our attention. Of ever growing importance is the realization that there can be no justification any longer for the many independent sovereignties that now mar the prospects of peace in days to come. Clearly the economic factor is not in line with such arrangement. The indication of the times is that perhaps that primacy of the international order which Professor Kelsen predicts is not indefinitely remote, even if a half dozen world wars should lie ahead before any considerable degree of international order will come to be. When that day arrives, what implications for the understanding of a human justice it will carry with it, cannot now be known. Perhaps only an intensification or extension of the old issues. Perhaps some new insight into the real and ideal nature of sovereignty and law. Whether these or other words be used to represent the vast integrative needs of present and future society, the problem will remain always unsolved, yet always on the way toward some degree of solution. It will demand always the best attention of the experts concerned, and in some of its important aspects the concern of an intelligent citizenry as well.

BIBLIOGRAPHY

ARONSON, MOSES J. "Roscoe Pound and the Resurgence of Juristic Idealism," *Journal of Social Philosophy*, VI, 47-83.
AUSTIN, JOHN. *Lectures on Jurisprudence*. 4th ed. 2 vols. London, 1873.
BARKER, ERNEST. "The Discredited State." *Political Science Quarterly*, February, 1915.

BRYCE, JAMES. *Studies in History and Jurisprudence.* 2 vols. Oxford, 1901, 1904.

CHEN, SU CHING. *Recent Theories of Sovereignty.* Canton, China: University of Illinois, Doctor of Philosophy thesis, 1929.

DEWEY, JOHN. "Austin's Theory of Sovereignty." *Political Science Quarterly,* IX (1894), 31 ff.

DICEY, A. V. *Introduction to the Study of the Law of the Constitution.* London: Macmillan Co., 1889, 1915, 1926. P. 577.

DICKINSON, J. "A Working Theory of Sovereignty." *Political Science Quarterly,* XLII, 524-48; XLIII, 32-63.

DUGUIT, LEON. *Les Transformations du droit public.* Paris: A. Colin, 1913. Trans. under title *Law in the Modern State* by H. and F. Laski. New York: Viking Press, 1919. P. 247.

—————. "The Concept of Public Service." *Yale Law Journal,* XXXII, 425 ff.

—————. "The Law and the State." *Harvard Law Review,* XXXI, 1 ff.

DUNNING, WILLIAM A. *A History of Political Theories ,Ancient and Medieval.* New York: Macmillon Co., 1902.

EMERSON, RUPERT. *State and Sovereignty in Modern Germany.* New Haven: Yale University Press, 1928.

ESMEIN, ADEHAR. *Elements de droit constitutionnel.* 6th ed. Paris: A. Tenin, 1914.

FOLLETT, MARY PARKER. *The New State,* chaps. xxviii-xxxii. New York: Longmans, Green & Co., 1918.

GARNER, J. W. "Limitations on National Sovereignty in International Relations." *American Political Science Review,* XIX, Feb., 1925.

GIERKE, OTTO F. VON. *Political Theories of the Middle Ages.* Trans. Maitland. Cambridge: Cambridge University Press, 1900. P. 197.

GURVITCH, GEORGES. "Major Problems of the Sociology of Law." *Journal of Social Philosophy,* VI, 197-215.

GREEN, T. H. *Principles of Political Obligation.* London: Longmans, Green & Co., 1921. P. 252.

HOBHOUSE, L. T. *Metaphysical Theory of the State.* London: Allen & Unwin, 1918. P. 156.

HOLLAND, THOMAS ERSKINE. *The Elements of Jurisprudence.* 13th ed., 1924. Oxford, 1880.

JHERING, RUDOLF VON. *Law as a Means to an End.* Trans. from the German *Der Zweck im Recht* by Isaac Husik. Boston: Boston Book Co., 1913.

KRABBE, HUGO. *The Modern Idea of the State.* Trans. from *Die moderne Staats-Idee* by Sabine and Shepherd. New York: Appleton & Co., 1922. P. 281.

LASKI, HAROLD J. *Foundations of Sovereignty.* New York: Harcourt, Brace & Co., 1921. P. 317.

—————. *The State in Theory and Practice.* New York: Viking Press, 1935.

LINDSEY, A. D. "The State in Recent Political Theory." *Political Quarterly,* I (February, 1914), 128 ff.

MATTERN, JOHANNES. *Concepts of State, Sovereignty and International Law.* Baltimore: Johns Hopkins Press, 1928.

MERRIAM, BARNES, and Others. *A History of Political Theories, Recent Times.* New York: Macmillan Co., 1924.

MERRIAM, CHARLES E. *History of the Theory of Sovereignty Since Rousseau.* New York: Columbia University Press, 1900.

POUND, ROSCOE. *Law and Morals.* McNair Lectures, 1923. Chapel Hill: University of North Carolina Press, 1924.

ROUCEK, JOSEPH S. "Political Behavior as a Struggle for Power." *Journal of Social Philosophy,* VI, 341-51.

SABINE, GEORGE H. "Pluralism: A Point of View." *American Political Science Review*, XVII (1923), 34 ff.

VINOGRADOFF, SIR PAUL. *Outlines of Historical Jurisprudence*. Oxford: Oxford University Press, 1920.

WILLOUGHY, W. W *The Fundamental Concepts of Public Law*. New York: Macmillan Co., 1924.

—————. *The Ethical Basis of Political Authority*. New York: Macmillan Co., 1930.

Chapter IX

RELIGION AND POLITICS

FLOYD A. CAVE

SECULARIZATION OF RELIGION

The Bearing of Religion on Politics.

Political thought is influenced by religion in two principal ways: (1) by political doctrines of religious thinkers as regards contemporary political forms and functions, and proposals for political reconstruction in terms of religious and ethical ideals; and (2) by the policies and activities of religious organizations in so far as they affect political processes and ideas. Present religious doctrines are in many respects radically different from those of the early 19th Century and show, in their transformation, the revolutionary affect of new scientific and naturalistic conceptions of the recent past. This section will deal with the background of changes which have tended to secularize modern religion. The second and third sections will consider recent reaction to this trend by Neo-realistic theologians, and resulting cleavages in religious thought and action. The fourth section will consist of an attempt to analyze and criticize contemporary ideas of the relations of church and state as associations.

Naturalism, Science, and Traditional Theology.

Modern science from the Renaissance to the present has been at work revolutionizing traditional theological conceptions. Scientific emphasis on the reality of natural physical phenomena and its success in dealing with it, together with agnosticism of science towards alleged spiritual realities not subject to objective proof, undermined the traditional theological dualism of natural and supernatural, matter and spirit. Rationalists turned to society itself for the explanation of man's nature, social laws, and processes. An optimistic belief in man's perfectability in society, given proper training and surroundings, replaced the established religious doctrine of the natural depravity of man since the Fall.

The enormous success of modern industrial techniques based upon scientific discoveries and inventions established the authority and prestige of science beyond question and compelled reconsideration of theological beliefs in conflict with it. Scientific naturalistic positivism with its agnostic attitude regarding hypothetical spiritual reality beyond experience was more and more forced upon religious thinking until eventually a large body of liberal Protestant clergymen had accepted its basic premises.

The Darwinian theory of evolution with its attempt at complete explanation of man's earthly biological origin and development from lower forms of life, seemed to render unnecessary and irrelevant the Biblical story of the Creation and cast doubt upon the whole Christian theology of the Fall, Redemption, and Salvation. On the other hand, uncritical acceptance of the Darwinian theory led optimists to overstress the possibility of progress, causing it to be viewed as an inevitable march towards a better world.

Critics began to demand that the Bible itself be subjected to scientific analysis. Lewis Wallis demonstrated that, far from being the inspired Word of God, the Bible is merely an historical record of the folk ways, struggles, and development of the Hebrew people. It has no program of political reform which could possibly apply to modern conditions.[1]

Scientific methods and conceptions began to be applied to human social relationships, including religion. Sociological writers analyzed the origins, characteristics, and functions of religion. Comte, Durkheim, Kidd, Ellwood, and Hobhouse exhaustively studied religion in its various aspects and concluded that moral standards are of social origin and that the function of religion is

---

[1] Lewis Wallis, *Sociological Study of the Bible* (Chicago: University of Chicago Press, 1912). Especially preface and introduction.

to teach, sanctify, and give emotional and rational justification to group moral standards.[2]

Calverton accepted the conclusions of Durkheim, *et al,* but contended that group moral standards are largely the work of ruling power groups. Hence religion is a means of rationalizing, justifying, facilitating and defending the class interests of dominant groups.[3]

H. E. Barnes makes a searching comparison of biblical doctrines with contemporary conceptions of science and finds them totally untenable. He concludes that agnosticism is the safest position regarding metaphysical matters and that religion must become a means of promoting higher social aims based on scientific findings.[4]

Barnes' position is essentially the same as that of Kidd, Ellwood, and Hobhouse. Scientific knowledge by itself, they say, is not enough to provide the emotional drive necessary to achieve the social goals which sociology and social science find are essential to the good life. The breaking down of traditional religious beliefs has led to widespread tendencies towards paganism, selfishness, and the use of force. Therefore, there must be a rapprochement between religion and science. Religion must be stripped of its mystery, supernaturalism and traditional theology. In their essentials, Christian doctrines and the principles of scientific social reform are the same. Both teach the necessity of voluntary subordination of individual will and purposes to the higher ends of the group: mutual service, mutual brotherhood, and good will.

---

[2] *Cf.* H. E. Barnes, Howard Becker, and F. B. Becker, *Contemporary Social Theory* (New York: Appleton-Century, 1940), pp. 838-841; B. Kidd, *Social Evolution* (New York: Macmillan, 1894), pp. 101-103, and *The Science of Power* (London: Methuen, 1920), p. 123; C. A. Ellwood, *Christianity and Social Science* (New York: Macmillan, 1923), pp. 38-40, and L. T. Hobhouse, *Morals in Evolution* (London: Chapman and Hall, 1923), pp. 493-497, 528.

[3] V. F. Calverton, *The Passing of the Gods* (New York: Chas. Scribner's Sons, 1934), pp. 12-17.

[4] H. E. Barnes, *The Twilight of Christianity* (New York: The Vanguard Press, 1929), preface and Ch. IX.

These principles, Kidd and Ellwood contend, are universally basic to successful and happy living in organized society. They may be attained through proper indoctrination of the young. It is the duty of the Church to arrest the dangerous spread of the Nietzchean doctrine of the superman by cooperating with social scientists in the achievement of this new form of social salvation.[5]

In summation, the following doctrines may be said to be fundamental preconceptions of Kidd, Ellwood, Hobhouse, and others of their school: (1) the traditional dualism of God and man is rejected as incompatible with modern scientific knowledge; (2) materialistic monism is also rejected as making for paganism, social predation, and emphasis on selfish individualistic aims for power and self; (3) natural science is shunted to one side and the basic principles of social science are postulated as in agreement with the fundamental doctrines of Christianity; (4) there is a tendency to idealize or personalize the Universe, *i.e.,* make it seem friendly to and in harmony with man; (5) God becomes a moving force in society's progress toward a perfect society, an immanent rather than a transcendant God; (6) religion loses its other-worldly and individualistic character and becomes ethical, social morality, founded upon scientific knowledge, vitalized by emotion; and directed to the service of social progress towards an ideal goal; (7) the older doctrines of Christianity are re-interpreted, *i.e.,* sin becomes disloyalty to humanity; salvation a life of love, service, and fellowship in society.[6]

This survey of the efforts of these scientific writers to reconcile religion and science raises the question as to whether they achieved either good religion or good science. No attempt is made to give a detailed account of just how the desired Utopia is to be achieved. Apparently, there is optimism that man is progressing inevitably towards it, yet the churches must bend every effort to bring it about. The doctrines postulated as social science,

---

[5] *Cf.* B. Kidd, *The Science of Power, op. cit.,* Chaps. 1, 2, 7, 8, and C. A. Ellwood, *Reconstruction of Religion* (New York: Macmillan, 1922), pp. 7-24, 34-37, 64-75, 94-117.

[6] See espec. C. A. Ellwood, *Reconstruction of Religion,* pp. 127-157.

on the other hand, instead of viewing the social scene objectively, reflect the one-sided conceptions of a particular school of social ethics.

Religion as a Motivating Force for Natural Competition and Survival of the Fittest.

T. N. Carver rejects the contention of Kidd, *et al.*, that the Darwinian theory of survival of the fittest does not apply to social evolution. On the contrary, he considers competition as basic to all social and economic progress. All life, he says, is a struggle for survival and only the fittest survive. Religion is valuable as an aid to promote enthusiasm and energy in production. Nations, as well as individuals, survive and dominate if they can out-produce other nations. Hence, the function of the Church is to discipline its members in the acceptance and application of the laws of survival.[7]

Weber shows that Calvinism gave emotional motivation to originators of the new Capitalistic methods and that the pietistic traits inculcated by Calvinism such as honesty, frugality, punctuality, and industry, sanctified business enterprise and became the rational basis of the profit system.[8]

Order.

Calverton's position is exactly the opposite of that of Kidd and his followers. Throughout its entire history in Western Civilization, he contends, religion has been employed to defend upper class interests, and thwart reforms, and as it stands, interposes a tremendous barrier to the achievement of a new social order. Man must cast off religion and use the limitless possibilities of science to achieve his reforms. Religion will disappear

---

[7] T. N. Carver, *The Religion Worth Having* (Boston: Houghton-Mifflin, 1912), pp. 9-64, 84-124.

[8] M. Weber, *The Protestant Ethic and the Spirit of Capitalism* (London: Geo. Allen and Unwin, 1930), trans. by Talcott Parsons, pp. 64-74.

as science proves its adequacy to control the environment, and the upper classes lose their privileged positions.[9]

The Social Gospel

The term social gospel has reference to the movement among liberal Protestant clergymen in America to readapt Christian doctrines to the new scientific theories of the 19th and early 20th Centuries, particularly the sociological conceptions of Kidd and his followers. Faced with widespread defections by workingmen, on the one hand, who resented domination of the churches by the wealthy; and by the educated classes, on the other, who, in the light of modern science, could no longer accept the outmoded conceptions of the old theology, liberal churchmen saw the necessity of directing the churches towards new theological constructions and social goals. The apparent success of scientific socialism stimulated them to devise a social program for the churches to meet its challenge. In effect, the new plan of salvation was to be redemption both of individuals and society through inevitable evolutionary progress to a Kingdom of God on earth.

Characteristic Conceptions of the Social Gospel Movement. Theology and Evolution.

Liberal theologians set to work to adjust new scientific doctrines to their religious views. Thus, to the Darwinian theory of evolution, they gave a teleological slant so that, instead of a theory of mutation, it became an inevitable progress towards the goal of Christian ethics. The Hegelian theory of the conflict of opposites in history resulting in a higher and higher synthesis until a perfect human order at one with the absolute is reached, was freely used. To these conceptions, organismic notions were added. Terms such as "superorganic" and "spiritual organism" were applied to the process of evolution. Man was said to be led by an "invisible hand" and to have a divine "instinct" to

---

[9] V. F. Calverton, *op. cit.*, preface, and pp. 14-17, 58-62, 76-86, 135-143, 189-196, 248-276, 278-279.

work for the Kingdom of God on earth. Progress became not only natural but divine. Yet, man through scientific knowledge could, putatively, guide the course of social evolution to the desired consummation.[10]

Rauschenbusch and others undertook to modify traditional theological doctrines. Under the new interpretation, God loses his other worldly character and becomes immanent in humanity, working through men and institutions to achieve his purposes.[11] Thus a tendency is shown to defy human relationships.

In the new view, Christianity must be linked with ethics and present-day problems. The doctrine of original sin is rejected—man is inherently good.

Sin becomes the conflict of individual selves with the common good of humanity (God). It originates in and is transmitted through man's animal instincts and passions and also through evil social institutions and traditions. Thus, there are superpersonal forces of sin and of good in conflict.[12] The forces of evil tend to hold back progress towards the ideal end.

The idea of Christ as God is rejected. The new emphasis is upon Jesus as the great teacher and example. Jesus' tachings are presumed to furnish a complete ethical guide to social conduct.[13] Personal salvation is interpreted to mean the complete subordination of selfish individual purposes to a life of social service for the common good. Prayer makes easier submission of individual wills to the service of humanity. The Crucifixion and the Resurrection are symbolic of supreme love and sacrifice in social service and of the possibility of man's attainment of a new world order.[14]

---

[10] W. Rauschenbusch, *Christianizing the Social Order* (New York: Macmillan, 1912), p. 30.

[11] W. Rauschenbusch, *A Theology for the Social Gospel* (New York: Macmillan, 1917), p. 49.

[12] *Ibid.*, pp. 46-47, 58-73.

[13] Sherwood Eddy, *Revolutionary Christianity* (New York: Willett, Clark & Co., 1939), p. 21.

[14] W. Rauschenbusch, *op. cit.*, pp. 96-98, 104-105, 261-273.

The Kingdom of God on earth, according to these writers, is a Utopian society, the goal of human progress, including all humanity, in which brotherhood, mutual service, democracy and equality will reign supreme.[15]

Progress Towards the Kingdom.

The ideal goal of liberal church doctrine, thus, becomes a perfect society of men to be achieved on this earth. The question then is how to attain it. The solution of perfection through personal salvation seemed to have failed, while new studies in psychology demonstrated the decisive importance of proper environment to character building. Attention of church reformers was thus turned towards social maladjustments which impede the development of personality and character, which all concede is the highest human value. Even the Cosmos is tending to become more personalized.[16]

Perfecting the environment by itself, however, is not enough. Materialistic socialism is bound to fail because of its omission of spiritual values. The socialist program of reconstruction must be combined with the personality values of religion.[17]

Nevertheless, the majority of liberal Protestant Churchmen came to see the primary need of eliminating the most extreme evils of the economic system if the Kingdom of God on earth was to be realized. Hence, leading writers among them began to lay bare these evils with devastating criticisms. They demonstrated how the profit system promotes greed, selfishness, dishonesty, and class conflict. The ownership of wealth creates a leisure class, and promotes snobbery, patronage, and waste. The earlier doctrine of stewardship, or even trusteeship, is ruled out

---

[15] Shailer Mathews, *The Social Teaching of Jesus* (New York: Macmillan, 1909), Chap. III.

[16] Shailer Mathews, *Christianity and the Social Process* (New York: Harper & Bros., 1934), p. 63.

[17] H. F. Ward, *Our Economic Morality and the Ethic of Jesus* (New York: Macmillan, 1930), p. 314 ff.

in favor of public ownership of capital and approximate equality of income.[18]

The competitive system, they show, produces cutthroat competition, excessive sales costs, and monopoly. The drive for profits means luxury for the few and poverty for the many, and leads to class warfare, exploitation of workers and consumers, economic crises, imperialism and war. Competition itself is condemned as a method, and the substitution for it of cooperation is urged. To eliminate exploitation of the workers by dictatorial employers, the use of cooperatives, or outright government ownership is favored.

All agree that the church has a special function to perform in achieving the aims of Christianity. Church members are exhorted to consider the sins of the Church in the past and to recognize the need to practice Christian ethics within the walls of the Church and in their daily lives as an example.[19] Above all, the church in the future must act as a leavening influence through its members who, themselves, have been converted and will in turn convert the world to the new gospel.

In their reformist attitudes, leading liberal churchmen vary, from the moderate stand of F. G. Peabody, who is inclined to tolerate the capitalistic system and to reject socialism as a solution (since, in his view, most businessmen are Christians and hence, most business life is redeemed), to Sherwood Eddy and H. F. Ward, who are frankly socialistic and even revolutionary in outlook. Both Eddy and Ward accept Marx's materialistic interpretation of history and both look upon the working class as the messianic class to lead the way towards the social goal. Ward accepts the necessity of revolution, but Eddy prefers evolution as the proper method.[20]

---

[18] Cf. Kirby Page, *Jesus or Christianity* (New York: Doubleday, Doran & Co., 1929), pp. 250-267, 298-301, and W. Rauschenbusch, *Christianizing The Social Order, op. cit.,* p. 155 ff.

[19] Kirby Page, *op. cit.,* Chaps. II-V.

[20] Cf. Sherwood Eddy, *Revolutionary Christianity, op. cit.,* pp. 140-170, and Ward, *Democracy and Social Change* (New York: Modern Age Books, 1940), pp. 80-200.

THE NEW REALISM: HORTON, NIEBUHR, BARTH AND DAVIES

The post-war period witnessed a decided religious reaction
to the soft, optimistic idealism of the social gospel movement
with its tendency to romanticize social change and to overlook
brute facts which opposed barriers to the march towards the
millenium. The savage conflict and its disillusioning aftermath,
raised profound doubts as to man's ability to create an ideal
society, or even a tolerable one. The above-mentioned writers
have been chosen as representative of this movement to return
to the realities of life as it is, and not as it ought to be. All manifest a disposition, not to complete pessimism, but to recognize
inherent defects in man's character which operate to postpone
the realization of an ideal life to an existence beyond the grave.
In effect, they return to the dualism of Christian theology,
though in terms of modern philosophical conceptions.

Characteristic Doctrines.

With one accord, these writers reject the typical doctrines
of the social gospel school. They show the unreality, in terms
of modern conditions of the idealistic theory of evolution to a
predestined Kingdom of God on earth.[21]

The doctrine of the immanence of God in society is condemned as an attempt to defy man and to create God in man's
image. Man, Barth contends, cannot construct out of psychology
or history a God worthy of his adoration.[22]

Man cannot save himself through progress or by his own
efforts. Led astray by science, men have turned to paganism, and
have precipitated the present crisis by defying themselves and
erecting a God-state.[23]

The scientific study of the Bible has led to unbelief and
weakening of the power of religion. Attempts of moralists to

---

[21] For example, see W. M. Horton, *Realistic Theology* (New York: Harpers &
Bros., 1934), Chap. 1, and pp. 24-30.

[22] W. S. Kilpatrick, "Karl Barth and His Times," *Christian Century*, VIII (Oct.
8, 1941), p. 1236.

[23] *Ibid.*, p. 1237.

combine religion and ethics has the same effect. The Bible must be restored as the Word of God and God, Himself, recognized as Absolute, beyond man's ability to know.[24]

Scepticism regarding the power of religion to overcome men's selfish passions and thus produce subordination to a common purpose is also strongly felt by these writers. Niebuhr denies the thesis of Kidd and Ellwood that religious evolution can be used to motivate radical social reforms. Hobhouse's argument that man's reason is gradually working to promote social harmony is also refuted. Man's social will-to-power is too powerful to be overcome completely by other moral or rational forces. On the other hand, both reason and religion may be employed to justify and rationalize selfish conduct.[25]

The doctrine of original sin is restored to theology. The real existence and persistence of sin as the principal cause of human ills must be recognized. Sin is the basic cause of the evils of the present capitalistic system and its existence as a disrupting force in human relations cannot be explained away by an easy theory of gradual evolution, through education and moral teaching, to a better world.[26]

Man is born sinful, says Barth, and his selfish will to evil and irrationality pervades all of his social relationships. Good will is transcendant and cannot exist in its pure form in this life.[27]

Man has capacity for progress, Davies admits, but this is offset by his destructiveness in modern warfare. As Niebuhr puts it, the will-to-power causes economic inequalities which result in class and national conflicts. Power can be balanced

---

[24] R. Birch Hoyle, *The Teaching of Karl Barth* (New York: Chas. Scribner's Sons, 1930), pp. 85-95, 114-119.

[25] R. Niebuhr, *Moral Man and Immoral Society* (New York: Chas. Scribner's Sons, 1932), Intro., and pp. 1, 32-42.

[26] W. M. Horton, *op. cit.,* pp. 42-62, 90-91.

[27] K. Barth, *The Word of God and the Word of Man* (New York: The Pilgrims Press, 1928), pp. 150-166.

only by power. Moral appeals are of little avail. Hence, conflict is inevitable—there is no solution for it in this world.[28]

Thus exhortations of modernists that men should follow the teachings of Jesus are in vain. Jesus' teachings are councils of perfection in a world of relative values.[29]

Christ, Barth insists, is the only way by which man can escape the consequences of his sinful nature by enabling him to cross the abyss which separates two incommensurable planes of existence. But the salvation which Christ offers is possible only to the few who are capable of throwing off the natural man and seeking him. It is available only to individuals, not to societies as a whole, and, when attained, does not give perfection in this life. The Christian man can do much to make life more livable but his hope of saving society is vain.[30]

Niebuhr supports this viewpoint by showing that the Church can act as a leavening influence to uphold standards of morality and help to mitigate the rigors of the power conflict but, in order to do so, must purify itself of desire for material things, cease acting as an apologist for the present order, and give up the delusion that the world is being redeemed through progress. The only adequate religion is qualified optimism which nerves men to struggle for perfection but to realize that it can never be completely attained.[31]

Like Barth, Davies argues that outward improvements have not changed the inner man. If he persists in his refusal of obedience to God, man is doomed to ultimate destruction. But men, as a rule, do not seek God. Hence, there is no possibility of a

---

[28] *Cf.* D. R. Davies, *The Two Humanities* (New York: Harper & Bros., 1940), pp. 45-46, and R. Niebuhr, *op. cit.*, pp. 314, 44-49.

[29] R. Niebuhr, *Does Civilization Need Religion?* (New York: Macmillan, 1927), pp. 60-63.

[30] K. Barth, *op. cit.*, pp. 167-173, 250.

[31] R. Niebuhr, *Christianity and Power Politics* (New York: Chas. Scribner's Sons, 1940), pp. 200-201, 213-219.

common salvation which will make possible a Kingdom of God on earth, or an earthly solution to the problem of conflict.[32]

POLITICAL DOCTRINES OF CHURCHES AS INSTITUTIONS
Relation of Church and State.

Throughout its entire history organized Christianity has claimed ethical and religious superiority over the state. The modern Catholic Church still relies upon the Thomistic analogy of the superiority of the spiritual over the material aspects of life—the Church being presumed to represent reason and morality, the state material force.[33]

Ideally, therefore, the temporal acts of the state should conform to the spiritual and moral needs of the citizen, and the state should accept direction by the church in all matters touching upon the spiritual and temporal welfare of citizens.[34]

Prostestant doctrine, in theory, does not differ materially from this. Calvinistic policy as taught and practiced in pre-Revolutionary New England reflects the same conception.[35]

Separation of Church and State brought about by the federal constitution compelled the Churches to readjust their policies somewhat and most Protestant creeds today provide that the Churches will not interfere in civil matters. Yet in practice, intervention of the Churches in political affairs is common-place and covers a wide range of activities.[36]

---

[32] D. R. Davies, *op. cit.*, pp. 53-60, 67-72, 236.

[33] R. Krannenberg, *Political Theory* (London: Oxford University Press, 1939), pp. 228-231.

[34] Leo XIII, "Imortal Dei," reprinted in M. Oakeshott, *The Social and Political Doctrines of Contemporary Europe* (Cambridge: Cambridge University Press, 1941), pp. 46-49.

[35] John Cotton, "Letter to Lord Say and Sele," reprinted in B. F. Wright, Jr., *Source Book of American Political Theory* (New York: Macmillan, 1929), p. 3.

[36] W. A. Brown, *Church and State in Contemporary America* (New York: Chas. Scribner's Sons, 1936), p. 154.

Catholics recognize formally the separation of Church and State in America but frankly prefer acceptance by the State of the Catholic Church as the established religion.[37]

Protestants agree that both Church and State are divinely ordained, that they should cooperate to redeem individuals and society; and that the Church is the pre-eminent instrument for this purpose; but are opposed to the establishment of religion. They lack also the advantage of the Catholic Church in having one unchangeable creed which is proclaimed by one highly integrated church; and a common conviction as to the proper steps to take to achieve their spiritual aims.[38]

But, to both Protestants and Catholics, the State is, ideally, an instrument of the Church to aid in its mission through the use of the State's temporal power.[39]

The facts do not bear out Catholic protestations that moral questions cover only a small part of the political field. Cardinal Manning's statement that politics are nothing more than the morals of society is undoubtedly much nearer the truth.[40] This overlapping of function, as Marshall shows, leads to inevitable conflict between the Roman Church and the State.[41]

Both Catholic and Protestant Churches have recently enlarged their conceptions of the responsibility of the Church for various defects of the social order. Speaking for Protestants, Calvert recognizes that expanding functions of the State are coming into increasing conflict with enlarged views of the Church respecting its role in redemption of the social order—a conflict which is testing the loyalty of citizens to Church and State.

---

[37] J. A. Ryan, and Moorhouse Miller, *The State and the Church* (New York: Macmillan, 1936), pp. 9, 14, 30-34.

[38] W. A. Brown, *op. cit.*, pp. 89-90, 116-117.

[39] George Seldes, *The Vatican, Yesterday, Today, Tomorrow* (New York: Harper & Bros., 1934), pp. 405-406.

[40] C. C. Marshall, *The Roman Catholic Church in the Modern State* (New York: Dodd, Mead & Co., 1928), p. 3.

[41] *Ibid.*

Where conflicts arise, he says, loyalty to God is primary, to the State secondary.[42]

The Protestant, Coffin, agrees with the Catholic, Manning, that religion covers all aspects of political life. By its very nature, he says, religion is totalitarian. Separation of Church and State, therefore, is no solution.[43] This tendency of religious theorists to subordinate the State to the Church in theory is reflected also in religious conceptions of liberty, democracy, and natural rights.

Liberty, Democracy, and Natural Rights.

Natural, unbridled liberty is condemned by Catholic doctrine. Man is not born free but must attain freedom, Maritain points out. Obedience to rightful authority is an act of reason and of freedom. The new democracy must be theocentric and based upon the development of spiritual personality under the guidance of the Church.[44] Liberal Protestants also regard individual self-assertion as sin and true liberty as submission of personal wills to social and religious ends.[45]

Though the Catholic Church repudiates the doctrine of natural rights as false, it insists upon its own inalienable right to exist as an independent association with an absolute right to teach and spread its doctrines and to control its property and internal affairs.[46] Protestant writers hold similar views.[47]

In a Catholic doctrine, all men are subject to the moral law in the exercise of their civil rights and in the expression of their

---

[42] H. P. Van Dusen, et al., *Church and State in the Modern World* (New York: Harper & Bros., 1937), pp. 162-164.

[43] *Ibid.*

[44] J. Maritain, *Scholasticism and Politics* (New York: Macmillan, 1940), pp. 78-106.

[45] Ante, p. 60.

[46] Leo XIII, *op. cit.*, pp. 50-51.

[47] H. P. Van Dusen, *op. cit.*, pp. 102-103.

private opinions. Freedom from restraint would lead to license and, eventually, absolutism.[48] In a Catholic State, there would be toleration in only a strictly limited form.[49]

Protestants are inclined to allow complete freedom of speech and press but emphasize the importance of the Church's function in forming public opinion and the desirability of teaching citizens to think "right".[50]

Catholic theorists frown upon democracy of the historical, or naturalistic type. The Pope has condemned the doctrine of consent of the governed. There is no political power, he says, but from God. No one can blind himself, hence the doctrine of consent is untenable.[51]

The Catholic writer, Neil, exposes the decadency of democracy in the United States. Current election evils, lack of discipline, grasping capitalism, lack of moral standards, and the religion debunking policy in the schools, all indicate, he says, democracy's decline.[52]

Catholics say they do not pretend to prescribe the form of government for the State so long as it conforms to the moral law. Yet, the foregoing analysis seems to indicate that they would prefer some other form than existing democracies. The Catholic hierarchy in Italy supported the dictatorships in Italy and Spain. However, some American Catholics have condemned Fascism and the absolute state as heresy.[53]

Liberal Protestant opinion either tends to identify democracy in its ideal form, i.e., a condition where men are considered as ends rather than means, and where liberty and equal-

---

[48] Cf. Ryan and Millar, op. cit., pp. 53-59, and Leo XIII, op. cit., pp. 50-53.

[49] Ibid., p. 60.

[50] H. P. Van Dusen, op. cit.

[51] Leo XIII, op. cit.

[52] Thomas P. Neil, "Democracy: The Threat from Within," The Catholic World, CLIV (February, 1942), no. 923, pp. 588-595.

[53] Cf. Wm. Teeling, The Pope in Politics (London: Lovatt Dickenson, Ltd., 1938), pp. 82-83, 123-130, and The Catholic World, CLIV, Jan., 1943, no. 934, p. 388, Editorial.

ity of opportunity prevail, with Christianity, or to regard them as having parallel aims and ends.[54]

Political Pluralism and the Churches.

American Catholic and Protestant spokesmen emphatically deny the theory of the absolute sovereignty of the State. Legal absolutism, Catholic writers say, leads logically to the God-State which asserts its pre-eminence over spiritual as well as material matters. Actually, the State is merely an association of families organized to secure strictly temporal ends, not an end in itself.[55]

Protestants point out that the State is limited in its appeal to interests and loyalties of the people, and in the fact that its laws and officials rest upon popular support. The Church, on the other hand, is divinely ordained and inspired and, therefore, has a right to resist wrongful acts of the State. Both Church and State are functional associations within the Community but even the Community is not absolute.[56]

The political pluralism of Catholic doctrine is external as regards the relation of Church and State but not internal in relation to either the Church or the State. Following advocacy by Pius XI, in 1931, of industrial Guilds which would include both employers and employees, Maritain proposes a graded order of associations presided over by the State. But the government would be organized on hierarchical levels and the executive independent of political parties and the legislature. Real authority would rest with popular elites subject to the restraining moral influence of the Church. These proposals bear a close resemblance to Fascist State organization.[57]

---

[54] Cf. C. J. Oates, "Democracy and Christianity," The American Scholar, X, no. 3 (Summer, 1941), pp. 325-336, and E. G. Jones, "America United, On What Level?" Christian Century, LVIII, no. 38 (Sept. 17, 1941), pp. 1139-1141.

[55] Ryan and Millar, op. cit., pp. 195-202.

[56] H. P. Van Dusen, op. cit., pp. 62, 71-80.

[57] Cf. Pius XI, Quadragesimo Anno, reprinted in Oakeshott, op. cit., p. 59, and J. Maritain, op. cit., pp. 112-116.

Previous analysis makes it clear that Church and State are not distinct associations with completely different functional objectives but rival organizations with objectives and ideologies at variance with each other at many points. In democratic states, organized religion, along with other interest groups, promotes its program through appeals to public opinion by means of church schools, study groups, religious associations, and propaganda of various kinds. In anti-religious dictatorships like Nazi Germany, the conflict between Church and State has broken out into open violence.

Nazis have sought to eliminate or take over all rival ideologies, including those of the Churches. Lutherans, under Nazi pressure, split into German Christians, who yielded and adapted their creed to Nazi doctrines, and the Confessional, of which Barth became the chief spokesman, which refused to give up its traditional tenets.[58]

When the Concordat of 1933 failed to protect them, the Catholic Church, relying upon its highly integrated and international organization, began a desperate struggle with the Nazis for survival.

In the Hitlerite view, National Socialism is the real German Church which aims at reconstruction of the Nation in terms of German ideals. Existing Churches should cooperate. If they fail to do so, they must be suppressed. Catholic authorities in turn, condemn Nazism as paganism, and urge their members to resist this assault upon the Church.[59]

Nazi theorists have cleverly applied modernist doctrines to their ends. God, they say, means the race-soul which is working out salvation for the German people on this earth. Christ is a German leader not a Jew, and all Jewish conceptions including the doctrines of love, humility, and mercy, are eradicated from so-called Christian beliefs. Judging from this, Barth seems justified in concluding that modernism leads to the God-State and

---

[58] *Cf.* R. Krannenberg, *op. cit.,* pp. 240-241, and K. Barth, *The German Church Struggle* (London: Kulturkampf Association, 1938), pp. 3-5.

[59] N. Micklem, *National Socialism and the Roman Catholic Church* (London: Oxford University Press, 1939), pp. 12-23, 35-47, 53-59, 76, 77.

that only adherence by the Church to the traditional gospel can prevent its absorption by the secular state.[60]

As Nazi encroachments on religion proceeded, Barth realized that there could be no place for the Christian Church in Nazi-dominated Germany. He, therefore, called upon all Christians to take up arms against the false messiah and the unjust state, of which Hitler is leader, which seeks to encompass mankind, body and soul, and to destroy man's liberties.[61]

Religious Education.

Both Catholics and Protestants seek to have the State provide religious instruction in state-schools under Church control. This failing, the Catholic Church has provided its own school system which it feels the state should support at least in part. Most Protestant Church, however, because they cannot afford to maintain schools of their own, do not favor this.[62]

Public Morals.

Most Churches feel an exceptional responsibility for public morals and have no hesitation about supporting or opposing political action involving such matters. The failure of the Church-supported experiment in national prohibition, however, discouraged further attempts, on their part, to impose morality on the community by law.[63]

The Catholic Church has tried to keep marriage and divorce under Church control and to prevent departures from traditional standards in divorce laws. Protestants have not taken so rigid

---

[60] K. Barth, *Credo* (London: Aberdeen University Press, 1936), pp. 137-143.

[61] K. Barth, *The Church and the Political Problem of Our Day* (New York: Chas. Scribner's Sons, 1939), pp. 30-43, 76-78.

[62] *Cf.* M. Oakeshott, *op. cit.*, pp. 54-55; P. J. Marique, *The Philosophy of Christian Education* (New York: Prentice-Hall, 1939), pp. 28, 67-69; M. Williams, *The Catholic Church in Action* (New York: Macmillan, 1934), p. 282, and Vernon McCasland, "Our Secularized Education," *Christian Century*, LVIII (Dec. 17, 1941), pp. 1576, 1578.

[63] W. A. Brown, *op. cit.*, pp. 124-125.

a stand but their tendency has been to oppose liberalizing of divorce laws.[64] Neither Protestant nor Catholic Churches have made an extended effort to adequately control or eliminate vice and prostitution through political action.

Social Justice and Economic Welfare.

The stand of the Federal Council of Churches in its "Social Creed of the Churches", condemning the unequal distribution of wealth, and advocating protection of women and children in industry, industrial democracy, equal rights for the workers, and social security, has been re-emphasized during the war. At a meeting of delegates of Protestant Churches at Delaware, Ohio, in 1942, private profit was rejected as the basis of our industrial order while preference for democracy in industry and the use of cooperatives as the principal form of production after the war was indicated. A similar position was taken by the Church of England at the Malvern Conference in 1941.

American Protestants have opposed military measures which they believe to be socially unjust. Thus, the Austin-Wadsworth National Service Act was opposed as a form of industrial slavery, and army courts which impose more severe sentences upon enlisted men than officers were severely criticized.[65]

In addition to supporting the "just" wage and the elimination of exploitation of workers in industry, the Catholic solution for industrial conflict is to organize strong, self-governing vocational groups containing both employers and employees to secure mutual cooperation, and to make property holders out of the workers, thus reducing or eliminating conflicts of interest.[66]

---

[64] Cf. Ibid., p. 125, and C. C. Marshall, op. cit., p. 225 ff.

[65] Cf. W. W. Tippy, Policy and Program of the Protestant Churches, The Annals CIII (September, 1922), p. 126 ff.; R. Fitzgerald, "The Christian Churches in the War," Fortune, XXVII (Mar., 1943), pp. 148-150, and Editorial, The Christian Century, LX, no. 42 (Oct. 20, 1943), pp. 1188-1190.

[66] Cf. Quadregesimo Anno (1939), op. cit., pp. 68-69, and R. Fitzgerald, op. cit., p. 154.

The principal function of the Church regarding matters of economic justice seems to consist in the molding of public opinion. Actual settlement of such issues must be left to the State.

Taxation of Church Property.

Church members generally approve of tax exemption for the Churches and resist all efforts to repeal such legislation.

The War and The Churches.

Before the outbreak of war, both Protestant and Catholic Churches organized extensive anti-war campaigns. They established study groups to analyze the causes of war, promoted discussion, and disseminated propaganda against war, and even in some cases, made non-participation in war a matter of discipline for their members.

Extremists among the Protestant clergy went so far as to advocate boycotts against the war system, refusal of obedience to laws requiring participation in war service, and even complete non-resistance to armed aggression on the hypothesis that unarmed peoples would not be attacked or harmed, by war-like neighbors.[67]

The liberal Protestant Clergy were in the main against the draft and intervention of the United States in the war. Many of them advocated immediate peace and disarmament. They condemned the steps taken by Roosevelt to prepare for war such as the destroyer deal with England and the move into Iceland. They contended that the Nazis as a whole were not really against religion, as stated by Roosevelt, but only certain German writers. War, they argued, would be much too costly and would require men and munitions far beyond even our means to supply. America's entry into the war would probably lead to Fascism at home, and Anglo-American imperialism and colonialism, therefore we should remain neutral.[68]

---

[67] A. J. Muste, *Non-Violence in An Aggressive World* (New York: Harper & Bros., 1940), Chaps. VII-VIII.

[68] See files of the *Christian Century* (Sept.-Nov., 1941), espec. Nos. 36-41, 45-58.

The Catholic Clergy also aligned themselves overwhelmingly against war. The Catholic World leagued itself with the America First movement. Like the liberal Protestants, Catholic spokesmen attacked the President as a war-monger and opposed America's entry into the war. They contended that the situation did not conform to the Catholic conception of a just war and that, therefore, we should remain neutral, but prepare to defend ourselves.

American aid to Russia was particularly condemned, especially our possible entry into the war as an ally of the Soviets. Stalin and the leaders of Russia, they said, are a clique of murderers. Communism and Christianity are arch-enemies and it would be suicidal to Christian civilization to make such an alliance.[69]

After Pearl Harbor, pacifist Churchmen were confronted with the dilemma of either standing by their anti-war doctrines, thus becoming guilty of disloyalty, or of supporting the war and thus seemingly repudiating their anti-war stand. After considerable hesitation, the bulk of them came out in support of the American war effort, though with reservations.

This change of attitude was rationalized by liberal Protestants by taking the position that a war in which your own nation is involved is an unavoidable necessity. To oppose it would be to aid the enemy; to support it is to condone unchristian acts, yet this is unavoidable since war is destructive of all morality. The fact that we are at war, they said, is a punishment for our sins—for our previous failure to set things right so that conflict could be avoided. It is God's judgment upon us. This theory seems to put more emphasis on man's free will than is justified by their doctrine that God is immanent and is working out his plan for mankind in history.

For Niebuhr, on the other hand, history is merely a setting for man's sinful struggles for power. This is not God's doing, for God transcends history and stands above all worldly strife. Man cannot perfect himself in history. The idea that he can achieve salvation through progress in this world is a delusion.

---

[69] See files of the *Catholic World*, CLIV, Nos. 919-921 (Oct.-Dec., 1941).

Evil is to be found on every level of civilization. On the other hand, there are elements of good in the world which the Fascist nations are trying to suppress. Both Barth and Niebuhr take the stand that the war is justifiable and necessary to destroy the forces of evil.[70]

Liberal Protestant Churchmen continued their attacks during the war upon policies tending, as they charged, towards Fascism. They condemned attacks by the government upon the constitutional rights of conscientious objectors and clergymen who defended them, and racial discrimination; particularly against the Japanese and Negroes. The Navy V-12 program was criticized for its usurpation by the state of the training of ministers.

In the field of foreign relations, British colonial policy was attacked as exploitative and the placing of colonies under some impartial international body advocated. Forcible reeducation of the Germans by the Allies was opposed, as was also the ruthless food blockade of Europe. Fear of post-war American imperialism in the Pacific was expressed. Exponents of the theory of power politics were condemned as was the theory itself. Churchmen placed their hopes in a world peace union, after the war which would limit national sovereignty, and provide an international police force to put an end to future wars. They seek representation at the peace conference to try to bring this about.[71] Extremists among the Protestant Churchmen demanded that the belligerents immediately lay down their arms and make a peace without victory.[72]

American Catholics found less difficulty in adjusting themselves to the war. As editorials in the Catholic World indicated, the attack on Pearl Harbor made this a just war which

---

[70] Cf. R. Niebhur, *Christianity and Power Politics,* preface and pp. 1-47, and "A Faith For History's Greatest Crisis," *Fortune,* XXVI (July, 1942), p. 100 ff., and "War as a Judgment of God," editorial, *Christian Century,* LX (Oct. 6, 1943), no. 40, pp. 1126-1128.

[71] See files of the *Christian Century,* LX, April-October, 1943.

[72] H. J. Cadbury, "The Validity of Religious Pacifism," *Christian Century,* LX, no. 52 (Dec. 29, 1943), pp. 1534-1535.

Catholics could support with good conscience. In fact, the war is not merely one of defense but for Christian ideals—democracy and the common man. But there must be no alliance with atheism. Therefore, the Catholic Church continues its opposition to Soviet Communism.

As for the peace settlement, Catholics here follow the Pope's pronouncement. Human freedom must be granted to all men. The special needs of each of various groups of people should be considered. National lines should be followed as closely as possible. The working class should be accorded its fair share in the business and government of the world. Adequate consideration should be given to racial groups. Impossible penalties should not be imposed. Progressive disarmament should be undertaken, and an international organization set up to enforce these principles. The United States should avoid trying to settle Europe's problems and abstain from imperialistic expansion after the war. Peace should be negotiated, not imposed by the victors.[73]

Criticism and Conclusion.

In the present situation ,the Churches find themselves in a dilemma. If they return to traditional theology, as Barth calls upon them to do, they are faced with gradual decline, and perhaps, ultimate extinction because of the growth of unbelief, and increasing reliance upon the conclusions of science. If, on the other hand, they attempt to make their ideology conform to the theory of evolution and the facts of science, they not only lost their religious authority, but their solutions to personal and social problems become subordinate to the superior experience and knowledge of statesmen and scientists. This applies also to their plans of post-war reconstruction, and their doctrines of progress towards a political Utopia.

By losing their hold on the mysteries of religion, the Church admits fallibility of judgment and exposes itself as an interest

---

[73] See *Catholic World,* CLIV, no. 922 (Jan., 1942), editorials, CLVI, nos. 934, 935 (Jan., 1943), editorials, and Thomas P. Neill, "Some Thoughts on the Peace," pp. 397-403.

group whose claims must be weighed along with those of other groups. The expanding powers and functions of the State are bringing it into open collision with the Churches and its jealous regard for the loyalty of its subjects makes opposition by Churches to its measures less and less tolerable.

In a practical political sense, Churches as political institutions are still forces to be reckoned with, but their ability to function as power groups will depend upon their capacity to hold their membership and to influence wide circles of public opinion.

SELECTED REFERENCES

Books

BERNHART, J., *The Vatican as a World Power* (London: Longmans, Green and Co., 1939), Trans. by G. N. Shuster. Depicts the Catholic Church as at war with totalitarian theories and objectives.

BROWN, F. J., HODGES, CHARLES, AND ROUCEK, JOSEPH S., *et al.*, *Contemporary World Politics* (New York: John Wiley and Sons 1940). Valuable for its chapters on Catholic and Protestant theories of international relations.

EDDY, SHERWOOD, *I Have Seen God Do It* (New York: Robt. M. McBride and Co., 1939). An optimistic statement of belief in the coming Kingdom of God.

HOBHOUSE, L. T., *The Elements of Social Justice* (New York: H. Holt and Co., 1922). Develops his theory of rational harmony in social relationships.

——————, *The Rational Good; a Study in the Logic of Practice* (London: Geo. Allen and Unwin, 1921). A theoretical exposition of his doctrine of rational harmony.

HOPKINS, C. H., *The Rise of the Social Gospel in American Protestantism*, 1865-1915 (New Haven: Yale University Press, 1940). Adequately surveys the rise and decline of the social gospel movement.

KIDD, B., *The Principles of Western Civilization* (New York: Macmillan, 1902). Traces the influence of the "emotion of the ideal" as a factor in subordinating of individual purposes to common social aims.

MATHEWS, SHAILER, *The Spiritual Interpretation of History* (Cambridge: Harvard University Press, 1916). An attempt to demonstrate that spiritual influences are molding history.

TROELSCH, E., *The Social Teaching of the Christian Church* (London: Allen and Unwin, 1931) Two volumes. Develops familiar modernist doctrines of Christianity.

WARD, H. F., *Which Way Religion?* (New York: Macmillan, 1931). Contends that Christianity must align itself with socialism if it is to remain a vital social force.

——————, *The New Social Order, Principles and Programs* (New York: Macmillan, 1920). Calls upon the Churches to work for the Kingdom of God on earth through the application of Christian principles to social problems.

Articles, Booklets, Pamphlets

Ascoli, Max, "The Roman Church and Political Action," *Foreign Affairs*, XIII (April, 1939), pp. 441-452. Summarizes influence of the Catholic Church in contemporary affairs.

Bedoyere, M. De la, "Christianity Now and After," *Atlantic*, 169 (April, 1942), pp. 451-458. Shows need of new spiritual awakening to values of democracy to prevent spread of Communism.

Cook, Stanley, "Communism and Christianity," *Contemp. Review*, CLX (Nov., 1941), pp. 282-287. Advocates compromise and reconciliation with Communism.

Corrigan, R., "The Rise of Secularism," *Catholic Hist. Rev.*, XXV (April, 1939-Jan., 1940), pp. 37-52. Attacks Modernism from the standpoint of Catholic dogma.

Fernsworth, L., "The Vatican in World Politics," *Va. Q. Rev.*, XVI (Autumn, 1940), pp. 485-498. Attacks Vatican Policies as pro-Axis.

Fitzgerald, R., "The Christian Churches in the War," *Fortune*, XXVII (Mar., 1943), pp. 119-121. Surveys the effect on Church ideas and policies of the war.

Furfey, P. H., "The Curse of Nationalism," *Catholic World*, CLVI, no. 936 Mar., 1943), pp. 652-657. Shows the danger of the Nationalistic State to the Church.

Jones, Stanley E., "Sponges on Spearpoints," *Christian Century*, 60, no. 34 (Aug., 1933), pp. 963-965. Attacks racial intolerance and oppression of backward peoples.

Strasser, Otto, "German Youth as a Post-War Problem," *Catholic World*, CLVI, no. 935 (Feb., 1943), pp. 652, 657. Christian Churches must reeducate German youth to Christian principles.

Rall, H. F., "The War and The Second Coming," *Christian Century*, LX, no. 33 (Aug., 1943), pp. 941-942. Salvation for man will work its way out in history.

Chapter X

AGRARIANISM IN POLITICS *

C. ARNOLD ANDERSON

"The agricultural interest of our country is so essentially connected with every other and so superior in importance to them all that it is scarcely necessary to invite to it your particular attention. It is principally as manufactures and commerce tend to increase the value of agricultural productions and to extend their application to the wants and comforts of society that they deserve the fostering care of Government."
—Jackson's First Message to Congress

The Paradox of Resurgent Agrarianism in an Industrial Age

The political strength of farmers has increased notably in the last generation—a fact often unnoticed by students of contemporary society. In eastern Europe the twentieth century has seen the culmination of a long struggle for recognition by the peasantry, and the revival of the Junkers. In the West, including the United States, farmers have refused to bow to their predicted fate of a minor element in national affairs. Rural people have adopted successfully city men's techniques for the protection of group interests. Doctrines of nationalistic self-sufficiency have induced in the public a willingness to subsidize the source of food and soldiers. For an understanding of the new trend we must also take account of the disillusionment from the failure of urbanism and industrialism to deliver their promised boons to mankind.

* Journal Paper No. J1216 of the Iowa Agricultural Experiment Station, Ames, Iowa. Project No. 795.

Agrarianism, like the ideologies of the other sectors of society, is at the same time a moral philosophy, a theory of history, and a formula of political tactics. This creed, attaining its most elaborate formulation when the agrarian order is no longer the economic basis of society, was previously no less fervently held, but more implicitly, and perhaps less defensively. Morally agrarianism is not merely a backward looking to a golden age but also an affirmation of values deep in our traditions that we wish to retain. Now that we have more extensive historical data for comparisons, the role of farmers in national life is clearer to scholar and layman alike, and the utopians of industrialism have lost some of their confidence under the impact of war and depression. On the level of politico-economic tactics, new devices in group organization are being adapted to slow down the drift of political power away from farmers. No longer appearing to other groups as illiterate, technically backward, and socially isolated rustics, farmers are able and eager to speak for themselves—however many pseudo-agrarians may wish also to be their spokesmen, whether for humanitarian or nationalistic reasons.

Reflecting the composite character of agriculture, agrarianism is the most complex of the philosophies espoused by the big groups in society. The farmer is laborer as well as enterpriser to an extent unusual among vocations, he is usually a capital owner and often a landlord. To a marked degree, therefore, farmers are at the same time an economic interest group, a social class, an estate (Stande), and a geographic section of the society.[1] No wonder agrarianism in politics displays many paradoxes. To illustrate: although farmers are less tightly organized politically, their political lobbies are often the most powerful. Farmers are traditionalists, yet often insurgent in politics. The belief and practice of economic individualism are deeply rooted in farming, yet in many nations agricultural policy

---

[1] P. A. Sorokin, C. C. Zimmerman, and C. J. Galpin, *Source Book in Rural Sociology.* (Minneapolis: University of Minnesota Press, 1930-32), Vol. 1, Chap. 27 (Comparison of Farmer-Peasants and Other Social Classes.)

manifests a more extreme departure from orthodox economics than policy in other spheres.

Even in a discussion limited to Europe and the United States it is difficult to reach broad conclusions since rural-urban relations have been changing at such different rates in different countries. It may be helpful to keep in mind two sets of parallels between European and American events.[2] First, both in eastern Europe recently and in the United States earlier, agrarian policy revolved around the land question and the instrument for its solution, political suffrage. Second, recently in both western Europe and the United States, the central problems have been price and market relationships.

The Place of the Political Among the Organized Activities of Farmers

Political action is only one form of collective effort by farmers, and the place of the political among all types of organized expression of interests differs for farmers from that in other sections of society. Farmers have become more alert to their need for collaboration as they have been drawn into closer relations with other groups, many of their programs being a reaction to the intrusion of influences from the city. The most definite of these disturbances have been those summed up in the term agricultural revolution, technology, and commercialization. Groupings of a folk character (on a family, neighborhood, or community basis) have remained important—less in the United States than in Europe—but the transformation of agriculture has been accompanied by the emergence of a complex array of special interest groups: some non-political (education, fraternal, technical, and economic), others political (direct action, lobbies, and parties).

Early in the 19th century in this country, as farming became more distinct from other ways of life, associations of farmers and artisans and later farmers' clubs appeared in numbers. In western Europe a larger proportion of activities were

[2] D. Warriner, *Economics of Peasant Farming* (New York: Oxford, 1939).

carried out through the more firmly established communities, while in this country with its successively transplanted communities more specialized groupings were called for. Whether founded by farmers or by gentlemen farmers and urban friends of farmers, education and sociability marked these groups. Fairs and state agricultural societies followed, many receiving public aid and in time often becoming state agencies.[3]

Widespread farmer participation awaited the conversion of these general societies into more specialized ones: horticultural, wool, dairy, corn, cotton, livestock societies.[4] General education programs languished until later in the century, particularly until the appearance of the forerunners of the extension service. After the Civil War, stimulated by their growing awareness of common problems resulting from the agricultural revolution, farmers began to link up their local clubs into general fraternal organizations. A parallel development occurred in Europe, with educational and technical and especially economic coöperative groups more prominent than fraternal; the Danish folk schools were a distinguished exception, however.

As the incompatibility of the tradition of farmer independence with the growing actual economic dependence became clearer, economic associations became more prominent on both continents. Political associations also appeared, less conspicuously in Europe, though peasant parties in Europe have proved more durable than in America. Farmers have been progressively less willing to remain the residual claimants and by a variety of tactics have forced their demands upon public attention.

The rising level of electoral participation of recent generations has been shared by farmers; their rate of increase in voting has been greater than that of the whole population. On the basis of Tingsten's more complete recent survey it appears that' we may still speak of higher urban rate of voting, however,

---

[3] P. H. Johnstone, *Old Ideals versus New Ideas in Farm Life* (Washington: Government Printing Office, United States Department of Agriculture Yearbook, 1940), pp. 116-166.

[4] E. Wiest, *Agricultural Organization in the United States* (Lexington: University of Kentucky, 1923).

rather than to rest with Sorokin and Zimmerman's verdict of not proven.[5] Farmers' votes usually count for more than their strict proportion by virtue of their geographic concentration. In the United States the combination of a growing frequency of voting with the key role of rural states in the swings of political sentiment has given the votes of farmers a per capita weight in excess of that of the rest of the population. Farmers may make their desires politically effective also by electing farmers to legislatures. Most legislative bodies, however, over the last century have contained a declining number of farmers. For example, Johnstone's tabulation shows that Iowa has had only 15 farmers in Congress out of 419 representatives from 1844 to 1938, and only 3 of these were elected after 1892. This decline in direct representation has not prevented farmers exerting strong pressures, particularly through lobbies, and in Europe also by alliances with clerical parties.

Farmers shift their participation between non-political and political groups with the fluctuations of economic conditions.[6] Educational, fraternal, and technical programs are less popular in depressions; political tactics gain in prominence. This changing pattern is distinctly in contrast with the thriving of labor unions in prosperity and shrinking in depressions; the contrast is related to the lesser suitability of economic weapons for farmers. In successive depressions the several farmers' educational and fraternal organizations have had to adopt a political program or drop out of the picture. Time after time "radical" programs have supplanted the general organizations that would not yield.[7] Similarly, direct action programs, such as milk-strikes and farm holiday movements, are largely depression phenomena.

---

[5] P. A. Sorokin and others, *op. cit.*, Vol. 2, Chap. 16 (Rural Political Organization, Parties, and Behavior). H. Tingsten, *Political Behavior: Studies in Election Statistics* (London: King, 1937).

[6] C. C. Taylor, *Rural Sociology in Its Economic, Historical and Psychological Aspects* (New York: Harper, 1933, 2nd ed.), Chap. 28.

[7] R. E. Wakeley, "How to Study the Effects of Direct Action Movements on Farm Organizations." *Social Forces*, XII (1933), pp. 380-5.

The two types of programs appear to recruit different types of followers—though in this respect the coöperative and other economic associations must be grouped with the political. The more prosperous farmers, the commercialized farmers contributing more than their share of produce sold on the markets, tend to favor the non-political and the commodity organizations. The poorer, relatively more self-sufficient, farmers are normally less often members of educational or fraternal groups, but they provide the strength of insurgent movements in politics.[8] And when the latter enter the political arena aggressively they are more prone to mix their agrarianism with racism and moralism and more likely to align with clerical parties. In the United States this contrast is also in considerable measure regional, the Eastern and Midwestern farmers holding more firmly to economic tactics and general farm organizations. It is not that the prosperous farmers are lacking in political mindedness; they are more prone to non-partisan political tactics, especially lobbying.

If we accept Johnstone's formulation of the agrarian creed as comprising economic independence, a belief that farming is the basic occupation, and a moral conviction that agriculture is the natural way of life—it is clear that farmers have been progressively less willing to believe in this creed passively and more determined to assert it and to implement it with political action. They have accepted the political weapons forged by other groups, concentrating first upon assuring the basis of their existence, the land. More recently they have improved upon the pressure group tactics invented by business to deal with their novel problems of prices and markets.

FARMERS AS TRUSTEES OF THE TRADITION OF INDEPENDENT ENTERPRISE — THE LAND PROBLEM

One of those great historical movements toward more equal distribution of land swept over eastern Europe after the last war

---

[8] D. J. Saposs, "The Role of the Middle Class in Social Development," in *Economic Essays in Honor of W. C. Mitchell* (New York: Columbia University Press, 1935), pp. 397-408.

affecting the lives of the majority of peasants on the continent.[9] While these changes had been in course earlier, the political instability associated with the war gave scope to long pent up desires for the right of independent operation and ownership. The programs were most drastic where the previous holdings had been most unequal, where the landlords had been most privileged, and where the pressures had been longest restrained. Not all of these programs were carried through. In some areas the peasantry lacked the organization to keep their plans in the center of national policy, and in some countries the aristocracy quickly regained their political preëminence. The revolutionary ideas of the early 19th century had not swept this area; feudalism had persisted, and as it decayed the landlords had been able to turn the situation to their own advantage. In the similar but earlier transition the peasants of western Europe, benefiting from their higher cultural level and proximity to markets, had come out of the transition with increased privileges.

In the recent upheavals the reforms were relatively mild in Bulgaria and Czechoslovakia where considerable economic and political emancipation had been going on. In Hungary, Poland, and Prussia the political advantages of the aristocracy sufficed to stop the movement before it was well begun. Rumania accomplished a major reallocation so that while before the war 40% of the holdings were over 100 hectares, afterwards only 10% were.[10] The land seizures during the opening months of the Russian revolution were also marked successes for agrarian reform.

The see-saw struggle of the last quarter century between the Russian peasants and the government was basically over land-

---

[9] P. A. Sorokin and others, *op. cit.*, Vol. 1, Chap. 7 (Social Stratification of the Agricultural Population); Chap. 9 (Types of Rural Aggregates and Forms of Land Possession). D. Warriner, *op. cit.*

[10] D. Mitrany, *The Land and the Peasant in Rumania: the War and Agrarian Reform* (1917-21) (London: Oxford, 1930). Also lecture notes on peasant movements.

holding.[11] The poorer peasants had promptly taken land for themselves, meanwhile beating down the differentiating tendencies of the richer peasants who had been the beneficiaries of Czarist reforms. Although the collectivization program took advantage of this enmity within the peasantry, that same program had to be suspended and modified more than once in order to concede the demands of even poor peasants for a bit of land under their own control and title to their livestock on which they bestowed their individual care. Whenever this land problem became stabilized even temporarily the market problem came to the fore in the rebellion against giving cheap food to the cities without equivalent return in goods. Mitrany describes the similar impasse in Rumania: previously when the peasants were legally freed from the land their labor was tied; when their labor had to be freed the land was tied; and when finally both were freed the market was tied.

In American history, the farmers have led a constant drive for political democratization, spurred by a tradition of the revolution won in the name of political equality and the opportunities of a pioneer country.[12] If American politics has been middle class politics, the farmer has been the backbone of that class. The right to the land has been a dominant theme in our history. The goal of a nation of small, independent, owning farmers came to be shared by all Americans. Actual settlers won priority over investors, squatters received preëmption rights, payments were eased, internal improvements were given lavishly so that no self-reliant man should be deprived of his birthright, a farm.

Nor has this ideal been given up. The outcome of the Civil War, the Homestead Act, and manhood suffrage settled the struggle of Northern yeomen farmers and slaveholders for control of the West. If the South has lagged, we may credit

---

[11] D. Warriner, *op. cit.* L. A. Owen, *The Russian Peasant Movement, 1906-17* (London: King, 1937). L. E. Hubbard, *The Economics of Soviet Agriculture* (London: Macmillan, 1939). N. S. Timasheff, "Structural Changes in Rural Russia." *Rural Sociology*, II (1937), pp. 10-28.

[12] C. Seymour, *How the World Votes: the Story of Democratic Development in Elections*, I (Springfield, Mass.: Nichols, 1918), pp. 209-34.

this largely to the race problem and the stronger feudal tradition. When the land question recurs from time to time in depressions and mortgages and credit become topics of agitation, the tradition remains vital. Its vitality shows also in determination to maintain the family-size farm, and in the steady direction of technical research to provide the machinery suited to such farms. With the industrialization of the country and the opening of urban and world markets to the farmer after the Civil War, agrarianism turned haltingly but definitely to the new focus, prices and markets.

SHIFT TO PRESSURE GROUP TACTICS AND GROWING DIVERGENCES WITHIN AGRICULTURE — THE PROBLEM OF PRICES AND MARKETS

The agrarian movements of the last 70 years in American politics were perhaps less a revolt of frontiersmen than a demand by capitalist farmers for the conditions of fair competition.[13] Though European countries had no frontier, yet the trend of agricultural policy in western Europe was not unlike ours. The farmer, especially in our Western states, had to pay high freight rates, he had to deal with market monopolies, he had given up live-at-home practices, and he needed abundant credit. In each wave of revolt a new set of states with these features took the lead, while older states which had once led the revolt were now producing crops of higher unit values that could carry the charges and which commanded a larger share of the consumers' price.

It is not often realized that most of the demands of the embattled farmers have been conceded substantially. It was the agrarian West and South that created the politically effective demand for a new deal of which the contemporary version is

---

[13] B. H. Wilcox, "An Historical Definition of Northwestern Radicalism." *Miss. Valley Hist. Review*, XXXVI (1939), pp. 377-94; C. C. Taylor, *op. cit.*; J. D. Hicks, *The Populist Revolt: A History of the Farmers' Alliance and the People's Party* (Minneapolis: University of Minnesota Press, 1931); V. O. Key, Jr., *Politics, Parties and Pressure Groups* (New York: Crowell, 1942), Chap. 3; F. E. Haynes, *Third Party Movements Since the Civil War with Special Reference to Iowa: A Study in Social Politics* (Iowa City: State Historical Society of Iowa, 1916).

an elaboration. What were those programs? Taylor lists the
successive complaints as railroads, money, grain exchanges,
monopolies, and tariff-price inequalities. As remedies farmers
proposed crop storage and loan facilities, pure-food laws, freer
coinage, control of packers and brokers, cheaper freights, aid
to coöperatives, research and information. And there were some
political demands, "so that the honest citizen could make his
opinions count": direct elections, initiative, election of judges.

The farmers' weapon was the third party or its threat. These
parties were populist, even without the name; they advocated a
system of regulated private property and profit, and that the
government should restrain impersonal agencies destroying the
substance of personal opportunity. From 1872 to 1892 and since
the last war farmers have been on the rampage politically, and
in nearly every election there was an agrarian third party. Even
when farmers lost an election, the major parties accepted some
of their policies lest they revolt again.[14] This agrarian influence
was greatest after long periods of declining prices, and in these
critical years all farmers worked together, drifting apart again
into sectional and commodity groupings when prices rose. The
seat of agrarian parties, as of insurgent votes, was mainly in the
West. While Jefferson's and Jackson's feats of uniting all
farmers have not been repeated, due to the aftermath of the
Civil War, nevertheless no party could win without support from
a large segment of Western farmers.

By virtue of this sectional concentration farmers have had
a disproportionate influence; the critical states being rural, the
average farmer's vote has weighed more than an urban vote.
This power is magnified by the structure of the Senate and by
the seniority principle which keeps the farmers' friends in key

[14] C. A. M. Ewing, *Presidential Elections: from Abraham Lincoln to Franklin
D. Roosevelt* (Norman: University of Oklahoma, 1940). A. N. Holcombe,
"Present Day Characteristics of American Political Parties." In E. B. Logan (ed.),
The American Political Scene (New York: Harper, 1938, 2nd ed.), Chap. 1 and
App. 1. L. H. Bean, *Ballot Behavior: A Study of Presidential Elections* (Wash-
ington: American Council on Public Affairs, 1940), p. 100. H. F. Gosnell,
Grass Root Politics: National Voting Behavior of Typical States (Same publisher,
1942), pp. 162-3. Notice particularly the similarity of American farmer insur-
gency and the violent swing of German peasants to Nazism.

positions on committees. In Congressional voting the same sectionalism appears, and here also farm representatives unite in depressions despite section or party and break apart again in prosperity, as Roach shows for a series of key issues.[15]

Though farmers have not forgotten their heritage of revolt, as 1932 and 1936 showed, they have been developing a preference for other political tactics, especially non-partisan lobbying. Politicians know they cannot win without farm support and farmers have learned how to apply pressures, but farm leaders also have learned not to rely on farmers' deserting traditional parties in sufficient strength to carry an election. Then, not all farmers recognize "where their own interests lie" and in the South large numbers never vote. By lobbying, a lesser strength can be made effective and the pressure from each sectional and commodity group mobilized with precision.

Thus agriculture has discovered more victories can be won by choosing direct and concrete aims. This method of limited goals is especially suited to satisfying the interests of classes of farmers rather than the mass and to the use of farm organizations rather than parties as spokesmen. It is these tactics and factors that have permitted the cotton lobby, the dairy lobby, the wheat lobby, to win their separate and often inconsistent ends by policies frequently benefiting only a fraction of the farmers.[16]

The shifting content of recent American agricultural policy reflects in part the relative political influence of different groups

---

[15] W. H. Nicholls and J. A. Vieg, *Wartime Government in Operation* (Philadelphia: Blakiston, 1943), Chaps. 4, 5. H. G. Roach, "Sectionalism in Congress (1870-1890)." *American Political Science Review,* XIX (1926), pp. 500-26.

[16] E. P. Herring, *Group Representation before Congress* (Baltimore: Johns Hopkins University, 1929), Chap. 7. H. H. Putnam, "A History of the Farm Bloc." *Manuscript Masters Thesis* (Ames: Iowa State College, 1941). There is a notable parallelism in German agrarian moves as described by A. Gerschenkron, *Bread and Democracy in Germany* (Berkeley: University of California, 1943).

of farmers.[17] Cheap credit, experiment stations, the extension
service, coöperatives, the AAA have been received more favorably by the more prosperous farmers. Relief, debt adjustment,
tenant loans, rehabilitation and resettlement, are of more value
to low income farmers. Significantly, it has been difficult to
mobilize support, after the worst of the depression had passed,
for this second group of measures. Farmers preferring the first
group are less numerous but more vocal and more likely to
vote.

This alteration in methods of protecting agriculture's interests occurred earlier in western European countries. Where the
farm population is small, agricultural policy is based largely on
interests of state. Farmers there retain some voting power, but
they benefit by national concern for the food supply. In other
countries as Denmark [18] and Scandinavia, the similarity to the
United States is greater. Peasant parties are prominent, but their
power is not mainly in the vote but as a focus of bargaining and
negotiation with other economic groups.

CONVERGENCE OF AGRARIAN PROGRAMS AND TACTICS TO THOSE OF LABOR AND BUSINESS

There was strong mutual identification of artisan and
farmer in the first part of the 19th century in the United States;
earlier urbanization and the antagonism of socialist theory led to
sharper alignments in Europe. The American agrarian programs
of the late 19th century often cordially endorsed labor demands;
but recently farm organization pronouncements on labor have
been more general and so qualified as to be aloof if not hostile.

[17] L. C. Gray, "Disadvantaged Rural Classes." *J. of Farm Econ.*, XX (1938),
pp.71-80. C. O. Rggles, "The Economic Basis of the Greenback Movement in
Iowa and Wisconsin." *Proc. Miss Valley Hist. Assn.*, VI (1912), pp. 142-65.
G. A. Lundberg, "The Demographic and Economic Basis of Political Radicalism
and Conservatism." *Amer. J. of Soc.*, XXXII (1927), pp. 719-32. J. A. Neprash, *The Brookhart Campaigns in Iowa, 1920-1926: A Study in the Motivation
of Political Attitudes* (New York: Columbia University Press, 1932).

[18] E. Jensen, *Danish Agriculture: Its Economic Development* (Copenhagen:
Schultz, 1937). This contrast between the individual-coöperative programs in
Denmark and the government aided programs in the United States deserves sys-
tematic investigation.

Even though laborers have become factory workers and farmers employers, the announcement of a farmers' institute as "a business meeting for business men" does not express the whole attitude of farmers toward labor.

When American farmers were asked in a recent poll whether they would prefer business or labor as a political ally, the preference was strongly for labor. No less significant was the preference of the "best informed", who are also the most prosperous, farmers for business. On the other side, polls show farmers to be the group least in favor, even less than urban upper income groups, of unions or their policies. There is therefore no rigid pattern of thinking in this area. Particularly in depressions are farmers and laborers likely to become allies, but differences within agriculture persist — Southern agricultural movements are typically more favorable to labor, and the Farmers Union more willing than other organizations to form alliances. Apparently labor representatives vote for farm measures more often than they receive help in return; perhaps labor has more to gain from the goodwill of farmers; certainly more laborers are farm reared while few farmers have been workers in the usual sense.

Despite the variety of opinion on this question, there have been few studies of actual working political relations. In Europe agrarian voters are steadily opposed to labor programs with a socialist coloring, and the socialists accepted the economic liquidation of farmers as a step toward the new economy. In recent years there has been some mutual support. For the United States, the only studies are those of Rice [19] in the early 20's when the farm bloc was active and could use help. He found that in one Congress the number of bills jointly sponsored exceeded chance and that more candidates were supported by both groups than would be expected. There was little agreement in most state legislatures, but more durable alliances of the two groups have persisted in some states.

---

[19] S. A. Rice, *Farmers and Workers in American Politics* (New York: Columbia University Press, 1924). W. Diamond, "Urban and Rural Voting in 1896." *Amer. Hist. Rev.*, XLVI (1940), pp. 281-305.

Relationships with business men are more complex. The two groups sometimes work together against unions, though frequently farm organizations rather than rank and file farmers have served as fronts for union-smashing drives. Farmers share the antagonism to "socialism". But the history of agrarian revolt is a struggle against business monopoly. This is not to say that farmers line up with small business, for the battle of local merchants and farmers has been a continuous one. The most adequate conclusion may be that farmers regard themselves as middle class and will work with whatever group calls itself middle class provided that group is not already regarded as hostile.

That farmers are individualists and supporters of private property while industrial laborers favor government ownership and socialism is a commonplace of the literature on political agrarianism.[20] This is a half-truth. It ignores the fact that in an industrial order the right to work is the equivalent basis of security with the right of property for the farmer. For the laborer, independence through property is an unrealistic ideal; it is practicable for farmers. It follows that the recurrent movements among farmers to protect their land rights have more than an incidental similarity to the loyalty of laborers to the unions which are their protection against arbitrary insecurity. Just as laborers desire their unions to be exempt from anti-trust prosecution, so in a commercialized agricultural market farmers demand exemption for their coöperatives.

Fair or parity prices, as was shown in the last section, have become prominent goals in farm policy; laborers too ask for a living wage. If "control of the job" is a prime aim of labor, market agreements serve the same end for farmers. As apprenticeship rules and minimum wage laws protect labor's income from being undermined, so production control and ever-normal granaries stabilize farm income. The similarities in tactics sometimes extend to details as when farmers carry out property destroying strikes. Or they may stage passive strikes, as when a

---

[20] Sorokin and others, *op. cit.* P. H. Johnstone, *op. cit.* R. Bauder, "Three Interpretations of the American Trade Union Movement." *Social Forces*, XXII (1943), pp. 215-224.

group of farmers held their livestock off the market in protest against wartime price ceilings. If generally farmers are more prone to political and laborers to direct and economic tactics, there are two reasons. Laborers cannot expect extensive public support of their requests unless labor is itself a major political element. On the other side, farmers require the coercive power of the state to carry out programs coördinating the activities of innumerable scattered individuals.

"Prices and markets have been as much the center of the farm movement as wages and hours have been for the labor movement. . . ." Taylor's succinct emphasis on parallels in policy deserves more study than it has received. The similarities are notable, and increasing. In both groups thinking runs in terms of prices, the wage rate and farm prices, rather than in terms of family income. In this emphasis on price lies the possibility that the traditional emphasis upon creating opportunities for individual attainment may give place to demands for hedging in the status quo.

FARMERS AS CUSTODIANS OF TRADITIONAL MORAL VALUES

Traditional values and practices, which persist longer in rural areas, are continually being brought back into urban and national life by migration, but also by the expression of these traditions in political programs of farmers.[21] This adherence of farmers to the customary is often greater in principle than in practice, however. Farmers speak for individualism and private property in voting against taxes, laws limiting the privileges of employers, and policies labeled as socialistic generally. But not infrequently they also vigorously sustain policies that drastically limit their own property rights and undermine the principles of capitalist economy.

On moral and humanitarian issues farmers are conservative in about the degree typical of the urban middle classes, but more carefully defending the rights of the common man than

---

[21] P. A. Sorokin and others, *op. cit.*, Vol. 2, Chap. 16. W. F. Ogburn and D. Peterson, "Political Thought of Social Classes," *Political Science Quarterly*, XXXI (1916), pp. 300-17.

the upper classes. They do not favor labor legislation: shorter day, social security, union privileges. They oppose lessening legal penalties, aid to "neglected and dependent" groups, changes in family law. They are strong advocates of prohibition.

Innovations in the political structure are viewed cautiously. Farmers in the United States have been an exception in part to this rule; while this caution normally prevails, agrarian parties have favored basic reforms as a means to correct farmers' economic disadvantages. Typically, except in periods of insurgency, party allegiances are firmer among farmers, as shown by less ticket-splitting or irregular voting.

American agrarianism is an exception moreover for a whole series of social reforms; while normally voting conservatively, yet a long list of measures were adopted first in the Western farm states. Bailey showed that for the whole following list of laws the leading states were Western: initiative and referendum, direct elections, recall, women's suffrage, prohibition, legalized sterilization, mothers' pensions, old-age pensions, workmen's compensation, child labor, minimum wages for women. It would seem that here we see the frontier influence as much as the agrarian. Cushman found that in Ohio farmers favored suffrage for women, apparently as a means to prohibition, but voted against permitting women to be eligible for public office.[22]

Farmers are distinctly nationalistic, but more in the isolationist than in the imperialist sense—except when imperialism is related to the land question as in this country in the last century. Crenshaw's study of the 1860 election showed that it was the rural areas, North and South, that stood for no compromise, while the cities in both sections favored the conciliatory parties. Nativist movements, as the Ku Klux Klan of the 20's, receive most of their support in rural areas. Friedrich found a distinct correlation of farm population and voting on the German referendum against the Young Plan in a situation where only the more nationalistic people turned out to vote. In recent years it

[22] T. A. Bailey, "The West and Radical Legislation." *Amer. J. of Soc.*, XXXVIII (1923), pp. 603-611; R. E. Cushman, "Voting Organic Laws." *Pol. Sci. Q.*, XXVIII (1913), pp. 207-29.

has been the urban labor groups rather than the peasants that have held out against fascist regimes. Particularly informative is Heberle's comparison of different types of farmers in Schleswig-Holstein; it was the areas of family-sized farms that gave the most whole-hearted supported to the Nazis, once that party had begun its rise. Finally, opinion polls in this country find farmers to be more determined to collect war debts, less willing to grant an international control over foreign trade, and most opposed to readmitting enemy nations to a new league.[23]

If farmers resemble other groups in accepting changes that clearly promise aid to their own interests and improvement of their status among the groups in society, at the same time they are the group providing the most extensive continuity in national traditions.

MUST FARMERS BECOME THE WARDS OF THE NATION?

"The political economists of the state must seek to adjust these differences between agricultural and industrial prices." This axiomatically-stated demand by Swiss peasants is typical of a growing theme in agrarianism, and it cuts to the heart of the question of the politico-economic relationships within every industrial nation. Such a doctrine can rest on two grounds. One can assume that agriculture is inherently weak politically and disadvantaged economically and that it is only equitable to grant protection; in a poll of American farmers a quarter believed agriculture needed help even if other groups did not. Or, one can conclude that agriculture is so indispensable to the nation for food and manpower that the remainder of the population must subsidize it; this inference rests on a prior premise of nationalism.

---

[23] O. Crenshaw, "Urban and Rural Voting in the Election of 1860," in *W. S. Holt Memorial Volume* (Baltimore: Johns Hopkins, 1941), Chap. 3; C. J. Friedrich, "The Agricultural Basis of Emotional Nationalism." *Public Opinion Quarterly*, I (1937), pp. 50-61; R. Heberle, "The Political Movements Among the Rural People in Schleswig-Holstein, 1918 to 1932." *J. of Politics*, V (1943), pp. 26, 115-41. Also unpublished manuscript: "The Ecology of Political Parties: An Analysis of Elections in Schleswig-Holstein, 1918-1932."

Farmers generally, and in lesser measure other vocations, believe their way of life to be basic to all others and themselves the moral custodians for society. In the United States they have not until recently asked special favors as farmers, contenting themselves with asserting that the economy was loaded against them and that fairness of competition should be reestablished. European farmers earlier took advantage of their contributions to national military power to ask preferential treatment. Not that American farmers have lacked government help; our land policy was one long series of bonuses to farmers. But the whole public approved because they assumed most people would be farmers, and ought to be.

The economics of the agricultural industry has undergone a revolution. Prices are no longer taken as given by the market but have become politically regulated by Congress.[24] This policy, long established in Europe, is in principle consistent with our pioneering in tariffs. But the extent of manipulation has now gone further in agriculture than in any other sector of the economy. The new approach is formulated in the concept of parity and the marketing agreements. But parity cannot be applied uniformly for all groups, else it would cancel out. Applied to one part, and given the possibility of changing the rules as political pressure dictates, the principle of parity undermines the foundations of the free economy in a peculiarly comprehensive manner—even more than monopolies or tariffs or minimum wage laws.

Market agreements are in some respects more destructive, for they permit a part of the farmers in an area to freeze out others from access to markets or to coerce others into accepting the structure of prices decided upon by the majority of farmers voting upon the agreement. This policy copies one of the most contested features of labor unions with the added feature that government agencies are active partners in the program. Certain prevailing attitudes of farmers make this government bless-

---

[24] For a complementary treatment of the factors encouraging a "managed economy", see the writer's paper "Sociological Elements in Economic Restrictionism." *Amer. Soc. Review*, August, 1944.

ing dangerous. A poll showed that while business men were 81% in favor of the government having the right during the war to tell them what to make and what to charge, and while laborers were 64% in favor of allowing government to control their jobs and hours and pay, only half of the farmers were willing that government should dictate crops and prices. And subsidies acquire a vested character as indicated by farmers' divergent opinion regarding proper channels for government investment in agriculture. Farmers were less in favor of choosing conservation and were much more in favor of direct subsidies and production control than the other groups polled—though farmers did rate conservation higher than subsidies.

If pressure groups bargain and negotiate, rather than fight as do parties, the shift toward lobby tactics has some benefits for the public. As programs must be administered by bureaus and bureaus must be staffed by experts, an agency like the Department of Agriculture can exercise discretion in guiding policies according to the public spirit of the officials, and it does force pressure groups to perceive more clearly the implications and limitations of their policies. There is also an undeniably democratic element in the effort to articulate farmers in local communities with central agencies so that policy may represent farmer opinion as well as the wishes of interest groups. Bringing interests and pressures into the open, in contrast to the method of tariff making, is constructive even if conflicts are made more visible.

This mediatory role of bureaus is distinctly limited, however, by the tendency of experts to be agricultural minded in origin and training. In many situations they may well be less judicial than a political appointee would be, for the latter must be responsible to diverse groups. This same unconscious warping occurs as well in agencies like the extension service that do not carry administrative responsibilities; here there has been a perceptible shift toward problems of legislation and business and away from the ideal of unbiased education. Withal, the Department of Agriculture has pioneered new types of relationship between public, legislature, and bureau.[25]

In the Western nations generally, then, agriculture has come into a preferred position in national policy. To a degree not enjoyed by other major groups in the economy (excepting in some countries the social security policies that are not welcomed by farmers), farmers are hedged about by policies warding off the full operation of the adjustive mechanisms of the economy. In the totalitarian countries, and in other nations in wartime, agriculture more recently has been forced to accept distinct limitations as the price of its privileges. The question is: will similar limitations be imposed in every nation in exchange for the privileges so widely asked by the spokesmen of farmers, if not by the farmers themselves? In the agricultural sector there are many features of the corporative state emerging even in countries not professing that philosophy. Farmers who fought so long against monopoly now have some of their own monopolies not merely tolerated by government but encouraged. Significantly, one farm organization in this country proposed that all farm programs be taken away from the USDA and put under state committees appointed jointly with the farm organization. It is unlikely that so flagrant a misuse of public power and funds would occur. More probable is a more active sharing by the central government together with more control over farmers. Herein lies the possibility that farmers might become the wards of the nation.

There are definite factors operating to check this tendency in the United States. A large majority of farmers belong to no farm organization and do not participate actively in the lobby tactics. These farmers, less prosperous generally, are realizing that their interests are divergent in many ways from those of the more vocal ones. They may gain allies from those prosperous and well educated farmers who have never approved of

[25] E. P. Herring, *The Politics of Democracy: American Parties in Action* (New York: Norton, 1940), pp. 384-5. J. M. Gaus and L. O. Wolcott, *Public Administration and the United States Department of Agriculture* (Chicago: Public Administration Service, 1940), pp. 83, 110, 197, 379, 393.

production control and special privileges. Leadership in agriculture may again be less exclusively channeled into pressure group tactics and instead revive political party agrarianism, in any case revive the older theme of opportunity rather than subsidy. Perhaps it is principally the state of international trade that will determine the drift toward or away from wardship for agriculture.

SELECTED REFERENCES

1. *Encyclopedia of the Social Sciences.* The articles on Agricultural Movements, American Farm Bureau Federation, Farmers' Alliance, Farm Bloc, Farmers' Organizations, Farmers' Union, Peasantry, give a useful and brief introduction to the subject.

2. EWING, C. A. M., *Presidential Elections: from Abraham Lincoln to Franklin D. Roosevelt* (Norman: University of Oklahoma, 1940). This book not only gives a concise picture of voting changes but is particularly useful for its data on the regional sources of strength for different types of minor parties.

3. GAUS, J. M., and WOLCOTT, L. O., *Public Administration and the United States Department of Agriculture* (Chicago: Public Administration Service, 1940). The authors trace the development of this unique agency, with insight into the economic changes and shifts in opinion that have molded its program and the special problems arising from the new types of public policy for agriculture.

4. GERSCHENKRON, A., *Bread and Democracy in Germany* (Berkeley: University of California, 1943). Against the background of the Junker's successful fight to preserve their uneconomic position before the last war, we are given a detailed analysis of agriculture's privileged position under the social democratic Republic, with many illuminating parallels to policies in other countries.

5. HOLT, J. B., *German Agricultural Policy 1918-34* (Chapel Hill: University of North Carolina, 1936). A more detailed description than that of the previous work, with more attention to sociological considerations.

6. JOHNSTONE, P. H., *Old Ideals versus New Ideas in Farm Life* (Washington: Government Printing Office, United States Department of Agriculture Yearbook, 1940). A lucid and dramatic account of the impact of the agricultural revolution upon ideology and practices. (See also the companion chapters by D. C. Wing on national farm organizations, and E. E. Edwards, "American Agriculture—the First 300 Years.")

7. MITRANY, D., *The Land and the Peasant in Rumania: The War and Agrarian Reform* (1917-21) (London: Oxford, 1930). This is the most detailed analysis of post-war reforms in southeastern Europe (outside Russia) and it shows clearly the half-way character of land redistribution without market reforms.

8. NEPRASH, J. A., *The Brookhart Campaigns in Iowa, 1920-26: A Study in the Motivation of Political Attitudes* (New York: Columbia University, 1932). While less informative on motivation than it appeared to be ten years ago, he careful dissection of votes by section and price shifts is unique.

9. NICHOLLS, W. H., and VIEG, J. A., *Wartime Government in Operation* (Philadelphia: Blakiston, 1943). The chronicle of manpower and farm price policy is supported by an analysis of the influence of Congressional structure upon the toleration of pressure tactics, especially by farmers. (For background material on the agricultural lobbies, see W. McCune, *The Farm Bloc* (New York: Doubleday Doran, 1943).

10. Public opinion polls. Wallaces' Farmer polls the farmers of Iowa bi-weekly and the Des Moines Register polls all groups in the state weekly. Wallaces' poll of May 15, 1943, for example, showed the discrepancy of farmer opinion and farm bloc policies. The National Opinion Research Center polls of March and June, 1943, dealt with internationalism. The Fortune poll often reports farm responses; see particularly the issues of April, 1940 and April, 1943. Gallup's reports are too numerous for detailed citation. The last three polls are cumulated in the Public Opinion Quarterly.

11. RICE, S. A., *Farmers and Workers in American Politics* (New York: Columbia University, 1924). This is still the most comprehensive monograph, but it needs to be brought up to date.

12. SCHULTZ, T. W., *Redirecting Farm Policy* (New York: Macmillan, 1943). Readers interested in economic phases of policy will find here a compact portrayal of the impasse in recent American policy.

13. SOROKIN, P. A., ZIMMERMAN, C. C., and GALPIN, C. J., *Source Book in Rural Sociology*, 3 vols. (Minneapolis: University of Minnesota, 1930-32). There is no comparable analysis and collection of readings on all phases of rural life, knowledge of which is required for understanding the political behavior of farmers.

14. TAYLOR, C. C., *Rural Sociology in its Economic, Historical and Psychological Aspects* (New York: Harper, 1933 ed.). The chapter on farmers' organizations is a most compact and perceptive treatment of all kinds of American movements. The author will soon publish a monograph on farmers' movements.

15. WARRINER, D., *Economics of Peasant Farming* (New York: Oxford, 1939). While limited as its title indicates, this survey of European farming types is valuable for its demonstration of the importance of other factors than land in determining peasant welfare and for its unusual treatment of Russian collectivization.

CHAPTER XI

MODERN UNIVERSALISM

MULFORD Q. SIBLEY

In what follows I shall examine the nature of modern universalism—the problem of enlarging the scope of community—as reflected, first, in humanitarianism; second, in the context of theories of progress; third, in the contrast between internationalism and cosmopolitanism; and finally, in the major tenets of pacifism. Quite obviously, such a discussion cannot be exhaustive—for the conflict between particularist and universalist ideologies has ramifications which touch on all phases of speculative endeavor. But an examination of this type can at least be illustrative.

HUMANITARIANISM

Humanitarianism is not exclusively a modern phenomenon—the ancient protests against gladiatorial combats rooted in a similar sentiment, for example—but it is probably safe to maintain that in no other period of the world's history has consciousness of, and concern for, human, indeed for all sentient suffering, been so widespread as during the past century and a half.[1] Characteristically, humanitariansm is optimistic regarding the future of humanity and particularly concerned for its physical well being. Spontaneous relief of hardships, protection of the weak by means of legislation, and a feeling of kinship with other animal life are marks of the modern humanitarian. Not infrequently his humanitarianism with relation to one object will conflict with humane attitudes toward another. Thus, he may

---

[1] See Crane Brinton, "Humanitarianism," *Encyclopaedia of the Social Sciences*, and Maurice Parmelee, "The Rise of Modern Humanitarianism," *American Journal of Sociology*, Vol. XXI (1915-16), pp. 345-59.

be an anti-vivisectionist and at the same time be genuinely concerned about the reduction of human suffering caused by disease. Politically, the humanitarian would distrust pleas which argue that large segments of the world's population must be starved, for example, in order to establish world order. Thus, during the Second World War the provisioning of starving populations residing in occupied territories, even at the risk of aiding indirectly the military enemy, became a leading plea of the humanitarian.

Three illustrations of modern humanitarianism immediately occur to one—nineteenth and twentieth century movements against slavery; the widespread consideration of the criminal's lot; and, to a degree not frequently realized, the growth of ideas which would more clearly define the duties of human society in relation to the beasts.

The history and ideology of the anti-slavery movement are well-known.[2] Here it need only be emphasized that all types of general political opinion have been associated with it—Tory, Liberal, and Socialist—a phenomenon which well illustrates the fact that what we call humanitarian sentiments have been held by men of the most varied social philosophies.

As for the growth of humanitarian sentiment with respect to the criminal, it need only be recalled that only about a century and a half ago, more than two hundred crimes were still punishable by death in Great Britain. Religious humanitarianism as represented by such groups as the Quakers, the philosophy of utilitarianism developed in Great Britain and the United States, and Continental European rationalism, have all had their part to play in prison reform and in century-long efforts to ameliorate the general lot of the criminal. In the twentieth century, of course, the decline of humanitarianism has not been without its effect here, as elsewhere. Capital punishment, for example, which for a time seemed to be on the way out, is being

---

[2] For accounts of the debate concerning the relation of a universalist ethic to slavery, see R. Coupland, *The British Anti-Slavery Movement* (London: Thornton Butterworth, 1933), and Earl L. Griggs, *Thomas Clarkson, the Friend of Slaves* (London: G. Allen & Unwin, 1936).

revived; and the general insecurity characteristic of the times, accompanied as it is by a decline in humanitarian professions, would seem to support the contentions of those who argue that humanitarian ideology flourishes only in times of relative prosperity and political security.

Reacting against the prevalent mechanistic theories of the seventeenth century which tended to think of beasts as merely machines with no emotional kinship to humanity, modern theories of the relationship between men and beasts have seen humanity and the beastly realm as bound by common suffering and in some respects a common destiny. The Earl of Shaftesbury, in 1711,[3] Adam Smith,[4] Francis Hutcheson,[5] and Jeremy Bentham [6] laid the groundwork for nineteenth and twentieth century conceptions.[7] Whether in theories of progress such as that of T. H. Huxley or in cosmopolitan politics such as that sketched out in H. G. Wells' *Men Like Gods* [8] there is an intimate connection between what one might call a horizontal extension of the idea of community to embrace all mankind politically, and a vertical extension, which would endow the beasts with many of the attributes of citizenship in that community.

The critics of humanitarianism have alleged, that it is by its nature ineffective in making fundamental changes. Because it is concerned with the immediate relief of suffering, it does not see that the nature of the world requires stern discipline and hardship for the effectuation of basic social and political organi-

---

[3] *Characteristics* (London: 1732).

[4] *Theory of Moral Sentiments* (London: Cadell and Davies, 1812).

[5] *A Short Introduction to Moral Philosophy* (Glasgow: Robert and Andrew Foulis, 1772), Bk. II, Chap. V, Section II.

[6] *Principles of Morals and Legislation* (Oxford: Clarendon Press, 1859), Chap. XVII, Section IV, pp. 310-311.

[7] For a good general account of the development of conceptions of beastly-human relations in a vital period see Dix Harwood, *Love for Animals and How It Developed in Great Britain* (New York: Columbia University Press, 1928).

[8] On Huxley see particularly his *Evolution and Ethics and Other Essays* (New York: D. Appleton and Company, 1899). On Wells, see Section III of this essay.

zation. Humanitarianism is thus short-sighted when it approaches the realities of politics.[9]

These observations involve questions of moral philosophy into which, unfortunately, we cannot go here.

II.
PROGRESS TO UNIVERSAL HARMONY

The idea of progress itself is a comparatively modern conception;[10] and the belief that the abolition of war, the establishment of a world harmony, and the spread of benevolence even into the beastly realm, were possible, is consequently a recent development. As with Condorcet in the eighteenth century,[11] not a few nineteenth and twentieth century writers seemed to imply not only that it was possible to bring about this Isaiah-like Elysium, but that it was inevitable. One might hasten the process by observing the "natural law" of progress; but even if one "violated" that "law" Progress would somehow have its way and a world of harmony would inevitably descend. The idea of original sin, so prominent in traditional Christian theology, is almost completely absent; and a reorganization of human political systems will allow the "law" to work without difficulty. Indeed, with one or two exceptions, few have ventured to criticize the general idea of progress even to this day.

It is possible to discern three contexts in which what might be called the universalist idea of progress has been elaborated. The first may be termed the Liberal, because it is associated with certain aspects of nineteenth and early twentieth century liberalism; the second is the biological, because it utilized the language of Darwinian or pseudo-Darwinian speculation; while the third is best denominated the proletarian, because of its association

---

[9] See Irving Babbit, "Humanists and Humanitarians," *Nation*, v.c. (1913), pp. 677-80, 704-06, and v. cl. (1915), pp. 288-89.

[10] J. B. Bury, *The Idea of Progress* (London: Macmillan, 1921).

[11] For his conception of a progress leading to the enthronement of the idea of Humanity and the subordination of all particular interests to that idea ,see his *Esquisse d'un Tableau Historique des Progrès de L'Esprit Humain* (Nouvelle Edition, Paris: 1797).

with conceptions closely identified with Karl Marx and his successors. Since the third is considered elsewhere in this book, no endeavor will be made to deal with it here.

1. *The Liberal Theory*

The general Liberal conception of progress stems from the rationalism of the eighteenth century. Appeal to men's reason and cast off all aspects of economic and political organization which inhibit its development, and the result will be peace and harmony throughout the world. On the whole, the Liberal idea of progress emphasizes the role of the economic in the achievement of its goal; and it is inclined to look with suspicion on the State. While admitting the need for political organization in an harmonious world, it trusts to a considerable degree the supposedly automatic law of a free economic world.

In part, its genesis can be discerned in the growth of the organized peace movement of the nineteenth century, which arose partly as an expression of the horror with which men viewed the cruelties of the Napoleonic Wars. Groups like the British Society for the Promotion of Permanent and Universal Peace gave impetus, no doubt, to schemes for the peaceful settlement of international disputes; for those proposals began to be made now with ever-increasing detail. International arbitration, conciliation, and even legislative and judicial bodies, were confidently proposed in the hundred years preceding the outbreak of the war of 1914, as steps in a process toward universal harmony, which tended to be looked upon as inevitable in any event.[12]

One conception of peace contended that free trade would automatically result in an era of harmony. A phase of the extreme *laissez-faire* philosophy of the nineteenth century, this view maintained that harmony would return to the world when men returned to "nature"—that is, to a state of affairs where

---

[12] Such schemes, for example, as William Ladd's *Essay on a Congress of Nations,* published in 1840, which sketched out an international organization embracing both legislative and judicial organs. For a general history of the peace movement see, A. C. F. Beales, *History of Peace* (New York: L. MacVeagh, Dial Press, 1941).

government is reduced to a bare minimum of action and men are free to seek their personal economic ends without interference. The expansion of trade which would ensue, both within and among nations, would, it was argued, promote such a degree of interdependence that men would no longer fight: their immediate interests would be too obviously impaired thereby. In examining the writings of such men as John Bright and Richard Cobden, for example, one is treated to the spectacle of the almost limitless growth of commerce, not only between the so-called civilized parts of the world, but also between "civilized" and "barbaric".[13] With commerce would come wealth, with the leisure which wealth provided, invention, with invention, greater production, which would in turn ensure yet greater commerce —and the circle would be re-initiated. Eventually, somehow, this process would inevitably propel the world in the direction of that minimum political organization which was grudgingly admitted to be necessary; but fundamentally peace was to enshroud the world because men were left "free" to pursue their own "personal" interests.

This particular application of the liberal theory of progress was at one time very widespread in Great Britain and the United States, and even in the twentieth century is not without at least implicit supporters.[14]

But with the twentieth century, the Liberal emphasis has shifted to a different area. It still remains essentially individualist in its general outlook, but is concerned primarily with demonstrating that many of the popular assumptions concerning international conflict are fallacious—particularly the assumption that war benefits any people economically. The most prominent exponent of this contention has been Sir Norman Angell.

To begin with, he maintains, the entities which gain or lose in warfare are *individuals*, and not *nations*. Ruthlessly he strips away the verbiage surrounding such expressions as "na-

---

[13] For an elaboration of Cobden's conception of progress see John A. Hobson, *Richard Cobden: the International Man* (New York: Henry Holt, 1919).

[14] For example, Cordell Hull, Secretary of State during the presidency of Franklin D. Roosevelt.

tional interests" or "national economic advantage" or "the fruits of victory". In his own words, he attempts to demonstrate [15] that the commerce and industry of a people no longer depend upon the expansion of its political frontiers; that a nation's political and economic frontiers do not now necessarily coincide; that military power is socially and economically futile, and can have no relation to the prosperity of the people exercising it; that it is impossible for one nation to seize by force the wealth or trade of another—to enrich itself by subjugations, or imposing its will by force on another; that, in short, war, even when victorious, can no longer achieve those aims for which peoples strive.

In the realm of territorial expansion, for example, he seeks to show that there is no discernible positive correlation between geographical size and individual incomes. In every instance, he contends, where (as in Great Britain), the per capita income is high in comparison with a smaller "power" (Bulgaria, for example), the cause can be shown to be, not the vast area of political control exercised by the former, but other factors largely unconnected with it. Contrariwise, many of the so-called "fourth-rate" powers, such as Denmark, afford far better livelihoods to their citizens than those nation-States whose vast expanse is said to bring to their citizens great wealth (Russia, for instance).

Conquest cannot benefit the victor. For without a cooperative population the resources which he desires to exploit will be useless; and if he should kill a large percentage of the "enemy" country's people, the market for his own goods will thereby be destroyed, or at least greatly reduced. To impose slavery on the conquered country is equally no solution, for slave labor is notoriously less productive than free labor.

The general tenor of the Angellian argument is to underline the importance of alignments which cross national boundaries, and concomitantly to reduce the role of military power in the promotion of economic well-being to zero. The interests

---

[15] *The Great Illusion* (New York: Putnam, 1933), pp. 59-60.

which workmen in Germany have in common with laborers in Great Britain are far more real than the ties which bind a member of the *junker* class to a Berlin carpenter, for example. True art by its nature must ignore national boundaries; and military might becomes an irrelevance, even a hindrance, for its maintenance.

The conclusions which he derived from his argument were for the most part negative. *If* men could be convinced that warfare would never achieve welfare, the world would probably evolve spontaneously in the direction of a sort of "peaceful anarchy", where, the implications of interdependence having been understood, nation-States would simply cease to use their power in military expeditions against one another.[16] Later, it is true, he comes to a more positive political implementation, and the element of automaticity is reduced; but he remains, nevertheless, in the tradition of the liberal theory of progress.

The Liberal conception of progress, including the doctrines of Norman Angell, have been criticized from a number of points of view in the twentieth century. It has been contended by Brailsford that the Liberals and their twentieth century successors failed to understand fully that, while "free trade in goods is an interest consistent with humanity",[17] when capital is exported from an industrial to an undeveloped country, imperialism, and hence war, cannot be far away. The Liberal theory of progress really represented particular interests which could best profit in a regime of peace; but when capital is sent abroad to "unexploited lands, those same interests discover that war may be useful in maintaining their investments—their privileged position. J. A. Hobson [18] is in substantial agreement with Brailsford: both point out that there is a positive correlation between imperialist expansion in the nineteenth century and the increase in exportation of capital, but no such relation between growth of trade

---

[16] In the 1933 edition, he admits that this was a "possible" implication of the original work as published in 1908. See pp. 53-54.

[17] H. B. Brailsford, *The War of Steel and Gold* (London: H. Bell and Sons, 1917).

[18] *Imperialism* (London: 1902).

and expansion. An obvious criticism of Norman Angell's thesis, then, is that while he points out correctly that conquest does not "pay", in the sense that the great mass of citizens benefit from it, it does definitely "pay", at least in the short run, if only the "interests" of a small group of investors be considered.[19]

A second major criticism of the Angellian thesis has been offered by R. G. Hawtrey,[20] when he points out that power, and hence the extension of sovereignty in the international sphere, is sought not only as a means to the end of general welfare but also desired as an end in itself. Economic well-being is cast aside in favor of the power of the State. While it is true that war does not benefit the great mass of men, the reason for the persistence of war is not only the non-recognition of that contention, but also the fact that political institutions as now established make it impossible to set up economic well-being as the end. Politics are anterior to economics, and not the reverse; power is both an end and a means. This Angell did not seem to understand.

2. *The Biological Evolutionists*

Probably the most persistent argument which modern universalists since the time Darwin have had to combat is the assertion that violent struggle, especially between Nation-States, is inevitable and even desirable because of certain biological "laws" which presumably apply in the area of politics. Walter Bagehot, Edward Grant Conklin, Karl Pearson, Sir Arthur Keith, and many others have elaborated this contention and so popularized it that comparatively few are acquainted with the literature which seeks to disprove it. The controversy has been, then, between the biological "particularists" and the universalists.

No member of the universalist school denies the reality of struggle, either in the past or at present; either in a cosmic "natural" sense or as specifically applicable to man. Thus, to T. H. Huxley, the development of Humanity in early days is a [22]

---

[19] *The War of Steel and Gold,* p. 164.

[20] *Economic Aspects of Sovereignty* (London: Logmans, Green and Co., 1930).

[22] *Evolution and Ethics and Other Essays* (New York: Appleton, 1899), p. 204.

continual free fight, and beyond the limited and temporary relations of the family, the Hobbesian war of each against all was the normal state of existence. The human species, like others, plashed and floundered amid the general stream of evolution, keeping its head above water as best it might, and thinking neither of whence nor whither. Spencer likewise asserts the never-ending violence of most past politics;[23] and his disciple, Benjamin Kidd, echoes him in different terminology.[24]

It is Jacques Novicow, however, who carries out the idea of universal struggle to the farthest extent—as a framework within which he foresees the eventual unification of the human race in peace and order. The whole universe, animate and inanimate, terrestrial and celestial, is a product of a struggle. For the universe consists of an infinite number of atoms "animated by perpetual movement and occupying limitless space".[25] Atoms form themselves into molecules, and these in turn into more complex systems. Diffused throughout space, none are eternal. They are perpetually combining, and recombining. The whole solar system is, in fact, an illustration of this conflict of bodies. At present they travel what are apparently permanent courses, but if a new body comes within the solar system, a crisis occurs. If the new entity is feeble it will be absorbed by the body which it strikes; on the other hand, if it is larger than the solar system, it will necessarily absorb the latter, and the old individualities which once composed it will be changed.

Now this general pattern is to be discovered throughout all the universe. All bodies are at war, so to speak, with other bodies. Some are being defeated constantly, while others as regularly are victors. The losers of the battle are absorbed—form new associations with the victors—and the battle begins anew.

---

[23] Herbert Spencer, *Principles of Sociology* (3 volumes, New York. D. Appleton & Co., 1890), II, Chap. I, Nos. 437-439.

[24] *The Science of Power* (New York: Putnam, 1918), pp. 204, 163-64.

[25] Jacques Novicow, *Les Luttes Entre Sociétés Humaines et Leurs Phases Successives* (Paris: Ancienne Libraire Germer Baillière, 1896), p. 2. Novicow's ideas are, of course, a part of that general stream of modern political thought founded upon a conception now no longer prevalent in physics—a conception which saw the universe as simply as infinite number of atoms in motion.

In the meantime, however, the new association has begun to differentiate within itself and a division of labor is the result. Animals are associations of cells of an extreme degree of complexity, and struggle amongst themselves, absorbing and reabsorbing, just as do atoms, molecules, and the units of the solar system. The result of this perpetual struggle among them is eventually the formation of new associations in the same manner as that prevailing elsewhere. Families, herds, flocks, States, and confederations constitute but the continuation of the process of a struggle, defeat, and agglomeration which occurs in Nature; in fact, they are a part of one and the same process. Atoms will forever struggle for existence; never will be state of definite equilibrium be reached, for matter by definition is movement, movement is struggle, and if struggle should cease, matter would no longer exist.

Applying this general doctrine to human societies the struggles between those societies select those which are best adapted to their environment, or, in other words, those which have the truest conception of the universe. For a nation, taken in its broad sense, is only an idea of the universe.

But the universalists' conception of struggle differs radically from that of those who used "Darwinism" to plead the inevitability and desirability of war. It differs in two respects: (a) the universalists deny that Nature is as "red in tooth and claw" as the apologists for particularism would maintain; and (b) even if it be admitted that there is a large element of waste and bloodshed in the "natural" struggle, the essence of the human community is such as to provide the potentiality for their abolition. Nature, it is maintained, does not know war as a method of struggle, except in the case of *homo sapiens* and the social insects. Wolves do not usually fight other wolves, or lions other lions. Intra-species warfare, therefore, is the exception rather than the rule. Instead, the struggle proceeds rather by adaptation: survival or failure to survive against the competition of "nature".[26]

But withal there is a terrible wastage in "nature". And it is just here that the potentialities of the human community differ from those of the "natural" order. For, as T. H. Huxley points out, while the cosmic process—Nature—demands self-assertion, the ethical process (which he postulates as that which emerges with man from the purely animal state), demands self-restraint.[27] It is not the task of man in society to conform to the cosmic prowess, but, like the Stoics, to combat it.

For most of the universalists, therefore, the struggle, while not exactly of the character often pictured—and, indeed, existing parallel to the widespread practice of cooperation—[28] becomes transformed radically when it reaches the human community. For Novicow, this is expressed in terms of time, for he looks upon his universal struggle as being essentially an endeavor to move more and more rapidly: to discard the slower and therefore irrational forms of conflict. Eventually, intellectual conflict is substituted for all other forms, and the process of history is seen to be but a clumsy effort to reach that goal.[29] War is not a eugenic device for the preservation of the more fit; but rather a dysgenic institution which preserves the least fit—and an extremely wasteful mode of carrying out the evolutionary process.[30]

T. H. Huxley himself has probably stated best the goal which thinkers of this school see for the history of the human

[26] See, for example, G. F. Nicolai, *The Biology of War* (translation by Constance A. and Julian Grande, New York: Century, 1918); P. Chalmers Mitchell, *Evolution and War* (London: John Murray, 1915); and Novicow's analysis, especially in *War and Its Alleged Benefits*, English translation by Thomas Seltzer (New York: Henry Holt, 1911). Physiologically, economically, intellectually, politically, and morally, Novicow points out, the pretended benefits of war vanish on analysis.

[27] *Evolution and Ethics*, p. 82.

[28] See the works of Prince Kropotkin, especially *Mutual Aid: A Factor of Evolution* (London: William Heinemann, 1910), for illustrations. Darwin himself pointed this out, but then Darwin was not a Darwinian.

[29] See *Les Luttes*, pp. 402-404, where he attempts to chart out graphically his idea of progress to the universal community.

[30] See especially the words of David Starr Jordan.

race. It is, he states, "an ideal *civitas Dei;* a state when, every man having reached the point of absolute self-negation, and having nothing but moral perfection to strive after, peace will truly reign, not merely among nations, but among men, and the struggle for existence will be at an end." [31]

III.
INTERNATIONALISM AND COSMOPOLITANISM

1. *Internationalism*

Internationalism may be said to be the postulation of a community in which the primary constituent entities will be Nation-States.[32] It asserts the value of the Nation-State culturally and politically—nationalism is not to be destroyed, but rather to find its fullest expression in internationalism. Thus, when Mazzini, the Italian patriot, came to expound his political ideas, he made the Nation-State the intermediary between the individual and Humanity; the entity to which the individual must look for a definition of his duties, and at the same time the organism through which the idea of Humanity could most vividly be transmitted to the individual.[33]

The general position of the internationalist may best be understood by examining what it involves in three different spheres—the more narrowly cultural, the legal, and the political.

In the first, that which has reference to the artistic and literary life, the internationalist emphasizes the necessity for the maintenance of wide variations; for only thus can all possible *nuances* of beauty and truth ever hope to find expression. And those diversities within the human race can best be encouraged by the continuance of historic national cultures, each of which

---

[31] *Evolution and Ethics,* p. 209.

[32] For a brief history of international thought see F. Melian Stawell, *The Growth of International Thought* (London: Thornton Butterworth, 1929). Christian Lange, *Histoire de l'Internationalisme* (Christiana: 1919) might also be consulted.

[33] Giuseppe Mazzini, *The Duties of Man and Other Essays* (New York: Dutton, 1915).

constitutes a matrix, so to speak, within which genius flowers. Abolish the comparatively intimate life of the national community (and a certain measure of political independence is necessary to maintain it), and artistic creativity is discouraged because it has no well-articulated cultural nexus with which it can associate. The world as a whole, it is argued, is too large and too remote to capture the imaginations of men: and without imagination genius cannot reach its apex.

From the viewpoint of law, the internationalist sees the world as a society of *nations,* and not a society of men. Incidentally, men come within the purview, and are affected by, international law. But that law is primarily concerned with the public relations of Nation-States. The whole development of the idea of international arbitration, not to speak of the theoretical bases of the Permanent Court of International Justice, illustrates this point.

Finally, in the political sphere, internationalist thought assumes the continuance of Nation-States as separate entities. Ideally, the boundaries of every State should be exactly coterminous with the limits of every "nation". Thus, when Woodrow Wilson, perhaps the most articulate internationalist the twentieth century has produced, enunciated his principles for a just peace, the idea of "self-determination" of peoples along presumably national lines was clearly stated.[34] In conformity with this theme, the political organs of the League of Nations acted only through and upon individual human beings. "Sanctions" for the prevention of aggression were to be carried out against Nation-States as entities, not against individual offenders. Votes in the political organization were to be cast by States and each State was to be the equal of every other. Unanimity was generally required.

Eventually, then, the internationalist looks forward to a community of Nation-States, each one of which will constitute a "person" within the wider society. While some internationalists believe that this community will have to be achieved through

---

[34] Cf. *The Public Papers of Woodrow Wilson: War and Peace, I* (New York: Harper, 1927), pp. 160-161.

the medium of regionalism—that is, internationalism on a regional basis must be made effective before it can be made universal [35] the end-result is substantially the same.

The official statements published by British and American statesmen during the first four years of the second World War seem to imply a nationalist-internationalist view of the world. Nation-States "raped" and "violated" by the "aggressor" are to be restored; and the right of "self-determination" of peoples is in theory exalted. In this official philosophy is witnessed the same tendency observable during the first World War.[36]

2. *Cosmopolitanism*

Cosmopolitanism is a criticism of internationalism. The values of independent nationhood which to the internationalist are so important are to the cosmopolitan undesirable. The distinction between internationalism and cosmopolitanism is thus fundamental. While the former envisions a society of nations, the latter looks forward to a society of men. While the former emphasizes the value of national States in the cultural sphere, the latter either minimizes it or is definitely hostile. On the legal side, the complete achievement of a cosmopolitan order would imply the destruction of international law; on the po-

---

[35] See, for example, R. F. Coudenhove-Kalegri, *Pan-Europe* (New York: Knopf, 1926); and Edouard Herriot, *The United States of Europe* (translated by R. J. Dingh, New York: Viking, 1930).

[36] Most of the "plans" for post-war reconstruction which have been prepared in the Second World War, are essentially international in tenor. For the most part, they recognize the need for a world structure which will permit peaceful change, provide equal economic opportunities for all "nations," and lead to a gradual reduction of armaments. But most of them are amazingly vague about the exact nature of the political organization required, implying, however—with some exceptions to be noted in the next section—that the primary units of governance are to remain nation-States. For contemporary pronouncements see the Preliminary Report of the Commission to Study the Organization of Peace, James T. Shotwell, editor, *International Conciliation*, No. 569 (New York: Carnegie Endowment for International Peace, April, 1941); William P. Maddox, *European Plans for World Order* (Philadelphia: American Academy of Political and Social Science, March, 1940); Commission to Study Bases of Just and Durable Peace of Federal Council of Churches, *A Just and Durable Peace—Data Material and Discussion Questions* (New York: Federal Council of Churches, April, 1941). But see C. E. M. Joad, *The Philosophy of Federalism* (London: Macmillan, 1941).

litical, the removal of the last vestige of nationalism in political
organization.

From one point of view the cosmopolitan is highly individualistic: distrusting all groups save the human race taken as
a unit, he sees himself as an entity confronted by the whole of
humanity—with the beasts, perhaps, as associate members—un-
mediated through nation or class or even family.

The full implications of the cosmopolitan idea can best be
understood if we examine briefly the conceptions of its most
prolific twentieth-century apologist, H. G. Wells.[37]

For him the problem of a future universal society revolves
about the possibility of a scientific elite arising to obliterate all
national and class divisions. On occasion it is simply the engineers, physicists, and chemists, who, disgusted with the irrationality of class and national conflict, use their crucial position
to assume power and impose rationality. At other times, the
"forward-looking" intellectuals of the world unite in what is
called an "open conspiracy" with a definite program of action
and an embryonic government, which, at the strategic moment,
takes charge of the affairs of the world after the bankruptcy of
the old national governments is clearly demonstrated.[38] Yet
again similar sensitive souls discover God the Invisble King,
who, associated as he is with the Spirit of Humanity, guides the
dull-witted and inspires the intelligent to achieve the World
State.[39]

Despite his reliance on reason, Wells despairs of its ability
to catch up with catastrophe. The nature of that final conflagra-
tion is not certain, but it may reduce the human race, both in

---

[37] Wells' *Experiment in Autobiography* (New York: Macmillan, 1934) is perhaps the clearest account of the growth of the cosmopolitan idea in an individual,
as his famous *Outline of History* (2 volumes, New York: 1920) is one of the
best modern interpretations of history from the cosmopolitan point of view. See
also M. H. Boehm, "Cosmopolitanism," in *Encyclopaedia of the Social Sciences,*
IV, p. 460.

[38] *The Open Conspiracy: Blue Prints for a World Revolution* (Garden City:
Doubleday Doran, 1928).

[39] *God the Invisible King* (New York: Macmillan, 1917).

numbers and in culture, to a status it has not known since the days of the cave man.[40]

A rationalistic humanist, Wells sets hardly any limit on the possibilities of producing economic goods and of human attainment in the cultural realm. In his most famous blue-print, *A Modern Utopia*,[41] the World State is a universal socialist commonwealth under the leadership of an intellectual elite known as the *samurai*. At first this governing group is a comparatively small part of the community; but with the spread of education and the achievement of complete political unification, the rigid tests for entrance into its closed order can be passed by an increasingly large portion of the world's population, until at last the *samurai* become practically co-terminous with the sum total of human beings.

In his most developed picture of what political, social, and economic unification can bring, *Men Like Gods*,[42] the traditional State itself has been cast off like the skin of a rattlesnake —but never to reappear. The world becomes "so unified, so understanding, so clarified and harmonized, that its advancing welfare and the vigour and happiness of the individuals reflect and complement each other".[43] Other-worldliness is to be replaced by a sort of social mysticism: "We shall live in the All and the All will live in each of us." [44]

The cosmopolitan theme has been re-played in limited form by such men as Clarence Streit,[45] who looks forward to a genuine federal union, first of the so-called democratic nations and ultimately, perhaps, of the world. Oscar Newfang, long before

[40] See, for example, *The War in the Air* (New York: Macmillan, 1908), and *The Shape of Things to Come* (New York: Macmillan, 1938).

[41] (London: Chapman and Hall, 1905).

[42] (New York: Macmillan, 1923).

[43] *The Anatomy of Frustration* (New York: Macmillan, 1936), pp. 93-94.

[44] *Ibid.*

[45] *Union Now* (New York: Harper, 1940). For a criticism of this work from the viewpoint of what the author calls socialism, see John Strachey, *Federalism or Socialism?* (London: Gallancz, 1940).

Streit, had sketched out a similar scheme.[46] Insofar as conceptions like these throw overboard the conception of national
States as primary entities in a world system, they may be termed
"cosmopolitan". But their limitations as compared with the
more elaborate suggestions of Wells and perhaps H. N. Brailsford [47] should be pointed out. Proposals like those of Streit and
Newfang confine themselves largely to legal and political statistics. They make no attempt to elaborate a theory of political
change in the context of the world problem, such as for example, one will find in certain of the writings of Harold Lasswell. They do not discuss the problem of political psychology—
for example, what social "myth" will constitute the best rally-
ing point around which, all lesser myths becoming subordinate,
the World State can be built.[48] They do not raise or attempt
to answer the very important questions which the necessity for
a common world *ethos* makes imperative. Nor do they pose the
problem of whether the world can unite in the absence of some
external opponent against whom its divisive factions could find
common ground. This is an issue which André Maurois thinks
a serious one; and he attempts to solve it by suggesting that if
humanity could be made to believe it was being attacked by
the moon, it might develop its sense of solidarity and the necessary institutions.[49]

But the cosmopolitan world has not been immune to the
thrusts of these critics who fear that unity in politics and economic organization might, if not guarded with extreme care,
lead to uniformity and lack of spontaneity in life as a whole.
A cosmopolitan order, they argue, in surrendering completely
to the ideal of conscious planning on a world-wide scale, might
well become a huge machine in which variety, other than that
officially planned by the World State, would wither away and

---

[46] In *The United States of the World* (New York: Putnam, 1930).

[47] In *Olives of Endless Age* (New York: 1928).

[48] See, for a discussion of this question, Harold Lasswell, *World Politics and
Personal Insecurity* (New York: McGraw-Hill, 1935).

[49] André Maurois, *The Next Chapter: The War Against the Moon* (New York:
Dutton, 1928).

die. The spirit of these criticisms has been captured in the twentieth century by Aldous Huxley who, with inimitable satire, has pointed out the horrors of living in a polity where human embryos are developed in bottles; where orgiastic exercises symbolize the complete absorption of the individual in the "all-in-all" which is the World State; and where individuals are so "conditioned" by the rulers as to remove the last elements of spontaneity.[50]

IV.

PACIFISM

To some the growth of pacifist thought spells the degeneracy of the human race.[51] To others it is looked upon as a sign of intellectual and moral vigor. But most would at least agree, probably, that its doctrines found a comparatively wide audience in the third and fourth decades of the twentieth century, when war and bloodshed were leaving their indelible imprints upon the consciousness of men.

Most critics usually distinguish between two different types of pacifism—the religious and the secular. The first couches its doctrines in the terminology of religious thought—whether that thought be Hindu, Buddhist, or Christian; while the latter uses language usually associated with psychology, sociology, secular philosophy, and political science. The underlying conceptions

[50] *Brave New World* (New York: Harper, 1932). One of the most beautiful discussions of what Plato might have termed the *idea* of separate nationhood as contrasted with the idea of a cosmopolitan order will be found in AE (George Russell), *The Interpreters* (New York: Macmillan, 1923).

[51] See, for example, Oswald Spengler, *The Decline of the West: Perspectives in World History* (translation by Charles F. Atkinson, 2 volumes, New York: Knopf, 1928), and William McDougall, *Ethics and Some Modern World Problems* (New York: Putnam, 1924). The former, of course, couches the thesis of degeneracy in historical language; while the latter employs psychological. Both, as might be expected, bracket cosmopolitanism with pacifism.

of both types are essentially the same, however, and a single analysis will, therefore, be largely applicable to both.[52]

War, pacifism contends, is an act so grossly incompatible with the achievement of harmony and a measure of equality, that none of the ideals which universalists share can ever be attained unless war as a method is abandoned. Historically, the pacifist points out, universalists have not been unwilling to utilize war in order to gain their ends; and the result has been for the most part, the perversion of those ends and the utter frustration of those who sought them. Slavery was an evil to the humanitarian of the twentieth century, and he was willing to use war to "abolish" it, but it is doubtful if the legal abolition of slavery effected during the Civil War was not more than counter-balanced by certain undesirable results flowing from that military conflict. Would the one-party system have fastened itself upon the South, for example, had it not been for the war? Would social inequality have been as great?

But why does war thus always tend to betray those who would use it for good ends? Primarily, because it cannot be conducted without turning upside down the system of values which humanitarians and universalists generally endorse. What is deprecated in the universalist view of life must be exalted in war; and what is exalted in humanitarian philosophies must be denounced in war. In war, killing becomes a virtue, and an over-tender conscience in relation to the enemy a vice; lying is made essential, truth-telling a hindrance; humility is frowned upon, vain boasting encouraged; hatred is subsidized, love (for the "enemy") anathematized. And the longer the war continues, the more firmly entrenched does this topsy-turvy system of values become; until at the end of the conflict the world is

---

[52] One of the best recent apologies for religious pacifism will be found in C. J. Cadoux, *Christian Pacifism Re-examined* (Oxford, England: Basil Blackwell, 1940). For a secular pacifist argument, with a bias in the direction of philosophical anarchism, see Bart. de Ligt, *The Conquest of Violence* (translation from the French by Honor Tracy, New York: Dutton, 1938). A recent general article is Mulford Q. Sibley, "The Political Theories of Modern Religious Pacifism," *American Political Science Review*, Vol. XXXVII (1943), pp. 439-454.

fortunate if it can create an order even approaching the justice and equity of that which existed before the war.

This is the negative statement of the pacifist position; and the inference is drawn that those who hold this view cannot possibly support any war, no matter what its avowed ends may be. Pacifists, therefore, refuse to perform any military service, although just what may be deemed to be military service—beyond actual fighting in the front lines—is interpreted variously by different individuals.

Pacifism has often been criticized on the ground that it is essentially an individual protest, individual non-cooperation, and hence, largely futile politically. Ethically it may be a satisfactory position; but politically, the critics maintain, it must remain largely ineffective. This criticism is justified with reference to many proponents of the pacifist position who have not thought through the political implications of their position. But it would be unfair to assert that modern pacifism does not see the political problem which it confronts. How can it be made effective politically? How, in other words, can it envision a pacifist State?

The pacifist answer to these questions takes the form of a theory of socio-political conflict which would, while eliminating the frustration inherent in the method of violence, yet provide a means for the attainment of the universalist society. Closely associated with the philosophy of Mohandas K. Gandhi and others sharing his general outlook, the pacifist means have been variously termed "non-violent coercion",[53] "war without violence,"[54] "passive resistance," or simply "non-violence."[5] Depending upon the situation involved, it might take the form of protest, of mass-meeting, of political agitation, of industrial

---

[53] C. M. Case, *Non-Violent Coercion* (New York: Century Co., 1923).

[54] Krishnalal Shridharani, *War Without Violence* (New York: Harcourt Brace, 1939). This is a study to some extent of Gandhi's general philosophy, as well as of the technique of the Indian Nationalist movement.

[55] Richard M. Gregg, *The Power of Non-Violence* (Philadelphia & London: Lippincott, 19355).

strikes, or of civil disobedience.[56] But whatever the means, violence must be eschewed. The means themselves are not original with those who call themselves "pacifists"—they have been used throughout recorded history and in modern times have a particularly close affinity to the ideology of the strike; but it is the pacifist who has seized upon them, developed them for his own purposes, and theorized about them to a much greater degree than others.

It should be emphasized that pacifism is not merely a protest against international war, but a repudiation of all violence in achieving socio-political goals. Revolutions, armed insurrections, civil wars, and even violent language must be renounced.[57] Pacifists must be organized and submit to discipline. Indeed, their training must be more rigorous than that of the army. Then, when they confront those who oppose them in the political sphere, their opposition will be wholly pacific—and hence immeasurably more effective than violent opposition could possibly be. The opponent will be utterly confused when he finds his armies, his armed police, and his strong men answered, not in kind, but by firm individuals who offer no physical resistance but who, on the other hand, refuse to obey the violent organization's orders to do what the non-violent resisters regard as evil.[58] Violent organization is at a tremendous disadvantage; it knows how to answer opposing violence, but its prestige will disintegrate when it discovers that it cannot provoke its opponents to physical resistance. Eventually, it will have to give up the attempt, and, by process of negotiation with the non-violent resisters, settle the controversy.[59]

---

[56] For the student of American political thought Thoreau's classic, *Civil Disobedience,* is an exposition worth careful reading.

[57] Gandhi particularly emphasizes language. For the development of his pacifist philosophy, see his *The Story of My Experiments with Truth* (Ahmedabad, India: 1927).

[58] Gregg, *op. cit.*

[59] This statement undoubtedly recalls to many minds Shelley's great poem, *The Mask of Anarchy.*

Pacifism thus should not be confused with passivism. Pacifism advocates—indeed, insists upon—resistance to what is looked upon as inequitable or as morally wrong. But the resistance must not be violent. Its metaphysical assumptions follow those of liberalism—no one party to a controversy knows the truth completely; and the best way to approach more nearly to a discovery of reality is through mutual discussion. Violence makes impossible real discussion and negotiation, and hence, cuts off our only possibility of removing the shadows which obscure our knowledge.

Society, therefore, is looked upon as essentially a community of consent. Violence destroys this community by attempting to rule without consent. Thus, to the pacifist, his means and the ultimate universal community are inseparable.[60]

Once pacifist organization is disciplined and perfected, it is possible to imagine its being utilized in many contexts. Opposition to invasion, to tyranny, to refusal of elementary civil liberties, could be carried on most effectively. And in the meantime, incipient organs of government could be developed within the pacifist itself.[61] Eventually, these embryonic devices could, in a world movement, become the nucleus of a World State erected upon pacifist foundations. Thus pacifism, which began as an individual negative protest against military service, becomes a positive theory of political means for attaining the cosmopolitan State.

Both negative and positive aspects of the pacifist philosophy have been attacked with vigor, although only two critics have thus far considered pacifist arguments with any thoroughness. Reinhold Niebuhr has attacked the pacifist case from the viewpoint of his own perspective in Christian theology and anthro-

---

[60] See Aldous Huxley, *Ends and Means* (New York: Harper, 1937).

[61] This is particularly emphasized by Shridharani, *op. cit.*, in the context of Indian opposition to British rule.

pology; [62] while the assumptions of John Lewis [63] are those of a Marxian materialist. In general, Lewis discovers two types of pacifism, the absolutist—based upon supposedly unequivocal prohibition of killing, war, and violence—and the utilitarian, which makes its criteria of right and wrong a matter of consequences flowing from the condemned acts. Neither type, Lewis argues, will bear the test of critical scrutiny.

It is beyond the space limitations of this paper to analyze more fully the philosophy of pacifist critics or to adjudge in any adequate manner as between pacifist and non-pacifist. It may be pointed out in conclusion, however, that the center of the controversy between them turns on the answer to two questions: (1) Can a sharp line of division be drawn between "violent" and "non-violent" acts on the basis of consequences? and (2) If so, what criteria can be developed to distinguish between violent and non-violent acts?

V.

SUMMARY AND CONCLUSION

Recent and contemporary universalism in politics has its historical rootage in the rationalism of the eighteenth century and in a re-emphasis of the traditional religious values of the western world. Universalist theories have been reflected in the growth of humanitarian thought, which, because of its basic belief in the essential kinship and dignity of humanity, is centrally concerned with the immediate amelioration of the lot of human beings and beasts everywhere, regardless of political harmony, whether the context of discussion be economic or bio-

---

[62] Niebuhr's criticisms, implicit and explicit, will be found in *Moral Man and Immoral Society* (New York: Scribner, 1932); *Reflections on the End of an Era* (New York: Scribner, 1934); and *Christianity and Power Politics* (New York: Scribner, 1940). Insofar as his criticism is theological, Niebuhr insists that Christian pacifism is over-optimistic. It fails to estimate correctly the power of sin, and assumes that the love-ethic of the New Testament can be realized here and now. The theological truth is rather that "The grace of God for man and the Kingdom of God for history are both divine realities and not human possibilities". *Christianity and Power Politics,* 21. See also *The Nature and Destiny of Man,* 2 vols. (New York: Scribner, 1941 and 1942).

[63] John Lewis, *The Case Against Pacifism* (London: Allen & Unwin, c. 1940).

logical; in internationalism and cosmopolitanism, with their diverse theories regarding the nature of the universal community; and in pacifism, with its emphasis on the determination of ends by the character of the means involved and its theory of social and political revolution.

In conclusion, it might be reiterated that this analysis has been merely suggestive and illustrative, not exhaustive and critical. To the serious student of politics it should constitute only a very brief introduction.

BIBLIOGRAPHY

ANGELL, NORMAN, *The Great Illusion* 1933 (New York: Putnam's, 1933). This edition of Angell's classic is particularly valuable because, while an abridgement of the original, it omits nothing essential and includes a discussion of the Angellian thesis as applied to the events of the thirties which constitute the real "beginning" of the Great War of 1939.

BECKER, C(8_ L., *The Heavenly City of the Eighteenth Century Philosophers* (New Haven: Yale, 1932). Professor Becker's acute insights into eighteenth century thought are very helpful in understanding the spirit of much contemporary humanitarianism and cosmopolitanism, so much of which roots in the "Age of Enlightenment".

BURY, J. B., *The Idea of Progress* (London: Macmillan, 1921). An attempt by the eminent historian to show the uniqueness of the idea of progress, so intimately associated with the thinking of the past hree hundred years while almost completely absent during the previous centuries of speculative effort. The relationship of the idea of progress to humanitarianism, internationalism, and cosmopolitanism is analyzed.

DE LIGT, BART, *The Conquest of Violence* (New York: Dutton, 1938). This is one of the most carefully constructed arguments for pacifism. The author, a Dutch anarchist, not only seeks to show that war cannot achieve "good" ends but also endeavors to demonstrate that there are other techniques, non-violent in character, which are efficacious.

GREGG, RICHARD M., *The Power of Non-Violence* (Philadelphia: Lippincott, 1935). This is the best theoretical exposition of pacifism. Written by an American lawyer who became interested in the Gandhi, this book is the author's statement of the case for non-violent resistance.

HUXLEY, ALDOUS, *Ends and Means* (New York: Harpers, 1937). Although not free of ambiguities and at many points wanting in clarity, this might be looked upon as one of the most beautifully expressed statements of what might be called a mystical, a political pacifism.

HUXLEY, THOMAS HENRY, *Evolution and Ethics and Other Essays* (New York: Appleton, 1899). This is still perhaps the best explanation of the social and political implications of Darwinian evolution.

JOAD, C. E. M., *The Philosophy of Federalism* (London: Macmillan, 1941). A brief treatment in pamphlet form of the general conception of a federated world. Joad is not so much concerned with the details, as with the relation of the idea to the several spheres of life.

LEWIS, JOHN, *The Case Against Pacifism* (London: Allen & Unwin, c. 1940). This is an elaborate and detailed statement of the argument against pacifism. The author is not too successful in much of his treatment, but at other points delivers several telling blows against pacifist armour.

MACGREGOR, G. H. C., *The Relevance of an Impossible Ideal* (New York: Fellowship of Reconciliation, 1941). This is an answer, couched in theological terms, to the views of Reinhold Niebuhr. The author, a Scotch theologian, attacks Niebuhr's position on the ground that it mis-states the relationship of traditional Christian thought to "perfectionist" ideals.

MACIVER, R. M., *Towards An Abiding Peace* (New York: Macmillan, 1943). One of the most suggestive works dealing with the possibilities of a world order following the Second World War. Unfortunately, MacIver is not too clear at many points in his argument. On the whole, the framework is internationalist rather than cosmopolitan.

NEWFANG, OSCAR, *World Federation* (New York: Barnes & Noble, 1939). Newfang, who for long has been a federationist as contrasted with an apologist for a league, states his argument most succinctly here.

RUSSELL, FRANK M., *Theories of International Relations* (New York: Appleton-Century, 1936). A general text-book analyzing theories of international relations from ancient to modern times. This is a comprehensive survey and the bibliographical lists attached should be helpful to the student.

STAWELL, F. MELIAN, *The Growth of International Thought* (London: Thornton Butterworth, 1929). A brief history of international doctrines since the eighteenth century. A short sketch, the major problems are treated in such a manner as to enable the student to see the picture as a whole.

STREIT, CLARENCE, *Union Now* (New York: Harpers, 1940). Streit's work has provoked more comment, and won more assent to the idea of world federation, than any work in the past forty years. Why this is true is difficult to discover. Oscar Newfang has elaborated the theory clearly years before, yet his work produced scarcely a ripple.

WELLS, H. G., *A Modern Utopia* (London: Chapman and Hall, 1905).

——————, *The Anatomy of Frustration* (New York: Macmillan, 1936).

——————, *The World Set Free* (New York: Macmillan, 1914).

——————, *World Brain* (Garden City: Doubleday Doran, 1938). Wells has been the most consistent exponent of the cosmopolitan ideal in modern times, and these works are among those which best exemplify his argument. The first and the third are novels.

WOOTTON, BARBARA, *Socialism and Federation* (London: Macmillan, 1941). Some writers, of whom John Strachey is one, look upon federation and socialism as antithetic conceptions. But the author of this pamphlet seeks to show that they are complementary instead.

Chapter XII

THE ELITE IN RECENT POLITICAL THOUGHT

FRANCIS G. WILSON

THE GOVERNMENT OF THE FEW

In 1909 James Bryce declared in his presidential address to the American Political Science Association that there had been in fact only one form of government—the government of the few.[1] This view could readily be argued in the more happy days of modern democracy, before the emergence of the present crisis. But even such a standardized axiom of twentieth-century political science cannot now be pressed with a smile of wisdom by those once sure that democracy was the final form of government in the history of progressive humanity. Indeed, the government of the few has become in part the symbol of political irresponsibility and the tyranny of organization. Even if the few rule in fact in the democracies, we do not desire to display too openly a condition which suggests that the difference of regimes is relative rather than absolute.

Ideally, however, students of politics have believed that the government of the best—necessarily the few—is the proper regime could it but be organized. Plato dreamed in his *Republic* of a just city to be governed by those who were the best, the most able, and the wisest. They were to be chosen by a rigid and life-long system of education, at each stage of which the unfit would be separated from the competent. True aristocracy is just this, the government of the best, of a ruling class dedicated to the common well-being and to the application in verity

---

[1] James Bryce, "The Relations of Political Science to History and to Practice," *The American Political Science Review*, III (February, 1909), p. 18.

of the highest principles of justice. If Plato sadly admitted that his city of justice was laid up in heaven, so have others who would construct an ideal society, which has been in many instances governed by the few. The history of utopian thought is replete with the dream of government which combines beauty and justice in the full sense of the words.[2]

Our concern in this chapter is with those ideas about the government of the few which have been expressed in fairly recent times. Democracy has been based on the principle of the day-to-day sovereignty of the people, the government of the many in the Greek or Aristotelian sense. Therefore, government of the few as a principle stands in some measure as a criticism, a rejection, or an improvement of democracy. It should be made clear, however, that the defense of the government of the few can be pressed as an improvement of democracy; the government of the few, say professional administrators or benevolent leaders of the masses, does not always stand in contradiction with the modern democratic conception of social organization. Thomas Jefferson, for example, believed that the natural aristocrats should rule, provided their power should come from the free suffrage of the people.

The ideas expressed above, however, are the exception rather than the rule. Many critics of democracy in the nineteenth century and our own have been believers in the government of the few because it was a way to escape from the perils of the government of the many. Some form of aristocracy was, therefore, the remedy for the weaknesses of democracy as it emerged from the European ciisis of the French Revolution. Sir Henry Sumner Maine in his *Popular Government* (1886) pointed out the fragility, the weaknesses and the unprogressive character of democratic government. Thomas Carlyle and other Victorians showed without reserve their contempt for the government of the masses; they were looking for ways in which the very limited British democracy of their day might be cir-

[2] J. O. Hertzler, *The History of Utopian Thought* (New York: The Macmillan Company, 1923).

cumvented and more responsible government instituted.[3] Frenchmen, like Faguet and Le Bon, were critical of the democratic
process;[4] in the United States writers like H. L. Mencken in
his *Notes on Democracy* (1926) enjoyed satirical criticism of
democracy, while others objected to the lack of standards in
democracy or the lack of intelligence in the electorate.[5] Or, if
we turn to an earlier period in American history, writers like
John Adams and James Kent were fearful of the results that
would follow the establishment in America of an unlimited democracy. Whatever the nature of these criticisms, however, the
trend of history during the nineteenth and early twentieth centuries has been toward an effort to realize the sovereignty of
the people. Democracy seemed, indeed, to Tocqueville in 1835
when he wrote his *Democracy in America* a providential fact,
that is to say, the universal trend was toward equality which
meant to him democracy. It may be added that Tocqueville as
an aristocrat had little taste for the new democratic age.

THE MODERN CRISIS

Democracy, therefore, has never been without its critics.
The prophets of doom have always been shouting at the masses
in the market place that they were moving toward destruction
in the name of democracy. Yet, if the implication of all this
anti-democratic criticism has been to support the government
of the few, that criticism seemed never able to give a convincing
program for the realization in practice of the government of the
few. The criticism was negative, or it looked with nostalgia to
an impossible restoration of the past. It could not propose a
means of restoring the government of the able or the best. While

---

[3] See Benjamin E. Lippincott, *Victorian Critics of Democracy* (Minneapolis: The
University of Minnesota Press, 1938).

[4] Émile Faguet, *The Cult of Incompetence,* translated from the French (London:
J. Murray Company, 1911); Gustav Le Bon, *The Crowd, A Study of the Popular
Mind* (London: T. Fisher Unwin, 1913).

[5] See Irving Babbitt, *Democracy and Leadership* (Boston and New York: Houghton Mifflin Co., 1924); N. J. Lennes, *Whither Democracy?* (New York and
London: Harper and Brothers Publishers, 1927).

certain groups have been proposed as candidates for the new ruling class, no general support for any program could be mustered. Thus the defenders of democracy have regarded criticism as a parlor luxury without much practical application to the triumphant march of the government of the many.

Today the situation has changed. The critics of liberalism have proposed, and in many instances established, regimes which negate the democracy of the last century and a half. Criticizing democracy is no longer a parlor game; it is part of the deadly conflict of politics. Those who speak against democracy today must accept responsibility for their words, for they are speaking for the regimes which in effective degree destroyed the popular system over large areas of the world. How did this change come about? An answer is hard to give, since any great transitional period in society is a complex result of even more complex causes. To state the importance of the crisis is less difficult; all intelligent minds know that it is great, and they know that the alternative to historic democracy must specifically be fought. The world crisis in regimes, the new world revolution as some say,[6] may be with us for generations, and only at the end of the long crisis can we say what the result will be for the democratic system around which, for example, the American tradition has grown. Within democracy itself the divisions of purpose have been acute, but in the twentieth century all men of good democratic will have come together against the greater enemy.

One of the central political symbols and organizations of power in the anti-democratic regime is the elite. It is to this idea and practice that we must now turn. Against the sovereignty of the people stands the sovereignty of certain kinds of elites. That the elite should govern, the few and the putative best, is accepted by those who stand against the traditional order of free men in a free state, enjoying a free economy, *i.e.*, a "capi-

---

[6] Herman Rauschning, *The Revolution of Nihilism* (New York: Alliance Book Corporation, 1939); *The Redemption of Democracy* (New York: Alliance Book Corporation, 1941); Robert C. Brooks, "Reflections on the 'World Revolution' of 1940," *The American Political Science Review*, XXV (February, 1940), p. 1 ff.

talistic" or private property system. Naturally, as democracies have tended toward a balance of political and economic forces, of cooperation and compromise between groups, the new regimes (totalitarian or authoritarian as one will) have tended toward dominance in the control of the state and the economy, and they have substituted effectively suppression for cooperation and compromise. As Carl Schmitt has urged, the central idea of the "political" is the antagonism between friend and foe.[7]

A concentration of political and economic power can exist only if there is a strong ruling class, having organization and integration within itself sufficient to overcome the latent and always emergent opposition. The elite is, in the twentieth-century crisis, the name given to the new ruling orders, which in all soberness have been organized to such a degree of effectiveness that other and older oligarchies in most instances will hardly bear comparison. That the masses are called upon to support the elite makes little difference; the unorganized masses cannot do otherwise except at the peril of their lives. Up to the outbreak of war, in 1939, the mass revolution against the authoritarian states of Russia (1917), Italy (1922) and Germany (1933) had not occurred. It has not shown its force against the one-party dictatorship of China, against the regime in Turkey, Spain or other countries in Europe and South America which cannot be assimilated to the democratic ideal of the great powers of Western civilization. The existence of these regimes constitutes the democratic crisis, a crisis which may last for generations.[8]

What can one say of the nature of these new elitist and totalitarian regimes? In other words, what is the nature of fascism, whether in Russia, Germany, Italy or other countries? The woods are full of theories, which we must mention briefly, though all of them imply some conception of the nature of historical movement and causation. None can deny, however, that the traditional democracies moved into the supreme conflict

---

[8] See Pitirim A. Sorokin, *Social and Cultural Dynamics,* 4 volumes (New York: American Book Company, 1937-1941).

of war against fascism in 1939; the greater democracies have turned their effort against the greater and more efficient fascism of Germany, using all the enemies of Germany, such as Russia, in order to preserve the free society, if they may, that has been theirs.

Socialist and communist movements were the first victims of the elite in fascist Europe, and therefore the followers of Marx tried first to organize in order to stem the new authoritarian tide. The communist United Front and Popular Front of 1935-1939 sought to unite socialists of all sects against fascism, while the Popular Front was an effort to unite all non-Marxians in the crusade. From 1939 to 1941 Russia and Germany seemed friends and these efforts were quietly put aside. On the other hand, with the Soviet-German War of 1941, the Russians have turned to the capitalist democracies for help to save the Workers' Revolution of 1917. Marxians have said that the true nature of fascism is the reaction of capitalism in crisis; the war against fascism is a continuation of the old war against the bourgoisie.[9]

For a time some democratic thinkers looked upon fascism as a weapon to be used primarily against the danger of the communist revolution. That conception has now changed, and the democratic, capitalistic societies, believe that fascism is against the ideal of a free economy; the denunciations of capitalism to be found throughout fascist literature have been taken seriously. On both the communist and the democratic sides, however, the argument has stressed the importance of ideology.

Another school is more interested in political process or pattern, and it has seen from the outset of warlike argument the similarity in oppression and tyranny between the Russian and the other totalitarian regimes. In passing, it may be said that all of these regimes, from Russia onward, have claimed to be truly democratic. Such uses of the term, however, cannot be accepted as they fall completely outside any reasonable historical context. If the importance of ideology in these regimes is denied, the process of authoritarian control becomes the focus of

---

[9] See Melvin Rader, *No Compromise* (New York: The Macmillan Company, 1939). See Chap. VI especially, for a discussion of the elite.

attention. The regime is based on techniques of control, and these techniques are equally to be deplored in all regimes and all are equally undemocratic in the extent to which they are used.[10] Whether the ideology of the regime is the Marxian conception of the new society as in Russia, the organic nation as in fascist Italy or the superiority of the Aryan race as in National Socialism, it is equally in contradiction with the Christian and democratic conception of the reasonable individual; and the techniques used by the elites in all these regimes go beyond the humane principle of compromise and democratic submission to the just decision of the people.[11]

THE NATURE OF ELITIST THEORY

We must now turn to a more detailed examination of the conception of the elite in modern political theory. What does the word "elite" mean? It is a French word which has migrated into other modern languages. It means in general a select group or a select few. In comparative government the term applies, narrowly, to the party members in the single-party authoritarian states. These party members have shown their fidelity to the cause, be it communism, fascism or national socialism. There are two senses in political theory in which the term is ordinarily used, one of these senses being descriptive and the other purposive, evaluative or normative.

ELITE AS A DESCRIPTIVE CONCEPT

The descriptive theory of the elite must be separated sharply from the normative, since in the former case it is merely, or seeks to be, a sociological or scientific conception. It is, in this view,

---

[10] See Karl Mannheim, *Ideology and Utopia,* translated from the German (New York: Harcourt, Brace and Company, 1936); Waldemar Gurian, *The Future of Bolshevism* (New York: Sheed and Ward, Inc., 1936); *Bolshevism, Theory and Practice* (New York: The Macmillan Company, 1932).

[11] See F. G. Wilson, "The Structure of Modern Ideology," *The Review of Politics,* I (October, 1939), pp. 382-399; "Political Suppression in the Modern State," *The Journal of Politics,* I (August, 1939), pp. 237-257.

merely a generalization drawn from the observation of the political and social behavior of men in organizations. Here we find the view expressed, like that of Bryce in 1909, that there is always in control a few leaders or rulers who may be called an oligarchy. The power of oligarchies may differ widely, just as their organization, closed or open, may vary widely. Likewise, the techniques of control may be variable and quite compatible with the democratic process, or, indeed, it may be argued that such is inevitably the nature of the democratic process itself. To say there is inevitably an oligarchy in well-organized groups does not condemn them; one might also say there is always a ruling class or order, as John Adams did, or, if one wishes, an elite that does in fact exercise the social or political power vested in the group as a whole. A sociological analysis of leadership does not mean the rejection of purpose or a denial of its effectiveness. It does not mean the denial of reform or social change. It may in fact be argued that a well organized leadership or elite is necessary if social reform or progress is to be achieved.

Such modern theories are realistic, that is, they seek to describe accurately the political process. They may be brought into the democratic system of sociology without making that system a denial of liberal government. These conceptions may advance the scientific explanation of what takes place in society. In a general sense elitist explanations may mean simply that social scientists have undertaken to see clearly just how the people attain any of their goals. To organize the people means to give them leadership. That leadership has laws or patterns which a sociological or Aristotelian examination of politics can reveal. From the democratic standpoint, to say there are elites or oligarchies in social, political and economic organization is not a denial of norms; it is a statement of conditions under which any norms must be realized. In the United States certain thinkers have accepted the concept of the elite in a descriptive sense, though it must be conceded that the term is European in origin, arising either from the French syndicalist thought of Georges

Sorel or the aristocratic and anti-democratic thought of conservatism.[12]

THE ELITE IN SOCIAL PROGRAMS

If we turn from more or less objective discussion of the notion of elites to the normative, polemical or programmatical side of the question, a variety of interpretations may be selected for treatment. But it is often difficult to separate the social program connected with the elite and the objective treatment of social organization. Continuous argument has prevailed as to whether Pareto's theory of the elite is an objective description of the facts of society or an argument for reactionary conservatism. In any case, many of the current elitist theories are associated with particular programs which are anti-democratic and authoritarian in implication. The nature of the elite approved or organized varies with the program or social theory involved.

Early in the present century Georges Sorel, then a leader of the revolutionary French syndicalist movement, insisted that the proletariat could attain its just ends only by the use of violence in the class struggle. Violence was, therefore, ethically justified and politically creative. Since the weapons of the workers are not properly parliamentary democracy and the bourgeois intellectualist theory of class reconciliation, the proletariat must

---

[12] See Harold D. Lasswell, *Politics, Who Gets What, When, How* (New York: McGraw-Hill Book Company, 1936); Edwin Mims, Jr., *The Majority of the People* (New York: Modern Age Books 1941), pp. 248 ff., especially 269, 273; F. G. Wilson, "A Theory of Conservatism," *The American Political Science Review,* XXXV (1941, p. 29 ff. It cannot be argued that the sociological acceptance of the elite in the United States is very general.

Among European writers who have fathered the principle of the elite, primarily as a descriptive concept, one should mention Gaetano Mosca, *The Ruling Class,* translated from the Italian (New York: McGraw-Hill Book Company, 1939); Vilfredo Pareto, *The Mind and Society,* translated from the Italian, 4 vols. (New York: Harcourt, Brace and Company, 1935). The "iron law of oligarchy" was argued in Robert Michels *Political Parties,* translated from the Italian (London: Jarrold and Sons, 1915).

Mosca stressed the existence of a ruling class in all societies. He analyzed the forms this class takes, but he insisted strongly on the juridical defense of the individual. Pareto argued the existence of elites based on wealth and power; one of his main contributions is the theory of the circulation of elites. Michels' data relates to socialist parties in Europe before 1914; he shows the existence of oligarchies in what one might presume would be thoroughly democratic social structures.

turn to the inherent possibilities of the class. But the class war was a training school; each strike demarked the able leaders, or proletarian elite, from the masses of the workers. The socialist movement must be led by the elite stratum which is produced by the class struggle, while conversely the masses of the workers must be inspired by the myth of the general strike, which may indeed come, and which will overthrow the whole capitalist structure. It has been said that the ideas of Sorel are the key to contemporary political theory. But no one can deny that Sorel's *Reflections on Violence,* in which these ideas are ramblingly presented, is one of the lasting books of our time.

The elite principle runs through much of socialist thought since the days of Marx and Engels. Marx believed that the proletariat was to be the future ruling class, and he stated at one time, for example, that the industrial proletariat was the "natural trustee" of the rural producers or peasants.[13] While the discussion of leadership has not formed a significant part of Social Democratic literature in Germany, or in the socialist thought of France and England, the Russian Revolution in 1917 changed this condition. For the Communist Party, *i.e.,* the Bolsheviks, in Russia has stressed the revolutionary role the proletariat will play in the organization of the new society once the revolution has been won. The most comprehensive statement of the problem of leadership in communist literature arises from the discussion of proletarian tactics,[14] but more narrowly the party, *i.e.,* the Communist Party with its limited membership, has been regarded as the "best of the proletariat", the vanguard of the whole movement. Thus the party constitutes not only the center of the

---

[13] This view was presented in *The Civil War in France,* Chap. III. See Karl Marx, *Capital, The Communist Manifesto and Other Writings,* edited by Max Eastman (New York: The Modern Library, 1932), p. 406.

[14] See V. I. Lenin, *The State and Revolution* (revised translation, New York: International Publishers, 1932); *"Left-Wing" Communism, an Infantile Disorder* (revised translation, New York: International Publishers, 1934). The whole literature of the United Front is, in a sense, a literature of the tactics of leadership.

governing order in the new society, but also the elite of the whole international proletariat.[15]

If we turn to the concept of leadership in the German National Socialist movement, a very different concept of the elite is presented. Instead of the broad foundation of the elite being the proletariat, it is the superior Aryan race. The folk state has implied the creation of institutions of leadership from this group, and under the Nazi regime strenuous training was provided for those who were to be the political leaders of tomorrow.[16] It cannot be said that in Italy organization of leadership was as complete as in Germany. In the first place, while German thought emphasized the folk, the "state" was made the supreme symbol in modern Italian thought. Naturally, the Fascist Party in Italy assumed a large share in the control of government, though as in Germany bureaucratic organization was continued in effect as a competitor with the party.[17] Training for leadership, culminating in party membership, characterized, however, the Italian program. A process of selection was operative from the early years in the schools until full positions of responsibility were attained by those best suited to the needs of the regime. A somewhat similar process must, it is believed, be characteristic of any revolutionary regime whether fascist or otherwise.[18]

---

[15] See Joseph Stalin, *The Foundations of Leninism* (New York: International Publishers Co., 1932), p. 106 ff. The Trotskyist criticism of the Stalinist regime in Russia has the same flavor. Trotsky has argued that the betrayal is in the ruling stratum, and that the Russian regime vitiated socialism by the creation of a privileged ruling class. See Leon Trotsky, *The Revolution Betrayed* (New York: Doubleday, Page and Company, 1937).

[16] *The Nazi Primer*, translated and edited by Harwood L. Childs (New York: Harper and Brothers Publishers, 1938); Adolf Hitler, *Mein Kampf*, translated from the German (New York: Reynal and Hitchcock, 1939); Alfred Rosenberg, *Der Mythus des 20. Jahrhunderts* (München, 1934); Frederick L. Schuman, *The Nazi Dictatorship* (revised edition, New York: Alfred A. Knopf, 1936).

[17] Fritz Morstein Marx, "Bureaucracy and Dictatorship," *The Review of Politics*, III (January, 1941), pp. 100-117.

[18] H. Arthur Steiner, *Government in Fascist Italy* (New York McGraw-Hill Book Company, 1938); see Benito Mussolini, "The Political and Social Doctrine of Fascism," *International Conciliation* No. 306 (1935); Alfredo Rocco, "The Political Doctrine of Fascism," *International Conciliation* No. 223 (1926).

Lawrence Dennis, an American fascist writer, has accepted the elite principle as the basis of the reorganization of society. See *The Coming of American Fascism* (New York: Harper and Brothers Publishers, 1936); *The Dynamics of War and Revolution* (New York: The Weekly Foreign Letter, 1940).

The programmatical conception of the elite involves therefore a selected base for the elite. What social group should be favored? In Russia the industrial worker has been regarded as the future sovereign of the world; in Germany the members of the Aryan race occupied this position; while in Italy the patriot member of the organic nation was chosen for power. In the United States, Dennis, for example, has been inclined to take the middle classes as the basis for the future elite. In the pre-1939 Polish Constitution, which recognized the elite, landowners and military men were given preferred treatment. Always the political philosophy of the movement will determine the direction taken by the conscious organization of the new elite. Elitist government is clearly the government of the few, but in the authoritarian countries the elite expresses a future social purpose, to be attained by the totalitarian or authoritarian organization of society.

There are suggestions, hardly clarified, that administrators or bureaucrats as receivers of the good society will constitute a responsible elite. The literature of modern administration has kept the principle of democratic responsibility to the masses of society, yet there is a belief also that the masses should accept the government of the expert. Many today believe that the future of good government in the modern state rests with the civil service, the efficient administration, rather than with the democratic devices of a past generation which attempted to throw the government directly back to the control of the people. In the extreme James Burnham called it in 1941 *The Managerial Revolution*,[19] a revolution in which a new diversified class of managers will control society and reorganize the property and legal system to its liking. Such a position for the managerial elite

---

[19] See also James Burnham, *The Machiavellians, Defenders of Freedom* (New York: The John Day Company, 1943).

would, however, deny responsibility to the people. The "science" of public administration may yet save society.[20]

What we reach, it would seem, in the discussion of the elite is the theory of the ruling class. How should the governing class be organized? From what social groups should the leaders of society be selected? To what extent can such a conscious selection be effective? We may mention briefly, for the augmentation of the discussion, a few other ideas in this perspective. The leaders of the Hamiltonian party in the United States were concerned with the organization of leadership, and it was said that manufacturers and merchants, as well as the more wealthy agriculturists, should be in this class. Southern thinkers from the early days of the Union until the destruction of southern leadership after the Confederate War were concerned with the share of the leaders of the South in the total governing order in the nation. As a minority group, they believed that the minority "elite" should have a veto or concurrent voice in the determination of national affairs. It may be, indeed, that under the attack of the mass state, the twentieth-century business man will find in southern thought many ideas to his liking.[21]

In view of the above discussion, it cannot cogently be argued that the elite principle means necessarily a dictatorship, in the sense of tyranny or autocracy. To argue for an elite of a certain character has often been a serious argument for the advancement of the public welfare. In fact it may be said that no modern defenders of the elite, whatever its social character, admit

---

[20] Luther Gulick and L. Gulick (editors), *Papers on the Science of Administration* (New York: Institute of Public Administration, 1937); Leonard D. White, *Introduction to the Study of Public Administration* (revised edition, New York: The Macmillan Company, 1940); *Trends in Public Administration* (New York: McGraw-Hill Book Company, 1933).

[21] We have no space to pursue utopian proposals for the organization of ruling classes. In general very few utopian conceptions from Plato to the present have believed in the sovereignty of the people. Higher standards or higher ruling orders have prevailed. Francis Bacon in his *New Atlantis* first proposed, it is believed, the sovereignty of an elite of scientists. Technocracy suggests an engineering elite, and others have proposed even that physicians or doctors should constitute the ruling class. *Cf.* H. G. Wells, *An Experiment in Autobiography* (New York: The Macmillan Company, 1934).

that they are supporting the exploitation of the people or the denial of the best interest of the nation or social group.[22]

The elite principle in Europe has, however, been chiefly acclimated in the anti-democratic and authoritarian systems. It has been deeply associated with the principle of the fascist dictatorship. As such it has been doctrinally connected with anti-liberal views, and with the practice of neo-Machiavellian politics. The theory of the elite in Sorel and Mussolini has been a justification of violence in politics and a phase of the use of totalitarian means. Here is, indeed, the modern version of Machiavelli's *Prince.* To many it is political realism gone to seed to such an extent that it is no longer political realism. The elite is the primary technique of the bloody revolution and its concomitant, the counter-revolution. It is reason of state, *ragione di stato,* gone lush.[23] The fundamental democratic criticism of elitism must be that it leads to a totalitarianism in means for the attainment of ends that are morally justified. Democracy must be a democracy of means if it is to be democracy at all. Dishonorable political means endangers the honorable political end.[24]

Cutting across the theories of the modern world which justify the elitist conception of politics, other thinkers have been oppressed with the mass movement. To some the mass movement is the greatest danger faced by modern civilization, for it is upon the mass movement that the new elite can be constructed and from which it draws its sustaining political support. For there is contempt of the masses in the minds of the elite, as well as fear; there can be little love.[25]

---

[22] *Cf.* Othmar Spann, *Der Wahre Staat* (Jena: Gustav Fischer, 1931).

[23] Historically, dictatorship has been a perfectly good democratic and republican device for meeting emergencies. In the Roman Constitution provision was made for extraordinary power for short periods, and it was a consul who was given this power. See Carl Schmitt, *Die Diktatur* (München, 1928); Friedrich Meinecke, *Die Idee der Staatsräson* (München, 1924); Frederick M. Watkins, "The Problem of Constitutional Dictatorship," in *Public Policy,* edited by C. J. Friedrich and E. S. Mason (Cambridge: Harvard University Press, 1940), p. 324 ff.

[24] *Cf.* Max Lerner, Introduction, *The Prince and the Discourses* by Niccolo Machiavelli (New York: The Modern Library, 1940).

[25] José Ortega y Gasset, *The Revolt of the Masses,* translated from the Spanish (New York: W. W. Norton Co., 1932); Johan Huizinga, *In the Shadow of Tomorrow* (New York: W. W. Norton Co., 1936); Emil Lederer, *State of the Masses* (New York: W. W. Norton Co., 1940).

In the United States we have had, perhaps, elites throughout our national history. However, Americans do not like the term except as descriptive of the social process, or as a means of analyzing the iniquity of world revolution which has swept out from Europe. We still regard the business man as important in our civilization, but we may, like Jefferson, turn to the education of the more competent as the solution of our difficulties. An elite based on education of the able may not in the end be undemocratic.[26]

BIBLIOGRAPHY

BALL, MARGARET M., "The Leadership Principle in National Socialism," *Journal of the History of Ideas,* III (January, 1942), pp. 74-93. A discussion of the intellectual history of the leadership theory in German thought.

BURNHAM, JAMES, *The Machiavellians, Defenders of Freedom* (New York: John Day Company, 1943). This book defends elitist writers, such as Sorel, Mosca, Pareto and others.

BURNHAM, JAMES, *The Managerial Revolution* (New York: John Day Company, 1941). An overall interpretation of the development of the modern bureaucratic state; an argument for the proposition that he new ruling class will consist of the managers of society.

CHILDS, HARWOOD L., *The Nazi Primer,* translated by Harwood L. Childs (New York: Harper and Brothers Publishers, 1938). A volume of useful source material on Nazi thought and on the organization of leadership in the Third Reich.

DENNIS, LAWRENCE, *The Coming of American Fascism* (New York: Harper and Brothers Publishers, 1936).

DENNIS, LAWRENCE, *The Dynamics of War and Revolution* (New York: The Weekly Letter, 1940). These volumes constitute one of the vigorous defenses of fascism for the United States, with an elaborated theory of a new elite.

GERTH, HANS, "The Nazi Party: Its Leadership and Composition," *The American Journal of Sociology,* XLV (January, 1940). A title descriptive of the clinical material contained in the article.

HITLER, ADOLF, *Mein Kampf,* translated from the German (New York: Reynal and Hitchcok, 1939). A "must" book for our time.

KAMMERER, GLADYS M., "The Political Theory of Vichy," *The Journal of Politics,* V (November, 1943), pp. 407-434. This article describes briefly the use of elitist ideas by the Vichy regime.

LASSWELL, HAROLD D., *Politics, Who Gets What, When, How* (New York: McGraw-Hill Book Company, 1936). An excellent analysis of the operations of politics from the psychological approach.

LIPPINCOTT, BENJAMIN, E., *Victorian Critics of Democracy* (Minneapolis: The University of Minnesota Press, 1938). This volume provides the English background of modern authoritarian thought.

---

[26] See John Gould Fletcher, "Education, Past and Present," in *I'll Take My Stand,* by Twelve Southerners (New York: Harper and Brothers Publishers, 1930

MICHELS, ROBERT, *Political Parties,* translated from the Italian (London: Jarrold and Sons, 1915). An argument for the "iron law of oligarchy" based on a study of European socialist parties.

MOSCA, GAETANO, *The Ruling Class,* translated from the Italian (New York: McGraw-Hill Book Company, 1939). A "realistic" argument by one of the late Italian students of government.

MUSSOLINI, BENITO, "The Political and Social Doctrine of Fascism," *International Conciliation,* No. 306, January, 1935. A primary statement of elitist and fascist thought.

ORTEGA Y GASSET, JOSE, *The Revolt of the Masses,* translated from the Spanish (New York: W. W. Norton Company, 1932). An attempt to explain what is happening to modern civilization.

PARETO, VILFREDO, *The Mind and Society,* translated from the Italian, 4 vols. (New York: Harcourt, Brace and Company, 1935). One of the more controversial works of our period, but a systematic presentation of one view of elite theory.

RADER, MELVIN, *No Compromise* (New York: The Macmillan Company, 1939). An excellent statement of the United Front period on fascism and elitist theory.

RAUSCHNING, HERMANN, *The Revolution of Nihilism* (New York: Alliance Book Corporation, 1939). An intuitive, personal study of the modern crisis of political institutions.

SOREL, GEORGES, *Reflections on Violence,* translated from the French (New York: B. N. Huebsch Company, 1912). The beginning of much that is modern in politics.

CHAPTER XIII

MILITARISM AND POLITICS

STUART PORTNER

The history of the twentieth century has been that of a world at war. The first forty years of the century have produced armed conflict devastating in the destruction of life and property beyond the proportion of any war in history. During these four decades, and at no time in history, have nations so armed them-selves in the contest to impose their will upon other nations. A new idea of a "nation in arms" has become a reality as the entire political, economic, and military structures of the nation have been welded into a single integrated pattern to better enable the nation to attain victory at war.

Economic nationalism, territorial ambitions, and the desire for power have been as fundamental causes of the war that broke out in 1939 as they were of the first World War. The forces motivating action in Germany during Hitler's ascendancy have been different only in outward manifestation and in language to that impelling Germany to seek a more significant portion of the world's territory in the days of William II. Mussolini's attempt to gain an empire for Italy has been but a modernization of the play inspired and produced by Crispi half a century previously, and has resulted in a disaster even worse than the Italian defeat at Adowa in 1896.

The problems of international relations remain what they have been from time immemorial, and fundamental among these problems is the desire to maintain what one possesses, or to gain what one does not possess but covets. Armed force is merely the instrument employed by nations to gain and maintain power. As Clausewitz has indicated, war is but an extension of politics, utterly disagreeable it is true, but a fact evidenced on innumerable occasions in the past and undoubtedly to be witnessed in the future. The democratic nations of the world have sought to avoid war during the last 25 years by not thinking of it. But it has been the pattern of things in the past that other nations will seek what we possess and will force us to return again and again to the realization that preparedness cannot be blithely waved aside.

It is absolutely fundamental for a nation to arrive at a clear conception of its place in the society of nations, to develop its international relations accordingly, and to augment its military establishment in order that it retain a respectable position in that society. It is further necessary that the people of the nation have a knowledge and an appreciation of the meaning of the nation's political and military position in order that they comprehend the significance of that position for them as individuals. Only by clear definition can one expect spirited support from the populace. The indecisive political and military philosophies of the democratic nations have twice brought them to the brink of disaster. The time is now more than passed when we must take active measures to protect our democratic institutions and prevent such catastrophes as occurred in France. It behooves us to maintain the armies we have created, for the military is the force protecting our institutions. We must not abdicate the responsibility handed us by our forebearers to preserve the democratic way of life.

The Military Situation, 1900-14

The nations of Europe at the turn of the twentieth century dominated the affairs of the world, notwithstanding the growing nationalistic movements and developing power of the United

States and Japan.[1] A spirited nationalism was evident throughout the continent as the new national states sought to expand territorial holdings and gain new markets and added prestige. By the beginning of the century, however, the entire habitable surface of the earth had been explored and partitioned and it seemed likely that henceforth any reorientation in colonial possession would be the result of armed conflict. Germany, in the full growth of its power, contested for international supremacy with a British Empire grown strong on decades of imperial domination. The Bismarckian opposition to overseas expansion had been dropped in Germany with the venerable prime minister, and the new imperial aspirations of the German people were well exemplified in the aggressive expansionist policies of William II. This expansionist zeal was reflected in governmental legislation for the building of a greater navy, in movements toward the obtaining of territory in Africa and the Far East, and was echoed in the exhortations of innumerable pan-German groups. Nationalism was a concomitant of the expansionist spirit in Germany, but was matched by an emotion similarly expressed throughout the greater part of the world.[2]

A most significant reflection of such developing nationalism was the rise of aggressive militarism in the major nations of the continent. Throughout all of Europe measures were adopted to secure defenses and make available all resources for a showdown

[1] Of value for a general review of the background of the European international situation at the turn of the century see E. Brandenburg, *From Bismarck to the World War* (London: Oxford University Press, 1927); S. B. Fay, *The Origins of the World War* (2 vols., New York: Macmillan Company, 1938); G. P. Gooch, *History of Modern Europe, 1878-1919* (London: Cassell and Company, 1923); R. J. Mowat, *Concert of Europe* (London: Macmillan Company, 1930); B. E. Schmitt, *The Coming of the War, 1914* (2 vols., New York: Charles Scribner's Sons, 1930); J. W. Swain, *Beginning of the Twentieth Century* (New York: W. W. Norton and Company, 1933).

[2] See Mildred S. Wertheimer, *Pan-German League, 1890-1914* (New York: Columbia University Press, 1924) for a study of German nationalism. For a general treatment of the nationalist trend see C. J. H. Hayes, *The Historical Evolution of Modern Nationalism* (New York: R. R. Smith and Company, 1931); Edward Krehbiel, *Nationalism, War and Society* (New York: Macmillan Company, 1916); Parker T. Moon, *Imperialism and World Politics* (New York: Macmillan Company, 1926); Ramsay Muir, *Nationalism and Internationalism* (London: Constable and Company, 1917).

struggle for domination. In Great Britain, Germany, France, Russia, Austria-Hungary, Italy, even in Turkey and the smaller Balkan countries military preparations were undertaken at a rapidly accelerated pace. During the thirteen years prior to the outbreak of the World War, Germany increased its regular army by close to two hundred thousand men. France made a similar increase of almost one hundred and fifty thousand men. Russia added four hundred thousand; Austria-Hungary expanded by one hundred and thirty thousand, and Italy increased its standing army by forty thousand.[3] Similar increases were made in naval craft, with Britain and Germany engaging in a naval race such as the world had never witnessed.[4]

There were added changes in the administration and the structural organization of the military and naval forces during this period. The other countries of Europe looked toward Germany, victor in 1866 and 1871 in the most important wars on the continent in more than 50 years, and followed the German pattern of the administration of military forces.[5] Provision was made for universal conscription in all countries of Europe, except Great Britain which adhered to its program of a long service volunteer army. Short-service, however, was the accepted practice in most European armies, in emulation of the German system which had been so markedly successful in the Franco-Prussian war. Provision was made for rapid mobilization in order that troops be brought into action at the earliest possible moment. Staff planning, inter-allied military conversations, more

---

[3] See *Armaments Year-Book*, 1928 (Geneva: League of Nations, 1928).

[4] For a discussion of the Anglo-German naval race A. R. Coloquhoun, 1912 *Germany and Sea-Power* (London: Sir I. Pitman Company, 1909); Henry B. Hanna, *Can Germany Invade England* (London: Methuen Company, 1912); A. S. Hurd, *The Command of the Sea* (London: Chapman Hall, 1912); A. S. Hurd and H. Castle, *German Sea-Power* (London: J. Murray, 1913). See also Percival A. Hislam, *The Admiralty of the Atlantic* (London: Longmans, Green, 1908); Captain J. Eardley-Wilmot, *Our Fleet Today* (New York: Charles Scribner's Sons, 1900); O. E. Schüddekopf, *Die Britische Marinepolitik, 1880 bis 1918* (Hamburg: Hanseatische Verlagsanstalt, 1938); H. F. Wyatt, *Britain's Imminent Danger* (London: Imperial Maritime League, 1912).

[5] See Hoffman Nickerson, *The Armed Horde* (New York: G. P. Putnam's Sons, 1940).

intensive and more practical training, and other developments became the universal fact. Arms production was increased, but no clear definition was made of the utilization of the total resources of the nation in armed conflict. The concept of the totality of war was not to be recognized until well into the World War, when it became evident that all elements of the national life must henceforth be employed to wage war.[6] But in 1913 military men, almost without exception, conceived of the coming war as a short war of movement, and preparations were made accordingly.[7]

Counter-balancing such preparation for war were the proposals of various governments for a limitation on arms production. Proposals for disarmament and for arbitration of international difficulties were made on numerous occasions during each year of the year 1900-13, and the internal legislation of several of the governments during the period is further evidence of the desire to avoid armed conflict.[8] During this period elements of every nation opposed the expansionist-imperialist trend, but all too frequently however such proposals were a facade for the most cynical practices in power politics. The Russian proposal in 1899 for a disarmament conference that led to the meeting at The Hague in that year has been seriously questioned, especially since the first great increases in the Russian navy were made by that nation during the previous year.[9] Subsequent declarations of pacificistic piety similarly were frequently covers for more dubious purposes.

---

[6] See especially the contribution of Walter Rathenau in H. Kessler, *Walter Rathenau, sein Leben und sein Werk* (Berlin: H. Kleman, 1928).

[7] H. A. DeWeerd, "Churchill, Lloyd George, Clemencau: The Emergence of the Civilian," in Edward M. Earle, editor, *Makers of Modern Strategy* (Princeton: Princeton University Press, 1943).

[8] On pacifism and the attempts at disarmament and arbitration see Norman Angell, *The Great Illusion* (London: W. Heinemann, 1910); A. P. Higgins, *The Hague Peace Conferences and Other International Conferences* (London: Stevens and Sons, 1904); J. B. Scott, *The Hague Peace Conferences of 1899 and 1907* (Baltimore: Johns Hopkins University Press, 1909).

[9] Harry Elmer Barnes, *Genesis of the World War* (New York: A. A. Knopf, 1926).

GERMANY

In Germany, as elsewhere throughout Europe during the first years of the century, systematic preparations were being made for war. The German Great General Staff, under the direction of the most highly competent students of the art of war, developed and trained an army and prepared military plans to carry out the politics of the Kaiser.[10] By the end of 1913, Germany had a regular army of 870,000 front line troops and could mobilize five and a half million men in the event of war. By that date, the foreign politics of the Kaiser having so bungled matters that Germany had only Austria-Hungary as a certain ally, it was obvious that Germany would be forced to fight a two-front war against Russia and France and would have to meet the challenge on the seas of the British fleet, the greatest in the world.[11] Schlieffen, the chief of the German Great General Staff, had anticipated hostilities against Russia and France and in his plans of 1905-06 laid the basis for this two-front war.[12] The

---

[10] For a study of the 19th century German Army see General C. von der Goltz, *Kriegsgeschichte Deutschlands im 19. Jahnhundert* (2 vols. Berlin: G. Bondi, 1910). See also P. Camena d'Almeida, *L'Armée Allemande avant et pendant la Guerre de 1914-18* (Nancy: Bergen-Levrault, 1919); A. F. Kovacs, *Nation in Arms and Balance of Power* (Dissertation, University of Chicago, 1937); H. G. Treitschke, *The Organization of the Army* (London: Gowans and Gray, 1914); L. R. G. Rüdt von Collenberg, *Die Deutsche Armee von* 1871 *bis* 1914 (Berlin: E. S. Mittler, 1922); J. Poirier, *L'Évolution de l'Armée Allemande de* 1888 *à* 1913 (Paris: L. Fournier, 1914).

[11] On German diplomatic history during this period see E. Brandenburg, *op. cit.*; O. Hammann, *Deutsche Welt Politik,* 1890-1912 (Berlin: R. Hobbing, 1925); W. L. Langer, *European Alliances and Alignments,* 1871-90 (New York: A. A. Knopf, 1932); K. Nowak, *Germany's Road to Ruin* (New York: Macmillan Company, 1932); Veit Valentin, *Bismarck's Aussenpolitik von* 1871-1890 (Berlin: Deutsche Verlaggesellschaft für politik, 1922); Veit Valentin, *Deutschlands Aussenpolitik von Bismarcks Abgang bis zum Ende des Weltkrieges* (Berlin: Deutsche Verlagsgesellschaft für Politik, 1921).

[12] On the Schlieffen plan see Eugen Bircher, *Schlieffen, Mann und Idee* (Zurich: 1937); W. Foerster, *Graf Schlieffen und der Weltkrieg* (Berlin: E. J. Mittler, 1925), and *Aus der Gedankenwerkstatt des Deutschen Generstabes* (Berlin: E. J. Mittler, 1931).

major weight of the German army was to be concentrated on the western front against Holland and Belgium. It was hoped that France would be set in motion against such a threat and would violate Belgium's neutrality by taking aggressive action before the German forced moved. By an enveloping attack through Belgium and Holland, Schlieffen hoped to avoid an expensive attack against the French fortification in his center and win a rapid victory. Russia was to be given free rein in the east, but Schlieffen hoped that the Russian forces might be sucked in precipitately and before completely mobilized and the German forces might be in a position to divide them at the Masurian Lakes and do battle there. Tannenberg was full justification of this plan.

Schlieffen was succeeded in 1907 by the younger Moltke, with whose adaptation of the plan for an offensive against France Schlieffen sharply disagreed.[13] The Schlieffen plan in adaptation was employed by the German forces at the opening of hostilities in 1914. In the west the Germans met with initial success, but failed to achieve the desired result of annihilating the French as the latter forces retreated in order. In the east the Grmans were more successful in their efforts against the Russians, but the general strategy of quick action and an immediate victory was not successful due to the inability to carry through in the west. The adoption of trench warfare put an end to the German hope for an annihilation of the French army. The new orientation to campaigns of long duration and against a determined opposition also was not successful, and Moltke was succeeded by others who similarly failed in their efforts to defeat the French-British combination.[14]

---

[13] See General W. Groener, *Der Feldherr wider Willen* (Berlin: E. J. Mittler, 1931) on the younger von Moltke.

[14] On the World War see the official histories of the belligerents, including the British, *History of the Great War, Military Operations, Naval Operations*; the French, *Les Armées Francaises dans la Grande Guerre*; and the German, *Der Weltkrieg*. The memoirs and diaries of leading military and civil leaders, like Churchill, Lloyd George, Ludendorff, Foch, Hindenburg, Falkenhayn, and others will give added color to the official studies.

GREAT BRITAIN

Matching the developing aggressive spirit of Germany by the end of the first decade of the twentieth century was a British nation which had become thoroughly alarmed at the rising German power.[15] The new British political and military commitments were founded upon a reorientation of foreign policy which witnessed Germany taking the place of foremost rival of Britain, rather than France and Russia. When William II turned down the proposals of Joseph Chamberlain for a military agreement in 1899, Britain began to seek elsewhere for the military support necessary to maintain the balance of world power. With the turn of the century Great Britain embarked upon a series of international agreements which saw her and her allies in a strong united position by the outbreak of the World War. In 1902 a military alliance was formed with Japan; in 1904 an agreement was entered into with France establishing respective spheres of colonial interests, and in 1907, following the vigorous stand taken by William II in the Moroccan crisis, an alliance was made with Russia. Though no military commitments were made in the 1904 entente with France, a series of military conversations between the chiefs of the respective military staffs of the two countries led to integrated staff planning. Vigorous military preparations were undertaken especially in the reorganization of the structure of the military establishment and the rapid expansion of the naval force.

Notwithstanding the fact that its geographic position made it a military base of great natural strength, and that it possessed a navy capable of keeping its communication lines undisturbed, it became apparent to the British early in the century that the

---

[15] On British foreign policy see Volume III of the *Cambridge History of British Foreign Policy* (Cambridge: University Press, 1923); G. P. Gooch, *A Century of British Foreign Policy* (London: G. Allen and Unwin, 1917); A. L. Kennedy, *Old Diplomacy and New* (London: J. Murray, 1922); Max Montgales, *British Foreign Policy and Sir Edward Grey* (New York: A. A. Knopf, 1928); A. F. Pilram, *England and the International Policy of the European Great Powers, 1871-1914* (Oxford, Clarendon Press, 1931); Spencer Wilkinson, *Britain at Bay* (London: Constable and Company, 1909).

army needed renovation.[16] The Boer War, among other matters had revealed a definite lack of trained staff officers, and fundamental planning and measures were adopted to rectify these and other faults. In 1904 reorganization of the army was begun with the formation of a general staff. The control of the army was placed in the hands of a council consisting of the Secretary of State for War, the Chief of the General Staff, the Adjutant General, the Quartermaster General, and the Master General of Ordnance. The War Office also was reconstructed and the Committee of Imperial Defense was established as an advisory aid to the cabinet. The numbers in the army were cut down and training made more effective. A reservist system was established that would permit the mobilization of a greater number of trained men, and through a program of territorialization such reservists could be mobilized rapidly and without great delay integrated into tactical units of the army. The staff colleges were enlarged, maneuvers expanded and made more practical, and the army became a small, but a cohesive and extremely hardstriking machine.

Equally significant were the advances made in the navy.[17] When it became apparent that there could be no equitable basis of negotiations with Germany on the limitation of naval construction, the British undertook a building program that easily kept it the leading naval power in the world by the outbreak of the World War. Under the direction of Sir John Fisher, ships carrying a greater burden of armor and having more devastating fire power than the ships of any other fleet were produced in number sufficient to maintain Britain's supremacy at sea. Following the crisis with Germany in 1911 the administration of the navy was likewise reorganized and Winston Churchill was named to head the naval staff.

---

[16] On the British Army see Major D. H. Cole and Major E. C. Preistley, *An Outline of British Military History* (London: Sifton Praed and Company, 1936); Colonel J. K. Dunlop, *Development of the British Army, 1899-1914* (London: Methen, 1938); Sir J. W. Fortescue, *History of the British Army* (14 vols., London: Macmillan Company, 1899-1930).

[17] See the autobiographical writings of Lord Fisher, *Records and Memoirs*.

FRANCE

France's international orientation throughout this century has been based upon the isolation of Germany. In the years prior to the first World War it was necessary to counter the position of the Triple Alliance; in the years following 1918 to hold Germany impotent. An alliance with Russia in 1893 was followed by agreements with Italy in 1900 and Great Britain in 1904 and re-sulted in the practical isolation of Germany.[18] Under the vigor-ous direction of Foreign Minister Delcasse, France initiated an aggressive foreign policy, one which continued even after Premier Rouvier was forced to drop Delcasse following the Moroccan crisis of 1906.

A similar aggressiveness was to be found in French military thought and preparations of the period. Interest in the scientific aspects of the art of war had been awakened in France in the seventies after the disastrous defeat at the hands of the Ger-mans, and that the interest was fanned to flame by the desire to avenge 1871[19] The military establishment was increased so that by 1913 France had a regular army of 720,000 troops and could mobilize four million trained men. Officer training was made more thorough and more practical, armament production in-creased, the navy concentrated in the Mediterranean and geared for action in that theater, and integrated strategy was developed through conversations with the Russian and British military staffs. The new feeling of confidence was to be noted in the military literature and plans of the period. Nowhere is this expressed more thoroughly than in the philosophy of attack current in the instruction at the French staff schools and in the writings of the

[18] See W. L. Langer, *The Franco-Russian Alliance*, 1890-94 (Cambridge: Harvard University Press); Graham Stuart, *French Foreign Policy*, 1898-1914 (New York: Century Company, 1921); Raymond Récouly, *De Bismarck a Poincaré* (Paris: Les Editions de France, 1932); R. P. Millet, *Notre Politique Exterieur de 1898 à 1905* (Paris: F. Juven, 1905); Christian Scheften, *D'une Guerre à l'Autre* (Paris: F. Alcan, 1920); F. L. Schuman, *War and Diplomacy in the French Republic* (New York: Whittlesey House, 1931).

[19] See Joseph Monteilhet, *Les Institutions Militaires de France*, 1814-1932 (Paris F. Alcan, 1932). See also D. D. Irvine, "The French Discovery of Clausewitz and Napoleon," *Journal of the American Military Institute*, IV (Fall, 1941), pp. 143-161; Stefan T. Possony and Etienne Mantou, "Du Picq and Foch: The French School," in Earle, editor, *op. cit.*, pp206-33.

military. The defensive philosophy of the immediate post Franco-Prussian War years, evidenced in the rebuilding of a system of fortifications, gave way to the thesis maintained by Foch and his disciples that the enemy not be permitted to move first and set the plan of campaign. The French-Russian agreement of 1913 calling for a two-front offensive was founded upon such a philosophy, but the French plans were thrown into confusion in 1914 by indecision as to the violation of Belgian neutrality. The Germans made the first move, crossed the Belgian frontier, and set the pattern of action throwing the French onto the defensive.

The military gave added fuel to the aggressive spirit by a splendid demonstration of ability in the colonies. By the turn of the century Galliéni and Lyautey were deep in their work of perfecting the French colonial military system which played so great a part in the concretizing and stabilizing of colonial administration[20] In Indo-China and Madagascar, Galliéni and Lyautey combined force and politics in achieving pacification and successful administration. Later in the century, in his thirteen years in Morocco, from 1912-25, Lyautey added further to the prestige and power of an army which already had attained eminence through its success in the World War.

Russia

Russia, formerly a member of the Triple Alliance, was a partner of France in international affairs by 1900 and had turned its ambitions from the Far East to the Near East after its defeat

---

[20] See Jean Gottman, "Bugeaud, Gallieni, Lyantey: The Development of French Colonial Welfare," in Earle, editor, *op. cit.*, pp. 234-59. Both Lyautey and Galliéni wrote extensively. See Galliéni, *Rapport d'Ensemble sur la Pacification, l'Organisation, et la Colonisation de Madagascar* (Paris: Lavauzelle, 1900) ; Lyautey, *Paroles d'Action* (Paris: A. Colin, 1927).

at the hands of the Japanese in 1905.[21] Fundamental in the new
pattern of Russian activity became its interest in the Balkans and
the Black Sea and Persian areas. Bungling diplomacy displayed in
inept attempts to play Germany, Britain, France, and Italy simultaneously resulted however in but little success in the advance toward domination of the Straits and the Balkans. The defeat of
1905 in a conflict against which such prominent and able statesmen as Baron Rosen and Count Witte had warned, revealed the
full ineptitude of the Russian military leadership and forced
changes in its administration and direction.[22] Under the direction
of Minister of War, Sukhomlinoff, the administration of the war
office was reorganized and staff conversations with the French
brought definite plans and a series of mobilization tests. In 1913
Russia had a regular army of over 1,200,000 and could mobilize
four and a half million men. It was obvious that in material
and in its system of service and supply, Russia was deficient; that
fact early became apparent during the course of the ensuing
conflict.

---

[21] On Russian foreign relations and military preparations see Langer, *Franco-
Russian Alliance*; Gregory Alesensky, *Russia and the Great War* (New York:
Charles Scribner's Sons, 1915); E. J. Dillon, *The Eclipse of Russia* (London:
J. M. Dent and Sons, 1918); S. Dobrovolsky, *Die Mobmlechlachung der Russisen
Armée* (Berlin: 1922); A. von Drygalski and Count von Zeppelin, *Russland, das
heer; die flotte* (Berlin: A. Scholl, 1898); M. T. Florinsky, *The End of Russia
Empire* (New Haven: Yale University Press, 1931); Lt. General N. Golovin,
Russian Army in the World War (New Haven: Yale University Press, 1931);
S. A. Korff, *Russia's Foreign Relations during the Last Half Century* (New York:
Macmillan Company, 1922); René Marchand, *Un Livre Noir* (Paris: Libraire du
Travail, 1922); S. D. Sazonov, *Les Années Fatales* (Paris: Payot, 1927); F .Stieve,
Izvolsky and the World War (London: G. Allen and Unwin, 1926); G. S. C.
Sydenham, *Russia's Sea-Power* (London: J. Murray, 1898).

[22] Baron R. R. Rosen, *Forty Years of Diplomacy* (2 vols., New York: A. A. Knopf,
1922).

ITALY

Notwithstanding the failure of its territorial ambitions in Ethiopia in 1896, Italy continued its quest for territory.[23] That desire forced Italy out of the orbit of the Triple Alliance and agreements were made with France in 1900 and 1902 and with Russia in 1909. The military establishment was put on a war footing under the premiership of Giolloti, and in 1911 using disorders in Tripolitania as an excuse for aggressive action, Italy went to war against Turkey and won Tripolitania and Cyrenaica. Italy's action against Turkey was further indication that it could not be counted as an ally in the Triple Alliance. The success in this war, however, did not lull the Italians into the false belief that they possessed sufficient strength to enter the World War. General Pirro refused to take over the war office in 1914 when insufficient funds were proposed for military preparations. Cadorna who took over as chief of staff in July, 1914 was amazed to discover that staff plans for war with Austria were almost uniformly defensive in character, and that little had been done to plan an offensive.[24] Caporetto for Cadorna was but a reflection of the fact that Italy was in no way capable of participation in a major conflict, even though more than a million and one-half trained men could be mobilized.

AUSTRIA-HUNGARY

Austria-Hungary in the decade and a half before the outbreak of the World War could mobilize close to two million men.

---

[23] On Italian foreign policy and military establishment see Jean Alazard, *L'Italie et le conflict Européen,* 1914-16 (Paris: F. Alcan, 1916); Lucien Dupain, *L'Administration Militaire Italienne* (Paris: Lavauselle, 1892); J. L. Glanville, *Italy's Relations With England,* 1896-1905 (Baltimore: Johns Hopkins University Press, 1934); R. Michels, *L'Imperialismo Italiano* (Milano: Società Editrice Libraria, 1914); Pietro Silva, *L'Italia fra le Grande Potenza,* 1882-1914 (Roma: P. Cremonere, 1931); A. N. Stieglitz, *L'Italie et la Triple Alliance* (Paris: Dujarric, 1906); A. I. Sulliotti, *La Triplice Alleanza,* 1882-1915 (Milano: Fratelli Treves, 1915).

[24] General L. Cadorna, *La Guerra alla Fronte Italiana* (Milano: Fratelli Treves, 1921), and *Altre Pagine sulla Grande Guerra* (Milano: A. Mondori, 1925).

With the substitution of Aahrenthal for Goluchowski, Austria-Hungary embarked upon a vigorous foreign policy.[25] Even more aggressive than the policy of the civilian chiefs of state was that maintained by Conrad von Hötzendorf, chief of staff and later inspector of the Army. Von Hötzendorf, a typical nationalistic fire-eater, called for aggressive action against Russia and Serbia in 1908 and 1909, and became so obnoxious in his opposition to the more tempered opinions of Aehrenthal that the Emporer was forced to remove him from office. Hötzendorf was not stilled, however, for he called for a war against Italy in 1912, and action by Austria-Hungary during the Balkan wars. The seeming passivity of the Germans during 1912-13 aroused his opposition, but this was not the first, nor was it to be the last time that these allies differed in their approach to international affairs.

UNITED STATES

The United States entered the World War with the smallest regular army of any of the major nations of the world. Essentially a naval power, it had maintained isolation while the European nations aligned themselves for the coming struggle for domination.[26] The isolationist character of the international policy of the nation was reflected in the belief that no nation could do battle against the United States, because of its insular position. That its position had changed somewhat with the acquisition of the Philippines was recognized, but no basic strategy was devised to meet the new contingencies. There were appropriations leading to an increase in our naval strength, but funds for

[25] For the foreign policy of Austria-Hungary see especially A. P. Pribram, *Austrian Foreign Policy,* 1908-18 (London: G. Allen and Unwin, 1923); and *Secret Treaties of Austria-Hungary,* 1879-1910 (2 vols., Cambridge: Cambridge University Press, 1920-22). See also Berthold Molden, *Alois Graf Aehrenthal* (Stuttgart: Deutsche Verlagsanstalt, 1917). On the military see F. Conrad von Hötzendorf, *Aus meiner Dienstzeit* (5 vols., Wien: Rikola Verlag, 1921-25); L. Dupain, *L'Administration Militaire Austro-Hongroise* (Paris: Lavauzelle, 1894); E. Kählig, *Osterreich Ungarn: das Heer; die Flotte* (Berlin: A. Schall, 1899); R. Krieger, *Die Enwicklung des Conrad'schen Offensivgedankens* (Stuttgart: W. Kohlhammer, 1934).

[26] See Brig. General John McA. Palmer, *America in Arms: The Experience of the U. S. Military Organization* (New Haven: Yale University Press, 1941).

the Army were limited. By 1913 there were less than one hundred thousand regulars in the American Army, a force considerably less than half the size of the second-rate Italian Army of that year. A realization of the inadequacy of the military force had been apparent during the war with Spain, but measures taken to correct the faults evident in that campaign were nowhere comparable to those adopted in Great Britain as a result of the performance of the British Army in the Boër War. Provisions were made for the integration of staff planning with the establishment of a General Staff in 1903, but internal administrative changes did not alter the fact that Congress, and the nation at large, was not disposed to support an adequate army, let alone one of consequence.[27] The War Department and the army proved its ability to perform during the World War, but in 1922 the army was reduced to a total of 146,000 volunteers on a 3-year service basis. In the years before the World War, as in the period 1919-40, the United States failed to appreciate the need for a policy of adequate military protection.

JAPAN

Japan emerged as a nation of power in international affairs during the first decade of the century with its success against the Russian forces. An army of 87,000 in 1900 was built to more than 250,000 before the outbreak of the World War. By diplomatic and by military demonstration it indicated that henceforth it would be a power to contend with.[28] Through successful alliances during the World War it was able to obtain island holdings in the Pacific which set the stage for the development of military and naval bases throughout the central and western

---

[27] F. L. Huidekoper, *Military Unpreparedness of the United States* (New York: Macmillan Company, 1915).

[28] On the foreign and military policies of Japan see A. L. P. Dennis, *The Anglo-Japanese Alliance* (Berkeley: University of California Press, 1923); J. C. Balet, *Le Japon Militaire* (Yokahoma: Kelly and Walsh, 1910); Captain J. Dubois de Saligny, *Essais sur la Guerre Russo-Japonaise* (Paris: Bergen-Levrault, 1913); Henry Dyer, *Japan in World Politics* (London: Blackie and Son, 1909); J. H. Gubbins, *The Making of Modern Japan* (London: Seeley, Service, 1921); Karl Haushofer, *Dai Nipon* (Berlin: E. S. Mittler, 1913); H. Labroue, *L'Imperialisme Japonais* (Paris: Delagrave, 1911).

expanses of that ocean. Increases in the army and navy, competent instruction, and heavy shipbuilding and armament production provided the facilities by which Japan could make its play for power in the thirties.

THE WAR OF 1914-18

The war that broke out in 1914 seemed inevitable then, and today, after thirty years, seems to have been even more emphatically so.[29] The forces in play for more than a decade could not be stayed, even though men in all the contesting countries tried desperately to prevent actual hostilities. The lightning victory sought by Germany was not obtained, and for four years of dreary position warfare the contesting powers failed to attain decision. The German High Command continued to play for the complete annihilation of the enemy, but were forced to a stalemate by the Allies. The latter effected unified command in the spring of 1918 after four years of ineffective staff relations. In the summer of 1918,—the Allies met a last German offensive, then sent about on counteroffensive and won the war.

The war proved almost all the experts wrong in their belief that it would be short, that actions would be highly mobile, that the offensive would be applied unremittingly—and in many another military matter that had been held as rule since the successes of the German armies in the sixties and the seventies. The war brought with it the introduction of new arms, new services, new facilities that had not been conceived of by military staffs prior to the war, but most significant was the realization that henceforth all resources of the nation, in manpower, industry, government and otherwise must be employed in a total effort to gain victory.

THE MILITARY SITUATION, 1919-44

The conclusion of hosilities brought a peace that satisfied no nation.[30] The United States government reverted to its tradi-

---

[29] See footnote 14.

[30] On the peace treaty see H. W. V. Temperley, *A History of the Peace Conference of Paris*.

tional isolationism, and the victorious powers in Europe sought by passive defensive strategy to retain the gains of the war. No dynamic policy was formulated to cover the obviously growing resentment in Germany and Italy. Instead of military preparations, both Great Britain and France lost themselves in the attempt to hold what they had won with the least expenditure of funds and manpower. The entire history of continental Europe for the twenty years between wars became the story of the steady retreat of the victorious allies before the rising dynamism of the totalitarian powers. In the demilitarization of the Rhine, the return of the Saar, the recreation of the German army, in the Ethiopian affair, in Austria, Spain, Czechoslovakia, did the allies seek to placate Hitler and Mussolini. Military preparations in Great Britain and France followed the political developments and left both nations sorely unprepared for the war that broke out in 1939.

FRANCE 1919-44

From the peace table and the insistence that Germany be completely subjugated, France sought to establish a *cordon sanitaire* about Germany and to force that nation to remain a subservient position. Armament control, the limitation on the size of the army, the provisions against short service and a reservist system, the prohibitions against the development of military aviation, and other devices written into the peace treaty were adopted as a means of keeping Germany from attaining the military primacy which it had held at the outbreak of the World War.[31]

The attempts at isolating Germany were furthered by a series of agreements with Great Britain, Russia, Poland, Czechoslovakia, Yugoslavia, and Rumania. The French military machine was maintained at a relatively high figure, so that the regular army had 666,000 in its ranks in 1928, 692,000 in 1937, and France could put more than five and one-half million men into the field in the event of war. A series of fortifications, the Maginot Line, was constructed with the intent of preventing

---

[31] See Arnold Wolfers, *Britain and France Between Wars* (New York: Harcourt, Brace and Company, 1941).

German penetration into France. But the size of the army and
the vaunted fortifications were false facades. A shortening in
the term of service, the departure from the army of many of the
most competent officers, failure to maintain armament production, inability to perceive the changing nature of modern warfare, and the terrific political wrangling between the parties of
the right and the left over the size of the army, its equipment,
and the nature of strategy and tactics, was such as to prevent
the French army from becoming a truly effective force.[32]

In its final analysis the failure of the French military was
founded upon the inability of the French to control their own
domestic economy. The task of domestic reconstruction following
the end of the war and the seeming inability of the nation to
attain a new dynamic meant formal abdication of her foremost
position in Europe. The paralysis gripping France during the
late twenties and thirties was as evident in the nature of its
military preparedness as in its confused political leadership. The
assurance of power was evident directly following the war, so confident a power that the French did not hesitate to send an armed
force into the Ruhr in 1923 over the question of reparations, gave
way in the thirties to the belief that stationary defenses, formidable artillery, and good luck would hold off the Germans.
The spring of 1940 proved otherwise.

Great Britain

The conclusion of hostilities brought relief to the British.
Domestic disturbances created by the inability of private industry
to take care of returning veterans were so severe that Lloyd
George was forced out of power in 1921. The conservative administrations of Bonar Law and Baldwin succeeded George, and
were in turn succeeded by MacDonald's first Labor government,

---

[32] See S. C. Davis, *French War Machine* (London: G. Allen and Unwin, 1937);
General M. E. Debeney, *La Guerre et les Hommes* (Paris: Plon, 1937); Monteilhet, *op. cit.*, General A. J. H. Mordacq, *Faut-il Changer, le Régime* (Paris: A.
Michel, 1935), and *Les Leçons de 1914 et la Prochaine Guerre* (Paris: Flam-
marian, 1934); Pertinax, *Les Fossoyeurs* (2 vols., New York: 1943); A. F.
Kovacs, "Military Origins of the Fall of France," *Military Affairs*, VII (Spring,
1943), pp. 25-40.

but in none of these administrations nor in any that succeeded them for the next fifteen years did there seem to be any full appreciation of the need for a proper military policy.[33] It was the fashionable belief that Britain did not need to fear military aggression and that the British navy and French army were sufficient to maintain for them dominant power in the European theater.[34] The naval strategy of the British continued to be the control of sea communications, but the German navy no longer being a menace, Great Britain entered into agreements with the United States and other powers whereby her fleet strength was reduced. The army abandoned the reforms of Haldane during the period of 1904-10 and returned to the old Cardwell system, with the British army at home being only for the purpose of replacements for the overseas garrisons. By 1936 the British army stood at 197,000 men, twenty-five percent less than it had been in 1900. Arms production was sharply curtailed as the burden of domestic relief cut deeply into the revenue of the nation, and the British retreated as vigorously from the thought of war as did the French. During the thirties the idea became widely current that Britain should engage only in defensive actions in the event of a war, in order that Britain not suffer such a loss in manpower as she had during World War I.

Britain, like France, attempted in ostrich-fashion to avoid recognizing that the expansionist policies being advocated by Italy, and Japan could lead to war. Appeasement, the desire to temporize, to avoid armed conflict was almost as fatal for Britain as it was for France. Only by superlative, dogged resistance was Britain able to come back after the disasters of May-June, 1940 to do contest with Germany.

ITALY

Diametrically opposed to the defensive, dispirited position taken by France and Britain during the two decades after the con-

---

[33] See Sir Guy C. Williams, "Changes in British Strategy," *Military Affairs*, VIII (Spring, 1944), pp. 7-14.

[34] On British foreign policy see G. P. Gooch, *British Foreign Policy since the War* (London: G. Bell, 1936). For an insight into the prevailing military philosophy of the period see especially the works of Liddell Hart, *The British Way in Warfare* (London: Faber and Faber, 1935).

clusion of World War I was the display of aggressiveness by the Axis powers.[35] Coming into power through a virtual *coup d'etat,* Mussolini, by the subjugation of all elements of the Italian populace to his will, effected a degree of unity not attained previously in the century by Italy. Designating himself as a new Caesar, he sought the establishment of a modern Italian Empire. The armed forces of the nation were developed to a strength they had never possessed and by 1937 there were 400,000 men in the regular army. Armament production was accelerated, the air force built to such proportions that it was recognized as outstanding in Europe for some time, and innovations made in naval craft so that the Italian fleet became in effect a latter-day version of the *jeune ecole* school of small, fast ships—capable of commerce and coast raiding in the Mediterranean.[36]

Italian military strategy was founded upon an expansionist political philosophy, and its orientation was according to that political bent. In 1934, by a show of strength against the rising Hitler, Mussolini indicated his pretensions to domination of Mitteleuropa as well as the Mediterranean. In the next year, he opened a successful campaign to avenge Adowa. He was temporarily successful in unseating Haile Selassie and further strengthened his position in developing his colonial enterprises in northern Africa. France and Britain stood by during the Ethiopian campaign. The revelations of the Hoare-Laval conversations, by

---

[35] For studies of Italian foreign policy during Mussolini's dictatorship see J. Ancel, *Les Balkans face à l'Italie* (Paris: Delagrove, 1928); G. A. Borgese, *Goliath, the March of Fascism* (New York: Viking Press, 1937); R. Cantalupo, *Fatti Europei e Politica Italiana, 1922-24* (Milano: Imperia, 1924); M. I. Currey, *Italian Foreign Policy, 1918-32* (London: I. Nicholson and Watson, 1932); Dino Grandi, *L'Italia Fascista nella Politica Internazionale* (Roma: Libreria del Littorio, 1930); M. H. H. Macartney, *Italy's Foreign Colonial Policy, 1914-37* (London: Oxford University Press, 1938); P. Agostino Orsini, *L'Italia nella Politica Africana* (Bologna: L. Cappelli, 1926); G. Salvemini, *Mussolini Diplomate* (Paris: B. Grasset, 1932).

[36] For a statement on the defense problem in the early twenties see Aldo Valori, *Probleme Militori della Nuova Italia* (Milano: Imperia, 1923). For an estimate of the Italian forces just prior to the outbreak of the Second World War see the League of Nations, *Armaments Year-Book.*

which both countries were revealed as being not unsympathetic to the Italian aggression, presented in bold relief the abject poverty of their position. The full significance of that renunciation was to be seen in the utter resignation at German-Italian participation in the Spanish civil war, in the overpowering of Austria and Czechoslovakia, and the inability to contest the rising Japanese threat in fashion other than to strengthen the British base at Singapore.

GERMANY

An even more spectacular success in overcoming internal resistance to his authority and then attaining position in international affairs was scored by Hitler after his ascension to power in Germany in 1933.[37] Liquidating opposition, Hitler coordinated the military and civil life of the nation by the most ruthless and undemocratic means, and went on to the domination and control of Europe. Hitler turned away from the expansionist colonial policies of William II and concentrated on a nazified version of the Bismarckian ideal of control of central Europe and preeminence on the continent. Such preeminence was to be followed by domination of the world.

Utilizing the military ideas of an *attaque brusqueé* set forth by von Seeckt, coordinating industry and the military on the basis of plans formulated by Walter Rathenau during the World War, employing propaganda techniques laid down by Ludendorff, Hitler was able to develop in Germany a unity of purpose and spirit that stood the army in good stead during the course

---

[37] On the growth of National Socialism see A. Hitler, *Mein Kampf* (Boston: Houghton-Mifflin, 1943); K. Heiden, *A History of National Socialism* (New York: A. A. Knopf, 1935); H. Lichtenberg, *The Third Reich* (New York: A. A. Knopf, 1937); F. L. Schuman, *The Nazi Dictatorship* (New York: A. A. Knopf, 1936); Hermann Ranschnigg, *The Voice of Destruction* (New York: G. P. Putnam's Son, 1940); Rohan d'O. Butler, *The Roots of National Socialism* (New York: E. P. Dutton, 1942).

of military campaigns such as no army had ever attempted in the history of the world.[38]

The German military forces, directed by Junkers, tended to its professional affairs and displayed its customary ability. The military strategy employed by Hitler and his military advisers utilized the time honored practice of disposing of one foe at a time. The strategy was successful in Austria and Czechoslovakia without the necessity of armed conflict. In Poland the German forces were able to annihilate the Polish army by powerfully combined air-ground operations, and in Denmark, Holland, Belgium, France, and Norway, similar power pushes won him quick victories. The initial successes gave way in the third to the fifth years of war to campaigns on the ground in Africa and Russia, and to a similar campaign in the air with the British and American forces. In 1943 Germany went on the defensive; in the spring of 1944 it was still in Russia and holding all her gains on the European continent except portions of Italy below Rome and sections of northern Esthonia, Poland and Rumania to which the Red army had penetrated. By this time the Germany army had lost heavily on the Russian and African fronts, but these losses were not decisive.[39] Through the utilization of industrial labor enslaved from all the conquered countries of Europe and through the employment of the forces of allies in military operations, Germany still retained great strength.

---

[38] For an appraisal of the new German Army see H. Rosinski, *The German Army* (New York: Harcourt, Brace and Company, 1940); Albert Müller, *Germany's War Machine* (London: J. M. Dent Sons, 1936). See also a fine summary on Hitlerian strategy by E. M. Earle, "Hitler: The Nazi Concept of War," in Earle, *op. cit.*, pp. 505-16; General H. von Seeckt, *Die Reichswehr* (Berlin: R. Kittler, 1933). On strategy and techniques see Karl Justrow, *Der Technische Krieg im Spiegelbild der Kriegserfahrungen und der Weltpresse* (Berlin: R. Claassen, 1938); General E. Ludendorff, *The Coming War* (London: Faber and Faber, 1938); E. Banse, *Wehrwissenschaft* (Leipzig: Armeen-Verlag, 1933); H. Foertsch, *Art of Modern Warfare* (New York: Veritas Press, 1940).

[39] For a statement of Germany on the defensive see H. A. DeWeerd, "Germany on the Defensive," *Yale Review*. Winter, 1943.

Soviet Union

For the Soviet Union throughout the period between wars, the basic political and military consideration was to remain at peace in order that the nation might develop its resources.[40] Having conquered the white forces in Russia, and concluded hostilities against the allied powers, Poland, and Finland, the Soviet Union set itself to the problem of industrialization and the realization of its natural potentialities. In international affairs throughout this period the Soviet Union became the arch-exponent of collective security. At the sessions of the League of Nations, and in diplomatic negotiations the Soviet Union sought such assurances from the nations of Europe, but they were not forthcoming.[41] The military orientation of the nation was founded upon its alliances with France and the Little Entente, and military preparations were prosecuted with a spirit seemingly equal to that in Italy and Germany. Conscription was maintained, armament production greatly accelerated, staff schools were established, and the army completely democratized in keeping with the general principles of the October revolution. Innovations in tactics and the use of special troops and material gave further evidence of the Soviet Union's intention of developing a first-rate army. Border clashes with the Japanese and a full-dress war with Finland gave Russian military leaders the opportunities to test men and material. By 1928, Russia had a regular army of close to 700,000 men, and could mobilize more than six million trained troops. In the next decade this number of men in the regular army was doubled and almost eight million trained men could be mobilized in the event of war.

In the summer of 1939 the Soviet Union broke with its allies to make terms with Germany, in what seemed to be an effort

---

[40] See Fedetoff White, *The Red Army* (Princeton: Princeton University Press, 1943); Erich Wollenberg, *The Red Army* (London: Secker and Warburg, 1940).

[41] On Soviet foreign policy see Maxim Litvinov, *Against Aggression* (New York: International, 1939); M. T. Florinsky, *Towards an Understanding of the U. S. S. R.* (New York: Macmillan Company, 1939); D. J. Dallin, *Soviet Russia's Foreign Policy, 1939-43* (New Haven: Yale University Press, 1942); F. R. Dulles, *Road to Teheran* (Princeton: Princeton University Press, 1944).

to gain time for further military preparation. When the Soviet Union did come into action in the summer of 1941, it displayed a military competence that few had expected of it. The generalship, quality of equipment and supplies, and ability and courage of the individual soldier were impressively demonstrated in the next three years of war.

UNITED STATES

The United States returned to a foreign policy of isolation after the conclusion of the World War.[42] The internal administration of the military establishment was defined in the passage of the National Defense of 1920, but the temper of the country was pacificistic and anti-military and the defense forces suffered accordingly. By 1922 the regular army had been reduced to 146,000 men, and by 1928 it was down to 136,000. Within the next decade it rose to 167,000. Peacetime naval production aspired to before the entrance of the United States into the World War was curtailed as this country took part in the program of naval disarmament started at the Washington Conference in 1921. Armament production declined to a fraction of wartime totals, and there were few advances in development and utilization of new equipment. It was not until the outbreak of hostilities in Europe in 1939 that the United States would take vigorous measures, for notwithstanding the growing power of Germany and Italy in Europe and the even more definite menace of Japan to the Pacific holdings of the United States, this country maintained a general policy of neutrality and isolation. These were decades of indecision for the United States, of eminent satisfaction with our position in the twenties and of concentration upon the domestic problems which beset the country in the de-

[42] See Pendleton Herring, *The Impact of War* (New York: Farrar and Rinehart, 1941) for a discussion of the effect of foreign policy upon military preparation. On recent U. S. foreign policy see C. P. Howland, editor, *Survey of American Foreign Relations,* 1928-31 (4 vols., New Haven: Yale University Press, 1928-31); U. S. Department of State, *Peace and War: United States Foreign Policy,* 1931-41 (Washington: Government Printing Office, 1942); A. W. Griswold, *The Far Eastern Policy of the United States* (New York: Harcourt, Brace and Company, 1938); R. L. Buell, *Isolated America* (New York: A. A. Knopf, 1940); A. W. Dulles and H. F. Armstrong, *Can We Be Neutral?* (New York: Harper and Brothers, 1936).

pression of the thirties. The nation had sought to turn its back upon the world, and remain secure behind two great oceans— a desire proven impossible in 1939 and for the future.[43]

JAPAN

In the two decades after the World War Japan embarked upon a program of imperial expansion as extensive as that ever undertaken by the most ambitious of European powers.[44] Throughout the twenties the army was developed and modernized, the navy perfected, and nationalism spread by spirited groups of young officers and ambitious industrialists.[45] In 1931 Japan struck in Manchuria and in short order was able to place that country under its domination. Six years later hostilities were opened against China and the Japanese army gradually forced the poorly equipped Chinese forces and the Chinese populace to retreat to the interior in order to continue the defense of their

---

[43] See Major G. F. Eliot, *Ramparts We Watch* (New York: Reynal Hitchcock, 1938); George T. Davis, *A Navy Second to None* (New York: Harcourt, Brace and Company, 1940); Johnson Hagood, *We Can Defend America* (New York: Doubleday, Doran, 1937); N. J. Spykman, *America's Strategy in World Politics* (New York: Harcourt, Brace and Company, 1942); H. Agar, *A Time for Greatness* (Boston: Little, Brown and Company, 1942); Hallett Abend, *Ramparts of the Pacific* (New York: Doubleday, Doran and Company, 1942); Seymour Harris, *The Economics of American Defense* (New York: W. W. Norton and Company, 1941).

[44] See J. F. Abbott, *Japanese Expansion and American Policies* (New York: Macmillan Company, 1916); Gregory Bienstock, *Struggle for the Pacific* (New York: Macmillan Company, 1937); G. Gothein, *Japans Expansionsdrang* (Zurich: Rascher Verlag, 1936); Nathaniel Peffer, *Japan and the Pacific* (London: H. Hamilton, 1935); A. M. Young, *Imperial Japan,* 1926-38 (London: G. Allen and Unwin, 1938).

[45] K. W. Colegrove, *Militarism in Japan* (New York: World Peace Foundation, 1936); E. E. N. Causton, *Militarism and Foreign Policy in Japan* (London: G. Allen and Unwin, 1936); M. D. Kennedy, *Some Aspects of Japan and Her Defence Forces* (London: K. Paul, Trench and Trubner, 1928); Ushisaburo Kobayashi, *Military Industries of Japan* (New York: Oxford University Press, 1922); Tsunekichi Kono, *Japanese Army* (Tokyo: 1929); Guchi Ono, *War and Armament Expenditures of Japan* (New York: Oxford University Press, 1922); Gotaro Ogawa, *Conscription System in Japan* (New York: Oxford University Press, 1921); O. Tanin, *Militarism and Fascism in Japan* (London: M. Lawrence, 1934).

country.[46] In 1941 Japan entered the second World War and within one year had control of major British, Dutch, and American possessions in the western Pacific.[47] The display of might by the Japanese army, navy, and air force came as a shocking surprise to the great majority of thinking people the world over. It was not until late in 1942 that the Allies were able to begin offensive action against the Japanese with an attack by American marines on Guadalcanal Island in the Solomons. By spring of 1944, the Solomons had been cleared of the Japanese, the Gilberts and Marshalls had been taken, and the United States Pacific Fleet had been able to shell Paramushiro in the Kuriles and Truk in the Carolines, but the Japanese still held the Dutch East Indies, the Philippines, Burma, the Malay Peninsula and many of the islands of the Pacific formerly under Allied control.

CONCLUSION

The past four decades have brought clearly to the mind of America the need for definite foreign and military policies. No longer are we able to isolate ourselves from the rest of the world and conceive of the oceans to our East and West as being adequate protection for all aggressors. Nor can we blithely accept events of political consequence anywhere, be it in deepest Africa or Asia, as outside the sphere of our interest. Modern transportation and communication, and an evolving economy that knows no national bounds, make it imperative that our diplomatic and military policies be reoriented in the light of the most recent developments. The second half of the twentieth century should witness the United States fully attaining its position of preeminence among the world powers.

---

[46] Seiji G. Hishida, *The Manchoukuo Question* (Tokyo: Maruzen Company, 1934).
[47] On Japan and World War II, see Hugh Byas, *The Japanese Enemy* (New York: A. A. Knopf, 1942); J. C. Grew, *Report from Tokyo* (New York: Simon and Schuster, 1942); Wilfrid Fleisher, *Our Enemy Japan* (New York: Doubleday, Doran and Company, 1942); O. D. Tolischus, *Tokyo Record* (New York: Reynal and Hitchcock, 1943).

BIBLIOGRAPHY

ALLEN, W. C., *War! Behind the Smoke Screen* (Philadelphia: Winston, 1929). War stripped of its glamour, with illustrations from the great conflict of 1914-1918.

ASTON, SIR GEORGOE GREY, ed., *The Study of War for Statesmen and Citizens* (New York: Longmans, Green, 1927). Lectures on the various aspects of modern war.

BERNARD, L. L., *War and Its Causes* (New York: Henry Holt and Co., 1944). A valuable survey of the militaristic theories. Bibliography, pp. 459-468.

COWAN, A. R., *War in World History* (New York: Longmans, Green and Co., 1929). Sets forth the essentially destructive influence of war on the progress of civilization.

CUSTANCE, SIR REGINALD NEVILLE, *A Study of War* (Boston: Houghton Mifflin Co., 1925). A sound discussion of the political and military aspects, by a British admiral.

FULLER, J. C. C., *The Reformation of War* (New York: E. P. Dutton, 1923). Pertinent discussion of the necessity of facing war as a permanent fact in human society.

HODGES, CHARLES, "Why War?", Chapter I in F. J. Brown, Charles Hodges, and Joseph S. Roucek, *Contemporary World Politics* (New York: John Wiley and Sons, 2nd printing, 1940), pp. 6-28. A short but brilliant exposition of the decline of our civilization.

HOWE, QUINCY, ed., *The Pocket Book of the War* (New York: Pocket Books, 1941). Chapters from outstanding current books on the present war.

ROUCEK, JOSEPH S., ed., *Contemporary Europe* (New York: D. Van Nostrand Co., 1941). A survey of Europe in relationship to world trends between the first and second World Wars.

ROUCEK, JOSEPH S., "War As a Symptom of Our Social Crisis," Chapter 20, pp. 591-608, in T. V. Kalijarvi, ed., *Modern World Politics* (New York: Thomas Y. Crowell Co., 1942). Also bibliography, pp. 606-8.

SCHUMANN, F. L., *International Politics* (New York: McGraw-Hill Book Co., 3rd ed., 1941). A brilliant exposition of the violent aspects of our modern civilization.

SHEEN, FULTON, *Whence Come Wars* (New York: Sheed, 1940). A discussion of the roots of war in human nature.

SPEIER, HANS, AND KAHLER, ALFRED, eds., *War in Our Times* (New York: W. W. Norton, 1939). A collection of valuables introductory studies.

WALLER, WILLARD, ed., *War in the Twentieth Century* (New York: The Dryden Press, 1940). One of the most useful works, prepared by specialists, on this topic.

WRIGHT, QUINCY, *A Study of War* (2 vols., Chicago: University of Chicago Press, 1942). A systematic and comprehensive study of the entire subject of war; with endless footnotes and references.

CHAPTER XIV

INTERNATIONAL LAW IN THE TWENTIETH CENTURY

PITMAN B. POTTER

International law constitutes, in this first half of the twentieth century, both a form of political thought, or a way of thinking about the universe (the world of nations), and also a device for managing the conduct of international relations. We shall approach the subject from both points of view, examine various aspects of the matter under both headings, and also try to reconcile these divergent elements into one whole.[1]

1. NATURE

The clearest identification of international law is to be had by reference to its content. This consists of general principles and detailed rules regulating the behavior of the nations one toward another,[2] individually or in groups, including unions of states and their agencies.[3] The question of whether sub-state entities, even down to the level of individual human beings, may properly be included in this system is, however, very much in dispute,[4] as is the exact content of the law itself. International law may, moreover, refer to the behavior of all states or other entities (general international law) or to that of any number of

---

[1] For fuller discussion of many of the points mentioned in this article, see the author's *Manual Digest of Common International Law* (New York: Harper, 1932), cited hereafter as *Manual,* especially Parts A, B, and D.

[2] G. G. Wilson, *International Law* (Boston: Silver, Burdett, 8th ed., 1922), Sec. 1.

[3] See below, Sec. 10, for fuller discussion, especially note 54.

[4] The same, at note 55.

states or other entities (special international law), the essential nature of the law being the same in the two cases but its practical importance varying somewhat according to the number of the parties involved and their importance.

A certain school of late nineteenth century political thought tended to define law in general as that which is enforced in case of attempted violation of its terms and to deny to international law the status of law on this account.[5] This criticism has lost much of its force today when it is seen that for much public law—and even private law—the facilities for enforcement are far from perfect, that the great bulk of obedience to law in all fields is voluntary, and that in the international field individual state enforcement bulks large even if community enforcement is lacking.[6]

The fact is that any branch of law dealing with social relations, whose essence is to be sought in its binding force, may derive that quality from more than one source. The law may be reliable in this sense because it is an accurate description of what the parties to it, for reasons inherent in their natures and their reactions, may be counted upon to do in given situations. It might be reliable because decreed by a superior authority with power of enforcement. Finally it might be decisive because accepted by the states themselves, and it seems to be the dominant opinion still today that this is the most solid basis of the binding force of international law.

2. Nomenclature

The term "international law" has almost entirely replaced another name, "the law of nations," formerly used to refer to the same body of material, although the latter term is still used

---

[5] W. J. Brown, *The Austrinian Theory of Law* (London: J. Murray, 1912), pp. 3, 50, 51 ff.

[6] See discussion of the bases and authority of international law, and its enforcement, below, Secs. 8, 11, 15.

by a few students who find it difficult logically to accept the younger concept.[7] At times the adjective "public" is inserted in front of the main words "international law"; [8] this is intended to indicate that the law referred to relates to the rights and duties of states, in contrast to what is at times called "private international law".[9] Apart from the fact that what is called "public" international law at times relates to sub-state entities, it is also the fact that "private" international law consists essentially of principles for resolving conflicts of law or jurisdiction among states over individuals, their activities, and their property, and hence itself constitutes one sector of public international law.[10] These features of the situation are present in the thought and in the languages of all the major Western countries.

3. PLACE

International law is to be distinguished from several other aspects of the international phenomenon. "International comity" does not purport to possess binding authority but consists merely of behavior based on courtesy; such is the execution by one country of judicial decisions rendered in another.[11] International relations" or "international politics" consist of the flow of political, economic, and other relations among states and their peoples, much of which is not regulated by law at all.[12] "International

[7] H. W. Briggs, *The Law of Nations* (New York: E. C. Crofts, 1938), pp. iii, 978; E. D. Dickinson, *A Selection of Cases and Other Readings on the Law of Nations* (New York: McGraw-Hill Book Co., 1929); and work cited below, note 24.

[8] A. S. Hershey, *Essentials of Public International Law and Organization* (New York: The Macmillan Co., 1927). This is very much more common among French and Spanish writers than among English or Americans; J. B. Scott and W. H. E. Jaeger, eds., *Cases on International* Law (St. Paul, Minn.: West, 1937), pp. lix-lxix.

[9] On private international law in general, see: J. H. Beale, *A Treatise on the Conflict of Laws* (Cambridge, Mass.: Harvard University Press, 1916).

[10] Potter, *Manual*, pp. 53-57.

[11] On the nature and extent of comity, see: Scott and Jaeger, p. 29, note 26.

[12] W. R. Sharp and G. Kirk, *Contemporary International Politics* (New York: Farrar and Rinehart, 1940).

organization" consists of the institutions and procedures utilized for the conduct and control of international relations; these institutions are regulated only in part by international law.[13] "International administration" is that part of international organization having as its function the application of international law and legislation.[14] Finally, "international government" consists properly of international administration where the element of cöercion is present; most international coöperation, organized as well as unorganized, is wholly voluntary in character, although international law enters into the picture at various points, as just indicated.[15]

4. HISTORY

By the beginning of the twentieth century international law was already a time-honored institution.[16] Traces of it are to be found in remote pre-Christian times, both in the Mediterranean area and in Asia.[17] The institution grew only slowly and fitfully in Antiquity, saw no great expansion in the Middle Ages, and only moderate growth in modern times prior to the last part of the nineteenth century. This long history was studded alternately with brief periods of rapid development (late sixteenth and early seventeenth century, early nineteenth, 1855-1875), interspersed with periods of comparative stagnation. By the opening of the present century, however, the concept of international law, its content, its practical employment, and the apparatus and technique therefor, had reached a high level.[18] Indeed so seemingly

---

[13] See in general the author's *Introduction to the Study of International Organization* (New York: D. Appleton-Century Co., 4th ed., 1935).

[14] See in general N. L. Hill, *International Administration* (New York: McGraw-Hill Book Co., 1931).

[15] See discussion between the present writer and another in *The American Political Science Review*, XXV (August, 1931), p. 173.

[16] There is no good comprehensive history of international law; see Potter, *Manual*, Part B.

[17] Hershey, Secs. 16-25.

[18] See J. W. Garner, *Recent Developments in International Law* (Calcutta, 1925).

well established was international law in thought, word, and deed, by the year 1900, that basic fallacies in its foundations and structure were unduly ignored.

Since 1900 international law has suffered a series of violent ups and downs. From 1900 to 1914 the story was one of increased growth and consolidation; in spite of several limited wars the rules relating to the conduct of hostilities were, on the whole, perfected rather than impaired, and the rules relating to international behavior in time of peace grew notably both in volume and in quality.[19] The law of war was badly shaken by the conduct of various belligerents in World War I, however, and this damage was not repaired afterward.[20] On the other hand, the law relating to normal international relations expanded very greatly and most beneficially in the period of 1919-1939, chieflly by the process of treaty-making or "international legislation".[21] Again today the law of war, or what was left of it in 1919 (and we have never known just what that was), is being revolutionized—or at least being challenged extensively and fundamentally—, and some of the principles of basic international relations (war and peace; right to remain neutral) also.[22]

5. ORIGINS

Without necessarily raising the problem of causation in all its logical and social aspects, it is important in any consideration of international law to inquire concerning the way in which that law comes into being. Both in primitive times (so far as any evidence reveals the true state of affairs), and in our own days, international law has originated from the desires of individuals and groups of individuals in the states which make the law and

---

[19] Same.

[20] J. B. Moore, *International Law and Some Current Illusions* (New York: The Macmillan Co., 1924), Chapters I, V, and references.

[21] M. O. Hudson, *International Legislation* (Washington, D. C.: Carnegie Endowment for International Peace, 1931).

[22] P. C. Jessup, "In Support of International Law," *American Journal of International Law,* XXXIV (July, 1940), p. 505.

from the response of public officials to such desires. At times the public official (Secretary of Foreign Affairs, Ambassador) will be expressing his own ideas of what should be done for the public welfare in this, that, or the other matter (settlement of disputes, commercial policy), but in most cases he will be trying to satisfy the demands of private interests. In a minority of subjects—disarmament, *e.g.*—something like pure state policy will decide the issue.[23]

6. Evolution

The changes through which international law has passed in the course of its history and in more recent decades are significant. These changes have related to the subject matters treated by the law, to its mode of formation, and to its application.

Thus international law began by treating of war and diplomacy, the earliest forms of contact between states.[24] Commercial and personal intercourse (navigation, travel and residence, trade) followed soon after. It was only in relatively recent times that matters such as postal and electrical communications, health, morals, and intellectual life came in for regulation, not to mention the more advanced aspects of economic and social problems (raw materials, finance, migration). Today the process of including more and more subjects in the scope of international jurisdiction goes on apace.[25]

The earliest international law was mainly based on custom and practice, supplemented by bipartite treaties. Only in the nineteenth century did multipartite conventions assume great importance. Finally, in the present century the promulgation of international law by majority vote—in international conferences—

---

[23] For a brilliant case study in the initiation of international law see J. E. Stover, *S. O. Levinson and the Pact of Paris* (Chicago: University of Chicago Press, 1943).

[24] T. A. Walker, *History of the Law of Nations* (Cambridge, England: Cambridge University Press, 1899), Sec. 30.

[25] P. B. Potter, "The Expansion of International Jurisdiction," in *Political Science Quarterly*, XLI (December, 1926), p. 546.

made its appearance, although it has not developed very extensively even as yet.[26]

Application of the law was at first left to individual states, acting on the international plane or in their internal administration (where a suitable occasion for application of international law often arises).[27] An exception is found in the application of the law by international tribunals, which made its appearance as early as 4000 B.C.[28] The latter mode of application of the law has been greatly expanded in the present century,[29] and has been supplemented by non-judicial international administration and even enforcement in case of need by sanctions of various types.[30]

7. SUBDIVISIONS

Along with the extension of international law in the present century to cover various new subjects, a traditional subdivision of the law, based on the alternative conditions of peace and war, with the status of neutrality forming either a third major division of the field or a subdivision of the law of war, has remained intact. The law of peace has always been regarded as the major and normal branch of the law, even in times when war was more frequent and more legitimate than it has recently become.[31] The law of war did, however, develop in such detail and importance in the sixteenth, seventeenth, and eighteenth centuries as to threaten to overshadow the law of peace. In the present century there has

---

[26] See C. A. Riches, *Majority Rule in International Organization* (Baltimore: John Hopkins University Press, 1940).

[27] P. Q. Wright, *Enforcement of International Law Through Municipal Law in the United States* (Urbana: University of Illinois Press, 1916).

[28] M. A. Tod, *International Arbitration Among the Greeks* (Oxford: Clarendon Press, 1913), p. 169.

[29] M. Habicht, *Treaties for the Pacific Settlement of International Disputes* (Cambridge, Mass.: Harvard University Press, 1931); M. O. Hudson, *The Permanent Court of International Justice, 1920-1942* (New York: The Macmillan Co., 1943).

[30] Hill, pp. 1, 46.

[31] H. Grotius, *On the Law of War and Peace* (1625), Bk. II, Chapters i, xxii; also Bk. III, Chapter XXV. On the frequency of war in modern times, see: Quincy Wright, *A Study of War* (Chicago: University of Chicago Press, 1942), p. 235.

been a tendency to deprecate this development and even to suppress this branch of the subject,[32] or—in very recent years, with the development of projects of international police action—to convert it into something else.[33] Similarly there has been a tendency to suppress the status of neutrality and the law expressing its implications—which developed most vigorously between 1793 and 1917 —, although the outcome here as in the preceding problem is still uncertain.[34]

8. BASES

During all of these developments two rival views respecting the fundamental basis of international law have striven for mastery and the contest still continues. One school of thought would base international law on what might be called a rational foundation, the other would derive its rules from what might be called a volitional source. Under the first should be entered the concept of international law as a reading of the will of a supernatural authority—even though the law would, in this case, embody the will of such an authority—, or as a transcription of the nature of man and of nations.[35] Under the second would appear the concept of international law as the product of the will of the nations or of the international community (called "the family of nations" in the time of the "law of nations", already mentioned).[36] The former type of law resides, latent, in the noumena

---

[32] C. G. Fenwick, *International Law* (New York: D. Appleton-Century Co., 2nd ed., 1934), pp. x, 27, 443. See contrary view presented by the present writer in Third Conference of Teachers of International Law, *Proceedings* (Washington, 1928), p. 95.

[33] Thus any international police force would doubtless be held to observation of the laws of war on land or sea. For a related problem see H. Wehberg, *Theory and Practice of International Policing* (Toronto: Macmillan, 1935), especially Chapter II.

[34] P. C. Jessup, *Neutrality: Today and Tomorrow* (New York: Columbia University Press, 1936); Quincy Wright, "The Present Status of Neutrality," *American Journal*, XXXIV (July, 1940), p. 391.

[35] E. Nys, "Development and Formation of International Law," *Ibid.*, VI (January, 1912), p. 1.

[36] On the Positivist school see note in Briggs, p. 23, and literature there cited.

of international life; the latter appears on the surface thereof. The second, or positivist theory, has, in general, won out over the first theory, although the latter is by no means entirely defunct and enjoys more or less of a revival whenever, as at the present moment, the nations seem to many observers to violate both transcendental and human wisdom in their activities.[37] Actually the positivist doctrine allows room for natural, if not divine, wisdom or law in its scope but insists that before the latter can become international law it must be adopted as such by the nations—a position which, however, does not go far enough to satisfy the theologians or the ethical philosophers.[38]

According to the dominant doctrine the basis of international law is the consent of the states.[39] This consent is in all but a small fraction of cases free and voluntary in character, but the doctrine does not exclude enforced consent.[40] Such consent—even when freely given—seems to certain observers to be but a weak reed on which to base law, as it may be given or withheld at discretion, and even revoked under certain circumstances,[41] but it has not proven unreliable in the vast majority of cases in the history of international relations. It also seems arbitrary and even vicious to other observers of the behavior of the states—it involves approval of whatever the latter choose to do, or so it seems [42]—but in the main international behavior is far from meriting such condemnation and it is difficult to see how any transcendental law or one not accepted by the states themselves can have much practical effect.

---

[37] C. J. Haines, *The Revival of Natural Law Concepts* (Cambridge, Mass.: Harvard University Press, 1930), deals chiefly with American Constitutional questions but throws much light on the general problem.

[38] Potter, *International Organization*, p. 160.

[39] *Ibid.*, p. 159; Briggs, p. 6.

[40] C. C. Hyde, *International Law* (Boston: Little, Brown, 1922), Sec. 493.

[41] Briggs, pp. 23-24, citing de Visscher.

[42] J. H. Ralston, *Democracy's International Law* (Washington, D. C.: Byrne, 1922), especially Chaps. I, VI, VII.

9. SOURCES

In view of the conceptions held concerning the nature or basis of international law it follows that the law emerges or flows from certain sources and is made manifest in certain materials which may be consulted for evidence of its content. The principal sources of international law are practice and agreement, practice itself embodying agreement and consent, and the latter extending from treaties to legislative action taken by less than unanimous consent in international conferences on the basis of an original agreement giving such bodies authority so to act.[43] The materials to be consulted for evidence of international practice include documentary materials and also historical writings of all kinds.[44] Similar materials yield evidence of international agreements—particularly the texts of treaties.[45] The decisions of judicial bodies, both national and international, serve as another expression of international consent through practice and enjoy in addition a certain degree of public authority which seems to buttress the binding force of these elements.[46] Finally, the writings of private jurists exercise a certain influence in this connection also although they have no authority in themselves.[47]

In this connection the concept of national or regional schools of international law, very prominent in recent times, must be noted.[48] An Anglo-American school is contrasted with a Continental Civil Law school.[49] American international law is distinguishable from European,[50] Asiatic from Occidental,[51] and so

[43] On the doctrine of the original agreement see note 57 below. It should be noted that "consent" is not mere self-limitation, however, in view of the presence of second, or other, parties.

[44] See Hershey, Sec. 15.

[45] League of Nations, *Treaty Series,* Geneva, 1920.

[46] See Briggs in general, and compilations by Cobbett, Evans, Fenwick, Hudson, Pfankuchen, Scott, etc., listed in Scott and Jaeger.

[47] Below, Sec. 13.

on. This is contrary to traditional principle,[52] and seems a passing phenomenon, but deserves careful watching.

It is at this point also that the highly special attitudes taken, more or less openly and more or less officially (but also somewhat hesitantly and tentatively), toward orthodox international law in totalitarian states must be cited.[53] In such quarters there has been some disposition to repudiate general international law in its entirety. On the other hand, fear of the consequences of such an action and inability to offer a convincing substitute have restrained such actions somewhat. In the result the totalitarian challenge to international law has been ineffectual, given the resistance of other peoples of the world to such anarchical doctrine or behavior.

10. PARTIES

As already indicated, independent national states are the normal or standard parties to international law, both in the making of the law and in holding rights and obligations under it. This automatically includes groups of two or more states, but international unions or federal organizations, and their agencies, seem to require still today a certain amount of special recognition or approval for this purpose.[54] Dependent territories and all other

---

[48] See below, notes 49, 51, 53.

[49] H. Lauterpacht, "The So-Called Anglo-American and Continental Schools of Thought in International Law," *British Year-Book of International Law,* XII (1931), p. 31.

[50] A. Alvarez, *International Law and related subjects from the point of view of the American Continent* (Washington, D. C.: Carnegie Endowment for International Peace, 1922).

[51] See articles by Ayusawa, Kamikawa, and Takayanagi in *Japan Weekly Chronicle,* July 11, August 22, and October 24, 1940, at pp. 57, 241, 524: courtesy of Dr. Harold S. Quigley.

[52] United States Supreme Court in Wilson v. McNamee, 1880, 102 U. S. 572, 574, quoting Cicero: "Nor is it (the law of nations) one thing at Rome and another at Athens, one now and another in the future, but among all nations it is, and in all times will be, eternally and immutably the same." So the United States Supreme Court in *The Scotia,* 1871, 14 Wall. 170, quoted in Briggs, p. 26: "That law (the law of nations) is of universal obligation and no . . . one or two nations can create obligations for the world" (p. 30).

[53] O. K. Flechtheim and J. H. Herz, "Bolshevist and National Socialist Doctrines of International Law," *Social Research,* VII (February, 1940), p. 1. Also Italian fascist document in *International Conciliation,* No. 306 (January, 1935).

[54] Clyde Eagleton, *International Government* (New York: Ronald Press, 1932), pp. 107, 379.

sub-state entities (government departments, corporations and other private organizations, groups of individuals, and individuals themselves) require such recognition still more. Classical theory and conservative thought still tend to restrict the system of international law, both as to its enactment and its application, to the states, but the drift of practice and independent thought seems overwhelmingly away from such a narrow view.[55] Doubtless such a development is calculated to render international law and its application more complicated, but it is at least possible that another result will also be to reduce the tension present when all international legal controversies are staged between sovereign nations, and to render the application of the law somewhat simpler and more effective.

11. AUTHORITY

Widely divergent views are held concerning the authority of international law both in the strictly logical and also in the practical sense of that question.

On the first point extreme critics hold that, there being no authority competent to give orders to sovereign states, or to enforce such commands, international law is not law at all but mere ethics or courtesy.[56] The reply is made that even the sovereign state may promise certain action or inaction and even, by an original agreement, consent to enforcement against itself in specified circumstances later. Such promises and submission may, in absence of special stipulations, and for adequate cause, be withdrawn, but unless so withdrawn are legally binding.[57] What is more decisive, this mode of action has proven adequate for all but the most abnormal and exceptional cases in international life. States give consent to be bound by international law by originally accepting recognition as states in the international community and

---

[55] C. Eagleton, "The Place of the Individual in the International Law of the Future," *American Journal of International Law*, XXXVII (October, 1943), p. 642, and H. A. Steiner, "Fundamental Conceptions of International Law," *Ibid.*, XXX (July, 1936), p. 414, Sec. III.

[56] See above, note 5. See also Lord C. J. Coleridge, in *The Queen v. Keyn*, 1876, as quoted in Briggs, p. 1.

[57] Potter, *International Organization*, pp. 257-273.

to various measures of revision of that law and its enforcement also.[58]

On the practical side the sceptic denies that international law actually controls state activity. It may be admitted that this is the most significant aspect of the matter but it is believed that inspection of the record will reveal that the states habitually conform to the law in all but a minute fraction of cases.[59] Certainly they claim to do so; they almost universally admit that they are bound by the law;[60] it is the *a priori* theorists who, almost alone, put forward the other view. In a few instances, not all in the field of war or similar situations, and mostly related to one or two countries, the law has been flatly defied in principle and practice in recent years, but such cases are very exceptional.[61] The most important comment to be made in this connection is the observation that there would be greater temptation to violate the law if the latter went further in its regulation of state interests, and for such a comment there is much justification but it does leave the existing situation as described above.

The most serious test cases concerning the binding force of international law in recent times arose, of course, in the years 1914-1918 and have arisen again in the years since 1931 or 1935 or 1939. In the years 1914-1918 the accepted rules of law concerning the conduct of hostilities on land, at sea, and in the air were often called in question or flatly violated. The same thing has happened in recent warfare in China, in Spain, in Ethiopia, and, finally, in all parts of the world. In addition, questions have been raised concerning the nature and existence of the very status of belligerency and/or peace or neutrality themselves.[62] These

---

[58] Sir Henry Maine, *International Law* (London: J. Murray, 1888), pp. 37-38, quoted in J. B. Scott, *Cases on International Law* (St. Paul: West, 1922), p. xiii.

[59] A. P. Higgins, *Binding Force of International Law* (New York: G. P. Putnam's Sons, 1910), p. 10; Moore, p. 300. Nor is it at all clear that states only obey the law in minor cases or disregard it lightly in to them important cases; the same, p. 301.

[60] Higgins, p. 7; Moore, pp. 300, 303.

[61] One recalls the "scrap of paper" attitude. See also material cited in note 53.

[62] See above, text at note 22.

testings of the law have occurred in spite of efforts to outlaw war, which, if juridically effective, would have had the incidental result of modifying the law of neutrality also.[63]

These episodes have unquestionably constituted the most serious challenges to the existence and authority of international law in over a century. Virtually nothing was done in the years 1919-1939 to define or repair the alleged ravages of the years 1914-1918 and war came again on a large scale without the student or the practitioner being able to feel sure just what the law was on a multitude of questions.[64] The potential damage to international law was very great but at least two comments must be made thereon. For one thing it is obvious that only one section of international law was involved here, namely, the law of war and neutrality, and this the abnormal, and, it is believed, the less permanent, section. Secondly, the violations in this sphere were certainly less numerous and extensive than alleged and in certain cases probably constituted, as had been the case in various alleged violations in history, merely the commencement of modification or even the positive development of the law.[65] We are far from knowing yet just how to evaluate the supposed violations of the law of war and neutrality of the past thirty years.

12. National Law

The relationship between international law and national law also provides a problem for both theoretical controversy and concrete practice.[66] One school holds that the two are distinct and that neither can contravene the other.[67] The position of international law within the individual state then depends upon the reception accorded to it by the latter, although the general ten-

[63] H. Wehberg, *Outlawry of War* (Washington, D. C.: Carnegie Endowment for International Peace, 1931), p. 83.

[64] See T. Baty, "Prize Law and Modern Conditions," *American Journal*, XXV (October, 1931), p. 625.

[65] J. W. Garner, "Violations of Maritime Law by the Allied Powers during the World War," *Ibid.*, p. 26.

[66] In general see the literature cited in the index volume of the *American Journal* for 1921-1940, under "International Law and National Law."

[67] On the dualistic school see Briggs, *op. cit.*, pp. 52-54, and literature cited.

dency of the dualistic school is to retain international law on the level of international relations exclusively.[68] The monistic school would regard national law and international law as an integrated whole, and would hold that international law is in itself binding within each individual state.[69] The latter phenomenon is, however, compatible also with a concept of international law as subordinate to national law, or as part of it, a concept which was, indeed, a common doctrine in certain countries in times past.[70]

The trend seems to be setting definitely in the direction of the monistic theory and in the direction of subordinating national law to international, and giving the latter application within individual states wherever appropriate.[71] This is a trend necessitated by conditions, events, and interests rather than abstract theory, although the proponents of the dualistic theory seem to be reluctantly acknowledging the facts, as, indeed, they well can do inasmuch as they rather than the monists have on the whole been the positivists in the premises. The startling result would follow that international law—even customary common unwritten international law—might override supreme national laws such as the Constitution of the United States, which in fact it has done on several occasions in the past.[72] Also that international law might be applied by the justice of the peace or the village traffic officer in suitable circumstances, which also is standard practice.[73]

---

[68] Whether demanding its enforcement in the national jurisdiction or not.

[69] Briggs, as cited above, note 67.

[70] "The law of nations . . . in all cases of international law is adopted into the municipal code of every civilized country": C. J. Best, in De Wutz v. Hendricks, 1824, 2 Bing. 314, quoted in Scott, *Cases*, p. 892; "International law is part of our law, . . .": Supreme Court of the United States in *The Paquete Habana*, 1900; 175 U. S. 677.

[71] Briggs, *op. cit.*, p. 54. The fact is that this controversy seems as artificial as that between "natural" and "positive" law, of which, indeed, it is a part. International law and national law emanate from different human sources (international or national action), not directly from one transcendent law of nature, but must be unified in their practical existence and application.

[72] Discussed in article by present writer: "Relative Authority of International Law and National Law in the United States," *American Journal*, XIX (April, 1925), p. 315.

[73] C. D. Burns, "International Administration," *British Year-Book*, VII (1926), pp. 54, 58.

13. SCIENCE

While international law grows by the processes indicated, students thereof attempt to discover its content and to record it.[74] In so doing they—both expressly and by implication—make suggestions to the states concerning the development of the law, as is inevitable. Finally, they attempt to codify the law—still unofficially—as will be noted later.[75]

The science of modern international law arose in the thirteenth and fourteenth centuries, simultaneously with the revival of the study of Roman law, the development of maritime law, and the institutionalization of both war and diplomacy.[76] It grew very slowly for six centuries, with occasional spurts around the end of the sixteenth and the early part of the nineteenth centuries. From 1855 to 1914, and again after 1919, the science and literature of the subject expanded and improved in quality more than it had in the six thousand years preceding that time, and extended to virtually all parts of the world, as had not been true previously.[77] This included both the basic phenomenon of the writing of treatises and also to the attempted codification (still unofficial) of the law, collection of source materials, instruction in academic institutions, periodical publications, and still other forms. In all this time the challenge brought to the law by the revolutionary changes taking place in international relations and even the threat arising from the repeated outbreak of war were largely met and assimilated, to the ultimate gain of the international legal system. In this process students and writers in the United States were more active than those of any other country.

---

[74] In general, Fenwick, *op. cit.*, chap. III.

[75] Below, Sec. 14.

[76] Hershey, *op. cit.*, Secs. 45-51 and p. 65, Note.

[77] For that matter the law itself was supposedly confined in its application to Europe until the early nineteenth century or later; see reference to "the Christian States of Europe," *La Jeune Eugénie*, 1822, 2 Mason 409 (Briggs, p. 9), and the titles of older works such as J. L. Klüber, *Droit des Gens Moderne de l'Europe* (Stuttgart: Gotta, 1819).

14. CODIFICATION

As a consequence of the way in which it is created and formulated, and of the form assumed by the science of international law, there is even greater need here for codification, or the systemic restatement of the law, than in most other legal fields. Events have not failed to respond to that need.[78]

Thus unofficial scholars have, as already indicated, essayed to set down the law of nations in systematic form. To some extent that is what these writers have been doing from the days of the obscure author of the *Arbre des Batailles* down to the present vintage. Various individual codifiers—Blutschli, Field, Fiore, Internoscia—followed this tradition in the nineteenth century and in the twentieth.[79]

Official codification began at the Congress of Vienna with the statement of certain rules concerning diplomatic rank.[80] This was followed, in 1856, by the Declaration of Paris, dealing with four items in the law of naval warfare. Through the last half of the nineteenth century the process continued, dealing mainly with the law of war, just as the earliest international law had done. The Second Hague Conference, the London Naval Conference, and other meetings carried the effort into the twentieth century, only to be interrupted by war in 1914.

American republics took up the task in 1917 and since that time various sections of the law have been so treated, under Pan-American auspices, in this hemisphere.[81] Under the League of

---

[78] Potter, *Manual,* pp. 45-33, 117-118 (and note 69), 187-188.

[79] J. C. Bluntschli, *Droit International Codifié* (Paris: Guillaumin, 1870, trans. from first German edition, of 1868); D. D. Field, *Outlines of an International Code* (New York: Diossy, 1876); P. Fiore, *International Law Codified* (New York: Baker-Voorhis, 1918, trans. from fifth Italian edition of 1915); J. Internoscia, *New Code of International Law* (New York: International Code Co., 1910); Potter, *Manual.*

[80] Above, note 78.

[81] A. S. de Bustamante, "The Progress of Codification of International Law under the Pan-American Union," American Society of International Law, *Proceedings* (1926), p. 108.

Nations efforts in the same sense led to a codification conference at The Hague in 1930, and an almost complete failure.[82] Since that time no progress in codification has been made in Europe although American efforts go on untroubled.

15. SANCTIONS

In all of the history of international law the problem of enforcement has never been absent.[83] Respect for the law has been yielded by the states to a large extent because of respect for principle and the obedience pledged in advance, and because of considerations of mutual convenience. But fear of retaliation has never been absent, and possible enforcement of the law by the party believing that its rights have been violated, a common characteristic of all primitive systems of law and government,[84] has always been present.

Recently the idea of community enforcement of international law, coupled with restrictions on, or abolition of, the individual state's right to possess arms and have recourse to force against another state, similar to the arrangements ordinarily set up in federal unions,[85]—whether of states all belonging to one nationality or to international leagues—has grown greatly in favor. Actually such provisions were found—both on paper and in practice—in various interstate or international organizations over the past three thousand years.[86]

This is not to say that the problem of international police action is not fraught with the greatest difficulties and dangers. But development in administrative procedure and technique in recent decades and in the technology of communications and transport may make the organization and use of both intermediate (administrative) and ultimate (physical) sanctions more practicable than at any time previously. It should be remembered

[82] M. O. Hudson, "The First Conference for the Codification of International Law," *American Journal,* XXIV (July, 1930), p. 447.

[83] See Wehberg as cited in note 33, above.

[84] A. S. Diamond, *Primitive Law* (New York: Longmans, Green and Co., 1935), in general, and especially p. 302.

[85] Constitution of the United States, Art. II, Sec. 3 and Art. I, Sec. 10 (3).

[86] E. Wynner, and G. Lloyd, *Searchlight on Peace Plans* (New York: E. P. Dutton, 1944), especially pp. 510 ("Enforcement") and 526 ("Sanctions").

that the real choice to be made, moreover, is not one between sanctions and no sanctions but between individual and collective sanctions, for the individual states are certainly not going to renounce
their right to take sanctions action against one another unless
and until community sanctions are available.[87]

16. FUNCTION

In the earlier decades or centuries of its existence no great
question was raised concerning the function or value of international law. Law was a familiar phenomenon in various spheres
of human life and it was assumed that the reason for having a
system of international law was obvious enough. In actual fact
such a question had not been considered at any length in other
social spheres either, down to the later nineteenth century. With
increasing reflection concerning all political institutions, however,
and particularly concerning various aspects of international relations, and with the appearance of new international institutions
which seemed to some to promise more progress in international
affairs than international law, the older institution now had to
justify its existence.

The students and authors of the law of war and diplomacy
at the birth of modern international law regarded it as an instrument for protecting the individual, civilian or soldier, against
the excesses of the enemy and the diplomat against indignity and
mistreatment at the hands of either the populace or the government of a foreign state.[88] In the first case the menace was envisaged not so much as coming from another individual soldier
as from the enemy state or the general institution and practice of
war. In the second case respect for the dignity of the sovereign
also played a part and finally the idea of facilitating international
intercourse was never entirely absent, and came, in the nineteenth
century, to dominate other considerations in the development of
the law of diplomacy.[89] These observations could be repeated

---

[87] See also the author's *Collective Security and Peaceful Change* (Chicago: The
University of Chicago Press, 1937).

[88] Grotius, as cited, Prolegomena, Sec. 28, and Book II, Chap. 18, Sec. 1.

[89] Fenwick, *op. cit.*, p. 369.

many times with reference to other sections of the law as well. In the earlier period the law was not regarded—or so it seems in retrospect—to any great extent as an instrument for protecting and furthering the interests and rights of the states, probably because the states were all too able and anxious to take care of themselves in those times.

In the twentieth century the function of international law has come to be viewed in a far broader light.[90] It is indeed regarded as an instrument for protecting national interests and rights but this is such a rudimentary concept of the role of the law that it receives little emphasis. The law is also still regarded as an instrument for restraining excesses on the part of states and their nationals, but the sceptical modern temper, plus, perhaps, a better understanding of the process of government in general, preclude exaggeration here. A few persons or groups regard international law as a means for establishing peace and justice in the world, and they, also not understanding the political process adequately, are bitterly disappointed at the failure of international law to attain this end.[91] Finally, other students of the problem realize that it is merely the function of international law to express the patterns of behavior which the states and their peoples wish to have followed; this in order that those patterns may be known and available for such use as can be prescribed for them in the international governmental system of the period. This however includes, in these later days, all that development of international organization and coöperation so characteristic of the time.

17. FUTURE

The future of international law obviously involves several problems which are neither simple nor unimportant. All that can be done here is to indicate those problems and to suggest a judgment concerning their probably desirable and practicable solution.

---

[90] H. Lauterpacht, *The Function of Law in the International Community* (Oxford: Clarendon Press, 1933).

[91] Ralston, work cited above, note 42.

Thus it does not seem likely that the international community, any more than the national, can dispense with the instrument of law for expressing its judgment and will and for regulating the relations among its members and its own organization and activity. The development of newer agencies in these departments renders the development of law more rather than less necessary.

Secondly, it seems both probable and desirable that international law should be expanded to regulate not only interstate phenomena but sub-state phenomena in so far as these are sufficiently important to the states to require to be so regulated. Whether the terminology of the subject is kept intact or modified to meet new conditions is of secondary importance.

Third, a growth in the emphasis on the law of normal international relations and a disemphasis on the law of war, or its conversion into a law of international police action, and the abolition of the status and law of neutrality, seem highly probable if not entirely certain.

Fourth, it appears that the formation of the law by multipartite conventions, and even by legislation proper (less-than-unanimous vote), will more and more overshadow the formation of international law by practice and the conclusion of bipartite treaties. In the international field the members of the community are so few that the general law need not leave great liberty of contract in their hands.

In all of this development it would seem open to conjecture whether the rational or the volitional principle would come to dominate. The former—a law following nature or supposed supernatural authority—is symptomatic of primitive human society, to be followed by something freer and more creative. It is not clear, however, that man can escape the fate of the ants and establish a new universe and a new law. The present-day strife between the neo-romantics and the liberals, atrociously garbled into a conflict between progressive dictatorial aristocracy and proletarian democracy, is an incident in the effort to find a solution for that problem.

There seems to be less doubt about the growing authority of international law. In spite of the German-Italian romanticism just mentioned, Bolshevik nihilism, and the trivial logical gymnastics of certain overtrained intellectuals of all races, the states and their component individuals and group find adaptation to general law more and more possible and useful. On this score the facts of real life are likely to predominate once more over morbid and irresponsible fantasy.

The integration of international law with national law, or the subordination of the latter to the former, is likely to continue, along with the integration of international organization and administration with national government. Again the force of events is likely to give the lie to the anarchy-mongers.

And we may at least hope for an improvement in the science of the law! First a more faithful statement of the law as it stands instead of much personal lucubration on what the law might be or should be. Then a much more intelligent calibration of ideas as to what the law should be with the facts of international life and society.

Codification of the law must be resumed and carried along— never to completion but always nearer to it. The sanctions of the law must be improved, whether this means an international police force, coöperative international police action, or subtler and less dramatic developments of a purely administrative and retaliatory type.

Certainly the life of the nations, and of the community of which they are members, cannot dispense with the instrumentality of law. That law has, after a very long history, and a very great growth and great promise of usefulness between 1855 and 1914, been recently grossly damaged and grossly neglected. It is high time that, thirty years later, this ancient yet ever-new form of international thought and action should be restored to its rightful place.[92]

---

[92] On the possible effects of atomic energy on international law and organization see editorial by present writer in *American Journal of International Law*, XXXIX, No. 4 (October, 1945).

BIBLIOGRAPHICAL NOTE

A number of the secondary works and collections of primary materials most useful to either the intelligent layman or the professional scholar in other fields who desires to become acquainted with present-day international law are cited in the footnotes to the text above. The more convenient works are cited with this end in view, not necessarily the most recondite.

Thus the most useful general treatise for American students seems unquestionably to be that of Fenwick, in spite of the peculiarities noted. The old work by Hershey is valuable for historical and bibliographical materials. The author's *Manual* gives a brief code statement of the substance of the law (full of the errors or debatable items inevitable in such a statement) as it will be found nowhere else. C. Phillipson, *International Law and Custom of Ancient Greece and Rome,* London, 1911, and Walker and Garner as cited are the best works available on the history of international law. Briggs and Pfankuchen are the most useful collections of judicial decisions and other documentary materials together with editorial notes and bibliography. Hudson is by far the most useful work on international legislation. The author's *International Organization* seems still to be the most useful introduction to that subject although now badly out of date; the similar works by Eagleton and H. Vinacke (*International Organization,* New York, 1934), should also be mentioned in this connection. So much for Hill on international administration.

The frequency of the references to the *American Journal of International Law* will testify to the value of the files of that periodical, as will the few references to the less voluminous *British Year Book.* References have been restricted intentionally to publications in English; in French the monumental *Receuil des Cours de l'Académie de Droit International* at The Hague contains enormous stores of material on both general and special aspects of both international law and international organization, not to mention international political and economic relations. No comparable repository exists in German, Italian, Spanish, or any other tongue.

Finally, the student is strongly urged to become acquainted with the more striking monographs cited above, particularly Beale (*Conflicts*), Habicht (*Treaties*), Hudson (*Court*), Lauterpacht (*Place*), Riches (*Majority*), Wehberg (*Policing*), Wright (*Enforcement*), and especially Moore (*Illusions*), a work of very debatable accuracy but great suggestiveness.

BIBLIOGRAPHY

Académie de Droit International (La Haye), *Receuil des Cours,* Hachette, etc., Paris, 1925-   . Rich depository of technical monographs on all aspects of international law and organization.

ALVAREZ, A., *International Law and Related Subjects from the Point of View of the American Continent* (Washington, D. C.: Carnegie Endowment for International Peace, 1922). Best sample of its class.

BEALE, J. H., *Treatise on the Conflict of Laws* (Cambridge, Mass.: Harvard University Press, 1916). Excellent introduction to the difficult field of private international law.

BRIGGS, H. W., *The Law of Nations* (New York: Crofts, 1938). The most useful collection of case and documentary materials with editorial notes and references.

EAGLETON, C., *International Government* (New York: Ronald Press, 1932). Another attempt, like that of Hershey, below, to combine international law and organization.

FENWICK, C. G., *International Law* (New York: D. Appleton-Century, 2nd ed., 1934). The most useful general treatment for American readers in spite of some "liberal" quirks.

GARNER, J. W., *Recent Developments in International Law* (Calcutta: University Calcutta, 1925). The only general history of the law in recent times.

HABICHT, M., *Treaties for the Pacific Settlement of International Disputes* (Cambridge, Mass.: Harvard University Press, 1931). Scholarly compilation and analysis for the years 1920-30.

HACKWORTH, G., *Digest of International Law* (Washington, D. C.: Government Printing Office, 1940). Comprehensive; thoroughly documented; official.

HERSHEY, H. S., *Essentials of International Public Law and Organization* (New York: Macmillan, rev. ed., 1927). Useful for historical materials and references.

HILL, N. L., *International Administration* (New York: McGraw-Hill, 1931). The only general treatment available.

HUDSON, C. O., *International Legislation* (Washington, D. C.: Carnegie Endowment for International Peace, 1931). Monumental collection of documents with thorough if too legalistic introduction.

HUDSON, M. O., *The Permanent Court of International Justice, 1920-1942* (New York: The Macmillan Co., 1943). Authoritative but critical.

JESSUP, P. C., *Neutrality: Today and Tomorrow* (New York: Columbia University Press, 1936). One of four volumes of a comprehensive treatment.

LAUTERPACHT, H., *Function of Law in the International Community* (Oxford: Clarendon Press, 1933). Searching and thorough; slightly over-legalistic.

MOORE, J. B., *International Law and Some Current Illusions* (New York: The Macmillan Co., 1924). Uneven and not entirely reliable but very suggestive.

PHILLIPSON, C., *International Law and Custom of Ancient Greece and Rome* (London: Macmillan, 1911). A brilliant and absorbing study with rich references.

POTTER, P. B., *Introduction to the Study of International Organization* (New York: D. Appleton-Century, 4th ed., 1935). Badly out of date but still most useful for its field.

POTTER, P. B., *Manual Digest of Common International Law* (New York: Harper, 1932). Especially useful for attempted code statement of the law; to be used with much critical scrutiny.

RALSTON, J. H., *Democracy's International Law* (Washington: Byrne, 1922). Good example of "liberal" ethical criticism of the law by one of its sworn friends and servants.

RICHES, C. A., *Majority Rule in International Organization* (Baltimore: Johns Hopkins University Press, 1940). Marks a revolutionary development; scholarly.

VINACKE, H., *International Organization* (New York: Crofts, 1934). Well balanced; sound; critical.

WEHBERG, H., *Theory and Practice of International Policing* (Toronto: Macmillan, 1935). A brief historical and analytical study, with references.

WRIGHT, QUINCY, *Enforcement of International Law Through Municipal Law in the United States* (Urbana: University of Illinois, 1916). Old; technical; thorough treatment of a crucial problem.

WRIGHT, QUINCY, *A Study of War* (Chicago: University of Chicago Press, 1942). Coöperative study of war in many phases; highly organized and indexed.

WYNNER, E., AND LLOYD, G., *Searchlight on Peace Plans* (New York: E. P. Dutton, 1944). Most useful compilation and digest, with indexes, of plans and experiments since 1933 A.D.

CHAPTER XV

POLITICAL GEOGRAPHY AND GEOPOLITICS

JOSEPH S. ROUCEK

World wars encourage, if they do not compel, global thinking. We are learning, under the impact of the present war, to look at the world geopolitically. The existing world order, generally speaking, is based on sea transportation and upon sea power. The world order which is coming into existence will most certainly be based on air transportation and land power. This seems inevitable, not merely because of the changes the airplane is bringing about, but because air power is most effective when planes are land-based.

The coming of the airplane has transformed political geography quite as completely as the building of the Suez Canal and later the Panama Canal once did.

If the first World War was a conflict between a power based on land and a power based on sea, the second is a struggle between a world order based on ships and a new emergent based on airplanes. The Nazi Germany had quite a start in her aggressive plans on her opponents by utilizing to a remarkable degree *Geopolitik*. It took some time before Geopolitics, in modified forms, has entered our own thinking.

But Germany did not invent Geopolitics. Germans merely took the concept seriously and applied it. Geopolitics is based on the realization that, in a world of unstable political forces, geography is the most important stabilizing factor. In this respect, *Geopolitik* is but a branch of "Political Geography".

POLITICAL GEOGRAPHY

If geography is "chiefly a study of the living conditions of mankind as affected by regional combinations of specific soil types—with production habits and possibilities, and landscapes effects that give every area its characteristic stamp",[1] what is Political Geography? Valkenburg calls it "the geography of state which provides a geographical interpretation of international relations".[2] After a study of many definitions of political geography Hartshorne[3] formulated it thus: "Political geography is the science of political areas or more specifically the study of the state as a characteristic of areas in relation to the other characteristics of areas." He divides it into two main schools; the first, defining political geography as the study of the relation between man's political activities organizations and natural environment; the second, chorography, defining it as the study of the areas of states in their external and internal characteristics. Accordingly the study of the political geography of a particular state would be as follows:

I. Descriptive Analysis of the State
    A. Description of the state as a whole
    B. Analysis of the internal structure of the area

II. Interpretation of the present area
    A. Relation to "kernal areas" and major limiting area
    B. Directions and character of territorial area and its problems

III. Appraisal of the present territorial area and its problems
    A. Degree of conformity with natural or cultural landscape areas, or with special population areas.
    B. "Harmonic" or "disharmonic" forms.

Vallaux propounds that "the life of political societies is determined, in part at least, by the natural frame in which they de-

---

[1] Isaiah Bowman, *The New World: Problems of Political Geography* (Yonkers-on-Hudson and Chicago: World Book Co., 1929), p. 13.

[2] Samuel van Valkenburg, *Elements of Political Geography* (New York: Prentice-Hall, 1939), VII.

[3] Richard Hartshorne, "Recent Developments in Political Geography," *American Political Science Review*, XXIX (October, 1935), pp. 785-804, 943-966.

velop: in what manner the soil, air and water . . . relate themselves to the collective action of man".[4] In other words, the proper field for political geography should be within the confines of geography.

THE DEVELOPMENT OF POLITICAL GEOGRAPHY

The relationship between geographic conditions and political and social events has been studied by such philosophers and historians as Herodotus, Hippocrates, Thucydides, Plato, Aristotle,[5] and the Moslems [6] in ancient times, and championed by Bodin, Montesquieu, Burke, Taine and Turgot in modern times,[7] as well as by our contemporary theorists. During that "Enlightenment" of the 17th and 18th centuries, geographic considerations were temporarily eclipsed by the doctrine of natural law with its search for ideal forms of the state institutions. However, political events such as the territorial wars stimulated by Europe's struggle for the balance of power, stimulated the interest in the relationship between geography and politics.[8] The net result of all the speculation of the time was, however, according to Dunning, that some relation was not made at all definite.[9]

A more definite development of political geography had to wait till a sufficient quantity of geographic field studies and an-

[4] George Vallaux, *Geographie Sociale: Le Sol et L'état* (Paris: O. Doin et fils, 1911), pp. 7-8.

[5] Otto Maull, *Politische Geographie* (Berlin: Barntraegar, 1925), p. 2; William A. Dunning, *A History of Political Theory, Ancient Medieval* (New York: Macmillan, 1902), pp. 82-3. Hippocrates not only showed the influence of the climate on the soil, but on the character of the people as well. Plato and Aristotle let geographic considerations be the basis of human action.

[6] William A. Dunning, *A Cultural-Historical Approach to National Integration* (New York: Holt, 1938), p. 280.

[7] William A. Dunning, *A History of Political Theory from Luth to Montesquieu* (New York: Macmillan, 1931), pp. 112-4. Bodin preached that each country must construct its institutions to fit its physical environment. Turgot was the first to name the systematic study of geographical conditions on politics as "political geography." Montesquieu elaborated the theory by maintaining that climate affects man through cultural and economic channels of life as well. Kant built up a political geography based entirely on physical geography.

[8] William A. Dunning, *A History of Political Theory from Rousseau to Spencer* (New York: Macmillan Co., 1926).

[9] William A. Dunning, *A History of Political Theory from Rousseau to Spencer*, p. 319.

thropo-geographical analyses were available for critical comparison.[10] These were provided through the great upswing of the study of geography at the hands of Carl Ritter and Alexander von Humboldt, generally considered the founders of modern geography.[11] Ritter was the first one to try to base conclusions of political geography on the growing body of physical geography, in contrast to the hypothetical work of the philosophic writers.[12] Ritter was interested in the influence of climate and terrestial relief upon human history, claiming that certain parts of the world were almost predestined for the historical role which they actually played. Humboldt never "swerved from geography and travelled all over the world to make observations upon physical geography". History he ignored, so occupied was he in classifying land forms which he demonstrated had a large influence on climate, animal and plant life and man himself.[13]

Nonetheless, the first systematic treatment of the subject of Political Geography did not appear till the very end of the century in the form of Ratzel's *Politische Geographie*.[14] Among geographers, Maull attributes this lag to the predominant natural-law orientation of German geographers which was unfriendly to an intensive study of political geography. Among historians, Vogel attributes the neglect of political geography to the predominance of the legal outlook. While historians (such as Dahlman, Waitz, von Treitschke, and von Ranke) dealt with states as units and, in the analysis of the elements of power, considered the geographic aspects of the state, they focused their attention on the inner-political, legal-constitutional aspects of the state, rather than on the behavior of states vis-a-vis one another and the foundations of the state in the conditions of nature.[15]

---

[10] O. Maull, *Politische Geographie,* p. 16.

[11] Richard Hartshorne, "The Nature of Geography," *Annals of the Association of American Geographers,* XXIX (1939), p. 209.

[12] *Ibid.*; Maull, *op. cit.,* pp. 16-17.

[13] Allan Nevins, *The Gateway to History* (Boston: D. C. Heath & Co., 1938), pp. 279-281.

[14] Friedrich Ratzel, *Politische Geographie* (Munchen & Leipzig: R. Oldenbourg, 1897).

[15] Walther Vogel, "Rudolf Kjellen und seine Bedutung fur die deutsche Staatslehre," *Zeitschrift für die gesamte Staatswissenschaft,* LXXXI (1926), pp. 211-14.

While, before Ratzel, political geography was merely concerned with the description and statistical analysis of states, as with Ritter, Ratzel set up a general theory of the effectiveness of geographic factors in the life and development of states, attempting to comprehend the development of states and the earth-determining course of their political actions.[16] In his organismic conception of the state, in his deterministic view of man as a powerless puppet in the hands of physical nature, in his dicta such as that "a struggle for existence is a struggle for space" and that organized societies constantly tend to expand until they reach the limits set by nature, Ratzel was the great forerunner of contemporary *Geopolitikers*.[17] His most important follower, from the standpoint of Geopolitics, has been Mackinder, who will be noted later. But it is important to notice Vidal de la Blache and Jean Brunnes who, as a reaction to the determinism of Ratzel, developed the concept of "Possibilism". The relationship between man and nature, they find, are a function of time as well as of place, and in this relationship man is far from being the passive recipient of forces emanating from nature; on the contrary, there is a mutual interplay of influences, and that of man on nature may be by far the greater one.[18]

It was not Ratzel but the Swede Rudolf Kjellen who became the Father of Geopolitics. This is largely due to certain political circumstances combining to give a sudden popularity to the writings of Kjellen during and after the first World War in Germany. The War stimulated the need for the development of social sciences in general, and popular as well as academic interests in political geography in particular. In Germany, under the blow

---

[16] Vogel, *op. cit.*, p. 221.

[17] For a summary of Ratzel's work, see: Franklin Thomas, "Some Representative Contributions of Anthropogeography to Political Theory," in Charles E. Merriam & Harry E. Barnes, eds., *A History of Political Theories Recent Times* (New York: The Macmillan Co., 1932), pp. 472-78. His contemporaries and followers, such as Bickle, Semple, Reclus, Huntington, Dexter, and Lowie do not, in the whole, concern us here and have been dealt with in *Ibid.*, pp. 457-507.

[18] Jacques Ancel, *Géopolitique* (Paris: Librarie Delagrave, 1936), p.17; Nicholas Spykman, "Geography and Foreign Policy," *American Political Science Review*, XXXII (1938), p. 30.

of defeat in war and the dissatisfaction with the territorial settlements of the Peace Conference, Political Geography was developed into the new "science" of *Geopolitik*. The Geopolitikers
never tire of emphasizing that the terrible fate of Germany in
the war and the alleged "geographic" blunders of her government
drew their attention to the subject of Political Geography and the
need for its existence.[19]

"DISCOVERY" OF GERMAN GEOPOLITIK

Although Haushofer's school of Geopolitik was known t
the European geographers from the very beginning, America
started to pay sudden attention to this German (or rather Nazi)
phenomenon only under the impact of World War II.[20] From
1941 to 1943 a flood of articles and publications appeared on
Haushoferism in the United States, nearly all of them merely
popularizing the ideas of Geopolitics already well-known to those
able to read German.[21] While Ewald Banse's *Germany Prepares*

---

[19] Closely related to the geographical background of *Geopolitik* is also the organismic concept of the state (see: Francis W. Coker, *Organismic Theories of the
State,* New York: Columbia University Press, 1910), the militaristic ideologies
(see: Alfred Vagts, *A History of Militarism,* New York: W. W. Norton, 1937),
pp. 11-18; Albert T. Lauterbach, "Roots and Implications of the German Idea
of Military Society," *Military Affairs,* V (Spring, 1941), pp. 1-20), and the
economic traditions of German Neomercantilism (Edgar Salin, "Romantic and
Universalist Economics," *Encyclopaedia of the Social Sciences,* V, p. 385; A. T.
Lauterbach, *Economics in Uniform,* Princeton: Princeton University Press, 1943;
Frank Munk, *The Legacy of Nazism,* New York: The Macmillan Co., 1943).

[20] Joseph S. Roucek, "World War II—A Survey of Recent Literature," *The Educational Forum,* IV (May, 1940), pp. 465-477, and *Ibid.* (May, 1941), pp. 461-
484. See: Charles Kruszewski, "Germany's Lebensraum," *American Political
Science Review,* XXXIV (October, 1940), pp. 181-183; Joseph S. Roucek, "German Geopolitics," *Journal of Central European Affairs,* II (July, 1942), pp. 180-
189; Johannes Mattern, "From Geopolitik to Political Relativism," *Essays in Political Science in Honor of W. S. Willoughby* (Baltimore: Johns Hopkins University Press, 1937), pp. 125-172; "Germany's Brain Trustee Produces Nazi
War Aims," *Life,* VII (November 20, 1939), pp. 62 ff. Edward Thermaenius,
"Geopolitics and Political Geography," *Baltic and Scandinavian Countries,* IV
(May, 1938), pp. 165-177, is a good example how foreign scholarship was
aware of Haushofer's designs.

[21] Joseph S. Roucek, "The Pseudoscience of Geopolitics," Chapter 21, pp. 609-
635, in T. V. Kalijarvi, *Modern World Politics* (New York: T. Y. Crowell,
1942), surveys the available literature up to 1942; the same applies to Johannes
Mattern, *Geopolitik, Doctrine of National Self-Sufficiency and Empire* (Baltimore:
John Hopkins Press, 1942).

for War (New York: Harcourt, Brace, 1934) was laughed at or disregarded in 1934, it had to be reissued in 1941, due to the publicity given Hitler's schemes, as evolved for him by Geo-politicians, by Hermann Rauschning's *The Revolution of Nihilism* (New York: Alliance, 1939). Among the better works paying attention to Haushoferism we can note the studies of Dorpalen, Hans W. Weigart, and Strausz-Hupe, and others.[22]

---

[22] Andreas Dorpalen, *The World of General Haushofer* (New York: Farrar & Rinehart, 1942); Hans W. Weigert, *Generals and Geographers* (New York: Oxford University Press, 1942); Robert Strausz-Hupé, *Geopolitics* (New York: G. P. Putnam's, 1942); A. W. Griswold, "Paving the Way for Hitler," *Atlantic Monthly*, CLVII (March, 1941), pp. 314-321; Konrad Heiden, "Hitler's Better Half," *Foreign Affairs*, XX (October, 1941), pp. 73-86; A. Pettenkofer, "Hitler Means to Destroy Japan," *Asia*, XLI (November, 1941), p. 653-660; H. W. Weigert, "Maps are Weapons," *Survey Graphic*, XXX (October, 1941), pp. 528-530; Hans Speier, "Magic Geography," *Social Research*, VIII (September, 1941), pp. 310-330; Andrew Gyorgy, "The Application of German Geopolitics: Geo-Sciences," *American Political Science Review*, XXXVII (August, 1943), pp. 677-686; Fritz T. Epstein, "National Socialism and French Colonialism," *Journal of Central European Affairs*, III (April, 1943), pp. 52-64; Isaiah Bowman, "Political Geography of Power," *The Geographical Review*, XXXII (April, 1942), pp. 349-352; Derwent Whittlesey, "The Role of Geography in Twentieth-Century War," pp. 78-87 in J. D. Clarkson & T. C. Cochran, *War As a Social Institution* (New York: Columbia University Press, 1941); Charles B. Hagan, "Geopolitics," *Journal of Politics*, IV (November, 1942), pp. 478-490; R. S. Nathan, "Geopolitics and Pacific Strategy," *Pacific Affairs*, XV (June, 1942), pp. 154-163; George Kiss, "Political Geography Into Geopolitics," *The Geographical Review*, XXXII (1942), pp. 632-645; Sigmund Neumann, "Fashions in Space," *Foreign Affairs* (January, 1943), pp. 3-15; Robert Strausz-Hupé, "It's Smart to be Geopolitical," *Saturday Review of Literature*, XXVI (February, 1943), pp. 4 ff.; Jean Gottmann, "The Background of Geopolitics," *Military Affairs*, VI (Winter, 1942), pp. 197-206; Ralph Turner, "Technology and Geopolitics," *Ibid,*' VII (Spring, 1943), pp. 5-15; W. J. Cahnman, "Concepts of Geopolitics," *American Sociological Review*, VIII (February, 1943), pp. 55-59; Paul Sweet, "Recent German Literature on Mittel-Europa," *Journal of Central European Affairs*, III (April, 1943), pp. 1-24; W. J. Cahnman, "Methods of Geopolitics," *Social Forces*, XXI (December, 1942), pp. 147-154; Philip W. Ireland, "Berlin to Bagdad up to Date," *Foreign Affairs*, XIX (April, 1941), pp. 665-70; F. L. Schuman, "Let Us Learn Our Geopolitics, "*Current History*, II (May, 1942), pp. 161-5; Leonard Engel, 'Geopolitics and Today's War," *Infantry Journal*, L (May, 1942), pp. 42-48; Isaiah Bowman, "Geography vs. Geo-Politics," *Geographical Review*, XXXII (October, 1942), pp. 646-658; Heinz Soffner, "Geopolitics in the Far East," *Amerasia* (January 25, 1943); "Poland in German Geopolitics," *The Polish Review*, III (December 6, 1943), p. 3; Andrew Gyorgy, "The Geophities of War: Total War and Geostrategy," *Journal of Politics*, V (November, 1943), pp. 347-362, etc.

CONCEPTS OF GEOPOLITIK

The original "science" of *Geopolitics* has been developed, nurtured, elaborated, and applied in Germany from the objective science of political geography, the study of political areas and their boundaries, capitals and other critical points and zones.[23] Modern political geography because of the turbulence and unrest of a changing status quo, split into two schools. In Great Britain, France and Italy geopolitical studies are not practiced although these motives animate their actions as states; in Germany Geopolitics has become a nationally orientated science with ideological, philosophical and moral aspects.

Definitions: Geopolitics can best be understood by quoting some definitions framed by its founders and adherents. Kjellen defined *Geopolitik* as the science of the state as a geographic organism or phenomenon in space.[24] Professor Karl Haushofer, editor of the *Zeitschrift für Geopolitik,* defined it as the science of political forms of life in their regional relationships, as affected by natural conditions and historical development.[25] These are relatively objective definitions. Others bring out the Geopolitiker's true bias, which attempts to assist the statesmen of their own country, by examining foreign country's spaces and stages of economics, the dependence of people's character development on the life, occupations and landscape of their country.[26] "To trace the basic forces of blood and soil in their fate determining effects is the task of the new science of Geopolitiks." [27] *Geopolitik* must be the nucleus of crystallization for a number of sciences,

---

[23] Derwent Whittlesey, "Political Geography: A Complex of Geography," *Education,* LV (January, 1935), pp. 293-98.

[24] Rudolf Kjellen, *Der Staat als Lebensform* (Leipzig: S. Herzel Verlag, 1917), p. 46.

[25] K. Haushofer, "Grundlage, Wesen und Ziele der Geopolitik," *Bausteine zur Geopolitik* (Berlin, Kurt Vowinckel Verlag, 1928), p. 17.

[26] Siegfried Passarge, *Die Erde und ihr Wirtschaftsleben, eine allgemein Verständliche Darstellung für Kaufleute, Volkswirte, Lehrer, Studierende der . . . Universitäten* (Hamburg, Hanseatische Verlagsanstalt, 1929).

[27] Walter Esehl, "Geopolitics im Unterricht," *Geographische Wochenschrift,* I (1933), p. 83.

demanding of them to "level out" and fit into" the philosophy of life of the German in the "Third Reich".[28] These are some of the more fanciful definitions. Haushofer and his students still insist nevertheless that *Geopolitik* is an empirical science.[29]

The chief difference between political geography and *Geopolitik,* the Geopolitikers claim, lies in the approach, respectively, static and dynamic. While Political Geography *describes* the boundary, *Geopolitics evaluates* it in the light of the requirements of the state. While Political Geography examines spatial *conditions,* Geopolitics examines spatial *requirements.*

MAJOR GENERAL KARL HAUSHOFER: FATHER OF
GERMAN GEOPOLITICS

The instigator of *Geopolitik* was Major General Karl Haushofer, a distinguished Doctor of Geography, Geology and History in civilian life. Born in 1869, Haushofer entered the military college where he was graduated with highest commendation. Thence he was ordered to the War Academy, where he was declared eligible for the general staff and where he taught until 1909, and then travelled extensively in India and Asia. His scientific preparation enabled him to make careful observations of the geography of the Far Eastern countries. At the same time he studied the German geographer Richthofen's publications on defense and military policy, drawing his own conclusions of the great role the Far East might play in world politics. He began to formulate, nebulously it is true, a plan for a new German order, basing it on the hypothesis that whoever made an alliance with Russia and Japan might rule the world.

In 1914 Haushofer received his Ph.D. degree from the University of Munich in geography, geology, and history, "with high-

---

[28] George Roder, "Der Geopolitische Gedanke in der Schule," *Ibid.,* p. 733.

[29] Karl Haushofer, Erich Obst, Hermann Lautensach, and Otto Maull, *Bausteine zur Geopolitik* (Berlin: Kurt Vowinckel Verlag, 1938), p. 27, gives their official definition as editors of the *Zeitschrift für Geopolitik*: "Geopolitiks is the science dealing with the dependence of political events upon the soil. . . . It aims to furnish the armature for political action and guidance in political life . . . Geopolitik must come to be the geographic conscience of the state."

est distinction." After World War I he returned from the front a general officer, only to be retired from active service. He was shifted once more from his career as an army officer to his career as a geographer, and was appointed in 1919 as lecturer on geography in the University of Munich. Here he was associated with numerous geographers, a few political scientists and publicists in the founding of geopolitics. In 1924 Haushofer started a seminar and, together with his followers, the monthly *Zeitschrift für Geopolitik* (Berlin, later Heidelberg). A series of geopolitical studies were soon published by its editors (E. Obst, H. Lautensach, O. Maull, A. Grabowsky, R. Hennig, and others).

During Hitler's incarceration at Landsberg on the Lech, Hess who was associated with Haushofer during the war and whose student he became at Munich, introduced the Führer to the General.[30] Haushofer's Wednesday afternoon visits with Hitler and Hess produced lengthy discussions on problems of world policy.[31]

When Hitler and Hess were released, late in 1924, Hess entered the service of his teacher Haushofer as an assistant. In 1925 Haushofer founded the German Academy, officially titled the Institute for Research in Germanism, whose task was to cultivate the intellectual relations between the *Vaterland* and German minorities abroad—a sort of Teutonic International of German splinter groups the world over. Upon Hitler's accession to power Haushofer was appointed to the Presidency of the German Academy at Munich, and his sons and his Jewish wife were decreed Aryan. A research organization called the *Laboratorium für Weltpolitik* (Laboratory for World Politics) was established in

---

[30] Hess wrote, under Haushofer, a study of Japan—*Japan and Espionage,* a 40,000 word thesis which may be regarded as the fundamental discussion for the Nazi intelligence service, according to Curt Riess, *Total Espionage* (New York: Putnam's Sons, 1941).

[31] Haushofer's influence on Hitler's concepts of foreign policy has been, however, exaggerated, according to Konrad Heiden, *Der Fuehrer* (Boston: Houghton Mifflin, 1944), p. 282. Hitler and Hess were certainly stimulated by their conversations with Haushofer and Hitler's "space as a factor of power" is Haushofer's expression. But *Mein Kampf* does not deal with foreign policy or military geography, but "with race, political education, the building of a spiritual force at home," and "Hitler always insisted on the predominance of domestic politics over foreign policy and held that the former determined the latter."

Munich and subsidized liberally, since Haushofer had persuaded Hitler that if the German people were to rise against the established post-war order they would have to know the strength and weakness of their enemies to the most minute details. The activities of this laboratory were published by the periodical *Zeitschrift für Geopolitik,* which became the outstanding German publication on foreign affairs. Its maps were issued under Haushofer's special supervision.

HAUSHOFER'S DOCTRINES

Haushofer's school developed a new type of military science based on a division of the world into great land and sea masses. It taught that while previously the power dominating the sea had dominated tne world, today this condition had been reversed. Immediately after the World War Haushofer had been of the opinion that the great battle fleets would gradually be transformed into "scrap iron" by growing swarms of U-boats and airplanes. Both planes and submarines depended for their power on land bases from which they could not stay away for any protracted period. But that is not the chief reason for the rising importance of the mainland in world politics. Through the development of the continental trade economy, the great inner spaces have become "less dependent on the coast"; in modern world politics, domination of the production centers is decisive, no longer domination of the trade routes.

Haushofer took for granted the decline of the British Empire, based on English domination of trade routes; all territorial relations, based on trade and especially maritime relations, would soon be broken. This would first happen in Asia with its great land blocks of China and Russia, and Japan would not necessarily be the winner in the "Eurasian space catastrophe". For Japan is also a power based on sea lanes; but today, Haushofer propounds, we stand "at the great turning-point in the favorable position of the island empires". Against this coming catastrophe he saw but one help, the early union of continental Europe. The great land mass, not control of the sea, is today the aim of high politics.

All in all, Whittlesey summarizes Haushofer's mold as developed by him and by his group, space concepts used by the geopoliticians: [32]

(1) *Autarchy.* This is the ideal that every political unit ought to be self-sufficient. Such a state following this program would be immune to attack from any enemy and would be able to threaten war and fight successfully.

(2) *Lebensraum.* The territory occupied by Germany should furnish Germany a living. *Lebensraum* (Living Space) is the *right* of Germany to find ample room for her population. If it cannot be done, then neighboring peoples should mutually adapt their economics so that they will supplement one another and enable all to earn a living—with Germany—of course—getting all the benefits. Since the tendency to regionalism ("large-area amalgamations") is blocked by the small states, it is Germany's duty to "free" them, since "small-area formations are forms of dissolution and evaporation". The small states have no other choice but to become voluntary protectorates of the resolute dynamic powers. Least of all can the small states with vast colonial possessions expect to hold their possessions while Germany is left to suffocate "through insufficiency of space". Germany is the leading "renovating power" of the world, forced to fight the "resisting" powers which are weak and inactive but hold obnoxiously onto possessions to which they have no right.

(3) *Panregions.* Germany's demands that her political area be extended to include all people of German origins (or of speech) have been traditional,[33] and reappear again in the geopolitical doctrines. A Germanic "culture area" and a Germanic "trade area" are inseparable parts of Germany's nature-given domain, and particularly east of Germany where can be found German settlements of earlier centuries scattered as linguistic enclaves

[32] Derwent Whittlesey, "Haushofer: The Geopoliticians," Chapter 16, pp. 388-411, in E. M. Earl, *Makers of Modern Strategy* (Princeton University Press, 1943), pp. 398-406.

[33] Derwent Whittlesey, with the collaboration of C. C. Colby and Richard S. Hartshorne, *German Strategy of World Conquest* (New York: Farrar & Rinehart, 1942).

in a region of Slavic and other non-Germanic languages. The world is to be divided into three or four "pan-regions", which would unify areas larger than the largest existing nations. Pan-America would be headed by the United States, Pan-Asia by Japan, and "Eurafrica" by Germany.

(4) *Land Power vs. Seapower.* Adopting Mackinder, the geopoliticians recognize the land mass Eurasia-Africa as the largest, most populous, and richest of all possible land combinations, and which may be thought of "as the principal island in the world ocean". The other continents are located on the periphery of this "world island" as a ring of smaller islands. The heart of this region is cut off from the oceans; there the rivers flow into the ice-blocked Arctic Ocean or lose themselves in inland seas and saltpans. This "Heartland" is the best possible base for land power, potentially greatest on earth. By dominating it, Germany would eventually be able to dominate the world.

(5) *Frontiers.* For the geopoliticians the boundaries are merely temporary halts of a nation in its march toward world domination. The nation has a right to "natural frontiers"; but since they may lie beyond the existing political borders, the process of accomplishing the needs of the *Lebensraum*—the war—might have to be used to bring about the realization of the extension of such frontiers. Hence, all the boundaries can be always utilized as standing excuses for war.

GEO-STRATEGY

A science named "geo-strategy" is the characteristic product of the theories of geopoliticians and of the strategy of war projected in a world-wide scale, extended from times of war to the brief periods of peace. It is an all-embracing science "ignoring strategic impossibilities and willing to exploit militarily any phase of human life, any reality of the natural or man-made world. It is a continuous, restless and relentless national strategy in which peace-time diplomacy and war-time military power are alike aimed at fighting the enemy".[34]

---

[34] Andrew Gyorgy, "The Geopolitics of War: Total War and Geostrategy," *Journal of Politics,* V (November, 1943), pp. 347-362.

German Geo-strategy redefined clearly the nature and main features of total war as a "permanent war preceded and followed by short and fitful periods of totalitarian peace". Modern war has four phases and three dimensions. Its various phases include: ideological, psychological, economic, and military warfare. To a former two-dimensional type of land-and-sea struggle is added the third dimension by an all-out mobilization of air power. It became totalitarian not merely in its ultimate goal of world conquest, but even in its methods, in an exploitation of all known human sciences and technological inventions.

While formerly military campaigns had been the beginnings of the struggle, geostrategists define them as the end of the struggle, preceded by ideological, psychological and economic war—as variant forms of the same power struggle. Thus total war has militarized peace and, paradoxically, to a certain extent demilitarized war itself. "In the Nazi chronology of events the beginning of military action merely means the successful conclusion of the first chapter, the preparation of a swift and possibly bloodless victory by psychological and economic, primarily *non-military* means." [35]   In this respect, propaganda is considered the best means of undermining the enemy's will to resist. Spying and fifth-column activities reach their climax immediately before the first military blow is struck against the already crippled and "softened" enemy.[36] Geopoliticians consider this last stage before hostilities as particularly important, because secret service and fifth-column activities "cannot be defeated or eliminated by mere military weapons". Important roles are assigned to the closely woven net of enemy secret service, fifth columnists, aroused minority leaders, and military spies, who act as secret, different inter-connecting links, "go-betweens" among the various branches and divisions of modern warfare.

---

[35] *Ibid.,* p. 353.

[36] *Cf.* Joseph S. Roucek, "Hitler's Propaganda as a War Weapon," *Educational Forum,* VII (November, 1942), pp. 67-83; Roucek, *The Axis Psychological Strategy Against the United States* (New York: New Europe, 1942).

PREDECESSORS OF GEOPOLITIK

Haushofer freely acknowledges his debt to both Friederich Ratzel, Sir Halford MacKinder, and in particular to Rudolf Kjellen, formerly Professor of Political Science in the Universities of Gothenburg and Upsala. It is generally agreed that Kjellen founded the science of *Geopolitik* and also invented its name.

Kjellen admits that he was a disciple of Friedrich Ratzel (1844-1904) and that he was influenced by Ratzel's *Politische Geographie* (1897).[37] Ratzel developed a general theory of the effectiveness of geographic factors in the life and development of states. To justify his theories philosophically he developed an organismic concept of the state which likened the struggle for existence to a struggle for space—*Lebensraum* ("elbow-room").[38] For him the state is bound to a particular *Lebensraum*, but in competition for space with other states and exhibiting individual characteristics of vitality or decadence. This concept was later seized upon by Geopoliticians. He maintained that every people must be educated up from smaller to "larger space conceptions" in order to prevent people from sinking back into the old "small space conceptions". He also stressed the importance of water power by maintaining that any power aiming to dominate the world must conserve its water ways: the world is 72% water and 28% land; thus oceans influence historical changes.

Kjellen accepted Ratzel's theories but reserved his reasoning in one respect. Ratzel's subject of study was "the influence of man on natural environment" But for Kjellen the subject of study was "the influence of natural environment on man". The latter problem belongs "to the sciences concerned with man, to psychology, ethnography, or to the political and social sciences". Directly this is realized, the science of Geopolitics is born.[39]

---

[37] *Cf.* Richard Hartshorne, "Recent Developments in Political Geography," *op. cit.*, for a good analysis of Ratzel.

[38] *Cf.* Robert H. Lochner, *Geopolitik, Its Nature and Aims* (Chicago: University of Chicago, M. A. thesis, 1941) is a penetrating study of the philosophical justification of Ratzel's theory.

[39] E. Thermaenius, *op. cit.*, is the best available study of Kjellen in English.

Kjellen, mentioning the new term for the first time, writes as follows: "In this wise Ratzel's political geography as also the main part of his anthropogeography are transferred from the field of geography into that of politics; I should like to call them geopolitics." [40] The term is defined by him as follows: "geopolitics is the theory of the State as a geographic organism or phenomenon in space, *i.e.,* as land, territory, area, or, most pregnantly, as country (Reich)."

It is also important to note that Kjellen was decidedly pan-German, particularly in his belief in the compass of Germany's "living space". His concept of Germany's *Mitteleuropa* included not only Central and Eastern Europe but also Scandinavia, Asia Minor and Mesopotamia as well.

Kjellen met Haushofer after World War I and both collaborated up to Kjellen's death in 1922. This partly explains that Geopolitics as a consciously applied branch of science exists only in Germany and Austria. But in Germany his *State as Organism* was already translated in 1917. His *The Great Powers* is the acknowledged Bible of German Geopoliticians. Carefully revised and enlarged by Haushofer and others, it has run to numerous editions. Haushofer, with his encyclopaedia knowledge, bold ecletism and "flair for publicity" developed and elaborated the concept of *Lebensraum* far beyond Kjellen's pedantic theory that world history is determined by geographic situations.

Although one of the most striking features of Haushofer's doctrine is its lack of rigidity and lack of fixed plan, it can be traced also to the early influences of the British geographer, Sir Alfred Mackinder, whose theory of seeing world policy as a match between Oceanic and Continental people is to be found in the "Geographical Pivot of History".[41] Sir Halford claimed that through the control of the "heartland" Eurasia, the conquering country could dominate not only the Old World but the World as a whole. Indeed many think that this idea led to Haushofer

---

[40] *Ibid.*, p. 166.

[41] Sir Halford MacKinder, "The Geographical Pivot of History," *The Geographical Journal*, XXXIII (April, 1904), pp. 434-37.

espousing the rapproachment of Germany and Russia in the summer of 1939. Mackinder maintained that world history has always been made by the press of the large landlocked peoples of Eastern Europe and Western Asia upon people settled on the ocean littorals of the land mass of Europe and Asia. In his book bearing the significant title, *Democratic Ideas and Realities* (New York: Henry Holt, 1919), while the Peace Conference was deliberating at Versailles, he urged the vital necessities of basing the new world order, not upon democratic sentimentalities, but upon the hard geographical and geopolitical facts underlying history. The chief lesson to be derived from these, in his opinion, was the vital necessity of preventing Germany and Russia from joining forces. These two powers were able to control the "heartland" to dominate not only the Old World but the world as a whole. He elaborated his theory further by designating the district he considered the "heartland" of expansion as a territory extending from the Volga to the Yangtze and from the Himalyas to the Arctic Ocean. This heartland could be so powerful because it would be invulnerable from the seapower of the surrounding oceans.

Haushofer adopted this theory as a line for Germany's striving for world power in terms of *Lebensraum*—a strategic area containing all advantages indispensable for a Germany at war against any great power or combinations of powers.[42]

EVALUATION OF HAUSHOFERISM

Recent studies indicate that Haushofer's reputation as the great geopolitician and as the founder of that study have been exaggerated.[43] If one compares Haushofer's works with Mackin-

---

[42] German authors recommend highly as an excellent introduction to Geopolitics J. Fairgrieve's *Geography and World Power* (New York: E. P. Dutton, 1915), translated into German in 1925 by Martha Haushofer, the wife of Karl Haushofer. This study is apparently quite independent of Kjellen and seems to have attracted the notice of German Geopoliticians rather late. It may be described as a very sketchy history of the world on a geographical basis, but bears the stamp of modern geopolitical ideas; these are especially obvious in the maps.

[43] Andreas Dorpalen, *The World of General Haushofer*; Hans W. Weigert, *Generals and Geographers*; Dewent Whittlesey (with the collaboration of Charles C. Colby and Richard S. Hartshorne), *German Strategy of World Conquest* (New York: Farrar & Rinehart, 1942).

der's *Democratic Ideals and Reality,* it appears that the German's fresh contribution is surprisingly small.[44] Haushofer is a popularizer who had debased geopolitics to the travel of highfaluting expansionist program and propaganda; he seems to have taken over the ideas of his predecessors without adding any valid concepts of his own. Haushofer's imperialism is most evident in his "dynamic" concept of the frontier; a boundary is not a fixed line, but the skin of an organism which tends to expand to inginity, like the frontiers of Lucretius' universe. Following the German romanticists and Kjellen, Haushofer thinks of the state as a biological organism, but few will consider this position an advance beyond Mackinder's. Of course Haushofer is a learned man and in some ways an extremely intelligent one. Individual statements of his have a prophetic ring today. Thus he anticipated the rapid fall of France and pointed out that the guns at Singapore faced the wrong way. In 1929 he described Pearl Harbor as a mousetrap. In a sense there are two Haushofers: at times he writes with notable moderation and objectivity, but more often his violent chauvinism distorts his considerable intelligence. He is brilliant though very erratic in his judgments of strategic situations; to the study of geopolitics as a whole his main contributions have been fanatic nationalism, a grim "Prussian" romanticism and an execrable style.

The popular belief that Haushofer was the "brains behind Hitler" is also in large part a mistaken one. One has merely to compare Haushofer's doctrines with Chapter XIV of *Mein Kampf*

---

[44] Other ideas can be traced also to non-Haushoferian thinkers. For instance, the concept of *Lebensraum* can be found in Grimm's epoch-making book *Volk ohne Raum* (*People Without Room*), a Pan-German classic since 1926. The term *Lebensraum* seems to have originated with Moeller van den Bruck, *Germany's Third Empire* (London: Allen & Unwin, 1931); see Gerhard Krebs, "Moeller van den Bruck: Inventor of the 'Third Reich,'" *American Political Science Review,* XXXV (December, 1941), pp. 1085-1106. List's ideas must be also noted in this connection: see: Edward Mead Earle, "Adam Smith, Alexander Hamilton, Friedrich List: The Economic Foundations of Military Power," Chapter 6, pp. 138-154, in Edward Mead Earle, ed., *Makers of Modern Strategy* (Princeton: Princeton University Press, 1943); this volume also contains a valuable chapter by Derwent Whittlesey, "Haushofer: The Geopoliticians," Chapter 16, pp. 388-411, and bibliography, pp. 542-543.

to see how sharp the opposition is. Haushofer is an apparently sincere admirer of Japan and has tremendous respect for the power of Russia; he was opposed to a military understanding with Italy and wished to ally Germany with the "colored" colonial peoples, believing that the British Empire was doomed. (The occasional racist remarks in Haushofer seem to have been inserted as protective coloring.) Hitler's original views were exactly the opposite. The alliance with Japan may mean that Haushofer's influence has modified Hitler's racist beliefs; more likely it was a matter of political expedience. After the Russo-German pact Haushofer's reputation rose dramatically, and Weigert speaks of the pseudo-alliance as a "triumph of Haushoferism". Perhaps it was, but there is no evidence that the influence of the geopoliticians was decisive. A strong faction in the Reichswehr had long favored an understanding with Russia, and Hitler himself was perfectly aware of the danger of fighting on two major fronts at once.[45]

To be sure, Haushofer and Hitler agree on the necessity of German expansion, the desirability of war, and the need for a large peasant population as the basis of state power, but such doctrines are the stock in trade of all Fascist publicists. The Institute for Geopolitics is only one of the many organs of planning and propaganda within the Nazi framework; it supplies some of the "brains" of German imperialism, but is by no means dominant.

Undoubtedly there are turns in geopolitics which nations must learn if they are to survive. The influence of land masses on history, the artificiality of our division of the world into continents, the strategic implications of the shape of the earth—all these will bear repetition. The difficulty is of course that geopolitics by its very nature tends to assume a nationalistic point of view. Even Mackinder, a humane and moderate person, writes as one who is first of all an Englishman. As Haushofer remarked, there is a German geopolitics, an English geopolitics, and so on; and Weigert warns against the hard-boiled American school now

---

[45] Henry C. Hatfield, "Haushoferism," *New Republic*, CVIII (February, 1943), pp. 155-158.

emerging. Obviously, geopolitics must first of all be purged of Haushoferism if it is to become a reputable study. Another weakness of the school is its tendency to underrate industrial strength in estimating the power of a nation—as well as the moral and psychological elements of the opponent. Like Haushofer, Mackinder relegates the Americas to a secondary position, since they are far from the "heartland". It might be well to require a thorough course in economics of all fledgling geopoliticians. Above all: unless the study is taken over by men of good will and with an international point of view it will continue to furnish guidebooks for bigger and better wars.

AMERICAN GEOPOLITICS

Geopolitics as a science has not found many adherents among the scientists of other countries,[46] who for the most part realize the "although geopolitics synthesized admirably new research, only geographical laws which were in accord with German ambitions of expansion were incorporated".[47] The Anglo-Saxon geographers have been recently aroused to the importance of geopolitics by the German effort—although Bowman's *The New World* bears no imprint of the pseudoscientific approach of the German geopoliticians and is really a scholarly and worthy interpretation of the political world. Recently Samuel van Valkenburg took up the "geopolitical" approach in his *Elements of Political Geography* (New York: Prentice-Hall, 1939), not succeeding very well, however, since Haushofer's approach must be understood in terms of Germany's imperialism and cannot be successfully applied through this American interpretation. On the other hand, Spykman's volume has been widely discussed and has

---

[46] Robert Strausz-Hupe, *op. cit.*, gives a brief sketch of geopolitical movements in other countries, which more scholarly sources have not as yet examined. Jaromir Korcak, *Geopoliticke zaklady Ceskoslovenska jeho kmenove oblasti (Geopolitical Foundations of Czechoslovakia and its Tribial Spheres,* Prague: Orbis, 1938), is a very interesting attempt to apply geopolitics to Czechoslovakia's development.

[47] Jaques Ancel, *Géopolitique,* p. 5.

had a mixed reception.[48] Mead points out that "it has been en-thusiastically hailed by those who feel, with justification, that, generally speaking, American professors and publicists have been living during the past twenty years in a dream world of their own creation and that they have misled themselves, their students, and the general public concerning the facts of life in a dynamic world. It has been violently denounced, on the other hand, as a primer for a new American Prussianism, which would base the policies of the United States almost exclusively upon the power factor, with almost cynical disregard of those human, psychologi-cal and moral considerations which frequently determine the course of history and which of necessity play a large role in the calculations of free men and free peoples." But not many spe-cialists in international relations can disregard Spykman as obvi-ously as they had Hodges, Fullerton, and a few others, whose "geopolitical" approaches were but "voices crying in the wilder-ness" before 1939.[49] But by 1939 the geopolitical approach be-came popularized. Bruce Hopper, for instance, wrote in 1941:

"The key to an understanding of the present titanic struggle must be sought in the forces of history which have perpetuated a disequilibrium in the No Man's Land of Eastern Europe . . . where Western and East-ern influence in European history have remained locked in stalemate."

Here we have an echo of Haushofer who terms that region "Zwischeneuropa" (Europe "In Between"). Derwent Whit-tlesey has attempted to describe the "areas of differentiation of the world's principal states and legal codes, in so far as these political phenomenas are formally established and their charac-

[48] Nicholas John Spykman, *America's Strategy in World Politics: The United States and the Balance of Power* (New York: Harcourt, Brace, 1942). Edward Mead Early, "Power Politics and American World Policy," *Political Science Quarterly*, LVIII (March, 1943), pp. 94-106, is probably the best critical evalua-tion of Spykman.

[49] Charles Hodges, *The Background of International Relations* (New York: John Wiley & Sons, 1931), and particularly Chapter V, "Environment and National Destiny," pp. 87-105, VI, "Barrier and Highway in World Life", pp. 106-132, and VII, "The Human Side of World Politics," pp. 133-160; Morton Fullerton, *Problems of Power* (New York: Charles Scribner's, 1919).

[50] Bruce Hopper, "The War for Eastern Europe," *Foreign Affairs*, XX (October, 1941), p. 18.

ter clean." [51] A curious similarity exists between the ideas propounded by Haushofer and American philosopher James Burnham.[52] Burnham stresses large contiguous areas as the units of "continental" political systems of the future. Modern technological discoveries have made the national state, colonial empires, and free world trade and chronisms, declared Burnham—voicing, perhaps unconsciously, Haushofer's convictions.[53]

BIBLIOGRAPHY

ANCEL, J., "The Political Geography of the East Baltic," *Baltic and Scandinavian Countries*, III (January, 1937), pp. 51-56; *Géopolitiques* (aris: Ancel, 1936); "Die franzosiche geographische Schule und die Geopolitik," *Zeitschrift für geopolitik*, XVI (1939), pp. 640-656, discusses geopolitics from the French point of view.

BOWMAN, ISAIAH, "Geography vs. Geo-Politics," *Geographical Review*, XXXII (October, 1942), pp. 646-58. To the President of the John Hopkins University geopolitics in German hands is an apology for theft.

CAHNMAN, W. J., "Concepts of Geopolitics," *American Sociological Review*, VIII (February, 1943), pp. 55-59. An able introduction into some of the principal concepts; "Methods in 'Geopolitics,'" *Social Forces*, XXI (December, 1942), pp. 147-154.

CHÉRADAME, ANDRÉ, *The Pan-German Plot Unmasked: Berlin's Formidable Peace-Trap of the "Drawn-War"* (New York: Charles Scribner's Sons, 1917). Still valuable today.

CRANWELL, J. P., *The Destiny of Sea Power* (New York: W. W. Norton, 1941). A forecast and a study of its influence on land and air power.

DORPALEN, ANDREAS, *The World of General Haushofer* (New York: Farrar & Rinehart, 1942). Valuable selections from the writings of the Haushofer school and some of its predecessors.

DOW, ROGER, "Prestor: A Geopolitical Study of Russia and the United States," *Russian Review*, I (November, 1941), pp. 6-19.

EAST, W. G., *The Geography Behind History* (New York: Nelson, 1939).

FAWCETT, C. B., *A Political Geography of the British Empire* (London: Ginn, 1933). Probably the best survey of its topic.

FAIRGRIEVE, J., *Geography and World Power* (London: University of London Press, 1915). Considers the relationship between climate and world power; should be studied in connection with Ellsworth Huntington's *Civilization and Climate* (New Haven: Yale University Press, 1924).

---

[51] Derwent Whittlesey, *The Earth and the State* (New York: Henry Holt, 1939), p. 591.

[52] James Burnham, *The Managerial Revolution* (New York: John Day, 1941).

[53] Geopolitical ideas can be also found in the great American naval strategist, Admiral Alfred T. Mahan, *The Influence of Seapower on History, 1660-1783* (Boston: Little, Brown, 1890), *The Influence of Seapower on the French Revolution and Empire* (Boston: Little, Brown, 1892), the writings of Homer Lea, *The Day of the Saxon,* and *The Valor of Ignorance* (New York: Harper & Brothers, new ed., 1942), R. J. Turner, and others.

GOTTMAN, JEAN, "The Background of Geopolitics," *Military Affairs*, VI (Winter, 1942), pp. 197-206. Looks for the background of geopolitics in writings of Montesquieu, Turgot, Fichte, Ratzel, Kjellen, MacKinder, Demangeon, etc.

GYORGY, ANDREW, "The Geopolitics of War: Total War and Geostrategy," *Journal of Politics*, V (November, 1943), pp. 347-362. One of the most valuable surveys.

HAGAN, CHARLES B., "Geopolitics," *Journal of Politics*, IV (November, 1942), pp. 478-490. Geopolitics is conceived here as a contemporary realization of power politics; a useful historical introduction into the world of ideas of those who attempt to find a deterministic principle controlling the development of states.

HARTSHORNE, RICHARD, "The Nature of Geography: A Critical Survey of Current Thought in the Light of the Past," *Annals* of the Association of American Geographers (Lancaster, Pa.), Vol XXIX, 1939; "Recent Developments in Political Geography," *American Political Science Review*, XXIX (1935), pp. 785-904, 943-966; "The Politico-Geographical Pattern of the World," *Annals of the American Academy of Political and Social Science*, CCXVIII (November, 1941), pp. 45-57. All Hartshorne's writings are indispensable for the understanding of political geography.

KERNER, R. J., *The Urge to the Sea* (Berkeley, Cal.: University of California Press, 1942). A geographic interpretation of the expansion of Russia by her great river-and-portage system.

KRUSZEWSKI, CHARLES, "Germany's *Lebensraum*," *American Political Science Review*, XXXIV (October, 1940), pp. 964-975.

MACKINDER, SIR HALFORD, "The Geographical Pivot of History," *Geographical Journal* XXXIII (April, 1904), pp. 434-437. One of the most influential scholarly lectures; Sir Halford brings his ideas up to date in "The Round World and the Winning of the Peace," *Foreign Affairs*, XXI (July, 1943), pp. 595-605, and *Democratic Ideals and Realtiy* (New York: Holt, 1919).

MATTERN, JOHANNES, *Geopolitik* (Baltimore: John Hopkins University Press, 1942). A competent survey of the various theories.

MEAD, E. M., "Power Politics and American World Policy," *Political Science Quarterly*, LVIII (March, 1943), pp. 94-106. Indicates to what extent Spykman's volume depends on Ratzel, Morton Fullerton, Ellsworth Huntington and others.

MILLS, C. A., *Climate Makes the Man* (New York: Harper and Brothers, 1942). A medical expert, utilizing his wide experience throughout the world, discusses the interrelation between man and his environment. He stresses the importance of the latter.

MUELDER, H. R. AND DELOW, D. M., *Years of This Land* (New York: D. Appleton-Century, 1943). American History interpreted as a response to our geographic environment.

NATHAN, R. S., "Geopolitics and Pacific Strategy," *Pacific Affairs*, XV (June, 1942), pp. 154-163.

NEVINS, ALLAN, *The Gateway to History* (Boston: D. C. Heath, 1938). See chapter X, "Man's Home and His History," pp. 272-78, for a survey of various theories of geographic determinism.

PEATTIE, RODERICK, *Geography in Human Destiny* (New York: Geo. W. Stewart, 1940). A study of the role played by geography in shaping the destinies of individuals, communities and nations.

POMFRET, J. E., *The Geographic Pattern of Mankind* (New York: D. Appleton-Century, 1935). An elementary text in human geography.

RENNER, G. T., *Human Geography in the Air Age* (New York: The Macmillan Co., 1942). A high school text by a well-known American geopolitician.

ROSINSKI, HERBERT, *The German Army* (New York: Harcourt, Brace, 1940). The interrelation of the German Army with the lief of the nation.

ROUCEK, J. S., "German Geopolitics," *Journal of Central European Affairs*, II (July, 1942), pp. 180-189. Summarizes various definitions.

RAUSCHNING, HERMANN, *The Revolution of Nihilism* (New York: Alliance, 1939). A rambling account of geopolitical theories; see particularly pp. 182 ff.

SCHUMAN, F. L., "Let Us Learn Our Geopolitics," *Current History*, II (May, 1942), pp. 161-165.

SIMS, N. L., *The Problem of Social Change* (New York: Thomas Y. Crowell, 1939), chapter VI, "Geographic Determinism," pp. 152-190.

SPEIER, HANS, "Magic Geography," *Social Research*, VIII (September, 1941), pp. 310-330. The use of maps by geopoliticians.

SPILHAUS, M. W., *The Background of Geography* (London: Harrap, 1935). A history of the growth of geographical knowledge which shows the great influence that geography has had on the development of mankind.

SPYKMAN, N. J., *America's Strategy in World Politics* (New York: Harcourt, Brace, 1942). The most able attempt to apply geopolitics to America's foreign politics; Spykman and Rollins, A. A., "Geographic Objectives in Foreign Policy," *American Political Science Review*, XXXIII (June, 1939), pp. 391-410, XXXIII (August, 1939), pp. 591-614.

STRAUSZ-HUPE, ROBERT, "It's Smart to be Geopolitical," *Saturday Review of Literature*, XXVI (February 6, 1943), pp. 4 ff. A brilliant survey of the whole field of geopolitics, as well as recent publications in this field.

SWEET, PAUL, "Recent German Literature on Mitteleuropa," *Journal of Central European Affairs*, III (April, 1943), pp. 1-24. Geopolitical ideas on Central-Eastern Europe.

TAYLOR, GRIFFITH, *Environment and Nation* (Chicago: Chicago University Press, 1936). A penetrating analysis of the regional geography of Europe.

THERMAENIUS, EDVARD, "Geopolitics and Political Geography," *Baltic and Scandinavian Countries*, IV (May, 1938), pp. 165-176. Published when hardly anybody in America paid attention to Geopolitics.

THOMAS, FRANKLIN, "The Role of Anthropogeography in Contemporary Social Theory," pp. 143-211, chapter 7, in H. E. Barnes, Howard Becker & F. B. Becker, *Contemporary Social Theory* (New York: D. Appleton-Century, 1940). One of the latest surveys of the field.

VIVES, JAINE VINCES, Espana: *Geopolitica des Estado y del Imperia* (Barcelona: Ediciones Yunque, 1940). An interesting adaptation of German geopolitical ideas and methods of interpretation to the history of Spain and her former empire.

WEIGERT, H. W., *Generals and Geographers* (New York: Oxford University Press, 1942). An analytical study of the nature and significance of German geopolitics and Haushofer.

WHITTLESEY, DERWENT, *The Earth and the State* (New York: Henry Holt, 1939). An able study in political geography.

WHITTLESEY, DERWENT, in collaboration with C. C. COLBY and R. S. HARTSHORNE, *German Strategy of World Conquest* (New York: Farrar & Rinehart, 1942). An analysis of doctrines and writings of the geopoliticians showing the historical background of Germany's plans for world conquest.

WILLIAMSON, J. A., *The Ocean in English History* (New York: Oxford University Press, 1942).

Chapter XVI

POLITICS AND SEMANTICS

G. S. PETTEE

"Nature, as we often say, makes nothing in vain, and mankind is the only animal whom she has endowed with the gift of speech."—Aristotle, *Politics,* 1253 a.

"The Greeks had but one word, *logos,* for both *Speech* and *Reason*; not because they thought there was no Speech without Reason; but no reasoning without Speech."—Hobbes, *Leviathan,* Bk. I, Chap. 4.

" . . . the word is a sacrament demanding the most delicate administration."—Ortega y Gasset, *Toward a Philosophy of History* (New York: Norton, 1941), p. 44.

"It will be the thesis of this book that disagreements of this kind—fundamental, doctrinal disagreements which seem to admit of no solution—are due not to stupidity or stubbornness, not even to an unscientific attitude towards the problems involved, but to an unscientific attitude towards language itself."—Hayakawa *Language in Action* (New York: Harcourt Brace, 1941), p. 8.

Semantics is in substance a new approach to the ancient questions concerning the relation of words to things, in other words, a new approach to many of the problems of the character of knowledge and of communication. The term is frequently taken in another sense, as if it referred simply to the misuse of words. This has led some of its followers to offer other names for it, generally with the familiar ending, "ology," which implies more immediately that it is a method and a field of investigation. But the name "semantics" is already so familiar that it would be best to continue to use it. The first two observations we must make concerning it are: that it is concerned with the nature and use of language, and that it is contemporary.

It is common in textbooks covering modern history down to the present, to adopt the same method and procedure for the examination of contemporary matters as for those of the more or less remote past. In works on the history of thought in particular an author will frequently analyze the inner structure, outline the development and observe the influence and effect of the thought of a contemporary writer by exactly the same method which he might apply to such historical figures as Machiavelli or Hobbes. He assumes that the evidence at hand is of the same value in the one case as in the other. But this is a false method when applied to very recent occurrences; for we know that there is always an interval between the time when a significant book is written and the time when a reasoned judgment of its value is possible.

Therefore, the most important thing which can be said to-day of the impact of semantics upon politics is that it is still too early to speak with assurance. Such a subject has never been dealt with contemporaneously in a fashion which could bear comparison with later research. In the case of semantics, its major writings, if one may make the risky assumption that they have been written, have appeared only since 1930.[1] The first fruits of the influence of semantics upon politics have therefore been very recent indeed, and must definitely be set down as first fruits only.

With this warning in mind we may plunge into the subject and do our best to obtain a fair perspective. In our judgment of what semantics has to say for itself, we must of course be guided

[1] For an introduction to the direct background of semantics and for the original use of the term, see Walpole, *Semantics, The Nature of Words and Their Meanings* (New York: Y. W. Norton, 1941). For most purposes it is convenient to date the general recognition of semantics from the publications of Ogden and Richards, *The Meaning of Meaning* (London: Kegan Paul Trench and Trubner, 1930). The popular use and misuse of the word followed the publication of Stuart Chase, *The Tyranny of Words* (New York: Harcourt Brace, 1938). The best introduction to the subject is Hayakawa, *Language in Action* (New York: Harcourt Brace, 1941).

primarily by what has been said and written. We may also, however, make some tentative guesses as to what consequences a sober observer might expect.

This requires that we examine a number of questions which need little attention in ordinary studies of the older history of political theory. First, of course, we must ask, What does Semantics mean? This is not a parallel question to such a question as, What does Mercantilism mean? Its own disciples are far from agreement upon the answer, and they are still alive. Hence, if semantics is a systematic group of ideas which we can describe with some confidence, we can do so only on the basis of the necessities of its own structure, and through deductions as to its implications. Any answers we give must be made in consciousness that we are entering a controversy between living men, and that our definition of semantics will be received with opprobrium by some of its reigning authorities. Secondly, in discussing the influence of semantics upon political thought, we must distinguish semantics as we may have defined it, from semantics as it has been influential, for the influence of a doctrine depends less upon its pure form than upon its communicated form, which may be a vulgarized or popularized version. Also we must distinguish the influence of semantics through its effect upon the mentality of political thinkers and writers from its effect upon political action and the secondary impact upon thought as thought in turn is influenced by events. We can also examine the reverse influence of politics and political thought upon semantics.

What does Semantics Mean?

The term, semantics, is free of an accumulated implications due to long use, but it is unfortunately liable to be defined by everyone for himself. It is at least a new method of study of the meanings of words, of the effect of words upon the concepts for which they serve as vehicles, and of the effect of language upon human communication. But this leaves plenty of margin for disagreement. Korzybski [2] for example, takes semantics as a new

[2] Alfred Korzybski, *Science and Sanity* (Lancaster, Penn.: The Science Press, 1933). Also his earlier work, *The Manhood of Humanity* (New York: Dutton, 1921).

system of thought including the whole ordinary field of psychology and philosophy, and much of neurology and physiology. This would make it a presiding all-inclusive study, and give it a position comparable to that of philosophy in the past. Walpole[3] on the other hand flatly rejects this position and insists that semantics is solely concerned with the meanings of words, in a sense which reduces it nearly to the status of philology. It is certainly so much at least. One is forced by these and other definitions to the observation that at the present time the compass of the subject depends upon the past background of a given writer; one familiar with modern propaganda will turn semantics into a new political theory based upon the relation of symbols to power, while one familiar with the history of science will make of it a new philosophy of science. All this is natural, since semantics is properly applicable to anything to which language itself is applicable; but it also illustrates the fact that writings on the subject are still more subjective than its claim to superior objectivity might lead us to expect.

The basic idea of semantics is that words, and hence language and logic, are arbitrary and relative. They should not be taken for granted. They are historically conditioned by their origins and development, *not* eternally given. If logic is a means of using language to develop truth from given premises, one might define semantics as the beginnings of a long needed general method for the scrutiny and derivation of premises themselves. Where logic takes verbal premises for granted, semantics begins by questioning the validity of the words.

If the roots of thought from which semantics has sprouted are traced, one may be puzzled where to stop. As with all innovations, its sources may be found almost as far back as one cares to seek. Certainly, for the modern world, the overthrow of symbols, the questioning of meanings, the effort to think in terms of what words refer to, instead of in terms of words themselves, has its roots at least as far back as the Renaissance. At a later time Galileo conducted a limited semantic revolution which

---

[3] Cited in note 1 above.

marked the birth of modern physical science. If one may summarize to an extreme degree, one may say that the growth of science has been a spreading application of thinking conditioned by a consciousness of the imperfection of symbols, or of thinking conditioned by a constant skepticism of words and concepts and a constant effort to readjust them to reality. All of the great political thinkers of the past few centuries, in so far as they have been iconoclasts, have been carrying forward by slower steps, for the study of society, the same process of rejection of older symbols and concepts.

Thus on the political side also the fairly rapid revision of concepts and symbols goes far back. Anyone who has read Plato's *Republic* knows that the meaning of such terms as "justice" has been under discussion for some time. Anyone who has studied the political problems involved in the trial of Mary Queen of Scots knows what a breach of the divinity that doth hedge a monarch was involved. The semantic issue was strong enough to make some good men of the time feel that murder would have been less scandalous than the mere idea of the trial of a sovereign. There can be no doubt that the execution of King Charles was a landmark of the further decay of the meaning of monarchy in Europe. Such events mark semantic changes, not for single thinkers, but for nations.

Aside from demonstrations of new faiths, there have been comments by writers of all literate ages which have suggested the outlook of semantics. Shakespeare's "A rose by any other name . . ." makes a nicely antique contrast to the modern story of the psychiatric patient who was so allergic to roses that she sneezed when she saw paper roses in a corner of the doctor's office. The breaking of the bondage to words and symbols has been remarked upon by Francis Bacon, Hume, and many another, in scattered comments. But such observations have only recently been followed up and developed as a conscious system.

The background of semantics must not be treated without attention to the development of a questioning attitude toward language which has characterized literature in this time. Gertrude Stein and James Joyce are the best examples, though there are innumerable others. "Debunking" as exemplified in the early nineteen-twenties by Menken was a narrow form of applied semantics. The recognition of the sins and foibles of others was a natural stage in the road toward a systematic account of the prejudices of all, including ourselves. In such a light, we must recognize semantics as a set of ideas with deep roots in the temper of the times, and distant origins in the temper and problems of the modern world. Though new in name, it is by no means a surprising development.

There are still other and more precisely definable roots as well. Psychology and anthropology, and the comparative study of institutions and customs, have brought to light, first, the existence of primitive psychology, and second, its survival in modern civilization. It is almost automatic to recognize the irrational and stupid ideas of savages, or the prejudiced outlook of other cultures or other times, and easy in the second place to transfer this critical recognition to the surviving stupidities in our own culture It required only a general rule for such recognition and rejection before a definite method could be developed for the analysis of the origins and conditions of superstition. We need hardly add that any such method must have a powerful impact upon existing political thought.

The idea that the meanings of words were determined when the language was in its origins, and have in many important cases been little changed, immediately suggests that much of our language reflects the mentality of a much earlier age than this. This is the basis of Korzybski's fundamental charge against logic, that we are still following a theory of how to use language which ostensibly mirrors cause and effect in the world of reality, but which actually ignores fatal faults in the structure of language itself. Moreover, this theory for the use of language dates from Aristotle. But also, language conditions all human communication and hence conditions society and the whole social process. If the language is imperfect, if language and logic are both out of date, their imperfections must have deleterious effects upon society. Correspondingly, if society is in a disastrous state, then we may well suspect imperfections in the conditioning system of communication. By recognizing such questions as these semantics promises not only to influence political or social thought, but to remake them.

Central Ideas.

The central perception of semantics, in its present development, is the one which Ogden and Richards [4] express through what they call "the triangle of Reference". This is simply the idea that words have meaning only in use, and that when a word is used there is always the user, the word itself, and the object or referent. In ordinary use the relation of word to referent is taken for granted, the word is reified, or taken by the listener as equivalent to the referent itself. This of course means just the opposite, the referent is taken by the user of the word as being equivalent to the word. Naturally if one learns to examine the relation between word and referent as a variable one, the assumptions implied in the words may become no less interesting than the logic of the argument. If what a speaker takes for granted, or wishes us to take for granted, is untenable, then his argument may be ignored forthwith. Examples foreign and domestic are too numerous for mention.

There are many familiar examples of the undying power of ideas which warp men's minds in despite of any reference to reality. Thus the Nazis have exploited deep set reflexes established around the word "Jew" in Germany and elsewhere. Thus also the Supreme Court of the United States, with no malice aforethought, has followed verbiage of the past in many of its doctrines, until finding itself in a strange position where the hiatus between word and referent has become too wide to swallow, it has been forced to follow new perceptions against old doctrine. The clearest instance is probably that of the too literal application of Marshall's famous dictum of the McCulloch case, "the power to tax involves the power to destroy," until only a few years ago a changed court escaped the language and restored the

---

[4] Cited in note 1.

narrowed principle of the decision. American constitutional law is without doubt one of the finest fields in which to investigate semantics, through a study of the longevity of false concepts, as well as through their eventual displacement. Many a bad old piece of legal wording fell vicitim in its day to the penetrating semantic weapons of Justice Holmes, with his alert eye for an "inarticulate major premise".[5]

At this point the idea might arise that semanticists would wish to do away altogether with such a source of trouble as language can be proved to be. Far from it, however, they all make their bows to the necessity of language for society, and not only as a reporting agent but also as a means of directing action. Human society and culture cannot continue, much less progress, except through constant communication.[6]

The claims of semanticists may be summed up best in the statement that the errors built into our language and the way in which we use it are a major cause of most of the social ills which affect mankind today, and can be recognized as direct inducements to stupidity and error. Even the mildest claims set semantics up as a new approach to the problems of the truth, and of how to use our minds and our language.

The Semantic Approach to Politics.

There are two different axes upon which the penetration of semantics into political action and thought may be measured. First, there is the wide vogue enjoyed by the simpler concepts in-

---

[5] The most immediate approach to the analysis of some of the strained doctrines of constitutional law may be found in the works of E. S. Corwin, especially *The Twilight of the Supreme Court* (New Haven: Yale University Press, 1934), and *The Commerce Power and States Rights* (Princeton: Princeton University, 1936). It is difficult today to select particular cases, to illustrate the eventual shift from an old and well established rule to a new one, because in the last ten years there have been so many such. The cases which ran the doctrine concerned with "Businesses affected with a public interest" into the ground, until its demise in the Nebbia Case, would make as good a series as any for study.

[6] ". . . communication as I understand it is, if not identical with, at least indispensable to, the cultural process." R. E. Park, "Reflections on Communication and Culture", *American Journal of Sociology*, XLIV (September, 1938), pp. 187-205.

". . . the fundamental cooperative act by which most of the higher animals survive: namely, communication by means of noises." Hayakawa, *Language in Action* (New York: Harcourt Brace, 1941), p. 10.

volved in the destructive analysis of contemporary folklore; second, there is what might be called the vertical thrust of the deeper techniques of probing the folklore of reason, and on the basis of such philosophical or methodological findings, recalculating many an old calculation for new conclusions. The former leads to a heightening of the technique and acrimony of controversy in this age without any direct effect on the solution of problems. The latter leads to the rejection and replacement of theories and concepts, many of which have been common currency beyond controversy for long ages.

The commonly recognized role of semantics is the narrow one which limits it to the function of a wrecking tool in controversy. This is readily illustrated by Max Lerner in his review of Thurman Arnold's *The Folklore of Capitalism*.[7] Lerner criticizes Arnold for concentrating on words and ideas rather than on economic realities. Somehow he missed the idea that it is only through words and ideas that we understand realities, and if Arnold's book has permitted readers to miss this, then Arnold's book has not quite explained the point of view which it adopts.

Mannheim,[8] on the other hand, illustrates the more fundamental approach to the relation between semantics and politics. He argues quite forcefully that superiority of realism lies neither in conservative "ideologies" nor in radical "utopias", but that the recognition of the universal relativity of past political thought paves the way for a new level of critical thinking.

It is important that this difference between the two approaches be recognized. One of the most hampering forces affecting the influence of the most fruitful innovation is the antipathy aroused by its exaggeration or by its cheaper forms. The world is now plagued by the parochial minds of those who proclaim this new gospel of semantics in the everlasting fashion of those to whom any new idea is a utopia. Thus the semantics which has the widest acceptance is the semantics which enables us

---

[7] Lerner's review is reprinted in his *Ideas Are Weapons,* (New York: Viking, 1939) p. 194. Arnold's best known book is the one under discussion, *The Folklore of Capitalism* (New Haven: Yale University Press, 1937).

[8] Karl Mannheim, *Ideology and Utopia* (New York: Harcourt ,Brace, 1936).

to detect the mote in our neighbor's eye. But the semantics which will be the most important is the semantics which enables us to recognize the beam in our own eye, and perhaps will enable us to see better than we have in the past.

Such a semantics must offer a lucid conceptual scheme for the analysis of the function of communication in culture, and therefore in politics. At present, some of the most interesting investigations are carried on by students of literature and philology. Other light has come from the deeper analysis of propaganda stimulated by Goebbels' inexplicable success. But very few students of semantics are well acquainted with both the philological and the sociological aspects, fewer still with the political and the scientific sides of the subject.[9] The emphasis most lacking in the texts is the analysis of just why words and communication are as important as the broad claims made for them. An analysis to replace the bare assertion that "semantics is important" must take not a linguistic, but a social-psychological approach. It must regard culture as a complex of channels of action, not of objects like pots and pans, but of ways of doing things like cooking, and disorder in the culture as conflicts of action.

Once this is done, the relation of culture to personality becomes apparent, since culture is the complex of directive channels for the actions of a society, and personality is the complex of the channels of action of an individual. Communication is then the means of implanting culture in a personality, and of maintaining it. Such an analysis makes it easy to trace the results of faults in the language in the maladjustments of persons and of societies.

In so far as semantics provides light in this otherwise dark field it serves as a real bridge between psychology and social science and can vitalize many fields of thought. This is semantics at its most ambitious and most promising, and also in its least

---

[9] The best introduction to the wider implications of the subject would be through the reading of a group of books covering several aspects. Hayakawa (cited in note 1, and Lynd's *Knowledge for What?* (Princeton: Princeton University Press, 1939), and Karen Horney's *The Neurotic Personality of Our Time* (New York: W. Y. Norton, 1937) are suggested as a combination.

understood form. It is semantics as the turbulent meeting ground between anthropology, psychology, sociology and science.
What Effect Has Semantics Had Upon Political Thought?

The immediate answer is that the effect upon political thought thus far has been almost wholly negative. Where a Thurman Arnold exploits it he uses it as a wrecking tool, and such a critic as Max Lerner is prompt to point this out. Lerner himself has also noted that the history of thought has a place for wreckers as well as builders, and that the former as well as the latter serve a useful task; but he remains impatient with those who do not join in building according to the plans which he feels are already drawn. He feels a degree of the same imperfection in Lynd's *Knowledge for What?*, which he holds is not destructive in the same sense as Arnold's book, but which "pulls its punches". The answer of a thoroughgoing disciple of semantics would be that the socialism of Max Lerner is at least as vulnerable to criticism as the faith in capitalism which he joins in deriding.

Lynd presents a much more general argument than that of Arnold, concerned to investigate not merely capitalism and its superstitions but all of the contradictions in our present culture, from capitalism to marriage, crime, city planning, war and neurosis. The ills of our present society are traced to the confusions of thought resultant from the faults of language, social contradictions are seen as arising out of mental contradictions. Though semantics is not made the major theme the whole argument owes much to semantics as a means of uniting psychology and sociology.

We find then, that there are several distinct aspects of the influence of semantics upon politics which we must take note of. Foremost, and rarest, is the re-examination of the general theory of politics, such as it is, in the light of an analysis of human communication and thought patterns. This may be found in at least rudimentary form in Mannheim.[10] A second is the application of semantics only as a means of refutation, simply to expose the irrational underpinning of some system of rationalizations which the

---

[10] Cited, note 8 above.

critic wishes to destroy. This is exemplified in Arnold's work already mentioned, or Rodell's.[11] A third which might be mentioned is the common effort to trace all political rationalizations to economic class interests. At first glance, this might seem to be a more general approach than the second one mentioned, since the second involves the attempt to expose only one ideology at a time, but actually it is not. Where the second, as typified by Arnold, attacks the rationalizations of only a single group, it does at least take a broad view of the cultural conditioning of those rationalizations, and does not exclude cultural inertia, nor put all its weight upon wishful thinking or hypocrisy in its account of the stubbornness of prejudice. The third type tends to exclude inertia from consideration, and sticks to a rationalistic account of self-interest as a factor conditioning thought, which is as open to attack as the theories which it attempts to expose.

Much more might be said of the applications of semantics to political theory than has been said here. But the three aspects of the influence of semantics which have been mentioned nearly sum up the case. The influence may be traced back as far as one pleases, to Voltaire or Nietzsche or Vaihinger. A summary of all the notable illustrations of the destructive criticism of the premises of others would be interminable. Lincoln Steffens' Autobiography[12] was a long account of attacks upon existing prejudice, and the gradual discovery that the theories of the reformers were almost equally as prejudiced. The world wide criticism of the Versailles Treaty and of the international structure built upon it, which preceded the rise of Nazism, gave rise to hundreds of books of the debunking variety.[13] At the same time literature has made capital of the same technique, holding the mirror up to life to show that reality does not match the conception. The disillusioned

---

[11] Fred Rodell, *Woe Unto You, Lawyers* (New York: Reynal and Hitchcock, 1939).

[12] *The Autobiography of Lincoln Steffens* (New York: Harcourt Brace, 1931).

[13] The best of the criticisms of the inter-war set-up is in E. H. Carr, *Twenty Years Crisis* (London: Macmillan, 1939). The same author's *The Conditions of Peace* (New York: Macmillan, 1943) is more recent, and an equally good example of the penetration gained by a systematic capacity to examine premises and evaluate them.

novels which followed the first world war, or such works as those of Steinbeck, or older ones by Sinclair Lewis or Upton Sinclair, or such plays as Tobacco Road, illustrate both the widespread use of this technique, and the fact that debunking has been for a generation a highly paid and widely pursued profession.

This brings us also to a recognition that some of the shallower aspects of semantics have such wide roots, as well as such old ones, that it is a very uncertain thing indeed to attribute such examples to the "influence" of semantics. Certainly Upton Sinclair was not influenced by Ogden and Richards and Korzybski, any more than Voltaire was. Rather we had best admit that here again we find that semantics appears as a natural product of a very general growth of techniques in the handling of ideas and criticism in the modern world, which has produced on the one hand a plethora of skillful critics, and on the other a new theory of the nature of concepts.

The Opposition.

The collapse of France in 1940, now so long ago, marked a complex crisis in the mentality of most of the world. For many it seemed to prove the fatal effects of questioning the foundations of a republic, and the misuse of the teachers' apportunity to cast doubts upon the premises of the established order, the demoralizing effects of destructive criticism. This precipitated a return to "fundamentals" by a great many of the leading critics of the previous decade, and a considerable production of recantations in the tone of *mea culpa*.[14] Such a reversal has much to tell us. First, like their predecessors, the many critics of the church who rushed back to the fold of Rome when the Reformation began to be serious, or the critics of the *Ancien Regime* in France who became *émigrés* from the French Revolution, these critics were only critics and had not yet caught sight of any positive alternative for the old order. They were skilled practitioners of the art of exposing

---

[14] Carl Becker and Archibald Macleish may be mentioned as examples. Becker, in his *Heavenly City of the Eighteenth Century Philosophers* (New Haven: Yale University Press, 1932) and Macleish, in such works as his *Public Speech* (New York: Farrar and Rinehart, 1936) took active parts in the criticism of existing prejudice in a period only a few years ago, but both have adopted a more conservative tone recently.

and destroying but not of building. This gives a clear test of the degree to which any of them may be taken as really exponents of semantics. It also gives us a clear demonstration of why semantics has been regarded with so much suspicion. Such critics talk of semantics, and stand before the world as examples of its influence, and illustrate only its destructive function. Those who distrust semantics have some reason to regard it as a social corrosive only.

This affords us a key to the character of the more serious opposition. This opposition comes from those who have been constant adherents of philosophical idealism, or Platonism, or whatever they chose to call it.[15] They may be roughly identified as those who are fond of a vocabulary featuring the terms "spirit" and "soul" and "idea" and "free-will", and utilizing a structure built from these in order to account for the vast realm of the unpredictable in human affairs. This school, resting its argument upon a profound impression of the inadequacy of determinism or materialism or nominalism, and therefore convinced of the validity of ideas as such, and of their timelessness and immunity to criticism, shows in all periods of history a tendency to conservatism founded upon a rejection of criticism. To the critics this always seems also a rejection of experience.

At any rate, there is a category of writers on politics and on literature whose opposition to semantics is clear cut, and clearly founded upon an idealist opposition to any assault by the forces of nominalism. This opposition is better understood by its own members than by the semanticists however, for the semanticists seldom show any appreciation of the real issues at stake. They generally regard such opposition as reactionary stupidity, when they of all people should be the first to understand its roots in the history of thought. Conservatism has an element of truth in the necessity of maintaining existing ideas in order that the culture can survive at all in time, even in order to be changed. This whole issue between the semanticists and their opponents gives us one more measure of the still undeveloped character of seman-

---

(October, 1940), pp. . . . .
[15] For an example see Mortimer Adler, "This Pre-War Generation", *Harper's*,

tics. Before it is fully grown it should give us, among other things, a sympathetic account of the nature and sources of conservatism.

Disillusionment.

The universal debasement of symbols of all kinds, both their loss of value and their general misuse, has been widely recognized as a characteristic of this age. All creeds and parties have learned to undermine the premises of their opponents. Each and all can see through the hollowness of all arguments but their own. And since culture is extremely complex, to see through and disbelieve all pretensions but one's own is to see through and disbelieve all but a small part of the communicated symbols of the time. There are also many, who have not only learned to distrust all others, but have come to trust nothing at all. However, few writers have expressed this in any general way; only a few poets and novelists, and a few writers on politics who recognize how the distrust of all pretensions arises out of the general dislocation of all standards of reference, and that the requisite is to find new methods and new standards.[16]

This universal distrust of truth is frequently referred to as a sad by-product of modern criticism, including semantics. There is no doubt that it frequently takes the form of demoralization. It is frequently traced in the first instance to the disillusionment which followed the first World War. Yet few of those who comment upon it recognize the first implication of disillusionment; that illusions are after all vulnerable to facts first, and only thereafter to criticism. People do not give up old symbols unless facts and criticism conspire together to undermine their faith. Conservatism commonly ignores this, and simply holds that the ancient truths must not be abandoned.

There is a plethora of catch phrases for the illness of the time. It has been called "The Retreat from Reason" and summed

---

[16] Irving Babbitt, *Democracy and Leadership* (Boston: Houghton Mifflin, 1924), and Jose Ortega y Gasset, *The Revolt of the Masses* (New York: W. W. Norton, 1932) are among the best examples.

up in other such titles as "Force or Reason".[17] The claim of semantics would be that far from being the cause of this general demoralization it is the most healthy reaction against it. This claim has not yet been fully justified, nor can it be disproved at present, one more indication of the early stage of growth of semantics. If it is true that semantics has thus far only helped to make confusion worse confounded, it is also true that this would be the case after the first introduction of truth into a turmoil of falsehood. But here again we must distinguish between the various levels of thought about language which bear the name semantics. It finds its widest diffusion in its shallowest form, and in this form it certainly, as Walpole has said, " . . . can be put to very queer ends by people who already had a gleam in their eye before they met it."

BIBLIOGRAPHY

1. *Background*:

GILSON, ETIENNE, *The Unity of Philosophical Experience* (New York: Charles Scribner's Sons, 1937). The two last chapters in particular throw an excellent perspective on the historical position of the present crisis in philosophy.

NIETZSCHE, FREDERICK, *The Genealogy of Morals* (1887); many editions; the Modern Library edition is convenient. Nietzche was probably the most extreme rebel against established shibboleths, and is frequently regarded as a forerunner of Nazism.

VAIHINGER, HANS, *The Philosophy of "As If"* (London: Kegan Paul Trench Trubner, 1924). Vaihinger's philosophy was less extreme than Nietzche's in its rejection of old concepts, and more rational in its exposition. He was probably the most direct anticipator of semantics.

2. *The Exposition of Semantics.*

CHASE, STUART, *The Tyranny of Words* (New York: Harcourt, Brace, 1938). The popular exposition, based largely on Ogden and Richards and Korzybski, which made semantics a popular term.

HAYAKAWA, S. I., *Language in Action* (New York: Harcourt, Brace, 1941). A very lucid and penetrating introduction to the subject.

KORZYBSKI, ALFRED, *Science and Sanity* (Lancaster, Penna.: The Science Press, 1933). A voluminous work and hard to read, but the broadest exposition of semantics and of its importance.

OGDEN AND RICHARDS, *The Meaning of Meaning* (London: Kegan Paul Trench Trubner, 1930). The first serious work on semantics; somewhat narrowly linguistic in approach.

WALPOLE, HUGH, *Semantics* (New York: W. W. Norton, 1941). A general exposition in very narrow terms.

---

[17] Lancelot T. Hogben, *The Retreat From Reason* (New York: Random House, 1938); Hans Kohn, *Force or Reason* (Cambridge: Harvard University Press, 1937).

3. Related Works.

BERDYAEV, NICHOLAS, *The End of Our Time* (New York: Sheed and Ward, 1933). An analysis which supplements Gilson on the character of the transition which the world is undergoing, and the consequent changes of meaning.

DINGLE, HERBERT, *Through Science to Philosophy* (Oxford: The Clarendon Press, 1937). An interesting parallel to some of Korzybski's arguments in different and simpler terms.

EINSTEIN AND INFELD, *The Evolution of Physics* (New York: Simon and Schuster, 1938). The best and most direct exposition of the history of physics, leaving interpretation to the reader, but very plain in its implications as to the character of science.

HORNEY, KAREN, *The Neurotic Personality of our Time* (New York: W. W. Norton, 1937). Written by an author who did not fully appreciate her own discoveries, it none the less provides on the side of individual psychology the beginnings of a recognition of social psychology.

4. Semantics and Politics.

ARNOLD, THURMAN, *The Folklore of Capitalism* (New Haven: Yale University Press, 1937). A brilliantly written diatribe on the nonsensity of modern American economic folklore.

CARR, E. H., *The Twenty Years Crisis* (London: Macmillan, 1940). The best reasoned explanation of the inter-war period and of the fallacious premises on which it was built.

DRUCKER, PETER, *The End of Economic Man* (New York: John Day Co., 1939). At attempt to isolate some of the objects of faith which are crumbling today, with the emphasis on economic beliefs.

FRIEDRICH, C. J., "The Deification of the State," *Review of Politics* (January, 1939). An article covering the overemphasis on the state, but not fully analysing why men defy the state as a semanticist might attempt to analyze the problem.

LYND, ROBERT, *Knowledge for What?* (Princeton: Princeton University Press, 1939). A very general analysis of the world crisis and of the cultural contradictions underlying it. If read in conjunction with a book like Hayakawa's there should be little difficulty in relating them.

MANNHEIM, KARL, *Ideology and Utopia* (New York: Harcourt, Brace, 1936). The most serious, if not the only serious examination of some of the problems and solutions presented to the sociologist or political scientist by some recent philosophical changes. Complements Horney in many ways on the basis of quite different evidence and reasoning.

MENDELSOHN-BARTHOLDY, ALBRECHY, *The War and German Society* (New Haven: Yale University Press, 1937). The final volume of the Carnegie series on the Frst World War, German Series, written with no consciousness of Semantics. But it gives a very objective account of the crumbling of meaning and belief in Germany in 1918.

RODELL, FRED, *Woe Unto You, Lawyers* (New York: Reynald and Hitchcock, 1939). Similar to Arnold's scope, not quite so successful in the effort at satire, but a fair summary of the more outstanding nonsense in the law.

ROUCEK, JOSEPH S., "Ideology as a Means of Social Control," *The American Journal of Economics and Sociology,* III (October, 1943), pp. 35-45; III (January, 1944), pp. 179-192; III (April, 1944), pp. 357-370; "A History of the Concept of Ideology," *Journal of the History of Ideas,* V (October, 1944), pp. 479-488. The latest synthesis of the material available on this field.

Chapter XVII

THE NATURE OF PUBLIC OPINION AND PROPAGANDA

JOSEPH S. ROUCEK

During the past few years there has been a marked increase in interest in the study of public opinion and propaganda. Universities and colleges have added courses in this subject to their curricula. A news reporting service has been established by Dr. Gallup, and a monthly report by *Fortune* magazine. Business organizations have added experts on public relations to their staffs and set up research departments to gather facts about public opinion.

As is to be expected, the literature has lagged behind the knowledge gained by practitioners in the field. Now this deficiency is beginning to be made up. We have been flooded in recent years with popular as well as scholarly studies which have tried to clarify the concepts of public opinion and propaganda or which have added to our knowledge of this field by detailed studies of some particular aspects of this problem. They show that there is scarcely a field of human activity in which propaganda does not operate. But, unfortunately, since World War I the world propaganda has often assumed an invidious connotation, less frequently, it is true, in the writings of serious students than in discussions of popular commentators. But even today the term is not too respectable a concept which to too many people savors of the sly and sinister.

The fact remains, however, that there is and always has been good and bad propaganda. We are all aware of Hitler's audacious advocacy of the colossal life in *Mein Kampf*. To us, indeed, that is a bad kind of propaganda. But we surely do not think of the public address of President Roosevelt as being bad propaganda,

354

or that the advertising manager for a commercial firm is a propaganda trickster. Hence, care must be taken to clarify the concept of Public Opinion and Propaganda [1]—always keeping in mind that the term is something to be studied rather than just defined.[2]

---

[1] Harold D. Lasswell, Ralph D. Casey, Bruce L. Smith, *Propaganda and Promotional Activities; An Annotated Bibliography* (Minneapolis: University of Minnesota Press, 1935), includes an essay by H. D. Lasswell on "The Study and Practice of Propaganda." Since 1937 B. L. Smith has continued the bibliography in *The Public Opinion* Quarterly (Princeton: Princeton University Press). In addition to the works cited hereafter, good introductions and summaries are: Harold D. Lasswell, *Public Opinion in War and Peace* (Washington, D. C.: National Education Association, 1943), and bibliography, pp. 46-50, 67-68; F. H. Allport, "Toward a Science of Public Opinion," *Public Opinion Quarterly,* I (1937), pp. 7-32; B. L. Smith, "Scientific and Semi-Scientific Literature on War Information and Censorship", *Journalism* Quarterly, XX (March, 1943), pp. 1-20; Leonard Doob, *Propaganda: Its Psychology and Technique* (New York: Henry Holt, 1935); Peter H. Odegard, *The American Public Mind* (New York: Columbia University Press, 1930); Bruce L. Smith, "Propaganda Analysis and the Science of Democracy," *Public Opinion Quarterly,* V (June, 1941), pp. 250-259; Kimball Young, *Source Book for Social Psychology* (New York: A. A. Knopf, 1930); W. B. Graves, Ed., *Readings in Public Opinion* (New York: D. Appleton-Century, 1928); R. D. Case, "Propaganda and Public Opinion," in Willard Waller, Ed., *War in the Twentieth Century* (New York: The Dryden Press, 1940); William Albig *Public Opinion* (New York: McGraw-Hill Book Co., 1939); etc. Among the classical books on public opinion are: James Bryce, *Modern Democracies* (New York: The Macmillan Co., 1921 and subsequent editions); A. Lawrence Lowell, *Public Opinion in War and Peace* (Cambridge: Harvard University Press, 1923); Walter Lippmann, *Public Opinion* (New York: Harcourt, Brace, 1922); A. V. Dicey, *Lectures on The Relation between Law and Public Opinion in England During the Nineteenth Century* (New York: The Macmillan Co., 1905).

[2] Cf.: Hadley Cantril, *Psychology of Social Movements* (New York: John Wiley & Sons, 1941), contains studies of "Two Thousand Plan," "The Nazi Party," "The Lynching Mob," and of such sectarian movements as "The Kingdom of Father Divine" and "The Oxford Group"; Handley Cantril, *The Invasion from Mars: A Study in the Psychology of Panic* (Princeton: Princeton University Press, 1940); H. L. Childs, *An Introduction to Public Opinion* (New York: John Wiley & Sons, 1940), pp. 89-102, analyzes the promotion of the New York Worlds Fair; Harwood L. Childs, Ed., *Propaganda and Dictatorship* (Princeton: Princeton University Press, 1936), deals with opinion management in totalitarian states; Edward L. Bernays, *Crystallization of Public Opinion* (New York: Boni and Liveright, 1923), is a summary of several campaigns by a public relations counsel; Alfred McClung Lee and Elizabeth B. Lee, *The Fine Art of Propaganda* (New York: Harcourt, Brace, 1939), is a valuable study of Father Coughlin's speeches; Ellis Elmer, Ed., *Education Against Propaganda* (Washington, D. C.: National Council for the Social Sciences, 1937, *Seventh Yearbook*), is a symposium on channels of communication and the teaching problems involved in public courses; James L. McCamy, *Government Publicity: Its Practice in Federal Administration* (Chicago: University of Chicago Press, 1939); Kent Cooper, *Barriers Down: The Story of the News Agency* (New York: Farrar and Rinehart, 1942); etc.

Too many of the writers who get tied up with definitions contribute nothing to this field except the purposeful obfuscation of the term.

THE FIELD OF PUBLIC OPINION

Our previous discussion indicates that there are few, if any, areas of human experience toward which the student of Public Opinion and Propaganda can assume an attitude of unconcern, for he must be interested in human drives and motives and the structure and mechanism of social conduct, and social statics. Public Opinions are largely products of report; hence, for the analyst of this field the comprehensibility and accuracy of communication lies literally at the root of his inquiry. More than this: as communication is part and parcel of all social life, it behooves those in every field of social science to give serious attention to any objective inquiry into its nature.

But above all, the student must always remember that his specific inquiry in which he is for the moment engaged is but a fragment, but one aspect of a larger whole to which it must somehow be related. Hence, careful students of Public Opinion, in order to understand the etiology of attitudes and the function of belief in society, must inquire into the foundations, both material and psychological, of civilization and the dynamic forces which give it life. Hence, attention to the problem of Public Opinion is now given by statisticians, psychologists, social psychologists, sociologists, journalists, legalists, and political scientists. For they all study the same problem from different angles. The sociologist stresses the significance of Public Opinion as a means of Social Control; the psychologist is interested in the role played by various inherited and environmental factors in the formation of personal opinion; the social psychologist in the effect of propaganda upon individuals and groups; the student of law and jurisprudence in the influence of public opinion upon public policy; the political scientist in its influence upon government and the influence of official as well as unofficial agencies of government upon it; specialists in journalism observe the methods whereby the newspaper as an agency of communication plays upon public opinion by disseminating news, opinion, and entertainment, and is, in turn, influenced by the cross-currents in public opinion.[3] In short, public opinion research and study today cut across and transcend the traditional lines separating social science departments and disciplines, for students of public opinion are in final analysis students of human thought and behavior. They all approach the same problem as specialists, as Political Scientists, Sociologists, Social Psychologists, Psychologists, Economists, Statisticians, Journalists and students of Jurisprudence, but all united, whether they realize it or not, as students of human belief and conduct. All their contributions describing the operation and functioning of public opinion are worthy contributions to the field; and the more precise and objective are their contributions the more they contribute to the scientific advancement of this field.

THE NATURE OF PUBLIC OPINION

It is well-known that directly a man starts to write on meaning and definitions of terms, he is usually doomed to produce some fine confused specimens of muddled expression. We do not propose to do this here, since we assume that Public Opinion and Propaganda is something to be studied rather than just defined.

Admittedly, Propaganda has a broad and fluid meaning. Basically it is but a modern form of the attempts to disseminate

[3] Areas of metropolitan newspaper circulation for 1920 and 1929 are outlined by R. D. McKenzie in chapter IX of *Recent Social Trends in the United States* (New York: McGraw-Hill Book Co., 1934); the physical network of communication facilities, and the flow of material through them, is summarized by Malcolm M. Willey and Stuart A. Rice, in chapter IV; Douglas Waples, Bernard Berelson, and Franklin R. Bradshaw, *What Reading Does to People* (Chicago: University of Chicago Press, 1940); Douglas Waples, *People and Print: Social Aspects of Reading in the Depression* (Chicago: University of Chicago Press, 1937); Edgar Dale, *Content of Motion Pictures* (New York: The Macmillan Co., 1935); Paul Lazarsfeld, *Radio and the Printed Page* (New York: Duell, Sloan & Pearce, 1938); Hadley Cantril & Gordon W. Allport, *The Psychology of Radio* (New York: Harper, 1935); Leo C. Rosten, *The Washington Correspondents* (New York: Harcourt, Brace, 1937); Leo C. Rosten, Hollywood (New York: Harcourt, Brace, 1941); Douglas Waples, Ed., *Print, Radio, and Film in a Democracy: Ten Papers on the Administration of Mass Communications in the Public Interest* (Chicago: University of Chicago Press, 1942); Harold L. Ickes, Ed., *Freedom of the Press Today* (New York: Vanguard, 1941); Malcolm M. Willey & Ralph D. Casey, Eds., "The Press in the Contemporary Scene," *Annals of the American Academy of Political and Social Science,* CCXIX (January, 1942).

interested information and to win adherents to special view-points. Such efforts are as old as human society. Their modern forms of pleading have been relabeled since the World War as "propaganda". It is built on the art and science of controlling Public Opinion by overwhelming insistence upon a point of it. Since Propaganda is the conscious effort to manipulate Public Opinion and sentiment, a technique of influencing and controlling Public Opinion, and hence, one aspect of the general framework of our topic, let us turn first to a consideration of Public Opinion.

Public Opinion is in the nature of a concensus arrived at on the basis of the predominating cross-currents of view that prevail in a given time or place (and as related to conflicting sentiments, convictions rooted in special interests, traditional prejudices, par-tial information rational and irrational discussion, and various other elements). It is a relatively homogeneous expression of preference by members of a group concerning issues which, though debatable, concern the group as a whole. A public opin-ion, therefore, implies the existence of a (1) public or a group of members which communicate among themselves on matters of common interest and concern; [4] (2) issues or matters of com-mon interest about which the members of the public communicate with one another and to some extent disagree (the issues being expressed by slogans or propositions, that is, by symbols); (3) leadership which formulates, publicizes, and concentrates atten-tion upon the issues which are important at a given time; [5] (4) and opinions which indicate the attitudes of the members of the public toward the issues and their willingness to acquiesce in ac-tion conforming to the predominant opinion. The essence of Public Opinion is controversy. It is true that opinion may become so accepted as to constitute, for the time, truth, and truth may become so contradicted by new observations as to become opin-

---

[4] H. D. Lasswell, *World Politics and Personal Insecurity* (New York: McGraw-Hill Book Co., 1935), p. 83: "The public is a situation in which persons with a common focus of attention are making debatable demands for action." See also Lasswell, "The Measurement of Public Opinion," *American Political Science Reveiw,* XXV (May, 1931), pp. 31 ff.

[5] Lasswell, *World Politics and Personal Insecurity,* p. 3, and others use the term "élite" popularized by Pareto.

ion.[6] But at a given time in a given group the distinction can usually be made. Truth is accepted as a fact; opinion only as a belief. Beliefs, it is obvious, in religions or propagandas are usually presented as historical facts; but, in so far as both the facts and the deductions from them are controversial, within any population, they lack the status of truth.[7]

Since public opinion presupposes public discussion, it might be assumed that it is for this reason non-existent in dictatorship. Although it is true that public opinion cannot find unhampered expression under dictatorial government, dictators still have to take into account public reaction. Their Ministries of Propaganda have the task of not only propagandizing the faith but also serving as listening posts.

It is well to distinguish individual opinion, even though it is uttered in public, from Public Opinion. The former remains essentially individual opinion, unless it represents the attitude of a significant group.

At this point it might be useful to make a distinction between the crowd and the public. "The crowd is to be regarded as a quasi-primary group of persons in direct contact, where the communication is vocal or directly overt."[8] The crowd is usually linked with mobility of population, the development innumerable audience situations, and with the development of what Park calls the "touch-and-go" relations of people. The public, on the other hand, may be conceived of as a relative temporary amor-

---

[6] See discussion of "facts and attitudes," in W. Wright and Carl J. Nelson, "American Attitudes Toward China and Japan, 1937-38," *Public Opinion Quarterly*, III (January, 1939), p. 57 ff.

[7] "The truth of propositions about matters of reason (means and causes) tends to make them believed. Universalization of belief on matters of faith (ends and intuitions) tends to make them true"—according to Quincy Wright, *A Study of War* (Chicago: University of Chicago Press, 1942), Vol. II, pp. 1085-6. Men want dogmatic certainty about everything, and so tend to expand unduly the latter category. Thus Albert Schinz, *Anti-Pragmatism* (trans. from French, Boston, 1909), p. xx, points out that pragmatism may have a place in the field of ethics, but "there exists a conflict between intellectual truth and moral truth, a conflict that all the rationalization of the world will not suppress."

[8] Kimbal Young and Douglas W. Obendorfer, p. 639, chapter 12, "Psychological Studies of Social Processes," in Harry E. Barnes, Howard Becker and Frances B. Becker, *Contemporary Social Theory* (New York; D. Appleton-Century, 1940).

phous, and quasi-secondary group, resting upon specific interests, upon certain voluntary choices and relations.

Much early writing on crowd and group behavior discussed "crowd consciousness", "mob mind", and other psychological concepts applied to "mass" phenomena (McDougall, Le Bon, Tarde, etc.). But today it is generally accepted that "crowd mind" is merely a universality of attitudes, ideas, and actions in a group of *individuals*: that there is no such thing as a "super-individual mind" determining crowd behavior, since a crowd is a collection of individuals influenced by interactions of individuals with each other and with surrounding objects.[9]

An opinion is a conclusion reached or a judgment formed in a problematical situation on the basis of an ideology, plus evidence and facts that are weighed or discussed. At best, an opinion is merely a crude representation of an attitude. An attitude is a tendency to act, positively or negatively, toward a value, or toward a total situation or a complex of values. It is an acquired predisposition to act in a certain way toward a specific object or a person or in a specific situation which calls for adjustment. As such, it includes all the neural and other physiological sets and postures toward a situation, and their psychological correlates (commonly known as "inclinations," "feelings," "prejudices," "bias," notions," "ideas," "fears," threats," and "convictions").[10] Thus, a man's attitude on Nazism means all that he

---

[9] We shall not enter upon the controversy over the objections raised against such units as "group" and "public" which are equally applicable to the individual as a unit. See George A. Lundberg, "Public Opinion from a Behavioristic Viewpoint," *American Journal of Sociology*, XXXVI (November, 1930), pp. 387-405, who points out, p. 396, that it is "just as permissible to speak of public opinion as of individual opinion and as permissible to speak of the thinking, feeling, and acting of a group as it is to attribute those phenomena to individuals. In both cases, these words merely indicate a deliberate technique through which the unit referred to achieves a tentative adjustment." See also: Charles Hartshorne, "Elements of Truth in the Group-Mind Concept," *Social Research*, IX (May, 1942), pp. 248-65.

[10] George A. Lundberg, *Social Research* (New York: Longmans, Green and Company, 1942), p. 212. For a good analysis of the hopeless confusion in current usage of the term "attitude", see Read Bain, "An Attitude on Attitudes," *American Journal of Sociology*, XXXIII (1928) pp. 940-7. Ross Stagner, "Attitudes," pp. 69-75, is a good survey with bibliographical references. Cf. also: L. L. Thrustone and E. J. Chave, *The Measurement of Attitude* (Chicago, The University of Chicago Press, 1929); G. W. Allport, "Attitudes," in Carl Murchison, Ed., *Handbook of Social Psychology* (Worcester, Mass.: Clark University Press, 1935), Chapter 17.

feels and thinks about Hitler, his clique, and the practices of Hitlerism, as can be deduced from some objectively observable behavior—his remarks, emotions, facial expression, and similarly. Obviously opinions can be expressed not only in vocal utterances; a facial or a bodily movement, a smile, a frown, a shake of the head, a pained expression, may reveal one's opinions and be more effective than uttered words. In effect such attitudes constitute "language"; when current in the group and conveying meaning to those able to "read" them, they are expressions of public opinions which influence conduct. But by far the greatest and most important of this attitudinal behavior is in the form of language; in its more complete form this behavior takes the language form of *opinions*. The fact that opinions or verbal behavior are frequently very unreliable guides to what a person would do in a concrete situation, does not destroy the value of the verbal behavior as an expression of attitude. This is due to the fact that "an expressed attitude is an opinion, but opinions do not necessarily express attitudes correctly".[11] The sociologists stumble, in particular, over the term *public*. Though it is agreed that there are numerous publics, much confusion exists as to what and how permanent a public is. Dr. Childs summarizes the quest for the meaning of this term when he declares that "the multiplicity of definitions of public opinion is really due to the effort of students to restrict the meaning of the term to some aspect of public opinion in which they are especially interested".[12] The word "public" implies no mystical entity which scarcely exists in reality. It is a term characterizing a group occupying a defined territory whose members discuss the same symbols.

All social groups are sociologically and psychologically similar in that they involve (1) a number of individuals and (2) interaction between the members. But they can be classified in various ways on the basis of some easily recognized, even if superficial, characteristics which distinguish one group from another. The

---

[11] L. L. Thurstone, "Attitudes Can Be Measured," *American Journal of Sociology,* XXXIII (1928), p. 533.

[12] Harwood L. Childs, *An Introduction to Public Opinion* (New York: John Wiley & Sons, 1941) p. 5.

basis of such a classfication, as in all classifications, is our immediate interest of purpose. If we are interested in the geographical aspect of a social grouping, we call it by such names as neighborhood, community, state, or nation. If our interest is chiefly in the basis of common beliefs, opinions, principles, creeds, or dogmas, we use such terms as sect, party or public. Hence, a public is any group which makes a tentative deliberate adjustment to any situation on which it acts—actively or by acquiescence. It follows of course, that a person may belong to as many publics as he has interest, and that a public may or may not coincide with physical, geographical, or political units. Furthermore, there are obviously numerous publics holding a state of opinions and beliefs over certain issues or matters where there is difference as well as agreement. When there is unanimity there is no opinion but folkways and mores. Public Opinion implies discussion, differences of opinion, and general conflict of ideas and attitudes. It is obvious that the range of differences, discussion and interest of Opinions of numberless Publics is world-wide, and that face-to-face gossip is supplemented and overridden by indirect gossip through newspapers, periodicals, movies, radio, motion pictures and all the means of communication.

The term, Public Opinion, then, in contrast to individual opinion, signifies some conviction, belief, or sentiment common to a group. It is but one of the many manifestations of the social mind—one of the many ways by which individuals think, will and feel together. A common impression that Public Opinion depends upon and is measured by the mere number of persons is far from accurate, for there are many publics. The question of unanimity or majority consent is of no immediate importance in defining Public Opinion. If the public for any reason acquiesces in the Opinion which finds concrete expression in a concensus, the concensus must be regarded as that public's decision regardless of whether a majority engaged in weighing the evidence.

Hence, it is obvious that there are many publics—as many as there are attitude-holding groups. These may be classified as to their location, economic or social status, physical straits, intellectual capacities, religion, race, nationality and the like.

Public Opinion, being the term describing the attitudes of individuals in groups toward other individuals, groups or objects, is, then, interested in the etiology of attitudes, the function they fulfill for various publics and individuals of which they are composed.

Opinion may be measured as to direction, intensity, homogeneity, and continuity with reference to symbols.[13] The opinions of groups vary greatly in all these dimensions. They are also affected by types of leadership, by methods of propaganda, and by economic, political, and other circumstances.

Various methods for measuring various states of public opinion have been applied. They include analysis of attitude statements from the press,[14] analyses of opinions of the man on the street,[15] and analysis of the opinion of experts. The latter method appears to be the most convenient and reliable.

SYMBOLS

Opinions are always expressed in symbols. While animals live in a world of things, a man is a dweller in two domains: he is an inhabitant of a world of objects, and he lives also in a world of symbols, which serve him as media of communication. This is the result of man's existence being absolutely dependent on the relationships of some society culture groups. Biological drives and cooperative efforts to gain their satisfaction for a group have exerted strong influences upon the development of cultures, but, added to these, there has been a development of mutual understanding and desires through the growth of symbols.

[13] Quincy Wright, *A Study of War* (Chicago: University of Chicago Press, 1942), vol. II, pp. 1087-8. See also Allen L. Edwards, "Four Dimensions in Political Stereotypes," *Journal of Abnormal and Social Psychology* (October, 1940), pp. 560ff. who substitutes the dimension "quality" for that of "continuity."

[14] James T. Russell and Quincy Wright, "National Attitudes in the Far Eastern Controversy," *American Political Science Review,* XXVII (August, 1933), pp. 550-76; Wright *A Study of War,* Vol. II, Appendix SLI, pp. 1472-1481.

[15] As in the Gallup, *Fortune* and other polls. See: George Gallup and S. F. Rae, *The Pulse of Democracy: The Public Opinion Poll and How it Works* (New York: Simon & Shuster, 1940).

Symbols are easily recognizable objects, sounds, acts, or other devices (words, writings, national flags, national emblems, hymns, music, poems, statues) which represent something other than itself and which ordinarily evoke ideas, actions, or things that are of social significance (the concepts of rank, ambition, doctrine, ideology, love, mythology). Hence, they are powerful methods and incentives of social control. The man who cannot remember what Marx's theory is can be moved into action by a symbolic slogan, "Workers of the world unite!"

Our will requires the guidance of imagination, and the limits of imagination make intermediate symbols essential. A symbol is always an intermediate answer to ultimate questions. For minds of limited grasp, as all human minds are, only an intermediate answer can be definite enough for practical purposes. Each group, each culture pattern, consists of common symbols, which are mutually shared and possessed by the members of the group. Individual ways of acting are alike because these individuals are guiding their behavior by a set of symbols they share in common. Symbols are especially important in communicating abstract or subjective experiences, such as ideas, purposes, attitudes, and feelings, from one person to another, because such experiences cannot be easily observed directly.[16] The fine arts may be considered symbolic systems with such communication as their prime purpose. A symbol, however, is related not only to the thing which it stands for but also to other symbols which elaborate the relationships of that thing (its symtactic meaning)

---

[16] The behaviorists have attempted to define such experiences by the description of nervous, glandular, linguistic, and other observed behaviors rather than by the description of his own introspections given by the person who has had the experience.

and to those who use the symbol and influence or are influenced by its use (its pragmatic meaning).[17]

Man is the creator of symbolic universes, and it is this ability to rise above the limitations of time and place which makes it possible for him to give to airy nothings a local habitation and a name. Man is the fabricator of culture because he can create a second world of imaginative constructions and give them concrete reality in material form. The very foundations of our society rest, in fact, on symbols. Paper "money" is a symbolic substitute for bullion, and this in turn is a symbol of "real wealth". The signing of a contract, the writing of a poem, the setting down on paper, and the playing of a symphony—these are all exercises of the expression and interpretation of symbols.

Since opinions are invariably expressed in symbolic forms, publics may be also classified in terms of their unifying symbols or slogans (Republicans, Jew, Catholic, American, Czechoslovak, Communist, New York, United Nations). These symbols help to identify and express the private wishes or fears of those who make up the public to which the symbols or slogans relate. As such they serve as the basis for united action and as shortcuts to understanding. In distinction to most crowds the public is usually supported by some more permanent, highly organized group such as a political party, a labor union, a subversive movement, and the like. Furthermore, the public, even more than the crowd, is influenced by culture patterns of the larger society in which it finds itself; it is thus linked with political democracy, capitalism, religion, nationalism, world revolution.

The study of symbols is one of the most important aspects of the knowledge of Public Opinion and Propaganda, for the manipulation of symbols—stereotypes, key words, phrases, songs,

---

[17] Charles W. Morris, *Foundations of the Theory of Signs* ("International Encyclopedia of Unified Science," Vol. I, No. 2, Chicago: University of Chicago, 1938) is a good description of the affective, intentional, connotative, emotive, or pragmatic meaning which relates the sign, sword, or symbol to the user, from the informative, extensional, denotative, symbolic, or semantic meaning which relates it to the thing designated; see also: C. K. Ogden and I. A. Richards, *The Meaning of Meaning* (New York: Harcourt, Brace, 1923); S. I. Hayakawa, *Language in Action* (New York: Harcourt, Brace, 1941); A. Korzybski, *Science and Sanity* (Lancaster, Pa.: Science Press, 1942).

images, pictures,—is the core of all manipulations of Public Opinion and Propaganda.

Public Opinion is formed by verbalized, beliefs, and convictions, which are essentially emotional, and their associated images and ideas. The amount of rational and scientific discussion is likely to be at a minimum, although in special groups, of course, opinion is occasionally based on fact and logic. But even the Public Opinion based on cold fact is usually in the end, incorporated into the larger scheme provided by emotional attitudes and values.

CHANGING CONCEPTS OF PUBLIC OPINION

Probably the oldest concept of public opinion, which is also the core of our democratic theory, is the thesis that man is a rational being who deliberates on the basis of logic and cool reason. This view is really but a continuation of the eighteenth and early nineteenth century doctrine of rational man. This liberal-democratic ideology was derived from the Christian philosophy "of which it was a reformulation in secular terms".[18] God the Father conceived as the Great Contriver or Author of the Universe endowed man with Reason, which would allow him to achieve perfection (salvation) by a progressive adjustment of his ideas, by the conflict of individual interests and ideas. This liberal conception of Reason was a cardinal notion of the eighteenth-century Enlightenment. Any man might, of course, act contrary to reason, but that would happen only when he would be misled by insufficient knowledge or corrupted by non-rational impulses. Inseparable from this idea of reason was the idea, so dear to the nineteenth century, of intellectual detachment, the idea of the objective, right-thinking man, which permitted at least a group of consecrated scholars to achieve a complete detachment from all bias, so that they could "determine the facts and let them speak for themselves" and derive therefrom significant rational conclusions.

[18] Carl L. Becker, *New Liberties for Old* (New Haven: Yale University Press, 1941), p. 20. Harold D. Lasswell, *Democracy Through Public Opinion* (Menasha, Wisconsin: George Banta Publishing Co., 1941) is a brilliant exposition of the thesis that "In America we can achieve democracy through public opinion."

This way of viewing man and his universe by Rousseau, Volney, Godwin and Shelley, Mazzini, and with qualifications even by Bentham and Mills, is no longer fashionable. "The rational, right-thinking man," as Max Lerner says, "has as surely ceased to be considered the center of the planetary system." This attack on the conscious reason of individual men as the motivating force behind things and events was already beginning to be outmoded in some philosophical and scientific circles when Marx formulated the communist ideology. The doctrine of the "unconscious" was developed by Hartman and Freud. The Darwinian theory of evolution had much to do with the spread of such ideas, with his theory that since there is no break in the chain of descent between man and other animal species, the behavior of man need not be assumed to be determined by forces radically different from those operating in the behavior of animals. Since the behavior of animals is largely impulsive and instinctive, it began to be asserted at the turn of the present century that human beings, too, have instincts, that human actions are, in considerable part, "non-rational" or "non-logical." [19]

Marx's doctrine gave another blow to the concept of "rationalism" with its insistence that the social structure at any time, together with its supercargo of institutions and ideas, is fundamentally conditioned by the economic factors of production and distribution, and that social change or progress, was the result not of a conflict of ideas but of a conflict of economic interests, a conflict between the ruling and the dispossessed classes. Here, again, the emphasis was switched from the importance of the persuasive force of ideas to the impersonal pressure of economic conditions.

Today it is generally accepted that Public Opinion is controlled by the sentiments and emotions, and that it expressed itself in terms of attitudes and sentiments largely emotional

---

[19] Among the prophets may be mentioned William James (*Principles of Psychology*, 1890), and William McDougall (*An Introduction to Social Psychology*, 1908). theories of instincts, Sumner's (*Folkways*, 1906) treatment of the influence of the folkways and mores on human behavior, Graham Wallas's (*Human Nature and Politics*, 1908), *The Great Society*, 1914, *Our Social Heritage*, 1921, *The Art of Thought*, 1926), emphasis on the non-rational character of most human behavior.

rather than intellectual. The idea that Public Opinion could arise out of "conditions of disinterestedness" is hardly believed in any intellectual quarters any more. Furthermore, Public Opinion is not a static, inflexible standard. It is itself the end product of innumerable influences that direct and mold it. Whether in a democracy or in dictatorship, Public Opinion is subject to an incessant battle of Propaganda. It is evoked and formulated by Propaganda.

PROPAGANDA

Public Opinion finds its expression in discussion of the opinions, beliefs, sentiments, ideas and notions of a particular public. It is circulated first by conversation and gossip: then by various modern organs of communication, especially the newspaper, radio, motion pictures, schools and churches. Notice, however, that these means of communication not only reflect the beliefs and convictions which are the results of direct social inter-communication but also arouse our prejudices, myths, and legends by their manipulation of symbols, by means of what is commonly known as Propaganda.

Until Mussolini and Joe Stalin and Adolf Hitler came along probably the most stupendous and effective propaganda job done in a given time in modern history was that of the Creel Committee, which mobilized American Public Opinion towards winning the first World War.[20] In the immediate post-war years, the potential uses and abuses of these organized efforts to propagate ideas and attitudes were fully revealed. Many laymen, as well as scholars, have since become acutely propaganda conscious. But there is nothing necessarily sinister about Propaganda, which may be—in spite of the cynics, and often is—an honest effort to convince others of what one believes to be true— a religious creed, a principle of public policy, or a scientific proposition. In fact, when broadly defined, this form of political action is obviously essential to the working of a democratic government. It is only so that conviction, first held by a few far-seeing persons, may become those of a controlling majority.

[20] James R. Mock and Cedric Larson *Words that Won the War* (Princeton: Princeton University Press, 1940).

Numerous attempts to give the term narrower meaning have resulted in an array of conflicting interpretations.[21] Doob observes two general approaches in the various definitions, the sociological and the psychological or socio-psychological. In the former, propaganda is viewed as a means of social control, and stress is laid either upon the *motives* underlying it or upon the *methods* by which it is carried on, or both. In the latter, the psychological approach, the effects upon the individual in terms of changing attitudes or some similar process are emphasized. A more composite definition resulting from a combination of these two approaches is likewise frequently found.

A number of authors, among whom Lumley and Martin[22] are fairly typical, regard propaganda as deceptive, self-interested, promotional activity that is always deliberate, wholly iniquitous, and something very distinct from education. Others, however, including Doob, Lasswell, Childs, and Miller take exception to this one-sided interpretation. They define Propaganda more in

---

[21] For summary discussions of various definitions of propaganda, see Leonard W. Doob, *Propaganda: Its Psychology and Technique* (New York: Henry Holt and Co., 1935), pp. 71-89; Frederick E. Lumley, *The Propaganda Menace* (New York: D. Appleton-Century Co., 1933), pp. 21-44. The best theoretical evaluation of such definitions is Harwood L. Child's, *An Introduction to Public Opinion* (New York: John Wiley and Sons, 1940), "What is Public Opinion", pp. 35-48, and "The Concept of Propaganda," pp. 75-88. See also Gorham Munson, *Twelve Decisive Battles of the Mind* (New York: The Greystone Press, 1942), Chapter 1, "What is Propaganda?" pp. 11-20; Charles R. Hoffer, "A Sociological Analysis of Propaganda", *Social Forces*, X (May, 1942) pp. 445-8; Harold D. Lasswell, Ralph D. Casey, Bruce D. Smith, *Propaganda and Promotional Activities on Annotated Bibliography* (Minneapolis: University of Minnesota Press, 1935), "Theories of Propaganda," pp. 31-43.

[22] Everett Dean Martin, *The Meaning of a Liberal Education* (New York: W. W. Norton and Company, 1926), pp. 45-65.

the original sense,[23] as the effort to influence the behavior of people on behalf of predetermined ends by shaping their ideas and attitudes.[24] It is not regarded as considered clearly distinguishable from education.

Many writers stress the deliberate character of Propaganda. But this invidious connotation is less attributed to Propaganda in the writings of serious students than in discussions by popular commentators, for the most acceptable definitions include within the term all activity which, intentionally or unintentionally, influences attitudes and controls behavior through suggestion. A usage similar to that which has been given a popularization by the Institute of Propaganda Analysis, which defines Propaganda as "expression of opinion or action by individuals or groups deliberately designed to influence opinions or actions of other individuals or groups with reference to predetermined ends".[25] Professor Childs agrees with this definition as "simply another way of stating that the word Propaganda refers to ideas, doctrines and opinions which are propagated for a purpose",[26] but points out that "It is only when the Institute proceeds to identify, analyze, and appraise propaganda that it departs from its announced objectives. In reality the Institute confines its investigations to propaganda which it considers bad. . . . Instead

[23] The term originated in 1622 when Pope Gregory XV established the "Congregatio de Propaganda Fide." This Congregation of Propaganda was in reality a committee of cardinals in charge of foreign missions. As the Latin gerundive of the verb meaning "to propagate," the term was used originally to designate that which should be propagated: namely, the faith. On the history of propaganda, see: H. E. Barnes, *A History of Historical Writing* (Norman, Okla.: University of Oklahoma Press, 1937); Gorham Munson, *Twelve Decisive Battles of the Mind* (New York: Greystone Press, 1942); P. A. Throop, *Criticism of the Crusade: A Study of Public Opinion and Crusade Propaganda* (New York: Swets and Zeitlinger, 1940); Philip Davidson, *Propaganda and the American Revolution* (Chapel Hill, N. C.: University of North Carolina, 1941); C. E. Merriam, *A History of American Political Theory* (New York: Macmillan, 1918); H. C. Peterson, *Propaganda for War* (Norman, Okla.: University of Oklahoma Press, 1939); Porter Sargent, *Getting us Into War* (Boston: Sargent, 1941).

[24] Doob, *op. cit.*, pp. 71-89; Harold D. Lasswell, "Propaganda," *Encyclopedia of Social Sciences*, XII, pp. 521-28.

[25] Institute for Propaganda Analysis, *The Fine Art of Propaganda*, edited by Alfred McClung Lee and E. B. Lee, p. 15.

[26] Harwood L. Childs, *An Introduction to Public Opinion*, p. 81.

of attempting to find out precisely why certain types of propaganda spread it merely tries to show that propagandists use certain devices or methods. It ignores the possibility that other and, from its point of view, good propagandists selected may use other techniques equally important. In other words, instead of coming to grips with the phenomenon of propaganda the Institute simply tries to prove that 'bad' propagandists use certain methods, thereby implying that only 'subversive' advocates use them. Instead of trying to find out something the Institute is merely trying to prove something. . . ." [27]

Obviously Propaganda may involve individual or group activity; its underlying motives may be selfish or altruistic; its methods may be veiled or open; its appeal may be made to the emotions or to the intellect; and the cause it promotes generally accepted or controversial. For Propaganda may be defined as "any ideas and doctrines which are intentionally propagated. To Propagate ideas is to advance, further, spread, transmit, disseminate, promote, and increase them".[28] Such a definition would not obstruct the vision of social scientists for it implies that Propaganda is neither good nor bad but must be judged in terms of its sources, objectives, methods and results. At its worst it degenerates into a vicious conspiracy of selfish cliques which employ deceitful methods to win support for ends inimical to public welfare—as exemplified by Hitler's gang. At its best it

[27] *Ibid.*, p. 82. Notice Max Lerner's criticism of the definition of Propaganda by the Institute of Propaganda Analysis (review of Harold Lavine and James Wechsler, *War Propaganda and the United States, in New Republic,* CIII (August 26, 1940), pp. 281-2, reprinted in Lerner's *Ideas for the Ice Age* (New York: The Viking Press, 1941), pp. 184-190. Another useful criticism of the Institute's conception of propaganda is that of Read Bain in *American Sociological Review,* VI (December, 1941), pp. 886-7. William Garber, "Propaganda Analysis—To What Ends?" *The American Journal of Sociology,* XLVIII (September, 1942), pp. 240-5, criticizes Lasswell's Institute's concepts of propaganda and concludes that "The proper way to understand the phenomenon of propaganda is not primarily through the study of the theoretical and psychological tricks employed, but rather by an analysis of the total social context of the propaganda under investigation, conceiving the whole as a dynamic field of stress and strains wherein the forces of propaganda plays its part . . . "

[28] Harwood L. Childs, "Propaganda," *Dictionary of American History,* IV, pp. 358-9; and *Introduction to Public Opinion,* p. 75.

may promote worthwhile community projects, World War II endeavors on behalf of the welfare of the United States, and, in general, contributions to the unity and preservation of our "way of life". Hence, the task of the specialist in this field is to study the operation of Propaganda rather than to worry about its definitions and the subjective connotation of the word; to throw light on the range, the method, and the purpose of Propaganda.

It ought to be borne in mind, however, that the following important elements form constitutent parts of Propaganda. (1) All such activity has a predetermined end in view; it involves a deliberate effort to get people to do or not to do a particular thing by various media available to the propagandist, from deeds to printed texts—by means of the printed word, oratory, the cartoon and motion picture, the awakening incident or by the demonstration by trial or pageantry. (2) Propaganda is an effort to convince, in contradistinction to efforts to simply give information. Propaganda always contains, however, information, true or false, but its purpose is not so much to increase the knowledge of those to whom it is addressed, as to induce them to accept some principle of action. As N. S. Timasheff puts it: "You can propagate faith or a political doctrine, but you cannot propagate pure mathematics." [29] (3) Obviously then, propaganda endeavors pertain to controversial subjects. (4) Propaganda is characterized by its orientation towards action, and the specific mode of manipulation in propaganda is to "dispel doubt" and to pretend "to the finality of truth".[30] (5) The methods used to accomplish these results tend to be veiled in some way or other so that they harmonize with the interests and cultural values of the groups being reached.

When fused together, these elements then yield a definition which states propaganda is the process of influencing attitudes in a veiled manner regarding matters of controversy within

---

[29] N. S. Timasheff, "Cultural Order in Liberal, Facist, and Communist Society," *The American Catholic Sociological Review*, III (June, 1942), pp. 63-72.

[30] R. E. Park, "Morale and the News," *American Journal of Sociology*, XLVII (November, 1941), p. 364.

a society for the sake of some principle of action pretending the finality of truth.

EDUCATION AND PROPAGANDA

Research has not succeeded in determining precisely in what essential ways education is distinguished from Propaganda. "It is true that the majority of writers in this field attempt to characterize as Propaganda those activities which manipulate misrepresentations or partial representations for the advantage of special interests." [31] But other students have discovered that education shares with Propaganda many traits in common; each purports to have a modicum of fact as a base, a regard for seeking as well as affirming "truth", a tendency to impose conclusions, and a conviction of reasonable finality and of general rather than factional ethical values. Lasswell points out that, even when education is conceived of as transmitting techniques, nevertheless, values are involved; [32] and certainly a large part of education is inculcation of traditional value attitudes or value dispositions, such as opposition or approval for persons, groups, ideas and policies. Nor can educators be absolved from spreading novel or debatable ideas or even subversive doctrines. This dilemma cannot be solved by appealing to symbols, such as the spirit of education; greater or less disinterestedness, open mindedness, opportunity for discussion, and freedom for competion of new ideas and practices. Furthermore, Education, just like Propaganda, serves basically as an instrument of social control; within the field of Education conflicting schools of thought contend for dominance within the educational system.[33] Interested individuals and groups within the public schools use Propaganda to win support for these general theories of Education, often joining

[31] S. S. Bittner, "Adult Education," *Encyclopaedia of Educational Research* (New York: Macmillan, 1941), p. 26; See also L. C. Kercher, chapter 26, "Propaganda and Educaation," pp. 579-603, in J. S. Roucek, Ed., *Sociological Foundation of Education* (New York: Thomas Y. Crowell, Co., 1942).

[32] H. D. Lasswell, Propaganda," *Encyclopaedia of the Social Sciences*, XII, pp. 521-7.

[33] For such schools, see William E. Drake, chapter 32, "Educational Sociology in Relation to Educational Theory and Practice," pp. 711-44., in Joseph S. Roucek, Ed. *Sociological Foundations of Education*.

with special pleaders for more limited aspects of the institution. Last but not the least, Education, as an agency of our fluid society, must practice indoctrination—one of the most important weapons of Propaganda.[34]

The school is, therefore, presented with something of a dilemma; democratic principles guarantee the right to propagandize; much of the resulting Propaganda makes wise choices very difficult; yet wise choices are essential to a healthy democracy. The best, then, that the school can do is "to provide as far as possible a positive education for reflective citizenship" [35] to promote the welfare of all people rather than the claims of organized interests, to foster realistic study and progressive elimination of the various social conditions which are harmful to our democracy and which promote irrationality and the acceptance of alien doctrines. In short, Education, as one of the Propaganda agencies of our Democracy, must promote general acceptance of values consistent with our democratic society.

The only possible distinction which possibly can be made between Propaganda and Education by accepting Lasswell's definition of Propaganda as the process of manipulating symbols so as to effect the opinion of a group.[36] Such a definition of Propaganda may be contrasted with Education, which is the process of manipulating symbols so as to affect the attitudes of an individual [37] (the totality of the attitudes of its members constitutes the culture of the group for the sociologist). The fact that Education as compared with Propaganda deals with the young rather than the mature, with the traditional rather than the novel, with techniques rather than values, indicates more profound influence upon personality and culture.[38] Propaganda and Education are

---

[34] Joseph S. Roucek, "The Essence of Educational Sociology, No Shangri-La in Educational Problems," pp. 21-3, in Roucek, *Sociological Foundations of Education.*

[35] Kercher, *op. cit.,* p. 599.

[36] Lasswell, *World Politics and Personal Insecurity,* p. 114; "Propaganda," in *Encyclopaedia of the Social Sciences,* XII, 521.

[37] G. S. Counts, "Education," *Encyclopaedia of the Social Sciences,* V. p. 403, defines education "as the induction of the maturing individual into the life and culture of the group."

[38] See Lasswell, *World Politics and Personal Insecurity,* pp. 251 ff.: "Propaganda," *op. cit.,* p. 522.

related, because opinion to some extent reflects attitudes and attitudes are to some extent influenced by opinion, but they are not ncessarily identical.[39] Attitudes, though originating in the drives of the individual organism, are given form by education, the process by which the culture of a group is developed and passed on to the rising generation. Propagandas, on the other hand, are addressed to the group, educational procedures to the individual. Propagandas try to influence public opinion and stimulate immediate social action through superimposing group objectives upon the individual consciences. Education seeks to influence private attitudes, thus building the individual personality and the group culture into an organic unity.

WAR PROPAGANDA

Never before had propaganda been resorted to on such an organized scale as during World War I and again in World War II, and by the practices of the dictators. Since the appearance of Lasswell's pioneer analysis,[40] we have seen numerous valuable studies devoted to that topic.[41] During the two armistice periods between the two world wars, the increased capitalization of modern war, changes in its techniques through industrial and technological advances and the rise of aggressive dictatorships have extended, in addition, the scope of wartime propaganda. To an even greater extent than World War I, World War II was fought not only on the land fronts, the sea front and those vast fronts of the air, but also on a fourth. This might be called the front of the human mind. On that front, Adolf Hitler won in the opening days of the World War resounding victories.

[39] See L. L. Thurstone, "Attitudes Can Be Measured," *American Journal of Sociology*, XXXIII (1928), p. 533.

[40] H. D. Lasswell, *Propaganda Technique in the World War* (New York: A. A. Knopf, 1927).

[41] G. G. Bruntz, *Allied Propaganda and the Collapse of the German Empire in 1918* (Stanford University: Stanford University Press, 1938); G. Creel, *How We Advertized America* (New York: Harper, 1920); C. H. Grattan, *Why We Fought* (New York: The Vanguard Press, 1929); *E. von Ludendorff's Own Story* (New York: Harper, 1920); W. Millis, *Road to War* (Boston: Houghton Mifflin, 1935); J. R. Mock, and C. Larson, *Words that Won the War* (Princeton: Princeton University Press, 1939); H. C. Peterson, *Propaganda for War* (Norman, Okla.: University of Oklahoma Press, 1939); G. S. Viereck, *Spreading Germs of Hate* (New York: Liverright, 1930).

Indeed, it was largely those victories, won in psychological warfare, which enabled him to conquer a continent. He had, to be sure, a mighty army, a large and ruthless air force and even a navy. But the war for their easy march through one country after another was prepared for them by staggering triumphs in political and psychological warfare. In six countries they did not have to fire a shot, so well was the ground prepared. In the others, until Hitler met his match in Russia, the German Army and Air Force met little opposition.

This war of the mind and of the nerves is one of the most remarkable developments in the endeavors to control Public Opinion toward the national cause as well as to promote public sentiment against the enemy. It more than ever accentuated the fact in the United States that we are living in the age in which Propaganda is used as an instrument of internal, international and global political strategy,[42] Nazism means all that he feels and thinks about Hitler, his clique.

---

[42] Joseph S. Roucek, "Axis Psychological Strategy Against the United States," *New Europe*, II (October, 1942), pp. 331-337, and "Hitler's Propaganda as a War Weapon, *Educational Forum*, VII (November, 1940), pp. 67-83; Derrick Sington & Arthur Weidenfel, *The Goebbels Experiment* (New Haven: Yale University Press, 1943); Kenneth Stewart, *News is What We Make It* (Boston: Houghton Mifflin, 1932); Edmond Taylor, *The Strategy of Terror* (Boston: Houghton Mifflin, 1940); Edmond Taylor, *The Strategy of Terror* (Boston: Houghton Mifflin, 1940); Serge Chakotin, *The Rape of the Masses*: *The psychology of Totalitarian Political Propaganda* (New York: Alliance, 1940), is written by Russian-born psysiologist who developed the Three-Arrow campaign against the Nazis in Germany; Harwood L. Childs and John B. Whitton, *Propaganda by Short Wave* (Princeton University Press, 1942); F. L. Bartlett, *Political Propaganda* (New York: Macmillan, 1940); Committee for National Morale, *German Psychological Warfare,* edited by Ladislas Farago (New York: The Committee for National Morale, 1941), is a critical, annoted survey and bibliography on this topic; C. Siepmann, *Radio in Wartime* (New York: Oxford, 1942); Harold Ettlinger, *The Axis on the Air* (Indianapolis, Ind.: Bobbs-Merrill, 1943); J. T. MacCurdy, *The Structure of Morale* (New York: Macmillan, 1943); Matthew Gordon, *News is a Weapon* (New York: Knopf, 1942); Sherman Dryer, *Radio in Wartime* (New York: Greenberg, 1942); Joseph Bornstein & Paul N. Milton, *Action Against the Enemy's Mind* (Indianapolis: Bobbs-Merrill, 1942); C. L. Hoag, *Preface to Preparedness*: *The Washington Disarmament Conference and Public Opinion* (Washington, D. C.: American Council on Public Affairs, 1941); Kenneth Stewart, *News Is What We Make It* (Bosto: Houghton Mifflin, 1943); James Morgan Read, *Atrocity Propaganda* (New Haven: Yale University Press, 1941); E. Malcolm Carroll, *Germany and the Great Powers,* 1866-1914: *A Study in Public Opinion and Foreign Policy* (New York: Prentice-Hall, 1939); O. W. Reigel, *Mobilizing for Chaos* (New Haven: Yale University Press, 1934); Bruno Lasker, *Propaganda From China and Japan*

PROPAGANDISTS AS INFLUENCED BY PROPAGANDA

One of the most interesting developments in recent years has been an influence on the propagandists as a result of the attention paid to Propaganda.[43] The present specialists in Propaganda in America seem to rely less on downright lies and on the hold over us by naïve stereotypes and more on factual and reasonable material. At any rate, their work is not at all as crude as the propaganda that we carried on during World War I. On the other hand contemporary Propaganda may be all the more insidious for that reason.

IMPROVED TECHNIQUES

In particular we must note here the recent advances in the functional etiology of attitudes as well as in the description of

---

(New York: American Council, 1938); H. L. Lasswell & D. Blumenstock, *World Revolutionary Propaganda and the United States* (New Haven: Yale University Press, 1940); Arthur Ponsonby, *Falsehood in War Time* (New York: E. P. Dutton, 1928); James D. Squires, *British Propaganda at Home and in the United States* (Cambridge: Harvard University Press, 1935); Marcus M. Wilkerson, *Public Opinion and the Spanish-American War* (Baton Rouge: Louisiana State University Press, 1932); Joseph E. Wilson, *Cuban Crisis as Reflected in the New York Press* (New York: Columbia University Press, 1934); Walter C. Sweeney, *Military Intelligence: A New Weapon in War* (New York: Stokes, 1924); Joseph S. Roucek, "Sabotage and America's Minorities," *World Affairs Interpreter*, XIV (April, 1943), pp. 45-66; and "Foreign-Language Press in World War II," *Sociology and Social Research*, XXVII (July-August, 1943), pp. 462-71; and "The 'Free Movements' of Horthy's Ekchardt and Austria's Otto," *The Public Opinion Quarterly*, VII (Fall, 1943), pp. 466-76; and "American Japanese, Pearl Harbor and World War II," *Journal of Negro Education*, XII (Fall, 1943), pp. 633-49; and "International Aspects of our Problems of Minorities," *World Affairs Interpreter*, XIV (October, 1943), pp. 307-26; and "The Sociological Weaknesses of Federation Plans for Central-Eastern Europe," *Journal of Legal and Political Sociology*, II (October, 1943), pp. 94-116; and *Misapprehensions about Central-Eastern Europe in Anglo-Saxon Historiography* (reprint, *Bulletin of the Polish Institute of Arts and Sciences in America*, II, January, 1944, pp. 353-70); and "Some Recent Illusions about Peace and War," *Social Education*, VIII (April, 1944), pp. 152-7; and "Public Opinion in the Totalitarian States: Its Revolutionary and Ideological Character," *Social Science*, XIX (April, 1944), pp. 87-93; and "Bulgaria and the Menace of Macedonia's Independence," *New Europe*, IV (November, 1944), pp. 25-29; and "Japanese Propaganda Among American Japanese and Negroes," *World Affairs Interpreter*, XV (October, 1944), pp. 305-312; etc.

[43] Bruno Lasker and Agnew Roman, *Propaganda from China and Japan* (New York: American Council, Institute of Pacific Relations, 1938): Charles W. Smith, Jr., "The Intelligence Factor in Public Opinion," *Journal of Politics*, I (August, 1939), pp. 301-311.

a measurement of opinion.[44] Here the studies of Thurstone, Pressey, Terman and Murphy among psychologists, and of Beyle, Gossnell, Gallup, Ogburn, Rice and others among political scientists and sociologists represent notable contributions to the study of Public Opinion. Psycho-metrics and socio-metrics are well on the way to becoming as rigorously scientific as physics and chemistry. Useful have been the many objective studies of balloting, with due allowance for the conditions at the time of the votes. Speeches, "movies," and entertainments of various sorts have been seized upon as opportunities for noting items provoking applause or negative responses. The sale of newspapers, periodical literature, and books, has been employed, and checks have been made upon precisely what people read in them. Curves of press opinion have been devised and employed to show the attitude of a public in one country toward other countries. Various checks have been made upon radio listening. Direct interviews and questionnaire polls have been taken of opinion or attitude on all sorts of topics. Today we have methods and techniques for investigations to permit their wide use. The main problem is of focusing the various methods upon different concrete communities, issues and sequence of opinion, in order to see what contribution may be made by each in rounding out an analytical comprehension of these concrete situations.

But the advances in this field must not prevent us from a definite conviction that much work is here yet to be done, since this work is only in a formative stage. Much of the emphasis is still on the improvement of techniques without so much concern for the social significance of what is measured. Commercial

---

[44] Concerning the brief poll interview method of determining public opinion, consult George Gallup & Saul Forbes Rae, *Pulse of Democracy* (New York: Simon & Schuster, 1940) ; for a compact summary of methods used to measure opinion, see chaptex X of William Albig, *Public Opinion,* and also Gardner Murphy, Lois Barclay Murphy and Theodore N. Newcomb, *Experimental Social Psychology* (New York: Harper, 1937) ; methods of isolating the effects of opinion in different factors, are discussed in Douglas Waples, Bernard Berelson, & Franklyn R. Bradshaw, *What Reading Does to People* (Chicago: Chicago University Press, 1940) and in Murphy; current opinion can be followed through polls, notably those conducted by the American Institute of Public Opinion (George Gallup), by *Fortune* magazine (Elmo Roper) and the National Opinion Research Center (University of Denver).

agencies have, after all, gone much further than scholars toward improving the mechanics of collecting individual opinions over wide areas.

BUSINESS, POLITICIANS AND NON-ACADEMICIANS

In the study of public opinion and propaganda, scholars cannot even start sharing honors with men of various vocations outside the academic field, and particularly political, business and commercial leaders. When a first class public relations man or politician writes a book with a reasonable degree of frankness, it is likely to contain valuable material for students of public opinion.[45] In the anti-World War period the development of Propaganda had already been promoted by popular education, manhood suffrage, the spread of democracy generally, the growth of capitalism, and the expansion of technocracy and industry. Public and special groups had long availed themselves of modern mechanical inventions to influence Public Opinion. Specialists in this field had been given the benefit not only of improved means of communication but also researches in social sciences, and particularly psychology and social psychology in understanding of how opinions and attitudes are formed, prejudices established and passions inflamed. Free education and the broadening of the base of political power in this country, as well as abroad necessitated an expansion of Propaganda in politics.

The ever-growing complexity of our culture has forced the representatives of specialized activities, many of them in conflict, to promote their business and political interests by hiring symbol specialists, giving rise to new specialists of this modern age—the press agent, the public relations council, the advertising

[45] E. L. Bernays, "The Revolution in Publicity," *Saturday Review of Literature,* XXIV (November 1, 1941), pp. 3ff.; Harold P. Levy, *A Study in Public Relations* (New York: Russell Sage Foundation, 1943); Benjamin Fine, *Educational Publicity* (New York: Harper, 1943); Averell Broughton, *Careers in Public Relations* (New York: E. P. Dutton, 1943); Richard J. Gabel, *Public Funds for Church and Private Schools* (Washington: Catholic University, 1937).

specialist, all interested in reaching individuals and groups with basic appeals designed to stir the common man to action.[46]

RECENT TRENDS

Contemporary developments have given impetus to the study of public opinion and propaganda. While James Bryce, A. Lawrence Lowell, Walter Lippmann, and others wrote penetratingly on the subject in an earlier period, the study of this field has, however, come of age only in more recent years when numerous detailed and specific studies have become available. Politicians, public relations men, psychologists, sociologists and journalists, as well as political scientists, are continually learning and revealing more about the forces that determine the composition and direction of public opinion and propaganda.

There are those who believe that there "is a steadily increasing awareness of the methods of propagandists and a corresponding decrease in the gullibility of the public", and that "despite threats and occasional set-backs, we move toward an increasingly rational public opinion in the modern world"; [47] a larger and more vociferous group is, on the other hand, convinced that man is dominated by non-rational motives, by his ideologies.[48] But here we approach the "new" field of Seman-

---

[46] S. H. Walker, & Paul S. Sklar, *Business Finds Its Voice* (New York: Harper, 1938), is a sketch of big business campaigns in answer ot the New Deal by two publicity men; E. Pendleton Herring, Jr., *Public Administration and the Public Interest* (New York: McGraw-Hill Book Co., 1936), summarizes private efforts to influence administrators; Harwood L. Childs, Ed., "Pressure Groups and Propaganda," *Annals of the American Academy of Political and Social Science,* CLXXIX (May, 1935); William Gellermann, *The American Legion as Educator* (New York: Columbia University Press, 1938).

[47] Charles W. Smith, "The Intelligence Factor in Public Opinion," *Journal of Politis,* I (August, 1939), pp. 301-311.

[48] See the bibliography, pp. 342-359, in Franz Alexander, *Our Age of Unreason* (Philadelphia: J. B. Lippincott, 1942), and such studies as: Joseph S. Roucek, "Ideology as a Means of Social Control," *American Journal of Economics and Sociology,* III (October, 1943), pp. 35-45 & ff.

tics and the Sociology of Knowledge which we cannot deal with here.[49] But the fact remains that the whole field of public opinion and propaganda is related to the whole field of social sciences and that, in a narrower sense, it is a problem of increasingly growing importance when we consider the mass character of our civilization, the growing improvements of our means of communication, the growing bitterness of social struggles for the distribution and control of power in internal and international affairs, and the recent discoveries in the field of propaganda as the means of persuasion.

BIBLIOGRAPHY

ALBIG, WILLIAM, *Public Opinion* (New York: McGraw-Hill, 1939). A standard introductory textbook to this field.

BIRCHALL, F. T., *The Storm Breaks* (New York: Viking Press, 1940). Foreign relations and the formation of public opinion by newspapers.

BIRD, G. L., AND MERWIN, F. E., *The Newspaper and Society* (New York: Prentice-Hall, 1942). A valuable collection of readings on public opinion, propaganda press freedom, and the newspaper at work in society.

BRUCKER, HERBERT, *The Changing American Newspaper* (New York: Columbia University Press, 1937).

CANTRIL, HADLEY and others, *Gauging Public Opinion* (Princeton: Princeton University Press, 1944). Studies done under Dr. Cantril's direction in the Office of Public Opinion Research at Princeton University.

CASEY, R. D., "Propaganda and Public Opinion," pp. 429-477 in Willard Waller, Ed., *War In the Twentieth Century* (New York: The Dryden Press 1940). A valuable survey.

CHILDS, H. L., *Propaganda and Dictatorship* (Princeton: Princeton University Press, 1939). On the operation of propaganda among and by the totalitarian systems.

CREEL, GEORGE, *How We Advertised America* (New York: Harper, 1920). How America built up its propaganda machinery in World War 1.

DESMOND, R. W., *The Press and World Affairs* (New York: D. Appleton-Century, 1937).

GALLUP, G. H., *Public Opinion in a Democracy* (Princeton: Princeton University Press, 1939); Gallup G. H. & Rae, S. F., *The Pulse of Democracy* (New York: Simon and Schuster, 1940). By the director of the Gallup Poll.

GRANDIN, THOMAS, *The Political Use of the Radio* (Geneva: Geneva Studies, Vol. 10, 1939).

GRAVES, W. B., Ed., *Readings in Public Opinion* (New York: D. Appleton-Century, 1928).

HARPER, M. H., *Social Beliefs and Attitudes of American Educators* (New York: Columbia University Press, 1927).

---

[49] Among other works, see: Karl Mannheim, *Ideology and Utopia* (New York: Harcourt, Brace, 1936; Talcott Parsons, *The Structure of Social Action* (New York: McGraw-Hill Book Co., 1937); H. Otto Dahlke, "The Sociology of Knowledge," chapter 4, pp. 64-92, in H. E. Barnes, Howard Becker & Frances B. Becker, *Contemporary Social Theory* (New York: D. Appleton-Century, 1940).

KING, C. L., *Public Opinion as Viewed by Eminent Political Theorists* (Philadelphia: University of Pennsylvania Lectures vol. 3, 1916, pp. 417-453.)

LASSWELL, H. D., *Propaganda Technique in the World War* (New York: Alfred A. Knopf, 1927). A study which inaugurated a trend of examination of this field.

LASSWELL, H. D., and others, *Propaganda and Promotional Activities* (Minneapolis: University of Minnesota Press, 1935). An indispensable annotated bibligraphy.

LAVINE, HAROLD AND WECHSLER, JAMES, *War Propaganda and the United States* (New Haven: Yale University Press, 1940.) A readable survey of the introductory phases of World War II.

LEE, A. M., *The Daily Newspaper in America* (New York: Macmillan, 1937). A valuable introduction to the history of the rise of America's newspapers.

LIPPMAN, WALTER, *The Phantom Public* (New York: Harcourt, Brace, 1920). One of Lippman's classic studies of public opinion.

MICAUD, CH. A., *The French Right and Nazi Germany* (Durham, N. C.: Duke University Press, 1943). A study of public opinion between 1933-1939.

MOTT, F. L., ed., *Journalism in Wartime* (Washington, D. C.: American Council on Public Affairs 1944). A discussion of wartime journalistic problems by American journalists.

MOTT, F. L., AND CASEY, R. D., *Interpretation of Journalism* (New York: F. S. Crofts, 1937).

NAFZIGER, RALPH O., *International News and the Press* (New York: H. W. Wilson, 1940). Bibliography.

ODEGARD, P. H., *The American Public Mind* (New York: Columbia University Press, 1930). One of the exploratory studies of this concept.

PARK, R. E., "News and the Power of the Press," *American Journal of Sociology*, XLVII (July, 1941), pp. 1-11.

RAUP, R. B., *Education and Organized Interests in America* (New York: Putnam, 1936).

RICE, S. A., *Quantitative Methods in Politics* (New York: Alfred A. Knopf, 1928).

ROBINSON, C. E., *Straw Votes* (New York: Columbia University Press, 1932).

SMITH, C. W., *Public Opinion in a Democracy* (New York: Prentice-Hall, 1939). A textbook dealing mainly with the operation of political parties.

WILKERSON, M. M., *Public Opinion and the Spanish-American War* (Louisiana State University, 1932).

WILEY, M. M. AND CASEY, R. D., Eds., *The Press in the Contemporary Scene* (*Annals* of the American Academy of Political and Social Science, vol. 219, January, 1942).

WILSON, F. G., "Concepts of Public Opinion," *American Political Science Review*, XXVII (June, 1933), pp. 371-392.

WOODWARD, JULIAN, *Foreign News and American Morning Newspapers* (New York: Columbia University Press, 1930).

Chapter XVIII

DEFENDERS AND CRITICS OF AMERICAN CAPITALISM AND CONSTITUTIONALISM: CONSERVATISM AND LIBERALISM

CARLTON C. RODEE

Probably the most important and controversial issue in American political thought since the opening of the twentieth century has been the proper relationship of government and business—of politics and economics. The problems of a maturing industrial society [1] have challenged America's statesmen and her political philosophers. As popular demands for reform resulted in steadily increasing governmental intervention to eliminate economic abuses and alleviate social inequities—as the era of Progressivism and Wilsonian "New Freedom" gave place to Franklin Roosevelt's "New Deal"—political theorists and men active in public life were led to scrutinize more closely the basic postulates of American political thought and to seek a new formulation of traditional concepts in the light of the conditions of the machine age.

Though stated in varying terms during different periods of controversy, the basic question is whether government ought to pursue a policy of economic non-intervention except where forced to remedy the most serious abuses, or whether it ought to take positive, aggressive, purposeful action to provide greater economic and social security, wider opportunities, and improved living standards for underprivileged groups and the people as a

---

[1] For a brief discussion of recent trends, see Stuart Chase, *The Road We Are Traveling*, 1914-1942 (New York: Twentieth Century Fund, 1942), especially Chapter 2.

whole. In other words, ought government to play the role of a mere policeman, or of an agency for the positive promotion of individual and group welfare? This question is often obscured beneath the verbiage of current controversy, but it is the fundamental problem of all modern industrial societies.

This basic issue involves many others. Can a democracy competently guide a collectivized society and remain a democracy? In what direction, and to what extent, should American governmental institutions and processes be modified in order to enable government to deal effectively with the problems of today? Is our constitution, a product of the eighteenth century, adequate to the tasks of government in the twentieth? [2] Should we modify such constitutional arrangements as federalism, the "separation of powers", "checks and balances", judicial review of legislation, strict limitations upon government? Ought we to view with alarm or complacency recent trends toward increased powers for the President and the administrative establishments, toward federal centralization, toward the expansion of governmental powers in general? If our government is to continue to extend its controls over economic life and to promote social welfare, what ought to be the structure of that government?

If, as many believe, there is a fundamental contradiction between our political democracy and the alarming growth of economic oligarchy resulting from corporate concentration, which trend will emerge victorious? Shall we push outward the frontiers of democracy, giving to the majority of the people greater powers to shape not only their political, but also their economic and social, future? Or shall we resist further democratization lest it lead us to socialism—or to communism? Shall we seek to preserve those features of our constitutional system which restrain the majority? Will the growing concentration of economic power culminate in the complete domination of government by

---

[2] See: Thomas H. Reed, ed., "The Constitution in the Twentieth Century", Annals of the American Academy of Political and Social Science, CLXXXV (May, 1936).

big business—a trend which many regard as already far advanced? Will this mean Fascism in America?[3]

An ideological battle is in progress between traditional and modern concepts of liberty, democracy, property, capitalism, individualism, "the American system." Is liberty, as we formerly believed, an absolute and natural right of the individual, upon which society may almost never encroach? Or is liberty to be regarded as relative to society's needs—highly desirable for both society and the individual, but necessarily subject, in our dynamic modern society, to increasing social control? Does liberty mean merely the absence of governmental restraint, or does it imply the presence of opportunity for its exercise,—opportunity provided, in many instances, by governmental intercession on behalf of underprivileged groups? *Whose* liberty should receive first consideration? Is liberty a monolithic unity, to be preserved or destroyed as a whole? Or are our liberties separable, so that we may restrict, say, certain manifestations of economic liberty while retaining in full measure our political and civil freedoms? Is the issue of liberty a matter of "all or nothing"? Around answers to these questions turns much of the controversy over increased governmental collectivism and national planning.[4]

THE DEFENDERS: THE CASE FOR CONSERVATISM

Recent and contemporary defenders of American capitalism and constitutionalism base their arguments upon various doctrinal foundations. Some reiterate the doctrine of natural rights or stress the Bill of Rights (rooted in that gospel); some rely upon the supposed "laws" of classical economics; some derive

---

[3] See President Franklin D. Roosevelt's message to Congress, recommending the strengthening and enforcement of the antitrust laws, in the course of which he said: "The liberty of a democracy is not safe if the people tolerate the growth of private power to a point where it becomes stronger than their democratic state itself. That, in its essence, is fascism—ownership of government by an individual, by a group, or by any other controlling private power". 75th Congress, 3rd Session, *Senate Document* No. 173 (April 20, 1938).

[4] For the classic statement of the traditional position—the "old" liberalism—see John Stuart Mill, *On Liberty* (1859) (London: Humphrey Milford, 1912, 1933); for the "new" liberalism, see George Soule, *The Future of Liberty* (New York: Macmillan, 1936); H. J. Laski, *Liberty in the Modern State* (New York: Harper and Bros., 1930); also see Dorothy Fosdick, *What is Liberty?* (New York: Harper and Bros., 1939).

their credo of economic individualism from the Darwinian theory of evolution through struggle; others adopt the historical or empirical approach, basing their case upon factual, practical considerations; still others draw conclusions from the field of human psychology.[5] A further line of defense is grounded upon legal and constitutional considerations. Some conservatives seem scarcely to go beyond mere name-calling, asserting that their principles are "sound", "traditional", and "American", while those of the reformers are "communistic", or "fascist"—or both.

In general, the trend of modern conservatism is away from dogmatism and toward empiricism. Private property and private economic enterprise are not frequently defended today on the ground that they are natural rights of the individual, but rather because they are said to produce desirable social results.

"Social Darwinism" is in decline but still somewhat influential. This doctrine is so named because its devotees have attempted to apply to human social and political relations Darwin's supposed thesis that the process of evolution from lower to higher organisms is the result of a struggle for existence which results in the "survival of the fittest". Writers of this school, especially Herbert Spencer and William Graham Sumner,[6] have drawn the conclusion that government must not intervene in the struggle for existence among men; to do so would retard the social progress which would otherwise ensue from the competition for survival, wealth, and power. Hence, government ought not to protect the weak from the strong, but should allow the "fittest" to survive and the "unfittest" to perish. Today, even the more "rugged" of the economic individualists reject the uncompromising, inhumane attitude of Spencer, who opposed all public education, poor relief, aid to industry or agriculture, or government operation of service agencies. The modern individualist usually accepts as necessary, or at least advisable, most existing

---

[5] See Chapter 18, *infra*.

[6] For a fuller discussion, see chapters 3, 12, and 21, *infra;* Francis W. Coker, *Recent Political Thought* (New York: D. Appleton-Century, 1934), pp. 390-404; Irving Babbitt, *Democracy and Leadership* (Boston: Houghton-Mifflin, 1924), chapter 6.

forms of governmental restraint and assistance, but opposes further steps toward what he terms "paternalism" or "regimentation".

Some recent studies by biologists tend to support the conclusions of Spencer and Sumner; these writers argue that public funds expended on the care of defectives must be provided by taxes which burden the capable members of society, while such humanitarian expenditures do not improve, but merely preserve and increase, the inferior stock. Thus these "biologic individualists" conclude in favor of a public policy of non-interference, because even the most extensive system of social services cannot alter the quality of human germ-plasm or make incompetents the equals of the more able members of society. These writers do not attempt to define "fitness", apparently regarding worldly "success" as a sufficient manifestation.[7] Their position involves a challenge to the liberal assumption that a favorable environment can reduce human inequalities.

Increasingly, modern defenders of economic individualism are adopting the empirical approach. While their writings often show traces of the doctrine of natural rights or of classical economic theory, their conclusions are usually based upon the claimed accomplishments of the capitalistic system and the presumed difficulty or impossibility of government regulation or management of economic enterprise. Instead of insisting upon absolute standards of right with regard to private property and governmental activity, their arguments stress the social utility of private property as an institution and the value of the acquisitive impulse to both the individual and society. They contend that private property is a mark of progress away from primitive communism, and that it has spread because of its social value and its great productive achievements. They oppose further governmental regulation, ownership, or direction of economic enterprise; this they term "regimentation", ultimately destructive of political and civil, as well as economic, liberty. They disapprove of governmental assistance to disadvantaged, unfortunate

---

[7] Coker, *op. cit.*, pp. 396-398, 405-407.

groups; this they call "paternalism".[8] They resist the tendency of recent public policy toward the reduction of inequalities of opportunity. Conservatives worship liberty, not equality, but they are more deeply concerned with the maintenance of economic liberties at present enjoyed by the more fortunate classes than with the extension of substantial economic, civil, or political liberties to the underprivileged. In general, they oppose reform, or, at best, urge caution and delay. American conservatives have a high regard for "business" but hold government and the "politician" in low esteem. They point to our high standard of living as irrefutable proof of the productivity, efficiency, and beneficence of economic individualism, giving little or no credit to our abundant natural resources and to the aid and encouragement provided by government. On the other hand, government is pictured as inherently corrupt ,inefficient and tyrannical.[9]

The defenders of economic individualism are often hesitant in their support for democracy. They distrust popular majorities, especially when these seek social and economic reform. They express misgivings about the tendency toward government by the "masses" or the "mob".[10] They endorse judicial review, praising the Supreme Court for invalidating legislation imposing new economic and social controls. When a conservative Court declared the major part of the New Deal legislative program unconstitutional, self-styled defenders of the Constitution hailed our highest tribunal for "preserving liberty" and for confining the federal government within its "proper" constitutional limits.

The conservative constitutional position may be summarized as follows: Governmental powers (especially those of the fed-

----

[8] But the conservative position on this point does not imply criticism of protective tariffs, subsidies to business, the railroads, etc., or other familiar forms of government support for private enterprise.

----

[9] See Herbert Hoover, *The Challenge to Liberty* (New York: Charles Scribner's, 1934) ; Ogden L. Mills, *Liberalism Fights On* (New York: Macmillan, 1936); Carl Snyder, *Capitalism the Creator* (New York: Macmillan, 1940) ; Ralph Adams Cram, *The End of Democracy* (Boston: Marshall Jones, 1937).

----

[10] Raoul E. Desvernine, *Democratic Despotism* (New York: Dodd, Mead, 1936) ; R. A. Cram, *op. cit.;* James M. Beck and Merle Thorpe, *Neither Purse Nor Sword* (New York: Macmillan, 1936).

eral government) must be construed very strictly; limitations
upon those powers, such as the "due process" and "equal protection" clauses, should be interpreted very broadly in order to
protect individual (and corporate) liberties against governmental encroachment. Social and economic reform should, so far as
possible, be left to the states; if certain problems clearly demand
uniform national legislation, the constitution should be formally
amended to sanction such extensions of federal power. The
Court ought to follow its own precedents in constitutional interpretation, instead of creating confusion by a series of reversals.[11]
Established constitutional principles such as the separation of
powers, checks and balances, and states' rights must be maintained against the New Deal threat of "Presidential dictatorship", "bureaucracy",[12] unconstitutional delegation of legislative
powers, and federal centralization.[13]

In conclusion, it may be said that the defenders of the
status quo in economics and politics are the liberals of the old
school who have become the conservatives of today. Viewing
government as the perpetual enemy of all liberty, they resist its
interventions even where the new restraints on the liberties of a

[11] In 1937, following the heated controversy over President Roosevelt's proposal to
enlarge the Supreme Court, the Court, before any changes occurred in its personnel,
reversed its position on virtually all of the important constitutional questions presented by the New Deal program. See the summary of these reversals in *The
New York Times*, May 30, 1937, Section 4, p. 7; also E. S. Corwin, *Constitutional
Revolution, Ltd.* (Claremont, Calif.: Claremont Colleges, 1941).

[12] Cf. the bitter fight in 1937 over the bill to reorganize the federal administrative
establishment in the interest of efficiency. See the *Report* of the President's Committee on Administrative Management (Washington: Government Printing Office,
1937).

[13] Beck and Thorpe, *op. cit.*; Hoover, *op. cit.*; Mills, *op. cit.*; Desvernine, *op. cit.*
Constitutional conservatism is nowhere more ably expressed than in the Supreme
Court opinions of Justices Sutherland and Butler. See especially *Adkins v. Chil-
dren's Hospital*, 261 U. S. 525 (1923). For temperate and scholarly discussions of
these constitutional issues, see Robert K. Carr, *The Supreme Court and Judicial
Review* (New York: Farrar and Rinehart, 1942: George C. S. Benson, *The New
Centralization* (New York: Farrar and Rinehart, 1941); J. Roland Pennock, *Ad-
ministration and the Rule of Law* (New York: Farrar and Rinehart, 1941); Harold
J. Laski, *The American Presidency* (New York: Harper and Bros., 1940); Edward
S. Corwin *The President, Office and Powers* (New York: New York University
Press, 2d. ed., rev., 1941), *Court over Constitution* (Princeton: Princeton Univer-
ity Press, 1938); E. P. Herring, *Presidential Leadership* (New York: Farrar and
Rinehart, 1940).

minority are designed to enlarge the area of effective freedom
for the greater number of citizens. They fear that a collectivistic
democracy will soon become totalitarian—and no democracy.
They see little likelihood of maintaining our civil and political
liberties if economic liberty is circumscribed or extinguished in a
planned society.[14]

Herbert Hoover speaks for many modern American conservatives when he identifies the extension of governmental economic controls with the "regimentation" characteristic of foreign
dictatorships, and when he ascribes our high living standards to
the American system of free enterprise. He combines almost all
of the favorite conservative themes; we must cling to the Bill
of Rights; any necessary alterations must be made only by formal constitutional amendment; governments have an insatiable
appetite for power; society cannot remain partly "regimented"
and partly free, and even partial regimentation will eventually
destroy democracy. To attempt "to solve the . . . problem of distribution of a hard-won plenty by restrictions . . . will abolish
the plenty". We must not "undermine the stimulants to individual effort" which are the basis of our productivity. To restrict
economic liberty will involve making government "master of
people's souls and thoughts"; "economic freedom cannot be sacrificed if political freedom is to be preserved." Moreover, the conduct of business by government would only give us the "least
efficiency". "It would increase rather than decrease abuse and
corruption, stifle initiative and invention, undermine the development of leadership, cripple the mental and spiritual energies
of our people, extinguish equality of opportunity, and dry up
the spirit of liberty and the forces which make progress." [15]

---

[14] See Francis G. Wilson, "The Prelude to Authority", *American Political Science
Review,* XXXI (February, 1937), pp. 12-27.

[15] Herbert Hoover, *The Challenge to Liberty,* pp. 190-193, 194-196, 197-199, 200-
201, 203-204. For a fuller statement of the view that collectivism and planning
are impossible in a democracy, see Walter Lippmann, *The Method of Freedom*
(New York: Macmillan, 1934), and *The Good Society* (Boston: Little, Brown,
1937).

THE CRITICS: LIBERAL AND OTHERWISE

Criticism of a society tends, by its very nature, to be more diversified than its defense. The attack upon the existing order in America has always been marked by variety. Twentieth century critics are no exception; they differ widely regarding both ends and means. Their disunity and confusion serve to weaken the forces of reform; their conflicts are of inestimable aid to conservatism. The more radical critics provide conservatives with an especially effective semantic weapon; by applying the term "radical", or "communist", or "fascist" to all critics, it is easy to discredit criticism and reform in general, and to defend the *status quo* silently and by indirection.

There is, however, one viewpoint which is shared in varying degrees by nearly all modern American critics of the existing order. That is their recognition and support of the trend toward collectivism. As the conservative position remains, in general, a defense of economic individualism and "free enterprise", coupled with restricted democracy and limited government, so the overwhelming majority of modern critics view individualism as an outmoded policy,—no longer just, efficient, or sufficiently productive. They start with the premise that our complex modern society is basically collective and interdependent; hence, today's problems, set in such a framework, can be effectively met only by means of collective (usually governmental) action.[16] The trend toward collectivism has been clearly discernible for some time.[17] Collectivists urge the accommodation of public policy to this dominant social trend.

Most but not all modern American collectivists believe that a more completely democratized and less restricted government can competently direct a collectivized society. In general, they have faith in popular majorities, and opposite what they consider the excessive limitations placed upon democratic govern-

---

[16] Certain groups favor cooperative or group action short of outright state intervention. See below, pp. 21-22.

[17] See Karl Mannheim, *Man and Society in an Age of Reconstruction* (London: K. Paul, Trench, Trubner, 1940); John Dewey, *Individualism Old and New* (New York: Milton, Balch, 1930).

ment in the United States. Believing that a modern democracy must be accorded wider powers if it is to survive the challenge of the machine age, collectivists reject the notion that political power is necessarily evil and insatiable.[18] In its place they affirm that "power is what you make it",[19] and that political power, if "democratically arrived at and democratically controlled" is very different from the power of a dictator.[20] The collectivist views the coercive powers irresponsibly wielded by the economic oligarch as far more to be feared than political power in the hands of the people themselves. Our reluctance to transfer economic powers to the democratic state is in part a fear of abandoning our traditions, but it is also, in part, a fear of the responsibility which we, as citizens, would thus be required to undertake.[21]

Advocacy of an increasingly collectivist policy by a more democratized state is, in the writings of most American collectivists, based upon empirical, rather than dogmatic, considerations. With few exceptions, they reject the dogmas of both conservatives and radicals without formulating their own. They favor public regulation of certain kinds of business enterprise (usually those of a quasi-public character), and a limited amount of public ownership (usually of monopolistic businesses), rather than outright and complete socialization of all production and distribution. They wish to aid workers and farmers, but do not advocate proletarian or agrarian domination of the state. They stress the necessity of governmental curbs upon certain manifestations of liberty without loss of faith in the value of liberty

---

[18] See Lord Action, *The History of Freedom, and Other Essays* (London: Macmillan, 1907.

[19] Max Lerner, "Power Is What You Make It", *The New Republic*, XCVII (Nov. 23, 1938), pp. 69-71.

[20] *Ibid.*

[21] Also see Max Lerner, *It Is Later Than You Think* (New York: Viking Press, 1938), and *Ideas for the Ice Age* (New York: Viking Press, 1941), especially Chapter 3; Thurman W. Arnold, *The Folklore of Capitalism* (New Haven: Yale University Press, 1937), especially Chapters 11, 12; Charles E. Merriam, *Political Power, Its Composition and Incidence* (New York: McGraw-Hill Book Co., 1934).

itself. Many urge the necessity of economic and social planning by the democratic state, yet do not contemplate such sweeping governmental regimentation of the individual as the Soviet and Fascist regimes have produced. Collectivists believe in the separability of liberty,—in the possibility of preserving political and civil liberties despite some necessary restraints upon economic freedom.[22]

The beginnings of modern American collectivism are to be found chiefly in the Progressive Movement. Progressives and Wilsonians sought "a newer individualism, a mean between socialism and *laissez-faire*, . . . designed to give the individual under new conditions the same kind of advantages enjoyed in a simpler day, . . . to place controls on certain practices of business, not to restrain freedom but to conserve freedom for a greater number".[23] The basic idea was to curb monopoly, outlaw anti-social business practices, and protect those who could not protect themselves. Progressives demanded basic social and economic security for all groups. Above and beyond such minimal governmental intervention, individual initiative was to remain the dominant principle. America was to be made safe for small, competitive businessmen, farmers, workers, and consumers.[24]

The "New Dealers" have revived and restated the principles of Progressivism, and have sought to achieve its goals through legislation. The New Deal program—unemployment relief, public works, conservation, social security, increased regulation of transportation and public utilities, aid to agriculture, labor legislation, reform of banking and stock market practices, the National Industrial Recovery Act,[25]—did not represent a radi-

[22] See Francis W. Coker, *Recent Political Though*, Chapter 20.

[23] Edward R. Lewis, *A History of American Political Though from the Civil War to the World War* (New York: Macmillan, 1937), p. 364.

[24] See Chapter 21, *infra;* Lewis, *op. cit.*, Chapter 8; also works by Croly, Weyl, and Theodore Roosevelt listed at the close of this chapter.

[25] For brief accounts of the New Deal, see Charles A. Beard and George H. E. Smith, *The Future Comes: A Study of the New Deal* (New York: Macmillan, 1933), *The Old Deal and the New* (New York: Macmillan, 1940); A. M. Schlesinger, *The New Deal in Action* 1933-1938 (New York: Macmillan, 1939); L. M. Hacker, *A Short History of the New Deal* (New York: Crofts, 1934).

cal departure from the reforms urged by Theodore Roosevelt and Woodrow Wilson. The attack on concentrated, monopolistic economic power was renewed.[26] The goal, as defined by President Franklin D. Roosevelt and his advisers, was not a new economic and political system, but the restoration of security, freedom, and opportunity for the majority of the American people under a reformed American system of private enterprise, subjected to necessary regulations imposed by democratic processes. President Roosevelt denied the charge that the New Deal was either Fascist or Communist; it was, he said, a combination of Theodore Roosevelt's Square Deal and Woodrow Wilson's New Freedom.[27] He stressed the interdependence of all groups in the new era of technology, and the necessity of governmental intervention to solve the nation's problems.[28]

A central idea in New Deal thought is the necessity of restoring the balance of our economy by enabling "every one to be reasonably prosperous".[29] This calls for action by government to effectuate price adjustments between the rigid and flexible parts of the economy—raising prices in the "area of flexibility" and raising production in the "area of rigidity".[30] Economic balance is necessary for the preservation of both our economy and our democracy; we must not allow a "small, inordinately wealthy class" to be built up.[31] Business is reminded of its social obligations and exhorted to join cooperatively in a "concert of interests" to promote the general welfare. New Dealers refute the

[26] See the *Hearings, Monographs,* and *Report* of the Temporary National Economic Committee to investigate the Concentration of Economic Power in the United States (75th Congress, Third Session, *Public Resolution* No. 113, Washington, Government Printing Office, 1938-1941).

[27] Franklin D. Roosevelt, *On Our Way* (New York: John Day, 1934), pp. ix-xi; see also his *Looking Forward* (New York: John Day, 1933) ; Rexford G. Tugwell, *The Battle for Democracy* (New York: Columbia University Press, 1935), p. 78.

[28] *Looking Forward,* pp. 267-169 (Inaugural Address, March 4, 1933).

[29] Beard and Smith, *The Future Comes,* p. 146.

[30] Tugwell, *op. cit.,* p. 84.

[31] Henry A. Wallace, *New Frontiers* (New York: Reynal and Hitchock, 1934), p. 121.

charge of "regimentation", citing the democratic processes established in the Agriculture Adjustment Act as proof of their preference for voluntary cooperative methods.[32] They insist that if all groups will work together—if the philosophy of cooperation, "the vital idea of the twentieth century," can supplant the philosophy of competition—then all of our contemporary problems can be solved without revolution, within the framework of democracy.[33] A "mature economy" can be managed by a democratic, cooperative commonwealth.[34] Much New Deal emphasis is placed upon stability and security, rather than upon adventurous, speculative economic opportunities,[35]—the "good life for all", rather than vast fortunes for a few. The New Deal openly recognizes the obligation of government to provide employment or relief for the innocent victims of economic depression. It also asserts as a principle that agriculture is entitled to equal treatment with industry. It acknowledges labor's right to organize without interference by the employer and to bargain collectively through representatives of its own choosing. It accepts large industrial combinations as an inevitable development and seeks to regulate them instead of attempting to destroy them. Through the entire New Deal program runs the idea of the mutual obligations of individuals and groups to one another; the centrifugal tendencies of excessive individualism are countered by a new emphasis upon the duties owed by the citizen to society.

On the side of constitutional theory, New Dealers have been generally critical of judicial review, though they do not, as often popularly supposed, desire its abolition. They assert that the Constitution is, in reality, very flexible and susceptible of widely varying judicial interpretations. New Deal reforms did not require "the slightest constitutional departure" from our established system.[36] Neither formal amendment nor a tortured con-

---

[32] Tugwell, *op. cit.*, pp. 195-199.

[33] Henry A. Wallace, *Whose Constitution? An Inquiry into the General Welfare* (New York: Reynal and Hitchock, 1936), pp. 321 ff.

[34] *Ibid.*, p. 318.

[35] Beard and Smith, *The Future Comes*, p. 163.

[36] Former Attorney-General Cummings, quoted in Beard and Smith, *op. cit.*, p. 155.

struction of the Constitution was necessary. The Supreme Court had, they point out, seldom been consistent in its views on major constitutional issues; it had not followed its own precedents closely. Changing times, problems, and philosophies of individual justices had led to sharp reversals in constitutional interpretation. Indeed, it would be salutary for the Court to abandon many of its precedent-built "principles" and "retreat to the Constitution" as originally conceived.[37] Not only the New Dealers themselves, but many eminent authorities on constitutional law have urged the removal of the judicial "gloss" from the Constitution's text.[38] They argue that it was not the Constitution itself which stood in the path of New Deal reforms, but a judge-made "constitutional law" fashioned chiefly from the economic and social predilections of particular justices who happened to constitute a majority of the Court. The earlier dissents of Justices Holmes, Brandeis, Stone, and Cardozo were viewed by liberals as pointing the way toward a better constitutional law.[39] When the Court, in 1937, abandoned its obstructionist attitude toward the New Deal program, and especially after the appointment of seven new and presumably liberal justices, New Deal criticism of the Court came to an end.[40] As Mr. Justice Jackson points out,[41] the Court inevitably tends to be a conservative institution because of the life tenure of justices and their legal training and background; hence, recurrent political controversy over the Court's "conservatism" is to be expected. In view of the political nature of judicial supremacy, such struggles cannot be avoided.

---

[37] See Robert H. Jackson, *The Struggle for Judicial Supremacy* (New York: A. A. Knopf, 1941), pp. 197 ff.

[38] Walton H. Hamilton and Douglass Adair, *The Power to Govern; The Constitution—Then and Now* (New York: W. W. Norton, 1937), pp. 185 ff. Edward S. Corwin, *Court over Constitution,* pp. 93 ff.

[39] For the semantic and symbolic aspects of the controversy, see Chapter 17, *infra;* Thurman W. Arnold, *The Symbols of Government* (New Haven: Yale University Press, 1935), *The Folklore of Capitalism,* especially Chapter 3; Ralph H. Gabriel, *The Course of American Democratic Thought* (New York: Ronald Press, 1940), Chapter 30.

[40] Indeed, in recent years, conservatives, not liberals, have indulged in such criticism.
[41] Jackson, *op. cit.,* p. 213.

New Dealers urge the modernization of our governmental machinery in the direction of increased federal powers, greater authority in the executive branch, wider use of "experts" in government, and the delegation of more quasi-legislative and quasi-judicial powers to administrative agencies. They contend that a "horse-and-buggy" government cannot operate effectively under modern conditions.

The most novel element in the New Deal is its emphasis upon the need for national economic planning,[42]—an emphasis stimulated by the hardship wrought during the great depression and by the urgency of prompt relief. New Dealers point out that modern technology has made possible an "economy of abundance", in which distribution, rather than production, is the chief problem.[43] We no longer need to provide the same economic incentives to capital accumulation and plant expansion that were required in an earlier era; we are able to produce more than we require. But the growth of concentrated economic power has led to artificial restrictions on industrial production, rigid prices beyond the reach of many consumers, and consequent inequities in distribution of both goods and income.[44] To remedy this situation, social planning is necessary. Huge modern corporations and trade associations are themselves engaging in business planning to circumvent the operation of the "laws" of economics and to increase their profits; such partial planning destroys what is left of the automatic character of the price mechanism and introduces further rigidity into the economic system. Overall planning by government in the public interest must coordinate or replace partial planning for personal and group enrichment. Such governmental planning would not ignore the possibility of improving the techniques of production, but would be chiefly concerned with "a wiser, more equitable distribution of the national income", with the maintenance of full production, full employment, stability, and security. Such societal planning is "well with-

[42] F. D. Roosevelt, *Looking Forward,* Chapter 2.

[43] *Ibid.,* p. 32.

[44] Tugwell, *op. cit.,* pp. 82-18.

in the inventive capacity of man" [45] and is entirely consistent with democracy; social goals and plans can be formulated through democratic discussion and decision, and can be democratically administered through the utilization of interest-group organizations in the enforcement process.[46]

The New Deal has actually attempted very little over-all planning. There has not been complete agreement concerning the extent to which national planning should be carried. Henry A. Wallace thinks that "precise detailed planning" is required only "with respect to natural resources and to certain rather small segments of our national life on an emergency basis".[47] This view is reflected in the preoccupation of the National Resources Planning Board with conservation problems, and in regional planning projects such as the Tennessee Valley Authority.[48] As to the method of planning, New Dealers agree on cooperation, a "partnership" between government and industry—*i.e.*, the processes of democracy.[49]

Outside the ranks of the New Dealers (though sometimes grouped with them as "brain trusters") are many distinguished social scientists—historians, political scientists, economists, philosophers—who are decidedly critical of the existing order. Among the historians, Carl L. Becker points to the basic problem of modern democracy—how to correct "the flagrant inequality of possessions and of opportunity . . . by the democratic method".[50] Warning of the dangers of communism and fa-

---

[45] F. D. Roosevelt, *Looking Forward*, p. 49.

[46] See Findlay Mackenzie, ed., *Planned Societies Yesterday, Today, Tomorrow* (New York: Prentice-Hall, Inc., 1937), especially the "Foreword," by Lewis Mumford and "The Prospects for General Economic Planning," by George Soule; George Soule, *A Planned Society* (New York: Macmillan, 1932) ; National Resources Board, *A Report on National Planning* (Washington: Government Printing Office, 1934) ; Stuart Chase, *Goals for America: A Budget of Our Needs and Resources* (New York: Twentieth Century Fund, 1942) ; Beorge B. Galloway and Associates, *Planning for America* (New York: Henry Holt, 1941).

[47] Henry A. Wallace, *New Frontiers*, p. 22.

[48] See H. W. Odum and H. E. Moore, *American Regionalism* (New York: Henry Holt, 1938).

[49] Beard and Smith, *The Future Comes*, pp. 148-150.

[50] Carl L. Becker, *Modern Democracy* (New Haven: Yale University Press, 1941), p. 67.

scism, and doubting whether social legislation alone can "validate" the system of free enterprise. Becker yet concludes, rather haltingly, that there is "no compelling reason" why "governmental regulation of economic enterprise should not continue even to the point . . . of a virtual . . . socialization of certain basic industries, without incurring the destruction of democratic institutions".[51] He hopes that there may yet be time to save capitalist-democratic institutions before they are overwhelmed by "the discord between the physical power at our disposal and our capacity to make a good use of it".[52]

A more optimistic view is taken by the political scientist, Charles E. Merriam. He believes that the "modern long-time trend is in the direction of democracy" and that the tasks of modern democracy will be made easier by the development of superior forms of public administration (including the growth of executive leadership), the spread of universal education, the modern "economy of abundance", the possibility of reconciling liberty and equality, and the growing acceptance of the idea that it is the function of the democratic state to distribute the gains of the nation among the masses to whose efforts these gains are really due.[53] He anticipates a moderate, planned collectivism based not upon dictatorial force but upon "consent, discussion, persuasion, . . . expert knowledge under the general guidance of the common judgment".[54] Merriam's optimism rests in large part upon his tendency to minimize the importance of economic problems and motivations, although he concedes that the "root problem" of democracy is the fair distribution of the gains of civilization.[55]

Among economists, there is an important and growing group which rejects classical economic doctrine and advocates a

---

[51] *Ibid.*, pp. 72, 91.

[52] *Ibid.*, p. 98.

[53] Charles E. Merriam, *The New Democracy and the New Despotism* (New York: McGraw-Hill Book Co., 1939), pp. 252-262.

[54] *Ibid.*

[55] *On the Agenda of Democracy* (Cambridge, Mass.: Harvard University Press, 1941), pp. 92, 100, 102-103.

considerable extension of public economic control. Alvin H.
Hansen is primarily a monetary theorist; in substantial agreement with the British economist, Lord Keynes, Hansen favors
a "functional" public fiscal policy—in other words, a program
of taxation, borrowing, and spending so planned and controlled
as to achieve economic balance and counteract the tedencies of a
capitalistic economy toward either inflation or deflation.[56] J. M.
Blair has pointed out the "functional weaknesses of capitalism,"
calling particular attention to the destructive implications of its
tendencies toward inflexible prices, restricted production, chronic
unemployment, and declining real wages.[57] A. A. Berle, Jr., and
Gardiner C. Means have drawn attention to both the alarming
growth of concentration in American industry and the divorce
between ownership and management in the modern corporation.
They call for a new legal approach to the corporate problem.[58]
George Soule urges, short of forthright national economic planning, a governmental fiscal policy which will provide public
channels for new investment to replace those no longer open
under the system of private intiative—in other words, more public enterprise, which will also offer salutary competition to private monopolies and maintain steady production and employment.[59]

The critical attitude toward recent tendencies in American
capitalism finds corroboration in the monumental studies of our
economy made by the Temporary National Economic Commit-

---

[56] Alvin H. Hansen, *Fiscal Policy and Business Cycles* (New York: W. W. Norton,
1941).

[57] J. M. Blair, *Seeds of Destruction* (1938).

[58] A. A. Berle, Jr. and G. C. Means, *The Modern Corporation and Private Property*
(New York: Macmillan, 1932); see also C. F. Ware and G. C. Means, *The
Modern Economy In Action* (New York: Harcourt, Brace, 1936).

[59] George Soule, *An Economic Constitution for Democracy* (New Haven: Yale
University Press, 1939). See also Seven Harvard and Tufts Economists, *An Eco-
nomic Program for American Democracy* (New York: Vanguard Press, 1938);
H. D. Anderson, *Taxation, Recovery, and Defense* (Temporary National Economic
Committee, Monograph No. 20) (Washington: Government Printing Office, 1941),
especially pp. 32-37; G. Colm and H. Tarasov, *Who Pays The Taxes* (T. N. E. C.
Monograph No. 3) (Washington: Government Printing Office, 1941); Stuart Chase,
Where's The Money Coming From? (New York: Twentieth Century Fund, 1943).

tee. In a series of forty-three monographs and approximately as many volumes of hearings, every phase of the economic system has been subjected to close scrutiny. The Committee's final recommendation, however, amounted to little more than a plea for stricter enforcement of the enti-trust laws and the elimination of a few corporate abuses. Despite the mass of evidence pointing to the need for increased governmental control of economic life, the Committee contented itself with the expression of pious hopes for a return to "free enterprise".[60]

The "neo-Marxist" school of criticsm includes such men as Harold J. Laski, Max Lerner,[61] and Norman Thomas. Professor Laski has grown increasingly pessimistic regarding the possibility of a non-violent transition from capitalism to socialism,[62] but he has recently voiced the hope that a "planned democracy" might be established now, while the challenge and exaltation of the present global war for freedom cause men to "live on the heights".[63] His "planned democracy" involves extensive, but not complete, socialization of the instruments of production; it will provide "positive", rather than "negative", freedom for the individual—"an environment in which the emergence of an integrated personality becomes possible for the mass of citizens."[64] Norman Thomas also advocates a "planned production for the use of all rather than an unplanned production for the profit of an owning class", possible only under social ownership of "land, natural resources and the principal means of production and distribution". Like Laski, Thomas hopes to establish socialism without revolution; he advocates compensation of expropriated owners. He insists that liberty is dependent on se-

[60] Temporary National Economic Committee, *Final Report and Recommendations* (Washington: Government Printing Office, 1941).

[61] See above, p. 10, notes 19, 20; p. 11, note 21.

[62] H. J. Laski, *The State in Theory and Practice* (New York: Viking Press, 1935).

[63] *Reflections on the Revolution of Our Time* (New York: Viking Press, 1943), Chapter 8.

[64] *Ibid.*, p. 408.

curity and that political and civil liberty will therefore be increased, not reduced, in a planned, socialistic democracy.[65]

Many liberal critics of the existing order fear the centralized power of the collectivistic state and urge other, non-collectivistic measures to meet present problems. Herbert Agar and Allen Tate advocate a redistribution of property—especially of land and other forms of property that possess "use-value" as well as exchange value. They do not simply propose a "back-to-the-land" movement, but they urge putting a stop to industrial and governmental centralization (which are interrelated) and returning to a simpler, earlier type of economy, even if it should prove less productive and efficient. The restoration of the independence of the individual through the wider distribution of property ownership is viewed as far more socially desirable than mere material productivity. Natural monopolies would be regulated by the government; other types of monopoly could be combatted by means of cooperatives. Agar and Tate fear both monopoly-capitalism and communism; seeking a middle course, they would in effect turn the economic clock back.[66]

Catholic liberals share this distrust of collectivism. The Right Reverend John A. Ryan urges a plan of self-government through organized occupational groups—a modern guild system —as an alternative to both state collectivism and monopoly capitalism. These occupational or trade organizations would include both employers and workers; each organization would adjust disputes and make plans within its particular economic field; there would be a national federation for each industry, and perhaps an over-all national economic parliament. The workers would thus share in the management of industry, if not also in its ownership and profits. Democratic economic planning would be fa-

---

[65] Norman Thomas, *After the New Deal, What?* (New York: Macmillan, 1936), pp. 157-158, 162-164, 178-185. The term 'neo-Marxist' has been applied to these writers because they seem to seek a middle ground between the present capitalistic system and "all-out" socialization, though they are nearer to the latter. For a more strictly Marxist viewpoint, see Lewis Corey, *The Decline of American Capitalism* (New York: Covici-Friede, 1934).

[66] Herbert Agar and Allen Tate, eds., *Who Owns America? A New Declaration of Independence* (Boston: Houghton Mifflin, 1936), pp. 80-109.

cilitated. The state would continue to play the role of arbiter and guide, but not that of initiator and dictator, although the plan includes some public ownership, where necessary to prevent or check private monopoly.[67]

Still another line of criticism is to be discerned in the works of philosophers, novelists, and other literary men. William Ernest Hocking defends the state against the disparagements of the old liberalism and champions it as an agency vitally concerned with the promotion of morality and justice—with "the making of men".[68] Theodore Dreiser, Sinclair Lewis, Ernest Hemingway, John Dos Passos, John Steinbeck, and other novelists have exposed the uglier side of our acquisitive society.[69] Lewis Mumford assails the abuses of technology under the capitalistic system, pointing to the brutalizing effect of routine and monotony upon the individual worker.[70] Poets, playwrights, and artists have for many years depicted the injustices of our politico-economic system, though as a group they have not advocated very definite reforms.

*   *   *   *   *   ...

The critics of American capitalism and constitutionalism have oscillated between optimism and despair. During the Progressive Era and the first years of the New Deal, the hopes of reformers ran high. Liberals felt reasonably certain that economic and social democracy could be achieved by the methods of political democracy,—that an enlightened, cooperative capitalism could be teamed with democracy for the achievement of the highest possible standards of living, both material and spiritual.

---

[70] Lewis Mumford, *Technics and Civilization* (New York: Harcourt, Brace, 1934), *Faith for Living* (New York: Harcourt, Brace, 1940).

[67] Rt. Rev. Msgr. John A. Ryan, *A Better Economic Order* (New York: Harper and Bros., 1935), pp. 175-190. For Protestant criticism of the *status quo*, see recent and current issues of *The Christian Century*.

[68] W. E. Hocking, *Man and the State* (New Haven: Yale University Press, 1926), pp. 151-174.

[69] See Merle Curti, *The Growth of American Thought* (New York: Harper and Bros., 1943), Chapters 27, 18.

The first World War put an end to Progressivism, despite the attempt to revive it in 1924.[71] A decade of reaction, cynicism, and materialism ended in the crash of 1929. Out of that crisis emerged the New Deal, a modernized version of Progressivism—empirical, more definitely collectivist, hopeful. But the New Deal failed to solve really basic problems—for example, unemployment. When the second World War began in 1939, the New Deal was virtually dead—its demise brought on by the stubborn, uncompromising resistance of American business and the loss of faith in reform on the part of the public and many of the New Dealers themselves. Twise in a single generation an era of reform had been succeeded by war, although in the second instance war was not the prime cause.

It may be suggested that the decline of liberalism—the loss of faith in reform—is perhaps a symptom of modern society's loss of faith in general. Modern man, in his "quest for certainty", has relied upon religion, science, reason, "progress", economic "laws", absolutism in philosophy and logic,—only to see these supports swept away one by one. The recent vogue of semantics tends to destroy even the prop of language. The loss of faith in the rationality of man undermines faith in the democratic process.[72]

There has undoubtedly been a connection between mass disillusionment and cynicism, on the one hand, and the rise of fascism, on the other. Even the certainty of servitude may sometimes appear preferable to intellectual and moral chaos. Recent years have witnessed the spread of an indigenous American fascism, the true extent of which cannot be accurately measured.[73] Its intellectual spokesman is Lawrence Dennis,[74] who bases his

---

[71] See John Chamberlain ,*Farewell to Reform*s *The Rise, Life and Decay of the Progressive Mind in America* (New York: John Day, 2d ed., 1933).

[72] See Chapter 18, *infra*.

[73] See, however, the "Fortune Survey," *Fortune*, XXVIII (November, 1943), pp. 10, 14, 20, 22, 26.

[74] Lawrence Dennis, *The Coming American Fascism* (New York: Harper and Bros., 1936), *The Dynamics of War and Revolution* (New York: The Weekly Foreign Letter, 1940).

case for fascism upon the supposed impossibility of further social and economic reform within the framework of a contracting
capitalism and the presumed irreconcilability of a planned economy with democracy.

Other writers also believe that a basic transformation is in
progress. James Burnham sees economic and political power
being transferred, in all advanced countries, to the "managers",
whom he identifies as the production managers in industry (not
the financial and sales executives) and the technicians, experts,
and "bureaucrats" in government.[75]

Is the present decline of liberalism merely a phase in a
politic-economic cycle or part of a long-term trend in which
sharpened social issues will leave no room for discussion, compromise, moderation, reconciliation—the methods of democracy?
We can only hope with Harold J. Laski that there will occur
"a refreshment and a reinvigoration of the doctrinal content
of liberalism",[76] involving new conceptions of property, liberty,
equality, education, and social planning. The epicenter of the
controversy between defenders and critics of the *status quo* has
already shifted from dogmatic to pragmatic grounds, from
sterile absolutes to fruitful compromises. Perhaps it is not too
much to hope that man's rationality will be equal to the challenge of a post-war world in which social planning and cooperation, both domestic and international, will be absolutely imperative.

BIBLIOGRAPHY

ARNOLD, THURMAN W., *The Bottlenecks of Business* (New Yokr: Reynal and
Hitchcock, 1940). A popular account, by a former Assistant Attorney-General of the United States, of business and labor practices which restrain
trade and adversely affect our economy; the case for restoration of the free
marke by means of improved enforcement of the antitrust laws.

——————, *The Folklore of Capitalism* (New Haven: Yale University Press,
1937). A study of the semantic aspects of law and economics; American
subservience to "magic words" which distort instead of describing the
actualities of corporate, financial, and legal relationships.

---

[75] James Burnham, *The Managerial Revolution; What Is Happening in the World*
(New York: John Day, 1941).

[76] Harold J. Laski, *The Decline of Liberalism* (No. 10 of the L. T. Hobhouse
Memorial Trust Lectures) (London: Humphrey Milford, 1940), p. 22.

BEARD, CHARLES A. AND MARY R., *The Rise of American Civilization,* Volume 3, *America in Midpassage* (New York: Macmillan, 1939). An integrated history of events, issues, and ideas of the past two decades.

BEARD, CHARLES A., *Public Policy and the General Welfare* (New York: Farrar and Rinehart, 1941). A plea for the restoration of ethics to its place in political thought and for a new balance in America between cultural liberty—hitherto neglected—and economic laissez-faire, which has been over-emphasized.

BEARD, CHARLES A., AND SMITH, G. H. E., *The Old Deal and the New* (New York: Macmillan, 1940). An excellent summary of the New Deal, with a splendid sketch of the economic and social trends which constituted its background. The New Deal is shown to be a "prolongation" of history, not a break with it.

BINGHAM, ALFRED M., *Man's Estate: Adventures in Economic Discovery* (New York: W. W. Norton, 1939). A plea for a continued and expanded New Deal, to include control over total purchasing power and new investment. These further steps are optimistically viewed as entirely possible *via* democracy and as likely to result in "economic democracy."

BURNHAM, JAMES, *The Managerial Revolution; What Is Happening in the World* (New York: John Day, 1941). An interpretation of the recent trends toward concentration of corporate control in the hands of management and of governmental power in those of skilled administrators. The thesis is that these business and governmental "managers" already possess the reality of economic and political power.

CHASE, STUART, *The Road We Are Traveling,* 1914-1942 (New York: Twentieth Century Fund, 1942).

——————, *Goals for America: A Budget of Our Needs and Resources* (New York: Twentieth Century Fund, 1942).

——————, *Where's the Money Coming From? Problems of Postwar Finance* (New York: Twentieth Century Fund, 1943). These are the first three in a series of six brief, popular reports on postwar problems. The first volume deals with recent trends, the second lists objectives and problems of postwar national planning, and the third is a simplified presentation of the Keynes-Hansen theories of money and public finance.

COKER, FRANCIS W., "American Traditions Concerning Property and Liberty," *American Political Science Review,* XXX (February, 1936) pp. 1-23. Provides a background of earlier American ideas against which to evaluate current programs of economic reform.

——————, *Democracy, Liberty, and Property: Readings in the American Political Tradition* ΛNew York: Macmillan, 1943), Parts 3 and 4. An excellent collection of readings, carefully selected and edited, covering the writings of leading Americans from John Winthrop to Franklin D. Roosevelt. Part III, "Government and Property Rights," is especially relevant here.

——————, *Recent Political Thought* (New York: D. Appleton-Century, 1934) Chapters 10, 11, 13, 14, 15, 19, 20. One of the most scholarly and comprehensive texts in the field, indispensable for further study of the present topic.

COYLE, DAVID CUSHMAN, *Brass Tacks* (Washington: National Home Library Foundation, 1936). One of a series of popular books on recent economic trends and problems, with a program of planned reform along New Deal lines.

CROLY, HERBERT, *Progressive Democracy* (New York: Macmillan, 1914).
—————————, *The Promise of American Life* (New York: Macmillan, 1909).
  Statements of the Progressive philosophy by one of its leading thinkers.

CURTI, MERLE, *The Growth of American Thought* (New York: Harper and Bros.,
  1943), Chapters 24, 25, 27, 28. An able and scholarly effort to present an
  integrated account of the development of intellectual life in America from
  colonial times to the present. The chapters referred to deal, respectively,
  with "Formulas of Protest and Reform," "The Conservative Defense,"
  "Prosperity, Disillusionment, Criticism" (the 1920's), and "Crisis and
  New Searches." An excellent bibliography is appended.

DOUGLAS, WILLIAM O., *Democracy and Finance* (New Haven: Yale University
  Press, 1940). Addresses and public statements of the author while serving
  as member and chairman of the Securities and Exchange Commission.

ELLIOTT, WILLIAM Y., *The Need for Constitutional Reform*: *A Program for National Security* (New York: McGraw-Hill Book Co., 1935). A survey, in
  the midst of the early controversy over the New Deal, of the problems of
  American industry and of the need for governmental control; a suggested
  program for overhauling our governmental system (along New Deal lines)
  in order to make it more effective.

EPSTEIN, ABRAHAM, *Insecurity*: *a Challenge to America* (New York: Random
  House, 1933, 1938). A standard work on the need for social insurance in
  the United States; a survey of social insurance plans in operation in foreign
  countries, together with a program for America.

GABRIEL, RALPH H., *The Course of American Democratic Thought*: *an Intellectual
  History Since 1815* (New York: Ronald Press, 1940), Chapters 25, 26, 28,
  29, 30. A history of American social and political ideas. The chapters cited
  cover progressivism, the post-Versailles era, the philosophy of Mr. Justice
  Holmes, and the "New American symbolism."

GALLOWAY, G. B., and Associates, *Planning for America* (New York: Henry Holt,
  1941). A symposium on economic and social planning in the United States:
  "its principles, practices, and problems; its achievements, present status,
  and potentialities."

HOLCOMBE, A. N., *Government in a Planned Democracy* (New York: W. W.
  Norton, 1935). A contemporary interpretation and evaluation of the
  National Industrial Recovery Administration in terms of the representation
  and reconciliation of classes and interest-groups in policy-determination and
  administration. "Middle-class politics" is advocated.

HOOVER, HERBERT C., *The Challenge to Liberty* (New York: Charles Scribner's
  Sons, 1934). A restatemnt of the principles of nineteenth-century liberalism,
  liberty being considered as an inseparable blend of civil, political, and
  economic liberties, and also as a natural right; a reply to the New Deal,
  schemes for national planning, etc. An uncompromising presentation of the
  supposed necessity of choosing between "liberty" and "regimentation".

JACKSON, ROBERT H., *The Struggle for Judicial Supremacy*: *a Study of a Crisis
  in American Power Politics* (New York: A. A. Knopf, 1941). A study of
  the Supreme Court controversy of 1937, preceded by a brief historical sketch;
  also an account of constitutional interpretations, 1937 to 1940.

JACOBSON, J. MARK., *The Development of American Political Thought*: *a Documentary History* (New York: The Century Co., 1932), Chapter 7. A book
  of readings, with introductory essays by the author; Chapter 7 is entitled
  "Government and Economic Institutions."

LASKI, HAROLD J., *Reflections on the Revolution of Our Time* (New York: Viking, 1943). An interpretation of the present war and its significance, including "the meaning of fascism," the internal and international conditions of democracy, "the threat of counter-revolution," and the author's view of the prospects for "freedom in a planned democracy".

LERNER, MAX, *Ideas for the Ice Age* (New York: Viking Press, 1941). A collection of essays discussing "varied aspects of a revolutionary era," in which emphasis is laid upon the necessity of strengthening democracy and enabling it to become dynamic and to use so-called "totalitarian" means.

——————————, *It Is Later Than You Think: the Need for a Militant Democracy* (New York: Viking Press, 1938, rev. ed., 1943). An argument for democratic collectivism,—to make "democracy militant enough, and collectivism democratic enough, to survive."

LEWIS, EDWARD R., *A History of American Political Thought from the Civil War to the World War* (New York: Macmillan, 1937), Chapters 8, 9, 12. A well-documented account, drawing heavily upon judicial decisions and political pronouncements as well as upon scholarly writings.

LIPPMAN, WALTER, *The Good Society* (Boston: Little, Brown, 1937).

——————————, *The Method of Freedom* (New York: Macmillan, 1934). These two books express the author's view that although laissez-faire is dead and private initiative inadequate to the maintenance of the modern economy, planned control by the democratic state is impossible.

MACKENZIE, FINDLAY, ed., *Planned Society: Yesterday, Today, Tomorrow* (New York: Prentice-Hall, 1937). A symposium on social and economic planning: its historical background, present necessity, political, philosophical and international implications; present prospects; planning in fascist and communist societies.

MERRIAM, CHARLES E., *The New Democracy and the New Despotism* (New York: McGraw Hill Book Co., 1939). A re-examination of the assumptions of democracy; the background of recent democratic theory; the challenge of the "new despotism;" the prospects for the new democracy.

MILLIS, M. H., AND MONTGOMERY, R. E., *Labor's Progress and Some Basic Labor Problems* (New York: McGraw-Hill Book Co., 1938). A text on some modern labor problems, e.g., the labor of women and children, the hours of labor, government regulation of wages, etc.

MOLEY, RAYMOND, *After Seven Years* (New York: Harper and Bros., 1939). An account, by one of the original "brain trusters" (later disgruntled and hostile), of the "birth" of the New Deal, the 1932 campaign, the bank crisis, the "hundred days," and other New Deal events, 1933-1938.

NATIONAL RESOURCES PLANNING BOARD, *National Resources Development Report for 1942* (Washington: Government Printing Office, 1943). Planning in war-time; suggested objectives and problems in the field of post-war planning; public works planning; planning for social security; trends of national income, employment, and consumption.

ROOSEVELT, FRANKLIN D., *Looking Forward* (New York: John Day, 1933). A compilation made from articles and speeches, principally those written and delivered during the 1932 campaign and including the Inaugural Address of March 4, 1933. Essentially a statement of New Deal aims.

——————————, *On Our Way* (New York: John Day, 1934). A sequel to *Looking Forward;* an account and interpretation of the legislative accomplishments of the first year of the New Deal.

ROOSEVELT, THEODORE, *Progressive Principles* (New York: Progressive National Service, 1913). Selections from addresses made during the 1912 Presidential campaign; also the Progressive National Platform of that year.

ROSEN, S. McK. AND L., *Technology and Society: the Influence of Machines in the United States* (New York:Macmillan, 1941), Part 4. An analysis of the extent of technological advance and its economic, social, and political consequences. Contains many tables, charts, and illustrations.

TEMPORARY NATIONAL ECONOMIC COMMITTEE, *Hearings*, Part I, *Economic Prologue* (Washington: Government Printing Office, 1938). A general survey, with many charts and tables, of recent trends toward economic concentration in the United States.

—————————, *Monograph No. 25, Recovery Plans,* by Arthur Dahlberg *et al.,* (Washington: Government Printing Office, 1940). An analysis of recent economic recovery plans under five headings: monetary reform, tax modifications, changes in the price mechanism, modification or extension of the structure of our business organizations, and more government ownership in the production and distribution of goods and services.

—————————, *Monograph No. 26, Political Power and Economic Pressures,* by Donald Blaisdell, (Washington: Government Printing Office, 1941). An excellent study of the organization and methods of various business pressure groups.

WEYL, WALTER E., *The New Democracy* (New York: Macmillan, 1912). A Progressive's statement of an industrial, political, and social program for American democracy.

Chapter XIX

POLITICS AND EDUCATION

FRANKLIN L. BURDETTE

The modern world witnesses the almost universal acceptance of the principle of compulsory school attendance. The interest, the authority, and the responsibility of the state in promoting and requiring education are everywhere recognized and applauded. Governments and educational systems are interdependent; thoughtful statesmen of every brand of political nomenclature turn their minds to the paramount necessity of training citizens to support the regime. The intimate relationships between politics and education are not new, of course. They are as old as the struggle for power, and yet they are as new as the accelerated tempo and the cataclysmic struggle of ideas in the twentieth century.

Educational theory is inescapably linked with political theory. The aims, methods, and facilities of education are profoundly affected by prevailing opinion about the means and ends of the state. In the many types of warfare which have characterized the twentieth century, education has been no less a battleground for power than has the area of practical politics. Political and educational theories have been intertwined in contemporary conflicts of ideas because they are aspects or facets of total patterns.

It is sometimes useful to oversimplify the conflicts of modern theory by placing them within two extremes: on the one hand, the autocratic, the authoritarian, the totalitarian; and on the other, the liberal, the self-expressive, and the democratic. Thus there are always frictions between educational motives which seek to perpetuate a system or to mold individuals to pre-conceived standards and those aims which emphasize progress through self-realization. There are always clashes between po-litical programs advocating authority and those demanding free-dom. But there are nuances which enter into and complicate every practical situation, which make simple classifications or types unrealistic, which often destroy sharp differences or divi-sions. The reconciliation of liberty and authority is no less a problem in education than in politics.

DEMOCRATIC EDUCATION

In democratic theory, the individual is of primary impor-tance. The functions of the state, protective, economic, educa-tional, are in his interest and are intended to promote his wel-fare. Moreover, the democratic state is dependent upon indi-viduals, its citizenry, for the operation and preservation of its institutions. Democratic government can be no better than it is made through the intelligence, education, and social morality of the people themselves. Free, public, universal education is therefore of fundamental significance, a political as well as social necessity.

The exact meaning of the term democracy is, among theo-rists, a matter of controversy; and the differences of opinion are not without influence in political and educational relationships. Specialists in politics are prone to define democracy as a form of government in which the people control policy; [1] professional educators usually think of democracy as a way of life in which freedom, opportunity, and reasonable security are implicit.[2] The

[1] See, for example, James Bryce, *Modern Democracies* (New York: The Macmillan Company, 1921), Vol. I, pp. 20-23; Edward M. Sait, *Democracy* (New York: The Century Co., 1929), p. 24; Charles E. Merriam, *What Is Democracy?* (Chicago: The University of Chicago Press, 1941), pp. 6-12.

[2] Publications of the Educational Policies Commission of the National Education Association are particularly valuable as summaries of democratic theory. See especially *The Unique Function of Education in American Democracy* (Washington: Educational Policies Commission, 1937); *The Purposes of Education in American Democracy* (1938); *The Education of Free Men in American Democracy* (1941). *Democracy and Education in the Current Crisis* (New York: Bureau of Publica-tions, Teachers College, Columbia University, 1940) presents a detailed creed of democracy.

legalist thinks in terms of governmental machinery, of majorities, of devices to administer faithfully the popular will. The social philosopher thinks of ends or purposes, which the legalist prefers to call the assumptions of democracy. To many educators, the identity of democracy with freedom and self-expression prohibits inculcation of decisions or conclusions; facts must speak for themselves. Other democratic educators contend that experiences by which men have found freedom through a form of government should be imparted, that understandings, beliefs, and loyalties should be indoctrinated for the sake of that freedom itself.[3]

The training of citizens for participation in democratic processes raises at once the delicate issue of equalitarianism. Leaders are indispensable to effective democracy, but their selection must not create an aristocracy of power if popular control of government is to be maintained. Selection on the basis of equal opportunity for equal talent is not a complete solution, even if the ideal of equal economic opportunity can be developed and preserved. Totalitarian states boast that their leadership is recruited from the best talent, whatever its origin. Democratic societies must guarantee that the power of leadership shall rest upon persuasion of electoral majorities. It is therefore imperative that the whole citizenry, leaders and followers, be educated in the highest standards of character, information, and judgment. The school is the foundation of the democratic order, and the progress of democratic politics is largely dependent upon the developing effectiveness of education.

Theories of administrative centralization and decentralization have divided the educational practice of democratic states. But democratic centralization, sometimes authoritarian in administration, does not prescribe the political views of pupils, parents, and teachers. It differs sharply from the character and purpose of totalitarian centralization. Democratic advocates of centralization submit that opportunities are equalized and that backward

---

[3] See Benjamin Floyd Pittenger, *Indoctrination for American Democracy* (New York: The Macmillan Company, 1941).

areas are afforded the advantages of progressive communities, that higher qualifications for teachers can be required, and that efficiency is promoted by uniformity of educational standards. Theorists who prefer decentralization question the accuracy of statements implying uniform quality of results under centralization, suggest that nominal efficiency may be purchased at the price of a mechanization which ignores the needs of the social environment, and demand that democratic policies shall encourage and promote the widely differing manifestations of genius which comprise a rich culture. The crux of the argument is not in the method of administration but in the result of the educative process, and many authorities believe that by either device, under proper conditions of cooperation, incentive, and freedom, a high caliber of participating citizenship can be trained.

Educational and political traditions in England, Switzerland, and the United States have established policies of decentralization in school administration. The English system is indirect, preserving a delicate balance of private initiative, local control and responsibility, and governmental interest in quality and standards. "Ostensibly a system without a system, apparently with no effort at all in design or accomplishment, it is in reality one of the most intricate and carefully adapted to the social and economic forces it must interpret."[4] In Switzerland the obstacles to civic cohesion have been enormous. Barriers of geography, language, and religion have been overcome by centuries of slow but remarkable progress. Swiss nationalism is bulwarked almost paradoxically by local allegiances, and the control of civic education rests understandably in the cantons. The principle of federal aid is employed, but the symbolism of citizen training is local as well as national. In the United States, the absence of a national system of education and the presence of decentralization even within the states have been conspicuous features, although there has been a trend toward the use of federal funds for educational purposes. Federal financing of

---

[4] Charles E. Merriam, *The Making of Citizens* (Chicago: The University of Chicago Press, 1931), p. 185.

education is advocated by numerous publicists and organizations. Great emphasis has been placed upon free schools as centers of civic training, and elaborate curricula have been developed, often by state legislation, for that purpose. In no other country has there been more formal emphasis upon education for democratic citizenship.

National systems of democratic education, employing highly centralized administration, have been notable in France, Belgium, the Netherlands, and the Scandinavian countries. French nationalism has enjoyed a high degree of geographic, ethnic, linguistic, and economic unity. Civic training has stressed French history as well as the political and social characteristics of French nationalism with uniformity and thoroughness. In the Scandinavian countries the centralized school systems are also notable for their freedom from political interference and for their influence in developing democratic citizenship. In most of the Latin American countries centralization of educational systems was inevitable before local governments had been established; and tradition, governmental organization, and financial requirements operate together to continue such arrangements. The inadequate distribution of elementary and the selective aspects of secondary education tend to accentuate aristocratic elements in society, setting up a distinction between the uneducated and the educated "which results in a sort of cultural *caudillismo* often indistinguishable from political *caudillismo*." [5] In China, where the educational system is nominally national, remarkable progress has been made despite unsettled conditions in a program of education "to the end that national independence may be attained, exercise of political rights may be made universal, conditions of livelihood may be developed, and in so doing, the cause of world peace and brotherhood may be advanced." [6] The Kuomintang, the

---

[5] "Introduction" by the editor, in I. L. Kandel, ed., *Educational Yearbook of the International Institute of Teachers College, Columbia University, 1942* (New York: Columbia University, 1942), p. xxv. The entire volume is devoted to education in the Latin American countries.

[6] Promulgation by the National Government in April, 1929, quoted in Chai Hsuan Chuang, "China," *Educational Yearbook, 1936,* p. 202.

only legal and the paramount political party of China, devoted to the principles of its late leader, Dr. Sun Yat-sen, has strongly supported a mass education program to eliminate adult illiteracy and to broaden Chinese political participation.

CATHOLIC DOCTRINE

The Catholic position regarding the state and education affects both democratic and totalitarian governments, although the latter perhaps more frequently disregard the influence of the Papacy. The long-established Catholic position is authoritatively stated in the Encyclical of Pope Pius XI on the Christian Education of Youth (*Rappresentanti in Terra,* December 31, 1929).[7] Education, it is held, belongs pre-eminently to the church; the family holds the mission and the right to educate; the state is endowed with the function of protecting and fostering education, respecting the rights of the church and the family. The child is not the mere creature of the state, declared the Pope, citing with approval the decision of the United States Supreme Court invalidating an Oregon measure intended to abolish parochial schools and to require attendance exclusively in public schools.[8] The Pope condemned any educational monopoly which forces families to make use of governmental schools. "The state can exact . . . that all its citizens have the necessary knowledge of their civic and political duties"; it may "reserve to itself the establishment and direction of schools intended to prepare for certain civic duties and especially for military service, provided it be careful not to injure the rights of the Church or of the family in what pertains to them."[9] Indeed, "the state has the duty of providing for the education of children, not only in order to make them good citizens but for their own welfare."[10]

---

[7] For the text, see Joseph Husslein, S. J., ed., *Social Wellsprings,* Vol. II: *Eighteen Encyclicals of Social Reconstruction by Pope Pius XI* (Milwaukee: The Bruce Publishing Company, 1942), pp. 89-121. It is also printed in *Current History,* XXXI (March, 1930), pp. 1091-1104.

[8] Pierce *v.* Society of the Sisters of the Holy Names of Jesus and Mary, 268 U. S. 510 (1925).

[9] Quoted in Husslein, *op. cit.,* p. 102.

[10] John A. Ryan, "The Pope's Encyclical on Education: A Catholic Interpretation," *Current History,* XXXI (March, 1930), at p. 1087. See *ibid.,* pp. 1089-90 for "A Protestant Comment" by Dean Luther A. Weigle of the Yale Divinity School.

Catholics are ordinarily forbidden to attend mixed schools, open to Catholics and non-Catholics alike, even if separate religious instruction is provided; and the official Catholic position suggests that in nations where there are different religious beliefs it is the duty of the state to allow free scope to the initiative of the church and the family, giving them such financial assistance as justice demands. Basically, Catholic theory suggests, the school should be "subsidiary and complementary to the family and to the Church"; it should form with them "a perfect moral union." [11]

TOTALITARIANISM

Totalitarian philosophies of education deny the principles of individual academic freedom. The state assumes a supervisory role for the social welfare which precludes individualism. Yet the several totalitarian aims, highly similar in practical effect, are not identical.

1. SOVIET RUSSIA

The educational objectives of Soviet Russia are proclaimed as Marxian in origin and in evolution. The present nature of the Soviet state is, in theory, temporary. The period of the proletarian dictatorship, although prolonged, will pass. When communism has reached full fruition, when society has become classless, the state will wither. In the meantime, during the present proletarian period, the problem of authority is that of destroying capitalism, creating new social organs, and constructing new ideologies. The state must employ every facility of education, formal and informal, to instill a communistic philosophy. The state must dominate education. The school cannot be outside the realm of politics; it must be molded and implemented by the proletarian dictatorship for the exclusive indoctrination of communism.

The communist does not conceive that his purpose destroys the genuine freedom of men; he contends rather that men are freed from the shackles of exploitation and superstition. A prominent Soviet educator declares, by way of considered sum-

---

[11] Husslein, *op. cit.*, p. 113.

mary, "that the aim of nurture and general instruction in Soviet Russia is to aid in the all-round development of a healthy, strong, actively brave, independently thinking and acting man, acquainted with the many sides of contemporary culture, a creator and a warrior in the interests of the proletariat and consequently in the final analysis in the interests of the whole of humanity." [12] The same writer, President of the Second State University of Moscow, contends that everywhere in bourgeois society church and state conspire to support a regime founded on exploitation of the poor. Engels and Lenin declare that non-human morality is a phenomenon of class oppression. Revolutionary socialists therefore denounce bonds between church and education. Education must be complete, in accordance with the ability of the individual.[13]

Soviet emphasis upon proletarian citizenship is conspicuous. The citizen must produce. The school is therefore closely related to production. The ideal citizen should participate in communist political activity, and to that end illiteracy must be liquidated. Socialist production and Marxian politics are the essence of Soviet education; there is no room for neutrality.

2. NATIONAL SOCIALIST GERMANY

Succeeding an era of educational liberalism, German National Socialism is its antithesis, denying belief in the importance of the individual as such. Opposition to liberalism is basic in National Socialist thought; individualism is conceived as leading only to a decline of society and civilization. The individual possesses no natural right; indeed, he has no existence except in the community. He is the creature of the community—the German people, the German folk. National Socialism denies that freedom is destroyed or suppressed; the very concept of individual freedom is an artificial doctrine of liberalism which separates man from the realities of his environment. Education therefore promotes the welfare of the German folk, inculcating

[12] Albert P. Pinkevitch, *The New Education in the Soviet Republic* (New York: The John Day Company, 1929), p. 28.

[13] *Ibid.*, pp. 25-31.

as an ethical ideal loyalty to the community. The National Socialist concept is not collectivist, for it opposes the idea that the community is an organization of individuals justified by social or cultural expediency. The community or folk is the basis of mankind, an organism precedent and superior to individuals.[14]

The fundamental characteristic of the people, the folk, is race. The state is a means rather than an end, a means to the self-realization of race and the preservation of its purity for the highest freedom and dignity of mankind. The state is an organ for the race or folk, by means of which political activity, the general will and welfare of the community, reaches its fulfillment. The character of National Socialism and its *Weltanschauung* ("world outlook," in reality nationalistic) have been formulated deliberately for the welfare of Germans.[15]

National Socialism is not only anti-individualist and anticollectivist, it is also anti-pluralistic. It repudiates the doctrine of autonomous organizations within society. It does not permit any other loyalty than to the state. Education must, therefore, be political education, and it belongs exclusively to the state. Neither the family nor the church has any right to the control of instruction. Education for citizenship must indoctrinate allegiance to the state; it must subordinate loyalty to the family, the church, and social organizations. "Education for the community, education for citizenship, and education for National Socialism are *all one thing*." [16]

The educational theory of National Socialism espouses the élite principle, whereby leadership for the state is guaranteed and trained. Leaders arise by natural selection, but very few are born for leadership. A select number, peculiarly suited by disposition, must be trained under rigorous discipline for that

---

[14] Walter Landé, "Basic Principles of National Socialist Education in the Third Reich," *Education for Dynamic Citizenship,* University of Pennsylvania School of Education, Twenty-fourth Annual Schoolmen's Week Proceedings (Philadelphia: The University, 1937), pp. 104-7.

[15] George Frederick Kneller, *The Educational Philosophy of National Socialism* (New Haven: Yale University Press, 1941), pp. 10-12, 34-38.

[16] Landé, *op. cit.,* p. 110; see pp. 108-12.

role. Because of the inequality of man, the rule of the majority is replaced by the rule of creative personality. It is the purpose of National Socialism to perpetuate itself.[17]

If the roots of National Socialism and its educational philosophy are not deep in history, they are consistent with German tradition. National Socialism is primarily an attitude demanding action, it is a revolution. But it is a nationalistic revolution, and it comports with many philosophic aspects of German nationalistic progress. Dr. Kneller has pointed out that the fashion of National Socialist theorists to cite precedents in great German philosophers is chiefly for the purpose of argument,[18] but it is true that significant nationalistic similarities are found in the works of such thinkers as Herder, Fichte, Hegel, Schlegel, Lange, Nietzsche, and Treitschke.

3. FASCIST ITALY

Italian Fascism, like German National Socialism, portrays the state as the organized will of the nation. The individual achieves moral personality only by identification with national culture. Freedom is found by voluntary service to the nation, and the national will must synthesize and unify the institutions of society. Education is its principal instrument and therefore must be secularized and embodied in the state.[19]

Earlier Italian education was predominantly influenced by doctrines of positivism, which emphasized acquisition of knowledge for its own sake. The school had therefore become separated from the realities surrounding the pupil. Fascism authorized the substitution of idealism as developed by Benedetto Croce and Giovanni Gentile. Empowered to organize Fascist educational reforms, Gentile gave the political theory of the regime a cultural form. Reality can be found, he taught, only in the human spirit; education must be through personal experience, it must be achieved through action. Within the limits neces-

---

[17] Kneller, *op. cit.*, pp. 62-67.

[18] *Ibid.*, p. 82; see pp. 83-139 for a discussion of philosophical backgrounds.

[19] Herbert W. Schneider and Shepard B. Clough, *Making Fascists* (Chicago: The University of Chicago Press, 1929), pp. 86-87.

sary for development of national culture, the schools, the teachers, and the pupils must be free to learn through their own experiences. Curricula were therefore not to be prescribed, but emphasis should be placed upon the study of heroes as symbols of the national spirit. While the idealism of Gentile was scarcely political, it could be turned to the uses of Fascism by relating the primacy of the human spirit to that national spirit in which individuals should find their expression. Upon the retirement of Gentile, however, the schools became more closely related to Fascism and to the indoctrination of Fascist ideology.[20] In 1939 the Fascist Grand Council issued the Italian Education Charter, which proclaims the integration of the schools with Fascist education for citizenship: "In the moral, political, and economic union of the Italian Nation which is being integrally realized in the Fascist State, the school, the essential foundation for the solidarity of all social forces, . . . develops the human and political conscience of the new generations." [21]

JAPAN

The schools of the Japanese Empire are highly centralized, facilitating strict governmental direction and prescription of uniform curricula. The social philosophy of Japanese education bears marked resemblances to the totalitarian ideologies of Germany and Italy. It is not individualistic but is based on the principle that the nation is a family and a social group. Education is designed so to develop the personality of the individual that he will serve the ideals of the national community. In practice, individualistic elements have often prevailed in education because of overpopulation, programs for training successful officials, and the conflict between ideals and facts.[22] The Japanese Bureau of Thought Supervision has striven to guide education in orthodox channels of interpretation and to exclude doctrines which may be considered dangerous to the state.

[20] I. L. Kandel, *Comparative Education* (Boston: Houghton Mifflin Company, 1933), pp. 457-62.

[21] Quoted in I. L. Kandel, *The End of an Era, Educational Yearbook,* 1941, p. 195.

[22] Kumaji Yoshida, "The Philosophy Underlying the National System of Education in Japan," *Educational Yearbook,* 1929, p. 452.

The policy of Japanese education is based on the Imperial Rescript on Education, also actually a code of morals, issued by the Emperor on October 30, 1890. A copy is given to every school in the Empire and is read on the anniversary of its issue and on other occasions. The source of education lies in virtue implanted, states the Rescript, by Imperial Ancestors and illustrated by generations united in loyalty and filial piety. "Ye, Our subjects, be filial to your parents, affectionate to your brothers and sisters; as husbands and wives be harmonious, as friends true; bear yourselves in modesty and moderation; extend your benevolence to all; pursue learning and cultivate arts, and thereby develop intellectual faculties and perfect moral powers; furthermore advance public good and promote common interests; always respect the Constitution and observe the laws; should emergency arise, offer yourselves courageously to the State; and thus guard and maintain the prosperity of Our Imperial Throne coeval with heaven and earth." [23]

Japanese nationalism lays stress upon the term morality. Any act contrary to morality is declared to be an offense against nationalism; policies which are worthy will be found to be clearly within the scope of nationalism. Advocates of internationalism who decry the sovereignty or need of state organization, for instance, are called proponents of cosmopolitanism, distinguished from true internationalism, and excluded. World brotherhood consistent with state organization need not be excluded; but since such brotherhood has not developed in the community of nations, Japan has sought to attain the principle of the family in a race of common history and tradition. [24]

Aristotle observed that "the citizen should be molded to suit the form of government under which he lives." Many contemporary thinkers are convinced that the forms of government in the world must be so molded that citizens may live in freedom and peace. But it is none the less clear, from the light of men's experience, that governments will seek, subtly or force-

---

[23] The text is quoted in Henry Lester Smith, *Comparative Education* (Bloomington, Indiana: Educational Publications, 1941), p. 369.

[24] Yoshida, *op. cit.*, pp. 457-8.

fully, with forbearance or with ruthlessness, to shape the civic concepts in the citizen mind. It is also true that the nature of education will ultimately determine the dogma of the state. Education and politics are inevitably complementary. Civic training and civic action are mutually both cause and effect.

SELECTED BIBLIOGRAPHY

BROOKS, ROBERT C., *Civic Training in Switzerland* (Chicago: The University of Chicago Press, 1930).

BRUBACHER, JOHN S., *Modern Philosophies of Education* (New York: McGraw-Hill Book Company, Inc., 1939).

Educational Yearbook of the International Institute of Teachers College, Columbia University (New York: Bureau of Publications, Teachers College, Columbia University, annual volumes since 1924). An important source of information on comparative education. The 1929 volume is devoted to the philosophies underlying the systems of education in England, France, Germany, Italy, Japan, and the United States.

GAUS, JOHN M., *Great Britain: A Study of Civic Loyalty* (Chicago: The University of Chicago Press, 1929).

HARPER, SAMUEL NORTHRUP, *Civic Training in Soviet Russia* (Chicago: The University of Chicago Press, 1929).

——————————, *Making Bolshevists* (Chicago: The University of Chicago Press, 1931).

HAYES, CARLTON J. H., *France, a Nation of Patriots* (New York: Columbia University Press, 1930).

KANDEL, I. L., *Comparative Education* (Boston: Houghton Mifflin Company, 1933). A textbook.

KNELLER, GEORGE FREDERICK, *The Educational Philosophy of National Socialism* (New Haven: Yale University Press, 1941). A comprehensive treatment.

KOSOK, PAUL, *Modern Germany* (Chicago: The University of Chicago Press, 1933).

LANDE, WALTER, "Basic Principles of National Socialist Education," *Education for Dynamic Citizenship* (University of Pennsylvania School of Education, Twenty-fourth Annual Schoolmen's Week Proceedings, Philadelphia: The University, 1937), pp. 103-114. A brilliant analysis of theory.

LEEBRICK, K. C., "Politics and Education," in Roy V. Peel and Joseph S. Roucek, eds., *Introduction to Politics* (New York: Thomas Y. Crowell Company, 1941), pp. 552-62. A survey of recent theories.

LINEBARGER, PAUL M. A., *The China of Chiang K'ai-shek* (Boston: World Peace Foundation, 1941).

MARRARO, HOWARD R., *The New Education in Italy* (New York: S. F. Vanni, Inc., 1936).

McGUCKEN, WILLIAM J., *The Catholic Way in Education* (Milwaukee: The Bruce Publishing Co., 1934).

MERRIAM, CHARLES E., *Civic Education in the United States* (New York: Charles Scribner's Sons, 1934). The sixth volume of the Report of the Commission on the Social Studies under the auspices of the American Historical Association.

——————————, *The Making of Citizens* (Chicago: The University of Chicago Press, 1931). A comparison of systems of civic education in eight nations; the summary volume in a series of studies in the making of citizens.

PINKEVITCH, ALBERT P., *The New Education in the Soviet Republic* (New York: The John Day Co., 1929).

REISNER, EDWARD H., *Nationalism and Education Since* 1789 (New York: The Macmillan Co., 1922). Historical background for the study of modern politics and education.

ROUCEK, JOSEPH S., *Sociological Foundations of Education* (New York: Thomas Y. Crowell Co., 1942). One of the latest and probably one of the sanest evaluations of the relationship between education and social action.

SCHNEIDER, HERBERT W. AND CLOUGH, SHEPARD B., *Making Fascists* (Chicago: University of Chicago Press, 1929).

SMITH, HENRY LESTER, *Comparative Education* (Bloomington, Ind.: Educational Publications, 1941).

Chapter XX

BRITISH POLITICAL THOUGHT

J. RUMNEY

The history of political ideas is essentially the history of conflicting interests, groups and classes within the state and between states. These ideas do not emerge in a vacuum. They are born from the interplay of numerous social forces acting in response to specific social problems that require solution. They are not, therefore, empty and bloodless categories, but important instruments for the shaping of theory and practice, implying political programs of action determined to preserve or change a social order. Modern political ideas only differ from earlier ideas in reflecting the technological temper of our age and in stressing concrete and practical aspects. In the following sketch it will not be possible to unravel the intricate connections between ideas and the social structure, especially those between the state and economic activities, but they should be kept in mind.

The Rise and Fall of Liberalism

The triumph of commercial and industrial capitalism brought about an essential cleavage between a new social class which owned all the means of production and a wage-earning class which was nominally free, but neither owned, nor was attached to the means of production. The dominant class is no longer an aristocracy of birth and land, but an aristocracy of factory and bank. With the conquest of economic power, it won political power. And this new revolutionary class, revolutionary until it was victorious, created an ideology more in harmony with its historical role. It vindicated the right of property and derived it from personal effort and initiative. Property it argued, was the nurse of virtue, and without it no incentive would exist for the performance of work. In religion, it stressed personal salvation and made a sharp distinction between the sacred and the profane, between the church and the market. It made both God and King into constitutional and limited sovereigns. It based philosophy and ethics on empiricism, and made morality into a personal matter. Indeed, it isolated and abstracted every aspect of human life from every other, as if to conform to the minute division of labour and specialization it had brought about.

This magnificent structure, so firmly and solidly founded, began to be undermined from many different directions in the middle of the nineteenth century. In science, Darwin, Huxley and Spencer established the theory of evolution, natural selection and survival of the fittest. True, their theories could be used to justify laissez faire and ruthless competition, or to make the survival of the fittest synonymous with survival of the richest. But they could also be used to justify a social organism, collectivism and planning. In literature, Arnold, Ruskin and Carlyle thundered against the "dismal science" which in amassing riches only increased poverty. It appeared that the invisible hand did not guide individual self-interest to the greatest happiness of the greatest number, and to retain Benthamism, therefore, John Stuart Mill had to change it beyond recognition. In religion agnostics such as Leslie Stephen or atheists such as Bradlaugh were vociferous. In jurisprudence Maine and Maitland reigned supreme. In social philosophy Green, Bradley, Bosanquet and McTaggart found consolation in Hegelian idealism. In sociology, a Comtean positivism held undisputed sway. In politics the Communist Manifesto proclaimed the end of a social order which had begun with Rousseau and the French Revolution and the beginning of a new one, with the liberation of the Fourth estate. Rousseau's opening sentence was "Man is born free, but everywhere he is in chains." The concluding sentence of Marx was "Workers of the World Unite, You have nothing to lose but your chains." Moreover, the restiveness and misery of the masses and the efforts of Lord Shaftesbury brought about the

Factory Acts and the beginning of a series of social legislation.[1] The negative state was slowly changing into the positive state. The comparative prosperity which characterized England as the first workshop of the world began to break in the 80's with increasing competition from other industrialized countries. There began a period of increasing social unrest and strikes, and the power of the Trade Unions was felt. Henry George awakened a new interest in the problem of poverty, and the idealism of Morris and the burrowings of the Fabians stimulated socialist thought. Morris, Walter Crane, Belfort Bax and Eleanor Marx formed the Socialist League, and Hyndman, Champion, John Burns and Harry Quelch the Social Democratic Federation. These movements and new currents of thought, as well as the increasing participation of the state in economic matters consequent upon the changing nature of capitalism, set up a challenge which liberalism found it difficult to meet—even the New Liberalism of Toynbee and Green. Liberalism, it appeared had performed its historic role, of removing the obstacles to individual freedom. But in freeing the individual, it had at the same time isolated and uprooted him. It had freed him *from* restraints but it had not given him the freedom *for* the kind of life an integrated society requires. Instead of government at a minimum, with the maximum degree of individual liberty, there is a tendency for government at a maximum with a minimum degree of individual liberty. In destroying the old Mercantilist state, Liberalism finds itself faced with another Leviathan, the Totalitarian State.

TUE NEW PSYCHOLOGY AND POLITICAL THOUGHT

The old associationist psychology had been pre-eminently suited to a period of economic liberalism and *laissez-faire*. It had regarded man as a rational being who always equated his good with his pleasure and therefore always strove to obtain the maximum of pleasure. The newer psychology of William James, Bergson, Nietzsche, and Sorel tended to the opposite

---

[1] Alison in his *Principles of Population* 1840, II, p. 206, observes: "While slavery existed the landlords were obliged to feed their slaves; but when that was done away with, it was necessary for government to feed them, *hence* poor laws."

extreme of regarding man as purely an irrational being. In England as early as in 1873, Bagehot in his *Physics and Politics* applied the principle of imitation to politics. In 1908 William McDougall (1871-1938) in *An Introduction to Social Psychology,* a book which went through numerous editions, and had a far-reaching influence on the social sciences, sees man as a bundle of instincts, and reason as their humble servant always alert to satisfy their demands for gratification. "Take away these instinctive dispositions" he writes "with their powerful impulses, and the organism would become incapable of activity of any kind; it would be inert and motionless, like a wonderful clockwork whose mainsprings had been removed, or a steam engine, whose fire had been drawn. These impulses are the mental forces that maintain and shape all the life of individuals and societies, and in them we are confronted with the central mystery of life, and mind and will." [2] In a later work *The Group Mind* (1930), McDougall applies his analysis to the behavior of groups such as crowds, armies, states, and postulates a group-mind, a collective consciousness, a supersensuous entity above and distinct from the minds of its members in their interrelations.

But where, we may ask, is the location of this mind, wherein it is embodied? This mystical view of society lends itself to the glorification of the state and to the complete subjection of the individual to it. The same objections may be raised to the theory of society as a social organism such as is found in Hobbes, Rousseau and Spencer and more recently in W. H. R. Rivers (1864-1922) in his book *Psychology and Politics* (1923), in Morley Roberts (*Bio Politics,* 1938), and Dendy (*Biological Foundations of Society*).

Following McDougall, there was a tendency to interpret all behavior in terms of instincts which were postulated *ad hoc* for that purpose. Was it religion? There must be a religious instinct? Was it war, there must be pugnacious instinct? Was it leadership, there must be instinct to lead and to follow. Instincts,

---

[2] William McDougal, *An Introduction to Social Psychology* (Boston: John W. Luce & Co., 1926), pp. 43-46.

however, do not explain anything, unless we can show how a particular instinct matures and what specific conditions must be present for it always to lead to some specific form of behavior. Thus W. Trotter in "The instincts of the Herd in Peace and War" attempts to unlock many and diverse social phenomena by means of the gregarious instinct, so that suggestion, conscience, morality are all to be interpreted by means of it; it is this instinct which makes each individual sensitive to the behavior of his fellows, suggestible to the voice of the herd, and creates that heavy uniformity and social pressure from which no individual can escape.

Graham Wallas (1858-1925), like McDougall has also exposed the irrational elements in human behavior, but he is no irrationalist. He exposes in order that the political scientist may take them into account in planning political institutions. In *Human Nature and Politics* (1908) he shows how important, habit and instinct, suggestion and imitation are in political life, and how unimportant is conscious reason. Elections are orgies in spell binding and party labels emotional symbols. In his later works (*Our Social Heritage,* 1921, and *The Art of Thought,* 1926) Wallas attempts to apply the new social psychology to the problem of social reconstruction. Our present political institutions, he argues, baffle and thwart the individual citizen and makes him incapable of continuous initiative. What is therefore required is a social therapeutics. He seeks a synthesis between Fabianism and Syndicalism, so that the greatest individual liberty is possible.

Two other writers, primarily sociologists, who have influenced psychological thinking on these matters are L. T. Hobhouse (1864-1929) who in *Mind in Evolution* (1901), and *Development of Purpose* (1913), shows that instinct and intelligence, cannot be sharply demarcated, indeed, that intelligence grows out of instinct, and that social evolution is correlated with the growth of purpose in social life; and Morris Ginsberg who in his *Psychology of Society* (1921), has given one of the most penetrating analyses of such topics as the role of instinct in society, the meaning of the group mind and the general will, the nature of public opinion and the psychology of organization and democracy.

In recent years there have been attempts to explain political phenomena in psycho-analytical terms. These attempts like those of the instinctivists are guilty of the error of singling out biological drives as explanations of complicated cultural phenomena. Thus revolutionaries are explained by their aggression to their fathers; Dictatorship is explained by terms of a revival of the parent-child situation; of a process of identification by which the ordinary citizen unable to exercise authority himself identifies himself with the dictator; and of a satisfaction of the sadistic and masochistic impulses by the existence of concentration camps. Such interpretations ignore social and historical factors and do not tell us why dictatorships arose at one particular time and not at another. One of the most interesting studies that has recently apepared is *War, Sadism and Pacifism* (1933) by T. R. Glover, wherein the thesis is presented that identical psychological forces lie back of pacifism and war, and that frustration and repression of impulses in early life engender an aggression whose natural outlet is violence and war. Still more recently an effort has been made to synthesize Marxism and Freudism, but without much success.[3]

SOCIOLOGY AND POLITICAL THOUGHT [4]

The development of biology and sociology brought about an evolutionary and sociological interpretation of the state which made impossible the excessive mystification and glorification of the state or the antithesis between the individual and society found in Rousseau, Hegel and Bosanquet. For this two major errors were responsible. The first was the identification between the state and society; the second was the confusion between the state as it is and the state as it ought to be.

---

[3] R. Osborn, *Freud and Marx. A Dialectical Study* (London: Gollancz, 1937).

[4] For the sociological view of the state, see: L. T. Hobhouse, *The Metaphysical Theory of the State* (London: G. Allen & Unwin, 1918); J. H. Laski, *The State in Theory and Practice* (1935); and his other works, such as: *Politics* (Philadelphia: J. B. Lippincott, 1931); *The American Presidency* (New York: Harper, 1940); etc.

Society is taken to include the whole complex of indeterminate relationship of human beings in contact. A society is a definite collection of individuals which possesses a certain permanency and whose members have definable relations to each other and who know their rights and duties to each other. The state emerges with its monopoly of compulsion within a society with the development of property war, and ordered government. Where the state expresses the general and widespread needs of the community, the government will be representative of the population within its territory. But where a certain minority or class is dominant within the state, the government will be representative of that class. The functions, therefore, exercised by the State will differ from age to age, and in accordance with the requirements of historical conditions. They may range from bare preservation of internal order and external defense, to the comprehensive scrutiny of every aspect of social life as in totalitarian states. To determine the functions of the state *a priori* as was done by the *laissez-faire* theorists, is therefore futile. Their efforts to circumscribe the activities of the state represented the desires of a triumphant middle class that wanted no interference in business. Now, on the other hand, especially in times of depression business is only too willing that the state should take over additional functions and set it on its feet again.

Even where the state has not been superimposed upon a society by conquest, but has grown up within it, its main sphere of action lies in fashioning conformity to externals only. It can compel obedience, but the obedience will only last as long as the state satisfies the needs and desires of its members. If it does not do so, sooner or later the people will revolt. The state may be overthrown but society as such will not, therefore, cease to exist; again, the state is an historical and changing phenomenon. There is no reason to believe that the present nation-state, for instance, is permanent, or that the absolute sovereignty with which it is now endowed, will remain its attribute forever, although it is true that present and immediate trends do not indicate any diminution of such sovereignty.

The exponents of the metaphysical theory of the state, have been, with all their "idealism" defenders of the status quo. The state, instead of being considered what it is now, is transformed into a self-conscious ethical entity, a self-knowing and actualizing personality that can do no wrong, to use Hegel's words. In this way, the state becomes an end in itself, overriding the rights of its citizens, and transcending the morality of the individual. Freedom consists in slavishly obeying the state, a view which leads to the absorption of the individual by the state, and one which is being uniformly enforced by totalitarian states.[5]

What the idealist philosophers really wanted to answer was the unity and cohesiveness of the state. That this unity exists, cannot be denied, but it must not be exaggerated. There is conflict as well as cooperation. Many factors are involved in this unity, such as suggestion, imitation, sympathy, the appeal to collective sentiments, and the inhibition of conflicting tendencies. In developed societies, the degree of unity will largely depend on the degree in which conscious aims are pursued by particular associations, and the extent to which conflicting interests may be adjusted. The same analysis applies to the state whose unity, in so far as there exist sharp economic antagonisms and class divisions is far from enduring. We can only tell how far it embodies a common will, when we scrutinize its property arrangements, its history and traditions, its system of rights, the formation of public opinion, its administration of law and many other social institutions.

---

[5] "It is easy to see in this Hegelian doctrine," G. D. H. Cole, *Some Relations between Political and Economic Theory* (London: Macmillan Co., 1934), p. 32, shrewdly observes, "the germ both of the Fascist-notion of the Corporative State and of that Christion social doctrine of corporation which preceded it by more than a generation. This notion of the Corporative State is, of course, utterly different—from the Syndicalist and Guild Socialist conceptions to which it bears a superficial resemblance. For the Syndicalist and Guild Socialist both set out from an acceptance of the notion of the class struggle, and armed at building up a type of federal society, based on functional groups which would issue, from the carrying through of the class struggle, to a successful termination in the institution of the classless society."

The Soveroign State

The decay of the old individualism which had regarded the individual as the unit for political purposes, and the economic and social transformations that were tending to bring about the monopoly state gave rise to a number of political theorists who sharply attacked state sovereignty and who took the group and not the individual as the unit for political organization. In spite of the many differences in social philosophy and outlook among them, they all unite in hostility to the growing power of the state and in asserting the personality of economic and professional groups. It is argued that only in group life does man find opportunities for the fullest expression of his social life. To single out the state, therefore, as most important association morally or in authority runs counter to experience. A legal act of the state is valid only in so far as the end it serves is morally acceptable. Rights and duties, it is claimed, attach to groups as such not because of legal fiat, because the state recognizes them, but because they are inherent in the group function. Barker, following Maitland and Glerke argues that throughout history, groups have always pressed their claims against the state, and that the situation has been one of "polyarchism" rather than of sovereignty. "At different times," he writes, "different societies may claim a final allegiance, and at the same time two societies or more may tug at the same heart-strains, with equally imperative demands." [6] To Laski, the state is but one group among many. It secures obedience only in so far as it responds to the needs of its citizens, otherwise it must face the challenge of being overthrown. Society is pluralistic and sovereignty therefore does not inhere in the state. Whenever conflict supervenes, that association which has the greatest moral appeal will receive allegiance. Throughout his writings there sounds a passionate plea for the freedom

---

[6] Ernest Baker, "The Discredited States," *The Political Science Quarterly* (February, 1915), p. 7. See also his *Political Thought in England from Herbert Spencer to the Present Day* (London: Williams and Norgate, 1915).

of groups and the full development of the human personality.[7]

Compared with Laski, the other pluralists adopted a moderate position. To Figgis the state is still the "communitas communitatum." Barker warns against carrying pluralism too far. "Any unqualified theory of the 'inherent rights' of associations is likely to do as much harm as the unqualified theory of the inherent or natural rights of the individual man once did" he writes. "No rights are so inherent that they have not to be adjusted to other rights; and by the process of adjustment they become socially controlled rights." The state, he argues, is necessary to adjust the relations of associations to each other and to their members and to ensure equality of law. Laski also modified his position in his later writings. With his proposal in the *Grammar of Politics* for the state ownership of basic industries, he reintroduces the state in paramount importance. And sooner or later, the logic of the pluralists position requires the re-introduction of the state in a supreme position. Groups in society have overlapping functions, nor can they be sharply demarcated as political, economic or religious and even the guild socialists must resort to a joint body, representative of all functional associations, and presumably endowed with coercive authority to carry out orders. But this compulsiveness and comprehensiveness is the essence of the sovereign state. A. D. Lindsay admits this uniqueness, but claims it is not sufficient to constitute a sovereign state. But if so, what is? If the state is to become an association like other associations, are the pluralists prepared to abolish compulsory taxation and citizenship?

Nevertheless, the pluralists served the useful function of showing that there is nothing sacrosant about the state, and that to find out where effective sovereignty as distinguished from legal sovereignty, actually resides, the total social structure of the state must be known. Their advocacy of decentralization and federalism is valuable. Their plea for the revivification of group life is not only a welcome protest against the glorification of the

---

[7] H. J. Laski, *Studies in the Problem of Sovereignty* (New Haven: Yale University Press, 1917); *Authority in the Modern State* (New Haven: Yale University Press, 1919); *Foundations of Sovereignty* (New York: Harcourt, Brace, 1921).

state and dogmatic legalism but a powerful solution to the domination of "mass-society"—perhaps the central problem of modern political life.

Another attack on the sovereign state came from the field of international relations, when it was realized that state sovereignty under modern conditions had become a primary cause of international anarchy. Without going into the specific arguments raised by these groups of writers (though, when Norman Angell argues that war does not pay, he appears to forget that it may pay certain groups) one fact overshadows all others and that is that economic functions can no longer be confined to state boundaries. They overflow group exclusiveness and state barriers, and this inescapable situation cannot be ignored in the relations between states in the contemporary world.[8]

While the pluralists were attacking the sovereign state, the Neo-Liberals in transforming the negative into the positive state, were actually bringing it about, and the period between 1905 and 1914 saw more social legislation than at any other period of history. Foremost among the Neo-Liberals was L. T. Hobhouse, the greatest of English sociologists, and a passionate advocate of freedom and social reform.[9] At the root of his social philosophy is his belief in the necessity of a personal and social harmony based on creative consent and cooperation. The common good implies rights, and rights are the necessary conditions for social welfare: The function of the state is to secure those social and economic conditions which will make possible the fullest realization of personality, and to remove all those obstacles which hinder the fullest liberty. But Hobhouse does not use this word

---

[8] See: G. Lowes Dickinson, *The International Anarchy* (New York: Century Co., 1926); and *War: Its Nature, Cause and Cure* (New York: Macmillan, 1924); Norman Angell, *The Great Illusion* (New York: G. P. Putnam's Sons, 1913); and *Human Nature and the Peace Problem* (London: Harper, 1935); C. D. Burns, *International Politics* (London: Methuen, 1920); J. A. Hobson, *Towards International Government* (London: Allen and Unwin, 1915); A. Zimmern, *Nationality and Government* (New York: McBride, 1913).

[9] L. T. Hobhouse, *Liberalism* (New York: Henry Holt, 1920); and *Democracy and Reaction* (New York: E. G. Putnam's Sons, 1905); and *The Elements of Social Iustice* (New York: Henry Holt, 1922); and *The Natural Good* (New York: Henry Holt, 1921).

in any abstract sense. He analyses liberty into civil, fiscal, personal, social, economic, domestic, local, racial, national international and political liberties, and argues that state action must be universal in its application to every citizen, and that where there is differential treatment, that itself must be justified in terms of the common good. His aim Barker points out was "to deepen Liberal thought: to reconcile its old conceptions with new social demands and a new social philosophy, to turn Liberalism from *laissez-faire* to a genuine sympathy with labor."

Another advocate of the positive state, and like Hobhouse influenced by Fabian ideas is J. A. Hobson.[10] In *The Crisis of Liberalism* he shows that the old *laissez-faire* Liberalism is dead and that the state must become an active instrument for changing social institutions in accordance with the needs of the individual. In *Economics and Ethics* he urges that the state render available to its citizens on equal terms such services as health, education and recreation, which the present private property system cannot undertake. To his school belongs Delisle Burns who, in *State and Industry,* advocates increasing participation of the state in economic affairs and the utilization by the state of Trade Unions for the public interest.

THE ATTACKS ON DEMOCRACY: FASCISM

The inevitable trend towards increasing state control, the new light which psychology had thrown on the irrational elements in social life, and the genuine disappointment resulting from the broadening of the franchise, which the earlier democrats had thought would create an educated and intelligent electorate, and especially the dislocation brought about by the war, stimulated a re-examination of the whole democratic process. Even in the 19th century there had been numerous attacks on democracy by such men as Stephen, Lecky and Maine. In the twentieth century the attacks came from both the right and the left, the former emphasizing the need for an aristocracy or elite, the latter the need for a redistribution of economic power with-

[10] J. A. Hobson, *The Crisis of Liberalism* (London: P. S. King, 1909.

out which political power is meaningless. In some cases both aspects were emphasized.

In *Conservatism,* Lord Hugh Cecil makes an appeal for faith and tradition without which orderly progress is impossible and a restoration of the powers of the House of Lords in order to provide a check upon a pressure-ridden Parliament.[11] Antony Ludovici, a follower of Nietzsche, divides mankind into those who rule by virtue of superior endowments, and those who are ruled. The best state, he argues, is that which is based upon this ineluctable difference. To change the institution of private property is to go against a fundamental law of nature. W. H. Mallock contends (*A Defence of Aristocracy,* 1915) that in the highly complex state of today only a few people have the time he suggests that democracy and oligarchy are to government as or equipment to deal with the technical problems, and therefore an oligarchy is essential. Democracy by itself cannot exist, and chlorine and sodium are to table salt. A powerful work on its negative and ethical aspects is Canon D. Maclaine's *Equality and Fraternity;* on the constructive side it is authoritarian and theological. Hilaire Belloc attacks both democracy and capitalism, which by creating an economic oligarchy create the "servile state." In other works he advocates a real monarchy, or a sort of Fuehrer who will eliminate the demagoguery and corruption inevitable in a democracy. R. H. Gretton (*The King's Majesty*: *A Study in the Historical Philosophy of Modern Kingship,* 1930), too, advocates a monarchy but his "King" is to be above party and faction who will not only mediate between contending interests but who will actively uphold the integrity of the state.

It is not necessary to review other criticisms against democracy. But it should be noted that many of the severest critics, unlike those mentioned, are motivated not by the desire to destroy democracy but by a desire to improve it, which would be the case with H. G. Wells and Bernard Shaw who have not been sparing in their criticism of contempory political institutions. The same applies to such critics as Lindsay, Ivor Brown,

---

[11] Lord Hugh Cecil, *Conservatism* (London: William and Norgate, 1912).

A. T. Hadley, Hearnshaw, Hobhouse, Hobson, Zimmern and Gilbert Murray and Bertrand Russell. Many of the criticisms have been indirectly and effectively answered by Bryce who in his monumental study of how democracy actually works, concludes that popular government has justified itself. "If" he writes, "democracy has not brought all the blessings that were expected of it, it has in some countries destroyed, in others materially diminished, many of the cruelties and terrors, injustices and oppressions of modern times." [12] The solution, to many of the defects, it has been pointed out, is not less, but more democracy, and especially the democratization of non-political institutions so that a vigorous public opinion can function. It is only in a democracy that people know where the shoe pinches; and people can only learn to be democratic by living in a democracy. Public opinion, as Morris Ginsberg points out, is important in being public, in controlling rather than initiating legislation. To have democracy there must be not only a high level of education but also social and industrial democracy.

There are three features which are common both to democracy and to fascist dictatorship and these are: the rise of powerful political parties, the emergence of popular leaders and the vague political programs of mass societies schooled and dulled by an impersonal machine economy. But fascism, neither as a political movement nor as a political philosophy made much headway in England. Perhaps because the extreme Tories had their own brand of fascism, and neither internal nor external conditions favored it at the time. The British Union of Fascists headed by Sir Oswald Mosley was a small party, influenced seemingly much more by the Italian than the German example, although Spengler minus his pessimism, looms large in its ideology. It proclaimed its abhorrence of the rank of materialism of the age, of Jewish and Marxist internationalism, and of the obsolete capitalistic system. A new social and economic order must succeed the present one which "philosophically—has been regarded

---

[12] James Bryce, *Modern Democracies* (New York: Macmillan, 1921), II, pp. 668-669.

by some as the last orgasm of an overmature and already senescent society." In his books (*Greater Britain,* 1933, and *Tomorrow We Live,* 1938), Sir Oswald Mosley advocates a comparative, integrative and authoritarian system, a disciplined and military consciousness and a complete overhauling of the present economic system in favor of the small capitalists as against the big capitalists. But the program is vague and nebulous. The turn of events did not allow Mosley making it more specific.

SOCIALISM IN ENGLAND

If liberty without an economic basis is an illusion, as many of the preceding thinkers have shown, what must be done? The different socialisms are attempted solutions to this question, all of them advocating, in some form or another the emancipation of capital from private ownership and the vesting of it in the community for the general benefit.

Fabian Socialism. From its inception in 1853, this movement has retained the ethical and religious elements of its predecessor the Fellowship of the New Life. In 1854 George Bernard Shaw became a member, and in the following year Sidney Webb. Among its members have been Mrs. Besant, G. D. H. Cole, Laski, Ramsay MacDonald, Sydney Olivier, R. H. Tawney, Graham Wallas and H. G. Wells. Through its Fabian Essays and Fabian Tracts it has had a tremendous influence on political thought and movement, helping in the formation of the Independent Labor Party and later on of the Labor Party. Essentially its philosophy is one of reform and the gradual transformation of the positive state into a socialist state. The crisis theory of capitalism's collapse and the class war, it rejects, and maintains that instead of increasing misery as Marx predicted, the lot of the masses is getting better. The root of evil in the present economic system is not the retention of surplus value by the capitalists but the fact that the owners profit exclusively from the values created by society. The Webb's writings are eloquent testimony to the influence of the Fabians and in this connection the new program of the Labor Party drawn up in 1918 and written by

Sidney Webb, the Constitution of a Socialist Commonwealth of Great Britain 1920 should be consulted.

Guild Socialism. Guild socialism is essentially an English brand of syndicalism. If it harks back to the medieval gild it looks forward to anarchist communism. It desires economic collectivism but is afraid of its threat to individual liberty. Influenced by the attacks of the pluralists on the omnicompetent state it is suspicious of a centralized bureaucracy. It urges therefore the functional decentralization of industry. Real freedom, it is argued, implies economic freedom and economic freedom implies self-government in industry.

It is not possible to discuss here in detail the different forms this theory took. A. J. Penty in 1906 in his Restoration of the Guild System urged a return to the medieval handicraft system, and pride in creation destroyed by the machine. From then onwards, the ineffectiveness of the Labor Party in Parliament, the growth of Syndicalism on the continent; and the movement of the Shop Stewards during the last war stimulated the movement anew. Its most important theorists have been G. D. H. Cole, A. R. Orage and S. G. Hobson, and to a lesser extent R. H. Tawney, Bertrand Russell and H. N. Brailsford. Since the movement relied on the Trade Unions to bring about this new functional order, it was necessary to get their support. But this, in general, was not forthcoming. The Trade Unions followed a Fabian line. As they grew in importance they began to be transformed from preparatory schools for the revolution into schools for social reform. Later still, as they began to take over many functions of the state, they became collaborators in the administration of the state. Their officials became sharply separated from the members. Moreover, the Russian Revolution of 1917 turned the attention of the guild socialists to more immediate possibilities.

Marxist Socialism. The Russian Revolution, the post-war depression, the emasculation of the Labor Party by the philosophy of gradualness, the darkening menace of Fascism all helped to bring about a revival of Marxian Socialism and to make it a

stronger force than the size of the Communist Party would indicate. In Marxian socialism there is a definite break with the re-
visionism of Bernstein, Kautsky, MacDonald, etc. There is the
frank acceptance of the class struggle and of revolution as a
"locomotive of history." The state is regarded as an instrument
of domination of one class over another; its abolition must entail
destruction of its machinery by force if necessary and the conquest of power by a revolutionary class which will seize the
means of production and use them for the benefit of society until
the state has withered away and a classless society brought into
existence.

Many of the ablest economists and political scientists avowed
their acceptance of the Marxian position. Foremost among them
were Maurice Dobb, H. J. Laski and John Strachey. Another
indication of the influence of Marx may be seen in the number
of critics who arose to attack his economic and political views.
Among these were A. D. Lindsay, F. R. Salter, G. D. H. Cole,
J. A. Hobson, Henry Clay, H. W. B. Joseph, Bernard Shaw and
others.

IMPERIALISM

Herbert Spencer as he examined the future towards the close
of his life was filled with a deep foreboding and gloom. He
saw signs of increasing militarism, imperialism and political
burglaries. He saw a movement toward increasing regulation
and government control. "Is the movement" he asked himself
"towards the ownership of each man by others or towards ownership of each by himself." Undoubtedly the tendency was spreading towards the subjection of the individual by the state or as he
called it the Great Leviathan.

He did not see the elements of change that were leading to
a different world, a world so delicately integrated that regulation
is necessary. He himself lived at a time when profound changes
were taking place in the economic structure of society, and the
balance between social classes was altering. The very same Industrial Revolution with its message of peace, abundance and
prosperity was inevitably leading to a frenzied search for colonies,

markets, competition and imperialism. His militaristic and industrial types of society were not distinct but were phases of a social order that contained the seeds of its own transformation.

But he did not, like the Fabians and others support the Boer War and other ventures, and since his time many have gone deeply into the whole problem of imperialism as perhaps the most important one facing England. J. A. Hobson in his classical study (*Imperialism,* 1902) shows that imperialism not only leads to war but makes more precarious the freedoms enjoyed at home. John Strachey believes (*The Menace of Fascism,* 1932) that when the monopolistic stage of capitalism is reached by each state it must turn outwards in search of the markets which its own development has destroyed at home. This necessity makes war recurrent and inevitable under capitalism.

Whether these analyses or correct this question will become of increasing importance after the war. The economic dependence of Great Britain on the outside world has affected the entire people's view of life, explains the hold of imperialism and the difficulties of the Labor Party in formulating a policy towards the Empire, and accounts for a foreign policy, that wishing to preserve peace at any price, sacrificed one vital interest after another but to no avail. And at the conclusion of the war will it be possible for England still to govern India and receive tribute from nearly all the world? And what are the prospects of democracy and liberty in the face of these threats and the economic transformation of England into a monopoly state?

BIBLIOGRAPHY

ANGELL, NORMAN, *The Great Illusion* (New York: G. P. Putnam's Sons, 1912); *Human Nature and Peace Problem* (New York: Harper, 1935). Classic works, the recent events proved that Sir Norman overestimated the "rationality" of humanity.

BARKER, ERNEST, *Political Thought in England. From Herbert Spencer to the Present Day* (London: Williams and Norgate, 1915). See also his: *National Character and the Factors of its Formation* (New York: Harper, 1927); *Church and State* (London: Methuen, 1930).

BURNS, C. D., *Industry and Civilization* (New York: Allen and Unwin, 1925).

BRYCE, JAMES, *Modern Democracies* (New York: Macmillan, 1921). A classic exposition by the former British Ambassador to Washington.

CARPENTER, NILES, *Guild Socialism* (New York: Appleton, 1922). A historical and critical analysis.

CECIL, LORD HUGH, *Conservatism* (London: Williams and Norgate, 1912).

COLE, G. D. H., *Guild Socialism Restated* (London: Parson, 1920); *Self-Government in Industry* (London: Bell, 1920); *Social Theory* (London: Methuen, 1920). Standard works by a leading English proponent of guild socialism.

DICEY, A. V., *Lectures on the Relation between Law and Public Opinion in England During the Nineteenth Century* (London: Macmillan, 1914).

DICKINSON, G. L., *Justice and Liberty* (New York: Doubleday, Doran, 1909); *The International Anarchy* (New York: D. Appleton-Century, 1926); *War: Its Nature Cause and Cure* (New York: Macmillan, 1915).

DUNNING, W. A., *Political Theories from Rousseau to Spencer* (New York: The Macmillan Co., 1920).

FIGGIS, J. N., *Churches in the Modern State* (London: Longmans, Green & Co., 1913).

GINSBERG, MORRIS, *The Psychology of Society* (New York: E. P. Dutton & Co., 1928). A sociological approach.

GREEN, T. H., *Principles of Political Obligation* (London: Longmans, Green & Co., 1921).

HOBHOUSE, L. T., *Metaphysical Theory of the State* (London: Allen and Unwin, 1918); *Liberalism* (New York: Henry Holt, 1911); *Elements of Social Justice* (New York: Henry Holt, 1922); *The Rational Good* (New York: Henry Holt, 1921.

HEARNSHAW, J. C., *Democracy at the Cross Roads* (London: Macmillan, 1919).

HOBSON, S. G., *National Guilds and the State* (London: Bell, 1920).

HOBSON, J. A., *The Crisis of Liberalism* (London: P. G. King, 1909); *Towards International Government* (London: Allen and Unwin, 1915); *Imperialism* (New York: J. Patt Co., 1902); *Incentives in the New Social Order* (New York: Seltzer, 1925); *Democracy after the War* (New York: The Macmillan Co., 1917); *Free Thought in the Social Sciences* (New York: The Macmillan Co., 1926).

JOAD, C. E. M., *Modern Political Theory* (Oxford: Oxford University Press, 1924).

LASKI, HAROLD J., *Studies in the Problem of Sovereignty* (New Haven: Yale University Press, 1917); *Authority in the Modern State* (New Haven: Yale University Press, 1919); *Foundations of Sovereignty* (New York: Harcourt, Brace, 1921); *A Grammar of Politics* (New Haven: Yale University Press, 1925); *Studies in Law and Politics* (New Haven: Yale University Press ,1932); *Democracy in Crisis* (Chapel Hill, N. C.: University of North Carolina Press, 1933); *The State in Theory and Practice* (New York: The Viking Press, 1935); *Rice of European Liberalism* (London: C. Allen Unwin, 1936).

LINDSAY, A. D., *The Essentials of Democracy* (Philadelphia: University of Pennsylvania Press, 1929); *The Modern Democratic State* (New York: Oxford University Press, 1944).

LECKY, W. E., *Democracy and Liberty* (London: Longmans, Green and Co., 1896).

MACDOUGALL, WILLIAM, *The Group Mind* (New York: G. P. Putnam's Sons, 1920).

MAITLAND, F. W., *Collected Papers* (Cambridge: Cambridge University Press, 1919).

WEBB, SIDNEY AND BEATRICE, *Industrial Democracy* (London: Longmans, Green

ROBERTSON, J. M., *The Meaning of Liberalism* (London: Methuen, 1912).

ROCKOW, LEWIS, *Contemporary Political Thought in England* (London: Parsons, 1925).

Rosen, S. M., *Modern Individualism* (New York: Harper, 1937).

Russell, Betrand, *Political Ideals* (New York: Century Co., 1917); *Freedom and Organization* (London: Allen and Unwin, 1934); *Roads to Freedom* (New York: Henry Holt, 1919); *Prospects of Industrial Civilization* (New York: D. Appleton-Century Co., 1923); *Principles of Social Reconstruction* (New York: Cnetury Co., 1920).

Tawney, R. H., *The British Labor Movement* (New Haven: Yale University Press, 1925).

Wallas, Graham, *Human Nature in Politics* (London: Constable, 1908); *The Great Society* (London: Macmillan, 1914); *Our Social Heritage* (New Haven: Yale University Press, 1921); *The Art of Thought* (New York: Harcourt, Brace, 1926).

Wells, H. G., *The Open Conspiracy* (London: Hogarth Press, 1930).

Webb, Sidney and Beatrice, *Industria lDemocracy* (London: Longmans, Green & Co., 1920); *The Collapse of Capitalist Civilization* (New York: Harcourt, Brace, 1923); *History of Trade Unionism* (London: Longmans, Green and Co., 1920); *A Constitutional for the Socialist Commonwealth of Great Britain* (London: Longmans, Green and Co., 1920).

Woolf, L. S., *Imperialism and Civilization* (New York: Harcourt, Brace and Co., 1931).

Zimmern, A., *Nationality and Government* (New York: Robert M. McBride, 1918).

Chapter XXI

FRENCH POLITICAL THOUGHT

R. A. SCHERMERHORN

The opening of the twentieth century found France in the throes of the Dreyfus affair, a tragi-comedy of little import in itself, but profoundly significant of the deep internal division between the forces of liberty and order. Forty years later the tramp of Nazi hob-nailed boots in the streets of Paris brought to an end the Third Republic, and behind the German victory appeared the same two spectres, each warring with the other for the allegiance of Frenchmen, neither able to conquer, or willing to yield. Defeat by default is the bitter fruit of rupture. And whatever France may become, it is certain that only a closing of the breach will enable her to assume her national leadership on the continent.

THE DREYFUS AFFAIR AND "LES DEUX FRANCES"

Unfortunately the roots of the schism lie deeper; they began their growth in 1789, with the revolution that settled everything and settled nothing. Few outsiders can understand the hypnotic influence of the French Revolution on her later political theory and the interminable debate between those who clamored to "complete" the revolution, and those who sought to restore the unity of France through authority. The touchstone of political thought became, not the needs of France in contemporary life, but rather—the orientation of policy or philosophy toward the Revolution, the Commune, the Church, or the Republic. Political myopia was transformed into wisdom, and the straitjacket of French experience into universal principle. At times the quarrel between authoritarians and libertarians flamed into open hostility as in the Dreyfus affair; again it led to the deepest apathy and resignation, with only the slumbering embers of contravention left—enough so that each side was determined to let nothing be accomplished by its opponents, even if it could not win anything for itself. History decreed that Germany should strike at the time of paralysis; but the crisis might have had a different denouement.

At the opening of the century, the line between Dreyfusard and anti-Dreyfusard was roughly the line between Republicans and radicals on the one hand, with Monarchists and clericals on the other. The latter were convinced that "it is better that one man die for the people" than to have the honor of France impugned by acquitting that one man; the former felt that society was based on elemental individual rights, and for these rights to be denied to one would be to deny them to all. With the triumph of the Dreyfusards (though Dreyfus was pardoned and never acquitted), events took a new turn. For a time, the enemy of France became the church, and the radical anti-clericalism of Combes resulted, not only in disestablishment, but in forbidding the freedom of teaching by requiring priests and secular clergy to secure state diplomas, and in making churches and theological schools actually state property. This set-back led to a new alignment of conservative forces, this time behind a militant nationalist ideal.

NATIONALISM

Brunetière, Bourget and Barrès (the "three B's") were the outstanding leaders in the renaissance of traditional thought, with much of their inspiration coming from De Bonald and De Maistre who led the attack against the Revolution a century before. The burden of their plea is for a strong state, based on authority, the superiority of the aristocracy, and a proper feeling for localism and provincial life. All these elements have been levelled by the vulgarizing tendencies of the Republic, a tyranny of the majority leading to mediocrity and dead-level uniformity. France has been weakened in the process. To regain her soul she must begin with a profound consciousness of her uniqueness and eschew universalism. Everyone who is French must begin where he is, in his own province, his own city, and his own country—to put *la patrie* above all other considerations, and be true to his own destiny. Organic instinct must triumph over mechanical reason and patriotism will be the fulfillment of the ideal. For a time, the *Ligue de la Patrie française* became the organ and embodiment of these ideas, but its influence was soon superseded by the more radical conservatism of the *Action Française*.

THE "ACTION FRANCAISE"

The founder of the new movement was Charles Maurras, a fanatical royalist with a strong paranoid trend. On all sides he saw France being "betrayed" by Jews, Freemasons, Protestants and radicals who would like nothing better than to see France weakened. Parliament was an organ of fools or rogues or both, and a parliamentary government will always be strong in criticism and vacillating in policy. Power does not belong to the people but to the state and the stability of the state is dependent on the continuity of executive will exercised by a monarch who acts with "responsible arbitrariness". The institution that embodies authority in proper measure is the Church, and ecclesiastical power reveals the kind of imperial command that is characteristic of the healthy state. Therefore, when France is purged, the Church must be restored to her rightful position of dominance as the basic institution of social control. However, Maurras was not a believer in Christianity but in clericalism. The accusation made against De Maistre was even more true of Maurras—namely, that he was "Catholique par tête, Français par coeur". Unblushingly he called himself a "Catholic atheist" and thought it fortunate that the simple gospel of early Christianity with its dangerous acquiescence in individual liberty had been neutralized by the saner, more robust action of the hierarchy. In spite of his disbelief in church dogma, his strong defense of ecclesiasticism as a way of action made him extremely popular with the priesthood and the laity, while at the same time his fierce attacks and advocacy of direct action against liberals of all stripes, led to fear of reprisals on the part of the government. By 1926 the Pope acted, by decree, and prohibited all Catholics from participating in the *Action Française*, and it lost much of its strength. At the same time it had served to consolidate the forces of nationalism, conservatism, clericalism and authoritarianism, and its supporters formed a reservoir of popular interest later tapped by the *Croix de Feu*, as well as fascist and semi-fascist organizations.

LIBERALISM

French liberalism was probably strongest in the nineteenth century when its polemics against tyranny of all sorts aroused a chord of response in all lovers of freedom. In Quinet's words, "The Republic rests above all in the Divine equality of all hearts. Let us have belief in the greatness of man and in the immediate inspiration of the young men of France. Pour out the concord of love, of equality, out of an overflowing heart." The resistance of Michelet and of Hugo against the cruelties of the Second Empire was an inspiring example. But with the firm establishment of the Third Republic, after the debacle of 1870, came responsibility. The cry for liberty had to be implemented by political action, and time would not wait. Theoretically, republican Liberalism was a doctrine of freedom for all, but the attaining of parliamentary responsibility led to fear of "excesses" in the direction of increased privileges for industrial workers. Historically liberalism had been *laissez faire*, and it now allowed itself to be maneuvered into a position of defending bourgeois freedom in the name of order and law, giving the Socialists and Marxists an opportunity to attack it as a form of partiality. Furthermore, the Franco-Prussian war had a profound effect upon all parties, and the republicans felt constrained to support the military arm, and to join in panegyrics of patriotism that were not always clearly distinguishable from the nationalism of the three B's, or even Maurras. To make the confusion more complete, the Liberals were traditionally anti-clerical, and their attacks on the church, often justifiable in terms of curbing an independent power, aroused not only opposition, but the accusation that they were untrue to their own principles of freedom.

Thus the Liberals took a vacillating attitude toward fundamental questions like the authority of the state and the spread of democracy or parliamentary reform. Alfred Fouillée took a highly cautious view of the whole matter. The legislator must take into account the interdependence of different elements in the social organism, and refrain from giving aid to one element if it injures another. Social reforms should not be undertaken without a clear popular mandate and although revolution is sometimes justifiable, it should reflect the "general will" and promote the common welfare. All of these are statements that provoke no disagreement from most thinkers, and yet give no clear guidance for action.[1] On the other hand, a middle-of-the-road liberal like Emile Faguet was more hostile to equalitarianism. He believes that the government should have a democratic element in a Chamber of its own, so that the thought of the people is open and not hidden; and an aristocratic element "so that all that admits of precision shall not be smothered by that which is confused". Competence should be recognized and given its true place in government, though it is not exactly clear what this true place is, whether in executive, administrative or judicial function. On the whole he seems to favor it in the magistrate, but how the aristocrat is to be chosen remains less certain. He is devastating in his criticisms of ordinary democratic procedure and believes that forms of government perish "from the exaggeration of the principle from which their merit is derived". And it is Faguet's attack, not his positive doctrine that has had the greater influence.

A more independent line was taken by the Neo-Kantian Renouvier, who is certainly liberal in his individualism, but strikes out a different approach in his insistence on solidarity. He declares that social philosophy must begin with the polarity of individual freedom on the one hand and the inevitable de-

---

[1] Fouillée is chiefly remembered for his eclecticism reflected in the view that the state is a "contractual organism" which is both "natural" and "artificial" at the same time. It is an "organism born of an idea; and since that common idea involves a common will, we have a . . . contractual organism."

mand of solidarity on the other. The purpose of the state, which is a contractual agent, is to assure justice for those individuals who exercise their sovereignty through it. There is no collective being called the state that has its existence apart from the individual members, or to which they can delegate their will. The social contract that originates the state is only a "quasi-social-contract" or a fiction, but it is a fiction "which has its real counterpart in the nature of things". The conception of natural law is therefore tacitly affirmed. As for the Church, it has placed itself outside the social contract by its assertion of spiritual domination which violates the freedom of the individual, and therefore the state is justified in curbing its power in line with the demands of freedom and justice. By keeping justice before it as the supreme demand, the state may find it necessary to interfere with the activities of the privileged, in order that others may have their freedom restored. This may take the form of income taxes, limiting inheritance, socializing banks and transportation, and extending a social security system. However, the state cannot be expected to displace the activity of the individual in this regard; the latter must have freedom of association for labor organization, organizing collectives, and enlarging the sphere of activity in industrial society. On the whole, the state may aid in this program, though it should not initiate it.

Moving further toward the left, we find the doctrine of "solidarisme" which had considerable influence in French thought at the turn of the century. Léon Bourgeois, who first popularized the conception, emphasized with Kropotkin the importance of mutual aid as the force in history, making society and the state possible. This solidarity arising from the process of mutual aid, eventually implies a relation of quasi-contract between the individual and the state, and the idea of benefits received instead of promises made. To be a citizen means to acknowledge benefits and to assume obligations. Duties predominate over rights—a truly positivist strain. Especially are these duties evident in the case of property ownership, and in the doctrine of Joseph Charmont (a later exponent of the view) when the state insists that owners of industrial property are liable for the health

and safety of their employees, this is not a restric
liberty of action but simply a reassertion of their
now assume new form, due to new conditions. T
this school later formed part of the theoretical f
the Radical Socialist party.

RADICALISM

Also represented in the ideology of Radical S
the writings of Alain and Anatole France. The fo
a time the representative par excellence for "radic
French Radical party which was formed in 1901.
spective of forty years later, it appears that the chie
of the radicals were negative. They stood for opposition to the
Army, the Church, and to the moneyed classes. With other
Dreyfusards, they formed The League of the Rights of Man
and of the Citizen to arouse France against the unholy alliance
among the forces of reaction. Alain himself was not a socialist
but he believed that the enemies of radicalism and socialism were
the same, and declared that the chief function of an aroused
electorate was to check the abuse of power by irresponsible officials, and by its vigilance prevent the usurpation of authority
by moribund parliaments and bureaucrats. The basis of this
theory is a firm belief in equality and the right of every citizen
to see to it that the laws are properly made, honestly administered, and directed towards the eradicating of economic inequality. Anatole France carried the banner of radicalism still
farther by a withering attack on militarism, by his insistence
that capitalism leads straight to warlike activities and the profession of the "butcher". War and economic exploitation are
the twin horrors of society and they both depend on the union
of capitalism with imperial and colonial expansion. Of course,
for Anatole France, the bitterest enemy was the church that
tried to stifle science, freedom and innocent enjoyment. Until
the church is brought low, civilization cannot expect to be free
in mind or in action; by its authority it has corrupted the natural
pity of man and turned it into slavish obedience. On the whole,
Anatole France is best remembered as a destroyer of shams, a

merciless critic of institutions, and an emotional believer in reason who recalls the days of the enlightenment. For him, no type of government is without its defects, and democracy is defended chiefly because it is the least faulty of all systems. Science, which gives man a new control over nature, and breaks the bonds of tradition, may bring improvement in the future. But his skepticism hardly allows much in the way of prophecy.

SOCIALISM

Allied with the Radicals in the leftist bloc were the Socialists. These were, in 1900, a loose working federation of Marxists and trade unionists who developed no distinct original theories. Under the leadership of Guesde, they expelled Millerand from the organization for participating in the cabinet of Waldeck-Rousseau, by voting "no" to the question, "Does the class-war permit the entry of a socialist into a bourgeois government?" Guesde, as the orthodox leader, worked for the increase of socialist representation in parliament with the idea that when the increase became sufficient, the socialist majority would then take over the state and make it an instrument of the workers. But this aim did not allow a socialist to accept a post in the cabinet—that would be "collaboration" instead of class war. This position Guesde held with grim strictness until 1914 when he took office in the "union sacrée" during World War I. Orthodox Guesdism was really orthodox Marxism, with only slight modifications. It may be described as an attempt to give the modern state a proletarian content, and political effort in the present was only a means to an end—the final revolution. Even at the time when a socialist majority was attained, it could hardly be expected that the bourgeois would submit without a struggle; but if the conflict did come, legitimacy would rightfully belong to the socialists.

The most influential of the socialist leaders, however, was Jaurès. Revisionist by conviction and diplomat by temperament, he served as the liaison agent between orthodox Guesdism and the parliamentary bourgeois. He stated clearly that the great democratic changes were sometimes accomplished by peaceful means, and sometimes by revolution. Universal suffrage was attained in France only by force of arms, in Germany it was conceded by an all-powerful monarchy, in England it was prepared for by a long succession of reforms. Therefore, socialism, hesitating between a pacific and revolutionary policy, should recognize that neither of them needs repudiation, but that events will dictate what is to be done. And, he added significantly, there has been no real gesture of revolution in France for thirty years (Commune of 1871). What was most notable was that Jaurès had the almost universal respect of all parties through his gift of reconciling opposing claims and yet maintaining fundamental convictions.[2] His murder on the outbreak of the World War left a gap in French life that has never been filled.

SYNDICALISM

Still farther to the left were the anarchists, and the syndicalists, the anti-politicals. Sharing the doctrine of class war with the socialists, these leaders finally captured the imagination of a part of the working class movement in 1895 when they convinced the Fedération des Bourses de Travail, a local association of trade unions, that revolutionary syndicalism was the wave of the future. A program was adopted that was both anti-capitalist and anti-bourgeois state. Syndicalism could not compromise with bourgeois institutions, whether economic or political; the workers were to perfect their organization and undermine capitalism in every way by sabotage, infiltration of the army, and calling strikes. At a favorable moment, when capitalism and the state are sufficiently weakened, the time would come for the General Strike, the great moment of liberation for the proletariat. The wheels of industry and government would come to a stop, the workers would seize the factories and set up a new order based on essential trades and occupations, while the state was left to die a natural death. Government was to be replaced by syndicates and a form of association set up without the need

---

[2] An exception to this was his former friend Charles Péguy (see below) who could not forgive his deviations and compromises.

of force to perpetuate its injustices, being a free alliance of the workers who belong together in functional orders.

Perhaps the syndicalist who captured the popular imagination most was Georges Sorel. Space is insufficient to present the various twists and turnings of his beliefs and allegiances which were many. He is chiefly known for his volume *Réflexions sur la Violence,* although his *Illusions du Progrès* is equally important. Although not a representative syndicalist, Sorel became better known because of the peculiar charm and force of his thought. His protest against the bourgeois and the state was a moral one, based upon his conviction that the anti-Dreyfusards, to which he early belonged, had eventually used their influence and moral superiority in political log-rolling and self-advancement. They became ensnared in the bourgeois illusion that progress was a law of life, a fantasy that stemmed from the equally fatuous bourgeois of the eighteenth century. Progress leads to complacent satisfaction and prevents man from seeing, with Bergson, that each moment is pregnant with possibilities and that he who dares can begin a new and fresh creation. This the bourgeois with their bulging bank accounts and their fear of upsetting the apple-cart can never know. It was what made the early Christian martyrs attack the ancient Roman order with perfect confidence, and win. The revolutionary movement can never become truly great until it grasps this truth and does not wait for history to do its work. Sorel ridicules Jaurès who believes in the simultaneous ruin of the capitalist spirit and the revolutionary spirit, so that he can eventually dance on the ruins. But this is because the notion of bourgeois progress and compromise has penetrated into the very ranks of the proletarians and socialists themselves. It is only cowardice in disguise, the cowardice of their limited and mechanical existence. The proletarian should realize that he is in daily contact with real existence and with the direct denial of all the illusions of the democrats and economists, in his warfare with the powers that be.

Reforms are not possible without a totally new order. Syndicalists propose to destroy the state, not live off it; they are one with Marx in refusing to replace one minority with another. They must therefore set themselves resolutely against all present organization,—they are anti-state, anti-patriotic, and anti-capitalist. In replacing the old world with a really moral order, they will revive the pure essence of battle. They can no more compromise with what exists than the early Christians compromsied, and the older Church Militant will be replaced by the Militant Socialism[3] of the future; the difference will be that proletarians will be ready to kill as well as to die. The popular mind lives on myths that present in symbolic form the hopes and desires of men; such was the myth of Christ's return. To keep the élan of the workers at fighting pitch, the Myth of the General Strike, will serve the same purpose. Every local strike will then be a smaller model of the apocalyptic day when the General Strike will liberate the proletarians from all servitude to the existing order, when they can, at one blow wipe out the whole rotten bourgeois system. The units of violence would be the syndicates, and though Sorel did not picture the future society clearly, he was sure of one thing: there would be no intellectuals, politicians or business leaders in it. Perhaps he saw some sign of this appearing in the Soviet government, for he added an apology for Lenin in the seventh edition of the *Réflexions,* closing with the words, "May I, before descending to the tomb, see the proud bourgeois democracies so triumphant today, humiliated (at last)." At the same time, it is significant that Sorel's frank apology for violence was one of the inspirations of Mussolini's Fascism in whose boldness Sorel saw some of his hopes realized. But Fascism's glorification of the state was anything but Sorellian.

CHARLES PEGUY

Parallel with the revolutionaries of the early twentieth century was another figure who began as a Socialist and ended as a freelance, in fact a leftist without party and a Catholic without the church, but most important of all, a man. We refer to Charles Péguy. Most of all he will be remembered as the per-

---

[3] In the *Illusions,* Sorel speaks of the society of the future as Socialism, in the *Réflexions* as syndicalism.

sonification of individual conscience, and yet his importance for political philosophy is unquestionable. Today in her hours of darkness, France turns again to him as to a light. Alexander Werth declares, that if France had any sort of spiritual guidance as the second World War broke, it could be traced to Péguy, who was known, however, by only a few, not the masses.[4] The same could be said of his influence during his own life time.

Péguy began life as a peasant and he remained faithful to peasant simplicity to the end. Leaving the church in his early school days, he became a Socialist and joined the Dreyfusards with abandon. His chief importance in the early years was as editor of a periodical, *Cahiers de la Quinzaine,* to which Jaurès, Sorel, Benda, Halévy, and Romain Rolland contributed. All of his own writings appeared first in this organ. First of all, he attacked destitution which he distinguished from poverty. The line between the two was absolute. In poverty, morality and even a touch of happiness was possible, never in destitution. To remove the destitute from their destitution is the first of all social duties and none can come before it. Liberty, Equality and Fraternity, the three watchwords of the revolution are themselves unequal in value. The first and last are of primary importance, while the second is a "Duty of convenience". It is fraternity that commands the body politic to lift all men out of destitution.

For Péguy, the evils of the capitalist order are mechanization and vulgarization and the killing of the joy of work. He protests, with Marx, against the dehumanization of man, but in quite different terms. He views with pity the workmen who sabotage and go on strike, whose arms and hands long to be occupied, whose minds and hearts are disgusted at the absurd necessity to injure their tools because the "bourgeois" have told them that this would bring the socialist revolution. It is the bourgeois who have corrupted everything, who have treated man's work as a thing to be bought and sold on the exchange, and the laborer accepted his status with a kind of dull finality.

Péguy's view of politics grew out of his disillusionment with

[4] Alexander Werth, *The Twilight of France* (New York: Harpers, 1942), p. 345.

the Dreyfusards, especially those who hesitated to come in until they saw how the tide was turning, and then capitalized on their success. All causes, he declared, begin with the mystics and end with the politicians. It was certainly true of the Revolution of 1789. No one can overestimate the first, fine, careless rapture with which the Republicans grasped for the ideal, least of all the youth of the twentieth century who forget that there was once a Republican mysticism, and that the heroes of the past must be matched by the heroes of the present. The degradation of mysticism into politics is a kind of social law, but politics can be wiped out, only by a new mysticism based on the same moral fervour. Hence, he opposed the *Action Française* not because it had enthusiasm but because it substituted hate and invective for moral ideals; it failed to face the primary task of the age, which is the destruction of destitution.

The influence of Bergson can be seen in Péguy as in Sorel. "The forces of knowledge really correspond to ourselves, while our vital forces are greater than ourselves . . . We are engaged in an immense action the end of which we do not see. Perhaps it has no end. This action will contain all possible surprises for us. Everything is great, inexhaustible."

Anti-semitism drew from Péguy unmitigated scorn. Israel asks only to live in peace and everywhere she meets the sword. Though the prophets arose in Israel, she herself "asks only this: to give the prophets no ground for prophecy". Every inch of her body aches with the wounds inflicted by others, chiefly Christians, and the sins of which she is accused are far more common to the followers of Christ.

Unlike many of the Socialists before 1914, Péguy was not a pacifist. "There is a well-known system which has always been called the system of peace at any price . . . where honor is cheaper than life . . . What madness to link together the Declaration of the Rights of Man with a Declaration of Peace. As if a Declaration of Justice were not instantaneously and in itself a declaration of war . . . I come not to send peace, but a sword."

His religion is individual and yet includes within it a strange solidarity. He thinks of all modern faith as a private belief hemmed in by a sea of unbelievers, and yet asserts that true Christianity is made up of sinners who are willing to hold hands out to each other. The only true Christian charity comes from Jesus himself, and consists of constant communion with the poor; it is the poor who are the favorites in the kingdom of God and it would be unfair if everyone did not have the right to be poor. On the whole, Péguy's religious writings are composed of a series of aphorisms, sometimes without logical inconsistency, but united by a kind of fierce and unwavering compassion for the underprivileged and an eternal submission to the demands of faith. All of his works show an intuitional rather than rational approach to social problems.

SYNDICALISM OF THE CIVIL SERVANTS

The various leftist factions became united behind a more nationalist program during World War I. Among the syndicalists, the movement toward a more moderate and less revolutionary position continued with a continuing belief in the new functional order of society where administrative management, whether in the economic or the political order, would eventually be taken over by those who were responsible for the daily operations of the organization. The majority group of the *Confédération Générale du Travail* gradually adopted this compromise with the existing order under the leadership of Léon Jouhaux and Maxime Leroy, while the minority split off to affiliate itself with the doctrines and organization of the Communist International under the name of the *Confédération Generale du Travaile Unitaire*. Jouhaux and Leroy with their followers remained anticapitalist but gave up the doctrine of violence, partly as a result of the war experience, and partly because of the conviction that the separation between management and finance in private economy weakened capitalism from within while arbitrary political demands conflicted with the regularity of public services in the same way; thus the politico-economic system would slowly strangle itself. The patent weakness and irrationality of this system that separated direction from efficient management would eventually become apparent to all, and in time the syndicate and *fonctionnaires* would take over the administration with the consent of the community and without class war.

Especially interesting to the student of political theory is the emergence of the new syndicalism of the civil servants. With the rise of industrialism, the state simply became another employer, like any capitalist. Under the old legal doctrine of the Republic, these employees were merely agents of the state and did not have any voice of their own; the bureaucracy should remain non-political and responsible only to the governing body. But with new conditions, the *fonctionnaires*, especially in the lower brackets, came to recognize that their position was insecure; it was often dependent upon the whim of some cabinet minister or politician who was interested, not in administrative duties efficiently accomplished, but in seeing to it that appointees were in line with the dominant political philosophy, or that places were filled with friends and hangers-on. The civil servants therefore came into direct opposition with the state which was always semi-authoritarian and monistic in theory as well as practice. The higher *fonctionnaires* had security and so sided with the Chamber, while the lower fonctionnaires were driven more and more in the direction of the trade union and syndicalist movement to protect themselves. They began to employ the strike as a weapon to the great alarm of the politicians. The jurists, upholding the traditional order, claimed that administrative syndicalism was not parallel with labor organization and that the state was not a civil employer; it was the supreme organ of the people, above all divisions and groups within the nation.

The dilemma arose from the peculiar growth of the French Republic. As Laski shows, the French monarchy was monistic, and no associations could exist without its permission. When the Republic was formed, it carried on this tradition, and even Rousseau felt that a loyalty to any intermediary body was a kind of disloyalty to the state. Not until 1884 did Waldeck-Rousseau allow freedom of association and not until 1901 was this firmly established. But although this was allowed for political parties and finally the labor syndicate, it came as a kind of *bouleversement* to the average Republican bourgeois that this same reasoning should be applied to civil servants themselves, even to the extent of bureaucrats allying themselves with plans for a general strike. In his eyes, this amounted to nothing short of treason.

Paul-Boncour, the spokesman with Leroy of civil service syndicalism, asserts that their doctrines are only the logical outcome of completing the Revolution, that it is now a question of extending previous principles to the economic as well as the political order. Functional groups must now maintain their relations with the state on the basis of free contract. Their interests, as well as their aims, are therefore so nearly identical with those of the syndicate, that for all practical purposes, they are one. And Leroy declares that the change of authority which syndicalism demands is a change from arbitrary power to technical science and functional competence in terms of the new network of organizations which is the real fulcrum of modern society. In essence it is a new federalism attempting to work on vocational rather than geographical lines, pluralistic and flexible enough to cope with the stresses and strains of mature industrialism. In a way it is a return to the older idea of Proudhon that the workshop will eventually take the place of the Government.

NEO-POSITIVISM

The federalist principle is given a more solid foundation by Léon Duguit whose postivistic interpretation of law is based squarely on Durkheim's conception of solidarity. Instead of an individual with rights and a person-state, governing in the name of these rights but with a sovereignty superior to them, he insists with Durkheim that the solidarity of the community is anterior to all law, and that society is a collection of groups, each with its own function, each with its own rules of service. These rules of service are the source of all law, and they need no defense in terms of "metaphysical" abstractions like sovereignty or rights. Solidarity imposes, first of all, duties, and the rules of laws that arise from these duties are simply the most expeditious techniques for realizing the functions of solidarity. In this way, the law is anterior to the state. It follows that the state is not a fictitious sovereign body or nation-person but a social organization resulting from the division of labor in which there are governors and governed; it is the instrument through which the needed rules of service (laws) are made and enforced, a convenient agency that finds its justification purely in the value of its activities in terms of group needs. It is a public service corporation consisting of a group of governing individuals and hence has no abstract sovereignty, though it may constrain the individual in the interests of public order. Nor is the statute a command of the state but a kind of organic rule of service which is modified to suit changing circumstances. The rule of *ultra vires*, so important for French law, is not based upon a plea that individual right is violated but rather that the organic rule of service has been cancelled.

The state as the collection of governing individuals must, however, see that all individuals in the community have the opportunity to develop their personal activities, and may therefore engage in many services that would ordinarily be called socialistic. But this arises again from the solidarity which does not "admonish" but is a "fact". Duguit extends this notion of solidarity to the wide variety of associations in civilized society, each of which has its proper function in cooperation with the others, and with the governing body which is simply another association. Thus he recognizes the essential principle of syndicalists.

INDEPENDENT THOMISM

Still partly in line with the federalists, but blending it with Thomist and Catholic overtones is Jacques Maritain. Although the leader of an "integral humanism" which is essentially a minority movement in Catholicism, Maritain has a greater hold on those who are turning away from secularistic values outside the faith than on the traditionalists who accept the usual inflexibilities of clericalism. Maritain believes that wisdom, not science, should rule. The state should be autonomous in its own sphere, while recognizing that it deals with purely intermediary or "infravalent" ends. Ecclesiastical dominance in temporal affairs is definitely gone—no longer can the secular sword serve the church as its unquestioning instrument. In its place will come freedom for man to realize his highest ends in a pluralism of association. The state will utilize the high offices of the church, and the church that of the state in a partnership of ends. Christian teaching will be given in its proper place at the apex of the curriculum because the state will recognize that the highest aim of man, salvation through personal freedom and through worship, will be the only effective moral security for social organization. In the spirit of free association, the state will ask religious societies to aid in works of charity and welfare.

In this pluralistic order there will be universal suffrage for both men and women and active political participation for all. Legislative and executive will be combined instead of "worn-out" parliamentarism, and as a representative body, will work closely with the governmental "organs" or bureaus which are "indirectly" elected. In one sense the state will be authoritarian, in that it will aim to preserve freedom by wisdom, recognizing that no freedom is absolute. True to the Thomist conception, it should govern in line with measures suitable for each association or order, and recognize as St. Thomas did, that in the atmosphere of social conflicts and contingencies, every kind of evil cannot be punished.

Coextensive with the pluralist state will come a new co-proprietorship in industry, in which the sense of belonging and sharing will characterize both workers and managers. Like the volutionaries, Maritain is definitely anti-capitalist, but for a different reason: the capitalist order has enthroned material ends without recognizing their extrinsic character. Economism along with politicism must be transcended by a new moral order. The false partiality of capitalism has either dehumanized or plutocratised the workers, thereby demeaning the nobility of the proletarian worker that Sorel so much desired. Economism has spelled tragedy for Sorel's principles, in which Maritain finds much of grandeur and dignity. Only when the trade unions of the future become permeated with theocratic humanism and a new sense of partnership in the direction of industry and the state, will the new moral order of the future arrive.

The management of states must be directed by a morality of its own, one which is uniquely oriented to the peculiar and special properties of group life. It is impossible to apply purely individualistic ethics to societies, and this is the truth in the Macchiavellian principle. Social life is the world of contingencies, of competing loyalties and of innumerable gradations of evil and of good, the realm of existence, not essence. Government must therefore know how to choose the lesser evil, without cynicism, but without apology, while never losing sight of the spiritual principles beyond the temporal order.

RUIN AND RENASCENCE

Through all the twists and turnings of political thought in the twentieth century appear the visages of *les deux Frances.* They appear with special clarity in the debacle of the late 30's when their roles were curiously reversed, as a result of the Popular Front when the Communists, Socialists, Radical Socialists and a few bourgeois liberals became the apostles of order, while the conservatives under the leadership of the *Croix de Feu,* the *Cagoulards* and the *Camelots du Roi* openly threatened a coup d'état. Yellow journals like *Gringoire, Candide* and *Le Jour* inflamed the public with feeling against the "enemies of France. 'To be a true patriot one must be' against communism, against the Popular Front, together with the enemies of the Soviet Union." The Nazis were doing what everyone wanted— namely, to protect Europe from the Red danger. When Czechoslovakia was abandoned, it was argued that France could give her no effective aid, that only the Russians could, and that France would therefore be aiding Russia at incommensurate cost to herself. "Rather Hitler than Léon Blum" became a popular catchword. On the other side of the ledger the trade unions made the task of their own government no easier; at the slightest sign of compromise they called strikes that interfered with armament and with public safety. Without these demonstrations, the course of political development might have changed, but it would only have put off the inevitable crisis. With the coming of Daladier the Right was appeased and the Left angered; with war coming closer, Daladier could now call upon the national spirit to condemn all strikes in the name of national security. But neither his followers nor his opponents any longer believed in France. They had faith only in their own ideology, in the Rightist program or the Leftist. The unity of the Republic in a National Government, proposed by Blum, had become utterly impossible. Parliamentarism was regarded by its friends with despair or pity, by the populace with indifference, by its enemies with scorn and contempt. Coupled with this was the insistence of Nazi propaganda that democracy was perishing of its own internal weakness, a judgment that was too uncomfortably near the facts. It is hard to avoid the suspicion that the final capitulation of Petain under the slogan of *La France aux Français* meant only a chance to buttress conservative France under the protection of foreign arms.

With the occupation came a new and wider awakening to the necessity for national unity, to a feeling that the whole was more vital than its parts. The De Gaulle Committee, which began as a movement of only one element in *Les Deux Frances,* with the watchword of the Republican revolutionaries, *Liberté, Egalité, Fraternité,* is slowly showing signs of amalgamation with more conservative forces in behalf of a united France under a Fourth Republic. With the allegiance of Maritain, the committee will surely bring in more Catholic elements. And if, in the Fourth Republic, the breach is healed between the irreconcilables, the temporary humiliation of France may yet prove her political future to be a new variety in unity without fatal chasms. There are unmistakable signs that political thought of the France of the future is today being reborn.

BIBLIOGRAPHY

Among the general works in English, the following will be found useful: E. P. Chase, Robert Valeau and Raymond Leslie Buell, *Democratic Governments in Europe* (New York: Nelson, 1935); F. W. Coker, *Recent Political Thought* (New York: Appleton Century, 1934); Herman Finer, *The Theory and Practice of Modern Government* (2 vols., London: Methuen, 1932; Raymond G. Gettell, *History of Political Thought* (New York: Century, 1924); A. Grandin, *Bibliographie générale des Sciences juridiques, politiques, économiques, et sociales de 1800 à 1925-6* (Paris: Recueil Sirey, 1926-39); J. T. Shotwell, ed., *Governments of Continental Europe* (New York: The Macmillan Co., 1940); Roger Soltau, *French Political Thought in the Nineteenth Century* (New Haven: Yale University Press, Co., 1931); Margaret Spahr, *Readings in Recent Political Philosophy* (New York: The Macmillan Co., 1935).

The readings on French liberalism may include Léon Bourgeois, *Solidarité* (3rd ed. Paris, 1902); Joseph Charmont, *La renaissance du droit naturel* (2nd ed., Paris, 1927); Emile Faguet, *The Cult of Incompetence* (tr. by Beatrice Barstow, London: Murray, 1911); Emile Faguet, *Questions Politiques* (1902); Alfred Fouillée *La science sociale contemporaine* (2nd ed., Paris, 1885); Alfred Fouillée, *Le socialisme et la sociologie réformiste* (Paris, 1909); Charles Gide and Charles Rist, *History of Economic Doctrines* (tr. by R. Richards, Boston, 1915); Henri Michel, *L'idée de l'état* (2nd ed., Paris, 1896); Charles Renouvier, *Philosophie Analytique de l'histoire* (1896); Charles Renouvier, *Science de la Morale* (1869); Charles Renouvier, *Uchronie* (*l'utopie dans l'histoire*) (Paris: Alcan, 1901); also articles by Renouvier in *La Critique Philosophique;* Guido Ruggiero, *The History of European Liberalism* (tr. by R. G. Collingwood, London: Oxford, 1927).

For French nationalism consult Maurice Barrès, *Scènes et Doctrines du Nationalisme* (1904); Paul Bourget, *Pages et Nouvelles Pages de Critique et de Doctrine* (1912-22); Ferdinand Brunetière, *Discours de Combat* (Paris: Perrin, 1903); Georges Guy-Grand, *La philosophie nationaliste* (n. d.); Jacques Maritain, *The Things That Are Not Caesar's* (tr. by J. F. Scanlan, New York: Scribner's Sons, 1930); Charles Maurras, *"L'Action Francaise" et la Religion Catholique* (1913); Charles Maurras, *Enquête sur la Monarchie* (1900); Charlotte Touzalin Muret, *French Royalist Doctrines Since the Revolution,* (New York: Columbia University Press, 1933).

The older Radicalism is represented by Alain (non de plume of M. Chartier), *Les Propos d'Alain* (1906 ff.); Alain, *La Politique Radicale* (n. d.); Anatole France, *Crainquebille* (Paris: Renaissance, 1903); Anatole France, *L'Eglise et La Republique* (Paris: Pelletan, 1904).

French socialism receives special attention in Jules Guesde, *Le Socialisme au Jour le Jour* (1905); Jean Jaurès, *Études socialistes* (1901); Jean Jaurès, *L'Organisation socialiste de la France, l'Armée Nouvelle* (1911); Georges Weill, *Histoire du Mouvement social en France* 1852-1910 (Paris: Alcan, 1911).

For Péguy's philosophy consult Daniel Halévy, *Charles Péguy et les Cahiers de la quinzaine* (Paris: Payot, 1918); Emmanuel Mounier, *La pensée de Charles Péguy* (Paris: Plon, 1931); Charles Péguy, *Basic Verities* (tr. by Ann and Julian Green, New York: Pantheon Books, 1943); Charles Péguy, *Notre Jeunesse* (Paris: Gallimard, 1933); Charles Péguy, *Oeuvres Choisis* 1900-1910 (Paris: B. Grasset, 1911); Jerome Tharaud, *Notre Cher Péguy* (Paris: Plon, 1926).

Syndicalism, both revolutionary and administrative, is represented in the following: Anton Acht, *Der moderne französische Syndikalismus* (Jena, 1911); Georges Guy-Grand, *La philosophie syndicaliste* (Paris, 1911); Leon Jouhaux, *Le syndicalisme et la C. G. T.* (1920); Harold Laski, *Authority in the Modern State* (New Haven: Yale University Press, 1919); Maxime Leroy, *Les Techniques nouvelles du syndicalisme* (Paris, 1921); Louis Levine, *Syndicalism in France* (2nd ed., New York, 1914); Georges Sorel, *Les illusions du progrès* (4th ed., Paris: Rivière, 1927); Georges Sorel, *Reflections on Violence* (tr. by T. E. Hulme: New York, 1914); Savel Zimand, *Modern Social Movements* (New York: H. W. Wilson, 1921).

Of special value for Duguit's positivism are Léon Duguit, *Le Droit social; le Droit individuel et les Transformations de l'état* (1908); Léon Duguit, *Law in the Modern State* (tr. by Frida and Harold Laski, London: Allen and Unwin, 1921); Léon Duguit, *Souveraineté et Liberté* (1922); *Modern French Legal Philosophy, Modern Legal Philosophy Series,* Vol. VII, pp. 237-344 (Boston: Macmillan, 1916).

Maritain has been extensively translated and the following English texts will do justice to his political thought, together with one French work: Jacques Maritain, *Christianisme et democratie* (New York: Éditions de la Maison française, 1943); Jacques Maritain, *Freedom in the Modern World* (tr. by R. O'Sullivan, New York: Scribners, 1936); Jacques Maritain, *The Rights of Man and Natural Law* (tr. by Doris C. Anson, New York: Charles Scribner's Sons, 1943); Jacques Maritain, *True Humanism* (tr. by Margot Adamson, New York: Scribner's Sons, 1938).

Other general works of value for French politics and philosophy are: Julius Benda, *The Treason of the Intellectuals* (tr. by R. Aldington, New York: W. W. Morrow, 1928); Edouard Berth, *Méfaits des Intellectuels* (1914); D. Halévy, *Apologie pour notre Passé* (Paris, 1908); D. Halévy, *Décadence de la liberté* (Paris, Grasset, 1931); D. Parodi, *La philosophie contemporaine en France* 2nd ed., Paris, Alcan, 1920).

Concerning political thought and the Fall of France, see Edouard Berth, *Das Kapital aux Réflexions sur la Violence* (Paris: Rivière, 1934); Albert Guérard, *The France of Tomorrow* (Cambridge: Harvard University Press, 1942; Jacques Maritain, *France My Country Through the Disaster* (New York: Longmans, Green, 1941); A. D. Sertillanges, *La vie française, Montreal* (Les Editions Variés, 1943); Yves Simon, *La grand Crise de la République française* (Montreal: Éditions de l'arbre, 1941); Alexander Werth, *The Twilight of France* (New York: Harpers, 1942).

ENGLISH WORKS

BENDA, JULIUS, *The Treason of the Intellectuals* (tr. by R. Aldington, New York: W. W. Morrow, 1928). A searching analysis of the perversion of intellectual and spiritual interests by narrow nationalism, opportunism and the *raison d'état*, with special reference to France.

BUTHMAN, WILLIAM CURT, *The Rise of Integral Nationalism in France* (New York: Columbia University Press, 1939). A solid and thoroughgoing account of French nationalistic theory from the Franco-Prussian War to the 1920's with detailed accounts of Maurras and the *Action Francaise.* Has extensive bibliography.

CHASE, E. P., VALEAU, ROBERT, AND BUELL, RAYMOND LESLIE, *Democratic Governments in Europe* (New York: Nelson, 1935). The section on French government and politics by Robert Valeur, pp. 261-556, is a judicious and sagacious review of the main structure of the French government as typified by the period of the 1930's.

COKER, F. W., *Recent Political Thought* (New York: Appleton-Century, 1934). Probably the most useful short compendium of European political philosophy from the mid-nineteenth century to the early 1930's. Arrangement is topical rather than national. Helpful bibliographic aids for each section.

PIERRE, COT, *Triumph of Treason* (Chicago and New York: Ziff-Davis, 1944). A review of the disintegration and fall of France from the Popular Front government to the Vichy regime. Rather strongly leftist with a journalistic flair for the *thèse de complot*. Well documented.

EHRMAN, HENRY W., "The Blum Experiment and the Fall of France," *Foreign Affairs, XX* (1941-42), pp. 152-164. Presents the thesis that the timidity of the Popular Front contributed to the weakening of French morale. An alternative to Cot's view.

FINER, HERMAN, *The Theory and Practice of Modern Government* (2 vols., London: Methuen, 1932). A comparative study of British, French, German and American government in terms of both theory and practical adjustment. For advanced students.

GETTELL, RAYMOND G., *History of Political Thought* (New York: Century, 1924). This volume gives a broad review of political thought from the ancient Greeks to twentieth century Europe. Chapters 26 to 31 will give a short general background which is useful for readers relatively unfamiliar with the field.

GUERARD, ALBERT, *The France of Tomorrow* (Cambridge: Harvard University Press, 1942). Lively political essays on the possibilities of new political trends in France, with especially provacative reading on democratic government without parliament.

JACQUES MARITAIN, "Religion and Politics in France," *Foreign Affairs* XX (1942), pp. 266-281. The best short survey of clericalism and anti-clericalism in France since the Middle Ages.

POL, HEINZ, *Suicide of a Democracy* (tr. by Heinz and Ruth Norden, New York: Reynal and Hitchcock, 1940). A highly readable account of internal political weakness in France from 1936 to 1940. From a refugee's perspective.

RICE, HOWARD C., *France 1940-1942* (Cambridge: Harvard Co-operative Society, 1942). A series of invaluable documents issued from pre-Vichy, Vichy, German, and Free French sources. Makes vivid the changing life of France in two turbulent years.

SHOTWELL, JAMES T., Ed., *Governments of Continental Europe* (New York, The Macmillan Co., 1940). Professor R. K. Gooch presents a first rate analysis of the government and politics of France, of which part III on politics and parties in the Third Republic will be of special value to students of French political thought.

SIMON, YVES R., *The Road to Vichy* 1918-1938 (tr. by J .A. Corbett and George J. McMorrow, New York: Sheed and Ward, 1942). A liberal French Catholic describes the fall of France in terms of shifting political alliances. He does not spare the clericals.

SOLTAU, ROGER, *French Political Though in the Nineteenth Century* (New Haven: Yale University Press, 1931). This book is more generous than its title indicates, since the third section is devoted chiefly to the twentieth century. Shows remarkable independence of judgment and excellent literary qualities.

SPAHR, MARGARET, *Readings in Recent Political Philosophy* (New York: The Macmillan Co., 1935). An important source book for those who have no access to first hand writings of modern political philosophers.

TISSIER, PIERRE, *Government of Vichy* (London: Harrap, 1942). One of the earliest and most authoritative accounts of Vichy's beginnings. Indispensable for the advanced student.

Chapter XXII

GERMAN PRE-NAZI POLITICAL THOUGHT

FRIEDRICH CARL SELL

A nation, for a long time known as averse to political radicalism, moving suddenly from extreme to extreme, this is the spectacle Germany has offered since 1914.

The rule of a constitutional crypto-absolutism and of feudal patronage was overthrown by a more turbulent than violent revolution, and this revolution was channelled into a democracy, run by inconspicuous middle class people without spectacular success, but in a decent way. In turn, this republic was wiped out, giving way to a state of such concentrated power as the Western world had never seen before and under a leadership of unequalled corruption.

Display of servility and excesses of released slaves alternated during that period. A similar lack of balance characterizes the swift changes in the intellectual and moral attitude of the Germans during the past century. From the idealism of the age of the great poets and philosophers, they plunged headlong into materialism, money making and militarism being the signature of the so-called Wilhelminian era. Its overconfident arrogance was followed by dejection and almost destructive self-criticism after the war.

Political thought, reflecting the mentality of the nation, showed a similar oscillation between opposites. In the Reichstag of 1930 there were thirteen political parties with conflicting interests and views, and it was a difficult task for a government to find a working majority. Much as their programs varied in detail, however, from an ideological viewpoint they can be divided into two opposite groups. It is not the age old conflict of conservatism and progress but one that reaches beyond the political sphere into the depths of *Weltanschauung,* the conflict between rationalism and irrationalism. It is reflected by the type of leaders that appear on the public stage, the intellectual who pleads with the arguments of reason, and the demagogue who appeals to emotional sentiment.

After the 19th century had seen an unprecedented victory of rationalism, countermovements sprang up toward its end. They grew in fields that had nothing to do with politics, in art, literature and philosophy, but they had one thing in common: the revolt against calculating rationalism. The brutalities of war produced a primitivism which, in association with some of the other rebellious tendencies, gradually gained ascendency during the post-war period until its final victory in Nazism. The conflict between rational and irrational forces is the story of political thought in Pre-Nazi Germany.[1]

Liberalism. The oldest of the rational movements, liberalism, has its roots in 18th century philosophy like the correlated schools of thought in other nations. The ideas of natural rights, civil liberty, the dignity of the individual, and the duty of the state to protect these liberties were greeted in Germany with the same enthusiasm as elsewhere. A specific form of liberation however, developed owing to the three different sources from which it was fed. One was the idealistic philosophy of the late 18th century, rating freedom as the supreme metaphysical ideal. Some of the finest thinkers were engaged in defining the rela-

---

[1] Practical political problems are not to be discussed here. They may, however, be listed as the objects that inflamed the ideological controversies. Chief problems in the pre-war period since 1900 were the building of a navy, increase of armaments, colonial difficulties and a reform of the finances. During the war, a controversy about war aims divided the nation, annexations or a negotiated peace of understanding being the main issues. Leftists were aroused by the conservatives' refusal to grant a fairer and more liberal franchise in Prussia. After the war, the constitution of the republic and the liquidation of the consequences of the war had to be decided. Socialism or democracy, acceptance or refusal of the peace treaty, fulfilment of or obstruction against its stipulations, isolation or international cooperation were the alternatives. As a major constitutional problem remained that of further centralization or increased independence of the member states.

tion of the free individual to the state. Kant, in distinguishing the sphere of legality and morality, attributed legality to the state and morality to the individual; Wilhelm von Humboldt reduced the authority of the state to a minimum of necessary protection of the individual. Even Hegel considered freedom as the highest ideal yet subordinated that of the individual to the infinitely more valuable freedom of the greater organisms, society and state. Thus he initiated the worship of the state which in the end was to destroy liberalism.

The second source was the opposition against absolutism in any form, either as the despotism of a foreign conqueror or of a native prince. Growing in the wars of liberation from Napoleon's rule it was strongly nationalistic.

The third source is to be seen in the self-assertion of the middle class which, as the dominating social and economic factor in the age of industrialization, demanded its share in the government. Liberation of bondsmen, abolition of guilds, municipal self-government, free trade were stations on its road to success.

No European country, however reactionary its government was, could avoid being affected by liberalism, the principle of "freedom limited by reason", as Leonard Nelson put it.

Twice liberalism in Germany had a chance of gaining political control, in the revolution of 1848 and in the Prussian conflict between king and parliament in 1862. Twice it failed, in 1848 because, after great initial success, it had to fight radicalism with the military help of the old powers, thereby restoring authority to them. In 1862 and the following years it was paralyzed by Bismarck's successes, as he, the great antagonist of liberalism, brought about the unification of Germany, one of liberalism's favorite ideals. The newly founded empire, though acclaimed by a large liberal party, was by no means liberal in its structure but rather a sort of crypto-absolutism. Nevertheless, substantial concessions to liberal principles were made, such as universal manhood suffrage and, most important, the assurance of legality in public and of legal protection in private life. Liberal too was the extensive freedom of speech and of the press.[2] The division of powers, that favorite principle of the 18th century, was ill-balanced with the heavier weight on the side of the monarchical government. A serious setback for liberalism was its being drawn into Bismarck's campaign against Catholicism and his persecution of the socialists which were contradictory to liberal principles.[3]

In the inverse ratio to liberalism's political impotence stood its cultural importance about 1900. Three generations of eminent scholars brought about a flowing of intellectual liberalism the main principles of which were independence from authority, objectivity and tolerance. In various ways and fields the emancipation from blind submission to traditional authority was achieved. A materialistic philosophy, based on the findings of science, did away with metaphysical speculation. Religion was considered as an anthropological phenomenon instead of a supernatural revelation. The bible, critically analyzed like any other historical document, in the eyes of some did not even prove the existence of Christ. A new liberal theology did not teach morals and devotion but history. Next to science, history indeed was the signature of this liberal age. It taught dispassionate objectivity but the human element behind it should not be overlooked. History means understanding and understanding means tolerance with all its beneficent and its dangerous implications. Dangerous in that it allowed forces, hostile to itself, to creep up like Nietzsche's revaluation of values and the dogma of the superman or the anarchy of values evident in the decadence of the *fin de siècle*. A positive and noble impulse of the incessant research of intellectual liberalism was its immanent zeal for truth, and this enabled that last school of great scholars to look beyond

---

[2] It is amazing to see what could be said and printed in public during the pre-war period. The attacks of "Simplizissimus", liberal satirical weekly, against the Kaiser and the ruling powers could not have been more pungent.

[3] This deepened the split between two liberal parties which had arisen over Bismarck's policy and never was closed: the National-liberals who subordinated domestic liberalism to power politics and the Progressives who upheld the liberal principles, moving in the direction of democracy.

the limits of pure reason, to discover and to appraise the working of incalculable dynamic forces against the progress of rational humanity. In history it is the never ceasing conflict between human decency and the lust for power, appearing in the costume of the *raison d'état*,[4] in sociology it is the "charismatic" leader, fanaticizing the masses to an extent which is incomprehensible to a soberminded spectator. The two liberals who understood best the nature of demonic powers were Freud and Max Weber. Freud forged the only weapon reason has to combat that menace, namely, rendering the demons of the subconscious innocuous by bringing their complexes into the light of the intellect. Max Weber explored the unknown region of the relations between moral and religious ideals and economic systems as well as the dynamic factors, active in the political life of the present and of the future. Indeed he was one of the leading minds in setting up new aims and political ideas to liberalism. The first aim was to take an active interest in the social problem and work for its solution. The days of aloofness and *laissez faire* had passed. This was realized first, about 1875, by a school of liberal economists, ridiculed as *Kathedersozialisten* who opposed the unqualified general prejudice against socialism.[5] They were instrumental in bringing about a social legislation but old social conditions. This was the conviction of Friedrich Naumann, of the masses since it concerned only the weak and did nothing to conserve the physical and mental strength of the strong. To make human beings out of the amorphous masses was a task that could not be performed by moral admonition and an ap-

---

[4] Friedrich Meinecke, *Die Idee der Staatsräson* (München: R. Oldenbourg, 1924).

[5] Protagonist of this phobia was Heinrich von Treitschke, Considering himself a national liberal, he called socialism an "offspring of naked sensualism" and the desire of moderate socialists to have talented boys from the proletariat granted an education "a sin against nature". "Whoever destroys the pious religiousness, the best thing the lower class has, acts as a criminal against society", therefore "ruthless enmity against socialism is imperative". "Socialism leads to cretinism".

The founder of the by no means uniform school of *Kathedersozialisten* was Gustav Schmoller, influential advisor to the governmennt in social legislation, the leading figure and most universal mind was Lujo Brentano, the most popular writer Werner Sombart. The *Verein für Sozialreform* was founded by the group and did valuable work.

peal to human idealism but only by economic improvement of social conditions. This was the conviction of Friedrich Naumann, the other outstanding liberal thinker of the age. He tackled that problem. The parties and groups which emphasized freedom and social justice, progressives and socialists, were more or less hostile to the actual state since they identified the state with its particular Germano-Prussian brand of feudal patronage.

Accordingly, they strictly opposed any increase in national power through military and naval armament or colonial expansion as this would serve only the interests of the ruling classes. They had to learn that the fundamental basis of any state, regardless of its constitution, is power. National power and democracy are by no means inconsistent and throughout his career Naumann strove to make the socialists understand this and to relinquish their principal obstruction, provided the existing state make it possible. This implied a liberalization of the present conditions, the last point of the new program. Democracy and monarchy are not necessarily antagonistic, Naumann declared, in particular, as the complexity of a modern state practically excludes a one-man rule. From absolutism to the British system of a parliamentary monarchy—along this line should German democracy develop.

These arguments were substantiated by the defects of the Bismarck system as liberal thinkers saw it.[6] By intentionally depriving the parliament of any real authority he had prevented any political leadership from growing. After his autocratic rule had gone Germany was administered by a bureaucracy, authorized but not controlled by the monarch. Only the parliament with proper power could exercise an effective control and, despite the handicaps of a bureaucratic party machinery, provide an opportunity for the rising of real political leaders.

The expectations and hopes staked on this program were divided. Max Weber saw the shortcomings of the parliamentary system very clearly, although he recommended it as the only

---

[6] Max Weber, *Parlament und Regierung im neugeordneten Deutschland.* in *Gesammelte politische Schriften* (München: Dr. Masken Verlag, 1921), p. 130 ff. The essay was written in 1917.

possibility to save the liberal ideals. Leopold von Wiese took a more optimistic stand. Liberalism, he said in 1917, is still eudaemonistic, optimistic and worldly wise, it considers human happiness a worth while goal, it is open to new ideas and opposed to any fanatical radicalism. It cannot work without confidence in men and therefore believes in a further democratization. Institutions, however, are less important than a new spirit that should influence the lessening of class differences and work for an international understanding.

The optimistic liberalism of 1917 had no inkling of being called into action very soon. Almost overnight, it found itself in a responsible position. For the revolution of 1918 which began as a mutiny of sailors and an agitation of radical socialists ended in the establishing of a democratic republic along strictly observed liberal lines. The constitution of Weimar, the "freest in the world," as Ebert, the first *Reichspräsident* called it, was extremely fair in protecting the rights of the minorities against the majority rule. Liberalism and democracy once, in 1848, had had a different meaning in Germany. Now they found their proper place with liberalism stressing the political philosophy, the Weltanschauung, and democracy defining the political system.

Liberalism had triumphed to an extent never dreamed of, without any preceding struggle and any real sacrifice. Just this presented a problem crucial to the fate of democracy. How should people be induced to like and to defend the new freedom for which they had done so little, how should democracy become a faith? In concentrating on this problem, post-war liberalism turned to education and to the younger generation as every new political power will do. In response to the international call for founding a better world, educational reforms of all kinds of schools were introduced, particularly in Prussia, and they were truly liberal.[7] The reform tried to lower the barriers between the older and the younger generation, abnormally high in the old

---

[7] The Prussian minister of education, Carl Heinrich Becker (1876-1933) was the finest personification of liberal idealism after Naumann's death in 1919.

educational system. Resentment against the traditional mental drill that had poisoned the youth of so many sensitive persons [8] ran high. The goal of the reform was high too, nothing less than the education of a new man, judged not by what he knows but what he is. Personality should count more than memory, spontaneity more than formalism, contact with actual life more than specialization in a remote field. Politically education is not interested in the ideas of German power but of a unified, though not uniform, German civilization. The differences of classes and traditions, of emotional nationalism and rational socialism, were felt more strongly than ever. They should be understood. "Our education should explain the causes of the natural contrasts and contradictions in the complex German chararacter, it should teach to comprehend, to love and thereby to overcome them." [9] Would youth respond to this call of liberalism which so strongly emphasized the will for compromising as an essential principle of a liberal policy? Some hopes could be placed upon the movement of the youth which had started soon after 1900 in opposition against the old school, the militaristic state, philistine society and general snobbery. Those *Wandervögel*, in returning to a simple natural life, enjoyed a new freedom and so did the progressive country boarding schools which introduced community selfgovernment. In October, 1913, the various groups of the movement, meeting on the Meissner, a mountain near Kassel, issued a common program: "The free German youth wants to shape its life according to its own decision, its own responsibility and with inner sincerity. Under any circumstances it stands for this freedom." Yet the hope, liberalism derived from this attitude, did not materialize after the war.

Liberty, in the post-war era, lost all appeal because there was too much of it. Gradually the younger generation moved away in the direction of discipline, organization and subordination, not to a schoolmaster but to a leader. Liberal education

---

[8] Outstanding liberal writers like Thomas Mann, Gerhart Hauptmann and Hermann Hesse speak with utmost bitterness of their school days.

[9] C. H. Becker, *Kulturpolitische Aufgaben des Reiches* (Leipzig: Quellen & Meyer, 1919), p. 48.

had hoped for a new humanism, a harmonization of disciplined intellect and emotional vigor. The humanism proclaimed by intelligent leaders of the younger generation, proudly hailed as a third humanism, was very different and had nothing in common with any liberal harmony or compromise. Sparta not Athens, political action not cultural luxuries, pessimism and resolution, not optimism and conciliation, such was the tenor of a program proclaimed with prophetic pompousness.[10] It revealed the failure of liberalism to win the youth and to arouse a general faith.

Socialism. Marxism, the most powerful political doctrine of modern ages, grew on German soil and bore certain features of the German mentality. The method of dialectic thinking was taken from Hegel, Karl Marx' respected teacher, and the bitterness of class feeling came from the impressions, Friedrich Engels, son of a wealthy industrialist, had received in his early days. This may explain why the Marxist doctrine, although drawing its examples from English conditions, took such deep roots in the German masses between 1870 and 1918. An ever-increasing number of workers believed in those well known principles: the historical materialism with economic conditions determining the course of history, the continuous class struggle and the expectation of its end through an ultimate victory of the proletarians which would institute a classless society. The accumulation of capital and the increasing pauperization of the proletariat will hasten the cataclysm if the proletarians of all nations join hands. Thus Marxism was unmistakably international and revolution minded. The novelty and cold grandeur of the idea fascinated the masses and terrified the possessing classes. No wonder it absorbed socialist thinking for a long time after initial objections had been overcome, objections rather to the feasibility of the plan than about the truth of its dogma. Ferdinand Lassalle (1825-1864), in the early sixties, had advocated a more realistic and more national policy. The labor class should not withdraw from the present state in hostility but gain influence

---

[10] Lothar Helbing (Wolfgang Frommel), *Der dritte Humanismus* (Berlin: Verlag die Runde, 1932).

within its frame in order to reform and control it eventually.
Lassalle even contemplated a temporary collaboration with reactionary Bismarck in a common front against the liberal bourgeoise. These ideas were overruled by strict Marxism in the
seventies and the antagonism between socialism and the German
state flared into the open through the persecution of the socialists by Bismarck from 1878 to 1890. His efforts to outlaw and
suppress ideas, led to no other result than a steady increase in
socialist votes and deputies since he did not dare to use the
methods of illegal killing and incarceration so familiar in our
age. Yet Lassallean realism had not died completely. About
1900 it became evident that some of Marx's prophecies had not
come true; neither had capitalism collapsed nor had the pauperization of the masses increased. Emigration, for instance, that
sure barometer of social standards, had decreased from more
than 220,000 in 1881 to a mere trickle of 17,000 in 1912. Wages
and living standards had gone up, labor unions and cooperative
stores had shown that even within the existing order the lot of
the proletarians could be improved. Thus, about 1890, a new
school of socialist thought undertook a revision of the Marxist
scheme.[11] It would be a mistake to wait in idleness for a swift
collapse of the bourgeois society. Active participation in the social legislation was imperative and this meant collaboration with
other parties as opportunities arose. No deviation from Marxist
principles, however, was planned with respect to the opposition
against militarism and imperialism. The same kind of revision-
ism appeared simultaneously in most of the other European
countries and was heatedly discussed at international meetings
with a peculiar result. Owing to the predominance of radical
orators at such occasions it was rejected in theory while quietly
carried out in the smaller European and some of the German
states.

The outbreak of the first world war confronted the socialist
party with a difficult dilemma. Orthodox Marxism would have

---

[11] Eduard Bernstein, *Die Voraussetzungen des Sozialismus und die Aufgaben der
Sozialdemokratie* (Berlin, 1899).

decided on a general strike in order to inhibit the mobilization. On the other hand, almost the whole nation including the working class was convinced that Germany was the victim of aggression on the part of Russian Zarism. Fighting against this reactionary power made it easier for the socialist party to cooperate with the rest of the nation and to vote for the war credits. A few weeks later, however, a fraction of inexorables reverted to the old dogma of proletarians having only one fatherland, the International, and being obliged to continue the class struggle. From now on Socialism split into three groups in Germany. A small group of consistent radicals, the nucleus of the communist party of later years, worked together with Lenin, Trotzki and the other still exiled Bolshevists. A second group, the Independent Socialists, adhered to the Marxist opposition against any war of the capitalists and imperialists, while the third group, by far the majority, drew nearer to the state though not without misgivings about the military censure, annexionist propaganda sponsored by the army and the weakness of the administration to carry out a solemn promise to reform the Prussian franchise.[12] They did not abandon the plan of future socializations but discarded the idea of a revolution very definitely.[13] Much against their will, they were compelled to join the revolution on November 9, 1918, in order to prevent the masses slipping away from their control. In those bleak days, however, they upheld an idea which was expressed in the official name of their party: social democracy. It would have been easy to establish a purely proletarian dictatorship after the Russian pattern, but they threw all the weight they had behind the demand for democracy although this might mean compromising with other classes and parties. In fact, socialist ideas in the Weimar constitution were few and incoherent.[14] Internationalism was reduced to the vague

---

[12] After the war, the pacifist wing of the Independents reunited with the moderate majority while the radical socialists joined the communists.

[13] "I hate the revolution like sin", declared Friedrich Ebert only a few days before its outbreak.

[14] Article 156 made provisions for a future socialization of private enterprises against adequate compensation.

demand that all stipulations of international law should be parts of the constitution.

During the era of the republic, social democracy was absorbed by the practical tasks of the day heeding neither theory nor slogan that might fanaticize the masses. The party functionary, not the demagogue ruled and a new type of unassuming rationalists took over, a type that counted upon the reasonability of men and relied on knowledge (their extraordinary respect for knowledge saved the existence of reactionary university professors at that time).[15] Political thought concentrated upon the economic problems close at hand. Only a small group of religious socialists felt the need for a moral supplement; what they thought and did differed but little from what Friedrich Naumann once had said about the humanization of the masses.

The communists were in an ideologically stronger position. Undiscouraged by their failure to bolshevize the revolution of 1918, they remained unswervingly loyal to the Marxist principles, as materialized in Russia. Only temporarily refraining from action they expected the world depression to lead to another imperialistic war at the end of which the world revolution would come, and they exploited the emotions, stirred by such hopes, to the fullest. Significantly enough, intellectuals signing the communist program were all artists, while the social-democrat intellectuals were scholars, voicing the opinion of the older generation.[16]

Rathenau. It is not an afterthought that the excessive rationalism of the social-democracy constituted a serious setback. Early warning had been given by Walther Rathenau, the most

---

[15] The leaders of the republic were the most honest ones Germany ever had. Men like Ebert, Bruening, Severing, Braun compare very favorably with the pretentious militarists and bureaucrats of the Wilhelminian era and the corruption of the Nazi leaders.

[16] In 1930 the social democrat party had more members aged 60 than 25.

brilliant and most tragic figure in modern German history.[17] His criticism was directed against both, liberalism and socialism, for the mechanistic and materialistic conception of life they had. Trusting in the infallibility of science, they have no ideal in which to believe and for which to fight. They struggle only about institutions. Nevertheless, being too much of a liberal and a socialist himself, he proposed a remedy. His book In Days to Come (1917) is the only comprehensive political philosophy and plan that originated in Germany between 1900 and the end of the war. Socialist was his idea of eliminating the plutocracy and the class struggle, not by a revolution but by cutting down the luxuries of the rich and raising the standards of living of the poor. Monopolies should be abolished as well as idleness and all available forces should be harnessed to the work of spiritual and material production. Equal opportunity in education should provide a really able leadership and break down caste barriers. The power of the state would increase beyond imagination so unemployment and poverty could be abolished. Trade and industries should be organized in groups, regulating their own affairs. It is indeed the picture of a totalitarian and corporative state which Rathenau painted.

Still he had some liberal ideals. The task of economy is not to increase welfare and to create equality but freedom, "next to love the most divinely sounding word in our language." Freedom from want, a chance for all, spiritual freedom and spiritual progress are his demands. Socialist intellectualism has neglected the well-spring of all genuine happiness, the heart.

---

[17] Walter Rathenau (1867-1922), industrialist, organizer, philosopher, statesman, did great service to his country. He saved Germany from early defeat by organizing the raw material supply in the beginning of the war which had been neglected by the military authorities, he warned against the unrestricted submarine campaign and the underestimation of Anglo-American power. ("Even if we control Europe from Petersbourg to Bordeaux we cannot force the Anglo-Saxon powers to make peace") and he warned against suing for an armistice because it meant surrender. As foreign minister he worked toward an understanding with the former enemies which would have prevented the total financial ruin in 1923. The collapse of the monarchy did not surprise him since the maladministration of William II was bound to come to a disgraceful end. By frankly admitting this view he incurred the hatred of anti-semitic nationalists who assassinated him as a "criminal parasite" in 1922.

After a century of mechanizing materialism the soul should be restored to its own right. "It is time for the day-break of the soul! what we create is created from a profound and unconscious impulse. We are living for that which we will. And what do we will? that which we neither know nor can know, but in which our faith is inviolable."

Rathenau was typically German in that he overrated the value of efficiency. He had no idea of the necessity of the brakes, put on by democracy in order to prevent such efficient monster states from becoming a menace to the rest of the world. Strange to see, Rathenau, fair, tolerant, liberal, prepared a political system which was put into life by racial fanaticism 20 years later and it was one of history's tragic ironies that he was to become one of the first victims of this fanaticism. He had kept his ear to the ground and realized the power of a new irrationalism but he believed this movement would be all to the good.

Political Catholicism. An intermediate position between rationalism and irrationalism was held by a party unique in the German political system, the Catholic Centre. It was based not upon common material interests but upon a common faith. Founded in defense of the rights of the Catholics which were threatened by the new Protestant empire, persecuted by Bismarck in the *Kulturkampf*, it had gained power steadily until, in the pre-war period, it held the balance between right and left, able to cooperate with both sides. For a long time it was concerned chiefly with averting injustice to Catholics. After 1900, a tension between the more conservative and the more democratic elements could be observed. "We must get out of the ivory tower," the progressives said, urging a closer contact with the intellectual and cultural life of the rest of the nation. The tension never relaxed though, toward the end of the war, the left wing was distinctly in the ascendency. But it never came to a break either, on the contrary, the tension was considered as a positive advantage, almost a principle since it provided a great flexibility. The Centre was the party of "and", not of "either or", they wanted religion *and* patriotism, Fatherland *and* mankind, Germany *and* Europe, centralization *and* particularism. These principles enabled the Centre to participate in any party constellation of the Weimar republic. They wanted the Christian principles to be applied in state and society, economy and civilization. Anti-extremist and anti-doctrinarian, they opposed any desperado nationalism.[18] The philosophy of political Catholicis mis considered to be rational though not of the 18th century type of doctrinarism but of that of Thomas Aquinas' realistic reasoning. Any myths of blood and race and supermen must be repulsive to that kind of thinking. Nevertheless, political Catholicism had an indirect contact with irrationalism through the medium of romantic tendencies. 100 years ago, the opponents of revolutionary liberalism had resorted to the mystic spirit of the middle ages, reviving medieval political ideals. After 1900, a new school of Catholic romanticism trod similar paths, opposing the soul-less democracy of the West and recommending a corporative state along lines between a Platonic republic and medieval guilds.[19] The permanent parliamentary crises in the Reichstag disgusted the Catholic groups of the movement of the youth as well as the rest and made them favor the idea of a strong government, a kind of conservative democracy, and adopt the ideal of a third Reich, as outlined by Moeller van den Bruck, the founder of a modern conservative ideology.

Conservatism. Conservatism, up to the World War, proved its name by not producing a single new political thought. The conservatives—aristocrats, bureaucrats, industrialists and the military caste—were content to wield the actual power in Prussia and the Reich without feeling the need for a new theoretical justification of their privileges. Conservative ideology was still that of the restoration period when Karl Ludwig Haller and Julius Stahl had preached the duty of subordination to the will of a sovereign who is selected by the grace of God, and had

---

[18] The Centre's resistence against Naziism was weakened by the efforts of the Vatican to come to an understanding with Hitlerism after the pact with Fascism had proved successful.

[19] Othmar Spann, *Der wahre Staat* (1923).

glorified the state as a guarantee of Christian principles, throne
and altar being interdependent. In practical policy, time and
again, some younger members of the aristocratic party split off
but on the whole the conservatives remained stagnant until they
were dislodged by the revolution which swept their unwritten
privileges away together with the monarchy. Only after the war
a new political thought appeared with the label conservative yet
it had little to do with the views of the Junkers. These were
called reactionaries, stagnant minds unable to create anything new.
Equally sterile are the revolutionaries who only destroy. Constructive is the true conservative who does not intend to revive
rotten institutions but develops the immanent strength of a nation and a country, conserving the very best things the eternal
creative spirit has bestowed upon them.[20]

As a matter of fact, the ways of the old reaction and this
new conservatism met very soon in that both embraced the idea
which was eventually to ruin them, nationalism.

Nationalism. German nationalism, the child of the Napoleonic wars and a brother of liberalism, had reached its legitimate
goal with the unification of Germany in 1870. Nevertheless, it
continued to grow despite intermittent setbacks, such as the
defeat in 1918, in three different ways, as imperialist chauvinism, as moral nationalism and as scientific expansionism.

Soon after 1870, nationalist ambition looked out for new
conquests. "The Germanization of our neighbors in the East
would be a worth while deed," declared Paul de Lagarde as
early as 1881. "May Russia be so kind and move some 300 miles
farther East to Central Asia. We need land in front of our
door. . . . If she refuses to do so she will force us to expropriate
her, that is to make war on her." [21] During the following decades, similar schemes of expansion were propagated by the Pan-
German League, founded in 1891. They included the Baltic
provinces and the Ukraine, Belgium, the Netherlands and Eastern

---

[20] Arthur Moeller van den Bruck, *Das dritte Reich* (1922).

[21] Paul de Lagarde (1827-91), *Schriften für Deutschland* (Ed. A. Messer, Leipzig:
Alfred Kroener, 1933), p. xxiv.

France with all the colonies of these nations.[22] As motifs for such exorbitant claims, copied by Hitler later on, were given the want of space for the surplus of population—emigration to America means losing the people for Germany and was bitterly denounced—and the rights of a superior race.

Here moral nationalism comes in. Lagarde and Julius Langbehn [23] founded what may be described as the German "cant". From acrimonious denunciation of their contemporaries both proceeded, illogically enough, to stating the moral superiority of the Germans on account of the profoundness of their feelings. They initiated a cult of German *Innerlichkeit* (inwardness) which became a stock phrase of educators and an obsession of writers, particularly after the last war. The sufferings of the Germans cried to high heaven while those of other nations, the Belgians for instance, were an inevitable result of circumstances and their own foolishness. At the bottom of this amazing partiality lies the more or less subconscious conviction that only Germans are really able to have deep sentiments and therefore are the only ones who are entitled to have them.[24] In a pseudo-scientifical way the *Innerlichkeit* was endorsed by Houston Stewart Chamberlain, the godfather of Hitler's racialism.

Silenced for a while by the defeat of 1918, Pan-Germanism returned in scientific disguise as *Geopolitik*, a political technique based upon the findings of geography, economy, anthropology, etc., which in a seemingly detached manner discussed the potentialities of future aggression. General Karl Haushofer, not the inventor but the organizer of *Geopolitik*, planned nothing less than German world control in this way. He is free from any moral cant since he is completely amoral. For this reason he is unable to appraise the moral reaction of the world to his plans, and fails in this respect as well as the moralists of *Innerlichkeit*.

Nihilism. Offended pride and frustration was frequent

---

[22] D. Frymann (Heinrich Class, President of the Pan-German League), *Wenn ich der Kaiser wär* (1908).

[23] Julius Langbehn (1851-1908), *Rembrandt als Erzieher* (1891).

[24] Best known of modern literary representatives of this cent. are Gustav Frenssen, William Schäfer and Hans Grimm.

among the soldiers who, returning from the battlefields, were unable to adjust themselves to civilian life again. They found an outlet in nihilism, and this mood of indifference and apathy was activated by Oswald Spengler. The fundamental thesis of his famous book *The Decline of the West* must have been a comfort to a disturbed mind: All civilizations must die according to the same laws of history. Our Western civilization has reached the last phase of old age when its creative productivity has ceased and only technical improvements may come forth. The future belongs to the technician and the warrior alone. Pungent was Spengler's critique of liberalism ("an affair for simpletons") and of socialdemocracy. True socialism, he said, could be found in old Prussianism and its unfathomable demonic spirit.[25] To call the Prussian despotism with its haughty treatment of the lower classes a socialism was certainly an amazing distortion of history on the part of Spengler but it made a deep impression upon the frustrated ex-soldiers who could not get away from the war. In Germany, this type was glorified. "The German front-line fighter is invincible and immortal," declared Ernst Jünger as if no other nation had fought in the trenches.[26] This monomania is the root of modern German militarism, determined far more by frustration and cant plus the cult of Prussianism than by the influence of the comparatively few Prussian Junkers.[27] Militarism and socialism were coupled; the militarized laborer, working for rearmament, marching toward decision is the man of the future. Individual happiness has no meaning, freedom of a liberal age is contemptible. "The new freedom of the individual is the knowledge to stand in a decisive place," cried Jünger. And the march has no aim. "There is no aim," stated Spengler. "Marx, that misguided ideologist, had an aim. But that is very stupid. Life has no aim. Mankind has no purpose. The existence of the world is a fact so auguste that a

---

[25] O. Spengler, *Preussentum und Sozialismus* (München: Beck, 1920).

[26] Ernst Jünger, *Der Arbeiter* (Hamburg: Hanseatische Verlangsanstalt, 1932).

[27] An extinction of the Junker caste would not destroy militarism which has expanded, morally and mentally, far beyond that class.

wretched happiness of the greatest number could never be an aim." It is obvious that such a military communism can work, march and die without a definite aim only if it is inspired by irrational fanaticism. It is utterly nihilistic, unreasonable, unintelligible. No wonder it should turn against the intellect itself.

Anti-Intellectualism. Here it is met by the whole array of anti-intellectualism. The great protest against the intellect had begun in Germany with Nietzsche. His brilliant style and the glittery variety of his thoughts have blinded the generation that came after him and everybody found something suitable in his philosophy. Politically Nietzsche would not fit into the Nazi pattern, anti-nationalist, anti-socialist and philosemite that he is. Nevertheless he has forged more weapons for them than anyone else. He undermined the reputation of the 19th century liberal world, contested the validity of Christian ethics and invented the superman of whom the master race is only the mass production. Above all, he discredited the intellect. In his view, it had spoiled the wonders of the Dionysian cult in ancient Greece and, through the medium of Socrates, has rationalized European culture ever since, leading it away from the sources of real life. Criticism of the intellect became outright condemnation among some literatures of Schwabing, the Mont Parnasse of Munich, Alfred Schuler and Ludwig Klages who gathered around the poet Stefan George. Here a regular theory of anti-intellectualism was drafted and, years later, published.[28] Body and soul form the natural polar unity of human nature. The intellect, intruding like a wedge, tries to disrupt the harmony and finally destroys the vitality of both. European history is the tragedy of the triumph of the intellect. What is needed to revitalize the power of true nature is a great catastrophe and the bohemiens of Schwabing revelled in dreams of a cosmic cataclysm as early as 1900. In human relations, complete submission and passionate devotion to the mastermind replaces understanding. On this basis

---

[28] Ludwig Kages, *Der Geist als Widersacher der Seele* (Leipzig: J. A. Barth, 1929-32). Socially and ideologically, the *bohème* of Schwabing was the birthplace of Nazism.

Stefan George designed the ideal of leadership and the response of the followers: "Plow over our bodies and nobody will ever call you to account." The words of an esoteric poet became a political fanfare through the youth-movement. George was hardly known to the public before 1914. After the war, his ideas spread and soon he exercised a political influence greater than that of any other German poet at any time. It was a fatal influence for it led straight to Nazism and the killing of any independent thought, political or otherwise.

BIBLIOGRAPHY

BERGSTRASSER, LUDWIG, *Geschichte der politischen Parteien in Deutschland* (Mannheim, Berlin, Leipzig: J. Bensheimer, 1924).

BERNSTEIN, EDUARD, *Evolutionary socialism: a criticism and affirmation* (Translated by Edith C. Harvey, London: Independent labor party 1909).

DEITERS, HEINRICH, *Die deutsche Schulreform nach dem Weltkriege* (Berlin: Robert Kämmerer 1935).

DORPALEN, ANDREAS, *The world of general Haushofer. Geopolitics in Action* (New York: Farrar & Rhinehart, 1942).

HEUSS, THEODOR, *Naumann, Friedrich, Der Mann, das Werk, die Zeit* (Stuttgart-Berlin: Deutsche Verlagsanstalt, 1937).

JUNGER, ERNST, *Der Arbeiter. Herrschaft und Gestalt* (Hamburg: Hanseatische Verlagsanstalt, 1932).

KAMPFFMEYER, PAUL, *Changes in the theory and tactics of the social- democracy* (Translated by Winfield R. Gaylord, Chicago: C. H. Kerr & Co. 1908).

LAGARDE, PAUL DE, *Deutsche Schriften* (Göttingen: Dietrichscher Verlag, 1892).

LANGBEHN, JULIUS, *Rembrandt als Erzieher. Von einem Deutschen* (Leipzig: C. L. Hirschfeld, 1890).

MOELLER VAN DEN BRUCK, *Das dritte Reich* (Hamburg: Hanseatische Verlagsanstalt, 3rd edition 1930).

NAUMANN, FRIEDRICH, *Das blaue Buch von Vaterland und Freiheit* (Königstein und Leipzig: K. R. Langewiesche, 1913).

NEUMANN, SIGMUNND, *Die deutschen Parteien* (Berlin: Junker und Dünnhaput, 1932).

RATHENAU, WALTHER, *In days to come* (Translated by Eden and Cedar Paul, London: George Allen and Unwin, 1921).

ROSENBERG, ARTHUR, *The birth of the German republic* 1871-1918 (Translated by Ian F. D. Morrow, New York: Oxford University Press, 1931).

RUGGIERO, GUIDO DE, *The history of European Liberalism* (Translated by R. G. Collingwood, London: Oxford University Press, 1927).

SCHMITT, CARL, *Römischer Katholizismus und politische Form* (Hellerau: Jacob Hegner, 1923).

SELL, FRIEDRICH C., "Intellecutal Liberalism in Germany about 1900," *Journal of Modern History,* XV (1943).

SELL, FRIEDRICH C., "Thomas Mann and the problem of Anti-Intellectualism," *Germanic Review,* XV (1940).

SOMBART, WERNER, *Socialism and the social movement* (Translated by M. Epstein, New York: E. P. Dutton 1909)

Spengler, Oswald, *The decline of the West* (New York: A. A. Knopf, 1926-28).

Spengler, Oswald, *Preussentum und Sozialismus* (München: Beck, 1920).

Weber, Marianne, *Max Weber, ein Lebensbild* (Tübingen: J. C. B. Mohr, 1926).

Weber, Max, *Gesammelte politische Schriften* (München: Drei Masken Verlag, 1921).

Weigert, Hans W., *Generals and geographers; the twilight of geopolitics* (New York: London, Oxford University Press, 1942).

Wiese, Leopold von, *Der Liberalismus in Vergangenheit und Zukunft* (Berlin: S. Fischer, 1917).

Chapter XXIII

SOCIAL AND POLITICAL THOUGHT IN LATIN AMERICA

HAROLD E. DAVIS

Thought in Latin America, in spite of century long striving for autonomy, is still in large part influenced by European patterns and, to a less extent, by those of North America. This is particularly true in reference to general philosophy. Leaders of social and political thought, on the other hand, and to a less extent writers dealing with moral philosophy and aesthetics, have in many cases marked out patterns of originality reflecting the American scene. This is particularly true in Mexico and Peru, the centers of great *mestizo* (Indian and white) populations and culture.[1] It is in the field of the sociology of politics or "American sociology", as it is usually termed in the universities, that Latin American social thought found its most valid expression. Developments in this general area will, therefore, receive considerable attention here.

Certain colonial influences may still be seen in the mind of contemporary Latin America, especially a theological orientation noticeable in the receptivity displayed for the neo-Thomism of Jacques Maritain and other tendencies emphasizing the historical philosophies of the Church.[2] Many of the strongest

---

[1] As will be pointed out later, several of the most significant contributions in the development of an American thought have come from Argentina, and important contributions may be seen in the works of Fernando Ortiz of of Cuba, and in those of Fernando de Azevedo, Afranio Coutinho, Gilberto Freire, Arthur Ramos of Brazil, and certain others.

[2] See: Risieri Frondisi, "Tendencies in Contemporary Latin American Philosophy," in *Inter-American Intellectual Interchange* (papers presented at a conference under the auspices of The Institute of aLtin American Studies of the University of Texas in 1943). For Brazil, see: Nelson Werneck Sodré, *Historia de la literatura brasileira* (Rio de Janeiro: Livraria José Olympi, 1940), and his *Orientacöes do pensamento brasileiro* (Rio de Janeiro, 1943).

tendencies, however, are directly traceable to reaction against that orientation. The eighteenth century and the Wars of Indepndence in the early nineteenth century brought French eighteenth century liberalism and the Enlightenment. English economic liberalism, especially that of Jeremy Bentham, also had considerable influence during these years.[3] French and English liberalism were in turn followed by German romantic liberal influences.

During the latter part of the nineteenth century social thought in Latin America became increasingly identified with positivism. Positivism, originating in the ideas of August Comte, excluded everything except natural phenomena, or the properties of things which could be known, in order to concentrate attention upon elements of "positive" knowledge which might be useful in the interpretation of social problems and as a basis for social progress. Essentially materialistic in its essence, it naturally tended toward close identification with Darwinian, Spencerian and other forms of evolutionary social thought.

Positivism came to the zenith of the popularity between 1880 and 1900, although its influence continued strong well into the present century, notably in Brazil. In Brazil, indeed, positivism became nearly an official philosophy of the Republic. The *Sociedade Positivista* was founded in 1871 under the influence of Benjamin Constant. In 1881 Miguel Lemos and Teixera Mendez founded the positivist church, *Templo da Humanidade,* still in existence. It was probably the greatest development of Comtian religious influence and ideas outside France, and its membership constituted an important part of the leadership of the republican revolution in 1889. The Brazilian flag, with its motto, *Orden e progresso* still proclaims to the world this Brazilian identification with the Comtian dynamics and statics.

To say that positivism was popular in Latin America means largely that Latin America was preoccupied with the social basis

---

[3] See: Alejandro Marure, *Efemérides de Centro-America.* James Mill's *Elements of Political Economy* and Jeremy Bentham's theories of law and government were taught in the University of Buenos Aires when founded (1821) by Rivadavia. See: L. L. Bernard, in *The Encyclopaedia of the Social Sciences,* I, p. 305.

of its moral, political, educational, and economic problems, as modified by the ideas of Herbert Spencer and John Locke.[4]

Positivism came to the zenith of its popularity between ing problems of the organization of national life which occupied the attention of most of the Hispanic nations during the nineteenth century.

Originally, of course, positivism was an instrument of the liberal forces intent upon building a strong lay society and state, and wished to bend the forces of traditionalism and colonialism to its purposes. To this end, Benito Juárez supported Gabino Barreda in his reorganization of the educational program of Mexico after the triumph of the liberal revolution in that country.[5] Since positivism was associated with the solution of these great national problems, it naturally had great political importance. It suited well the growing spirit of nationalism, and at the same time provided the dominant classes with a well oriented philosophy of prestige and "scientific" character with which to meet the impatience of more radical reforming tendencies. The leading chairs of philosophy in the universities were, accordingly, held by positivists.

The Díaz regime in Mexico furnishes a good example of this identification of positivism with a regime emphasizing "scientific progress" and gradual evolution in order to prevent "revolution". Justo Sierra was the high priest of positivism in the University, and later in the Ministry of Education, "the popularizer of the positivist theory in art and life." [6] By the end of the nineteenth century, however, national political stability was

---

[4] José Vasconcelos, *Ulises Criollo,* p. 195.

[5] See: W. H. Calcott, *Liberalism in Mexico* 1857-1929 (Berkeley: University of California Press, 1931) ; Leopoldo Zea, *El Positivismo en Mexico* (Mexico: El Colegio de México, 1943), pp. 45 ff.; Justo Sierra, *Evolución Política del pueblo Mexicano* (Mexico: La Casa de España en Mexico, 1940; published originally by J. Ballesca with other works under the title *Mexico, su evolución social*).

[6] José Vasconcelos, *Ulises Criollo,* p. 197. Vasconcelos writes that his studies varied from rigid Comtian though to Spencerian evolutionism. The sociology of Le Bon, Worms and Gumplowitz was just beginning to enter the universities of his student days (ca. 1900). He remained, he says, "sumiso a Comte que prohibe las aventuras de la mente y las excluye del periodo científico que profesamos." (p. 174).

well achieved in most of the Latin American states, economic and demographic changes were presenting new national and international problems, and new movements of social protest found their ideological bases in conflict with the dominant positivism.

The great historical production in Latin America during the last half of the nineteenth century reflects likewise this achievement of national political stability. In Mexico it produced Lucas Alemán, Manuel Orozco y Berra and Joaquín García Icazbalceta; in Peru, Manuel de Mendiburu and Pedro Paz Soldán; in Chile, Claudio Gay, Diego Barros Arana, Benjamín Vicuña Mackenna, Miguel Luís Amunátegui, José Toribio Medina, and Gonzalo Bulnes; in Argentina, V. F. López, Manuel Bilbao, Bartolomé Mitre, Antonio Zinny and Vicente G. Quesada; and in Brazil, João Manoel Pereiro da Silva, José da Silva Paránhos and Manoel de Oliveira Lima. This history was nationalistic, but it was also reminiscent, stock-taking. It really represents a continuation of the social and political philosophy of the movement for independence.[7]

The Venezuelan, Blanco Fombona, about the turn of the century, studied the conflict of classes in his *Evolución política y social de Hispano America.* Francisco Bulnes of Mexico painted a pessimistic future for Latin America in its relations with the United States in his *El Porvenir de las Naciones Hispano-Americanas.* At the end of the century Octavio Bunge of Argentina likewise gave a pessimistic psychological-social analysis of the mixed racial basis of Latin America in his *Nuestra América.*

As positivism lost ground, Latin American interest in philosophy in general became more intense, showing itself in increased publications, a steady increase in the number of university chairs, and in the search for new autonomous patterns of thought.[8] In some cases the reaction was anti-"practical" and anti-"scientific", as in the growth of Neo-Thomism, and the in-

---

[7] See L. L. Bernard in *The Encyclopedia of the Social Sciences,* I, pp. 308-9.

[8] See especially Risieri Frondizi in *Handbook of Latin American Studies* (Cambridge, Mass.: Harvard University Press, 1940), No. 5, pp. 418-427.

fluence of Jacques Maritain, or in the earlier absolutism of
George Christian Krause and other German idealistic tendencies.

Most of the tendencies of European thought of the contemporary period are reflected in America. Unamuno and Ortega y Gassett naturally have exercised considerable influence,
and the latter's *Revista de Occidente* is particularly important
as the medium through which many American readers made the
acquaintance of German philosophical speculation.[9] Marxian
thought comes to represent an increasingly important influence
upon such men as José Ingenieros, Alfredo Palacios, Aníbal
Ponce, Carlos Mariátegui, Haya de la Torre, Vicente Lombardo
Toledano, and Juan Marinello.[10]

Socialist movements of course found their way into Latin
America from Europe in the late nineteenth century. Development was especially marked in Argentina, Brazil and Chile, and
was associated with the move for organization of labor. Since
the last World War Communist parties have been organized and
have participated in elections in Mexico, Cuba, Chile, Uruguay,
Argentina, Peru, Ecuador and Costa Rica. The older Socialist
groups have in most cases continued their separate existence.
Particularly notable is the existence of a strong indigenous socialism within the official Revolutionary Party in Mexico, a
socialism largely without international ties and older than the
the Russian Revolution.

The most distinctive reaction against positivism, however, if
not the strongest, is the tendency to turn to American soil and
to the mixed demographic pattern of America, as Sarmiento and
his contemporaries in Argentina did half a century before, for a

---

[9] See Francisco Romero "El Pensamiento hispanoamericano", *Philosophy and Phenomenological Research,* IV (December 1943) p. 132.

[10] Juan Marinello edited *Revista de Avance* (1927-31), *Revista Politica* (1931) *La
Palabra, Masas* and *Mediodia.* See also his *Literatura hispanoamericana* (Mexico:
University of Mexico, 1937). See Lombardo Toledano's *La doctrina socialista y su
interpretación en el artículo 3° constitutional* (1934). Lombardo Toledano was the
founder of the Workers University of Mexico. Among the writing of Alfredo
Palacios might be noted his *El socialismo y las reformas penales* (Buenos Aires:
Claridad). See: Alpiano Vega Cobiellas, *Interpretación: Juan Marinello Vidaurreta*
(La Habana: Cultural, S. A., s. f).

realistic and practical social and political philosophy keyed to the problems of the American scene and interpreting that scene in patterns of generalizations independent of European schematic systems.[11]

The basis for this tendency was laid within the patterns of positivist thought in the development of the study of American and national sociology. This framework has frequently embraced the most constructive Latin American thought dealing with national political, economic, educational and racial problems. Beginning with the work of Esteban Echeverría it continues through that of Alberdi and Sarmiento and that of the positivists of the middle and late nineteenth century to that of contemporaries such as Raúl A. Orgaz (Argentina), Oliveira Viana (Brazil), José Antonio Arze (Bolivia), Augustín Venturino (Chile), Augusto Mijares (Venezuela) and Manuel Gamio (Mexico). This tendency has been an outstanding characteristic of Latin American thought in and out of the universities.[12] Its most exaggerated expression has been given, probably, by Juan Augustín García

---

[11] Especially to be noted in this connection are the writings of Luis Alberto Sánchez, particularly his *Vida y pasión de la cultura en América* (1935); José Ingenieros, *La evolución de las ideas argentinas* (2 vols., 1918-1920)—although Ingenieros remains essentially a positivist; Ricardo Rojas, *Eurindia* (Obras, V, 1924); Francisco Gavidia, *La formación de una filosofía propia o sea Latino-Americano* (San Salvador, 1931), reproduced in *Discursos, Estudios y Conferencias* (San Salvador: Biblioteca Universitaria, 1941); Carlos Mariátegui, *Siete Ensayos de interpretación de la realidad Peruano* (1927); Afranio Coutinho's "Some Considerations on the Problem of Philosophy in Brazil," *Philosophy and Phenomenlogical Research, IV* (December, 1943), pp. 186-195; Francisco Romero in *Ibid.*, p. 133; Leopolod Zea, *El positivismo en México* (México, 1943) and the review of the latter volume by F. Giner de los Ríos in *El Noticiero Bibliográfico* (Mayo, 1943); Humberto Palza S., *El hombre como método* (San Francisco: ed. del autor, 1941), p. 197, discusses problem of true culture for Hispano-America and believes the mestizo is the key. Elías Entralgo y Vallina (1903-) (Cuba), *El fenómeno social latino-americano* and *El pensamiento político-social en la América latino*. Coutinho agrees with Sánchez in pointing out that an American philosophy is not a substitute for but a way to find a more universal philoosphy.

---

[12] Recent renascence of social thought in Latin American parallels the renascence of Spain and Portugal which set in after the Spanish American war, and especially after the publication of Costa y Martínez, *Reconstitución y europeización de España* (Madrid, 1900). See Fernando de los Ríos in *The Encyclopaedia of the Social Sciences,* "Introduction: The Social Sciences as Disciplines," VIII, "Spain and Portugal."

(1862-1922) of Argentina, who stated sociology as a science uniquely national.[13]

The Mexican Revolution and Peruvian *Aprismo* have stimulated the development of such thought, as well as the development of young aggressive intellectual and political leadership animated with such social concepts. Yet it is worth noting, in passing, however, that Mexico has not produced a matured social interpretation of its Revolution or an adequate political theory of revolution. The revolution of 1930 in Latin America stimulated several attempts at such a theory,[14] and considerable historical argument has taken place in Mexico concerning its revolution, as will be noted later.

A number of Latin American writers are currently interested in the social and political ideas of Bolívar. Victor Andrés Belaunde has written on *Bolívar and Political Thought of the Spanish American Revolution.*[15] José Vasconcelos has written of *Monroismo y Bolivarismo;*[16] Augusto Mijares and José Rafael Mendoza of Venezuela have also treated his ideas at length in the search for an American basis for political and social

[13] See his *Introducción al estudio de las ciencias sociales argentinas* (1899), *La ciudad indiana* (1900), and his *Historia de las ideas sociales argentinas* (1915).

[14] See especially Alfredo Colmo, *La revolución en la América latina* (Buenos Aires, 1932); Ricardo Rojas, *El radicalismo de mañana* (Buenos Aires, 1932); J. N. Matienzo, *La revolución de 1930 y los problemas de la democracia argentina* (Buenos Aires, 1930.) Alfredo Poviña in his *Historia de la Sociología en Latino America*, p. 52, mentions a number of Argentinian sociologists who have concerned themselves with the sociology of revolutions, taking their cue from German studies. Professor Alberto Rodriguez gave a course of lectures on the subject in the University of Buenos Aires in 1930 and published a study *El sentido de las revoluciones* in 1931. Raúl Orgaz wrote a series of articles on the subject in *La Prensa*. Alfredo Poviña presented a doctoral thesis, *Sociología de la revolución* at the University of Córdoba (1929) published 1932. Rodolfo Rivarola published (1932) in *La Nación* a series of articles "Ciclos de ideas fuerzas en la historia argentina". Antonio M. Grampone published his *Filosofía de las revoluciones* in 1932. José Varona, earlier, had commented on the revolutions of his day as sterile since they did not open the road to social revolution. He foresaw the forces of socialism and Caesarism (communism and fascism) coming like hurricanes. D. Agramonte in Medardo Vitier *el al, José Varona* (Habana, 1937), pp. 253-254. The views of José Vasconcelos are expressed in many of his writings, especially in *Qué es la revolución?* (1937).

[15] Johns Hopkins University Press, 1938.

[16] Santiago, 1934.

thought. This tendency should not be confused with the current interest of certain groups in Chile, Argentina, and elsewhere in glorifying such "strong men" as Diego Portales and Juan Manuel Rosas.

Some of the best thought of Latin America has been in the field of public law and especially international law. The study of social and political problems carried on as American sociology was frequently a product of the law faculties and grew out of the study of the philosophy of law. L. L. Bernard has pointed out that this great interest in public law in Latin America is traceable to the struggle for self government.[17] The close connection between the practice of law, government service and teaching the social studies has contributed likewise to this interest. Social sciences in Latin America originated as branches of law—*derecho natural, derecho publico, derecho criminal*—taught by lawyers in the law faculties. Positivism tended to convert this interest in public law into an interest in sociology and sociological jurisprudence.[18]

Latin American constitutions are a good expression of political thought on a practical level. Early constitutions were based on fundamental concepts of natural rights and economic individualism. Recent constitutions, and there have been a considerable number since 1917, reflect changes more in harmony with contemporary patterns of social thought.

Mexico's constitution of 1917 has had great influence. Its Article 27 tends to subordinate private property interests to those of the state acting for the general welfare. Provisions in new constitutions in Brazil, Bolivia, Colombia, Cuba, Ecuador, Uruguay and Venezuela also tend in this direction. The new constitutions likewise tend to place further restrictions on freedom of contract, and to lay broad bases for programs of social security. Labor is specifically set forth as a social duty and function, along with the duty of the state to promote its efficiency, including that of agricultural labor, by protective measures and

---

[17] L. L. Bernard, *Encyclopaedia of the Social Sciences,* I, pp. 306-7.

[18] Harry Elmer Barnes and Howard Becker, *Social Thought from Lore to the Science of Society* (Boston: D. C. Heath & Co., 1938), pp. 1122-1123.

by technical education. Property is represented as a social function. Most of the new constitutions postulate that the state must assure its citizens a minimum of well-being compatible with human dignity.[19] Probably the most original Latin American development in constitutional thought is that expressed in Baltasar Brum's *El ejectivo colegiado* (1925), an exposition of the theory behind the institution of the collegiate executive in the Uruguayan constitution of 1917 adopted under the leadership of José Battle y Orodoñez. In a new application of the principle of the balance of powers, a cabinet representative of both majority and minority parties was introduced as a means to end the bitter and frequently bloody partisan strife for national political power, while at the same time retaining the strong executive which seemed to grow out of the needs of the Latin American situation.

The struggle for political stability and independence also helps explain the great interest in international law. International law was taught in most Latin American universities by the end of the nineteenth century, although interest in the subject is traceable as far back as the publication of Andres Bello's *Principios de derecho internacional* in 1840. Outstanding contributions to the body of international law are represented by Luis M. Drago, Carlos Calvo and Baltasar Brum.

The Drago doctrine or principle that no state has a right to intervene in the affairs of another in order to collect economic obligations of that state to nationals of the former became a part of the Inter-American system by action of the Pan-American Congress at Montevideo (1933-34). By the Calvo Clause foreign capitalists doing business in another state undertook not to have recourse to their governments to protect their interests under a concession or contract with the government of the state in which the business was being transacted. Calvo also preceded Drago in the formulation of the principle which bears the latter's name.

---

[19] J. C. Zamora, "New Tendencies in Latin American Constitutions," *Journal of Politics*, III (August, 1941), pp. 276-296; Moises Poblete Troncoso, "The Social Content of Latin American Constitutions," *Social Forces*, XXI (October, 1942), pp. 100-106.

Under the Brum principle, enunciated during the first World War, an American state will treat another American state at war with a non-American state as a non-belligerent. In the Rio de Janeiro Conference (1942) the foreign ministers of the American republic recommended this principle to all the American governments. The contribution of Joaquim Nabuco to international law of the Americas and the outstanding contribution of the Count de Rio Branco to the development of arbitration in America should also be noted.[20]

A number of Latin Americans played important roles in the League of Nations. José Carlos de Macedo Soares of Brazil and Narciso Garay of Panama and to hers have contributed to the discussion of the relations of South America to the League.[21] The well known work of Manuel Ugarte, *Destiny of a Continent*,[22] although principally a polemic against Yankee imperialism, is notable for its interpretation of Latin America in the international scene. Among the other Latin Americans who have made significant contributions to the literature of international law and relations may be mentioned: Manuel de Oliveira (Brazil), Ernesto Quesada (Argentina), F. García Calderón (Peru), Victor Andrés Belaunde (Peru). Baltasar Brum and Pedro Erasmo Callorda have written outstanding books urging an American league of nations.[23]

Neo-Thomism apparently has many followers in Brazil although no outstanding spokesman. In Argentina it is represented by Octavio Nicolás Derisi and others in the Catholic

---

[20] Mario Monteiro de Carvalho, "Joaquim Nabuco," *Bulletin of Pan American Union* (February, 1934), pp. 127-133; F. W. Ganzert, "A Biography of Joaquin Nabuco," *Hispanic American Historical Review* (February, 1937), pp. 99-100); J. P. Cologeras, *History of Brazil* (Chapel Hill, N. C.: University of North Carolina Press, 1939), p. 193. See also: A. Roberto de Arruda Botelho, *Le Brésil et ses relations exterieures* (Paris: Mazarines, 1935), pp. 217-223.

[21] José Carlos de Macedo Soares, *Brazil and the League of Nations* (Paris, 1928), Narciso Garay, *La república de Panamá en la liga de las naciones* (Mexico, 1928).

[22] English translation by J. Fred Rippy (New York, 1925).

[23] Baltasar Brum, *"The Peace of America* (Montevideo, 1933) ; Pedro Erasmo Callorda, *Idea de una liga que responde a los conceptos panamericanos del Congreso de Bolívar* (Habana, 1928).

School of Philosophy and Theology at San Miguel. Mario Alzamora Valdez and Juan Lituma of the Catholic University in Lima represent this tendency in Peru. In the Catholic University of Chile it was formerly represented by Clarence Finlayson, recently of Notre Dame University. In Mexico, neo-Thomism finds its outstanding Latin American spokesman in Oswaldo Robles.[24] On the whole, neo-Thomism, while influencing religious social thought, has not exercised great influence on social and political thought in general, except where it has been exploited for political purposes. The liberal influence of Jacques Maritain seems in part to counterbalance a tendency in some quarters to identify neo-Thomism with *Hispanidad.*

ARGENTINA

Of all Latin American countries, Argentina has the greatest intellectual tradition. In the field of socio-political thought, Domingo F. Sarmiento, Juan B. Alberdi, Esteban Echeverría, Mariano Moreno, and Bernardo Monteagudo exercised an influence in the formation of the Argentine mind which cannot be duplicated in any other Hispanic American country. Their influence is still apparent in many ways in Argentina today.

Positivist thought was strongly represented by Francisco Ramos Mejía (1847--1893),[25] José María Ramos Mejía (1844-1914), and, in the early years of this century, by José Ingenieros (1877-1925), physician, psychologist, criminologist, sociologist and founder of the *Revista de Filosofía.* This *Revista* (founded 1915) holds an important place in the history of social thought in Argentina and all of Latin America. No other Latin American review published over so long a period of time has so consistently

---

[24] See Octavio Nicholás Derisi, *Los fundamentos metafísicos del orden moral* Buenos Aires: Instituto de filosofía, Facultad de filosofía y letras de Buenos Aires, 1941); Clarence Finlayson, *El primer aspecto ontológico del Ser* (Universidad Católica Bolivariana, No. 22, agosto—sept. 1941, p. 264-270); Oswaldo Robles, "Esquema de ontología tomista", *Filosofía y letras* (Mexico) (1941, No. 3.), pp. 35-45, pp. 199-208, and his "La Metafísica de la causa y el principio de finalidad" in *Abside,* (enero, 1941) pp. 38-47, (feb., 1941), pp. 126-132, and (marzo, 1941) pp. 189-195. See also *Handbook for Latin American Studies,* 1941.

[25] See his *El Federalismo argentio* (Buenos Aires, 1889), and his posthumous *Historia de la evolución argentina* (Buenos Aires, 1921).

concerned itself with the formulating of American culture and the solution of American problems.

Ingenieros became a member of the literary circle of Rubén Darío when the later came to Buenos Aires in 1897 shortly after the publication of his *Azul*. In company with the poet, Leopoldo Lugones, and with the support of Darío, he began publication of *La Montaña* and initiated the first important youth movement in Argentina.[26] For many years he remained the central intellectual figure in Argentine reform movements. Ingenieros represents positivist thought modified under the influence of the Argentine tradition, with elements of economic determinism derived from Marxian socialism and with biological and psychological interpretations related to Darwinian and Spencerian thought. Yet he is also distinguished for his search for idealistic or "spiritual" values within the structure of scientific materialism.[27] In his *Proposiciones relativas al porvenir de la filosofía* he set forth the view of ideals as "inexperiential hypotheses conditioned by experience and varying with the function of the experiential medium."[28] In line with the Argentine tradition from Echeverría to Sarmiento, he gave a great impetus to the study of national sociology and to the sociological interpretation of Argentine political thought.[29] The combination of a vast territory, fertile soil, temperate climate, and white race destined Argentina to become the center of the future neo-Latin race, he believed. He believed that a new spirit had been born in Latin American

---

[26] On Ingenieros, see especially, Sergio Bagú, *Vida ejemplar de José Ingenieros* Buenos Aires: Claridad, 1936), p. 35 ff. See also Alfredo Poviña, *Historia de la sociología en Latino-America* (Mexico: Fondo de cultura económica, 1941), p. 44 and *passim*. Ricardo Levene, the eminent historian-sociologist develops his thesis of the hispano-Indian origin of the social and juridical thought of Argentina in "Notas para la historia de las ideas sociales y jurídicas Argentinas," *Revista de la Universidad de Buenos Aires* (Julio-Septiember, 1943), pp. 34-46.

[27] In this connection, see his *El hombre mediocre,* his most widely read and influential work in *Obras Completas* (edited by Aníbal Ponce, Buenos Aires: N. J. Rossi, 1930-1936, 23 vols.; also Santiago de Chile: Ediciones Ercilla, 1937).

[28] Buenos Aires, 1918.

[29] See especially his *La evolución de las ideas argentinas* (Buenos Aires, 2 vols., 1918-20), and his *Sociología Argentina* (Madrid, 1913—the fifth edition of a work which first appeared as *El determinismo económico en la evolución americana* (Buenos Aires, 1901); the seventh edition was published in 1918.

youth during the years following the last war, and fired this youth with his own enthusiasm for an ethical, social, and political renovation of the Latin American peoples.[30]

Aníbal Ponce (1898-1938) was probably Ingenieros' outstanding disciple. In a brief life—he died at the age of forty—he crowded in a lifetime of accomplishment for an ordinary scholar.[31] Psychologist and psychiatrist, he shared the direction of the *Revista de Filosofía* with Ingenieros for a time. His chief contributions were in the field of psychology, but like Ingenieros he sought constantly to renew in Latin American youth the enthusiasm for social and political leadership which animated Sarmiento and the other early Argentines.

Alejandro Korn (1860-1936) is typical of the idealistic and metaphysical tendencies which began to appear in opposition to the materialism and realism of postivist thought near the end of the last century. He was one of Argentina's and Latin America's outstanding philosophers.[32] Korn was influenced particularly by Kant, Hegel, Schopenhauer and Bergson. To "scientific" thought he opposed metaphysics and a search for spiritual values. Starting with consciousness as the basis of all reality, he found time, space, and casuality derived from consciousness and without reality of their own. Abandoning determinism, he advocated a theory of freedom, particularly in the realm of ethics, where freedom of choice gives rise to ethical values. He has numerous followers among Argentine scholars today.

Neo-Thomism, as already stated, is strong in Argentina, centering in the Catholic School of Philosophy and Theology at San

[30] See: Sergio Bagú, *op. cit.*, p. 205.

[31] See: Aníbal Ponce, *Obras Completas* (Buenos Aires: El Ateneo, 1938—); Sergio Bagú, "Aníbal Ponce," *Nosotros* (August, 1938), pp. 3-11; and Luis Reissig, "Significación de Aníbal Ponce en la cultura argentina," *Claridad* (June-July, 1938). Among his works may be noted particularly *La gramatica de los sentimientos* (1929); *Sarmiento, constructor de la nueva Argentina* (1932); *El viento en el mundo* (1933).

[32] Publication of Alejandro Korn's complete works has been undertaken by the University of La Plata. Volume I was published in 1938, vol. II in 1941 and vol. III in 1940. On Korn see "Alejandro Korn, Philosopher of Argentina", *Panorama* (Division of Intellectual Cooperation of Pan American Union) (August, 1937), pp. 1-4, and Risieri Frondizi, *op. cit.* pp. 39-41.

Miguel. The journal *Stromata* is a vehicle of their views, as is to a certain extent *Sol y Luna*, except that in the latter a political turn is more likely to be given to the ideas. Yet here, too, as already noted, important neo-Thomists like Astrada are to be found who have not lent themselves to any political tendency.

The search for autonomous American thought has had a vigorous exponent in the literary critic, Ricardo Rojas. His *Eurindia* sets forth an "aesthetic founded on the historical experience of the American cultures".[33] Adopting in general an anthropological view of culture which leaves a large place for mystic or spiritual values, he feels that "Latin" America, although it has developed its culture more slowly than Anglo-Saxon America, will soon surpass the latter because of its "greater generality in aesthetic creation". Political autonomy he sees as merely an instrument for the use of the collective personality of the nation. The achievement of spiritual autonomy must precede its translation into philosophy and art.

A recent penetrating study of the geographic basis of Argentine social and political life, in line with the Sarmiento tradition, is Ezekiel Martínez' *Radiografía de la pampa*.[34]

BRAZIL

As already noted, positivist thought is more persistent in Brazil than anywhere else in America, although here as elsewhere there are strong counter currents. Luís Pereira Barreto (1840-1923) was the outstanding Brazilian positivist during the early years of this century, and Ivan Mario Lins is probably the most distinguished contemporary representative.[35] Fernando de Azevedo represents a positivism modified especially under the influence of Durkheim. As Director of the important Institute of Education in Sao Paulo he has been in a position to exercise considerable influence in educational thought. His *Principios de*

---

[33] Subtitle of volume *Eurindia,* Vol. 5, *Obras de Ricardo Rojas* (Buenos Aires: La Facultad, 1924).

[34] (Buenos Aires, 1943).

[35] Guillermo Francovich, *Filósofos Brasileños* (Buenos Aires: Losala, 1943). Barnes and Becker, *From Lore to Science,* pp. 1120-34.

Sociología published in 1935 is largely an introduction to positivist sociology but his *Sociología Educacional* shows more influence of contemporary currents of thought, and is perhaps the most influential book of social import to come out of Brazil in recent years.[36] Education is conservative by nature, he urges, closely linked with the state, and with definite political ends. Its purpose is to form men who conform to a certain ideal of man and life which dominates a given society or civilization, men who participate in political parties as a means to the conquest of political power to achieve a social-political program. His work ends with an analysis of the role of the school in achieving national unity, of patriotism and of public opinion, which is the regulating force controlling education.

The decline of positivist thought in Brazil, perhaps even more than elsewhere, brought a strong recurrence of thomistic thought. The influence of Jacques Maritain has been especially strong. Brazilian scholarship has also become increasingly concerned with the study of the country's negro population and the negro influence on national life and culture. Arthur Ramos in his *As Culturas Negras do Novo Mundo* and his *O Negro brasileiro* is concerned with negro patterns of ideas, the negro influences on the Brazilian mind. Gilberto Freire, on the other hand, in his *Casa Grande e Senzala*, *Sobrados e Mucambos* and his *Nordeste*, has attempted a comprehensive understanding of collective life in relation to its habitat.

In spite of all the literary activity of Brazil, there has been no recent adequate expression, on a philosophic level, of the great economic and social changes through which this rapidly expanding nation is obviously going. Nor has the revolution of 1930 and the subsequent regime found an adequate social interpretation. Sergio Buarque de Holanda in his *As Raíces do Brazil*, perhaps comes nearest.

PERU

Peruvians have been outstanding in their contributions to

---

[36] (São Paulo: Companhia Editore Nacional, 1940) ; it was also published in Spanish (Mexico: The Fondo de Cultura Económica, 1942).

contemporary Latin American thought. Among the outstanding figures may be mentioned Alejandro O. Deústua, José Carlos Mariátegui, Victor Raúl Haya de la Torre, and Luis Alberto Sánchez. Deústua represents the influence of Bergson and the idealistic reaction against positivism. His influence has been greatest, perhaps, in the field of aesthetics, but his theory of freedom, eloquently expounded in opposition to the determinism which had ruled positivist thought, has inspired Peruvian youth in recent years, and has had wide effect throughout Latin America.[37]

Mariátegui has made one of the strongest and most vital formulations of the theoretical basis and the practical approach to the solution of the socio-economic problems of Indo-America through political action. Studying the political and intellectual leaders and problems of Europe just after the last war, he evolved a theory of political leadership and social renovation for Peru. Strongly influenced at first by Marxist ideas,[38] he turned in the last days of his brief life to elements more largely indigenous to the soil of Peru. His *Siete ensayos de interpretación de la realidad peruana* became in many respects the program of the present *Aprista* movement, but its influence can also be seen in the social policies of present-day Peru.

Both Mariátegui and Haya de la Torre, the present leader of *Aprismo*,[39] were influenced by Marxism, the latter somewhat less than the former. Both have been more concerned with concrete programs of social action than with rigid critique of theory. Both represent the search for motives and forms of ideas in the American scene. Yet, in spite of this predominantly scientific

---

[37] Among his works may be noted: *La teoría de los valores; Sistemas de moral; Las ideas de orden y libertad en la historia del pensamiento humano; Historia de las ideas estéticas; Estética general; La cultura nacional* (Lima, 1937) ; *La estética de José Vasconcelos* (Lima, 1939).

[38] *Defensa de Marxismo* (Madrid) ; *La escena contemporánea* (Lima, 1925) ; *Siete ensayos de interpretación de la realidad peruano* (Lima, 1928) ; *Ideología y política en el Perú* (Madrid). See: Bazan Armando, *Biografía de José Carlos Mariátegui* (Santiago, 1939).

[39] Two works may be noted particularly: *Por la emancipación de la América Latina* (Buenos Aires, 1927) ; *A Donde va Indoamérica?* (Santiago de Chile, 1936).

and pragmatic tone in their thought, they have been concerned also with spiritual elements in the indigenous contribution to the pattern of Peruvian life, culture and problems.

Luis Alberto Sánchez is probably the most brilliant contemporary figure in Peruvian letters and one of the outstanding minds of America. He, too, has identified himself with the search for an American philosophy, including a philosophy of social action adequately related to the vital problems of the American scene. Like that of Ricardo Rojas, his approach was at first aesthetic, and even yet may scarcely be said to constitute a great addition to purely theoretical social or political thought. However, his influence among students and scholars in the other Americas has been tremendous, and as literary editor for the important publishing house of Ercilla in Santiago, during his years of exile, he has exercised great influence on the course of ideas. His *La vida y pasión de la cultura en América*, and his *La literatura en Perú* are particularly worthy of note for their social import. More recently, his prize-winning essay, "Latin America in the Post-War World," has received wide attention.[40]

CUBA

At the turn of the century José Varona (1849-1933) typified the currents modifying positivist social thought. It was he, in part, who led Menéndez y Pelayo to comment that Cuba was the hispanic nation which had produced the most vigorous philosophy.[41] In general, he opposed traditionalism and concerned himself instead with social interpretations of all aspects of Cuban life. He was greatly influenced by his study of English thought and retained from it many concepts that were in general utilitarian and pragmatic. Yet he was not satisfied with the theories of moral sentiment of Shaftesbury and Butler, nor with social Darwinism and the social evolutionism of Spencer. He also o-

---

[40] *La vida y passión*, etc. (Santiago de Chile, 1935); *La literatura en Perú* (Buenos Aires, 1939); see also: *America, novela sin novelistas* (Santiago de Chile, 2nd ed., 1940). The essay was published in *Tomorrow* (New York), III (April, 1944), pp. 8-12.

[41] Elias Entralgo, Medardo Vitier y Roberto Agramonte, *Enrique José Varona*, Vol. I, *Obras de José Varona* (La Habana: edición oficial, 1937).

posed the formalism of Kant and the absolutism of George Christian Krause, then becoming exceedingly popular in Cuba, and the neo-Hegelians—in general any schematic and systematic philosophy. Complete naturalism left him also dissatisfied, and he spoke of nature, seen without prejudice, as "the very image of chaos".[42] In general he achieved a relativistic position, and is particularly distinguished for his formulation of notions of relativism in reference to justice, wisdom and liberty.

Fernando Ortiz has been called the most "realistic and useful man of his times". Certainly his studies of African influences in Cuban culture and socio-economic relationships has directed thought and attention to the basic ethnological problems of a large part of Latin America as few others have done.

Cuba also provides one of the outstanding Latin American exponents of Marxist thought in Juan Marinello. His influence has been great, but characteristically shows itself largely in literary and educational activities.[43]

VENEZUELA

Few nations of America have gone through such a sudden, dramatic and far-reaching change from dictatorship to a regime of liberty and stability as has Venezuela since the death of Juan Vicente Gómez in 1935. A renascence in education has been accompanied by new vitality and optimism in social thought, previously limited, except for a few distinguished exiles, to sterile historical and biographical writing, largely in an adulatory vein. Augusto Mijares, in a series of penetrating studies, criticizes both the sociological explanations of the American scene offered by the great Argentinians, Sarmiento and Alberdi, and the more pessimistic views of the positivists who later rationalized militarism and dictatorship. His own view of the

---

[42] *Ibid.,* p. 98.

[43] For example, in his *Contrapunteo cubano del tabaco y el azúcar,* he indicates sugar and tobacco as "the two most important personages in the history of Cuba." (Habana, 1940). For Cuba, see also F. Peraza y Sarausa, *Indice de la revista de Cuba* (Habana: Biblioteca Municipal, 1938) ; *Indice de la Revista Cubana* (Habana: Biblioteca Municipal, 1939) ; *Indice de Cuba Contemporánea* (Habana: Biblioteca Municipal, 1940) ; and Medardo Vitier, *Las ideas en Cuba* (Habana, 2 vols., 1938).

possibilities of achieving democracy in Latin America by intelligent political action is optimistic. Mijares still apparently reflects many positivist ideas, but his voice is notable particularly
for the confidence he expresses in the ability of Latin American
leadership to solve American problems with American ideas.[44]

MEXICO

As previously noted, positivism, represented in the towering
intellectual figure of Justo Sierra, dominated social and political
thought in Mexico at the turn of the century. Already, however,
counter tendencies had begun, representing Boutroux, Bergson,
William James, Marxism and other such outside influences. A
nucleus of students and young professional men, the *Ateneo de
Juventud*, was the center of this tendency, a group with some
affinity to the other groups of Latin American youth which Rubén
Darío was firing with some of his enthusiam for cultural and
social self-realization. Included, among others, were the Domini-
can, Pedro Henríquez Ureña, Antonio Caso and José Vasconcelos, the two latter particularly destined to exercise profound
influence on the tumultous course of the subsequent Mexican
Revolution, as well as upon Latin American thought in the widest sense.[45]

Antonio Caso (1883-   ) is distinguished particularly for
the polemics against positivism with which he initiated his teaching at the University of Mexico. Alfonso Reyes writes that it
was Caso's eloquent attack which drove positivism from the
Mexican scene.[46] Influenced particularly by Bergson, Caso stands
in general for a philosophy of broad humanism. He has been
the channel through which most of the present generation of
Mexicans made their first acquaintance with contemporary

---

[44] *La interpretación pesimista de la sociología Hispano-americana* (Caracas, 1938);
Hombres y Ideas en América (Caracas, 1940).

[45] See: Francisco Romero, "Tendencias contemporáneas en el pensamiento Hispanoamericano," *Philosophy and Phenomenological Research*, IV (December, 1943), pp.
127-134.

[46] Alfonso Reyes, *Pasado Immediato* (Mexico, 1941); *El Noticiero Bibliográfico*
(October, 1941); A. Poviña, *Sociología en Latinoamerica*, p. 126.

European tendencies in thought. His influence has been correspondingly great. Ever since he has been for many Mexicans a steady point of orientation in the midst of changing orientations of the Revolution. Caso has not evolved a systematic philosophy of his own. He has, however, been an eloquent and influential spokesman for the general view that all social phenomena should be interpreted on a cultural basis. In this generally humanistic tendency one most readily perceives the basic resemblances to the thought of Bergson and Meyerson.[47]

José Vasconcelos (1882-   ) has had, perhaps, a greater popular influence, partly because of his stormy role in Mexican politics and cultural circles, and partly because of the prestige derived from his extensive travels in Europe, Asia and North and South America. The Mexican Ulysses originally responded to the same generally humanistic and anti-positivist influences which led Antonio Caso and the *Ateneo de Juventud* to revolt against Comtian positivism "which prohibits adventures of the mind and excludes them from the scientific age". Vasconcelos records in his Autobiography the dawn of his revolt and his own early tendency to seek a mystic, unifying basis for a philosophy.[48]

There is probably no more controversial figure in Latin American thought. He is polemical, his pen and tongue sharpened to keen and biting invective. At the same time he is sensitive to the cross currents of contemporary thought and social change. He is inconsistent, even self-contradictory. He is keenly critical of Americanists, "indigenists" and regionalists who look

---

[47] See: A. Menendez Samará, "Apuntes sobre la filosofía en Mexico," *Letras de Mexico* (15 enero, 1941), for influence of Antonio Caso. See also: R. Frondizi in *Inter-American Intellectual Interchange,* cited above, pp. 43-44; A. Poviña, *op. cit.,* pp. 126-129; and F. Romero, in *Philosophy and Phenomenological Research, loc. cit.* Among Caso's published works may be noted especially: *Problemas filosóficos* (1915; *Discursos a la nación mexicana* (1922) ; *El concepto de la historia universal y la filosofío de los valores* (1923) ; *Sociología* genetica *y sistemática universay y la filosofía de los valores* (1923) ; *Sociología genetica y sistemática* (1925) and subsequent editions; *El acto ideatorio* (1934) ; *La filosofía de la cultura y el materialismo historico* (1936) ; *Meyerson y la fisica moderna* (1940) ; and *El peligro del hombre* (1942).

[48] *Ulises Criollo,* p. 174. "But what is the secret of the soul?" he asks (p. 185). Vasconcelos' debt to Bergson appears in his "Bergson en México," *Filosofía y letras* pp. 239-253. Reproduced in *Homenaje a Bergson* (Mexico, 1941).

for an autonomous American thought, as well as of Marxism. Vasconcelos has produced not exactly a philosophical system, but a pattern of thought which comes nearer than most contemporary Latin American thinkers have come, perhaps the nearest of any, to bearing the stamp of originality.

His *Don Gabino Barreda y las ideas contemporáneas* was one of the earliest direct breaks with positivism in Mexico.[49] In his *Bolivarismo y Monroismo* he attempted to express an Ibero-American sociology which would transcend the conflict subject-object and the relation of individual to individual, incorporating dissimilarities in an organic and absolute whole. In his *Indología* he sought the philosophy necessary to achieve the high ambition of the Americas—the New World, confident of its future. In his *De Robinson á Odiseo* he expressed the need for a philosophic expression and for moral-intellectual leadership for the Mexican Revolution.

Vasconcelos is consistent in his defense of democracy, yet he attacks the Mexican concept of "permanent revolution" as an admission of defeat on the part of those who do not know how to use force to overthrow illegitimate oppression and reconstitute society on sound economic and elevated moral bases.[50]

It is in his *Ethics* and his *Aesthetics* that the mystic element appears most strongly. Ethics is discipline of life, he reasons. Morality is what leads us to transcend the disorder and chaos of life. His interpretation of the world has become tragic in these works ("joyful pessimism"). The aim of the moral law is spiritual redemption and integration with the Absolute. His

---

[49] (Mexico, 1910).

[50] See his *?Que es la revolución?* (1937). Among other works of Vasconcelos, in addition to the study of Gabino Barreda and the others cited above, are: *Monismo estético* (1919); *La raza cósmica* (1925); *Indología* (1927); *Tratado de metafísica* (1929); *Etica* (1932); *Bolivarismo y Monroismo* (1935); *Estética* (1936); *Historia del pensamiento* (1937); *Breve historia de Mexico* (1937); *Manual de filosofía* (1940); *Estudios Indostanicos*. The volume of selections from Vasconcelos, edited with prologue by Genaro Fernandez McGregor and published (1942) by the Secretaría de Educación Pública, Mexico, as the first volume of *Pensamiento de América,* is very useful although marred by lack of adequate bibliographic data.

Estética has been destructively criticized by the great Peruvian philosopher of liberty, Alejandro Deústua.[51]

The middle 'thirties were marked in Mexico by an historical argument over the Revolution, sometimes assuming a tone of great vindictiveness. In reminiscences, biographies, newspaper articles and a few more tempered historical works, followers of Madero, Carranza, Obregón, Cárdenas and other leaders exchanged charges and counter-charges. Little of this literature of controversy achieves the level of broad social and political interpretation of the Revolution, although it does serve to focus more clearly the divergent social views of the principal protagonists and their philosophies. The stimulus which seemed to come to the development of Mexican thought at this time may not be entirely unrelated to this historical controversy, a controversy which apparently has not yet run its entire course.[52]

At about the same time Spanish refugees began to bring a new impetus to social thought in Latin America, and particularly in Mexico and Peru. In the Catholic University in Lima, for example, Alberto Wagner de Reynal now represents the phenomenology of Husserl and the existentialism of Heidegger, recently point out by Risieri Frondizi as the most rapidly spreading tendency in Latin American thought.[53]

José Gaos, Juan D. García Bacca, Joaquín Xirau and others constitute a particularly brilliant group in Mexico. Here the *Colegio de Mexico* and the *Fondo de Cultura Económica* have been responsible for a great increase of philosophical study along several lines. They have published many basic social and philosophical studies, as well as translations of important foreign works not previously available in Spanish. Particularly not-

---

[51] Alejandro Deústua, *La estética de José Vasconcelos* (Lima, 1939).

[52] Of special interest from the standpoint of interpretation are: J. Vasconcelos *¿Que es la revolución?* (1937), Blas Urrea (Luís Cabrera), *Veinte años despues* (1938), J. M. Puig Casauranc, *El sentido social del proceso historico de Mexico* (1936), Manuel Gamio, *Hacia un Mexico nuevo* (1935), Alfonso Teja Zabre, *Panorama historica de la revolución mexicana* (1939), Moises Saenz, *Mexico Integro* (Lima, 1939). Alfonso Teja Zabre's work is distinguished by a rather strict economic determinism.

[53] See *Handbook of Latin American Studies,* and F. Romero, *op. cit.*

able are the *Fondo's* publication of translations of such works as Husserl's *Meditaciones cartesianas* (1942), Alfred Weber's *Historia de la cultura* (1941), Karl Mannheim's *Libertad y planificación social* (1942), and his *Ideología y Utopía* (from the English edition by Louis Wirth, 1941).

Joaquín Xirau represents the Husserl-Heidegger tendency of thought in Mexico. José Gaos represents an influence which has extended itself to a considerable group of students with which he has established various kinds of contact. They represent in general an historical approach to social thought which interprets ideas in space and time relationships to the culture to which they are related. Notable in this group is Leopoldo Zea, whose *El positivismo en México* has recently appeared.[54] Some of the ideas of this group may also be read in *Del Cristianismo y la Edad Media by* Leopoldo Zea, Edmundo O'Gorman, José Luis Martínez, Gustavo Pizarro, Tomás Gurza, Antonio Gomez Robledo, María Ramona Rey, Pina Juárez Frausto and José Gaos.[55]

URUGUAY AND CHILE

Carlos Vaz Ferreira, Rector of the University of Montevideo, holds an important position in Latin American thought. He has contributed several volumes on significant social problems. Baltasar Brum's contribution to constitutional and international law has been mentioned earlier. Another Uruguayan contribution of some distinction is Antonio M. Grompone's *Filosofía de las revoluciones* (1932).[56]

Alberto Zum Felde, in his *Proceso histórico del Uruguay*[57] gives an anthropological-economic analysis of Uruguayan social history, emphasizing Guaraní-Quechua cultural elements and the influence of cattle on national culture.

Augustín Venturino of Chile was singled out by Barnes and Becker as one of the outstanding students of society in Latin America. Making an ecological or anthropo-geographical ap-

---

[54] Leopoldo Zea, *El positivismo en Mexico* (Mexico, 1943).

[55] Leopoldo Zea, *El positivismo en Mexico* (Mexico, 1943).
[56] See: Poviña,*op. cit.*, pp. 115-6.

[57] (Montevideo, 1930).

proach to the analysis of Chilean society, he has studied, in a series of volumes, indigenous and colonial culture in Chile and the conflict and amalgamation of races in America.[58]

SUMMARY

The dominant social thought of Latin America still bears many strong marks of nineteenth century positivism. This is particularly true of the sociology taught in many of the law Catholic circles and has provided receptive ground for neo-faculties of the universities. Theological interest is great in Thomism as represented by the influence of Jacques Maritain and others.

Marxism has numerous representatives, of course, but strict Marxian thought has received no great emphasis in recent years. Alfredo Palacios of Argentina is perhaps the outstanding representative. Mariátegui and Haya de la Torre came briefly under its influence, and many Mexican intellectuals have flirted more or less with it, although it can scarcely be said to have become the dominant characteristic of their thought. There are, of course, outright Marxists like Marinello and Lombardo Toledano. Socialism has many political adherents and Marxist thought in Latin America, as elsewhere in the modern world, has exercised a profound influence on social and political thought, particularly upon historical interpretation.

The vogue of Dilthey, Spengler, Weber, Simmel, Durkheim, Husserl and Heidegger has lent itself to a generally sociological approach to problems of knowledge. In many cases, *e.g.*, Francisco Romero and Ernesto Quesada of Argentina, this approach tends to assimilate to the Latin American preoccuption with American or national sociology, that is with thought on a practical social and political level. This thought, however, is frequently based upon an affirmation or a profound intuition *á la* Bergson of the unity of spiritual, moral and material factors, and coupled with a strong belief in moral and social freedom.[59]

---

[58] *Sociología primitiva chileindiana,* (2 vols., 1927, 1928); *Sociología Chilena* (1929); *Sociología general americana* (1931). See: Barnes and Becker, *op. cit.,* pp. 1125-1127.

[59] On this point, see: Francisco Romero, *op. cit., p.* 133.

This fusion may be seen particularly in the thought of Alejandro Deústua. Yet, in this cardinal emphasis upon concepts of liberty, a Deústua, a Sánchez, an Azevedo, a Coutinho, a Vasconcelos, an Antonio Caso, a Francisco Romero and a Carlos Vaz Ferreira may find common ground with a John Dewey, a Whitehead or a Santayana. Direct influence from the United States has been small in recent years, except in the fields of education and sociology, probably because larger numbers of Latin American students have come to the United States for advanced study in these fields. The influence of William James is to be noted occasionally,[60] and much current thought, especially that following the search for autonomous patterns, or following the influence of phenomenology and existentialism shows many points of resemblance or contact with pragmatic and circumstantial or relativistic tendencies in North American thought.

Hispanic or Hispanic-American unity has exercised a great attraction for many Latin Americans during recent decades. It has frequently colored social and political thought. Stimulated at first by the renascence in Spain and Portugal which followed the Spanish American War,[61] it rested, of course, on cultural ties which united the Ibero-American peoples, the importance of which seemed to be emphasized by political disunity and instability. "Yankeephobia" and "Yankee imperialism" contributed to its development. Rubén Darío gave great impetus to this movement for cultural unity, and such writers as Mariátegui, Haya de la Torre, Vasconcelos and others have at one time or another sought to further it on the basis of racial and cultural concepts such as "Indoamerica" or a "cosmic race".[62]

Contemporary *Hispanidad* has given a decidedly different turn to the tendency, because of its closer identification with certain European tendencies, especially tendencies of traditional-

---

[61] Fernando de los Ríos, "Spain and Portugal," in "Introduction, The Social Sciences as Disciplines," in *The Encyclopaedia of the Social Sciences,* I; see footnote 12.

[60] As in the writings of Antonio Delle Piane (1864- ?) Argentine who played an important part in the attack on positivism, formulating an idealistic sociology. See his *William James* (Montevideo: A. Monteverde y Cía., 1943).

[62] John E. Engelkirk's article in *Hispanic Unity* (before 1890).

ism, since the Spanish Revolution. *Hispanidad* has tended to divert its ideological basis to political ends, of course, frequently involving tendencies like neo-Thomism which have little or no connection with the political objectives of *Hispanidad*. As a result of these changes, and particularly of the support of *Hispanidid* by the Franco government, the liberal *Americanistas* and *indoamericanistas* have tended away from their previous interest in Hispanic unity toward either a more intense nationalism or a broader internationalism.[63]

BIBLIOGRAPHY

There is no good comprehensive treatment of the subject in English. The best sources are the works of the Latin Americans referred to in the footnotes. Such one volume histories of Latin America as those of Mary W. Williams, J. Fred Rippy and David Moore are useful for general background, and the following references will be of value to the reader in English.

BARNES, HARRY ELMER, AND BECKER, HOWARD, *Social Thought from Lore to Science* (New York: D. C. Heath and Company, 1938), (2. II, p. 1120-1134. Generally useful, but based on the limited literature in English.

BELAUNDE, VICTOR ANDRES, *Bolívar and Political Thought of the Spanish American Revolutions* (Baltimore: Johns Hopkins University Press, 1938). One of the best contemporary interpretations of the Liberator's ideas by a distinguished Peruvian scholar.

BERNARD, L. L., in *Encyclopaedia of the Social Sciences,* I, pp. 301-320, "Introduction"; Part Two: "The Social Sciences as Disciplines," ix, "Latin America;" "The Development and Present Tendencies of Sociology in Argentina," *Social Forces* VI (1927), pp. 13-17. Still one of the most useful references.

CALCOTT, W. H., *Liberalism in Mexico,* 1857-1929 (Berkeley: University of California Press, 1931). An authoritative treatment of the subject.

CRAWFORD, WILLIAM REX, *A Century of Latin American Thought* (Cambridge, Mass.: Harvard University Press, 1944). This book, which should fill a long felt need, was not yet available as this chapter was being written.

DIFFIE, BAILEY, *"The Ideology of Hispanidad,"* Hispanic American Historical Review (August 1943), pp. 457-482.

ENGELKIRK, JOHN E., "El Hispanoamericanismo y la Generación de 98," *Revista Iberoamericana, II* (November 1940), No. 4. A careful statement of a movement which has influenced political thought in Latin America profoundly.

EULAU, HEINZ H. F. "The Ideas behind Brazilian Integralism," *Inter-American Quarterly,* III (October, 1941), pp. 36-43. A brief summary.

FLETCHER, W. G., "Aprismo Today—An Explanation and a Critique," *Inter-American Quarterly,* III (October 1941), pp. 14-20. Chiefly an analysis of the effect of the European crisis on Aprismo.

---

[63] See: Bailey Diffie, "The Ideology of Hispandidad," *Hispanic American Historical Review* (August, 1943), pp. 457-82.

FRONDIZI, RISIERI, "Tendencies in Contemporary Latin American Philosophy," *Inter-American Intellectual Interchange* (Austin, University of Texas, 1943), pp. 35-48.

GARCÍA CALDERÓN, FRANCISCO, *Latin America, Its Rise and Progress,* (tr. by Maill, London: T. Fisher Unwin, 1913). A well known historical treatment, notable for the author's analysis of the problems in the political development of the Latin American nations.

Handbook of Latin American Studies, especially volumes for 1939 (pp. 418-427), 1940 (pp. 453-462), and 1941 (pp. 550-558) contain bibliographical notes on recent philosophical studies of importance by Risieri Frondizi.

HAYA DE LA TORRE, VICTOR RAUL, "Inter-American Democratic Front," *Free World,* IV (November, 1942), pp. 150-152. A discerning but brief comment by the leader of Peruvian *Aprismo.*

INMAN, SAMUEL GUY, *Latin America, Its Place in World Life* (New York: Harcourt Brace, rev. ed., 1942). The author's broad acquaintance with the writers of Latin America, their works and their ideas, makes the book useful in many ways.

Philosophic Abstracts, Dagobert G. Runes, ed., contains useful references, especially in the issues since 1940.

Philosophy and Phenomenological Research, LV (December, 1943), published by Inter-American Conference of Philosophy held at Yale University, April 30, May 1, 1943. Printed in Spanish and English.

the University of Buffalo, Buffalo, N. Y., reports the proceedings of the first

POVINA, ALFREDO, *Historia de la sociología en Latinoamérica* (Mexico: Fondo de Cultura Economica, La Casa de España en México, 1940). A book of fundamental importance for the subject.

TORRES-RIOSECO, ARTURO, *The Epic of Latin American Literature* (New York: Oxford University Press, 1942), is useful for the ideas of important literary figures.

TRONCOSO, MOISES POBLETE, "Social Content of Latin American Constitutions," *Social Forces,* XXI (October, 1942), pp. 100-106, points out the similarities in provisions and social outlook of the new constitutions since 1917.

ZAMORA, J. C., "New Tendencies in Latin American Constitutions", *Journal of Politics,* III (August, 1941), pp. 276-296. Indicates how the tradition of liberalism has been modified by new social concepts of property, contract, social security and economic nationalism.

Chapter XXIV

CENTRAL-EASTERN EUROPE

W. J. EHRENPREIS

Differing in their racial origin, historical role and constitutional set-up, the Central-Eastern European nations have two common characteristics which distinguish them, as a group, from their neighbors to the west: they had all entered upon the path of industrial development much later than Western Europe; as a result of this lag, the peasantry is still the potentially dominant factor in their national life. Czechoslovakia and Austria have reached a high level of industrial development and have therefore achieved a certain degree of equilibrium between agriculture and industry (in time of peace); Poland and Hungary were steadily advancing toward a similar condition, but Yugoslavia and Roumania have hardly begun to emerge from the agricultural stage. However, irrespective of the marked differences in the level of industrialization, the common pattern is plainly visible.

In all these countries the peasantry has only recently become free and, to some extent, land-owning. The process of agrarian reform was not yet completed by the outbreak of the war. Every step towards the greater freedom of the peasant and agrarian reform had to be made against the strong opposition of the old land-owning class, which, in many instances, was able to use political power to suppress and combat the peasants' aspirations. Hence, the basic social conflict of the Central-Eastern European countries: peasant vs. landowner. This conflict is still fundamental, even where social and economic development has brought forward other, more apparent, conflicts, conflicts which may have given rise to more abundant political literature, as in

the case of the class struggle between workers and capitalists
which developed after the introduction of the capitalist pattern
of industrial production.

Superimposed upon and partly arising from these social
conflicts (peasant vs. landowner and worker vs. capitalist), was
the national conflict: native vs. foreigner (usually vs. foreign
ruler, such as the German or the Russian; the Turk may here
be disregarded, for Turkish domination was almost over at the
beginning of the Twentieth Century). Because of its far-reaching implications, the national conflict was able to overshadow
the social conflicts: hence, the amount of political thought and
writing devoted to national problems.

The problem of Austria offers striking illustration of this
emphasis on the national question. Because all the nations discussed in this chapter were either wholly or in part under
Austria's domination (before 1918), or at least in some way
dependent on it, the Austrian problem assumed paramount importance in all political discussion. Few thinking persons could
avoid admitting that the peoples which found themselves under
Austria's banner had a number of interests in common; geography, history, economic development and reasons of security—
all these created the basis for a community of interest. On the
other hand, the old Hapsburg Monarchy's glaring incapacity to
utilize and emphasize these positive elements which might have
united and bound the Danubian peoples, and its insistence on
granting parasitical rights and privileges to certain groups and
nationalities gave rise to much thought on what should have
been done—but was not. This was the reason for the numerous
plans to reform the Hapsburg Monarchy, without which few
Danubian political thinkers would have regarded their work as
complete. After the downfall of the Hapsburgs, the concept of
the Monarchy as a unifying factor was replaced by that of the
Danubian Federation.

Thus, in a nutshell, the basic problems of XX Century political thought in the Central-European nations have been as
follows: the struggle for agrarian reform, the struggle for so-

cial and industrial reform, and the problem of full national sovereignty vs. regional coordination. Insistence on a democratic solution to these problems has been an equally essential element in the political thought of these nations.

The writings of the various political thinkers discussed here reflect these problems both directly and indirectly. It would be difficult, within the space available, to provide a more detailed picture. The following pages, therefore, can be no more than a general outline and guide.

AUSTRIA

Since 1900, Austria has twice changed her political status as a nation. Prior to 1918, Austria was one of the two constituent parts of the Austro-Hungarian Empire of the Hapsburgs. It consisted of many countries and regions which had come under Hapsburg rule by various methods in the course of centuries, most of them at a time when nationality was not an all-important element in political life. When, in the Nineteenth Century, the national state became the basis of all political systems, the Austrian question emerged. The German element was dominant in Austria both because the Austrian State was essentially of German character and because no other national group was numerically stronger; at the same time, however, the various nationalities of Austria began to show strongly centrifugal tendencies. After the establishment of a German Empire, separate from Austria, the problem of the latter's national organization assumed a different character.

The "Language Dispute" in Imperial Austria.

In Austria the Twentieth Century was heralded by extremely violent political strife between the German and the non-German elements of the population. This strife was complicated by the fact that in many of the country's regions the population was not nationally homogeneous; as a result, the national or, as it was then called, the "language" [1] dispute which was stirring the entire country was repeated on a small scale throughout many of its provinces. The intensity of these conflicts had all but paralyzed the efficiency of the Austrian State: the central legislature, and many of the provincial legislatures as well, were unable to discuss any other matter and became a veritable battlefield whenever questions bearing on the "language dispute" were raised. The subsequent strengthening of executive power and of the military circles was a direct result of the deadlock in the legislative bodies.

Small wonder, then, that the foremost Austrian political thinkers of the time devoted much of their effort to the question of cooperation between the various nationalities. This was due not only to a desire to settle the question, but also to the need to remove the stumbling block which prevented the functioning of constitutional processes by paralyzing the legislative branch of the government.

A man to whom both aspects of the problem were equally important was *Karl Renner* (1870-   ). Known primarily for his part in active politics—he was a Socialist deputy in the Austrian Parliament and, for some time, head of a Socialist Administration—and for his book on the introduction of Socialist elements into the capitalist economy [2], he was also one of the most eminent theoreticians in the field of national problems. One of his earliest contributions in that field was "The State and Parliament", [3] in which he advocated the transformation of the political organization of Austria into a novel form of government which he called "A Federal Republic with Monarchical Leadership." While old Austria existed, he untiringly sought argu-

---

[1] At that time many people believed in the permanence and stability of the Hapsburg Monarchy. They were unwilling to admit anything as disturbing as "national" strife among its subjects. Since most of the strife centered about the question of what language was to be used in official life, the dispute was euphemistically called "the language dispute."

[2] Karl Renner, *Economic Life and Socialization* (Vienna, 1924, in German).

[3] Karl Renner (under the pen-name of Rudolf Springer), *The State and Parliament* (Vienna, 1901, in German).

ments to back this thesis and carried on extensive research work with that aim in mind.

He proposed a detailed plan for such reorganization in his book, "The Struggle of the Austrian Nations for their State." [4] This book sharply criticized the Austrian administration which, Renner asserted, had failed to convince the peoples of Austria that Austria was their common state. Only those elements of the population which owed personal allegiance to the Austrian Emperor (the nobility, the bureaucratic circles, the officers of the regular army and the higher clergy) considered Austria their own state. The non-German elements either looked towards their brethren who lived in independent national states, or planned to rejoin those of their co-nationals who lived under other foreign rule in order to jointly seek to achieve national independence. Even some of the Austrian Germans looked to Germany as the Empire to which they would rather adhere to.

In view of these facts, Renner advocated a reorganization of Austria along the lines of national autonomy, permitting all its subjects to govern themselves and leaving only the usual attributes of federal authority in the hands of the central government. Renner realized, however, that this solution would not answer the problem of the Austrian regions in which the population was mixed. For these, he devised a novel system, based on two institutions: national registration and cultural autonomy.

According to Renner, citizens of different tongues living in the same province were not likely to clash upon problems unrelated to those of nationality; these could properly and peacefully be arranged by common discussion. Controversy, however, was likely to develop in the discussion of such problems as that of education, for each national group would naturally seek to achieve the dominance of its own language in the school system. Renner therefore suggested that the legislative bodies of bilingual provinces allot lump sums for education, to be divided

---

[4] Karl Renner (under the pen-name of Rudolf Springer), *The Struggle of the Austrian Nations for their State* (Leipzig, 1902, in German) ; a revised edition of this book appeared as *National Self-Determination as Applied to Austria* (Leipzig, 1918, in German).

into shares in proportion to the numerical strength of each national group. Thereafter, the legislative body would suspend joint sessions, its members separating according to their national origin. Each national group would then decide for itself how its share of the funds voted for educational purposes was to be spent to fulfill its specific needs without any interference from other national groups.

The number of deputies of the various national groups were to be proportional to their numerical strength and elected, whenever possible, in nationally homogeneous constituencies in order to prevent the degeneration of election campaigns into struggles between national groups. Thus, for example, instead of the election of two members-at-large in a mixed county, or the division of the county into two territorially separate constituencies, each of the members would be elected by citizens using the same language. In order to determine the relative strength of the various national groups in mixed areas, their inhabitants would have to register as members of one or the other national group.[5] This register would be called the "national cadaster". This system, some of the elements of which had been proposed even before Renner advanced his ideas, could also be applied to the local and provincial administrations; indeed, several Austrian provinces adopted many of its features, while other provinces made it obligatory for their bilingual communities.

These proposals were once more developed at length in two later books by Renner; in one of these, "The Basis and Development of the Austro-Hungarian Monarchy,"[6] he supported his views by an impressive array of historical and constitutional argument. In some of his other books, Renner attempted a more popularized presentation of his concept of national autonomy.

---

[5] This registration would be somewhat similar to the party registration system in New York State, with the difference that national registration would be much more general than party registration (some persons have even advocated a compulsory national register), and that the various groups would be considered as separate constituencies for purposes of the general elections.

[6] Karl Renner (under the pen-name of Rudolf Springer), *The Basis and Development of the Austro-Hungarian Monarchy* (Vienna, 1906, in German).

The first World War broke out before Austrian reform could be achieved. Renner was a keen observer of the disastrous impact of the war upon Austria. Another book, "Austria's Renewal," [7] was the result of his observations and reflections. Subsequently, Renner once more returned to the problem of nationalities. His book, "Germany, Austria and the Peoples of the East," [8] is a summary of his ideas of what Austria could have achieved among the non-German peoples of Central Europe had her policy been based on justice and reason.

Austro-Marxism and Catholic Corporationism.

Monsignore Ignaz Seipel (1876-1932) was another keen student of the national problem in Austria. Best known for his part in active politics after the first World War,[9] he had also done some important research work on national problems, which he approached from the Catholic point of view. The results of his research and reflections were published after the downfall of Hapsburg Austria,[10] which doubtlessly colors the final presentation, but it is easy to observe that his argument does not materially differ from that of Renner, whatever other differences the two men may have had on related matters.

In addition to his interest in economic and social problems, Msgr. Seipel also held strong views on constitutional questions. These questions became increasingly pressing after 1918, when the German lands of the former Hapsburg Empire were set up as the new Federal Republic of Austria. Seipel played a prominent part in the shaping of Austria's Republican constitution and in the discussion of its amendments. He was one of the first European statesmen to attempt to introduce the Catholic point

---

[7] Karl Renner, *Austria's Renewal* (Vienna, 1916, in German). Part of the material of this book had appeared earlier in various periodicals.

[8] Karl Renner, *Germany, Austria and the Peoples of the East* (Berlin, 1922, in German).

[9] He was Austria's Federal Chancellor, an office corresponding to that of Prime Minister, for many years.

[10] Ignaz Seipel, *The Spiritual Basis of the Minority Problem* (Leipzig, 1925, in German).

of view on corporate representation [11] into practical constitutional law. It should be noted, however, that it was not until the promulgation of the Fascist Constitution of 1934 that Seipel's views on this matter gained acceptance in Austrian constitutional law.

Austria's most important political thinker in the Twentieth Century was unquestionably Otto Bauer (1881-1938). Bauer was a prominent political figure and the leader of the Austrian Socialist Party. This circumstance often obscures the fact that he was, primarily, a theoretician. He was a very prolific writer on a variety of subjects related to political, social and economic theory and practice. We shall, however, mention only a few of his books.

Otto Bauer was best known for the part he played in the discussion between Democratic Socialists and Communists which agitated the European Labor Movement between the two World Wars and which was probably more than anything else responsible for the Fascist successes in various European countries. He advanced a solution of his own, rejecting the thoroughly undemocratic elements of Communism and eliminating the obsolete aspects of the Democratic Labor Movement. Bauer's proposals in this direction were generally accepted by Austrian Socialists (his views became known as "Austro-Marxism"). This solution found a wide response throughout the Labor Movements of Europe. However, because of the general repugnance of Communist ideas to the organized workers, and the unwillingness of Labor's office-holders to relinquish any of the obsolete elements of their ideology and organization, the differences between Socialists and Communists became so deep that they could no longer be bridged.[12]

---

[11] Ignaz Seipel's views on this question are developed in *The Austrian Constitutional Struggle* (Vienna, 1930, in German).

[12] Some of Otto Bauer's most characteristic writings on this problem are: *Bolshevism or Social Democracy* (Vienna, 1921, in German; *The Road to Socialism* (Vienna, 1921, in German); *The Austrian Revolution* (Vienna, 1923, in German).

Bauer also wrote extensively on economic problems.[13] In his last book, "The Illegal Party," [14] he summarized the experiences of the clandestine struggle of Labor and democratic parties, which had been driven underground under Fascist rule, and attempted to discover some general rules governing the development of illegal movements.

Another outstanding representative of the Austro-Marxian school was Max Adler (1873-1937). Deeply involved in the study of the psychological and ethical aspects of society and their relation to Marxian economics,[15] Adler was also a keen student of the effects of democracy in the field of politics on the economic and social order. While Max Adler was by no means the first theoretician to proclaim that political democracy as such does not result in social justice (as some of the earlier Socialists believed), he strongly opposed the thesis advanced by the Communists during the period of 1922-1932, which urged that political democracy was a sham and that workers had nothing to gain from it. Max Adler undertook an extensive writing project in order to demonstrate that while political democracy and social justice are not identical, it is only under conditions of political democracy that the struggle for social justice can be waged effectively.[16] This position, reasonable as it seems now, was by no means widely recognized in Europe in 1925 or 1930, and it required much energy to work for its acceptance. While the general realization of its truth has come about as a result of the experiences of the democratic movements of Europe under Fascist and Nazi rule, it was Max Adler who had prepared the theoretical ground for it. Adler's last book, "The Riddle

---

[13] Otto Bauer's most important books on economic problems are *Social-Democratic Agrarian Policy* (Vienna, 1926, in German) ; *Rationalization—Success or Failure?* (Vienna, 1931, in German).

[14] Otto Bauer, *The Illegal Party* (Paris, 1939, in German).

[15] Max Adler, *Marxian Problems* (Berlin, 1913, in German; *Politics and Morals* (Leipzig, 1918, in German) ; *Kant and Marxism* (Berlin, 1925, in German) ; *Marxism, the Workers' Philosophy* (Berlin, 1926, in German) ; *Textbook on Economic Materialism* (Berlin, 1930/32, 2 Vols., in German).

[16] Max Adler's most important books on this question are: *Political and Social Democracy* (Berlin, 1926, in German) ; *The Worker's Fatherland* (Berlin, 1929).

of Society," [17] is devoted to purely sociological problems.

CZECHOSLOVAKIA

(A) *Masaryk—Philosopher-President.* Twentieth century political thought in Czechoslovakia developed under the influence of Thomas Garigue Masaryk (1850-1937), for many years Professor at Charles University in Prague and eminent statesman.

Masaryk was the first Czechoslovakian thinker to formulate political theory and pursue practical politics on a sociological basis. In this he differs fundamentally from earlier Czech political thinkers who tended to take a historical approach and to whom historical experience alone dictated the course to be taken in the future. Masaryk began his career with purely sociological works,[18] many of which were and still are of far-reaching importance in that field. It was only later that his sociological writings began to assume a distinctly political cast. He did not, however, limit himself to theoretical contributions to the social and political sciences, but entered practical politics as well, and it is probably for his activities in that field that he will be best remembered by posterity. After many years as a Progressive Czech member of the old Austrian Parliament, Masaryk assumed leadership in the Czechoslovakian struggle for independence during the First World War and became Chairman of the Czechoslovakian National Committee in Paris. When Czechoslovakia was liberated, he was elected President of the Republic, a post in

---

[17] Max Adler, "The Riddle of Society" (Vienna, 1936, in German).

[18] The best available survey in English is: Joseph S. Roucek, "Masaryk as Sociologist," *Sociology and Social Research,* XXII (May-June, 1938), pp. 412-420. See also: Roucek, "President Masaryk of Czechoslovakia," *Current History,* XXXI (March, 1930), pp. 1109-1112, and "Internationally Minded State," *World Unity,* VI (April, 1930), pp. 43-49; and "Thomas Garigue Masaryk as Politician and Statesman," *Social Science,* VI (May, 1932), pp. 272-278; and "Thomas Garigue Masaryk—Advocate of International Justice," *World Order,* L (April, 1935), pp. 12-14; and "Eighty-fifth Birthday of President Masaryk," *Social Science,* X (April, 1935), pp. 201-202; and "A Great Teacher, Democrat and Statesman: Dr. Thomas Garigue Masaryk Reaches his Eighty-Fifth Birthday," *World Affairs Interpreter,* VI (April, 1935), pp. 81-91. The most important of Masaryk's early sociological work was *Suicide as a Social Phenomenon in Modern Civilization* (Vienna, 1881, in German).

which he remained, and here he advocated the principles of reform and evolutionary development of society. His own political activities during the Czechoslovak struggle for independence, however, show that he did not reject revolutionary methods whenever they offered the advantage of rapid achievement of desirable changes. This again demonstrates Masaryk's realism: whenever a given course was preferable from a long range perspective, he unhesitatingly pursued it even if it was in seeming contradiction to his expressed views until his resignation in 1935; at that time the title of President-Liberator was conferred upon him.

It is important to keep in mind Masaryk's political activities to properly evaluate his political and sociological work. His writings reflect Czech (and, subsequently, Czechoslovakian) political and national conditions. Before the First World War Czechoslovakia was under the domination of the Austro-Hungarian Empire, and its leaders were principally interested in directing their social energies, as well as their research and investigations, towards promoting national interests. Everything in the field of culture and sociology was measured by the standard of national utility. By the same token, Masaryk's writings were characterized by practical aims rather than by emphasis on theory. His primary methods in sociology were observation of common daily phenomena; deductions from statistical tables, and analysis of historical trends which carefully avoided the pitfall of excessive preoccupation with details. The sociological conclusions he reached in his studies he immediately put to practical application in the field of politics.

Masaryk's first important contribution to political thought was his "Social Question." [19] The strong influence upon this work of Marxian theory is especially evident in its recognition of the effect of economic development upon history and politics. But Masaryk went beyond that. Unlike many contemporary philosophers and theoreticians who chose to completely reject Marxism, he felt that the basic Marxian concept should be broad-

---

[19] *Social Question* (Czech editions, Prague, 1892 and 1935; German edition, Vienna, 1899; Russian edition, Moscow, 1900).

ened; he did that by showing that evolution is determined by numerous complex elements and that its causes cannot be reduced to a single social force. Incidentally, in doing so, Masaryk remained closer to Marx than to some of the latter's pupils and followers.

It was Masaryk's basic thesis that politics, law, morality, art and science are all the result of underlying social developments and of economic conditions. But he also regarded psychological and emotional factors, and particularly religious factors, as of equal importance in the determination of these various aspects of social and ideological life. Masaryk was profoundly concerned with religious questions and devoted several works to the problem of religion and the church.[20]

As years went by, Masaryk's interest in political problems became deeper and deeper. While retaining his place as one of Europe's foremost sociologists, Masaryk took an ever more active part in politics; this developing interest was reflected in the changing topics of his books.

For more than half a century before the First World War the question of Russia's relations with and influence on the Slav peoples of the Austro-Hungarian Empire was one of great importance to these peoples. Pan-Slavism, as voiced by Czarist Russia at that time, had many attractive features for the Slav peoples, which were relegated to a third-rank place in the multinational Hapsburg Empire. For some of them, who, like the Czechs or Slovaks, were all subject to Austria-Hungary, Russia's ascendancy promised independence under her protection; for others, like the Yugoslavs, it bore the promise of reunion with those parts of their nation which were already independent.

On the other hand, however, the internal political conditions of Czarist Russia acted as a strong repellent, particularly among the progressive sections of the Austrian Slavs. Almost all the Polish subjects of the Hapsburg Empire, as well as a

---

[20] *The Battle Over Religion* (Prague, 1904, in Czech); *Introduction to the Most Recent Philosophy of Religion* (Prague, 1905, in Czech); *The Intelligentsia and Religion* (Prague, 1907, in Czech); *Science and the Church* (Prague, 1908, in Czech).

considerable section of the Ukrainians, were strongly opposed to Pan-Slavism, chiefly because of the treatment suffered by their brothers under Czarist domination. Pan-Slavism thus became a highly controversial question among the Austrian Slavs, while profounder minds were weighing the Russian problem from the point of view of Russia's relations with the rest of Europe and the part which Russia would eventually play on the Continent.

It was to these questions that Masaryk devoted one of his most important works, the famed "Russia and Europe," [21] which presented a concise and brilliant evaluation of the whole future of Czechoslovak-Russian relations. At about the same time Masaryk published an important contribution towards the theory of functional democracy, *The Difficulties of Democracy*.[22]

During the First World War, when Masaryk was abroad, directing the Czechoslovakian struggle for independence on the side of the Allies, he lectured on "The Problem of Small Nations in Europe's Crisis" at London University, in October, 1915, and on "The Slavs Among the Nations" at the Sorbonne, on February 22, 1916. Both these lectures were subsequently published in book form.

Masaryk's most important political work, however, was *The Making of a State*,[23] written when he was President of the Czechoslovak Republic. In this book he formulated his views on most of the pressing political problems of that time, as well as his ideas on philosophy, history and various sociological problems.

One of Masaryk's basic political and sociological tenets was the necessity to maintain a middle course between extreme individualism and extreme collectivism. He characterized this position as "critical realism." While firmly insisting upon the concept of the individual as the basic unit of society, Masaryk also stressed the role of what he called the "subsidiary organizations" within society. He believed that relations between individuals and

---

[21] *Russia and Europe* (first published in German, Jena, 1913; Czech edition, Prague, 1919-1921; American edition, under the title of *The Spirit of Russia* (New York: The MacMillan Co., 1919, 2 vols.).

[22] T. G. Masaryk, *The Difficulties of Democracy* (Prague, 1913, in Czech).

[23] T. G. Masaryk, *The Making of a State* (New York: Stokes, 1927).

these intermediate organizations, as well as the relations of the latter with each other, are the determining factors in the development of social phenomena. For him the value of philosophies was inseparable from their repercussions in cultural and national life. The manner in which they work out in practice is the essential test.

Masaryk has been rightly called the founder of Czech sociology, for he was the first man in Bohemia to concern himself systematically and on a scientific basis with both concrete sociological questions and the methods of sociological study. From the world-wide standpoint, he is the only example of a scholar-sociologist of modern times who was able to apply successfully his sociological principles and theories to currents of national and international problems.

(B) *Eduard Beneš—Political Thinker and Statesman*. Masaryk's most famous follower is Dr. Eduard Beneš, Professor of Sociology in Charles University, Prague, and an outstanding political collaborator of the late President during the struggle for Czechoslovakia's independence and during the latter's years in office. Czechoslovak Minister of Foreign Affairs from 1918 to 1935, Dr. Beneš succeeded Masaryk as President of Czechoslovakia, an office which he still holds.

Though a sociologist of distinction, Beneš is primarily interested in politics. To him, the social sciences are an essential basis for practical politics; he believes that, in order to achieve true understanding, a statesman must know how to analyze social conditions and systematically observe their development. Realistic analysis of social phenomena is all-important to democracy, for irrational intuition and emotional motivation are elements which spell destruction to democratic government. Beneš arrived at these conclusions by way of logical deduction; historic events have long since proved their correctness.

Dr. Beneš is an extremely prolific writer and limitations of space preclude mention of any but his most important contributions to political thought and science. Born an Austrian subject, Beneš was at one time interested in reform of the Hapsburg Empire along federal lines. His first work, *The Austrian Problem and the Czech Question*,[24] was devoted to this problem. From the specific problem he proceeded to the more general question of nationality which was then widely discussed in Austria; his "The National Question" was an important contribution to that discussion.

Subsequently, he devoted several volumes of his *Short Outline of the Evolution of Modern Socialism* (1911) to problems connected with socialist theory and development; a study of *The Party System* followed in 1912. The latter is an excellent analysis of the sociology and functioning of political parties. Again, Beneš achieved understanding of the part played by political parties in democracy far in advance of most of the other continental European sociologists. Shortly afterwards, Beneš published another book, *War and Culture* (Prague, 1915). Since the publication of that book, Beneš has devoted his principal activity to practical politics.

Having little time for theoretical studies, Dr. Beneš, however, continued to write. His post-1918 works have combined a strictly sociological approach with a profound understanding of the political problems of the day.[25]

Dr. Beneš' best works are in the field of political sociology. He regards politics as a social activity aimed at adjusting the social environment to human needs and aspirations. Democracy aims at social adjustments which will increase general welfare and satisfy general needs, hence its preferability to other forms of government.

In political theory, as well as in practical politics, Dr. Beneš has shown himself a worthy successor to Masaryk.

---

[24] (Paris, 1908, in French).

[25] The most important of Benes' works since 1918 are: *The Meaning of the Czechoslovak Revolution* (Prague, 1923); *World Revolution and Our Revolution*, published in America as: *My War Memoirs* (Boston: Houghton Mifflin, 1928); *Foreign Policy and Democracy* (Prague, 1923); *Democracy Today and Tomorrow* (New York: The Macmillan Co., 1939). The best short discussion of Benes' ideas in English is: Joseph S. Roucek, "Edward Benes as a Sociologist," *Sociology and Social Research,* XXIII (September-October, 1938), pp. 18-24; and "Edward Benes," *World Unity,* XIV (June, 1934), pp. 136-146 (reprinted in Social Science, X (April, 1935), p. 200; and "Fiftieth Anniversary Birthday of Dr. Edward Benes," *World Affairs Interpreter,* V (July, 1934), pp. 154-158.

(C) *The Followers.* The political philosophy of Masaryk and Beneš was dominant in Czechoslovakia throughout the twenty years of the country's independence. The practical social philosophies of most of the Czechoslokavian political parties were based on various aspects of their teachings; the ideological differences between these parties, on the other hand, were but the political expressions of various economic interests. Only small groups remained outside of the influence of the thought of Masaryk and Beneš, and the importance of these groups in politics was steadily dwindling. They produced no political thinker worth of mention.

The two leading social thinkers who emerged in Czechoslovakia during the years of its independence are both indebted to Masaryk, they are Dr. J. L. Fischer [26] and Dr. I. A. Blaha.[27] Both excel in concrete analysis of practical historical and political situations on the basis of methods which have become characteristic of Czechoslovak social science. Jan Mertl is another outstanding Czechoslovak political sociologist who concentrated his efforts on the analysis of Parliamentary government and the party system. His studies have shown how the failure of social groups to constantly adjust their ideology to current needs produces a time-lag between practical politics and ideological development. His chief works [28] are devoted to these problems. More recently, he has studied the impact of totalitarian trends on democratic states, showing that the latter also tend to concentration of political power, even while they jealously retain the

[26] J. L. Fischer, *The Future of European Culture* (Munich, 1929, in Geran) ; *The Crisis of Democracy* (Brno, 1935, in Czech) ; *The Third Reich* (Brno, 1932, in Czech).

[27] For a survey of Blaha's work, as well as of the other Czechoslovak thinkers, see: Joseph S. Roucek, *The Development of Sociology in Czechoslovakia* (unpublished M. A. thesis, New York University, 1937) ; Roucek, "Sociological Periodicals of Czechoslovakia," *American Sociological Review,* I (February, 1936), pp. 168-170; and "Czechoslovak Journals," *Ibid.,* II (April, 1937), pp. 270-271; "Trends in Educational Sociology Abroad," *The Educational Forum,* III (May, 1939, pp. 488-494; and "Concepts of Education in Czechoslovakia," *Review of Educational Research,* IX (October, 1939), pp. 377-380; etc.

[28] Jan Mertl, *The Political Parties* (Prague, 1931, in Czech) ; *Parliamentary Ideology and Our Times* (Prague, 1933, in Czech) ; *Ideology in Contemporary Politics* (Prague, 1934, in Czech).

people's unqualified right to criticize and to periodically determine which persons or groups are to exercise that power.[29] An American-Czechoslovak political sociologist, Joseph S. Roucek, has been a prolific contributor to American as well as European journals and has published and edited numerous volumes in the field of political science, history, sociology and educational sociology.[30] His main emphasis has been on the problems raised by the relationship of "what is" to "what ought to be" in the field of social sciences, and on the re-interpretation of politics and international events from the standpoint of power relationships.

HUNGARY

The most important political problems faced by twentieth century Hungary have been the national question and the agrarian question. Both were inherited from the nineteenth century. Most of the other political problems in Hungary were minor in comparison and dependent on these fundamental questions for their solution.

Hungary underwent a far-reaching change in its national organization in the latter part of the nineteenth century. For many centuries it had been a heterogeneous agglomeration of various peoples (Magyars, Slavs, Rumanians), living in the Middle Danube Valley and held together by common loyalty to the Hungarian Crown, but using Latin as the official language in order to facilitate mutual understanding. In the latter half of the

---

[29] J. Mertl, *The Concentration of Political Power,* is devoted to this problem.

[30] See: Patricia Pinkham, "Joseph S. Roucek," *The Slavonic Monthly,* I (July, 1944), pp. 7-9. Among Roucek's numerous works, the most widely used have been: *Contemporary Roumania and Her Problems* (Stanford University: Stanford University Press, 1932); *Our Racial and National Minorities* (with F. J. Brown, New York: Prentice-Hall, 1937); *Contemporary World Politics* with F. J. Brown and Charles Hodges, New York: John Wiley & Sons, 1939); *Politis of the Balkans* (New York: McGraw-Hill Book Co., 1939); *Introduction to Politics* (with R. V. Peel, New York: Thomas Y. Crowell Co., 1941); Roucek, Ed., *Contemporary Europe* (New York: D. Van Nostrand Co., 1941); Roucek, Ed., *Sociological Foundations of Education* (New York: Thomas Y. Crowell Co., 1942); *The Poles in the United States of America* (Gdynia: The Baltic Institute, 1937); *The Axis Psychological Strategy Against the United States* (New York: New Europe, 1942); etc.

nineteenth century, however, Hungary became a Magyar State,
which tried to capitalize on the loyalty of the non-Magyar population (nearly two-thirds of the total population of Hungary at
that time) to historical Hungary in its effort to foster Magyar-
dom and to bring about the Magyarization of the non-Magyar
elements. This policy had merely antagonized the latter; after
the defeat of the Central Powers in the First World War, the
non-Magyar areas of Hungary broke away to join nations with
which they were ethnically connected, carrying along, in the
process, considerable portions of Magyar-inhabited territory.
Hungary's whole-hearted support of Hitler's New Order in
Europe has earned her the restoration of these lost lands and
also of some non-Magyar territory, leading to a revival of the
national problem.

Hungary's agrarian problem has not changed in the twentieth century as often as her national problem. In 1944, as in
1900, more than half of the arable land is owned by a few hundred landlords, while the rest is divided among several thousand
so-called medium estates, also owned by the gentry, and millions
of petty peasant holdings. The great landlords and the lower
gentry are the masters of the country whatever the external form
of the government, and their whole policy is directed towards
the preservation, or even extension, of the existing agrarian
regime.

The national and the agrarian questions are closely linked,
for in the non-Magyar parts of Hungary the Magyars were the
landlords, while the peasants were usually Slavs or Rumanians.
When these areas were detached from Hungary, Czechoslovakia
and Rumania carried out agrarian reforms which transferred the
land to the peasants. This, of course, was detrimental to Magyar
interests and was one of the reasons for Hungary's uncompromising opposition to the territorial adjustments effected after the
First World War.

Among the Magyars themselves, voices demanding recognition of the national and social aspirations of the non-Magyars
were raised even before 1914. After 1920, the same voices urged
friendly collaboration with the nations which had absorbed some

of the formerly Hungarian territory. But these reasonable voices were drowned by floods of nationalistic argument which asserted that Hungary's social system was her most precious legacy from the past and demanded that the historic integrity of the country be restored regardless of the rights of non-Magyar populations. To administer the country, however, men had to be found who, while sharing the views of the dominant reactionary nationalists, would yet be acceptable to the Western European conservatives and liberals who constituted the political leadership of Europe after the First World War.

A leader who fitted into this pattern was found in the person of *Count Stephen (Istvan) Bethlen* (1874-   ). Bethlen is not a writer and it is necessary to study his speeches in order to discover the dominant ideas which prevailed in Hungarian politics between 1920 and 1944.[31]

Bethlen presented himself as a Conservative and tried hard to convince the English Conservatives that he was their Hungarian counterpart. He characterized himself as an advocate of "gradual progress." He also explained that this did not mean that he was a diehard Conservative, and defined his concept of "gradual progress" as "a modern and gradual evolution on the basis of ancient and venerable traditions";[32] he advised his followers never to retrogress from democratic achievements, for that would generate disappointment and subsequently weaken the country. His favorite slogan was, "Slow and gradual progress is the only way forward." But, lest he be considered too radical, Bethlen always made it plain that he was apprehensive of the possibly injurious effects of undue extension of public freedom in Hungary. Throughout his years of office, Bethlen's activity was directed at paving the way for a territorial readjustment in favor of his country and at strengthening conservative elements everywhere, at the expense of the democratic forces.

---

[31] Although Bethlen himself served as Prime Minister only from 1921 to 1931, his views are representative of the entire period in question.

[32] Quoted from: Gustav Gratz, *"Count Stephen Bethlen," Hungarian Review,* III (1937); The author is a political friend of Bethlen.

Strongly opposed to every idea represented by Bethlen is
Oscar Jászi (1875-   ), at present in the United States. One
of the leaders of Hungarian liberalism,[33] he has written a number of books on the modern history of his country.[34] His most
important contribution to political thought, however, are his
ideas on the problem of nationality. He has always advocated
a Hungary which would in effect be a federation of the peoples
living within the historic borders of that country; each nationality
would enjoy complete autonomy within its geographic area.
Discussing the various methods of achieving national autonomy
and securing friendly collaboration among the heterogeneous
population of his country, Jászi has criticized the projects advanced for Austria some time earlier by Karl Renner. The latter's plan provided for complete separation between the administration of cultural and educational activities of each national
group (to be exercised by central bodies at large throughout
the country on the basis of national cadasters) and the administration of other activities (exercised by regular local administrative bodies on a purely geographical basis).[35] Jászi, on the other
hand, argued that national autonomy cannot be effective without some territorial basis and shaped his proposals accordingly.

After the First World War, questions of national autonomy
ceased to be urgent in Hungary, for it became practically homogeneous from the national point of view. Jászi's major interest
turned to problems of the political and social organization of
Hungary. He wrote a number of papers on these questions, but,
having chosen voluntary exile after the establishment of Ad-

---

[33] He held office in the short-lived and ill-fated government of Michael Karolyi,
the only democratic administration Hungary has ever had (October 30, 1918-
March 13, 1919).

[34] The most important works of Oscar Jászi are: *Revolution and Counter-Revolution
in Hungary* (London: King, 1924); *The Dissolution of the Hapsburg Monarchy*
(Chicago: University of Chicago Press, 1929); *The Breakdown of Dualism and the
Future of the Danubian States* (Vienna, 1918, in German).

[35] This is the essence of Renner's proposals concerning the national set-up of Austria,
as they appear in his *National Self-Determination as Applied to Austria* (a revised
edition of his earlier *The Struggle of the Austrian Nations for their State*). These
proposals differ from those which are advanced in the earlier edition of Renner's
book.

miral Horthy's reactionary rule, he was unable to take active part in Hungarian politics. Jászi is a strong advocate of a federation of Danubian peoples. His proposals in this direction were developed in his "Break-Down of Dualism and the Future of the Danubian States."

Another thinker along the same lines is *Rustem Vambéry* (1874-   ), author of "The Hungarian Problem," [36] a masterly analysis of the background of the political situation in Hungary. Vambéry's main thesis is that only agrarian reform and the establishment of democracy in Hungary can create the conditions for friendly relations with its neighbors and with such non-Magyar populations as may remain within Hungary's borders.

POLAND

While in nineteenth century Poland political thinking was often divorced from political action, in the twentieth century these two elements have almost always gone hand in hand. Nearly all political thinkers of any importance were also leaders in political action, some of them wielding considerable influence upon the course of affairs and on the shaping of practical politics.

Of the great number of political writers in twentieth century Poland, we shall limit ourselves to those who were truly creative and who commanded a considerable following. In a few instances, we may ignore the latter qualification and include certain writers of creative and original mind whose ideas had won no immediate followers.

Polish political life and thought in the twentieth century has been dominated by two main currents: Progressivism (including Socialism) and Nationalism. As a result of historic circumstances (the struggle for independence up to 1918 and, again, since 1939), Polish Progressives and Socialists always were strongly aware of national problems; on the other hand, Polish Nationalism contained certain social elements for some time be-

---

[36] Rustem Vambéry, *The Hungarian Problem* (New York: The Nation, 1942); "Nationalism in Hungary," pp. 77-85, in *The Annals* of The American Academy of Political and Social Science, CCXXXII (March, 1944).

fore the national-social movements made their appearance in
most European countries. However, this overlapping of component elements did not lessen the antagonism between Socialism and Nationalism, since the two were sharply contradictory
in their basic concepts.

While Progressivism (in both its major expressions: Socialism and Peasant Populism) and Nationalism had gained the
adherence of mass movements, a third current remained limited
mostly to the older generation of the intellectual elite. In the
twentieth century, Polish Conservatism and old-fashioned Liberalism—both stemming from nineteenth century Positivism—were
rapidly disappearing, although their leaders still played an important part in Poland's intellectual life and produced ideas, some
of which became popular, but only after adoption by one of the
mass movements.

Progressivism and Socialism. In Polish Progressivism, Socialist thought undoubtedly occupied the first place; many brilliant intellectuals contributed towards its development at the end
of the nineteenth and the beginning of the twentieth century.
It may be said that almost all Polish intellectuals of that period
passed through the Socialist stage, although most of them abandoned it sooner or later. Despite serious ideological differences
within the Socialist camp, a common denominator for the various
Socialist schools was provided by the presence of *Prof. Ludwik
Krzywicki* (1859-1941). A sociologist of high standing,[37] Krzywicki was, above all, an educator who exercised a powerful influence on several generations of intellectuals. Most of his political
writings, which had appeared in numerous scientific journals and
pamphlets, were collected in the "Sociological Outlines."[38] His
scientific method of deducing political conclusions from economic

---

[37] Ludwik Krzwicki was Professor of Sociology at the Free University in Warsaw,
as well as founder and President of the Institute of Social Economics, an independent research organization. He is the author of an impressive array of writings
on sociological, statistical and philosophical questions, and of papers devoted to
Marxian analysis. His most important sociological works are: *Primitive Society and
Vital Statistics* (Warsaw, 1922, in Polish), and Social Psychology (Warsaw, 1890,
in Polish.)

[38] Ludwik Krzywicki, Sociological Outlines (Warsaw, 1923-4, in Polish).

data and social research is in the best tradition of Marxian sociology, but it also profits from contemporary developments in that science.

Another brilliant Polish Socialist thinker of the early twentieth century was *Kazimierz Kelles-Krauz* (1872-1906), one of the leaders of the Polish Socialist Party and author of many works in the field of politics, economics and sociology,[39] some of which (among them the most important ones) were published posthumously. His political views were stated more clearly in "Democracy and the Modern State," [40] and in "Political Writings." [41] In order to obtain a complete picture of Kelles-Krauz' ideas in the field of politics one must also read his "Historical Materialism." [42]

It is difficult to understand the essence of Kelles-Krauz' argument without some knowledge of the discussion which agitated Polish Socialists in his time. Most of them argued that Poland's national independence must be secured first and that only within the framework of a national state can Socialism be fought for without endangering the future of the nation.[43]

The other Socialist school of that time attacked this point of view, arguing that Poland as a national state was gone forever and that attempts to revive it would upset existing economic balances and relations, paving the way for permanent depression and resultant reaction; it also asserted that the national future of the Poles would best be safeguarded by victorious Socialist revolutions in the states which had partitioned Poland, rather than by a Polish national state which might not be Socialist. This school

---

[39] Kelles Krauz' most important sociological work was *A View on the Development of Sociology in the XIX Century* (in Polish and French, 1903).

[40] Kazimierz Kelles-Krauz, *Democracy in the Modern State* (Cracow, 1907, in Polish).

[41] Kazimierz Kelles-Krauz, *Political Writings* (Cracow, 1908, in Polish).

[42] Kazimierz Kelles-Krauz, *Historical Materialism* (Cracow, 1908, in Polish).

[43] Boleslaw Limanowski (1835-1935), a Polish historian whose principal achievements date to the XIX century, was the first to introduce Polish socialists to the idea of national independence. His main political work is *The Nation and the State* (Cracow, 1906, in Polish). He also wrote several important books on the history of Polish democracy.

often boasted of its Marxian orthodoxy and attacked Polish
Socialists who advocated national independence as non-Marxian
romantics and utopians.

Kelles-Krauz, attempting to resolve this controversy, showed
that, from a strictly Marxian point of view, the advocates of Polish national independence were right. He pointed out that as
long as Poland was not an independent national state, Poles of
all classes shared the common antagonism against the partition-
ing Powers, and that this interfered with one of the essential
premises of the struggle for Socialism—the consciousness of the
class-struggle among the workers. By constant emphasis on this
approach, both in theoretical writings and in current political
propaganda, Kelles-Krauz brought about its wide acceptance.
He realized, however, that the absolute and complete independence of Poland (as well as of other nations) would lead to an
armament race. He was also one of the first writers to expose
the influence of cartels on international politics. In his paper,
"Socialism and European Peace" (1903), he proposed a federal
organization of Europe, implying limitation of national sovereignties and control of international cartels as a means of eliminating
the undesirable aspects of national independence. He regarded
this as a preliminary step to the introduction of Socialism in
Europe.

Another Polish Socialist thinker of importance was *Feliks
Perl* (1871-1927). Primarily a historian,[44] he was a strong proponent of the thesis that national independence should be a preliminary step towards Socialist reconstruction in Poland. He early
realized, however, that certain Polish Socialists, including Pilsudski,[45] were gradually rejecting the idea that Poland's independence was to be achieved by a democratic or revolutionary process, and placing their hopes instead upon underground military
organization. Perl warned that such an organization meant incipient militarism which might subsequently dominate Poland.[46]

---

[44] Feliks Perl was the author of *A Short History of the French Revolution* and of
A History of the Socialist Movement (1910 and 1932, in Polish).

[45] Pilsudski, at that time, was one of the leaders of the Polish Socialist Party.

[46] See: Feliks Perl, *Patriotism and War* (in Polish).

He continued to point out the dangers of militarism after Poland had become independent and he had been elected deputy to the Polish Parliament.

Two other prominent Polish Socialist thinkers deserve mention: *Leon Wasilewski* (1870-1935) and *Mieczyslaw Niedzialkowski* (1894-1940). Both are best known as active political figures. Wasilewski was the first Minister of Foreign Affairs in the restored Polish Republic, and Niedzialkowski was the parliamentary leader of the Socialist Party. Wasilewski, however, was also a prolific writer on historical subjects and a keen student of the problem of nationalities. He studied Karl Renner's ideas on national autonomy and cooperation and sought to adapt his proposals to Polish conditions. He devoted especial attention to the problem of the Ukranians, White Russians and Lithuanians in Poland.[47] The results of his research and the conclusions he reached were summarized in his "Nationality Problems in Theory and Practice."

Niedzsialkowski's writings were mainly journalistic,[48] but he also wrote two books which expressed the ideological position of Polish Socialism between the two World Wars. In his "Socialist Theory and Practice in the Face of New Problems," [49] Niedzialkowski was particularly concerned with the dangers of dictatorship. He early recognized the dangers of totalitarianism, inherent in both the incipient Fascism of the years in which the book was written and in Russian Bolshevism. He also wrote that the direction of technological developments made it unlikely that manual workers would become the majority of the population in any country where they had not yet achieved that status; it was therefore necessary to win the professional and lower middle classes to Socialism, or, at least, to secure their sympathy, in order to prevent their becoming the mass base for Fascism. Time has

---

[47] Leon Wasilewski, *Nationality Problems in Theory and Practice* (Warsaw, 1929, in Polish).

[48] He was Editor-in-Chief of the Socialist daily, *Robotnik* (*The Worker*).

[49] Mieczyslaw Niedzialkowski, *Socialist Theory and Practice in the Face of New Problems* (Warsaw, 1926, in Polish).

shown the correctness of Niedzialkowski's analysis. In "Roads
to Socialism," [50] Niedzialkowski emphasized the democratic character of the Polish Labor Movement and declared that democracy
is an essential element of Socialism.

On the fringes of Polish Socialism a powerful thinker appeared at the turn of the century in the person of *Jozef Edward
Abramowski* (1868-1918). His early writings were devoted
mainly to psychological and ethical problems.[51] In that field he
was, like Freud and Janet, among the originators of the psychology of the subconscious. Starting from that, he proceeded to examine the psychological and ethical prerequisites of Socialism.
Two of his most important works [52] were devoted to these problems. Defending the concept of ethical anarchy, which was the
basis of his social thinking, he opposed the sovereignty of the
state whatever its class character. His "General Conspiracy
Against the Government" [53] advocated the overthrow of the government and extolled the method of non-violent struggle. This
method, as formulated by him, consisted of the repudiation by
the citizens of all governmental institutions and the organization,
in their stead, of free associations. He urged the substitution of
community pressure for police force, neighborhood referees for
state judges, free schools for public schools, and even home-
grown tobacco for commercial tobacco, on which tax had to be
paid.

In Abramowski's time the government institutions which he
opposed were those of foreign powers [54] and that lent his views
certain political weight. Today, when Poland is once more under
foreign domination, Abramowski's teachings enjoy a considerable
revival of influence and may be considered the theoretical basis

---

[50] Mieczyslaw Niedzialkowski, *The Roads to Socialism* (Warsaw, 1934, in Polish).

[51] J. Edward Abramowski, *Theory of the Elements of Psychology* (in Polish, 1899).

[52] J. Edward Abramowski, *Socialist Problems* (in Polish, 1899). "Ethics and Revolution," (in Polish, 1899).

[53] J. Edward Abramowski, *General Conspiracy Against the Government* (in Polish,
1905).

[54] Russia, Prussia and Austria, which had partitioned Poland in the XVIII Century.

for the policy of "boycotting" the authorities of occupation. Emphasizing the free will of social groups, Abramowski became the theoretician of the cooperative movement in Poland.[55] Through social cooperation, based upon the principle of free will, Abramowski visualized social rehabilitation, achieved in the spirit of democracy. Although his ideas have exercised considerable influence, Abramowski's works are hardly known outside the narrow circle of scholars interested in the problems with which he dealt.[56]

Polish Populism, politically represented by the Peasant Party, was the second wing of Polish Progressivism. One of its outstanding leaders was *Stanislaw Thugutt* (1873-1941), who was also one of the leaders of the Polish Cooperative Movement. Thugutt is well known as a writer on cooperative problems. While Abramowski delved into the depths of the human mind in search of psychological prerequisites for social development along cooperative lines, Thugutt was a writer on practical cooperative questions. His most important books in that field are: "Studies in Cooperative Legislation," [57] and "An Outline of Cooperative Philosophy." [58] He also wrote many articles on political questions for numerous publications; selections from most of them were published in 1943 (together with his autobiography) under the title, "Stanislaw Thugutt's Selected Writings." [59]

During the years preceding the present war, the Peasant Party was steadily growing in strength. Serious research work was undertaken by several writers in an effort to provide it with a theoretical basis. The writings of the Czechoslovak writer on agrarian problems and political figure, Dr. Milan Hodza, were used as a model upon which a young economist, *Stanislaw Milkowski* (1910-   ), based his Polish agrarian theories. The

---

[55] J. Edward Abramowski, *The Social Philosophy of the Cooperative Movement* (in Polish, 1907).

[56] Abramowski's collect writings on political and social problems were published as *Sociological Contributions* (Warsaw, 1924/28, 4 volumes, in Polish).

[57] Stanislaw Thugutt, *Studies in Cooperative Legislation* (Warsaw, 1931, in Polish).

[58] Stanislaw Thugutt, *An Outline of Cooperative Philosophy* (Warsaw, Second Edition, Warsaw, 1934, in Polish).

[59] (Glasgow, 1943, in Polish).

latter's book, "Agrarianism," [60] contained many interesting features.

Nationalism. Polish Nationalist thought lacks the breadth of Polish Progressivism. It is best represented by *Roman Dmowski* (1864-1939), outstanding Nationalist thinker and leader. A biologist by profession, he soon turned to writing. After the granting of a Constitution in Czarist Russia in 1905 (he was a Russian subject before Poland recovered her independence), he was elected to the Russian Parliament (Douma). When, during the First World War, he lost his initial hope that Russia alone could defeat Germany, he came to Western Europe, where he cooperated with the French. Subsequently, he was Polish delegate at the Versailles Peace Conference. Elected to the Polish Parliament, he returned home after the signing of the Peace Treaty, but played a relatively inconspicuous part in active politics, limiting himself to the role of theoretician and leader of the National Party. He maintained considerable organizational influence in the latter until his death, often determining the course taken by the party.

Before embarking upon political writing, Dmowski wrote some important sociological works.[61] His first and most important political work, "The Thoughts of a Modern Pole," [62] published in Lwow, in 1903, contains a complete summary of his ideas. Dmowski's later contributions were chiefly additions to his basic works, in which he noted new developments, interpreting them according to his original tenets and seeking in them new substantiation of his position. Some of his later writings [63] were devoted to current political problems, in the discussion of which Dmowski participated.

---

[60] Stanislaw Milkowski, *Agrarianism* (Warsaw, 1935, in Polish).

[61] Roman Dmowski, *Emigration and Settlement* (Lwow, 1900, in Polish); *Polish Youth Under Russian Rule* (Lwow, 1895, in Polish).
[62] Roman Dmowski, *Thoughts of a Modern Pole* (Lwow, 1903, republished 1904, 1907, and 1933, in Polish).

[63] Roman Dmowski: *Germany, Russia and the Polish Question* (1908, in Polish); *Problems of Central and Eastern Europe* (London, 1917, originally written in English); *The Decay of Conservative Thought in Poland* (1914, in Polish).

Writing at the turn of the century, Dmowski followed in the footsteps of the earlier Polish political writers and began with a study of the causes of Poland's downfall in the eighteenth century. Not unlike many other thinkers, he found that abuse of individual liberty at that time had undermined the security and cohesion of the State and was to a great extent responsible for Poland's catastrophe. But, where many other writers, pursuing this argument further, felt that this abuse consisted of allowing the upper-class gentry too much liberty, while the other classes had too little, or none, Dmowski came to condemn all individual liberty in the field of politics. At the time of the writing, this point of view was nothing but antiquated; later, however, it acquired new significance, permitting Polish Nationalists to claim that Dmowski was the originator of twentieth century authoritarianism.

Dmowski violently condemned what he called "doctrinaire humanitarianism" and asserted the supremacy of national interest over considerations of human rights. His opposition to liberty and humanitarianism brought him into sharp conflict with the democratic currents in Poland [64] and later with the Socialist movement. Practical considerations and the logic of everyday politics led Dmowski to become the bitterest enemy of the Polish Socialist Movement. But his greatest hatred was directed against Jews and Free Masons. The occupational distribution of Jews in Poland created many of the conditions which encouraged the development of anti-Semitism, but it was not until Dmowski's times, and, to a great extent, as a result of propaganda [65] conducted by his political friends, that anti-Semitism began to assume serious proportions in Poland.

Another object of Dmowski's hatred were the Free Masons. This secret order had never had a very large membership in Po-

---

[65] Anti-Semitic propaganda was one of the few political activities open to Poles under Czarist rule. Dmowski made full use of this opportunity. He urged Gentile Poles to boycott Jews economically and socially.

[64] Despite this antagonism, he chose the name of "National-Democratic" ("Endek") for the political party he helped to create. The word "Democratic" was dropped from the title much later.

land, but Dmowski conceived the idea of linking the Free Masons and the Jews and of using them as joint scapegoats for all the misfortunes suffered by the Polish nation. His obsession with Free Masonry made him suspect everyone he disliked of being a Free Mason and ascribe Masonic influence to every political move which displeased him.

In foreign policy Dmowski was an ardent adherent of Pan-Slavism and an irreconcilable foe of Germany. At the time when he was active in Russian politics as a member of the Douma, he advocated home-rule for Russian Poland as a means of eliminating Polish-Russian antagonism, which made the Poles cool to Pan-Slavic propaganda. He strongly opposed the Polish political movements which worked for Poland's independence, and permitted his political friends to characterize Polish revolutionaries as "bandits." As a Deputy to the Douma, he voted for conscription and military expenditures and persuaded his political friends to vote likewise. It was only after the Russian revolution that Dmowski began to favor Polish independence. As Polish delegate at the Versailles Peace Conference, he opposed the Polish statesmen who advocated dismemberment of Russia and the creation of buffer states between it and Poland; he argued that Poland's greatest enemy was Germany and that Poland could not afford to permanently antagonize Russia.

During the years between the two World Wars Dmowski was an attentive observer of the rising totalitarian trends. He instantly realized the affinity between his views and Italian Fascism and even introduced certain changes into his party's organization along the Fascist model. But he opposed German Nazism, although it carried out in Germany a program almost identical with that which he advocated for Poland. There were two major reasons for Dmowski's opposition to Nazism: his old distrust of all things German, and the anti-Catholic elements in Nazi ideology (Dmowski was a consistent supporter of the Catholic point of view in national life).[66] Younger members of Dmow-

---

[66] Dmowski himself was a philosophical Positivist. Although he returned to the Catholic Church only a short time before his death, he consistently supported the Catholic forces in national life throughout his career. Chiefly for reasons of political expediency, he carefully kept his views on religion to himself.

ski's party, who did not remember the Polish struggle for existence under German rule before 1918, were more ready to admit their ideological kinship with Nazism; Dmowski strongly opposed this tendency and it is mainly due to his influence [67] that there have been no serious collaborationists among the Polish Right during the present occupation of Poland by the Germans.

Dmowski's visit to Japan had a considerable effect upon him. He was especially impressed by "Shinto," the Japanese State religion based on ancestor worship and the concept that the Japanese throughout the generations are but a single entity—eternal Japan. He also admired the fanatical devotion of the Japanese to their country and their readiness to discard all personal feelings and rights for the sake of the national interest as interpreted by their Government.[68] He immediately recognized how close his own views on humanitarianism were to those prevailing in Japan. He took over the concept of "eternal Japan"; modifying it to suit Polish conditions, he grafted it onto his own political theories and turned it into the chief stock-in-trade of Polish nationalism.

Conservatism. The Conservative school of political thought, dominant in Poland in the latter part of the nineteenth century, suffered a decline in the twentieth century, but was still able to produce outstanding thinkers and intellectual leaders. Because the most prominent Conservative thinkers at the end of the nineteenth and the beginning of the twentieth century lived in Cracow (most of them were Professors at the Jagellonian University in that city), the Conservative school became known as the "Cracow School."

One of the leading representatives of this school was *Stanislaw Estreicher* (1869-1940), Professor of Law at the Cracow University and prominent member of the Conservative Party. He exerted his influence mainly through the editorial column in the Conservative paper, CZAS (The Time), which he wrote daily

---

[67] Dmowski died several months before the outbreak of the present war, at a time when its issues were already clear to all who possessed any political foresight.

[68] He described the impression which Japan made on him in *Ex Oriente Lex* (1904).

throughout most of his active life. He was a strong advocate
of legality and opponent of what he called "premature" social
reform; in the years after 1930, he became increasingly preoccupied with totalitarian trends. His attitude towards the latter
contrasted that of many other conservatives: in Fascism, he saw,
first of all, a menace to liberty and legal order. His best and
most effective papers and addresses were those in which he attacked the influence of Fascist ideologies.

Wladyslaw Leopold Jaworski (1865-1930) was also Professor of Law at the Cracow University and was active in practical politics for many years. As a political writer, he is best known
for his book, "Legality and Agrarian Reform," [69] in which he
strongly attacked the proposals for compulsory agrarian reform.
Jaworski argued that, since protection of property is one of the
chief functions of the State, the latter cannot force anyone to
relinquish his property, even if it is willing to pay for it. The
government, according to Jaworski, may only take over property
needed for the operation of public utilities; as for agrarian reform it should be confined to voluntary sales of land by landowners directly to the buyers.

Radically differing from the Conservatives in his political
conclusions and practical politics, but sharing both their positivist
heritage and their original belief in the possibility of reforming
Hapsburg Austria, was the Democrat *Konstanty Srokowski*
(1878-1937), a journalist who was intensely interested in the
problems of nationality. An Austrian subject before the First
World War, he took active part in the discussions of these problems, which agitated Austria at that time. For some time he
advocated the transformation of Austria into a federation of its
various nationalities, only to abandon this plan when it became
obvious that it was incapable of attainment. In independent
Poland his interest turned mainly to problems of foreign policy:
he was an uncompromising advocate of Poland's collaboration
with Great Britain, France and Czechoslovakia. A keen observer

---

[69] Wladyslaw Leopold Jaworski, *Legality and Agrarian Reform* (Cracow, 1922, in Polish).

of Russian affairs, Srokowski early recognized the authoritarian character of the Soviet State, but urged cooperation with it against the German threat. His most important books were: *National Problems, In the Capitol of the White Czar,* [70] *The Decline of Austrian Imperialism,* [71] *The Turning Point,* [72] and *The Soviet Elite.* [73]

*   *   *   *   *

No survey of Polish political thought in the twentieth century would be complete unless *Jozef Pilsudski* (1867-1935) is included. As a young man he was exiled to Siberia for pro-Polish political activities directed against the Czarist Government. Afterwards he joined the Polish Socialist Party and was one of its leaders for many years. Gradually, however, he became estranged from the Socialist movement, for he insisted on preparing for the revolutionary struggle by organizing an underground army, while other Socialists chose the method of mass political action. This rift grew with the years, until Pilsudski could no longer be considered a Socialist. As the creator of the Polish Legions (during the First World War) which became the nucleus of the Polish Army, Pilsudski exercised a decisive influence upon the latter. After serving as the first Chief of State of the restored Polish Republic, as Minister of War in various cabinets, Inspector General of the Polish Armed Forces, and Marshal of Poland, he withdrew from politics in 1923. In 1926 he staged a comeback by means of a coup d'etat. From that time until his death Pilsudski was the virtual dictator of Poland, although he consistently refused to accept any office that would correspond to his true position.

Pilsudski was a very prolific writer, but most of his work consisted of articles for various periodicals and short pamphlets. His more important writings were devoted not to political ideas, but to the history of the underground Socialist Movement [74] and

---

[70] Konstanty Srokowski, *In the Capital of the White Czar* (1903, in Polish).

[71] Konstanty Srokowski, *The Decline of Austrian Imperialism,* (1913, in Polish).

[72] Konstanty Srokowski, *The Turning Point* (1916, in Polish).

[73] Konstanty Srokowski, *The Soviet Elite* (1923, in Polish).

to military history.[75] To discover Pilsudski's political ideas it is
necessary to read his many contributions to various periodicals,
his addresses, press interviews, occasional pamphlets and similar
material.

The analysis of Pilsudski's political thought after he left the
Socialist movement presents a complicated problem. There is
hardly any doubt that he sincerely regarded himself as a democrat, although most of what he did in practical politics, or permitted to be done under his authority, was definitely anti-democratic. While Pilsudski blocked any attempt to introduce overtly
totalitarian political forms in Poland, he not only violently attacked, but also jailed his opponents in the legislative bodies who
attempted to carry out such elementary legislative functions as
control of public funds, or who insisted upon the independence
of the judiciary. Pilsudski simply attacked these things as "parliamentary abuse," often couching his remarks in the most filthy and
offensive language. As a matter of principle, Pilsudski rejected
parliamentary control of foreign policy and of military expenditures and organization; he considered these matters as belonging
purely within the province of the executive branch of the government.

A nearly complete collection of Pilsudski's writings and addresses was published in 1937.[76]

RUMANIA

Rumania's economic and social backwardness has been the
chief reason for the almost complete lack of independent political
thought in that country. Her oppressed and poverty-ridden past
provided no incentives for inquiry into the possibilities of evolving native political institutions. Rumania's law was shaped upon
French and Belgian models; when totalitarianism became the
fashion after 1930, she turned to Germany and Italy for new
patterns. But whatever nation's institutions were copied, the dif-

---

[74] Josef Pilsudski, *Underground Literature* (Cracow, 1903, in Polish).
[75] Pilsudski, *My First Battles* (written 1917, published in Warsaw, 1925, in Polish);
The Year 1920 (Warsaw, 1924, in Polish).

[76] (Warsaw, 1937, in Polish, 10 vols.).

ferences between its economic and social development and that of Rumania were never taken into account.

Despite the impressive names of Rumanian political parties (Liberal, National-Democratic, Progressive), they were never anything more than cliques clustering around various politicians; moreover, the party which happened to be in office at election time was invariably reelected by overwhelming majorities which set the pace for future totalitarian "plebiscites."

The only political groups which have had definite ideologies and represented popular interests were the Socialists and Communists, who derived their inspiration from Marx, and the National-Peasant Party. However, while the Marxian parties were never strong, the National Peasant Party is influential among the peasant masses and presents the only hope of a brighter future in Rumanian politics.[77]

The very backwardness of Rumania presents a host of problems which demand a high degree of statesmanship for their solution. The agrarian problem is the only one which has been partially solved (by a series of laws promulgated between 1917 and 1923); all others have been disregarded while personal rivalries rule political life and polemical pamphlets take the place of political thought. Few ideas have ever awakened nation-wide response in Rumania: one of these was the idea of Great Rumania, realized in 1919 by means of the union of all Rumanian-speaking territories (including considerable portions of non-Rumanian lands!); the other is general anti-Semitism and the propaganda for the seizure of Jewish property.

The agrarian problem has been and still is the basic Rumanian problem. It has been analyzed in masterly fashion by David Mitrany, whose most important book on the question is *The Land and the Peasant in Rumania*.[78] The nation's problems have also been studied by Joseph S. Roucek; his book on *Contemporary*

---

[77] The leader of the Rumanian Peasant Party is Dr. Juliu Maniu.

[78] David Mitrany, *The Land and the Peasant in Rumania* (New Haven, Conn.: Yale University Press, 1930).

Rumania and her Problems [79] presents an outline of Rumania's history and political problems and discusses her constitutional and political organization.

Since a considerable part of Rumania had belonged to the Austro-Hungarian Empire prior to 1918, the proposed solutions for the national problems of that empire had also been widely discussed among the Rumanians of Austria and Hungary. In the course of these discussions, Aurel Popovici, a Rumanian who was then a subject of the empire, contributed to the birth of the federal idea in the Danubian Basin by proposing the organization of a Danubian empire, composed of fifteen semi-sovereign states connected by federal links. Such an organization, he felt, should be achieved through the efforts of national movements among the Danubian peoples and established within the framework of the Hapsburg Empire. [80]

YUGOSLAVIA

Because of historical developments, the Yugoslav peoples have in many respects lagged considerably behind the Central European peoples. Until the turn of the present century they were still in the stage of tribal organization (the Serbs) or in the earliest stage of the development of national consciousness (the Croats and the Slovenians). Their political thought reflects these conditions.

---

[79] Joseph S. Roucek, *Contemporary Roumania and Her Problems* (Stanford University: Stanford University Press, 1932).

[80] Aurel Popovici, *The United States of Great Austria* (Vienna, 1906, in German). For additional information on Roumania's political thought, see: Joseph S. Roucek, "Sociology in Roumania," *American Sociological Review,* III (February, 1938), pp. 54-62; and "Roumania and Bulgaria," *Phi Delta Kappan,* XXII (November, 1939), pp. 83-86; and "The People's University-Professor Iorga's Experiment at Valenii-de-Munte," *School and Society,* XXXV (January 2, 1932), pp. 19-21; and "The New Educational System of Roumania," *Ibid.,* XLVI (October 23, 1937), pp. 537-538; and "Social Forces Behind Rumanian Politics," *Social Forces* X (March, 1932), pp. 419-425; and *The Politics of the Balkans* (New York: McGraw-Hill Book Co., 1939), pp. 26-54; and "Romanian Peasant and Agriculture," *Journal of Geography,* IV (October, 1932), pp. 279-287; and "The Political Evolution of Roumania," *Slavonic and East European Review,* X (April, 1932), pp. 602-615; and "New Tendencies of Roumanian Politics," *Social Science,* VI (October, 1931), pp. 374-381; and "World War II and the Balkans," *Social Education,* V. (March, 1941), pp. 187-189.

Almost all their political literature up to the nineteenth century was either of polemical character or violently nationalistic There were few writers who dealt with political questions dispassionately and objectively, and most of these confined themselves to analyzing concrete situations from a historical point of view.

It was only well within the twentieth century that anything comparable with the political literature of other European nations made its appearance in the present Yugoslav territory. The first Yugoslav political sociologist, both original and articulate, was Tihomiri Gjorgjevic, Professor of Ethnography at Belgrade University; his most important works were published under the title, *Our National Life* (Belgrade, 1930).

Another political thinker of importance was Mirko M. Kosic, Professor at the Belgrade and Subotica Universities. While devoting much of his energy to the study of sociological theory and methods, as well as to acquainting Yugoslavs with the works of the most prominent European sociologists (he translated them and encouraged translations by others), Kosic also participated actively in sociological research, publishing several monographs in that field. His research work on rural conditions and his conclusions stimulated and influenced the development of the agrarian ideology in the Serbian part of Yugoslavia.

Antun Radic's (1868-1919) ideas and writings had an even stronger effect on the development of the agrarian ideology in Croatia. His basic idea—today common to agrarian movements throughout Europe—was that peasants, who are the original producers of material goods, should wield political power commensurate with their economic position and use it to bring about a new, humane, equitable and peaceful world. This basic concept was taken over by his brother, Stjepan Radic, the creator of the Croatian peasant movement which has played and will certainly

continue to play an important role in Yugoslavia's political
life.[81]

BIBLIOGRAPHY

BARNES, HARRY ELMER, AND BECKER, HOWARD, *Social Thought from Lore to
Science* (Boston: D. C. Heath, 1938, 2 vols.). Contains most valuable
section on the various Central-Eastern European countries.

BENES, EDUARD, *Democracy Today and Tomorrow* (New York: The Macmillan
Co., 1939). Benes' review of the various experiments in democracy and
his hopes for the future.

DYBOSKI, ROMAN, *Poland* (London: E. Benn Ltd., 1933). Although out of date,
still one of the best introductions to the topic.

For Your Freedom and Ours, edited by Manfred Kridl, Wladyslaw Malinowski
and Josef Wittlin (New York: Frederick Ungar Co., 1943). Selections on
the Polish progressive spirit through the centuries.

JASZI, OSCAR, *The Dissolution of the Hapsburg Monarchy* (Chicago: University
of Chicago Press, 1929). Indispensable for the understanding of the history
of the region.

MASARYK, THOMAS GARIGUE, *The Making of a State* (New York: F. A. Stokes Co.,
1927). Indispensable for the understanding of Masaryk's political theories.

MITRANY, DAVID, *The Land and the Peasant in Rumania* (New Haven: Yale University Press, 1930). The best available introduction to the peasant mentality
of Eastern Europe.

MUNZER, JAN AND MUNZER, ZDENKA, *We Were and We Shall Be* (New York:
Frederick Ungar Publishing Co., 1941). For the forces in Czechoslovakia's
history.

ROUCEK, JOSEPH S., *Contemporary Roumania and Her Problems* (Stanford University: Stanford University Press, 1932). Covers all the political thought
of the country's development.

VAMBERY, RUSTEM, *The Hungarian Problem* (New York: The Nation, 1942). A
liberal interpretation of Hungary's past and present.

---

[81] For additional information, see: Joseph S. Roucek, "The Development of
Sociology in Yugoslavia", *American Sociological Review, I* (December, 1936),
pp. 981-988; and "Educational Work of Yugoslav Sokols," *School and Society,*
XXXVIII (September 16, 1933), pp. 375-77; and "Educational Reforms of
Yugoslavia," *Ibid.,* XXXVI (July 30, 1932), pp. 150-3; and "The Development of
the Educational Structure of Yugoslavia," *Ibid.,* XL (August 25 1934); pp. 250-53;
and "The Social Character of Yugoslav Politics," *Social Science,* IX (July, 1934),
pp. 294-304; and *The Politics of the Balkens,* pp. 55-83. "A challenge to Peace-
makers," *The Annals* of the American Academy of Political and Social Science,
CCXXXII (March, 1944), is devoted entirely to the ideologies of nationalism of
each country of Central-Eastern Europe.

CHAPTER XXV

PRE-FASCIST ITALIAN POLITICAL THOUGHT

JOSEPH ROSSI

A series of events that took place in Italy at the turn of the century determined the trend of political thought that was to prevail in the country until the rise of Fascism. These events were: the final collapse of the reactionary policy of the conservative parties, the victory of the "evolutionary" or "reformist" branch within the Socialist Party, the inception of the Catholic political movement, and the rise of two extremist schools of thought, the syndicalist and the nationalist, which questioned the immediate programs, the ultimate ideals and, especially, the democratic parliamentary method of the liberal state.

These events were closely connected with one another. The excessively repressive measures of the conservative government in the nineties alienated the lower middle class which swung to the left, supporting Liberals and Socialists. The Socialists, sobered by the persecutions suffered, and mollified by the middle class' sympathy, gave a limited support to the new government that promised to respect scrupulously the constitutional liberties and to look with favor upon the immediate economic and political aspirations of the proletariat. This liberal-socialist alliance, which threatened to quicken the process of secularization of the State, frightened the Catholics into a limited participation in the political struggle, from which they had abstained for thirty years because of a papal prohibition. This alliance was also strongly opposed by a small but highly articulate minority in the Socialist Party, the Syndicalists, who looked upon it as a betrayal of the socialist creed, while another small and vocal group, the Nationalists, protested bitterly against it, as a progressive surrender of the ruling classes to socialism.

One might say that, at the beginning of the century, the hospitable edifice of the Italian liberal state housed within its walls the majority of the Italian people; at the portals of the right and left wings of the building, neither completely in nor completely out, stood the Catholics and the Socialists; while on the grounds outside stood the Nationalists and the Syndicalists, refusing theoretically to go in, and demanding a new building. In the following pages an analysis will be attempted of these five political trends,—liberal, Catholic, socialist, syndicalist, and nationalist. It is to be noted that these movements did not originate in Italy, and that when they made their appearance there, the inspiration and guidance came from abroad,—the Liberals looking to England, the Catholics to Germany and Belgium, the Socialists to Germany, the Syndicalists and Nationalists to France.[1]

THE LIBERALS

The high-water mark of Italian liberalism was reached during the first two decades of the present century, when the fundamental principles of liberalism were finally accepted even by leading members of the conservative parties. Di Rudinì was one of the leaders responsible for the repressive measures of the late nineties; yet in 1907 Nitti, a "radical," or left-wing Liberal, considered Di Rudinì, a "sincere radical spirit," who for many years had found himself more in agreement with the Extreme Left than with the Right.[2] Sonnino, another conservative leader, had advocated, toward the end of the century, a reform abolishing parliamentary control over the government;[3] yet, a few

---

[1] The Italian forerunners of some of these movements exerted no appreciable influence. Italian socialists, for instance, drew inspiration and guidance from Bakunin, Malon, Marx, and later, Sorel, not from Russo and Pisacane. The only indigenous political movement, Mazzini's republicanism, by the beginning of the century had withered into insignificance.

[2] F. S. Nitti, *Il partito radicale e la nuova democrazia industriale* (Torino-Roma; Società Tipografica Editrice Nazionale, 1907) pp. 41, 42.

[3] Gaetano Mosca had proposed this type of constitutional reform a few years earlier. Cf. G. Mosca, *The Ruling Class* (New York: McGraw-Hill Book Co., 1939), pp. 262-265.

years later, he admitted that such a change was impossible, and when in charge of the government he always adhered strictly to the traditional parliamentary procedure.[4]

The most representative man of Italian liberalism in the twentieth century was Giovanni Giolitti. Five times Prime Minister between 1892 and 1921, he dominated the political stage without any serious challenge from 1903 to 1913. Not being a theorist, he never gave a detailed exposition of his views on government, and was accused by his opponents of unprincipled opportunism. He was an opportunist, however, only in that he preferred to concentrate on what was possible to achieve at a given time, and was distrustful of detailed blueprints of political action. A statement of his principles can be easily derived from the *Memoirs* he published in 1922 after his last Ministry.[5]

The State, according to Giolitti, was to be "the impartial guardian of all classes of its citizens."[6] He believed that all the forces in the country should be represented in parliament, and find there their expression and balance;[7] accordingly he encouraged the participation of the Socialists in the political life of the country, just as he later likewise encouraged the participation of the Catholics. He believed also that the State ought to raise the economic, cultural, and political status of the lower classes; but,—and this was typical of Giolitti,—he advocated this progressive policy not on the ground of abstract justice, but rather as a useful expedient for good and safe administration. He argued that the improvement of the economic conditions of the lower classes and their greater participation in the political life of the country was good business and wise politics at the same time: it was good business, because "the active participation in every form of progress on the part of all the people is

---

[4] B. Croce, *A History of Italy* (Oxford: The Clarenden Press, 1929), pp. 203, 217-218; also G. Giolitti, *Memorie della mia vita* (Milano: Treves, 1922), pp. 149-150, 237.

[5] "Giolitti's corruption," was not really peculiar to Giolitti or to Italian political life.

[6] G. Giolitti, *op. cit.*, p. 165.

[7] *Ibid.*, p. 610.

closely connected with the increase in wealth in a country"; [8] it was wise politics, even for a Conservative, because a repressive policy would give plausibility to the arguments of subversive leaders who pointed to revolution as the only way out for the masses.[9]

The aid of the State in this elevation of the working classes was to consist in favoring an increase of their political power through a gradual broadening of the franchise, and in maintaining strict neutrality in their conflicts with capital,—conflicts which, due to the relatively rapid pace of the industrialization of the country, and to the effectiveness of socialist propaganda, were quite frequent during the first decade of the present century. As early as 1892, at the time of his first ministry, Giolitti felt that in economic conflicts between capital and labor, the action of the government should be limited to maintaining order and trying to mediate the conflict.[10] Later, commenting on the difficulties of the last conservative government, he reiterated his belief that "the only fair and useful role of the government in these struggles between capital and labor is the exercise of a pacifying and at times mediating action," and that "in case of strike the government should intervene only in one case, namely, to insure freedom of work" to those who do not care to strike.[11] He maintained that the "Chambers of Labor," the workers' unions, had as much right to government recognition as the Chambers of Commerce, the capitalists' associations;[12] and he reminded those who clamored for government intervention to prevent wage levels from rising too high, that the government did not intervene when wages were too low.[13]

Giolitti stood by this principle of neutrality even at the time of the two most serious crises of the pre-fascist period,—

---

[8] *Ibid.*, p. 309.

[9] *Ibid.*, p. 308-310

[10] *Ibid.*, p. 88.

[11] *Ibdi.*, p. 166.

[12] *Ibid.*, p. 167.

[13] *Ibid.*, p. 166.

the general strike of 1904 and the occupation of the factories in 1920 and 1921; and in both cases he saw the wisdom of his policy vindicated by the final outcome of those revolutionary attempts. Discussing the occupation of the factories, he stated:

"From the very first I had the clear and precise conviction that the experiment could only prove to the workers the impossibility of achieving their aim *i.e.,* to operate the factories by themselves since they lacked capital, technical personnel, and commercial organization, especially for the purchase of raw material and the sale of the products they should be able to manufacture. Because of this fact, the incident looked to me like a repetition, in different form and under different conditions, of the famous experiment in general strike of 1904 which caused so much fright and later revealed its own inanity; and I was firmly convinced that the government should follow a similar line of action, that is, should allow the experiment to take place up to a certain point; thus the workers would be convinced that their aims could not be realized, and the leaders could not shift on others the responsibility for the failure." [14]

Still in keeping with this principle of neutrality, after the war Giolitti looked with favor on the organization of groups, like the Fascist, opposed to socialism, feeling that if some socialist leaders thought that the time had come for the violent overthrow of the bourgeois state, it was well that they experienced the violent reaction of the class they planned to dispossess.

In the economic field, Giolitti believed the State should intervene when essential services were neglected or poorly provided by local units of government or private initiative. Thus, during his regime, the State purchased and expanded the national railroad system, established a state monopoly on life insurance, and set up a system of national control and financing of elementary education.

In foreign policy Giolitti's ideas were dominated by the preoccupation of maintaining peace, almost at any price, because peace was what the country needed for her industrial development and her domestic political consolidation. For this reason he was in favor of maintaining the old alliance with

---

[14] *Ibid.,* p. 598.

Germany and Austria,[15] pursuing at the same time a policy of
friendship with England, France, and Russia, to make clear
that her membership in the Triple Alliance was not directed
against any other power.[16] Not a heroic course, but the only
one that Italy could follow at the time.

To Giolitti, politics was a matter of careful and judicious
administration, not one of inspired leadership. When new proposals were presented to him he scrutinized them from the
standpoint of possible realization, not from one of lofty principles and aspirations. Once a law advocated by him was criticized,
because it did not fit an ideal condition; he replied with the
analogy of the tailor who has to make a suit of clothes for a
hunchback,—and therefore with a hump in the coat.[17] He dis-
trusted enthusiasm and rhetoric, and carefully repressed any leaning in that direction.[18] In spite of the shortcomings of his
leadership, so often stigmatized as dull, grey and uninspired,
it should be pointed out that "Giolitti's period" was the period
of greatest economic prosperity and political liberty that Italy
had achieved in modern times.

THE CATHOLICS

In 1874 the Church forbade Italian Catholics to participate
in the elections, and in compliance with this prohibition many
Catholics sent to the Pope their unused ballots following the
national election of 1876.[19] But after a few years militant Catholics became divided over the interpretation of this papal injunc-
tion. One group held it to express an attitude of absolute and
permanent intransigence, and felt that the formula "Neither
voters, nor candidates" was to be applied until the state was
forced to come to terms with the Church, by either fear of revo-

---

[15] *Ibid.*, p. 221.

[16] *Ibid.*, pp. 479-480.

[17] *Ibid.*, p. 319.

[18] He knew the whole *Divine Comedy* by heart; yet, when a line from Dante slipped
from his lips during a parliamentary debate, he apoligized to the surprised and
amused Chamber, promising it wouldn't happen again. Cf. C. Sforza, *Makers of
Modern Europe* (Indianapolis: Bobbs-Merrill, 1928) p. 237.

[19] E. Vercesi, *Il Movimento cattolico in Italia* (Firenze: La Voce, 1923) p. 124.

lution,[20] or foreign intervention.[21] The other, in a more conciliatory temper, under the slogan "Preparation in abstention," looked
forward to a time when the Church would permit the exercise
of their rights as citizens, and believed it was necessary meanwhile to prepare for such an eventuality by keeping in close
touch with the masses. As the State showed no sign of collapse,
the conciliatory view became prevalent.

The work of preparation went through three successive
stages,—economic, syndical, and political. During the first stage,
the Catholics set up a large number of credit institutions and
other financial institutes, "organized on the pattern of the ecclesiastical hierarchy," which served as "a bond . . . to hold the
Catholic masses loyal to the direction of the party." [22] In the
second stage, alarmed by the spreading of socialist organizations, and encouraged by the famous encyclical *Rerum novarum*
(1891), they engaged in the organization of mixed syndicates
or "Corporations," designed to bring together in one union both
employers and employees, though, on account of the reluctance
of the employers, only workers were actually organized,[23]—
mostly agricultural laborers, share-croppers, peasant farmers, and
artisans.

The third stage was also determined by their concern over
the increasing strength of the Socialists, which forced in 1904
a partial relaxation of the papal veto. As a matter of fact many
Catholics, including clergymen, had been disregarding it for some
time. As early as 1886 priests in Giolitti's congressional district
went to the polls.[24] In 1900 King and Okey observed that
"many felt with the Turin Clerical, who said that no Papal veto
could prevent him from carrying water when the house was on
fire." [25] In 1905 Catholics took part in local elections, and a

---

[20] *Ibid.*, p. 125.
[21] Sforza, *op. cit.*, pp. 332-333.
[22] E. Vercesi, *op. cit.*, p. 233.
[23] *Ibid.*, p. 244.
[24] Giolitti, *op. cit.*, pp. 41-42.
[25] B. King, and Th. Okey, *Italy Today* (1901, new ed., London: Nisbet, 1909), pp.
48-49. An excellent discussion of the social and political activities of the Catholics
in pp. 46-60.

few years later Catholic candidates competed for seats in Parliament. The relaxation of the papal veto, however, was still only partial. The Church discouraged the formation of a Catholic Party patterned after the German center, preferring to have, as the formula expressed it, "Deputies who are Catholic but not Catholic Deputies;" and it likewise opposed the radical *National Democratic League,* led by Romolo Murri, a young priest who combined strict orthodoxy in theology with revolutionary ideas in politics.[26]

In 1919 a Catholic political party was organized under the name of Partito Popolare Italiano (Italian Popular Party). A committee, headed by Luigi Sturzo, issued an appeal to the country and submitted a program of political action. An analysis of the program and appeal shows that the new party was leaning slightly toward the Left. In the field of international relations it stood for Wilson's principles,—with support of the League of Nations, the principle of nationality, general disarmament, freedom of the seas, abolition of secret diplomacy, and so on. In domestic policy, it demanded freedom of teaching, of religion, of syndical organization, government decentralization, electoral reforms including an elective Senate, proportional representation, vote to women, and a series of other reforms dealing with the fiscal, tariff, and agrarian systems of the country.[27]

The new party was remarkably successful at the polls, winning about 20% of the seats in the Chamber of Deputies. In its political action, however, it was handicapped by the difficult situation of post-war Italian politics, and by an internal conflict of tendencies.

The Socialists, who constituted the largest group in the Chamber of Deputies, refused to participate in any Ministry; the Catholics therefore had to collaborate with liberal groups, if there was to be any government at all. Some of the liberal

---

[26] Eventually Don Murri won a seat in Parliament, and was excommunicated. Giolitti welcomed him to the Chamber with the ironic epithet of "Chaplain of the Extreme Left." B. Croce, *op. cit.,* p. 223.

[27] Text of the appeal and program in E. Vercesi, *op. cit.,* pp. 146-152. An English translation of the program in L. Sturzo, *Italy and Fascism* (London: Taber & Gwyn, 1926), pp. 91-94.

Prime Ministers, however, once assured of the collaboration of the Catholics, tried to win the passive support of the Socialists, on the principle, perhaps, that if you hold a bird in hand, it might be worth while to go after the bird in the bush. This was especially true of Nitti and Giolitti. Nitti's partiality to the Socialists gave rise to the witticism that he had the Catholic Party as a wife, and the Socialist Party as a mistress.[28] Giolitti preferred to consult with socialist rather than with Catholic unions on matters relating to labor policies.[29] Because of this attitude the Catholics were repeatedly thrown to the opposition, causing those frequent Cabinet crises which were the outstanding feature of post-war parliamentary life in Italy.

There was the problem of conflict of tendencies within the party. The clerical conservative group was more in sympathy with the aims of the old conservative Right than with the program of reforms advocated by their party, while these same reforms appeared too tame to the left wing of the party which was only one shade less "red" than the Socialists. The unity of the party was preserved for a time by the skill and energy of Sturzo, who was in the position of the strong man in the circus, holding back two teams of horses pulling in opposite directions.[30] The rise to power of Fascism precipitated the situation: the conservative group was absorbed by the Fascist Party which adopted some points of their program, and the Catholic Party was dissolved.

The Socialists and Syndicalists

The Socialist Party, first organized in 1892, was in the beginning essentially an intellectual middle class movement both in leadership and membership. The party had been preceded by, and became heir to, a number of socialist and workers' move-

---

[28] L. Sturzo, *op. cit.*, p. 98.

[29] Sturzo, *op. cit.*, p. 98-99.

[30] There was considerable grumbling against Sturzo's "dictatorship"—It was said that the Catholic Party, contrary to appearances, did not have one hundred Deputies and one Secretary, but really one Deputy and one hundred Secretaries. E. Vercesi, *op. cit.*, p. 189.

ments of various and conflicting tendencies. Of these the most important were Bakunin's anarchism (1865-1874), Malon's "integral" socialism (1874-1880), the Milanese Workers' Party (1880), and Marxian, "scientific" socialism (1891). These heterogeneous antecedents explain in part the internal struggles that plagued the Italian Socialist Party throughout its existence.

On the wave of an anti-conservative reaction, the Socialist Party rode to its first notable electoral victory in 1900, gaining 33 seats in the Chamber of Deputies. Under the leadership of Turati the Party became an important group in Parliament, and Giolitti made a working agreement with it, offering to sponsor a number of reforms in exchange for support of his Ministry. Shortly after, however, a revolutionary group, the Syndicalist, rose within the Party to challenge this policy of collaboration. A see-saw battle was fought in the Party conventions from then on between evolutionists and revolutionists. In 1904 the Syndicalists forced the passage of a resolution condemning the support of a bourgeois government, but four years later the Reformists gained the upper hand, and the Syndicalists were expelled; in 1912 Mussolini, at that time a socialist of syndicalist tendencies, had a group of Reformists expelled, but two years later Mussolini was himself expelled. After the war the contrast reappeared, first between Socialists and Communists, then between Reformists and Maximalists. By the time the Fascists suppressed it, Socialism in Italy had already split into three separate parties.

What was the basis of the contrast between Reformists and Syndicalists? In 1900 the Socialist Party approved a "maximum program," stating the ultimate goal of the party, and a "minimum program," listing the reforms of more immediate possible realization. Both programs and a report that went with them were prepared by a committee of three, one of whom was Filippo Turati, the outstanding exponent of reformism.[31]

The "maximum program" stated that workers could achieve their emancipation only with the socialization of the means of production, and that the party proposed to work toward that

---

[31] Programs and report reprinted in R. Michels, *Storia critica del movimento socialista in Italia* (Firenze: La Voce, 1926), pp. 212-222.

goal by engaging in a twofold struggle: an economic struggle, led by trade unions, directed at the immediate improvement of the workers' lot, and a political struggle, led by the Party itself, aiming at the conquest of the local and national government organs, "to change them from means of oppression into instruments of economic and political expropriation of the ruling class." [32] The "minimum" program listed a series of reforms,—political, economic, fiscal, and administrative: freedom of speech, press, and association; universal suffrage with proportional representation; administrative decentralization; renunciation to militarism and colonial conquests; a vast program of social and labor legislation; nationalization of essential services and national resources; extension of educational opportunities; abolition of indirect taxation, etc., etc. Of these two programs the "minimum" was to be considered the actual platform of the Party, while the "maximum" was to serve only as a sort of political compass pointing the direction in which they intended to travel.

Since a considerable portion of this program could be realized,—as indeed was being realized—under the liberal government of Giolitti, the Socialist Party changed from a revolutionary group to a reform pressure group. It was felt by the Reformists that the establishment of a socialist society could be achieved only in stages. During these stages more and more power was to be transferred from the bourgeoisie to the government, while the proletariat was to develop gradually the qualities necessary to take and hold those powers themselves. The revolution was to come only at the end, in a remote fullness of time, to crown this slow process of socialization, not at the beginning. The Italian proletariat was still immature, and nothing could have been more disastrous for the country and the Party, than their premature assumption of power, whether achieved by force or by winning a majority in parliament.[33] In addition it was felt that capitalism was still in its infancy in Italy, and a long way off from that over-development which would make the Revolu-

---

[32] *Ibid.,* p. 213.

[33] *Ibid.,* pp. 232-247.

tion inevitable; therefore there was a long path of reforms along which they could travel with sympathetic bourgeois groups.

Turati reiterated these ideas in the post-war period, in opposition to the Communists and the Maximalists [34] who advocated the immediate seizure of power by revolutionary means. In 1919 he warned them that "nothing so imperils the maximum program as the illusion to realize it without the minimum program, that is, without the necessary gradual transitions;" [35] that disaster was inevitable if the Socialist Party were to take over the government, because the masses were bound to be disappointed in their exaggerated expectations,[36] and might even be turned to counter revolution by hunger, if the capitalist states boycotted socialist Italy.[37]

He further points out that to speak of revolution was both illogical and dangerous. If the masses were ready and eager for a socialist state, they would undoubtedly give the socialist candidates an overwhelming majority at the next elections,— which would make revolution unnecessary. If, on the other hand, the masses were not so disposed, a revolution would establish, as in Russia, not the dictatorship of the proletariat, but a dictatorship of a few men over, and perhaps against, the proletariat, —which was not what they desired.[38] In addition, this appeal to violence was a dangerous game because it might be taken up by the "enemy," and turned against them. And in 1919, when Fascism was hardly out of swadling clothes, he prophetically warned:

"They do not take us seriously enough now; but a time will come when it is convenient for them to take us seriously, and then our appeal to violence will be taken up by our enemies who are one hundred times better armed than we, and parliamentary action, economic organizations,

---

[34] Those who thought the time had come for the realization of the "maximum" program without further delay.

[35] G. Lazzeri, *Filippo Turati* (Milano: Caddeo, 1921), p. 183.

[36] *Ibid.*, pp. 216-217.

[37] *Ibid.*, p. 191.

[38] *Ibid.*, pp. 199-202.

Socialist party will be crushed for a long time . . . To speak continuously of violence, and then to postpone it, is the most absurd thing in the world. It serves only to rouse, to arm, even to justify our opponents' violence, a thousand times stronger than ours. It is the ultimate stupidity a party can attain, and implies a real renunciation to any revolution whatever." [39]

The moderate, evolutionary theories of the Reformists were severely criticized by the Syndicalists, who saw in them the marks of a middle class mentality which was creeping into the socialist ideology, and deadening the revolutionary spirit of the masses. This syndicalist group had been organized in 1903 within the Socialist Party, under the influence of French Syndicalism. From their French brethren, and especially from Georges Sorel whose works were popular in Italy even more than in France, Italian Syndicalists drew the principles of the bourgeois contamination of orthodox socialism, of the political capacity of the syndical organization, of the necessity of the use of violence, and of the value of the general strike as a means of training the masses for revolution. [40]

Arturo Labriola, at that time a brilliant young economist and one of the leaders of the syndicalist movement, made the charge that Reformist Socialism was in reality a conservative party, because its interest in reforms led it to uphold the domination of the class from which the reforms were expected. [41] He expressed the suspicion that the Reformist movement represented an attempt of the middle class to capture and domesticate socialism, [42] and use it, not to achieve the substitution of the bourgeoisie by the proletariat, but to interest the proletariat in the support of the present State. [43] And he found supporting evidence for this suspicion in the fact that almost the whole socialist leader-

---

[39] *Ibid.*, p. 206.

[40] For the relationship between French and Italian Syndicalism *cf.* R. Michels, *op. cit.*, pp. 323-328.

[41] Arturo Labriola, *Riforme e Rivoluzione Sociale* (Milano: Società Editoriale Milanese, 1904), pp. 85, 104.

[42] *Ibid.*, p. 251.

[43] *Ibid.*, p. 115.

ship was made up of middle class professional men [44] whose constant effort was to minimize any conflict between socialist ideals and the interests of the middle class.[45]

On many points the Syndicalists took a view diametrically opposed to that of the Socialists. They rejected the idea of an eventual socialist conquest of parliament, holding that parliament, being an institution created by the bourgeoisie as an instrument of their domination, would not be suited by a proletarian society which was to create its own organs of control. Consequently, while the Socialists gave great importance to parliamentary activities, the Syndicalists proclaimed that "the proletariat can consider the parliamentary regime only as a means of political agitation, and a school in which to learn the management of collective affairs." [46] While the Socialists worked for reforms that would place the working class under the protection of the State, the Syndicalists maintained that the working class "does not wish to be under the protection of the State, but wishes rather to eliminate all State influence on the course of its own evolution toward the abolition of capitalism." [47] And again, while the Socialists welcomed the aid of sympathetic groups of the middle class, the Syndicalist emphatically rejected any support from "those intermediate classes (small landowners, professional people, clerical workers) who, not having a class interest to advance in the movement, try to use this movement for ends which are either in contrast or merely at variance with those of socialism." [48]

---

[44] *Ibid.*, p. 227.

[45] *Ibid.*, p. 101.

[46] *Ibid.*, p. 14.

[47] *Ibid.*, p. 211.

[48] *Ibid.*, pp. 253-254.

The Syndicalists instead, to quote Labriola once again,

"strike at . . . the political constitution of the State and aim to replace it with the complete and integral government of the working class . . . Their action is designed to demolish the existing state both in the mind of the masses and in the social organization. They demand and force changes which increase the destructive power of the proletariat, and at the same time decrease the power of resistance of the State. They are not under the illusion that the rise to power of the working class can be accomplished by substituting proletarian to bourgeois personnel,— leaving the machinery of the state intact. They feel that it is quite unlikely that the destruction of the existing political machinery can be accomplished by the use alone of that very machinery (elections, use of the central and local power, control of propaganda). They do not wish to increase the strength of the State by granting to it additional authority to repress the individual and social life (system of state intervention, nationalization of industry, etc.). On the contrary, they wish to reduce it to the very limit. The constructive activities they engage in are directed to vitalize the organs which are to replace the political state (professional syndicates, corporations in charge of public services, etc.). And, meanwhile, they limit their practical political action to a destructive criticism of government institutions; therefore, they refuse any share in the administration of the state, whether it be in the direct form of participation in the government itself (ministries), or in the indirect form of support of a bourgeois government's policies. They postpone the work of positive socialist legislation to the day when the working class has succeeded in breaking the machinery of the bourgeois state. It is very likely that that day will be preceded by a long period of systematic collective violence similar to that which accompanied the French Revolution, but of which it is impossible to predetermine the duration, the occasion, and the modality." [49]

This view of absolute intransigence prevailed in the Socialist Party only for a short time. As stated before, the Syndicalists were expelled in 1908,—with some of them, like Labriola, continuing their political activity as independent socialists, others, like Forges-Davanzati and De Ambris, drifting toward Nationalism. A good many Syndicalists, however, remained in the party, submitting to its discipline but keeping the revolutionary spirit alive within it. This revolutionary spirit flared up high anew after the war with evident traces of syndicalist ideology,—al-

---

[49] *Ibid.*, pp. 116-117.

though for a time Italian revolutionary socialists were under the spell of the Russian myth, while syndicalist principles were active in the Nationalist and Fascist parties. Signs of syndicalist ideas can be detected, for instance, in the effort of the strikers to keep up the production during the occupation of the factories in 1920-21, as well as in the attempt made in 1922 by the socialist labor unions to reach an understanding with the National Syndicalism of D'Annunzio's legionaries.

The high-water mark of socialism was reached in Italy right after the war when socialist candidates captured 154 of the 508 seats in the Chamber of Deputies. Its positive influence, however, was not proportioned to its actual strength. The forces of the Reformists and those of the Revolutionists were so nearly equally balanced that the Party was paralyzed and, like Buridan's ass between the two equal heaps of hay, could not move in either direction, with the result that when the Fascist onslaught came, it was unable to employ effectively in its defense either legal or violent means.

THE NATIONALISTS

The nationalist movement lasted altogether about twenty years. Starting, as an intellectual movement, with the publication of the review *Il Regno* (The Kingdom) in 1903, it became Italian National Association in 1910, and Nationalist Party in 1914. After the march on Rome, in 1923, it was merged with Fascism to which it contributed the bulk of its doctrine.[50] At first it was strictly an intellectual movement, finding its expression exclusively in books and reviews. Its basic principles were derived from the nationalistic doctrines of Barrès and Maurras and the syndicalism of Georges Sorel,—though some of its early exponents liked to point out that their campaign was based on the teaching of two contemporary Italian thinkers, Mosca and

---

[50] For the general background of the Nationalist movement, *cf.* B. Croce, *op. cit.*, pp. 237-255, 264-269; G. Volpe, *L'Italia in cammino* (1927) (Milano: Treves, 3rd edit., 1931), pp. 141-171; P. M. Riccio, *On the threshold of Fascism* (New York: Casa Italiana Columbia University, 1929), pp. 147-175.

Pareto.[51] It was free from racial exclusivism, as shown by the fact that three of its seven founders were Jews.[52]

It started out as a defender of the middle class against the invadence of socialism. Not of course of a middle class affected itself by a democratic mentality, the "tender, sugared, buttered," middle class, full of sympathy for those who wished to destroy it;[53] but of a strong middle class, conscious and jealous of its rights, ready to defend itself, to oppose violence with violence, to answer strikes with the lock-outs, to set up strike breakers' organizations in answer to the organization of labor unions.[54] It decried parliament, "the fetish of a God of foreign importation,"[55] the "central tumor . . . that festers on the nation," and hoped to see it replaced with "the free organization of workers and industrialists."[56] It was, naturally, against socialism, considered "what is basest, most vulgar, most overbearing in the animal man," which "in the name of Liberty wishes to enslave men, in the name of the Idea concerns itself with filling bellies, in the name of Equality sets up the tyranny of a demagogic oligarchy."[57] During this early period Nationalist propaganda gained many sympathizers among the members of liberal parties; later, however, as the movement acquired greater political consciousness, it began an active campaign not only against Socialism, but also against Democracy, Liberalism, and Freemasonry, laying exclusive claim on the loyalty of its adherents.

The outstanding leader, indeed the founder, of the movement was Enrico Corradini. He was its most authoritative spokes-

---

[51] G. Prezzolini, "L'Aristocrazia dei briganti," in G. Papini & G. Prezzolini *Vecchio e Nuovo Nazionalismo* (Milano: Studio Editoriale Lombardo, 1914), p. 38.

[52] R. Michels, *op. cit.*, p. 195.

[53] G. Papini, and G. Prezzolini, *op. cit.*, pp. 9, 93.

[54] *Ibid.*, pp. 95 ff.; 119. Some of these anti-labor suggestions were made after the general strike of 1904 which aroused very widespread resentment.

[55] *Ibid.*, p. 75.

[56] *Ibid.*, pp. 80-81.

[57] *Ibid.*, p. 23.

man, and, therefore, the one to turn to for a statement of the Nationalist doctrines.

Corradini criticized liberalism for remaining strictly political when new parties, like the socialist, were deriving a tremendous force from the economic content of their programs; for failing to defend the middle class,—its own class; for failing to react even when socialism, in order to strike at the bourgeoisie, was threatening the vital interests of the nation itself.[58] He condemned political socialism for its programmatic opposition to the State, and for its internationalism, although he looked with sympathy on some phases of its economic program. He admired the success socialism had achieved in awakening the latent energies of Italian proletariat, and offered this achievement as a model to the Nationalists, whose task was to rouse the whole nation as the Socialists had the working class.[59] Syndicalism, with its far greater emphasis on economic organization, found even more favor in his eyes. He approved of the scheme of organizing the country like one large syndicate, provided class solidarity stopped at the frontier, and the Italian worker realized he had more in common with his employer than with his fellow workers abroad; and provided also he supported Italy, a proletarian country, in her competition with bourgeois capitalistic neighbors.[60]

The highest form of human solidarity, according to Corradini, is achieved neither in the class nor in humanity but in the Nation. The Nation is not merely the sum of individual citizens at any given time, but it is a living organism, a mystical body embracing all past, present, and future generations, of which the individual is an ephemeral part, and to which he owes his highest duty. The Nation fulfills its mission by the creation of a civilization, "the supreme fruit, the supreme flower of all its history, of all its efforts through the centuries," and which is the contribution it owes to the civilization of humanity. Thus a series

---

[58] E. Corradini, *Discorsi politici* (Firenze: Vallecchi, 1923), pp. 185-187, 237.

[59] *Ibid.*, pp. 360, 363, 191, 213, 109.

[60] *Ibid.*, pp. 218, 60-61, 223, 100.

of transcendental relations is established,—between the individual and the Nation, the Nation and a national civilization, and the national civilization and the universal civilization of all mankind.[61]

The State is the visible, historical manifestation of the Nation. The individual is subordinated to it.[62] In its relation with its citizens the State is neither bourgeois nor proletarian; it is national. It favors the collaboration of the classes, a collaboration which in a first moment might be the result of class struggle, but which eventually will be achieved through organization and integration of the conflicting forces. In contrast with the Socialists,[63] the Nationalist Party emphasized the importance of foreign policy over and above domestic policy. Many problems for which Liberals and Socialists sought solutions at home, such as emigration, the backward condition of the Southern provinces, were, according to the Nationalists, essentially problems of foreign policy.[64] They advocated colonial expansion and opposed all sorts of pacifisms,—"the sentimental pacifism of the middle class," "socialist pacifism," and "plutocratic pacifism,"—insisting that "war is organic in the human nature of human society," and that in history the "oases of peace" correspond to areas of extinction of ethnic energy.[65]

During its twenty years of existence Nationalism campaigned actively in support of the occupation of Lybia, the annexation of Dalmatia, and D'Annunzio's expedition to Fiume. After the March on Rome, it merged with Fascism of which it considered itself a forerunner, and nationalist leaders like Rocco and Federzoni held high rank in the Fascist hierarchy.

---

[61] *Ibid.*, p. 206.

[62] *Ibid.*, p. 242.

[63] "Among the Socialists, with the exception of Salvemini's *Unità* [a review] . . . few were interested in foreign policy." G. Lazzeri, *op. cit.*, p. 80.

[64] E. Corradini, *op. cit.*, pp. 96, q.

[65] *Ibid.*, pp. 163, 165, 175.

The Crisis

Before 1914 liberal groups had an unquestioned control of Italian parliament. The socialist and syndicalist strength at that time never exceeded ten percent of the total; the Catholics had only a few members in parliament, and no "Catholic" parliamentary group; the Nationalists for the first time in 1913 had two Deputies. Thus a liberal ministry could always count on a solid majority in the Chamber,—a situation to which the skillful and not over-scrupulous electoral and parliamentary manipulations of Giolitti contributed materially.

After the war popular discontent, war weariness, economic maladjustment, and many other factors brought about a radical shift in the proportional strength of parties in the Chamber,— the process being aided by a further broadening of the franchise and the adoption of proportional representation. In 1919 the Socialist and Catholic parties, both opposed to liberalism, won about one-half of the seats,—the other half being divided among a variety of groups, going from the reactionary Agrarians to dissident Socialists. That marked the end of the Liberal State in Italy. The peculiar internal situation of the two largest parties left the Liberals in a shaky control of the government for three more years. Nevertheless, the Liberal State as Giolitti conceived it,—the impartial arbiter of the conflicting forces in the country,—was already dead, because the "conflicting forces" had grown too strong, and the "arbiter" had become too weak.

BIBLIOGRAPHY

AMENDOLA, GIOVANNI, *La Democrazia* (Milano: Corbaccio, 1924). Articles and speeches upholding the democratic principles against Fascism.

BONOMI, IVANOE, *From Socialism to Fascism* (London: Hopkinson & Co., 1924). A discussion of the defeat of Italian Socialism by an ex-socialist and former Prime Minister of Italy. Quite critical of socialist tactics.

CORRADINI, ENRICO, *Discorsi Politici* (Firenze: Vallecchi, 1923). Propaganda speeches in behalf of Nationalism by the founder of the movement.

CROCE, BENEDETTO, *A History of Italy: 1871-1915* (Oxford: The Clarendon Press, 1929). Defending the liberal viewpoint.

GIOLITTI, GIOVANNI, *Memorie della mia vita* (Milano: Treves, 1922). An account of Italian politics by the dominant figure in pre-fascist political life. English translation by E. Storer, London, 1923.

KING, BOLTON, AND OKEY, THOMAS, *Italy To-day* (1901) (London: Nisbet, new ed., 1909). An excellent account of the condition of Italy at the beginning of the present century.

LABRIOLA, ARTURO, *Riforme e Rivoluzione Sociale* (Milano: Società Editoriale Milanese, 1904). A spirited criticism, from the syndicalist standpoint, of the evolutionary theories in the Italian Socialist Party.

LAZZARI, GEROLAMO, *Filippo Turati* (Milano: Caddeo, 1921). A character sketch of the leader of reform socialism, with an ample selection of his articles and speeches for the period 1914-1920.

MICHELS, ROBERTO. *Storia critica del movimento socialista italiano* (Firenze: La Voce, 1926). The story is brought up to 1911. The author has syndicalist sympathies.

NITTI, FRANCESCO S., *Il Partito Radicale e la Nuova Democrazia Industriale* (Torino-Roma: Società Tipografica-Editrice nazionale, 1907). A criticism of the left wing liberals, for their lack of clear cut principles and incoherent action. Later, in the post-war period, the author was Prime Minister.

PAPINI, GIOVANNI, AND PREZZOLINI, GIUSEPPE, *Vecchio e Nuovo Nazionalismo* (Milano: Studio Editoriale Lombardo, 1914). Reprints of articles contributed by the authors to Corradini's Nationalist Review *Il Regno*. Later the authors opposed the nationalist movement.

RICCIO, PETER M., *On the Threshold of Fascism* (New York: Casa Italiana Columbia University, 1929). A doctoral dissertation discussing the cultural and political movements that foreshadowed Fascism.

SFORZA, CARLO, *The Makers of Modern Europe* (Indianapolis: Bobbs-Merrill, 1928). Sketches of several leading political figures of post-war Italy. The author was minister of foreign affairs in the last Giolitti's Cabinet.

STURZO, LUIGI, *Italy and Fascism* (London: Faber & Gwyer, 1926). The post-war political crisis related by the leader of the Catholic Party.

VERCESI, ERNESTO, *Il Movimento cattolico in Italia* (Firenze: La Voce, 1922). The story of the Catholic movement from a conservative standpoint. Lukewarm toward Don Sturzo.

VOLPE, GIOACCHINO, *L'Italia in Cammino* (1927) (Milano: Treves, 3rd ed., 1931). The history of the last half century told with a pro-fascist slant.

Chapter XXVI

FAR EAST

PAUL H. CLYDE

The past century has been for the Far East an era of total revolution—economic, social, and political. The society which will emerge from this chaos of change has not as yet taken shape. This is particularly true of the political structure. It may be granted that the machine and the factory have already given us a rather definite pattern for Asia's material, industrial future, yet the political and social pattern within which industry and the machine must operate is as yet embryonic. It is common practice to refer to the westernization of the Far East. In point of material things this westernization has been very real. The railroad and the radio do not change their shape because they operate in a Chinese or Japanese landscape. However, this is not necessarily true when one considers the "political westernization" of Asia. Constitutionalism, liberalism, democracy, socialism, fascism, and communism have also found a place in this same oriental landscape, but, unlike the railroad and the radio, their shape is being changed by the new environment. The political thinking of a Rousseau or a Jefferson flourished against a background of European feudalism, mercantilism, and divine right absolutism. The political thinking of a Sun Yat-sen or an Ito struggles against a background not only of western ideologies, but also, and perhaps more significantly, against a background of Confucianism or Shintoism and military feudalism.[1]

---

[1] Hu Shih, *The Chinese Renaissance* (Chicago: The University of Chicago Press, 1934), ch. I for a discussion of types of cultural response.

CHINA

China, during the past century, has been creating a new civilization drawing its inspiration not only from her own Confucian cultural heritage but also from the machine-age civilization of the West. The process has already involved three stages in the development of her political thought: (1) resistance to western civilization, (2) ardent appreciation, and (3) the appearance of doubt and indecision.[2]

RESISTANCE

Traditionally, Confucian China was a society rather than a state. Government as the West understands the term was minimized because controls were exercised through the people's understanding of virtue and propriety rather than through constitutions and the enforcement of inflexible laws. International affairs presented few problems, because China, the Middle Kingdom, dominated by cultural means all the lesser members of the Confucian society of peoples by whom she was surrounded. In a word, "the Chinese were not aware of their realm as a nation-state."[3] Herein lies the explanation of China's long resistance to the legal, political philosophy of the western trader and diplomat. The 19th century was preeminently a period of Chinese opposition to western concepts of sovereignty, government, and international relations.[4]

ARDENT APPRECIATION

Out of this period of resistance there emerged at the close of the 19th century a revolution in political thought. Confucianism appeared to be bankrupt in the face of the western impact. The new political and social philosophers looked with ardent

[2] In this discussion I acknowledge my great debt to the writings of Hu Shih who is of the company of China's greatest contemporary political and social philosophers.

[3] P. M. A. Linebarger, *Government in Republican China* (New York: McGraw-Hill Book Co., 1938), p. 3.

[4] For comprehensive surveys of the movement see H. M. Vinacke, *A History of the Far East in Modern Times* (New York: F. S. Crofts, 4th ed., 1941), chs. I-III; P. H. Clyde, *A History of the Modern and Contemporary Far East* (New York: Prentice-Hall, 1937), chs. II, V-VIII, XII-XIV.

appreciation to the Occident. The new trends were suggested as early as the 70's when Kuo-Sung-t'ao, scholar and first Chinese minister to the Court of St. James, remarked that: "Confucius and Mencius have deceived us." This was among the first significant admissions that "there was more than one way [the Confucian] of governing a civilized country." [5] In the same period, Wang T'ao, the scholar-editor who assisted James Legge in the English translation of the Confucian classics, praised the British political system as embodying "the best ideals of our classical antiquity" In 1894, a young southern Chinese, Sun Yat-sen by name, was idealizing "the scientific, technological, and democratic culture of the West." [7]

These suggestive beginnings took more formal shape in the political philosophy behind the abortive "hundred days" of reform of 1898. K'ang Yu-wei (known to his disciples as "Nan-Hai") was the leader of this movement. A Cantonese, who had enjoyed a classical education and held the degree of *chin shih* (doctor of philosophy), had read though perhaps not deeply in western literature, departed radically from conventional interpretations of the Classics, stressed the most democratic ideas of Mencius, headed a new school whose curriculum included western learning, and finally proposed a constitutional monarchy retaining the young Manchu emperor. [8] Closely associated with K'ang but of greater mental stature was Liang Ch'i-ch'ao, editor of a political journal (1903) called *The New* [Renovated] *People*. Liang's gospel was that China must acquire those characteristics which had made the West strong; civic as distinct from private morality, nationalism, the consciousness of human rights and liberties, a sense of duty, the martial spirit, and pride

[5] E. R. Hughes, *The Invasion of China by the Western World* (London: A. and C. Black, 1937), p. 107. A decade earlier, Tseng Kuo-fang, who saved China from the T'ai-p'ing rebels, had said: "Even they [the Occidentals] also have some of the virtues of a gentleman." Hu Shih, *op. cit.*, p. 33.

[6] Hu Shih, *op. cit.*, pp. 33-35.

[7] Hu Shih, *op. cit.*, p. 36.

[8] M. E. Cameron, *The Reform Movement in China 1898-1912* (Stanford University: Stanford University Press, 1931), pp. 24-25, 183; R. F. Johnston, *Twilight in the Forbidden City* (London: Gollancz, 1934), ch. I.

in economic independence. Here was a prophet of Victorian individualism and liberalism.[9]

This program could at best be only a partial answer to China's need. China's political and social hunger had become complex in the extreme, and this complexity is reflected in her greatest contribution to contemporary political thought. This is the *San Min Chu I,* the political and social ideology of Sun Yat-sen, founder of the Chinese Republic. Sun's doctrines are a re-interpretation of Confucianism and an adaptation of certain western political ideologies. The "three principles," tri-*min*-ism, all center in the Confucian social concept of the Chinese word *min* (people). *Min tsu* (race-determination) is Sun's theory of nationalism, of the race as an effective state, applying its traditional, Confucian ethical and social philosophy through western organization and techniques. *Min ch'üan* (democracy), Sun's second principle, was not merely a reflection of the high-tide of democratic enthusiasm in the Occident, but was also inherent in much of the philosophy of Old China. Finally, *Min shêng* ("people" plus "generation" or people's living) has been loosely interpreted as socialism. In Sun's mind it seems to have meant the greatest material welfare to the whole people rather than a particular political or social *ism.*[10] In 1927 the *San Min Chu I* became the official state dogma of *Kuomintang* China.[11]

Other exponents of western thought include: Ch'en Tu-shiu and Wu chih-hui of the early republican period (1912-23) who eulogized science, technology, and democracy; and Liang Shu-ming who thought of western civilization as a necessary but a temporary detour to a new and essentially Chinese civilization.

THE APPEARANCE OF DOUBT AND INDECISION

Meanwhile the occidental ideals which were influencing so deeply the new China were themselves challenged in the West.

---

[9] Hu Shih, *op. cit.,* pp. 36-38.

[10] Kyoson Tsuchida, *Contemporary Thought of Japan and China* (London: Williams and Norgate, 1927), pp. 223-228; Linebarger, *op. cit.,* pp. 41-44.

[11] *Kuomintang* or National People's Party (from three Chinese words meaning "country," "people," and "party,") is the power behind the present National Government of Chiang K'ai-shek, and regards itself as the custodian of Sun's philosophy—a claim which does not go unchallenged within China.

Were nationalism, liberalism, parliamentary government, and democracy an expression of western socio-political genius or merely ingenius political tools by which the strong exploited the weak? Was the war of 1914-1919 the beginning of the end of western civilization? Were the Russian revolutions a sign of a new society or merely a repudiation of all save materialism? Had the West become a chaos of error? These are but suggestions of the doubt and indecision which since 1919 have troubled the political thought of China.

Thus between two world wars the political philosophy of leaders in Chinese thought has struggled between extremes. In 1919 the old liberal, Liang Ch'i-ch'ao, reversed himself as he saw what seemed as "the imminent bankruptcy of scientific civilization." Pamphleteers among China's student-politicians decried capitalism and imperialism in economics and government demanding a Marxian and an agrarian revolution for a society controlled by laborers and farmers. Even many of the old-line liberals whose work had created the Republic began to question democracy and to turn toward "the newer tendencies of fascism and other forms of dictatorship." [12] Left wing theories, represented principally by the Chinese communists, gained greatly in influence after 1936 since the communists were an important factor in forcing the popular united front against Japan, and because "the Chinese peasantry welcomed a regime [the communist] antagonistic to the National Government," a regime which "offered them a decent place in society and a hope of

---

[12] Hu Shih, *op. cit.,* p. 42. This statement was made by Dr. Hu in 1933. In Feb., 1944, Madame Sun Yat-sen, widow of the founder of the Republic, said: "Reaction and fascism in China are strong. . . . This is proved . . . by diversion of part of our national [*Kuomintang*] army to the task of blockading and 'guarding' the guerrilla areas, by the fact that some still hold private profit above the national interest, by the oppression of the peasantry and the absence of a true labor movement. . . . Some Chinese reactionaries are preparing to destroy a democratic sector in our struggle." (*Time,* Feb. 14, 1944, p. 37). In terms of political thought Madame Sun's words were a direct attack on the totalitarianism of Chiang K'ai-shek's *China's Destiny,* 1943 (in Chinese), which significantly the National Government had not released for English translation or for direct quotation abroad. (*Fortune,* Oct., 1943). See also Agnes Smedley, *Battle Hymn of China* (New York: A. A. Knopf, 1943).

something better than blueprints of social reform." [13] Indeed the outbreak of the undeclared Sino-Japanese War (1937) came at a time when Chinese political thought was confused by ideological conflicts of great intensity. Many of China's intellectuals recognized that the problem for China's contemporary political philosophers, presented by these conflicts, was not to find some alien foundation which would preserve the *Kuomintang* dictatorship or to pave the way for an era of Marxian communism. Rather it was to revive and build upon the socio-political ideas of Sun Yat-sen—ideas which unlike imported ideologies, whether fascist or communist, portray a China modern in both politics and economics yet fortified by permanent virtues of her own Confucian heritage of social and ethical principles.

The hope that such a China is already in the making rests on the extraordinary contributions made by her present generation of intellectuals. In the past twenty-five years "a complete revolution has been brought about in almost all the fields of historical research once monopolized by the old scholars." [14] Many Chinese have been awakened to the fact that the western scientific approach to the study of the humanities and the social sciences is not a thing alien to Chinese intellectual tradition. What is more, that remarkable movement which has been called the Chinese Renaissance, which has fostered a new literature in the language of the people, drew its leadership from among mature Chinese students *"trained in the old cultural tradition."* It is notable that the men and women of this Renaissance are humanists. Their goal is emancipation not suppression, individual liberty and dignity not bondage. They look toward "the new birth of an old people and *an old civilization."* [15]

JAPAN

Japanese civilization in the broadest historical sense has been built to a very notable degree on alien cultures. During most of her history, certainly from the 5th to the 18th century,

[13] H. S. Quigley, *Far Eastern War 1937-1941* (Boston: World Peace Foundation, 1942), p. 14.

[14] Hu Shih, *op. cit.,* p. 75.

[15] Hu Shih, *op. cit.,* p. 44. Italics are mine.

Japan drew heavily upon the wealth of Confucian China.[16] Since the middle of the 19th century, western civilization has all but transformed completely the material face of Japan, and has also influenced, though in lesser degree, her intellectual outlook. Nevertheless, modern and contemporary Japan is not primarily a political descendant of China's Confucian thought or of western 19th century liberalism. To be sure, the literature of Japan's socio-political thought from as early as the 5th century is replete with commentaries on the Confucian virtues, and, since the establishment of constitutionalism in 1899 with the whole political vocabulary of liberalism and democracy, not to mention fascism and communism. Yet the realities of her dominating political thought during the past ten years have been peculiarly Japanese.

DISTORTIONS OF CONFUCIAN DOCTRINE

In two vital ways Japanese political philosophy has since early times changed and distorted some of the fundamentals of Confucian political thought. It is true that in a general sense Japan, like China, has accepted the basic concepts which hold: that society is more important than the individual, that all men are by nature unequal, that politics is synonymous with ethics, that government by man is superior to government by law, and that the patriarchal family is the ideal state.[17] In China, however, there were certain democratic safeguards. Although the Chinese emperor was a theocratic sovereign who ruled because he possessed the mandate of heaven," it is notable that heaven might deprive an unworthy sovereign of the mandate. It thereupon became the duty of his subjects to be disloyal, to rebel, to overthrow the unworthy ruler, and to replace him by a virtuous sovereign. Furthermore, in China, the highest and most coveted honors in society and government were reserved for the civilian-scholars, the *literati*. These men, comprising the ruling class, owed their position not to any accident of birth but to a

---

[16] Sir George Sansom, *Japan: A Short Cultural History* (London: The Cresset Press, 1932), in particular chs. IV-IX.

[17] R. K. Reischauer, *Japan: Government—Politics* (New York: Thomas Nelson and Sons, 1939), pp. 21-33.

system of competitive examinations for which in theory at least every educated person was eligible. Japan, in contrast, distorted these principles to create "a line of emperors unbroken through ages eternal." She thereby produced a theory of absolute loyalty, Confucian in its base but wholly lacking in Confucian safeguards. In addition, the guardians of this theory of patriotism, the historic Japanese ruling class, were not scholars selected by competitive examination but feudal warriors who ruled by force of arms and by hereditary title.[18]

THE 19TH CENTURY REVOLUTION

The opening of Japan to western intercourse in mid-19th century, coinciding with the rise of a powerful mercantile class, precipitated the downfall of the shoguns, of feudalism itself, and thus paved the way for the creation of a new Japan based not on feudal clan loyalties but rather on a unique nationalism inspired by the restoration of the emperor to *de facto* power.[19] The Restoration leaders sought in creating a unified and nationalistic Japan to preserve their power by directing the absolute loyalty of a people toward a sovereign who was to be regarded as the descendant of the gods, and whose will was to be interpreted as that of "the state." [20]

This new political structure and the theories on which it rested were devised and evolved by men who were political theorists and office holders at one and the same time. In 1867

[18] Sansom, *op. cit.*, chs. XIV, XV, XVII, XIX, XXI.

[19] H. S. Quigley, *Japanese Government and Politics* (New York: The Century Co., 1932), ch. II, for a full discussion of the Restoration.

[20] For conflicting interpretations of the theory of imperial powers, see: Quigley, *op. cit.*, pp. 67-68; Reischauer, *op. cit.*, pp. 167-169; G. E. Uyehara, *The Political Development of Japan 1867-1909* (London: Constable and Co., 1910), p. 19; Tomio Nakano, *The Ordinance Power of the Japanese Emperor* (Baltimore: The Johns Hopkins Press, 1923), p. 5ff; H. Sato, *Democracy and the Japanese Government* (New York: The Arbor Press, 1920), p. 1; E. W. Clement, "Constitutional Imperialism in Japan," *Proceedings,* Academy of Political Science, VI, p. 325; U. Iwasaki, *Working Forces in Japanese Politics* (New York: Columbia University, 1921), ch. II. The Japanese doctrine postulating the identity of the emperor and the state is known as *kokutai.* Championed by Professor Shinkichi Uesugi and others,, the doctrine was combatted with some success for twenty years by the great liberal scholar Professor Tatsukichi Minobe.

before the abolition of feudalism, most of them were *samurai* (military-feudal retainers) of the Western clans (Satsuma, Choshiu, etc.).[21] These men who engineered the Restoration (1867) and the formal abolition of feudalism (1871), enveloped the new Japan with the theory of unqualified loyalty to a "divinely descended" emperor in such a way that "the modern Japanese state was deliberately established on a foundation which unified government and religion."[22] The ancient mythology of prehistoric Japan was resurrected where convenient to provide the ultimate sanction for a theory of divine right absolutism. State *Shinto* (the way of the gods) was revived and developed to serve a particular political end: namely, to justify belief in the omnipotence of an emperor whose throne was bequeathed by "the Heavenly Deities and the Great Ancestress."[23]

Twenty-two years after the Restoration, the Emperor Meiji presented his people with a constitution (1889). It was the work primarily of a younger generation of the former *samurai* class who had been trained by the Restoration leaders and who remained true to the theory of theocratic absolutism which the latter had promoted. These men not only created the constitution, but also directed and controlled its functioning for some thirty years (1889-1918). The document which they devised was clearly a product of "Japanese political principles under the cloak of representative institutions."[24]

------

[21] Typical examples include: Takamori Saigo, Toshimichi Okubo, Koin Kido. Reischauer, *op. cit.,* p. 64.

[22] D. C. Holtom, *Modern Japan and Shinto Nationalism* (Chicago: University of Chicago Press, 1943), p. 5. See in particular also Holtom's use of *Kokutai no Hongi* [Fundamental Principles of the National Structure] (Tokyo: Ministry of Education, 1937).

[23] Holtom, *op. cit.,* p. 6. Note also Holtom's discussion of elements of universalism in State *Shinto* and its relation with *Hakko-ichi-u* (the World under one roof) the central principle of Japanese foreign policy.

[24] Uyehara, *op. cit.,* p. 110; Reischauer, *op. cit.,* p. 75. The more influential of the men who shaped and controlled the working of the constitution came later to be known as the *Genro* (elder statesmen): Hirobumi Ito, Aritomo Yamagata, Kaoru Inouye, Iwao Oyama, and Masayoshi Matsukata.

THE STRUGGLES OF LIBERALISM

Although the framers of the constitution had no intent to create a liberal parliamentary government, they recognized both the practical expediency of western political forms, and the necessity of placating the growth within Japan of western political thought, particularly liberalism. Indeed three major currents of western thought acquired significant influence in Japan following the Restoration: English utilitarian free thought, French social liberalism, and German political absolutism. At his Mita School (Keio University), Yukichi Fukuzawa taught that "Heaven does not create man above man, nor man under man." [25] Masanao Nakamura introduced concepts of subjective morality based on Christian standards. After 1880 French liberalism found a congenial setting in the intellectual turmoil of the post-Restoration era. It inspired the platform of the first political party the *Jiyuto* (Liberal Party, 1881), and in part prompted the Imperial Rescript promising a constitution and a parliament in 1889. Rousseau's *Social Contract* had already been translated by Tokusuke (Chōmin) Nakae. Montesquieu and Voltaire were read widely, while for a brief period Kimmochi Saionji, one of the greatest of Japan's liberals, reflected the democratic spirit in his *Eastern Free Press*. English as opposed to French political influence was seen in the appearance of the second political party, the *Rikken Kaishinto* (Progressive or Reform Party, 1882) with a parliamentary program somewhat more conservative than that of the *Jiyuto*.[26]

Reaction, inspired by government, was, however, already at work. The indigenous nationalistic and absolutist trends were strengthened by German influence. Many Japanese were already turning to the writings of Stein, Gneist, Bluntschli, Jhering, and others. Ito drafted the constitution under the spell of Bismarck and Prussia.[27] On the eve of promulgation of the constitution,

---

[26] Tsuchida, *op. cit.,* pp. 21-29.

[25] Fukuzawa was the most distinguished intellectual of those who sought westernization at the time. *The Autobiography of Fukuzawa Yukichi* (Tokyo: Hokuseido Press, 1934).

[27] Quigley, *op. cit.,* p. 40.

Ito and Yamagata banished from the capital more than 500
liberals, a move designed to extinguish all social and democratic
thought.[28] The constitution was thus introduced in an atmosphere
of Bismarckian constitutional imperialism. For nearly three
decades this influence, fused with State *Shinto,* was sustained as
the orthodox political philosophy. As a result most liberal political thought was driven into the literary channel of the political
novel. Ryukei Yano in his *Keikoku Bidan* glorified the democratic zeal of heroes of ancient Greece. Tokaisanshi in his *Kajin-
no-Kigu* presented his hero standing in deep reverence before
the Liberty Bell in Philadelphia.[29] Yet, it would be easy to overestimate the influence of such works, particularly in view of the
fact that a new and in part spontaneous resistance to European
thought had already set in before the turn of the 20th century.
This movement paraded under the banner of "Preservation of
national [Shinto] virtues." As early as 1892 Christianity was
attacked by Tetsujiro Inouye on the ground that it did "not conform to traditional Japanese ideas concerning the State." [30]

Nevertheless, Japan of the early 20th century appeared to
be moving toward a responsible parliamentary government. From
1918 until 1932 the party politicians as spokesmen of the new
and powerful industrialists were in power.[31] Liberals hailed it
as the dawn of *kensei no jodo* (period of normal government).
In 1918 precedent was broken when Takashi Hara, a commoner,
became prime minister. Manhood suffrage was achieved in 1925.
Significant as were these changes they by no means represented
the extreme left wing of Japanese political thought. While academic philosophers followed neo-Kantian individualism and remained aloof from the so-called practical political problems of
society, many of the younger professional political and social
scientists were turning to socialism as the answer to new prob-

---

[28] Tsuchida, *op. cit.,* p. 29.

[29] Tadao Kunitomo, *Japanese Literature Since 1868* (Tokyo: Hokuseido Press,
1938), pp. 13, 23-28.

[30] Tsuchida, *op. cit.,* p. 32.

[31] Reischauer, *op. cit.,* ch. VI.

lems arising from Japan's industrialization and the consequent disintegration of the traditional family system.

Left Wing Theories

The foundations of a new political and social philosophy had already been laid in the late Meiji and early Showa eras (c. 1910-1920). Odo Tanaka demanded a sweeping reinterpretation of Japanese philosophy. Kōjirō Sugimori saw the need for a new evaluation of political theory in the light of Japan's industrialization and social needs. His basic politico-ethical concept described man as "a free agent." Jirō Abe found in "freedom" his ideal society. Reikichi Kita advocated a democracy and "the right of revolution." [32] By 1920 political thinkers outside of government had swung far to the left. Some of these men were critics who shunned the ideological approach, such for example as Manjiro Hasegawa, who attacked the concept of the state based on Shinto mythology. In Takanobu Murobuse's *The Downfall of Civilization* (1923) there was the clear reflection of Spengler's influence. Sakuzo Yoshino and Tokuzo Kukuda were direct in their attacks on the controlling oligarchy and bureaucracy.[33]

From these critics it was but a short road to the advocates of socialism. Although socialistic pamphlets appeared in Japan as early as 1881, it was not until 1901 that the Social Democratic [Marxian] Party was formed by Denjirō Kōtoku, Iso Abe, and Sen Katayama. Suppression of the party by government was not surprising for its philosophy of pacifism made little popular appeal during the era of two wars, the Russo-Japanese 1904-5 and the World War 1914-19. Radical societies and their publications were banned almost as rapidly as they appeared while socialist and anarchist leaders were put to death with little discrimination. After 1919, however, Marxian doctrine gained rapidly in popularity. *Capital* was translated in full by Motoyuki Takabatake. The Russian revolutions found their chief Japanese spokesmen in Toshihiko Sakai and Kin Kamakawa. Hajime Kawakami while yet a member of the faculty of the Imperial

[32] Tsuchida, *op. cit.*, ch. VII.
[33] Tsuchida, *op. cit.*, ch. VIII.

University began in 1919 a socialist periodical, *Studies in the Social Problem*. In 1923 students of Waseda University under the leadership of Professor Ikuo Oyama campaigned against the introduction of military training. Gradually this post-war peace movement became identified with general progressive and socialistic movements. Professor Sakuzo Yoshino of the Imperial University of Tokyo led in organization of the *Shakai Kagaku Rengokai* (Intercollegiate Association for the Study of Social Science).[34] Thus the fusion of pacifism and socialism appeared as a challenge to the orthodox political philosophy of the oligarchy and to the tradition of militarism which had survived the collapse of feudalism.

"DANGEROUS THOUGHTS" AND THE REVIVAL OF MILITARISM

The revival of militarism, particularly notable since 1925, progressed hand in hand with the growth of chauvinistic and reactionary societies whose philosophy may best be described as "Japanese fascism." The elements of this political creed defy ready definition. They frequently present a self-contradictory hodge-podge of imperialism, patriotism, religious [Shinto] nationalism, social reform for peasants and workmen, political reform of the parliamentary parties, and, in some circumstances, their abolition. Some fascist societies stressed social reform; others were anti-social; while some were mere gangs of political assassins masquerading as the enemies of "dangerous thoughts," a phrase designed to encompass any idea associated with individualism, liberalism, democracy, and communism. Most powerful were the military societies that controlled the youth movement, that reflected the chauvinism of the Imperial Young Officers' League (*Kokoku Seinen Shoko Domei*), and championed the principle of *iaku no gunmu* (supreme command) through which the armed services were removed from all civilian control.[35] It was the incoherent political philosophy of these groups

---

[34] K. W. Colegrove, *Militarism in Japan* (Boston: World Peace Foundation, 1936), p. 15. Influential organs of the press (Tokyo: *Asahi* and Tokyo *Nichi Nichi*) supported this anti-militaristic movement.

[35] Colegrove, *op. cit.*, pp. 16-41; G. C. Allen, *Modern Japan and Its Problems* (New York: E. P. Dutton, 1927), ch. III; E. E. N. Causton, *Militarism and Foreign Policy in Japan* (London: Allen and Unwin, 1936), ch. III.

that paved the way for the undeclared China war, which, in turn, made possible the military dictatorship under General Hideki Tojo. The ideology of the militarists, best expressed by General Sadao Araki, rested on two points: *Toa-shugi* (East Asianism or Japan's mission), and the idea that Japan faced a crisis created by enemies both at home and abroad. The ideology of Japanese militarism is developed at length in Araki's *Nippon Rikugun no Seishin* (Spirit of the Imperial Japanese Army) published in 1932, and Mosaburo Suzuki's "Evolution of Military Ideology," in *Kaizo,* September, 1935.[36]

PHILOSOPHICAL BASIS OF JAPANESE FASCISM

Japanese militarism and fascism have made heroic efforts to provide themselves with an ideological foundation resting on oriental political philosophy. Japanese architects of the new State of Manchoukuo made a determined effort to convince the conquered inhabitants that Japan came to restore the Confucian politico-moral principle of *Wang Tao* (the way of the Sage-King). Yet it was significant that Japanese philosophers of the *Wang Tao* school, Chikao Fujisawa for example, spoke of Mussolini, Hitler, and Mosely as "playing consciously or unconsciously a role much akin to that of the Sage-King." [37]

THE POLITICAL PHILOSOPHY OF KODO

The Confucian principle of *Wang Tao* in its disguised and Japanized form appears today in the Japanese political philosophy of *Kodo.* If *Kodo* may be defined at all it is a concept of the Sage-King created spontaneously by the life-giving force of the Universe—the king who reveals the *tao* or way.[38] It is the creed of Japanese totaliarianism, of what Japanese reactionaries delight to call "the fundamental character of the Japanese State." [39] It is the denial of liberalism, of democracy, of political parties,

---

[36] Colegrove, *op. cit.,* p. 75; and appendix for list of Japanese army pamphlets.

[37] Chikao Fujisawa, *Japanese and Oriental Political Philosophy* (Tokyo: Daito-Bunka-Kyokai, 1935), p. 217. Note in particular chs. V and VII.

[38] Fujisawa, *op. cit.,* p. 274.

[39] Fujisawa, *op. cit.,* p. 232.

of parliamentary government, and even of the Japanese constitution itself. Under it constitutional guarantees become a fiction. It is the philosophical sanction for the emperor's divine right absolutism, for Japan's unique mission of conquest, for all the tenets of State *Shinto* national, and finally for the military dictatorship which dates from Hideki Tojo's rise to power in 1941.

CONCLUSION

In conclusion then, it may again be emphasized that political thought in the Far East of the 20th century has not as yet created a clear and compelling ideological pattern for the future. In an era of complex revolutionary trends and changes this is but natural. Nevertheless, the evidence is not wholly negative. Contemporary China does not appear to have lost the timeless element of her Confucian heritage: resistance to the arbitrary use of irresponsible power whether from within or from without. The principle of the Mandate of Heaven under new names and operating through new institutions may yet be a powerful force in creating a future China of free men. It is clearly inherent in the ideology of Sun Yat-sen. There can be little doubt that Dr. Sun laid the intellectual foundation for future China's political, social, and economic structure. Whether those who claim to be his intellectual descendants will prove true to this trust remains to be seen.

The assurance offered by the history of Japan's political thought is not so encouraging, for Japanese thinking, unlike Chinese, can boast no great and long tradition.[40] Yet it would be a mistake to assume that Japan is incapable of entertaining liberal concepts of human dignity and freedom. In the light of her historic background the surprising thing is not that free political thought was crushed, but rather that it spoke so loudly in the late 19th and early 20th centuries. Perhaps in generations to come there will be Japanese who will acknowledge with pride the work of liberals who were not less great because their numbers were few.

---

[40] Tsuchida, *op. cit.,* p. 190.

BIBLIOGRAPHY

HISTORY OF POLITICAL THOUGHT

BODDE, DERK, "A 'totalitarian' form of Government in Ancient China," *Far Eastern Leaflets* (1942), No. 5. A discussion of the state of China.

CHIANG K'AI-SHEK, *All We Are and All We Have* (New York: John Day, 1943). Speeches and messages since Pearl Harbor: *Resistance and Reconstruction* (New York: Harper, 1943). Messages during China's six years of war 1937-43.

China's Leaders and Their Policies (Shanghai: China United Press, 1935). Messages to the Chinese people by Chiang K'ai-shek and Wang Ching-wei.

HOLCOMBE, A. N., *The Chinese Revolution* (Cambridge, Mass.: Harvard University Press, 1930). Revolution considered as a phase of China's regeneration.

HSU, L. S., *The Political Philosophy of Confucianism* (New York: E. P. Dutton, 1932). An Interpretation of the social and political ideas of Confucius, his forerunners and his early disciples.

HU SHIH, "The Exchange of Ideas Between the Occident and the Orient," *Contemporary China*, I (1941), No. 12; *Historical Foundations for a Democratic China* (Urbana: University of Illinois Press, 1941).

JOHNSTON, R. F., *Confucianism and Modern China* (London: Gollancz, 1934).

KOTENEV, A. M., *The Chinese Soldier* (Shanghai: Kelly and Walsh, 1937). An effective analysis of the military philosophy of modern China.

LIANG CH'I-CH'AO, *History of Chinese Political Thought* (London: K. Paul, Trench, Trubner, 1930). Treats the early Tsin period.

MACNAIR, H. F., *The Real Conflict Between China and Japan* (Chicago: University of Chicago Press, 1938). An analysis of opposing ideologies.

PEFFER, NATHANIEL, *China: The Collapse of a Civilization* (New York: John Day, 1930).

THOMAS, ED., *Chinese Political Thought* (New York: Prentice-Hall, 1927). In particular chapter IV for the historic Chinese concept of the State, chapter XIII on Chinese democracy, and chapter XVI on political theory in practice.

TSENG YU-HAO, *Modern Chinese Legal and Political Philosophy* (Shanghai: The Commercial Press, 1930).

WANG, T. C., *The Youth Movement in China* (New York: The New Republic, 1927). See chapters VII-XI on the literary renaissance, the anti-military and anti-Christian movements.

POLITICAL THEORY AND GOVERNMENT

BLAND, J. O. P. and BACKHOUSE, E., *China under the Empress Dowager* (Peking: H. Vetch, rev. ed., 1939).

CHENG, S. G., *Modern China* (Oxford: Clarendon Press, 1919).

CH'EN, KENNETH, "Yuan Shih-k'ai and the coup d'etat of 1898 in China, *Pacific Historical Review*, VI (1937), pp. 181-187.

HEDIN, SVEN, *Chiang Kai-shek* (New York: John Day, 1940).

HSIEH, PAO-CHAO, *The Government of China 1644-1911* (Baltimore: The John Hopkins University Press, 1926).

JOHNSTON, R. F., *Twilight in the Forbidden City* (London: Gollancz, 1934). Chapter I on the reform movement of 1898.

LA FARGUE, T. E., *China and the World War* (Stanford University: Stanford University Press, 1937). Chapters VII, VIII for China's political program at the Paris Peace Conference, 1919.

QUIGLEY, H. S., "The National Government of China," *American Political Science Review*, XXIII (1929), pp. 441-449; "The Chinese Constitution," *Chinese Social and Political Science Review*, IX (1925).

T'ANG LEANG-LI, *The Inner History of the Chinese Revolution* (London: Routledge, 1930); *Wang Ching-wei* (Peiping: China United Press, 1931). A political history and biography written before the break between Chiang and Wang.

VINACKE, H. M., *Modern Constitutional Development in China* (Princeton: Princeton University Press, 1920).

WALES, NYM, *China Builds a Democracy* (Shanghai: Kelly and Walsh, 1941). A study of co-operative industry.

WU CHIH-FANG, *Chinese Government and Politics* (Shanghai: The Commercial Press, 1934).

ON SUN YAT-SEN

HSU, L. S., *Sun Yat-Sen: His Political and Social Ideals* (Los Angeles: University of Southern California Press, 1932).

LINEBARGER, P. M. A., *The Political Doctrines of Sun Yat-Sen* (Baltimore: John Hopkins, 1937).

RESTARICK, H. B., *Sun Yat-Sen* (New Haven: Yale University Press, 1931).

SHARMAN, LYON, *Sun Yat-Sen* (New York: John Day, 1934).

SUN YAT-SEN, *Memoirs of a Chinese Revolutionary* (London: Hutchinson, 1918). Sun's program of national reconstruction. *San Min Chu I* (Shanghai: Institute of Pacific Relations, 1927); *The International Development of China* (New York: G. P. Putnam's Sons, 2nd ed., 1929).

KUOMINTANG VERSUS COMMUNISM

BISSON, T. A., "Ten Years of the Kuomintang: Revolution and Reaction," *Foreign Policy Association, Reports*, VIII (1933), No. 25; "The Communist Movement in China," *Ibid.*, IX (1933), No. 4.

FIELD, F. V., "The Recent Anti-Communist Campaign in China," *Far Eastern Survey*, IV (1935), No. 16.

KUN, BELA, ED., *Fundamental Laws of the Chinese Soviet Republic* (London: Martin Lawrence, 1934).

ISAACS, H. R., *The Tragedy of the Chinese Revolution* (London: Secker and Warburg, 1938).

PRICE, M. T., "Communist Policy and the Chinese Nationalist Revolution," *The Annals* of The American Academy of Political and Social Science, CLII (1930), pp. 229-240.

SMEDLEY, AGNES, *China's Red Army Marches* (New York: International Publishers, 1934).

SNOW, EDGAR, *Red Star Over China* (New York: Random House, 1938).

TROTSKII, LEV, *Problems of the Chinese Revolution* (New York: Pioneer Publishers, 1932).

WILLIAM, MAURICE, *Sun Yat-Sen vs. Communism* (Baltimore: Williams and Wilkins, 1932).

WOO, T. T. C., *The Kuomintang and the Future of the Chinese Revolution* (London: Allen and Unwin, 1928).

WU CHAO-CHU, *The Nationalist Program for China* (New Haven: Yale University Press, 1929).

JAPAN
HISTORY OF POLITICAL THOUGHT

ARIGA, N., "L'idée de soveraineté dans l'historire du Japan," *Compte rendu du I-er Congres International des études d'Etrême-Orient à Hanoi,* 1902, I (1903), pp. 52-55.

FUJISAWA, RIKITARO, *Recent Aims and Political Development of Japan* (New Haven: Yale University Press, 1923).

KAWAI, TATSUO, *The Goal of Japanese Expansion* (Tokyo: Hokuseido, 1938). See for the so-called philosophy of *musubi.*

KAWAKAMI, K. K., *The Political Ideas of Modern Japan* (Iowa City: University of Iowa, 1903).

KEENLEYSIDE, H. L., and THOMAS, A. F., *History of Japanese Education* (Tokyo: Hokuseido, 1937). For the political philosophy behind the educational system.

TOKUTOMI, IICHIRO, "The Life of Yoshida Shoin," Asiatic Society of Japan, *Transactions,* XLV (1917), pt. I.

POLITICAL HISTORY AND GOVERNMENT

CLEMENT, E. W., *Constitutional Imperialism in Japan* (New York: Columbia University Press, 1916).

FAHS, C. B., *Government in Japan* (New York: Institute of Pacific Relations, 1940).

FUJII, SHINICHI, *The Essentials of Japanese Constitutional Law* (Tokyo: Yuhikaku, 1940).

IWAWAKI, UICHI, *The Working Forces in Japanese Politics . . . 1867-1920* (New York: Columbia University Press, 1921).

IYENAGA, TOYOKICHI, *Constitutional Development of Japan 1853-1881* (Baltimore: John Hopkins University Press, 1891).

KITASAWA, NAOKICHI, *The Government of Japan* (Princeton: Princeton University Press, 1929).

KAWABE, KISABURO, *The Press and Politics in Japan* (Chicago: University of Chicago Press, 1921).

MCLAREN, W. W., *A Political History of Japan During the Meiji Era, 1867-1912* (London: Allen and Unwin, 1916).

NORMAN, E. H., *Japan's Emergence as a Modern State* (New York: Institute of Pacific Relations, 1940).

TAKEUCHI, TATSUJI, *War and Diplomacy in the Japanese Empire* (Garden City: Doubleday, Doran, 1935).

POLITICAL PARTIES

IIZAWA, SHOJI, *Politics and Political Parties in Japan* (Tokyo: Kenkyusha, 1938).

COLEGROVE, KENNETH, "Labor Parties in Japan," *American Political Science Review,* XXIII (1929), pp. 329-363.

HUDSON, G. F., "Political Parties in Japan," *Nineteenth Century,* CVII (1930), pp. 792-96.

KATAYAMA, SEN, *The Labor Movement in Japan* (Chicago: C. R. Kerr, c. 1918).

KOHNO, MITSU, *Labour Movement in Japan* (Tokyo: Kenkyusha, 1938).

NATIONALISM

NITOBE, I. O., *Bushido: The Soul of Japan* (Philadelphia: Leeds and Biddle, 1900).

OKAKURA, KAKUZO, *The Awakening of Japan* (New York: The Japan Society, 1921).

SMITH, BRADFORD, "The Mind of Japan," *Amerasia,* VI (1942), pp. 7-14.

WILDES, H. E., *Aliens in the East* (Philadelphia: University of Pennsylvania Press, 1937).

LIBERALISM AND DEMOCRACY

SANSON, SIR GEORGE, "Liberalism in Japan," *Foreign Affairs,* XIX (1941), pp. 551-60.

HIRAO, YAGORO, *Social Policy in Japan* (Tokyo: Kenkyusha, 1937).

KATAYAMA, TETSU, *Woman's Movement in Japan* (Tokyo: Kenkyusha, 1938).

MIYAOKA, TSUNEJIRO, *Growth of Liberalism in Japan* (Washington: Carnegie Endowment for International Peace, 1918).

SPINKS, C. N., "The Liberal Myth in Japan," *Pacific Affairs,* XV (1942), pp. 450-56.

COLEGROVE, KENNETH, "Parliamentary Government in Japan," *American Political Science Review,* XXI (1927), pp. 835-52.

MILITARISM, FASCISM, COMMUNISM

BISSON, T. A., "Japan's 'New Structure'," Foreign Policy Association, *Reports,* XVII (1941), pp. 26-36.

BYAS, HUGH, *Government by Assassination* (New York: A. A. Knopf, 1942).

CROW, CARL ED., *Japan's Dream of World Empire* (New York: Harpers, 1942). On Tanaka memorial.

HINO, ASHIHEI, *Wheat and Soldiers* (New York: Farrar and Rinehart, 1939).

KONO, MITSU, "Japan's Proletarian Movement," *Contemporary Japan,* V (1937), pp. 577-86.

KUMAGAI, TATSUJIRO, *The Japan Young Men's Associations* (Tokyo: Kenkyusha, 1938).

STEIN, GUNTHER, " 'Totalitarian' Japan," *Foreign Affairs,* XVI (1938), pp. 294-309.

TANIN, O., and YOHAN, E., *Militarism and Fascism in Japan* (New York: International Publishers, 1934).

Chapter XXVII

SPAIN

ALFREDO MENDIZABAL

It would be an impossible task to consider Spanish political thought in isolation from the profound reality in which it dramatically holds forth. But, on the other hand, it would be erroneous to believe that this reality—which certainly conditions political thought to a certain extent—determines it in the sense of forcing it to take one definite direction. Very frequently, on the contrary, political ideas which take their course and fall into the category of guiding principles, are opposed to the events which give rise to them, and above all, to immediate interests. The Spaniard is reactionary, in the etymological sense of the word; he proceeds from reaction, and is guided, not by his own personal interests, but by moral motives of justice and exalted love of liberty; but his enthusiasm for the latter is much greater than his capacity to administrate it.

The classical theater and literature of the 16th and 17th centuries in general were already infused with certain themes of political justice, equality of all before the law, dignity of the human person, which were derived from Vitoria and from the Spanish school of natural law. The drama of Calderon and Lope de Vega, because it is a drama of the people and for the people, continues to enjoy popularity in our times, through characters such as Segismundo in Calderon's *La Vida es Sueño,* because as the modern poet Salinas tells us: "Through the mouth of Segismundo, the maltreated man of all time speaks, all the men who have been given life but not liberty, all the socially chained. In Segismundo, what you call the under-dog speaks. And it is very curious to realize that right in the midst of the Catholic monarchy of Spain, the most absolute and aristocratic of all, a monarchial and Catholic poet makes a character utter the most violent and persuasive defense of man's right not only in life, but to liberty." [1]

When Lope de Vega states in *Fuente Ovejuna* his resistance to oppression, an essentially political problem, he solves it with tyrannicide, with reasonings which translate into popular language the doctrines of certain jurists and theologians, applicable to a situation of extreme despotism when all legal procedures have been exhausted. And Lope was not only a clergyman but a member of the Inquisition.

The conflict between the individual and State has seriously arisen in Spain at many moments in her history; and it is necessary to be thoroughly acquainted with the political psychology of the Spanish people in order to understand the deep roots of their attitude before, outside or against the State. A very strong sense of justice usually guides the Spanish, although at times they are badly oriented. If Goethe has been reproached for preferring injustice to disorder, the opposite attitude can be attributed to the Spanish. They are in favor of what they believe just, even though the existing order may be violated. Nobody has pointed out this passion as well as Cervantes. The ideal of the knight errant is anarchistic and utopian, responding to private initiative outside of the State. Don Quixote works as if the State did not exist, but is inspired with just and elevated incentives: protection of the weak, defense of honor, against everything and everybody. His madness is a sublime madness, but it is nothing other than the exasperation of a sense of justice and independence which leads him to catastrophic situations. And it can even be said that he looks for catastrophe as a solution to his chimerical undertakings. In any sense, he is concerned with principles and not with consequences; he judges action according to intention, without ever calculating results; with the rectilinear logic of the man who is not mad

---

[1] Pedro Salinas, *Reality and the Poet in Spanish Poetry* (Baltimore: John Hopkins University Press, 1940).

because he has lost his reason, but because he has lost everything else and kept only his reason, his bare reason.

ON NATIONAL POLITICAL PSYCHOLOGY

More than a century ago, Spain introduced to the world
a new use for an old adjective, the "Liberal" Party. Actually,
the least widespread attitude in Spanish politics is the liberal
attitude, for the characteristic mark of Spanish politics has been
violence. For this reason, the very exaggerated pendular rhythm
of Spanish life creates the impression of perpetual revolution
and reaction, all leading to a sorry state of anarchic dissolution.
Each Spaniard is too much concerned with his individual self
to have much feeling for the community. What has been called
Spanish individualism—and this is today a matter of general
knowledge— is a sign of a strong *personalism* in the best and
in the worst sense of the term. And the element which hinders
the collective life of Spaniards—their intransigence—is a result
of profound convictions which are so deep-rooted, so essential,
and so bitter that the people heroically sacrifice their lives for
them—and also the lives of others, which is more deplorable.
For a Spaniard, living is not important. Nor is dying. It is the
manner of living and the manner of dying which is important.
And the clash between the diversified concepts of life develops
into violence in Spain, for dissidence soon becomes irreducible
opposition. Instead of going off in divergent directions, different lines of thought take closely parallel routes and forever seek
each other out, to confront and affront each other.

This constant presence of the antipodal is peculiar to Spanish psychology. Every man defines himself and asserts himself
in his own being by contrast with his opposite, whose mere existence excites and incites him; and yet he deeply feels the necessity for this provocation. The struggle against dissidence assumes gigantic proportions in periods of hyper-sensibility. The
combative spirit of the Spaniard leads him to create his opponent,
even to invent him when he does not exist (thus did Don Quixote
battle the windmill), for the mere pleasure of destroying him,
even when it is he who, in the end, is bested in the fight. Thus

anti-communism and anti-fascism preceded and in some way provoked the appearance of totalitarian parties, which sprang up
as a reaction to the forces combatting totalitarianism. The Spaniard reaches extremes of enthusiasm beyond all measure, but his
enthusiasm is generally *against* something, rather than *for* it. His
fury is an exalted form of his fervor. His love of liberty is so
exasperated that it leads him to extreme anarchistic positions,
and is so exclusivist that it denies all others the rights he claims
for himself. After the turbulent period following the fall of
Isabella the Second, which witnessed an ill-fated attempt at a
new dynasty, embodied in Amadeo of Savoy, and an ephemeral
First Republic which lasted barely two years, the Bourbon restoration, in the person of Alfonso XII, initiated a period of a certain
stability. Two parties pacefully succeeded each other in power,
the Conservative and the Liberal. The Constitution of 1876 was
democratic within limits and moderately liberal, and gave some
hope for securing public tranquility. Spain was thirsty for this
after sixty-five years of struggle for independence and liberty,
including the Napoleonic war, the tyranny of Ferdinand VII,
the Carlist wars, military "pronunciamientos" and Republican
cantonalism. But the nation, so eager for calm, had through
disillusionment lost her ideals. Canovas, the Conservative leader,
artificer of the restoration, was imbued with a spiritless pessimism. And Sagasta, the leader of the Liberal Party, uttered
these pessimistic words: "I do not know where we are going,
but I do know this, that wherever it is we shall lose our way."
There were only slight shades of difference between the parties,
and compacts between their respective leaders—who enjoyed
power and in turn—made suffrage a mere fiction. Voting was organized and results were determined in the Home Office, by
means of agreements and bargaining between the central power
and the local agents of the politicians, or "caciques," who suited
their own desires in managing the electoral body. Their methods
were far from wholesome; thus usury, for example, served as a
common economic-political instrument. They took full advantage
of their local influence at Madrid; and in their own districts they

exploited the protection which they received from the central government.[2] The country had lost its élan. Spaniards—it has been said—"accustomed to living for great and spectacular ends, and declined when the bourgeois ideal of work, perseverence and duty became the only one which could create or hold together society."[3]

At the end of the 19th century, a great shock upset the comfortable inertia of the complacent Spaniards, the Spanish-American War. This, with its disastrous consequences—the loss of Cuba, Puerto Rico and the Philippines, aroused a bitter national self-consciousness in the so-called generation of '98. Its thinkers provoked an intellectual movement whose influence not only has put its stamp upon their period, but fostered liberal and republican sentiment lasting until now. After losing the last vestiges of its distant colonial empire, the Spanish people found itself left with a denuded Spain, stripped of that world importance the memory of which had created in the average mind a mirage of continuity of past glories. Now there was only Spain herself, pared to the bone. From this national disaster some leading people learned a lesson of humility and asked themselves: At heart, what is this bereft country? And, in consequence, what is the task set before Spaniards? Rethoric was at an end. The pessimism of the generation of '98 was an active and constructive pessimism, although it has appeared harmful to many. Now cut down and reduced to herself alone, Spain had to arise, rebuild, seek new, life-giving directions and ideals, intellectual, social, and political. It was like an awakening, after dreams of grandeur and anxious nightmares. Spaniards had to examine their conscience and decide to work for the dawn of a new day which should be fertile or sterile, according to their own efforts.

Throughout the regency of Mary-Christine and the reign of

---

[2] *Cf.* Joaquin Costa, *Oligarquia y caciquismo como la forma actual de gobierno en España* (Madrid, Ateneo, 1902).

[3] Gerald Brenan, *The Spanish Labyrinth.* An account of the Social and Political Background of the Civil War (New York: The Macmillan Book Co., 1943), p. 12.

Alphonso XIII, a considerable effort to revive the country was made, especially by men such as Antonio Maura and José Canalejas, the leaders of the Conservative and the Liberal Parties which alternately ruled the State. Moret and the Count of Romanones, Liberals, and Dato and Sáanchez Guerra, and Conservatives, contributed also to launch Spain on the high seas of history. A wise and progressive social legislation was enacted after the creation of the Institute for Social Reforms (1903) devoted to officially promote this undertaking. But citizens remained generally apathetic to active public life. Antonio Maura's efforts to awaken the political conscience of the masses influenced only a limited minority. Suffrage was made obligatory in order to avoid electoral absenteeism. Nevertheless oligarchy and caciguism continued to supplant popular will. Good laws did not suppress bad customs.

Meanwhile unrest grew in the working class as well as in the Army. Revolutionary strikes disorganized industrial production, above all in Catalonia, where opposition of classes became more acute than in other regions, and legal means in the hands of incompetent authorities proved themselves incapable to solving such a problem. In addition, since 1917 the "Juntas of Defence" came into action in the form of syndicates of Army officers. These openly flaunted civil authority and caused the downfall of every government which showed any strength at all or which endeavored to keep the Army within the limits of its duties. Thus a secret military power was built up. True, the Army did not govern, but hindered others from governing. Gradually the political foundations of an already ailing country were being undermined. The Army was preparing to challenge civil power, and was awaiting a favorable opportunity.

SOCIAL MOVEMENTS

The founding of the Socialist Party in Madrid in the year 1879 gave form to the socialist movement. From the outset, it was inspired by the ideas and tactics of Lafargue and Guesde. The first nucleus was formed by a group of typesetters, with Pablo Iglesias at their head. *El Socialista,* the newspaper representing their views, was founded in 1886 with a very limited capital indeed: 927 pesetas, painfully collected bit by bit. Two years later, the "Unión General de Trabajadores" (UGT) arose, independent from the Party, but transmitting the Party's views to the socialist unions. Spanish socialism, incorporated in the Second International, underwent in 1920 a crisis, precipitated by those who wished to enter the Third International. After a very bitter struggle with the pro-communistic majority, the report of Prof. Fernando de los Rios prevailed and the Congress of the Party rejected Moscow's conditions. The dissenters, together with certain Anarcho-Syndicalists founded the Spanish Communist Party whose first inspiration was predominantly Trotskyite. But, up to the time of the Civil War, communism did not really have mass support in the country. Although its work of agitation and propaganda was effective in attracting many intellectuals, dissenters from other movements, students, and fanatics, the workers in general mainly followed Socialist and Anarcho-Syndicalist trends.

With the socialist domain as far as external discipline is concerned, but outside of the internal discipline of Marxism, Professor de los Rios' ideological position is of special interest. Starting from a humanist conception of history, he arrives—by way of ethics—at a personal interpretation of socialism as "a moral imperative which takes root in the very heart of the human problems." [4]

According to him, "capitalist subversion consists of the degradation of the eminent dignity of man and of the meaning of life and in its shadow "fade away the most beautiful and elevated esthetic, ethical and religious values." To combat this perversion it is necessary to revive and kindle within each man and within the community the individual and common essence of the spirit and "socialism must return to its spiritual foundations." [5]

[4] Fernando de los Rios, *Mi viaje a la Rusia soviética* (Madrid: Caro Raggio, 1921), p. 10.

[5] De los Rios, *El Sentido Humanista del Socialismo* (Madrid: Morata, 1926), pp. 402-403.

De los Rios is opposed to the class struggle as a formula
and as it is advocated by the Marxists, since from this struggle
"there cannot—directly and congruously—derive a social policy
and, therefore, social law. The struggle is thus a fact but not
a norm.[6]

To dogmatic and static marxism Professor Besteiro opposes
a "critical and dynamic" marxism. To the communist interpretation of marxism, which claims to be the only authentic one,
and conceives of "political action as a revolutionary struggle"
leading to dictatorship of the proletariat and destruction of the
mechanism of the capitalist state, Besteiro opposes the reformist
conception of the social-democrats, whose tactics presuppose "political action within the framework of democratic institutions
created by the bourgeoisie with the assistance of the proletariat." [7]

Spanish anarchism, and especially the peasant anarchism,
was inspired by Bakunin from the outset. The anarchist mentality has influenced most of revolutionary movements, and the
strong discipline imposed by Socialism and later by Communism
clashed perpetually with the anarchistic tendencies of the Hispanic temperament. The program of 1872 called for the abolition of classes, of individual property and of hereditary wealth
and the replacement of the political and overbearing State by a
simple administrative organization for public services. The tech-
nic of direct action by means of terrorism was inspired by the
anarchist Congress of London, held in 1881. There, resolutions
were passed accepting "propaganda by deed" as a useful method
and urging members to "pay more attention to the technical and
chemical sciences." But these methods were later replaced by
direct union action through partial strikes ending to disorganize
the system of production, and having in mind the myth of the
"general, total strike." This phase of "anarcho-syndicalism" has
been performed in our century, especially from 1910 onward.
In that year, the "Conferación Nacional del Trabajo" (CNT)

---

[6] *Ibid.*, pp. 226-7.

[7] Julian Besteiro, *Marxismo y Antimarxismo,* a speech made upon his entrance
into the Academy of Moral and Political Sciences (Madrid: Fráfica Socialista,
1935), pp. 33, 122-3.

was established. In 1927, the Anarchists founded the "Federación Anarquista Ibérica" (FAI) which, from then on, inspired the direct and open actions of the unions, whilst it protected itself by clandestinity and a halo of mystery.

The Catholic Social movement, initiated as far back as 1861, was for many years closely connected with the clergy, but finally gained independence in 1912 when the "Federación Nacional de Sindicatos Católicos Libres" was founded. Nevertheless, they prospered only in certain northern provinces. Generally scorned by the Socialists and Anarchists, they did not even have support from Catholic elements. It would be interesting to study their trajectory, along with that of the intellectual group of social reformers belonging to the "Christian Democracy" which wished to infuse society with the spirit of the Encyclicals of Leo XIII and Pius XI.

Experiment in Dictatorship

The period between 1923 and 1930, covered by the dictatorship of General Primo de Rivera, is a critical period for the country's political institutions. By the coup d'état of 1923, Spain's legal regime, the constitutional monarchy, was abruptly changed to an absolute monarchy; when Alfonso XIII, before the military insurrection led by Primo de Rivera, dismissed his own Government which proposed sanctions against the insurgents, and surrendered complete power of the State to the General who had started the rebellion against it, the monarchy committed suicide. Henceforth it had no basis, and in its place there was arbitrarily established a dictatorship modeled more or less on the one which had been established by Mussolini in Italy a year before. The constitution was abolished and not replaced by any fundamental law. The break with tradition was complete. Political parties suppressed, a single Party was formed and a militia (the *Unión Patriótica* and the Somatén), the Army, which for long years had, through its conspiracies, made impossible the work of numerous governments, was invested, through generals and officials, with civil and administrative functions. All popular liberties were abolished. And it was then, in reaction,

that the Spaniards' political consciousness began to awaken from
its apathetic lethargy. From the moment when civil liberties and
essential rights (for which so many citizens had so little use)
were taken from them, they began to acquire consciousness of the
necessity for liberty. A political idea, at the outset, linked to
certain representative figures, was spread in spite of censorship
of the press and correspondence and notwithstanding suspension
of the freedom of assembly and association for political purposes. The conscience of the citizenry grew during those years
of oppression until it finally crushed the dictatorship in 1930 and
in 1931 overthrew the monarchy which during that period had
been its accomplice.

It is not necessary to look for a political idea, a structural
theory of the State either in the declarations or in the acts of
the dictatorship. Primo de Rivera, who perhaps thought in good
faith that he had saved the country from the dangers—which
certainly existed—of a latent anarchism, was himself of anarchistic temperament, in his lack of mental discipline, and totally
ignorant of what the governing of a State implied. For him the
country was like an immense barracks, under his command; and
the citizens had to abstain from thinking and, above all, critical
thinking, and convert themselves into obedient and submissive
automatons. Since the great majority of intellectuals were opposed to the dictatorship, Primo de Rivera did not have among
his collaborators men capable of organic political thinking. This
was a period of mental deficiency in the ruling class and of
fermentation of ideas and passions in the mass of the people,
guided by thinkers and politicians, who continued to publish
clandestinely. The universities, until in 1929 the dictator pro-
ceded to their closure, could fill the function of orientating youth;
this gave to the new generation a premature maturity and an impulse to rebelliousness which the dictatorship itself was the first
to encourage—as a natural reaction.

The retirement of the political leaders gave to many of
them a halo of dignity. It should be recalled that the persecutions of the non-conformists were not bloody, that the dictator
was incompetent but not cruel. This combination of defects and

qualities hastened his ruin. He tried, upon various occasions, to find a way out of what he himself had previously closed. And when the fall of the system was already inevitable it was the King who tried to save himself, abandoning the dictator. But the unpopularity of the monarchy was tied up with opposition to the dictatorship. The latter had hardly fallen when popular democratic sentiment came forth as republicanism, or more precisely, anti-monarchism.

THE REPUBLICAN MIND

The advent of the Republic in 1931 was a biological fact which the monarchy, in its last stage, did not dare resist. It was necessary to fill the vacuum which the collapse of institutions had created; and since the constitutional monarchy had not existed since 1923, and the absolute monarchy which had supplanted it had shamefully crumbled, there was no other solution but the Republic, which had to build on ruins.

Perhaps one of the greatest errors of the leaders of the new republican parties was that of looking too much to the liquidation of the past, the vengeance against the past, instead of undertaking the task of founding a new legal order. Against the absolutism of the last years a new democracy arose; but also a stubborn demagogy. This danger was not taken enough into consideration, with the exception of certain political leaders such as Alcalá Zamora and Miguel Maura, who tried to give to the rising institutions a purely liberal content, essentially conservative; and at certain occasions men of the left such as Azaña and socialists as Besteiro, De los Ríos and Prieto who tried at times to check demagogy.

The Constitutional Cortes of 1931 were for many a great hope followed by deep disillusion. From the great number of intellectuals, especially the professors and writers, who had been elected deputies [8] one might have expected mature political thinking leading to the building of a coherent system. But frequently valuable contributions of first rate minds were eclipsed and destroyed by the demagogic attitude of the different parties. In

---

[8] In a Parliament of 473 members, 123 were lawyers, and 50 university professors.

parliament a good speech by Ortega y Gasset, whose ideas—
like those of the incomparable thinker Unamuno—had had such
an influence on the change or regime, would be applauded; but
at the hour of decision the votes of the majority generally took
a direction opposed to reason. The obstructionism of rightist
groups, because of their animosity towards the Republic, and the
overpowering passion of the leftist groups, inclined to revolt
and lacking self-control, often thwarted the noble efforts of
thinkers in search of practicable solutions acceptable to the majority of Spaniards. The most valuable ideas were crushed by
more forceful ideologies and quiet deliberation was often crippled by hasty decisions, if not by action of the masses, too much
inclined to violence. There was more of a tendency to think of
the positions which they wished to defend or obtain for themselves than to think of the regime which they had to build.

The strictly liberal position was nevertheless supported by
some—unfortunately not enough—political leaders and thinkers
who remained faithful to the principles theoretically proclaimed.
Among them should be remembered the attitude of the philosopher Ortega y Gassett, whose ideas had so much contributed to
the birth of the new regime.

Ortega claims for liberal democracy as the political doctrine
which has represented the loftiest endeavor towards common
life, carrying to the extreme the determination to have consideration for one's neighbor. He considers it as the prototype of
"indirect action" instead of the form of "direct action" assumed
by the masses. Liberalism is defined by Ortega: "that principle
of political rights, according to which the public authority, in
spite of being all-powerful, limits itself and attempts, even at
its own expense, to leave room in the State over which it rules
for those to live who neither think nor feel as it does, that is to
say as do the stronger, the majority. Liberalism—it is well to
recall this today—is the supreme form of generosity; it is the
right which the majority concedes to minorities and hence it is
the noblest cry that has ever resounded in this planet. It an-
nounces the determination to share existence with the enemy;
more than that, with an enemy which is weal." But Liberalism

in its whole purity appears to Ortega too much paradoxical, refined, acrobatic, and even anti-natural to be accepted by the human species. He confronts the human anxiety to get rid of it, and he concludes: "It is a discipline too difficult and complex to take from root on earth. Share our existence with the enemy! Govern with the opposition! Is not such a form of tenderness beginning to seem incomprehensible?" [9]

A less optimistic attitude within the Liberal school is that of Madariaga.[10] According to him, liberal democracies have suffered in their evolution from a popular conception of liberty which is both too absolute and too general; and "any revision of the liberal-democratical system must begin with a revaluation of liberty which will define and condition it more strictly and will recognize that, far from its being a boon to all men, it is a burden to many." [11] Madariaga's thought is much more liberal than democratic. He believes that the immense majority of our ills are due to mental anarchy and its material effects. The people "have no vision." "The people's instinct is blind and insecure. Any demogagic leader will be able to draw it astray." All that can be expected of the people is "vitality, resilience, enthusiasm, a ready, but not sure, instinct for primordial and essential things." As "a mass," it is "passive and plastic, though at times this mass be inflammable, it will not ignite of itself; the sparks must come from outside, from a leader who by the mere fact that he leads ceases to belong to the people and, whatever his blood, manners, education or political tendency, belongs worthily or unworthily, to the aristocracy." Thus, the social function of the people is no more than "chorus-like." The bourgeoise in the social design incarnates—according to Madariaga—"intelligence, a middle formation with an essentially executive and technical function." "But the higher activities of the community are incumbent on the aristocracy." He attributes to this "much misused word"

---

[9] José Ortega y Gasset, *The Revolt of the Masses*, p. 83, English translation (New York: W. W. Norton, 1932).

[10] Salvador de Madariaga, *Anarchy or Hierarchy* (English translation, London: Allen und Unwin, 1937).

[11] Op. cit., chapter I, p. 33.

a new meaning, even though this meaning "happens to be the oldest and most accurate of all." The statesman is here considered as "a sculptor of peoples. He is to the politician what the artist is to the craftsman." [12] Madariaga concludes that "the natural and necessary form of the State is that of a unanimous organic democracy." The second adjective is indeed better explained than the first one, and in the system proposed can be seen influences of Platonism and enlightened despotism.

THE CONSTITUTION OF 1931, THE BILL OF RIGHTS AND THE RELIGIOUS QUESTION

The Constitutional Cortes, elected after a bloodless revolution, were capable of giving to the country a fundamental code inspired by Spanish experience and constitutional reforms effected in other countries in preceding years. Two constitutions, in particular, were taken into consideration: those of the German and Czechoslovakian republics. The provisional government appointed a Consultative Juridical Commission, in the framework of which eminent jurists of independent spirit devoted themselves to the study of formulas which could be applied to the rising Spanish Republic. The result of their work was the preliminary draft of a constitution which was to serve as the basis for discussion in parliament. But the parliamentary commission formed by the Chamber to prepare the draft which was to be the subject of debate took quite a different direction from that of the jurists. The latter had drawn up and perfected a text which was apt to receive the support of all liberal Spaniards. The deputies, on the contrary, arrived in the Cortes after an electoral campaign for the most part demagogic, and by virtue of an easy republican socialist victory over the ruins of the old parties of the monarchy and the dictatorship and the impotence of new groups. These groups, though not openly republican, did not dare to declare themselves anti-republican and, in the popular enthusiasm for the new regime, had not yet found their orientation or propaganda possibilities.

---

[12] Salvador de Madariaga, *op. cit.*, pp. 153-59.

The Constitutional Cortes, in a natural reaction against the rightist dictatorship which the country had just experienced, leaned definitely towards the left, and a Jacobin tone often echoed in their deliberations and in their votes. This lack of balance would have been corrected if the new moderate republican party, under the leadership of Alcalá Zamora and Maura had been supported either by the conservative classes or by the neutral mass. But reactionary elements by no means desired the consolidation of the new regime. The preferred, by their indifference, to allow it to take an extreme left direction in order to be able later to criticize this extremism to which they themselves contributed in a negative way. Thus, both through the activity of one group, and the inactivity of the other, the Republic tended too much to become the tool of the republicans alone, and for many of them an instrument of revenge.

Of the 473 deputies of the elected parliament, 407 belonged to the parties of the victorious coalition (201 republicans of different leftist groups, 114 socialists, 64 Catalan and Galician autonomists and 28 Right liberal republicans). The opposition, counting only 66 members became intransigent and therefore ineffective. When article 26 of the constitution, which the Catholics considered an abuse of power and an act of persecution, was put to a vote, the moderate republicans went over to the opposition and their leaders Alcalá Zamora and Maura resigned from the cabinet. The parties of the right, at that moment, made the mistake of withdrawing from the Chamber in defiance of the regime, and placing themselves outside of the constitution instead of procuring, through legal channels, the revision of anti-liberal measures, such as Alcalá Gamore and Maura and their party favored, while resting on constitutional republican ground.

There existed in parliament, however, a conflict between liberal tendencies on the one hand and Jacobin, sectarian or socialist tendencies on the other. The socialists having wanted to define the regime (art. 1) as a Republic of Workers, the decisive vote added to this "of all types"; this was an attempt to limit the implications of the first text which aroused suspicions of Bolchevist tendencies. The Catalan, Basque and Gallician autonomists would have liked a "federal" Republic; after a lengthy discussion a compromise was reached between the unitarians and the federalists—"an integral State, compatible with municipal and regional autonomy." "Integral" was, however, an ambiguous term, and it had been chosed precisely because of its rather vague meaning, which cast aside the qualification, if not the idea, of centralization. The same is true of the property system: the socialists did not succeed in passing the principle of socialization of property, but they did manage to introduce it as a threat: "property can be socialized, public services as well as resources affecting common interests can be nationalized (art. 44). Without being effective, from the desired point of view, this created insecurity among the people who felt they were threatened. The regime to a certain extent provoked its own enemies, who stopped at defensive, while preparing for an offensive. The only domain in which Jacobin extremism struck hard and fast and was that of the role of religion in civil society —precisely the one which would create the most ferocious opposition because the liberties of the members and of the institutions of the church, to which belonged almost all Spaniards, was attacked.

If change had been limited to the guarantee of independence of the State from the church, secularization of the Republic, that alone would have constituted a radical reform in a country where until then Catholicism had been the official religion and the State supported the cult and the clergy. As a matter of fact, the purely liberal articles had not provoked any protests, and equality of all Spaniards before the law (art. 2), the declaration that "no legal privilege can be founded on filiation ,sex, social class, wealth, political ideas or religious beliefs" (art. 25) established principles which the country willingly accepted. And article 3 "the Spanish State has no official religion" was also accepted without any resistance. But against this spirit of freedom which was reaffirmed in article 27: "Freedom of conscience and the right to freely profess and practice any religion are assured; none shall be forced to officially declare his religious beliefs; religious condition will not constitute a modifying circumstance of civil or political personality," article 26 showed a sectarian criterium which denied the general principles and instituted anti-Catholic persecution which the founders of the Republic had opposed. This subjected all religious confessions to a law of exception, dissolved the Jesuit Society and nationalized its property, and threatened other congregations with the same measure by subjecting them to control which made their existence precarious and difficult. If the interdiction of business and industry were in agreement with canonic dispositions and could only serve to make the life of congregations more in keeping with religious spirit, the interdiction of teaching was considered as an attack upon the liberty of an entire group of citizens, and precisely because of their religious situation, in contradiction with the principal stated above. This measure of exception was to create serious difficulties for the republican state, which was not in a position to replace what it suppressed. While it was officially estimated that 8,000 elementary schools, costing the state 170 million pesetas had to be created, the budget allowed only a credit of 25 million. As for secondary education, the closing of 250 religious establishments employing 2,050 instructors (1150 of whom held university titles) was counterbalanced only by the creation of 77 official establishments employing 611 instructors. Immediate substitution thus proved to be impossible, but sectarianism imposed it. As an aftermath, and an ironic stroke of fate, the Jesuits who were the first to be attacked, became, as a result of the dissolution of their congregation, the only members of a religious order which could continue to teach, since it was no longer recognized as such by the State.

Besides these principles of exception determined by anti-religious fervor, the constitution contained liberal provisions common to all modern constitutions: guarantee of habeas corpus (arts. 28-29), non-extradition of political-social offenders (art. 30), liberty of domicile, circulation and emigration (art. 31), inviolability of correspondence (art. 32) liberty in choice of profession and exercise of industry and commerce (art. 33), free expression of thought (art. 34), right of petition (art. 35), freedom of assembly, association and organization of labor (arts. 38-39).

Electoral equality is established for men and women over 23 years of age (art. 36). In addition any differentiation based on sex is abolished (art. 40) and as far as marriage is concerned, a foreign woman who marries a Spaniard has the choice of retaining her own nationality or adopting her husband's (art. 23). Double nationality is provided for naturalized Portuguese and South Americans, Brazilians included (art. 24). In the international domain Spain denounces war as an instrument of national politics (art. 6) and the State accepts the universal norms of International law, incorporating them into its own positive law (art. 7), which establishes the supremacy of treaties over internal law.

Marriage, according to article 43, is based on equal rights for both sexes, and can be dissolved by mutual consent or upon request of one of the parties, upon presentation of a just cause. Parents have the same duties to children born out of wedlock as to those born legitimately. Laws will provide for investigation of paternity. No mention of legitimacy or illegitimacy is made in government records. The State assists the sick and the aged, protects maternity and childhood and will adopt the Geneva declaration or child's bill of rights. (Here they go as far as to make legal and constitutional a document of private initiative.)

Work, in its various forms, is considered a social obligation in article 46. The Republic will assure workers a proper existence. An entire series of protective measures of the rights of the worker are provided for in this article, which constitutes an index of social legislation; protection of peasants and fishermen is also provided for in article 47. The defect of these constitutional affirmations is perhaps their prolixity, but the writers wanted to show a definite orientation and put the State on the road to social reform, a desire which is not to be criticized.

In brief, the Constitution of 1931 wants to be liberal, and is in its principles, although not as far as religious life from the civil point of view is concerned. As far as everything else is concerned, the constitution is equalitarian and of a definitely social and progressive nature. On the whole, it represents a very marked advance on the road to political, social and economic democracy, and it would suffice to remove certain provisions which are in contradiction with the spirit of liberty, in order to make it more consistent and to eliminate the causes of dissent, which it so unnecessarily created, in a text which must become acceptable to all.

Alcalá Zamora, whose ideas incarnated the juridicial spirit of the new republicanism and whose attitude had been decisive in the introduction of the new regime, severely criticized the tendencies of the constitution and its partiality in certain questions. "The Constitution," he said, "was directed contrary to national reality. It tried to legislate according to party theories, feelings or interests, without giving the slightest thought to he realiy of national community life, without paying the slightest amount of attention to what was being legislated for Spain, as if she were rising anew, or as if the constitution were to be applied to another country." The original proclamation of the regime was distorted in the Constitution. Spain wanted to live united, and not to destroy itself; to keep to an ideal of resurgence and not of destruction and extermination; to an ideal of love and happiness, and not of hate and sorrow; an ideal of brotherhood and not partisanship, of harmony and not civil war.[13]

The so-called *Law for the Defense of the Republic*, promulgated while the draft of the constitution was being discussed, and evtended as an appendix to the text of the latter, really suspended most of the rights which the constitution had recognized. The incompatibility between the two texts was patent and should have been noted by the republicans themselves who were not blinded by the party spirit, and by all genuine liberals.[14]

The opposition between extremists of the right and those of

---

[13] Niceto Alcalá Zamora, Los defectos de la Constitución de 1931 (Madrid: Espinosa, 1936), pp. 44-49. In this book the former president of the Republic denounces the errors made in the domain of religious politics (pp. 87 ff.) and in the adoption of a system of unicameral legislature (pp. 109 ff.).

[14] Cf. Nicolás Pérez Serrano, *La Constitución Española* (Madrid: Revista de Derecho privado, 1932); an excellent serious critical analysis by a professor of public law.

the left was accentuated in terms of acute violence during the entire republican period, and the struggle lost its mere ideological and polemical nature to culminate in the catastrophe of the civil war, incited by the military insurrection which had only to adopt the fascist program and methods of the Falange.

FASCISM IN SPAIN

What breed of Fascism has been established by Franco and the Phalanx? It would be impossible to call it Spanish Fascism, for, despite its nationalistic claims, it is an imported product, submitted from the very beginning to the supervision of the major Fascist regimes, German and Italian. It is a typical phenomenon of imitation, an adaptation of foreign forms, symbolically clothed in a guirse taken from Spanish history and totalitarian phraseology disguised in traditional formulae.

From the outset, as in other countries, Fascism appears as a defensive reaction against a state of disorder and serious upheaval which Fascism itself contributed to produce. Fascism called itself revolutionary, "the National Revolution," because of its counter-revolutionary aims served by violent means. The political fascist phase succeeded the predominantly military one. Phalangists and Trationalists constituted the ideological nucleus of the rebellion against the Republican State. But their programs were far from being similar. The aggressive fascism of the former was not fitting in with the ultraconservative traditionalism of the latter. Nor did they agree on the religious question, a major one for the Spaniards. The traditionalists represented a monarchical-clerocratic conception, whereas the Phalangists upheld the supremacy of the fascist State over the Church and tried to make use of social force possessed by Catholicism (in the same way as the "Action Française): thus Catholicism was to be used in support of the nationalist movement, and the acceptance of this point of the Phalangist Program [15] by the Spanish church had inevitably to compromise the hierarchy. Having previously condemned the rebellion against the Republic and urged the Catholics to remain loyal to constituted power, "even in those cases

---

[15] No. 25: "Our movement incorporates the Catholic sense—of glorious and predominant tradition in Spain—for the national reconstruction."

where its holders and representatives have abused it"; for "it is not by a seditious and violent attitude that Christians will remedy those ills which weigh them down." [16] Almost the entire body of Spanish bishops accepted and upheld the rebellion at its outset.

The traditionalists, who at the beginning of the civil war, were, with the Falange, the staunchest supporters of the political military insurrection, understood only at the end that they had sacrificed themselves for a cause that was not their own; the predominance of the Falange only reduced their program to mere verbal evocation. Traditionalism, says one of its modern representatives, is not a political party, but a complete system of civilization which embraces every unit ranging from the family to the Cortes and from the individual to the state.[17] What has really characterized Spanish traditionalism is its opposition to liberalism and an archaically paternalist conception of monarchy. The joint defense of the throne and the altar has led ardent Catholics to consolidate religious institutions with already worn out political forms. Its double inspiration, French and Spanish, springs from De Maistre, Bonald, Le Play, La Tour du Pin; and on the peninsula from Donoso Cortes during the last century and Vázques de Mella during the present one: two great parliamentary orators who abhorred parliamentarism. Traditionalism is monarchist and authoritarian, without being totalitarian; from this difference arises its dissension with fascism, which attempts to monopolize and control for the State man's entire spiritual life. Today traditional tendencies are again springing up in certain semifascist theories such as Corporatism.[18]

Franco tried to accomplish the political program of the Phalange. The traditionalist motto: "God, Country and King"

---

[16] "Collective Declaration of the Episcopate," December 20, 1931.

[17] Salvador Minguijón, *Al Servicio de la Tradición* (Madrid: Morata, 1930), p. 278.

[18] Cf. Joaquín Azpiazu, *El Estado corporativo* (Madrid: Editorial Razón y Fe, 1940) ; *El Estado Católico* (Burgos: Rayfe, 1939). The author supports the thesis of the union of church and state in the latter book (pp. 27-28, 41), dissenting from fascist formulas (without calling them by their name) of absorption by the state of personal life (pp. 141-46) and approaches the French doctrine of personalism; he searches—with no luck-for an interpretation of totalitarianism which will save him from heterodoxy, and finally leans towards traditionalism (p. 160).

was opposed by the phalangists with their "One Fatherland: Spain, one State, one Leader: Franco," thus is completely explained. Then, what a kind of of State? The answer came soon: the totalitarian State. In order to establish it, a decree of April 18, 1937, set up the compulsory unification of the various elements which upheld the military forces; this was " in order to put an end to the war" (which was anyway to last for two more years). All these various ingredients ere to be incorporated in with the Phalange as the "only Party." The regime started by the insurgents who were occupying territory had all the essential characteristics of Fascism. There was one party whose interest was confused with the national interest. All political liberties were suppressed. The official ideological dogma was anti-democracy imposed through violence and persecution of all non-conformists. The reign of terror was inspired by that of the "Gestapo." The centralfiles listing the "suspects" reached no less than two million names (according to official declarations).

What are the legal bases for "the new State"? From whom have those in power received their prerogatives? A "Council of National Defense" was set up in Burgos in July 1936 by several insurgent military leaders. It functioned as a Council of generals until September 29 of that year. On that date, their rebellious comrades made General Franco "chief of the State." As a matter of fact all those generals had sworn their allegiance to the Republican Government at the beginning of the regime, and reaffirmed their loyalty to the Popular Front Government a few months before their revolt. On October 1, 1936, Franco, exercising the functions which his co-insurgents had so liberally conferred upon him, was thus enthroned by General Cabanellas: "I confer upon you the absolute powers of the State." And Franco formally declared: "Spain is organized according to a vast *totalitarian* concept." From then on, he was to be the "Caudillo": the equivalent of the Italian Duce and the German Fuehrer. A Decree of August 4, 1937, established the Phalange as the organ of the State: a "militant movement, to inspire the Spanish State." Such a decree determined the organic structure of both of those: Phalange and State. The "Caudillo" was to be over all. According to his own statement, he was the "personification of all values and honors." As leader, he had absolute authority, and was responsible only to God and History. He even gave himself the right to name his own successor. The National Council of the Phalange is completely chosen by the "Caudillo" who can at any moment replace it. This body is modelled on the Grand Fascist Council in Italy, and meets once a year. As a permanent delegation of the Council, to second the "Caudillo," a Political Council of twelve members was set up, six of them were appointed by the "Caudillo" and the other six by the Council from its own members, which actually means that they were also chosen by Franco. The entire political life of the nation and the entire social organization was entrusted to this organ of the totalitarian regime.

Such is the State, the shadow of State—a State in name only —which has emerged from the ruins of the civil war. Without the adherence of the citizens, and actually in the face of their opposition, this State suppresses all the rights of citizenship. Imposed by force and maintained by terror, it masters the bodies and souls of the Spanish people. One of the definers of the system characterizes it as follows: "Fascism, Hegelian absolutism, can not only establish itself in Spain, but it must do so . . . We have the right to be more papist than the Pope; likewise we may also be more Fascist than Fascism, for our fascism must be perfect, absolute. Fascism is a religious concept, as Mussolini has written. Spanish Fascism will therefore be the religion of Religion." [19] The dogmatic State is a very demanding divinity which places itself above God. It invades a realm in which even the Church has proclaimed freedom for its believers. The most peculiar statement in this direction was made by the Home Minister, R. Serrano Suñer on April 3, 1938: "There is a realm which we have taken over completely: it is that which is constituted by problems left by God to free discussion by men. Since we do not want any more disputes in Spain, these problems are solved definitely by the national movement embodied in the Phalange."

---

[19] José Pemartin, *España como Pensamiento,* in *Antología de Acción Española* (Madrid: Burgos, 1937), p. 401.

In the light of the principles of political philosophy, the totalitarian fascist regime set up in Spain lacks the most essential bases of legitimacy. In the light of mere political prudence, it causes one to foresee the most violent turmoil. Waving a flag of national unity, it is actually the most separatist form that one can imagine. And it carries a ferment of anarchy, since it does not recognize the fundamental principles of every legal power and it discredits all notion of the State in the eyes of the citizens.

Today, as in the past, the tendencies of Spanish political thought show an excessive polarization around positions whose respective roots have one principle defect: the absolute state power advocated by one party and absolute individual liberty preached by the opposing party. Almost everything in Spain which is genuinely revolutionary grows out of an anarchist attitude and uses anarchist methods. Almost everything which tries to be conservative or reactionary proceeds from an open or disguised fascist attitude and uses and accepts totalitarian methods. Too frequently the struggle to retain or to acquire control of the State moves thought to take pragmatic positions which obscure its potential clarity. The technical necessities of such a struggle in a period which does not cease to be constituent because it does not at any moment attain sufficient stability to have itself accepted as constituted, make impossible a normal political life and the building of a coherent system which would assure the functioning of the State and the essential liberties of its citizens. A violent pendular rhythm produces alternating catastrophes in civic life and extreme reactions which disturb the equilibrium of oscillations in the zone tempered by equal liberty for all, a great society. When, during each swing of the pendulum there appears an opportunity to moderate the rhythm and reduce it to regular hope dawns, only to be promptly shattered by the reality of the following day. The crisis in political thought in Spain is the result of the limited number or the limited strength of true liberals. Many of those who call themselves liberal are so only when they find themselves oppressed; and they cease to be liberal as soon as they gain power. On the right or on the left, men of extreme ideologies fight for the conquest of power and its benefits more

than for the triumph of their theses which are reduced to too!
and arms of struggle. And there is always lacking a sufficiently
large group of men who conceive of service to Liberty as a new
knightly chivalrous institution and who are capable of the difficult heroism which the cause of justice requires.

BIBLIOGRAPHY

Alcalá, Zamora Niceto, *Los Defectos de la Constitución de 1931* (Madrid: R. Espinosa, 1936). Strong criticism from a juridical and conservative republic
point of view, by the first President of the Second Republic.

Azaña, Manuel, *Una Política* (*1930-1932*) (Bilbao:: Espasa-Calpe, 1932); *En el
Poder y en la Oposición* (*1932-1934*) (Bilbao: Espasa-Calpe, 1934); *Mi re-
belión en Barcelona* (Madrid: Espasa-Calpe, 1935); *Discursos en Campo
Abierto* (Madrid: Espasa-Calpe, 1936). Political thought of the Prime Minister and later President of the Republic.

Azpiazu, Joaquín, *El Estado Corporative* (Madrid: Editorial Razón y Fe, 1940).
Explanation of the modern theories and organization of corporatism. *El Estado Católico* (Burgos: Ediciones Rayfe, 1939). A blueprint of a religious
conception of the state, trying to conciliate authoritarian (not totalitarian)
fascism and Catholicism, by a Jesuit under the Falange regime.

Besteiro, Julián, *Marxismo y Antimarxismo* (Madrid: Grafica Socialista, 1935).
Revisionist attitude on Socialism.

Brenan, Gerald, *The Spanish Labyrinth* (New York: The Macmillan Co., 1943).
Well-informed and generally impartial account of the social and political
background of the Civil War.

Costa, Joaquín, *Oligarquía y Caciquismo como la forma actual de gobierno en España* (Madrid: Ateneo, 1902). On collective political psychology.

Eliseda, Marques de la, *Fascismo, Catolicismo y Monarquía* (Madrid: Fax, 1935).
Extreme rightist monarchist position.

Ganivet, Angel, *Idearium Español* (Granada: El Defensor, 1897). A very influential work on political thought at the beginning of this century.

Giménez, Caballero Ernesto, *Genio de España* (Madrid: La Gaceta Literaria, 1932);
La Nueva Catolicidad (Madrid, 1933). Two deeply fascist-imperialist books
whose main thesis nourished the falangist ideology.

Hamilton, T. J., *Appeasement's Child* (New York: A. A. Knopf, 1943). Criticism
of Franco's regime, methods and policy.

Ledesma, Ramos Ramiro, *Discurso a las Juventudes de España* (Madrid: Ediciones
"La Conquista del Estado", 1935). A wholly fascist diatribe against Demo-
liberalism.

Lema, Marqués de, *Cánovas el Hombre de Estado* (Madrid: Espasa-Calpe, 1931).
The life and ideas of the father of Bourbon Restoration and the founder of
the Conservative Party.

Madariaga, Salvador de, *Anarchy or Hierarchy* (London: Allen and Unwin, 1937).
Criticism of Democracy; favors a new liberal aristocratism. *The World's Design* (London: Allen and Unwin, 1938). *On International Organization*.
Spain (London): J. Cape, 2nd ed., 1942). Political and social criticism of
contemporary history.

Mendizábal, Alfredo, *Aux origines d'une tragedie* (Paris: Desclée De Brower,
1937; English translation: *The Martyrdom of Spain*, New York: Charles
Scribner's Sons, 1938). An analysis of political ideologies and methods
through the troubled period preceding the Civil War.

Minguijón, Salvador, *Al Servicio del Tradicionalismo* (Madrid: Morata, 1930). An outline of traditionalist doctrines in France and Spain.

Morato, Juan Jose, *El Partido Socialista Obrero* (Madrid: Biblioteca Nueva, 1st ed., 1918, 2nd ed., 1931). A history of Spanish socialism, its struggle and aims.

Ortega y Gasset, José, *The Revolt of the Masses* (New York: W. W. Norton, 1932). A philosophical essay on the accession of Masses to Power and its implications. *España Invertebrada* (Madrid: Caple, 1921; translated as: *Invertebrate Spain*, New York: W. W. Norton, 1937). *Rectificación de la República* (Madrid: Revista de Occidente, 1931). An objective criticism upon the first steps of the regime.

Pemartín, José, *Qué es 'lo Nuevo."* (Madrid: Espasa-Calpe, 1940). A handbook of the Falangist doctrines.

Pérez, Serrano, Nicholás, *La Constitución española de* VTDV (Madrid: Revista de Derecho privado, 1932). A scholarly work on legislation and criticism.

Posada, Adolfo, *Derecho político comparado* (Madrid: Suárez, 1906). *Teoría social y jurídica del Estado: el Sindicalismo* (Buenos Aires: J. Menéndez); *La Sociedad de las Naciones y el Derecho político: Superliberalismo* (Madrid: Caro Raggio, 1925); *La Crisis del Constitucionalismo* (Madrid, 1925); *La Reforma Constitucional* (Madrid: Suárez, 1931). Work written by a very learned specialist in Public Law.

Primo de River, José Antonio, *Obras completas* (Madrid: Editora Nacional, 1939-41, 2 vols.). Speeches and articles by the founder of the Falange.

Recaséns, Siches Luis, *El Poder constituyente* (Madrid: Morata, 1931). On constitutional problems at the time of the transition from monarchy to republic.

Redondo, Onésimo, *El Estado Nacional* (Barcelona: Ediciones F. E., 1939). A violent diatribe against Freedom and the Rights of Man.

Ríos, Fernando de los, *El Sentido Humanista del Socialismo* (Madrid: Morata, 1926). A Philosophic and liberal revision of the socialist thought.

Romanones, Conde e, *Las Responsbilidades políticas del Antiguo Régimen* 1875 *a* 1923 (Madrid: Renacimiento, 1923). Criticism of contemporary history, by the former leader of the Monarchist Liberal Party. *Sagasta o el Político* (Madrid: Espasa-Calpe, 1930). About the leader of the Liberal Party after Restoration. *Notas de una Vida,* 1868-1912 (Madrid: Renacimiento, 1928, 2 vols.). Political life under the Monarchy.

Ruiz Castillo J., *Antonio Maura* (Madrid: Biblioteca Nueva, 1917).

Silió, César, *Maura* (Madrid: Espasa-Calpe, 1934). This, as well as the previous study, are well-informed books on the life and political thought of the great statesman of Spain.

Serrano, Suñer Ramón, *De la Victoria y la Postguerra* (Bilbao: Ediciones F. E., 1941). Some speeches of the fascist-minded inspirer of Franco's regime.

Smith, R. M., *The Day of the Liberals in Spain* (Philadelphia: University of Pennsylvania Press, 1938). On the Republican conjuncture.

Vázques de Mella, Juan, *Ideario* (Madrid, 1930, 3 vols.). *Política Tradicionalista* (Barcelona, 1932, 2 vols.). Traditionalist thought by the last leader of Carlism.

CHAPTER XXVIII

SCANDINAVIA

T. V. KALIJARVI

The political thought of Scandinavia during half a century, condensed to twenty pages, results inevitably in the submergence of individuals and sometimes of whole schools of thought. And, that is the case unfortunately in this chapter on Scandinavian political thought. It would be helpful to analyze the philosophies of such writers and thinkers as Honkasalo, Sundberg, Kjellen, Undén, Malmgren, Hammarskiöld, Grundtvig, Heiberg, and Snellman; but space will not permit.

WHAT IS MEANT BY SCANDINAVIA

Scandinavia, sometimes called Fennoscandia, includes Sweden, Denmark, Norway, and Finland. These four countries stretch from the Atlantic Ocean to Lake Ladoga and include the Danish territory jutting northward from the continent of Europe.[1] They are relatively poor, with extensive coast lines, and in the case of Norway and Sweden filled with many mountains.

For many generations there were only two countries in the area, namely, Denmark and Sweden. Norway remained a part of Sweden until 1905, when she achieved her independence by amicable means. In 1809 Russia succeeded in taking Finland from Sweden and held it as a part of the Russian empire until 1918, when Finland won her independence. Except for Finland the whole area houses people who are of the same ethnic stock and whose languages and dialects are grounded in the same basic roots. Finland, due to the long years of association with

---

[1] For a brief summary in English see Joseph S. Roucek (ed.) *Contemporary Europe* (New York: D. Van Nostrand Company, Inc., 1941), pp. 456-500.

Sweden, has a large population of Swedish speaking people. For centuries the official language of the country was Swedish, and during the Russian regime the Finnish people looked to Swedish associations as preferable to the Russian. Thus, although of different racial stock, the Finnish people approach their political problems in the same manner as the other three Scandinavian peoples.

Each country possesses its own particular individuality and national pride, which are reflected in its institutions, thinking, and life. Thus during recent times there has been one set of forces operating towards the union of the Scandinavian states, and another set of forces tending towards nationalistic individualism and particularism. So strong have the latter been during the twentieth century, due to the recent achievement of statehood by Finland and Norway, that any thought of union among them has been considered unrealizable. Thus in spite of considerable agitation during the truce of 1918-1939 particularism prevailed.

It took the present conflict to drive home to Scandinavians in all circles that there were many advantages in a union. When Russia attacked Finland, the thought was voiced in Sweden and Norway that the "Finnish case is our problem" (Finlands sak är vår!). When Germany invaded Norway and Denmark the feeling was the same in Sweden. Thus in the dark hours of 1940 a real, tangible feeling of Northern unity was transferred from the philosophical and legalistic realm to that of public opinion and governmental circles.[2] This feeling of unity is consistent with a commonality of race, language, literature, and thought. All of these people possess in common an almost brooding introspection which makes them view their problems in much the same manner.

CHARACTER OF SCANDINAVIAN THOUGHT

There is a basic core of conservatism, which runs through all Scandinavian thought. It is sometimes difficult to appreciate this fact in view of the great strides forward, socialistically, of

[2] Sven-Erik Bergh, (editor), *Sverige i Dag* (Stockholm, A/B Ljus Förlag, 1941), pp. 1-9

these people. Yet, it must not be forgotten, if one wishes to understand Scandinavian political thought. To these people the time honored, the traditional (urgammal), is as powerful and binding as the common law of England.

It is this conservative element which often voices criticism of the ease with which the Scandinavian people yield to outside influences. Although their political thought grew originally out of prehistoric societies and peoples, yet its development has been shaped by Dutch, Scotch, Walloon, Baltic, Finnish, and German migrants. It has been particularly moulded during more recent times by the Anglo-Saxon, French, German, and Italian influences. Even the few Jews, who have migrated into the area have been absorbed without any trace of racial feeling, so that they have been indistinguishably absorbed into the body politic (to become "good Swedes and citizens" (goda svenskar och medborgare).[3]

In spite of this there are certain basic ideas from which all political thought goes out. They do not seem to be dictated so much by the form of government[4] as by long, mutual associations and environment. They include a love of personal freedom especially as it pertains to government activity, value placed on protection against political influence, and a deep and abiding respect in many circles for the church.

Without further evidence it must be clear that the Scandinavian peoples do not take enthusiastically to philosophies such as those of Germany, Italy, and Russia, which challenge or break down the traditional and which terminate independent institutions. For over a century and a half life on the pattern of an army has held no appeal, and particularly so when it takes the form of prohibitions against free organizations, press, petition, and speech.[5] Freedom of organization is regarded as a folk right

---

[5] *Sweden A Wartime Survey* (New York: The American Swedish News Exchange, Inc., 1943), chapters 2, 20, 21, and 22.

[3] *Svensk Ordning och Nyordning* (Stockholm: Bokförlaget Natur och Kultur, 1943), pp. 17-37. The following pages may also be of interest, 38-77.

[4] Norway, Sweden, Denmark are monarchies, Finland a democracy.

and community liberty is a larger aspect of this same right. There are few people who do not belong to one or more organizations.

One oustanding exception to this conservative control was the red revolution in Finland at the end of the last war, when the communistic element, spurred on from the east, proposed to overturn and reconstitute the whole Finnish life on the Bolshevik basis. How strong the conservative strain was may be seen in the bloody quelling of that revolt by the majority of the Finnish people.[6]

THE SOCIAL CHARACTER OF SCANDINAVIAN POLITICAL THOUGHT

It may be paradoxical on the surface that in spite of the conservatism just discussed, the Scandinavian people are among the most progressive socialistically. Perhaps that is why one will look in vain among them for a second *Republic* of Plato, the legalistic emanations of a Jeremy Bentham, the world program of a Kant, or the cynical discourses of a Machiavelli. The key to Scandinavian political thought lies in the anonymous flood of broad social movements, most of which are the products of the last fifty to seventy-five years.

Whether it is the country, the climate, or the people which cause it, the Scandinavian people have learned to meet modern conditions of life by developing their social institutions in such a way as to preserve their society intact and so to broaden their liberties. In general their democracies are based upon modern systems of education, co-operative organizations for buying, selling, and credit, expert advice, and research.

It is not surprising, therefore, that Denmark has been called a social laboratory;[7] but this same title can easily fit any of the other three countries. The social programs are of cardinal importance. They are based upon the principle that the state exists

---

[6] See Henning Söderhjelm, *The Red Insurrection in Finland in* 1918 (London: Harrison and Sons, N. Y.) for a summary.

[7] See Peter Manniche, *Denmark a Social Laboratory* (Copenhagen: C.E.C. Gad, 1939).

for individual welfare, and not the reverse. State and group organizations exist to raise the individual. The most realistic and helpful organizations are temperance, consumer, and trade union societies. These organizations with the social aid of the state reduce the special aids demanded by individuals. They cannot be frozen into any fixed pattern because society is constantly changing. However, the social objectives do remain the same and can be summarized as (1) the improvement in the well being of the people, (2) the raising of the standards of living, and (3) an increase in opportunities for individuals and classes.

The reasons for such an approach to political problems are not obscure. For the most part these countries are poor in resources and rigorous to live in. Their prime problem will always be the elimination of poverty, and the solution of this problem will call for all forms of aid for the needy based on dispersion of social burdens as far as possible on society at large. The problem of the individual must of necessity be considered a community problem. Thus it is that every form of assistance will be tried and developed before resort to the poor or alms house will be undertaken. This is especially true in the case of the aged and the sick. All of these countries have advanced systems of old age pensions. The benefits may be small compared with our own social security payments; but when they are added to the income from a few hens and cows they are real aids and make self-respecting livelihood for a retired worker and his wife. Similarly health insurance, sick care, unemployment compensation, maternity care, and care for needy children are logical parts of the social action and thinking of the North.[8] Forces such as these of necessity will be the determiners of the political thinking of the peoples upon whom they work.

SOCIAL LEGISLATION

One of the most forward looking social programs is that of Denmark, which was largely codified into its Act of 1933. It was

[8] See: *Svensk Ordning och Nyordning*, p. 93; *Social Work in Oslo-Norway* (Oslo: Municipality of Oslo and the Travel Association of Oslo and Environs, 1939); Iisakki Laati, *Social Legislation and Activity in Finland* (Helsinki: Oy Suomen Kirja, 1939); and Peter Manniche, *Denmark a Social Laboratory*.

passed as the result of agitation which had steadily grown since the Child Labor Reform Act of 1873 was passed. The Act of 1933 covers child labor, women labor, social insurance, public relief, industrial accident insurance, unemployment relief, sickness insurance, invalidity insurance, and old age pensions. It also provides that in certain cases all political rights may be lost, particularly in the cases of alcoholics, prostitutes, and tramps.[9] This act had a far-reaching influence, particularly on Sweden, and it represents a highly enlightened conception of the state's social responsibilities.

However, it is only a part of the picture. To it must be added many other regulations governing sanitation, child welfare, housing, and labor relations.[10]

Sweden has modeled many of her present laws on social problems on the Danish pattern, although she has a long and distinguished social history of her own. As for Norway, she too has many similar regulations including poor relief, social insurance, industrial accident insurance, unemployment compensation, accident insurance for fishermen and seamen, health insurance, old age pensions, mother's pensions, relief for crippled children, aid to the blind, home building associations, farmer's relief, price protection, factory inspection, relief for the homeless, labor mediation, pure food regulations, aid to invalids and cripples.[11]

As for Finland, she too in a series of statutes has demonstrated progressive thought and philosophy on social questions. Her laws governing destitute, children, paupers, and mentally deficient are outstanding. Most of the regulations in behalf of labor are purely voluntary. Poor relief is subject to regulation by the State Department of Welfare. Assistance is provided for mothers based partly on social and partly on general consideration. Care of the blind, deaf-mutes, and cripples has been en-

---

[9] Peter Manniche, *Denmark a Social Laboratory,* Chapter V. and the Danish Statistical Department, 1934), pp. 132-139.

[10] See *Denmark* 1934 (Copenhagen: Royal Danish Ministry for Foreign Affairs).

[11] *The Norway Year Book,* Per Vogt, editor (third issue, Oslo: Sverre Mortensen Förlag A/S, 1838), pp. 146-171.

lightened. So, too, has the state program of public health.[12]

In summary, taken in conjunction with co-operatives, which are discussed later, this social progressivism represents not only Sweden's famous middle way, but also that of the whole North. In normal times the budget of the Department of Interior of Sweden, which deals with social matters, is almost twice that of national defense.[13] So also is the case of Denmark,[14] while Norway and Finland have more modest appropriations for social purposes than do Sweden and Denmark. The significant fact, it may be repeated, is that the state and local government structures are built about these services. The reasons for state existence, the ambit of state authority, the nature of governmental activities, the relationships between government and the individual, the character of justice particularly so-called social justice, the scope of liberty, and the whole socio-political concept are determined substantially by these socialistically conditioned ideas. To a very large extent, therefore, the political theory of the North is its social theory.

CO-OPERATIVE MOVEMENT

For reasons already given the Scandinavian people have fastened upon co-operative societies to further their well-being. Influenced during the latter half of the nineteenth century by the English and German co-operative experiments, the Danes, then the Swedes and Norwegians, and finally the Finns, began the establishment of co-operative societies. Since then the movement has grown to tremendous proportions until the Scandinavian countries are without question the world's most prominent examples of widespread adoption of co-operative societies covering buying, selling, producer activities and consumer interests. To mention only a few of the types of co-operatives without attempting to allocate them to countries, there are: co-operative dairy societies, purchasing societies, joint stock companies, bacon fac-

[12] See *Finland Year Book* 1939/1940, edited by I. Leiviskä (Helsinki: Oy Suomen Kirja, Ltd., 1939), pp. 106-115.
[13] See The *Sweden Year-Book,* 1938 (Stockholm: Almquist & Wiksells Boktryckeri A.-B., 1938), pp. 29-30.
[14] See *Denmark* 1934, p. 55.

tories, export societies, banks, egg export societies, cattle export societies, butter export societies, feed purchasing societies, cement factories, coal societies, sanatoria societies, wholesale societies, insurance societies, fertilizer societies, credit unions, agricultural engineering societies, rural electrification societies, and timber societies.[15]

While the loadstone of this type of enterprise is profit or economic saving, they have developed into institutions of great power and control. They are means of social and political liberation as well as ways of realizing profit. Through their press and communications control, they are powerful pressure groups determining governmental action both on national and local bases. Factory, farm, and distribution control are effective means for the realization of most political and social objectives. Indeed, as may be readily appreciated, the activities of the co-operatives are extended to the field of foreign affairs, thus entering into every level of political activity. Thus, no political analysis of the North is complete without, for example, taking into consideration the Swedish Kooperativa förbund, the Finnish Pellervo Society, the Danish Central Coooperative Committee, and their many concomitant organizations.

In Sweden, for example, there were 700 societies in 1941 with a membership of 740,000, which is a little more than 10 per cent of the people. These societies did about 10 per cent of the country's retail business. In this case the moving spirits have been journalists and workers. When the Kooperativa förbund was formed in 1898 it was closely linked to the Social Democratic party; but since then the cooperative societies have moved farther from partisan politics assuming at every opportunity a position of neutrality.[16] Originally many people eschewed the society because they considered it to be an effort on the part of the working man to better his condition without resorting to socialism.

---

[15] See Peter Manniche, *Denmark a Social Laboratory,* especially chapters I and II; also Henry Bakken, *Cooperation to the Finnish* (Madison, Wisconsin: Mimir, 1939). The latter has excellent references and is devoted to the development of the cooperative movement in Finland.

[16] *Svensk Ordning och Nyordning,* p. 63.

TEMPERANCE MOVEMENT

Closely integrated with the broad social movements which have been discussed is that of temperance, which has been agitated for the last half century or more in all four countries. Strongly influenced by the temperance movements in England and the United States, the first steps were taken in Sweden in 1880 since which time the movement has grown until it numbers many hundreds of thousands [17] in all of the countries. Many of the people are members of more than one temperance group. For a while there was keen rivalry between the Social Democratic party and the temperance movement. The reason for this friction is not clear, but it may have been that both appeared at about the same time and appealed to the same type of people. The original activities of the temperance people were carried on by the so-called liberal parties, but since 1910 most of the temperance people have entered the ranks of the Social Democratic and other parties.

The movement for prohibition was strong at the time the United States adopted it. Finland adopted prohibition; Sweden did not try; Norway after an advisory plebiscite began a control of all save wine and found for trading purposes that it was not feasible to put into effect; and Denmark does not seem to have been particularly concerned. But even though Denmark may not have adopted prohibition, the problem is considered in the same light as by the other Scandinavian countries, for there are some 126,000 Danish people mustered into temperance societies and there is a special state consultant on temperance.

FREE CHURCH MOVEMENT

In Denmark, Norway, and Sweden until the middle of the nineteenth century all citizens were required to belong to the state church (Lutheran). First in Denmark in 1849 and later in Sweden and Norway revolts against the church controls occurred taking their inspiration from the Anglo-Saxon countries. In Sweden the first free church people were the Baptists and Metho-

---

[17] More than 300,000 in Sweden in 1938

dists, and in 1878 P. P. Waldström led in the development of the
Mission Federation. The free church movement was but a reflection of powerful influences working for democratic and religious freedom.

At first the Social Democratic party with its original Marxian
basis was openly hostile to the church, but it long since abandoned this attitude and more and more church people have joined
its ranks. Today no particular opposition to the state church is
to be found in any of the countries, and further there is no particular antipathy between the church and other sects as are to be
found in the states.[18] However, the church in the case of the
four countries is one of the most powerful influences in the state,
and its thinking on social, temperance, and other questions has a
far-reaching influence.

WOMEN'S RIGHTS

It is not surprising in countries with such advanced social
views that the subject of women's rights has been of the keenest
interest, and that it was in Finland that the first complete parliamentary enfranchisement of women took place. This granting
of the right to vote to women took place in Finland in 1906-
1907, in Norway provisionally in 1910 and fully in 1936, in
Sweden in 1919-1920, and in Denmark in 1915. It should not
be forgotten that even though the vote was won on the dates
mentioned, women had been active in local and many other
affairs for a long time before their victory at the polls. Among
other fields they had distinguished themselves in education, trade
unions, and social affairs.

The women, however, since the vote has been achieved have
not taken advantage of it alike in all of the countries. In Norway
they have been slow to seize upon their new-found rights.[19] Perhaps this was due to a very conservative strain. In Finland on
the other hand there were 16 deputies in Parliament in 1939,

---

[18] For a useful discussion of this point see *Svensk Ordning och Nyordning*, p. 62.
Also see the chapters on religion and the church in the yearbooks referred to in
the previous references.

[19] See *The Norway Year Book*, p. 143-146.

while women play an important part in communal life and administration.[20] Between these two positions are those of the Swedish and Danish women.

However, it would be a mistake to assume that merely the franchise is the determination of the political interests and activities of Scandinavian women. They participate in administration and have been particularly active in the promotion of maternity assistance, mothers pensions, and child protection. They are organized into many direrent kinds of local societies, sometimes as in the case of Finland's Suomen Naisten Kansallisliitto, Finish Women's National League, the feminist organizations are coordinated by a special body. They in turn are coordinated by the North European Committee for six large feminist groups.

Women therefore are an important element in Northern politics and their views and programs have determined the action of governments. They undoubtedly play a part in the socialization of the political thinking which has been stressed previously.

VIEWS OF FREEDOM

Consistent with what has already been said, the Scandinavian people regard freedom both personal and constitutional as a product of the proper type of culture developed over a long time and achieved only through much sacrifice and cost. And yet, it is not difficult to demonstrate the influence on present Scandinavian concepts of liberty and freedom of American, English, and especially French thought and ideas. The French Revolution and the Bill of Rights left a deep impression particular on the Swedish thinking.[21]

It would be a mistake because of this to conclude that the thoughts of Rousseau, Locke, and Jefferson are the Scandinavian thoughts on freedom and liberty. Moreover, they do not follow Franklin Roosevelt's negative improvisations on the theme of freedom. Freedom to the Scandinavians has many facets, only a

---

[20] See *Finland Year Book* 1939/1940, pp. 361-372.

[21] See *Svensk Ordning och Nyordning*, pp. 50-51.

few of which are: (1) freedom of the individual, (2) freedom of the nation in the world, (3) freedom of groups and classes, and (4) freedom of the minority from majority tyranny. This thinking also considers that it is essential, as Harald Hjärne says, to protect the individual against organizations which affect his living conditions and home life. As yet no state has recognized that large groups are a threat through competition to the individual, to classes, and even to the state itself. Freedom among other things means the ability to work, to hold property and to share with other people.[22]

Once again freedom truly understood is not limited to the ethical concepts of Plato, the political moderation of Aristotle, nor the burning slogans of the French Revolution. It is a socio-politico-economic term meaning the ability to do certain things and applies not only to a single individual but also to classes, groups, and states.

DEMOCRATIC IDEAS

It is now possible to discuss briefly some of the Scandinavian ideas of democracy. In general democracy is a means for giving to the masses full political rights based upon a correlative assumption of responsibility by those who exercise the rights. Democracy means a common feeling of freedom. But it also means freedom of union activity, freedom of food and supply organizations, and freedom to organize with a minimum of interference from the state. True democracy dictates state aid in the achievement of the best possible living conditions. It is not merely a limited number of political rights nor a particular form of governmental organization. The real test is the freedom surrounding the individual.

When one remembers the Russian domination of Finland and the efforts at russification prior to 1918; when one recalls that even in spite of the reforms in Sweden following 1809 personal freedom was considerably restricted; when one appreciates that the industrial revolution and its concomitants came late to

---

[22] See Nils Herlitz, *Svensk Frihet* (Stockholm: P. A. Norstedt & Söners Förlag, 1943), pp. 44-45.

these lands; and when one remembers that at the turn of the century Sweden seemed on the verge of a revolution [23] the strides forward in political thinking are all the more remarkable in respect to democratic concepts.

Obviously this concept of democracy lies somewhere between the political purism of Anglo-Saxon ideas and the state socialism of Germany and Italy, and the communism of Russia. It is truly a middle way and one which has worked effectively answering some of the most urgent problems of a changing society.

SWEDEN, AN EXAMPLE

Because all of the countries here under discussion went through social movements of great importance having great and powerful significance not only for themselves, but also for their neighbors, this discussion would be incomplete if some effort to show how those changes occurred were omitted. For that reason it may be well to look at Sweden as an example.

After the defeat by Russia (1808-1809), the King lost power to the Riksdag, which was reorganized on drastically more democratic lines in 1866, when the suffrage and representation were broadened. At that time over 85 per cent of the people were peasants and rooted to the land. This was the time when the Swedish industrial revolution was taking place. Within a short time thereafter between 40 and 50 per cent of the people became engaged in handicrafts or manufacturing. This movement was accompanied by pressure from the peasantry, which had gone into the cities, the free intelligentsia, and women demanding emancipation. It was under these pressures incidentally that the church control was weakened and new sects permitted to come in. [24]

Demands for reforms grew, and Swedish history at that

---

[23] Crowds marched through the streets singing "Sons of Labor" and the "Internationale". This was the juncture at which Hjalmar Branting stepped to the fore (1897) and became the parliamentary leader for labor. The culmination was the political strike of 1902 lasting 3 days and involving 120,000 laborers. Labor success can be dated from 1909 when universal suffrage, proportional voting, age limitations, and similar measures were passed.

[24] *Svensk Ordning och Nyordning*, pp. 20-23.

time, just as today, was not so much the writings and the expressions of individual philosophies of revolutionary character as it was a socio-political movement of a whole people demanding curbs on the church especially in the field of education, temperance laws, constitutional reforms, and the democratization of work. The latter took the form of demands for : (1) parliamentarism, (2) equality of social groups in the lower house, and (3) universal suffrage. In addition it was accompanied by the struggle for freedom of the press and communal autonomy. Although the common rights of man were age-old in Sweden, they were rapidly taking on a new meaning.

These demands were reflected in the thinking and platforms of political parties which were taking on their current form. The first party to organize, as might be expected, was the Conservative; but the most significant from the present standpoint was the Social Democratic party, organized in 1889 on a frankly Marxist basis calling for the general socializing of productive means accompanied by a plank calling for equal voting or free franchise. About 1900 the Liberal party demanding social reforms appeared, strongly influenced by Karl Staaff (d. 1915) and English politics. These two parties, more commonly known as the Left, drove through most of the social reforms of this century.

As most of the objectives of the Social Democratic party were achieved, they tended to lose their radical character and have more recently taken on the form of a doctrinnaire reform party. Yet, it is significant to remember that these were the parties, which lay behind the program of socialization, which we have touched upon in some of its broader political aspects. The main emphasis has always been the achievement of everything possible for the working class.

Recent party history shows how completely the socializing victory has been won and how a new conservatism is creeping into the party system of Sweden. In the Lower House the Right had 37 members in 1921, 50 members in 1933, and 32 in 1943. The Peasant party has remained constant at about 20 members through the years. The Social Democrats as they have grown more conservative have increased their numbers from 50 in 1921 to 80 in 1943. The Liberals and Independents have dropped from 40 members in 1921 to 15 in 1943. The same trends may be discerned in the Upper House, except for the Right, which has dropped from 70 members in 1921 to 42 members in 1943. Thus the Social Democratic party which reflects Swedish political thought during the last twenty years shows that it is bending towards greater and greater conservatism with an emphasis on the social program.[25]

This same revolt against old institutions and a demand for more progressive social institutions may be traced in each of the other three countries. And, although each possesses its own peculiar history, parties, and experiences, the trends are the same and the Social Democratic party in all countries except Norway has been the bearer of the torch. In all four countries until the outbreak of the present conflict the same trend to conservatism was to be observed. Of course, what will happen after the present war ends remains to be seen.

NATIONALISM

One subject remains for brief discussion before bringing this chapter to a close. As was seen in another connection strong particularism and nationalism have marked the feelings of these people. That has been especially true of both Norway and Finland, perhaps most of all in the case of Finland. Independence in both cases was preceded by long years of agitation centered about language, culture, and institutions and accompanied by a flood of fiery literature. Men like J. Steen in Norway and John Vilhelm Snellman in Finland were both leaders and voices of their people.[26] The language problem in different guises was basic in both instances, although the question of establishing a standard basic Norwegian language was considerably different from the conflict between Finnish and Swedish in Finland.

[25] *Supra cit*, p. 26.
[26] See: John H. Wuorinen, *Nationalism in Finland* (New York: Columbia University Press, 1921), pp. 83-239; also *The Norway Year Book*, 1938, pp. 43-58.

Sweden and Denmark, having had their independence much longer had not been spurred on to intense nationalism until the occupation of Norway and Denmark by Germany and the war by Russia upon Finland. It would appear that recent events will perhaps have a double-barreled effect upon the Scandinavian lands. On the one hand it is driving them into a union for their mutual protection, and at the same time it is intensifying their nationalism.

INTERNATIONALISM

This is interesting since these states were among the strongest supporters of the League of Nations and the system of collective security. They resorted to the League and Court machinery at every possible turn. They were disappointed in the development and had moments when they regretted that they had not chosen a different course.

It may be recalled that in the First World War the Scandinavian states with the exception of Finland, which had not yet won its independence, chose a course of neutrality refusing to be drawn into the war on either side and accommodating themselves by rationing and otherwise to life under a blockade. Then when the League was established they had the choice of repeating that program in any war which might ensue and thus keep out of the European game of power politics in which at the best, even jointly, they were only a medium-sized pawn. Thus many hard-headed thinkers felt it unwise to enter into the system of collective security. Sweden felt that way after her experience with the Åland Islands, and Finland, after her treatment in the East Carelian case.

Yet they cast their lot with the League and the peace machinery and remained staunch in its support to the end. With the exception of Sweden, they have found that neither alternative can guarantee security. Around these points some of the most significant political thought in the North is revolving today.

CONCLUSION

Scandinavian political thought is contained in social experiments, thoughts, legislative acts, and parties. While the countries possess individual characteristics, their political experiences and reactions possess a central theme and thread, which can be properly described as Scandinavian socio-political thought. Theirs is a middle program lying between free enterprise state programs and communistic state socialism. In the present international turmoil the old international philosophies of neutrality and collective security are inadequate and these four states are confronted with the necessity for a more workable and realistic policy and philosophy.

BIBLIOGRAPHY

BAKKEN, HENRY H., *Cooperation to the Finnish* (Madison, Wisconsin: Mimir, 1939). Excellent discussion in English of Finnish co-operative movement, containing much reference material.

BERGH, SVEN-ERIK, (editor), *Sverige i Dag* (Stockholm: A/B Ljus Förlag, 1941). A symposium by several outstanding Swedish authorities discussing the current situation in Sweden.

Frihet och Samhälle (Stockholm: Albert Bonniers Förlag, 1943). An excellent series of essays on Swedish democracy and freedom.

HARTMANN, J. S., *Sveriges Riksdag under Fem Arhundraden* (Stockholm: Albert Bonniers Förlag, 1935). A short essay on the Swedish Riksdag.

HASTAD, ELIS, *Det Moderna Partiväsendets Organisation* (Stockholm: Albert Bonniers Förlag, 1938). A terse discussion of the Swedish party organization with considerable theory.

HASTED, ELIS, *Partierna i Regering och Riksdag* (Stockholm: Albert Bonniers Förlag, 1938). A further discussion of the same subject.

HERLITZ, NILS, *Svensk Frihet* (P. A. Norstedts & Söner Förlag, 1943). An analysis of the Swedish conception of freedom.

LAATI, IISAKKI, *Social Legisaltion and Activity in Finland* (Helsinki: Cy Suomen Kirja, Ltd., 1939).

MANNICHE, PETER, *Denmark a Social Laboratory* (Copenhagen: C. E. C. Gad, 1939). An excellent and interestingly illustrated discussion of agriculture, cooperative societies, social legislation, and education in Denmark.

MUNTELL, HENRIK, *Svensk Rättsradition* (Stockholm, Albert Bonniers Förlag, 1942). A brief summary of Swedish legal backgrounds.

Social Work in Oslo-Norway (Oslo: Municipality of Oslo in collaboration with the Travel Association for Oslo and Environs, 1939). An excellent summary of how the social philosophy is given practical application in a specific community.

SOLVEN, ARNOLD, *Svensk Arbetsfredspolitik* (Stockholm: Albert Bonniers Förlag, 1940). Swedish labor politics.

Svensk Ordning och Nyordning (Stockholm: Bokförlaget Natur och Kultur, 1943). A symposium of essays on the political problems of Sweden.

THERMAENIUS, EDVARD, *Sveriges Politiska Historia, efter* 1809 (Stockholm: Albert Bonniers Förlag, 1937). Swedish political history since 1809 in summary. Well done.

Sweden a Wartime Survey (New York: The American-Swedish News Exchange, Inc., N. D.). Several essays on Sweden today.

WAHLSTROM, LYDIA, *Den Svenska Kvinnorörelsen* (Stockholm: Albert Bonniers Förlag, 1939). A summary of the Swedish feminist movement.

For facts the following yearbooks will be found helpful:

Denmark 1934 (Copenhagen: Royal Danish Ministry for Foreign Affairs and the Danish Statistical Department, 1934).

The Finland Yearbook 1939/1940 (Helsinki: Oy Suomen Kirja, Ltd., 1939).

The Norway Year Book (third Issue, Oslo: Sverre Mortensen Förlag A/S, 1938).

The Sweden Year-Book 1938 (Stockholm: Almquist & Wiksells Boktryckeri-A.-B., 1938).

A

B

* Compiled by Alice Hero, Hofstra College.

E

F

H

K

L

S

W

Y

Z